A Dictionary of Phonetics and Phonology

Lto   1996

Written for students of linguistics, applied linguistics and speech
therapy, this dictionary covers over 2,000 terms in phonetics and
phonology. In addition to providing a comprehensive yet concise
guide to an enormous number of individual terms, it also includes
an explanation of the most important theoretical approaches to
phonology.

Its usefulness as a reference tool is further enhanced by the
inclusion of pronunciations, notational devices and symbols, earliest
sources of terms, suggestions for further reading, and advice with
regard to usage.

R. L. Trask is Lecturer in Linguistics in the School of Cognitive and
Computing Sciences at the University of Sussex. His previous publications include *A Dictionary of Grammatical Terms in Linguistics*
(1993), *Language Change* (1994) and *Language: The Basics* (1995).

A Dictionary of
Phonetics and Phonology

R. L. Trask

London and New York

First published 1996
by Routledge
11 New Fetter Lane, London EC4P 4EE

Simultaneously published in the USA and Canada
by Routledge
29 West 35th Street, New York, NY 10001

© 1996 R. L. Trask

Typeset in Times by Florencetype Ltd, Stoodleigh, Devon

Printed and bound in Great Britain by Clays Ltd, St Ives plc

British Library Cataloguing in Publication Data
A catalogue record for this book is available from the British Library

Library of Congress Cataloguing in Publication Data
A catalogue record for this book has been requested

ISBN   0–415–11260–5 (hbk)
0–415–11261–3 (pbk)

Contents

Figures

Preface

This dictionary is intended primarily for students and teachers of phonetics and linguistics. Like its companion volume, *A Dictionary of Grammatical Terms in Linguistics*, this dictionary focuses on just one major area of the linguistic sciences and tries to provide detailed coverage of that area.

Of course, it is not possible to include every single one of the many thousands of terms which make an appearance somewhere in the phonological literature, but the nearly 2,000 terms which are defined here should include virtually every term you are likely to encounter outside the most specialized monographs.

The larger part of the dictionary is devoted to terms which have been in existence for some time and which look likely to remain in use for the foreseeable future: *alternation*, *apical*, *contour tone*, *creaky voice*, *obstruent*, *rule loss*, *sandhi*, *vowel harmony*.

Though articulatory phonetics naturally features very prominently in these pages, acoustic and perceptual phonetics are not neglected, nor is general speech science: *Action Theory*, *acoustic filter*, *cochlea*, *duplex perception*, *electromyography*, *formant*, *quantal vowel*, *transition*.

The terminology of classical phonology is well covered, including the terms used by the Prague School, by Daniel Jones and by the American Structuralists: *archiphoneme*, *biuniqueness*, *diaphone*, *EPD*, *juncture phoneme*, *privative opposition*.

Classical generative phonology is abundantly covered: *absolute neutralization*, *exchange rule*, *Halle's argument*, *systematic phoneme*. Among more recent developments, Autosegmental Phonology and Metrical Phonology are treated in particular detail: *demibeat*, *deforestation*, *dumping*, *iambic reversal*, *No-Crossing Constraint*, *timing tier*. But the principal terms from nearly all the major developments in phonology in the last two decades are also defined: *coronal underspecification*, *Derived Environment Constraint*, *feature geometry*, *hot feature*, *Prosodic Hierarchy*, *subjunction*, *via rule*.

Distinctive features are covered in great detail. Summaries of some half-dozen feature systems are given, and many dozens of individual features are defined.

There is ample coverage of the phonology of English: *dark l, Estuary English, Great Vowel Shift, Received Pronunciation, rhotic accent, Trager–Smith system, velar softening.* Terms specific to other languages are included if they feature prominently in the literature: *Grassmann's Law, liaison, radoppiamento sintattico, rendaku, seseo, soft mutation, yer.*

I have made a point of including a number of terms largely confined to the older philological literature, since these are often maddeningly difficult to look up elsewhere: *anlaut, cacuminal, implosive position, surd, tenuis.*

There is a good deal of coverage of phonological change and variation, both traditional terms and recent ones: *apocope, Bill Peters effect, chain shift, lexical diffusion, reversal of merger, rhotacization, umlaut.* Given the current importance of metrical ideas in phonology, traditional terms from metrics are well covered: *crasis, masculine rhyme, synizesis, tetrameter, trochee.*

For many entries there are multiple definitions; competing and conflicting usages are noted and described, and recommendations are often provided; examples of troublesome terms are *breathy voice, dorsum, flap, heavy syllable, hypercorrection, prosody, tone.* As far as possible, I have tried to identify the original sources of the terms, and for many of the more important terms I have suggested further reading.

The alphabetical order used is one which ignores both hyphens and spaces between words. Thus, for example, *provection* precedes *P-rule*, while *off-glide* precedes *off rhyme*, which precedes *offset phase.*

The pronunciation given is that typical of the south of England. Speakers of other varieties of English will, I hope, find little difficulty in making any necessary adjustments.

In an enterprise of this kind, it is no doubt inevitable that there will prove to be a few errors and omissions. If you find any, I shall be pleased to hear about them. You can write to me at the School of Cognitive and Computing Sciences, University of Sussex, Falmer, Brighton BN1 9QH, UK, or e-mail me at larryt@cogs.susx.ac.uk.

Acknowledgements

I should like to thank Julia Hall, Emma Cotter, Alison Foyle and Caroline Cautley of Routledge for encouraging this book and for putting up with several exasperating delays along the way. To Dick Hudson I am indebted for getting me into the linguistic lexicography business in the first place. Two anonymous readers, and later Richard Coates, John Goldsmith and most especially Max Wheeler, read and commented on early drafts of varying sizes; I am grateful to all of them, and I have managed to incorporate most of their comments into the final version. I regret that Goldsmith's 1995 book appeared too late to be taken into account in preparing the dictionary; this book contains useful further reading on many of the entries in the dictionary. I am further indebted to Kasia Jaszczołt for making available to me a body of unpublished work in Optimality Theory. And, as always, I am deeply grateful to Jenny Potts for an impeccable job of copy-editing.

Naturally, I owe an enormous debt to all my fellow linguists, past and present, whose works I have combed for terms and definitions. Among those phoneticians and linguists of whose work I have made particularly heavy use are David Abercrombie, John Anderson, Stephen Anderson, Sheila Blumstein, Philip Carr, J. C. Catford, Noam Chomsky, John Clark, Alan Cruttenden, David Crystal, Peter Denes, Jacques Durand, Eli Fischer-Jørgensen, Victoria Fromkin, D. B. Fry, Hans Giegerich, A. C. Gimson, John Goldsmith, Morris Halle, Richard Hogg, Larry Hyman, Daniel Jones, Francis Katamba, Michael Kenstowicz, William Labov, Peter Ladefoged, Roger Lass, John Laver, Philip Lieberman, C. B. McCully, Elliot Pinson, Peter Roach, Iggy Roca, Alan Sommerstein, John Wells and Colin Yallop – though these names certainly do not exhaust the sources I consulted.

Needless to say, none of these people bears any responsibility for any shortcomings the dictionary may prove to have.

The author and publisher would like to thank the following for permission to reprint copyright material: *Figure A1*: from D. B. Fry (1979) *The Physics of Speech*, p. 56 and p. 77, by permission of Cambridge University Press; *Figure C1* and *Figure P1*: from J. C. Catford (1977) *Fundamental Problems in Phonetics*, p. 143, p. 145

and p. 185, by permission of Edinburgh University Press; *Figure V1*: from William Labov (1994) *Principles of Linguistic Change*, vol. 1: *Internal Factors*, p. 205, by permission of Blackwell. Every effort was made to clear permission of all figures reprinted in this dictionary, and the publisher would be very happy to hear from the copyright holders whom we are unable to trace.

Abbreviations

abstr. n.	abstract noun
adj.	adjective
ant.	antonym
CF	combining form
cf.	compare
EPD	*An English Pronouncing Dictionary* (Jones 1917)
n.	noun
OEP	*An Outline of English Phonetics* (Jones 1918)
pl.	plural
sg.	singular
SPE	*The Sound Pattern of English* (Chomsky and Halle 1968)
v.	verb
vi.	intransitive verb
vt.	transitive verb

Guide to pronunciation

The pronunciation represented is that of the south of England.

/p/	pop	/z/	zoos	/ɜː/	bird
/t/	tot	/ʒ/	measure	/ɛə/	bare
/k/	cook	/m/	mum	/ə/	banana
/b/	bib	/n/	nun	/æ/	bat
/d/	did	/ŋ/	sing	/ɑː/	bard
/g/	gag	/l/	lull	/ɒ/	pot
/tʃ/	church	/r/	ray	/aɪ/	bite
/dʒ/	judge	/w/	way	/ɑʊ/	bout
/f/	fife	/j/	you	/ɔː/	bawd
/θ/	think	/iː/	beat	/ɔɪ/	boy
/s/	sauce	/ɪ/	bit	/əʊ/	boat
/ʃ/	shush	/i/	city	/ʌ/	but
/h/	hay	/ɪə/	beard	/ʊ/	put
/v/	verve	/eɪ/	bayed	/uː/	boot
/ð/	either	/e/	bet	/ʊə/	poor
				/u/	influence

Diacritics

Raised bar primary stress: /əˈkuːstɪk/
Bar below syllabic consonant: /kənˈdɪʃn̩/

Words from other languages are transcribed with the ordinary symbols of the International Phonetic Alphabet.

A Dictionary of
Phonetics and Phonology

A

abbreviatory convention /ə'briːvieɪtri kənvenʃən/ *n.* Any notational convention which allows two or more distinct but seemingly related statements to be written as what appears to be a single statement by combining common elements. The object of such a convention is the **conflation** of related **rules** into a **rule schema**, thereby gaining **economy** by avoiding restatement. Among the conventions which have been widely used in phonology are **braces**, **parentheses**, **angle brackets**, **mirror-image environments** and the **alpha notation**. Analysts differ as to whether these conventions should be regarded as representations of an underlying reality or merely as descriptive conveniences with no theoretical standing.

abduction /æb'dʌkʃən/ *n.* The moving apart of the **vocal folds**. *V.* **abduct**. Ant. **adduction**.

ablaut /'æblaʊt/ *n.* (also **vowel gradation**, **apophony**) 1. A morphological process expressed by a change in the quality of a vowel within a root or stem for purely grammatical purposes, with the vowel alternation typically serving as the only exponent of the grammatical distinction. English examples include the inflectional patterns exhibited by 'strong' verbs like *sing/sang/sung* and *write/wrote/written*. The term is most usually applied to such phenomena in the older Indo-European languages, in which it was grammatically central: Latin *tegō* 'cover' but *toga* 'toga', Greek *legō* 'read' but *logos* 'word', Latin *sedeō* 'sit' but *sodālis* 'companion'; but it is also sometimes applied to similar phenomena in other languages. Ablaut differs from **umlaut** only in its historical source: originally, 'ablaut' was applied to cases of vowel alternation for which no phonetic motivation could be identified. See also *e*-**grade**, *o*-**grade** and **zero grade**. 2. A historical change by which such an alternation comes about. Coates (1994) recommends restricting 'ablaut' to sense 2 and using 'apophony' for sense 1. He also suggests the term 'consonantal apophony' for those instances of Celtic **mutation** in which no overt trigger is present.

abrupt release /ə'brʌpt/ *n.* (also **instantaneous release**, **abrupt offset**) 1. The phenomenon in which a complete oral closure is released suddenly, without perceptible friction noise. Abrupt release is the property that distinguishes **plosives** from corresponding **affricates**. 2. (**abrrel**) See **instantaneous release**.

absolute bleeding /ˈæbsəluːt/ *n*. The relation between two ordered rules A and B in which the earlier rule A destroys all possible cases to which B could apply, leaving B without function. See **bleeding order**.

absolute feeding *n*. The relation between two ordered rules A and B in which the earlier rule A creates all the possible inputs to B. See **feeding order**.

absolute final position /pəˈzɪʃn̩/ *n*. The position of the last segment in an **utterance**, before a following pause; utterance-final position.

absolute initial position *n*. The position of the first segment in an **utterance**, after a preceding pause; utterance-initial position.

absolute neutralization *n*. An analysis which posits an underlying contrast which is never realized phonetically on the surface. Such analyses have most often been invoked to account for an observation that some single segment exhibits two distinct and conflicting types of behaviour. A famous example concerns Hungarian **vowel harmony**. In general, a Hungarian word consists entirely of back vowels or entirely of front vowels, but the front vowels /i/ and /e/ are anomalous, behaving (as expected) like front vowels in some words but like back vowels in others. The analysis of Vago (1973) accounts for this anomaly by positing the two additional back vowels /ɯ/ and /ɤ/, unattested on the surface, which participate normally in vowel harmony and then merge unconditionally (absolutely) with /i/ and /e/, respectively. Absolute neutralizations were an important if highly controversial feature of **classical generative phonology**, but were generally prohibited in **Natural Generative Phonology** and its successors by the **Alternation Condition**. Useful summaries of the issues can be found in Hyman (1975: 3.3.5), Sommerstein (1977: ch. 9) and Lass (1984: ch. 9); Lass (1984: 234) enumerates the most important papers. See also **abstract segment**. Kiparsky (1968b); an extension of **neutralization**.

absolute slicing hypothesis /ˈslaɪsɪŋ/ *n*. The claim that speech can be exhaustively divided into a linear sequence of segments. Accepted by most earlier theories of phonology (though not by **Prosodic Analysis**), this claim is generally denied by **non-linear** approaches. Goldsmith (1976).

absolute threshold of hearing /'θreʃhəʊld/ *n*. The intensity at which sound is just distinguishable from silence, commonly taken for reference as a value of 10^{-16} watts per square centimetre, arbitrarily but conveniently equated with a value of zero **decibels**.

absolute universal *n*. A **universal** which holds for every single natural language without exception, hence, a statement which partially defines the notion 'natural language'. Among the absolute universals often suggested in phonology are 'Every language has both consonants and vowels' and 'Every language has at least one high vowel'. Cf. **statistical universal**.

absorption /əb'sɔːpʃən/ *n*. The phonological phenomenon in which the end point of a **contour tone** is lost when immediately followed by another tone which is identical to the end point of the contour. For example, if **HL** represents a high-to-low contour tone and **L** a low tone, the sequence **HL L** might undergo absorption to yield **H L**. Such absorption is a common phenomenon in tone languages. Cf. **spreading**, and see the **Obligatory Contour Principle**. Hyman (1973); Hyman and Schuh (1974).

abstract /'æbstrækt/ *adj*. (of an analysis) Characterized by the use of an **underlying form** which is significantly different from the surface form. Except perhaps for the most extreme versions of **American Structuralism**, all theories of phonology permit some degree of abstractness, but abstract analyses flourished in a particularly unconstrained way within **classical generative phonology**. For example, *SPE* represents *reduction* underlyingly as re=duke+æːt+iVn and *courage* underlyingly as kᵈorægᵈe, with a long sequence of phonological rules applying in each case to derive the surface form. **Absolute neutralizations** represent another striking kind of abstract analysis. See Lightner (1975) for a defence of extreme abstractness. *Abstr. n.* **abstractness**.

abstract feature *n*. A proposed **distinctive feature** for a particular language which lacks any clear phonetic motivation but which serves to distinguish a class of segments which unexpectedly pattern together in that language. For example, in many dialects of Basque, the coronal consonants /t s ś ts tś n l/ all palatalize after a high front vowel, but the coronals /d r rr/ do not. There being no clear phonetic basis for the distinction, one might conceivably distinguish the two groups by means of an abstract feature, say, [+P] for the first group and [–P] for the second. Most analysts, however, regard such abstract features with distaste. See Clark and Yallop (1990: 314–315) for some discussion. See also **cover feature**.

abstract segment *n.* In an analysis employing **absolute neutralization**, a segment posited as underlyingly present which never shows up overtly on the surface. For example, some analyses of French set up an abstract word-initial segment /h/ which, like any consonant, blocks *liaison*; having done so, the segment then disappears (merges with zero), accounting for the failure of certain words which are vowel-initial on the surface to undergo liaison.

abstract sound *n.* A conception of varying nature invoked frequently in the development of phonetics and phonology in the early twentieth century, notably by Daniel Jones in his refinement of the **phoneme** concept. Trubetzkoy (1939) distinguishes abstract sounds of the first level (hypothetical phonetic targets for the slightly varying individual phones occurring in different tokens) and those of the second level (**allophones** of a phoneme).

abstract suffix *n.* An abstract element, conveniently if somewhat arbitrarily regarded as an affix, posited in some analyses to account for the derivation of such forms as *kiss* (noun) from *kiss* (verb), *belief* (noun) from *believe* (verb) and *record* (noun) from *record* (verb), or possibly the other way round. See also **zero morph**, **conversion**.

acatalectic /eɪkætə'lektɪk/ *adj.* (of a line of verse) Possessing the full number of syllables in the final foot. *Abstr. n.* **acatalexis**. Ant. **catalectic**.

accent /'æksənt/ *n.* 1. A particular way of pronouncing a language, seen as typical of an individual, a geographical region or a social group. Every speaker of a language necessarily speaks it with some accent or other. 2. [*non-technical*] A popular term for an accent in sense 1 which happens to be regarded as striking or unfamiliar by the person making the judgement. 3. (also **word accent**) Particular prominence attached to one syllable of a word or phrase by some phonetic means such as **stress** or **pitch**. 4. A particular system for assigning prominence to certain syllables of words or utterances, such as the **stress accent** of English or the **pitch accent** of Japanese. 5. An occasional synonym for **sentence stress**. Bolinger (1951). 6. See **lexical accent**. 7. [*non-technical*] A loose term for a **diacritic**, often especially for a diacritic written above a letter, such as the **acute accent**. *Adj.* **accentual** /ək'sentʃuəl/.

accent I *n.* The unmarked **tone** pattern of Swedish and Norwegian, characterized by a single fall in pitch and conventionally marked by the symbol ´, as in Swedish ´*anden* 'the duck'. Cf. **accent II**.

accent II *n.* The marked **tone** pattern of Swedish and Norwegian, characterized by a fall–rise–fall in pitch and confined to certain words with initial stress, conventionally marked by the symbol `, as in Swedish `*anden* 'the spirit'. Cf. **accent I**.

accent d'insistance /aksã dẽsistãs/ *n.* [French: 'tone of insistence'] A particular, highly marked **intonation** pattern in French, characterized by high pitch and exaggerated length and loudness attached to a syllable which would not normally carry a stress, and expressing some kind of emphasis.

accented *adj.* (of a particular syllable, mora or nucleus) Assigned particular prominence by the presence of a stress or pitch **accent** (sense 3).

accent range /reɪndʒ/ *n.* That proportion of an individual's total **pitch range** within which the **intonation** pattern of a particular **nuclear tone** is enclosed. Variation in the most usual accent range (in particular, raising the upper boundary) is typical of many **marked** intonation patterns. Cruttenden (1986).

accidental gap /æksɪdentəl 'gæp/ *n.* A possible word which is phonologically well formed in every respect but which happens not to exist, such as /blɪk/ in English. Cf. **systematic gap**. Swadesh (1935).

accommodation /əkɒmə'deɪʃn̩/ *n.* 1. (also **coarticulation**) Modification in the articulation of a segment for the purpose of easing a transition to a following segment, as when English /k/ is fronted before a front vowel or glide (*key, back yard*), or when /t/ shifts from alveolar to dental before a dental fricative (*eighth*). Cf. **spreading**. See also **allophone**. 2. The behaviour of a speaker who (consciously or unconsciously) adjusts her/his speech towards (or less usually away from) the speech of an interlocutor or of a surrounding social group. See also **adaptation**.

acephalous /eɪ'sefələs/ *adj.* (of a line of verse) Lacking the first syllable expected according to the regular metre. *Abstr. n.* **acephalexis** /eɪsefə'leksɪs/. Greek: 'headless'.

ach-**Laut** /'axlaʊt/ *n.* The voiceless back fricative occurring in German after back and low vowels, as in *ach* 'alas', *Buch* 'book', *lachen* 'laugh' and *acht* 'eight'. Textbooks usually describe this as a velar [x], but many speakers use a uvular [χ]. The *ach*-Laut is in complementary distribution with the *ich*-**Laut** if and only if morpheme boundaries are taken into account.

achromatic /eɪkrəʊ'mætɪk/ *adj*. In the analysis of vowels in some **privative** systems, notably **Dependency Phonology**, lacking the cardinal properties of **palatality** and **labiality**; high in **sonority**, such as the vowel [a]. Ant. **chromatic**.

acoustic /ə'kuːstɪk/ *adj*. 1. Pertaining to **acoustics**. 2. Pertaining to sounds, especially speech sounds.

acoustic analysis *n*. The determination, for a **complex sound**, of its component **frequencies** and their **amplitudes** (**intensities**). The result of the analysis is conveniently displayed in an **acoustic spectrum**. For a sound which varies with time, the time dimension may also be displayed; this is the kind of display produced by a **sound spectrograph**.

acoustic assimilation *n*. A type of **assimilation** in which acoustic characteristics are assimilated, rather than (as more usually) articulatory ones. Lass (1984: 176) cites the example of certain varieties of Austrian German in which front vowels are rounded before a velarized lateral. There is no articulatory basis for this, but there is an acoustic one: both velarization and lip-rounding produce 'low tonality' – specifically, lowering of the second and third formants – and it is these formants that are being assimilated.

acoustic correlate /'kɒrəleɪt/ *n*. (of an articulation) An observable acoustic characteristic which is typical of, and to some extent diagnostic for, that articulation, particularly as evidenced in a **sound spectrogram**. For example, Ladefoged (1975: 180) cites the following (approximate) correlates: a **velar** articulation shows a high locus for the second formant and a common origin for the second and third formant transitions, while a **nasal** consonant shows a formant structure similar to that of a vowel but with nasal formants at about 250, 2,500 and 3,250 Hz.

acoustic cue /kjuː/ *n*. Any acoustic characteristic of a segment which aids in the recognition of that segment in speech. Such a cue is essentially the perceptual effect of an **acoustic correlate**.

acoustic energy /'enədʒi/ *n*. The energy transmitted by a sound wave, in phonetics usually by a speech wave. The energy of a speech wave is very small by most standards; according to Denes and

Pinson (1993: 140), speaking normally for one second produces only 200 ergs of sound energy, while keeping a 100-watt bulb lit for one second requires a billion ergs. Only about 0.05 per cent of the energy carried by the airstream flowing out of our lungs is converted to sound energy in speech, but the human ear is so sensitive that this is quite adequate.

acoustic feature *n*. A **distinctive feature** which is related primarily to an acoustic characteristic of a segment, rather than to an articulatory characteristic. The earliest work in distinctive features by Jakobson and his colleagues, such as Jakobson *et al*. (1952) and Jakobson and Halle (1956), emphasized acoustic features like **compact**, **grave**, **flat**, **voiced** and **strident**. With the publication of *SPE* in 1968, acoustic features mostly gave way to the **articulatory features** of that work, though **strident** and **grave**, and perhaps also **flat**, have continued to find some use. See **Jakobson–Halle feature system**.

acoustic filter *n*. Any device which allows certain frequencies of sound waves to pass through while suppressing the passage of other frequencies. Most familiarly, the resonating cavities of the vocal tract act as acoustic filters; varying the configuration of these cavities changes the frequencies which are preferentially passed, and hence the quality of the resulting sound.

acoustic impedance /ɪmˈpiːdəns/ *n*. A measure of the total tendency of a medium to oppose the passage of sound waves through it. If one tries to pass a sound wave from one medium to another of very different impedance, most of the sound energy will simply be reflected at the boundary. For example, little sound could be passed from the air-filled middle ear across the **oval window** to the fluid-filled inner ear if the **eardrum** and **auditory ossicles** were not present to reduce the impedance mismatch.

acoustic invariance /ɪnˈværɪəns/ *n*. A theory of speech which holds that invariant acoustic patterns or properties corresponding to phonetic features are directly derivable from the speech signal – invariant, that is, with respect to individual variations in the size and shape of the vocal tract, to the rate of speaking and to variations in the immediate phonetic environment. See Stevens and Blumstein (1981) and Blumstein and Stevens (1981) for presentation of the evidence and Lieberman and Blumstein (1988) for a brief summary.

acoustic nerve /nɜːv/ *n.* See **auditory nerve**.

acoustic phase *n.* The fifth of the seven **phases of speech**, in which sound waves produced by vibrating air in the speaker's vocal tract travel through the air to reach a hearer's ear.

acoustic phonetics *n.* The branch of **phonetics** which deals with the physical characteristics of the sound waves which carry speech sounds between mouth and ear. Acoustic phonetics makes heavy use of a battery of electronic instruments, perhaps most notably the **sound spectrograph**; these days it also makes considerable use of computers for analysis and modelling. See Fry (1979), Ladefoged (1962), Lieberman and Blumstein (1988), Borden and Harris (1980), Pickett (1980) or Kent and Read (1992) for an introduction.

acoustics *n.* The scientific study of sound and sound waves. *Adj.* **acoustic**, rarely **acoustical**.

acoustic spectrum *n.* A graphical representation of a (typically complex) sound in which **amplitude** is plotted against **frequency**. The resulting graph shows the relative contribution to the overall sound made by every component frequency. The two graphs in Figure A1, from Fry (1979), illustrate the spectrum of a clarinet note (middle C) and that of the vowel [iː].

acoustic stability /stə'bɪlɪti/ *n.* The property of a speech sound whose acoustic and perceptual characteristics are little affected by small variations in the articulation used to produce it. For example, the vowels [i] and [u] are far more acoustically stable than [e] or even [a]. In tests, acoustically stable segments are recognized far more consistently than others. See also **quantal vowel**.

acoustic wave *n.* See **sound wave**.

acquisition of phonology /ækwɪ'zɪʃn̩/ *n.* The process by which a child learning a first language gradually acquires adult control over the phonological system of the language, usually passing through a series of characterizable stages on the way. See Yeni-Komshian *et al.* (1980) for a comprehensive review, Smith (1973) for a famous case study, Locke (1983) for the relation between acquisition and phonological change and Ingram (1989) for a review of disability in acquisition.

across-the-board /əkrɒs ðə 'bɔːd/ *adj.* Exceptionless; applying in all circumstances throughout an entire language.

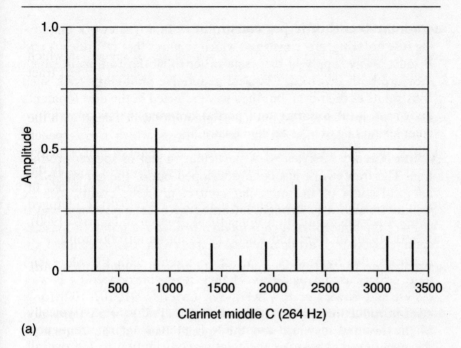

(a)

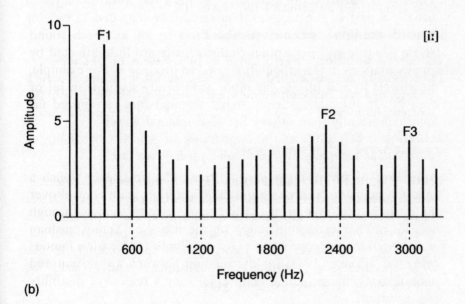

(b)

Figure A1 The acoustic spectra of a clarinet note (a)
and of the vowel [iː] (b)

across-the-board ordering constraint *n.* In a framework employing **rule ordering**, any **constraint** which requires that two rules A and B must always apply in the same order in all derivations in which they are both involved. **Classical generative phonology** took such constraints as the norm, but they were rejected in the developments known as **local ordering** and **partial ordering** in favour of more complex and flexible ordering constraints.

Action Theory /'ækʃən/ *n.* A particular model of speech production. The framework has been developed out of the general physiological study of the muscular control of cyclic events such as walking; hence it is strongly informed by neurophysiology, and it stresses the concept of a *coordinative structure*, a group of muscles acting together. Particularly associated with the Haskins Laboratories, the framework contrasts markedly with the older and more widely used **Translation Theory**; it was introduced by Fowler (1980) and Fowler *et al.* (1980). See Laver (1991: 107–109) for a brief introduction, Laver (1989) or Nolan (1982) for a comparison of the two frameworks, and the special issue of the *Journal of Phonetics* (14:1, 1986) for a debate.

active articulator /'æktɪv/ *n.* In the articulation of a consonant, the lower of the articulators involved in forming the constriction (most usually a part of the tongue), conventionally regarded as moving towards the upper **passive articulator**.

actualized notation /'æktʃuəlaɪzd/ *n.* In **Glossematic phonology**, a phonetically underspecified representation for a segment which undergoes a systematic **alternation**, corresponding fairly closely to the **morphophoneme** of the American Structuralists. Cf. **ideal notation**.

actuation /æktʃu'eɪʃn̩/ *n.* The appearance of a particular change in a particular language at a particular time. *V.* **actuate**.

acute /ə'kjuːt/ *adj.* In the **Jakobson–Halle feature system**, a **distinctive feature** defined as 'exhibiting a concentration of energy in the upper frequencies of the spectrum', interpreted as representing a non-peripheral (dental, alveolar, palato-alveolar, palatal) articulation. The specification [acute] corresponds approximately to the *SPE* specifications [+coronal] for consonants and [–back] for vowels. *Abstr. n.* **acuteness**. Ant. **grave**.

acute accent *n.* The diacritic ´, conventionally used in various orthographies and transcription systems for a variety of purposes. It was first used in Ancient Greek orthography to mark one of the distinctive pitch accents of that language. In French, ⟨é⟩ represents a different vowel quality from plain ⟨e⟩, and in Polish ⟨ś⟩ represents a different sibilant from ⟨s⟩. In Spanish, the acute accent represents an irregular word stress. In the IPA, the acute accent is used to mark a high level tone. Cf. **grave accent**, **circumflex accent**. Latin *acutus* 'sharpened', an impressionistic label for the perceptual effect of the Greek pitch accent it denoted.

Adam's apple /'ædəmz æpəl/ *n.* The visible projection of the **thyroid cartilage** of the **larynx** at the front of the throat, usually far more prominent in men than in women. Translation of Hebrew *tappūah hāādām*.

adaptation /ædæp'teɪʃn̩/ *n.* The process by which a speaker consciously adjusts her/his speech towards a different variety perceived as more desirable, as when a speaker of a regional accent attempts to produce something approximating to **Received Pronunciation**, or when a **non-rhotic** American speaker attempts to acquire a **rhotic accent**. See also **hypercorrection** (both senses) and **accommodation** (sense 2). *Adj.* **adaptive** /ə'dæptɪv/.

adaptation rule *n.* A systematic modification, expressible in the form of a **phonological rule**, consciously introduced by a speaker attempting **adaptation**. For example, a Briton trying to acquire an American accent might add a rule deleting the glide /j/ after a coronal consonant and before /uː/, generally producing the correct result. An American trying to acquire a British accent, however, would face problems: adding the opposite rule, inserting the glide in this environment, would produce the correct result with some words, like *dew*, but the wrong result with others, like *do*.

ADC /eɪ diː 'siː/ *n.* See **analog-to-digital converter**.

addition of rules *n.* See **rule addition**.

additive interference /'ædɪtɪv/ *n.* [*rare*] See **feeding order**. Chafe (1967).

adduction /æ'dʌkʃn̩/ *n.* The moving together of the **vocal folds**. *V.* **adduct**. Ant. **abduction**.

adenoidal /ædə'nɔɪdəl/ *adj.* [*non-technical*] A label frequently applied to a **voice quality** distinguished by an unusually low degree of **nasalization**, resulting either from obstruction of the nasal cavity (as by mucus or swollen tissue in a person with a head cold) or from the speaker's propensity to hold the velum in a consistently high position, thus reducing air flow through the nasal cavity (as in the speech of Liverpool).

adequacy, levels of /'ædɪkwəsi/ *n. pl.* Any of various sets of criteria for evaluating formal grammars, some of which can be plausibly invoked for judging phonological descriptions. The best-known criteria are those of Chomsky (1964): a description achieves *observational adequacy* if it correctly predicts all the data; it achieves *descriptive adequacy* if it also expresses all *linguistically significant generalizations*. A theoretical framework achieves *explanatory adequacy* if it also provides a principled basis for choosing among competing descriptions which achieve descriptive adequacy. Chomsky (1957) proposes a different characterization: a description is *internally adequate* if it correctly accounts for the data; it is *externally adequate* if it also exhibits generality, economy and simplicity. See **criteria for phonological analysis**.

Adjacency Principle /ə'dʒeɪsənsi/ *n.* (also **locality**) In **Government and Charm Phonology**, a fundamental principle: a governor (head) must be linearly adjacent to its governees (dependents).

adjunction /ə'dʒʌŋkʃən/ *n.* 1. In **Dependency Phonology**, the relation between two adjacent elements one of which linearly precedes the other within the overall structure. Cf. **subjunction**. 2. In some frameworks, a procedure invoked in order to augment a syllable, often in violation of the **Sonority Sequencing Principle**, for example to account for both occurrences of /s/ in English *spits*. *V.* **adjoin** /ə'dʒɔɪn/. Levin (1985).

admissible /əd'mɪsəbəl/ *adj.* Permitted by the ordinary phonological rules of a language. Thus, for example, an admissible consonant cluster is one not violating any constraints imposed by the **phonotactics** of a language. Some (not all) analysts consider that certain phenomena which actually occur may nevertheless not be admissible, so that, for example, since English does not normally permit word-initial clusters of fricatives, the cluster /sf-/ occurring in *sphere* and *sphinx* would not be regarded as admissible. *Abstr. n.* **admissibility**. Ant. **inadmissible**.

adoptive RP /ə'dɒptɪv/ *n.* In the classification of Wells (1982), a version of **Received Pronunciation** used by adults who did not speak RP as children. Adoptive RP may blend almost imperceptibly into **mainstream RP**, but is often distinguished by a lack of command over informal and allegro characteristics typical of native RP speakers.

adstrate /'ædstreɪt/ *n*. With respect to a particular language, a second language of comparable prestige which is spoken side by side with it in a largely bilingual community and which has some effect upon it. It is sometimes suggested that the English of South Africa, for example, is influenced phonologically and otherwise by Afrikaans. Cf. **substrate**, **superstrate**.

advanced /əd'vɑːnst/ *adj*. 1. (of an articulation) Articulated with the tongue position closer to the front of the mouth (than some reference position). In the IPA, an advanced articulation is transcribed with the diacritic [₊]. 2. In the study of phonological change, denoting a pronunciation which appears to be innovating with respect to a competing but more conservative pronunciation, often especially when the competing forms in question appear to be part of a process of **drift**. Ant. **conservative**.

advanced RP *n*. In the classification of Gimson (1989), a variety of **Received Pronunciation** exhibiting some innovations with respect to **conservative** and **general** varieties of RP and often associated particularly with younger upper-class speakers. The precise characterization of advanced RP is a matter of controversy.

advanced tongue root *n*. See **ATR**.

aerodynamic myoelastic theory of phonation /ɛərədaɪ'næmɪk/ *n*. The universally accepted explanation of **phonation**. In this view, air passing up through the glottis forces the vocal cords apart, allowing the air to pass between them; the resulting pressure drop caused by the **Bernoulli effect** forces the vocal cords to close again. The rapid repetition of this sequence constitutes **voicing**. See van den Berg (1958, 1968). Cf. **neuro-chronaxic theory of phonation**.

aerodynamic phase *n*. The fourth of the seven **phases of speech**, in which the air in the vocal tract is set into motion by the movements of the vocal organs.

aerometry /ɛə'rɒmɪtri/ *n*. See **electroaerometry**.

affection /ə'fekʃən/ *n*. A term applied in historical philology, particularly in respect of Celtic languages, to any of various historical developments in which the quality of a vowel is partly assimilated to ('affected' by) the quality of a vowel in a following syllable. Welsh, for example, historically exhibits both *i*-affection (raising before /i/) and *a*-affection (lowering before /a/); the conditioning vowel often disappeared later. Examples: *bardī > *beirdd* 'bards'; Latin *pāpilio* > *pebyll* 'tent'; **butā* > *bod* 'be'; Latin *grammatica* > *gramadeg*. The term **umlaut**, used in the Germanic languages, means the same as 'affection'.

affective form /ə'fektɪv/ *n.* A linguistic form which has undergone some kind of deliberate phonological modification (very often **palatalization**) for the purpose of expressing some particular attitude on the part of the speakers, most commonly one of warmth or affection. For example, Basque *zoko* 'corner' has an affective form *xoko* or *txoko*, roughly, 'familiar place' or 'little place of my own', and *zuri* 'white' exhibits an affective form *txuri* in *Txuri-Urdiñak* 'the White-and-Blues', nickname of the football team Real Sociedad.

affix /'æfɪks/ *n.* A **bound morpheme** which can only occur attached to a word or stem. Affixes may be **derivational**, like *-ness* and *pre-*, or **inflectional**, like plural *-s* and past-tense *-ed*. Affixes are divided into **prefixes, suffixes, circumfixes, infixes, superfixes** and **transfixes**; see also **parafix, interfix**. *Adj.* **affixal**.

Affix Rule *n.* The putative rule which accounts for the stress shift induced by the addition of certain English affixes, as illustrated by *dialect/dialectal, anecdote/anecdotal* and *theatre/theatrical*. Chomsky and Halle (1968).

affricate /'æfrɪkət/ *n.* (rarely also **affricative** /ə'frɪkətɪv/, **affricated stop**) A consonant whose articulation involves a complete oral closure followed by a comparatively slow release with perceptible friction noise. English examples include the [tʃ] of *church* and the [dʒ] of *judge*. An affricate is most often regarded as a single segment (though see Roca 1994: 4 on the English affricates), but it can usefully be thought of as a plosive immediately followed by a homorganic fricative, and the IPA symbols for affricates take advantage of this fact. *Adj.* **affricated** /'æfrɪkeɪtɪd/; *abstr. n.* **affrication**. Latin *affricatus* 'rubbed against'.

affrication /æfrɪ'keɪʃn̩/ *n.* 1. The **fricative** release of a stop; the property of an **affricate** which distinguishes it from a **plosive**. 2. A phonological process in which a plosive acquires a fricative release, as in the realization of /t/ as an affricate [tˢ] in the speech of London. See Laver (1994: 363–374).

age-grading /'eɪdʒgreɪdɪŋ/ *n.* The phenomenon in which a speech variable operating at a high level of social awareness is modified throughout a speaker's lifetime, so that the variable shows a clear correlation with age even in the absence of **generational change**. Labov (1994).

airstream /'ɛəstriːm/ *n*. In speech, the movement of air through the **vocal tract**, or through some part of it. An airstream is essential for the production of any speech sound. See **airstream mechanism**.

airstream mechanism /'mekənɪzm̩/ *n*. (also **initiation**) Any of the various ways in which a stream of moving air can be produced within the vocal tract. The three principal mechanisms are **pulmonic** (involving lung air), **glottalic** (involving pharynx air) and **velaric** (involving mouth air). Each of these may produce an **egressive** (moving outward) or an **ingressive** (moving inward) airstream, resulting in six possible airstreams. Of these, the pulmonic egressive mechanism is by far the most widespread, but the glottalic egressive and glottalic ingressive mechanisms are also well attested, and the velaric ingressive mechanism occurs in some languages. There is also the highly unusual **oesophagic egressive** airstream mechanism.

Aitken's Law /'eɪtkən/ *n*. A general rule governing the distribution of the phonetic length of certain vowels in Scottish accents of English. It says: a vowel is phonetically short unless it is followed by a morpheme boundary, a voiced fricative or /r/, in which case it is long. See McMahon (1991). Aitken (1962); Lass (1974).

Aitken's vowel *n*. The vowel /ë/, occurring in many Scottish varieties of English, in which it contrasts with both /ɪ/ and /ɛ/. Lexical incidence of this vowel varies enormously, but many speakers have it in *never*, which rhymes with neither *river* nor *sever*. Aitken (1962); Lass (1974) or Abercrombie (1975).

aliasing /'eɪliəsɪŋ/ *n*. A phenomenon which can occur during the **digital processing** of acoustic signals. If the *sampling* frequency is too low, the high-frequency components of the signal will be misinterpreted, producing spurious frequencies which distort the quality of the sound after reconversion to analog form; this is aliasing. See Denes and Pinson (1993).

allegro /ə'legrəʊ/ *adj*. (of speech) Rapid and fluent, and hence exhibiting the phonological processes typical of connected speech. Ant. **lento**. From the musical term *allegro* 'rapid', from Italian *allegro* 'lively'.

allegro form *n*. A reduced form which is typical of rapid or casual speech, such as *'Sright* ('That's right'), *'Cha doin'?* ('What are you doing?').

alliteration /əlɪtə'reɪʃn̩/ *n*. The repeated use of the same initial consonant sound in a string of words in a connected text: *The burghers of Brighton briskly bundled the belligerent boatmen back* *to Brest.* Cf. **consonance**, and see **assonance**. *V.* **alliterate**; *adj.* **alliterative** /ə'lɪtərətɪv/.

allochrone /'ælǝkrǝʊn/ *n.* Any positional variant of a **chroneme**. Jones (1950).

allomorph /'ælǝmɔːf/ *n.* (also **alternant**) One of two or more surface forms which are assumed by a single **morpheme** in varying circumstances. The negative prefix *in-*, for example, exhibits several allomorphs in such words as *indecent, impossible, irrational* and *ignoble. Abstr. n.* **allomorphy** /'ælǝmɔːfi/; *adj.* **allomorphic** /ælǝ'mɔːfɪk/. Nida (1948): Greek *allos* 'other' + *morphē* 'form'.

allophone /'ælǝfǝʊn/ *n.* 1. One of two or more phonetically distinct segments which can realize a single **phoneme** in varying circumstances. For example, the English phoneme /t/ may be realized phonetically as aspirated [tʰ] in *tin*, as unaspirated [t˭] in *stand*, as dental [t] in *eighth*, as nasally released [tⁿ] in *cotton*, as laterally released [tˡ] in *bottle*, as glottalized [ʔt] in *hit*, and possibly in other ways, depending upon the particular accent. The set of realizations used by a speaker constitute the allophones of the phoneme /t/ in that speaker's speech. For two phones to be classed as allophones of a single phoneme, they must exhibit **phonetic similarity**, and they must not be in **contrastive distribution**. See further under **phoneme**. Note: This is the prevailing sense of the term; the following senses, however, are also well attested in the literature. 2. An allophone which is a positional (conditioned) variant of a phoneme, as opposed to a free variant. 3. An allophone which is conspicuously different from other allophones of the same phoneme; this is the sense intended when a particular phoneme is said to have, say, 'three allophones'. 4. [*obsolete*] See **phone**. *Abstr. n.* **allophony** /ə'lɒfəni/; *adj.* **allophonic** /ælə'fɒnɪk/. Whorf (1938).

allophonic transcription *n.* A **phonetic transcription** which includes no information beyond the marking of the major **allophones** of phonemes.

allophonic variation *n.* The phonetic variation exhibited by a single **phoneme** in varying phonological environments; see the example under **allophone**.

all-or-none contrast /ɔːlə'nʌn/ *n.* In the study of **intonation**, a binary contrast imposed by the analyst upon a corpus of data, such as in the common classification of all falling patterns in English into **high falls** and **low falls**. Cf. **gradient**.

allotone /'ælətəʊn/ *n.* Any positional variant of a **toneme**. Jones (1950).

alpha /'ælfə/ *n.* 1. See under **alpha notation**. 2. In some **privative** theories, a phonological **component** |α| posited as equivalent to the specification [+ATR], the specification [–ATR] being represented by a separate component R. Anderson and Ewen (1987).

alpha notation *n.* An **abbreviatory convention** which allows the conflation of two rules which differ only in the values assigned to binary features at two (or sometimes more than two) points. The notation uses a Greek letter (a **feature coefficient**) as a variable ranging over the values + and –; the variable must of course assume a single value on any one reading of the resulting **rule schema**. For example, the **soft mutation** of Welsh may be broadly described by the following two rules:

[–cont, –nas, –voi] → [+voi, –cont]

(a voiceless plosive becomes voiced), and

[–cont, –nas, +voi] → [+voi, +cont]

(a voiced plosive becomes a fricative). These may be conflated by means of the alpha notation:

[–cont, –nas, α voi] → [+voi, α cont]

Similarly, the following schema states that a word-final nasal is syllabic if it follows a non-syllabic segment but non-syllabic otherwise:

[+nas] → [α syll] / [–α syll] ___ #

When additional such variables are required, succeeding letters of the Greek alphabet are used. The following schema states that a nasal segment assimilates completely in place of articulation to a following segment:

$$[\text{+nas}] \rightarrow \begin{bmatrix} \alpha \text{ ant} \\ \beta \text{ cor} \\ \gamma \text{ high} \\ \delta \text{ back} \end{bmatrix} / \_\_\_ \begin{bmatrix} \alpha \text{ ant} \\ \beta \text{ cor} \\ \gamma \text{ high} \\ \delta \text{ back} \end{bmatrix}$$

Zwicky (1970) suggests an extension of the alpha notation to cases like α[–cons, +voc] to represent the **disjunction** of [–cons, +voc] and [+cons, –voc], but this extension has not been generally accepted.

Another rarely encountered extension of the alpha notation is illustrated in the following rule posited for Zulu: [–son, α cont, β hsp] $\rightarrow$ [–cont, $\alpha\beta$ hsp, α delrel]. Here the notation '$\alpha\beta$' means 'the algebraic product of the values of α and β'.

Labov (1994) extends the alpha notation to describe sound changes in progress: in his system, a statement of the general form [z feature] $\rightarrow$ [$z+\alpha x$ feature] means that the existing value z of some feature is incremented or decremented by an amount x, depending on whether a has the value +1 or –1. Halle (1962).

alpha-switching rule /ˈswɪt͡ʃɪŋ/ *n*. See **exchange rule**.

alternant /ˈɔːltənənt/ *n*. 1. See **allomorph**. 2. One of two or more segments which participate in some **alternation** (sense 1). For example, English /e/ and /æ/ are alternants in such pairs as *sane/sanity*, *state/static*, *grave/gravity*, *profane/profanity* and *deprave/depravity*. Bloomfield (1933).

Alternating Stress Rule /ˈɔːltəneɪtɪŋ/ *n*. The putative rule which accounts for the stress pattern in the majority of English nouns of three or more syllables; these usually have **primary stress** on the **antepenult** and **secondary stress** on the **ultima**: *pedigree*, *baritone*, *antelope*, *hypotenuse* and *formaldehyde*. Certain words are exceptions: *Tennessee*, *kangaroo*, *chandelier*. Cf. **Main Stress Rule**. Chomsky and Halle (1968).

alternation /ɔːltəˈneɪʃn̩/ *n*. 1. A synonym for **allomorphy**, but one often preferred for instances in which the variation is systematic in nature, such as the [s]/[z]/[ɪz] alternation in the English plural morpheme (*cats/dogs/boxes*), or in which it is confined to a single segment, as in the [k]/[s] alternation observed in *electric/electricity* or the [aɪ]/[ɪ] alternation in *divine/divinity*. Bloomfield (1933: 207ff.) classifies alternations as *phonetic* or *suppletive*, as *automatic* or *grammatical*, and as *regular* or *irregular*; to these Hockett (1958: 277ff.) adds a contrast between **internal** and **external sandhi**. 2. The phenomenon in which a single word or morpheme exhibits **free variation** in a particular position between two segments which normally **contrast**. For example, *economics* can be pronounced with either /iː/ or /e/ in the initial syllable. See also **asymmetric alternation**. *V.* **alternate**.

Alternation Condition *n*. The principle that obligatory neutralization rules may not apply to all occurrences of a morpheme – In other words, it prohibits such analyses as underlying /piːn/ for the non-alternating *pine*, while allowing underlying /iː/ for the alternating *divine ~ divinity*. This principle is designed to constrain abstract analyses and specifically to prohibit the **diacritic use of phonological features**. It was succeeded by the **Revised Alternation Condition**. Kiparsky (1968b, 1973b).

alveolar /ælvi'əʊlə/ 1. *adj.* Pertaining to the **alveolar ridge**. 2. *adj.* (formerly also **gingival**) (of an articulation) Involving the alveolar ridge as the upper articulator. In this usage, often short for one of the more specific terms **apico-alveolar** and **lamino-alveolar**. 3. *n.* A consonant articulated in this way, such as [s], [d] or [n]. 4. In the **Ladefoged** and **Williamson feature systems**, one of the eleven possible values of the feature **articulatory place**. Ultimately from Latin *alveolus* 'small cavity', referring to the tooth sockets.

alveolar ridge /rɪdʒ/ *n.* (also **alveoli**, **alveoles** /ælvi'əʊliːz/, **alveolar arch**) The bony ridge behind the upper teeth, important in the articulation of **alveolar** consonants.

alveoli /ælvi'əʊlaɪ/ *n. pl.* 1. The tiny air sacs which make up most of the spongy tissue in the lungs. 2. See **alveolar ridge**. Latin *alveoli* 'small cavities'.

alveolo-palatal /ælviəʊləʊ'pælətəl/ 1. *adj.* (of a segment) Articulated in a position which is further back than **palato-alveolar** but further forward than **palatal**. An alveolo-palatal articulation might more systematically be called a lamino- or dorso-prepalatal articulation, as recommended by Catford (1988). The term is little used except in connection with the fricatives [ç] and [ʑ], when these need to be distinguished from the palato-alveolar fricatives [ʃ] and [ʒ], as in Polish. 2. *n.* A segment so articulated. 3. *n.* or *adj.* [*rare*] (of a segment) Articulated in a position which is further back than **alveolar** but further forward than **palato-alveolar**. 4. *n.* or *adj.* [*obsolete*] A former synonym for **palato-alveolar**. NOTE: The last two senses should be avoided.

alveopalatal /ælviəʊ'pælətəl/ *n.* or *adj.* 1. [*rare*] A cover term including both **palato-alveolar** and **alveolo-palatal**. 2. See **palato-alveolar**. NOTE: This second use, while not rare, is objectionable.

ambidependency /'æmbɪdɪpendənsi/ *n.* In **Dependency Phonology**, the structural relation in which a single vertex terminates more than one dependency arc – in other words, in which a single element occupies more than one position in the dependency structure.

ambisyllabic /æmbɪsɪˈlæbɪk/ *adj.* (of a consonant) Simultaneously forming part of two consecutive syllables, such as the /k/ of *ticker* or the /t/ of *petrol*. In *petrol*, for example, the presence of /t/ in the first syllable is shown by the occurrence in that syllable of the **checked vowel** /e/ (and in some accents by the **glottalization** of the /t/), while its presence in the second syllable is shown by **devoicing** of the /r/. The existence of ambisyllabic consonants poses problems for some theories of syllable structure, but it has been addressed with some success within **Metrical Phonology**. *Abstr. n.* **ambisyllabicity** /æmbɪsɪləˈbɪsɪti/.

American Structuralism /əˈmerɪkən/ *n.* A distinctive version of **structuralism** developed in the United States in the 1940s and 1950s, strongly influenced by the work of Leonard Bloomfield, though it is clear that Bloomfield would not have approved of some of its more extreme characteristics. The American Structuralists (or 'post-Bloomfieldians') were often fieldworkers struggling to describe and record the dying languages of North America; they attached great importance to developing efficient and reliable techniques for analysing, describing and transcribing unfamiliar languages. Partly as a consequence, they were sometimes perceived by European linguists as hostile to theory, while they themselves occasionally sneered at the Europeans as 'armchair theorists'. The Americans championed the **(autonomous) phoneme** as the fundamental unit in phonology, and often preferred the term **phonemics** to **phonology**. They eventually developed a view of phonology distinguished by a remarkable battery of doctrines, including the **separation of levels** and the conditions of **biuniqueness**, **invariance**, **linearity** and **local determinacy**. Motivated by a particular view of what constituted a scientific approach to language, these doctrines frequently compelled analyses which were inelegant and counter-intuitive; the introduction of **juncture phonemes** and **morphophonemes** provided only partial relief. But perhaps the single characteristic most objected to by a later generation of phonologists was the structuralist emphasis upon **representations** at the expense of **rules** (generalizations); beginning with Halle (1959), which presented the celebrated **Halle's argument** against structuralist doctrines, this priority was reversed, and within a few years **generative phonology** had supplanted American structuralist phonology as the mainstream in the United States. See Anderson (1985: chs 10–11) or Fischer-Jørgensen (1975: ch. 6) for an account of American Structuralist phonology, Makkai (1972) for a collection of classic papers, Stark (1972) or Huddleston (1972) for a more general account of American Structuralism, and Newmeyer (1986) for an account of the confrontation between structuralism and generative linguistics. See also **criteria for phonological analysis**.

American transcription *n*. An important **phonetic alphabet** (sense 1) developed in the United States in the first half of the twentieth century, the only significant alternative to the **International Phonetic Alphabet**. Designed by and for fieldworkers using type-writers, the American system differs from the IPA in a number of respects, but primarily in its avoidance of specially designed char-acters; it prefers to use ordinary Roman letters with diacritics instead. For example, the American system uses [š ž č ǰ] for IPA [ʃ ʒ tʃ dʒ] and [ü ö] for IPA [y ø]. There is no 'official' version of the system, and hence there is some variation in use. The American system continues to be used in the United States, but it appears to be slowly giving way to the IPA. See Pullum and Ladusaw (1986) for a comparison of American and IPA usages, and Abercrombie (1985) for an account of the competition between the two systems.

amphibrach /'æmfɪbræk/ *n*. A metrical **foot** consisting of three sylla-bles in the order unstressed–stressed–unstressed, or, in **quantitative metre**, short–long–short, as in the word *consider* or the verse *Remember, remember the fifth of November*. Greek *amphibrakhys* 'short at both ends'.

amphimacer /æm'fɪməsə/ *n*. (also **cretic foot**) A metrical **foot** consisting of three syllables in the order stressed–unstressed–stressed, or, in **quantitative metre**, long–short–long, as in the name *John McGraw* or the phrase *jingle bells*. Greek *amphimakros* 'long at both ends'.

amplification /æmplɪfɪ'keɪʃn̩/ *n*. The process of increasing the **inten-sity** of a sound and hence its perceived loudness. In human hearing, amplification is performed chiefly by the **auditory ossicles** of the middle ear. Amplification is also performed electronically for a number of purposes. *V*. **amplify** /'æmplɪfaɪ/.

amplifier /'æmplɪfaɪə/ *n*. Any device, most familiarly an electronic one, which increases the **intensity** of a sound and hence its perceived loudness.

amplitude /'æmplɪtjuːd/ *n*. That characteristic of a **sound wave** most directly related to the **intensity** of the associated sound and hence, in a complex manner, to the perceived loudness. Amplitude may be expressed in terms of the displacement of the vibrating medium from its rest position or, for a sound wave in air, in terms of the pressure of the air.

anacrusis /ænə'kruːsɪs/ *n.* 1. One or more unstressed syllables at the beginning of a line of verse, before the reckoning of the normal metre begins. 2. One or more unstressed syllables at the beginning of an utterance; in English, such syllables are often pronounced very rapidly and strongly reduced. Sense 2: Cruttenden (1986). Greek *anakrousis* 'a pushing back'.

anacusis /ænə'kjuːsɪs/ *n.* Total **deafness**. Cf. **hearing loss**. Greek *an-* 'without' + *akousis* 'hearing'.

analogical extension /ænə'lɒdʒɪkəl ɪk'stenʃən/ *n.* A process in which a morphological pattern occurring in some words or forms is extended to others in which it was not historically present, as when earlier English *help/holp/holpen* was remodelled to *help/helped/helped* under the influence of the more frequent pattern illustrated by *love/loved/loved*. The development of *dive/dived* in American English into *dive/dove* by analogy with verbs like *drive/drove* illustrates analogical extension in the opposite direction.

analogical levelling *n.* A process by which a morphologically irregular paradigm resulting from regular phonological change undergoes **analogy** in such a way as to remove the irregularity. The following example shows the phonologically regular Old French reflexes of the present-tense forms of the Latin verb meaning 'love' and the morphologically regular modern French forms derived by levelling of the stem-vowel alternation:

	Latin	*Old French*	*Modern French*
1sg.	ámo	aim	aime
2sg.	ámas	aimes	aimes
3sg.	ámat	aimet	aime
1pl.	amámus	**amons**	**aimons**
2pl.	amátis	**amez**	**aimez**
3pl.	ámant	aiment	aiment

analog model /'ænəlɒg mɒdəl/ *n.* Any mechanical, electrical or computational device which models the behaviour of a system of interest (such as the vocal tract) by using easily manipulated and measured quantities which are related mathematically to one another in the same way as the quantities important in the system of interest. For example, the physical quantities force (**F**), mass (**m**) and velocity (**v**), which are important in the study of air movement through the vocal tract, are related by Newton's law of motion (where **dv/dt** is the rate of change of velocity with respect to time): **F = m (dv/dt)**. The electrical quantities voltage (**V**), inductance (**L**) and current (**i**) are related mathematically in the same way: **V = L (di/dt)**. Hence the behaviour of a suitably designed electrical circuit can provide valuable insights into the behaviour of moving air in the vocal tract, and is far easier to study. See Lieberman and Blumstein (1988) for a brief introduction to analog modelling in speech, Flanagan (1972) for a comprehensive account of electrical analog modelling. NOTE: The American spelling 'analog' is often preferred in Britain to the British spelling 'analogue' for the terms entered in this dictionary.

analogous environments /ə'næləgəs/ *n. pl.* Similar but not identical environments in which can occur two phonetically similar segments whose phonological relationship is at issue. In English, for example, it is very difficult to find **minimal pairs** for [ʃ] and [ʒ], but the occurrence of these sounds in such analogous environments as *pressure* and *pleasure* (a **near-minimal pair**) is usually taken as adequate evidence that they must be assigned to different phonemes, since assigning them to a single phoneme would result in an impossibly complex distribution. Pike (1947a).

analog signal *n.* A **waveform** which varies continuously, so that, as it passes from one value to another, it passes through all values in betweeen. An ordinary sound wave is an analog signal. Cf. **digital signal**.

analog-to-digital converter /kən'vɜːtə/ *n.* (**ADC**) An electronic device which converts an **analog signal** to a **digital signal**. It does this by sampling the analog signal at very frequent intervals. According to the *Sampling Theorem*, if the signal is sampled at a frequency not less than double the frequency of its highest-frequency component, no information is lost, and the original signal can be exactly reconstructed from the samples. ADCs are the basis of modern high-quality sound recording and reproduction.

analogy /ə'nælədʒi/ *n.* The process by which a form or pattern is altered so as to conform to another form or pattern existing in the language. Examples: Middle High German *wort* 'word', pl. *wort* has been remodelled in modern German to *Wort*, pl. *Wörter* on the analogy of nouns like *Lamm* 'lamb', pl. *Lämmer*, in which the alternation results from regular phonological developments in

German; the French numeral *quatre* 'four' has for some speakers acquired a final liaison consonant [z] by analogy with *deux* 'two' and *trois* 'three', in which the liaison consonant is historically regular; after the regular **rhotacism** of intervocalic /s/ had converted early Latin *honos* 'honour', genitive *honōsis* into the morphologically irregular *honos*, *honōris*, the first form was analogically altered to produce the classical forms *honor*, *honōris*. As can be seen, the operation of analogy often disrupts the effects of regular phonological change. See also **analogical extension**, **analogical levelling**. *Adj.* **analogical**.

analysis-by-synthesis /ə'næləsɪs baɪ 'sɪnθəsɪs/ *n.* An analytical procedure in which the receiver compares an incoming signal to one or more internally generated signals; when a match is found, the receiver has succeeded in analysing the incoming signal as equivalent to the known characteristics of the internally generated match. This approach underlies the **motor theory of speech perception**. Halle and Stevens (1959).

analysis–synthesis system *n.* See **vocoder**.

anapaest /'ænəpest/ *n.* (also **anapest**) A metrical **foot** consisting of two unstressed syllables followed by one stressed one, or, in **quantitative** verse, of two short syllables followed by one long. The form is illustrated by the phrase *to the back of beyond* and by Clement Moore's famous poem: *'Twas the night before Christmas, and all through the house . . . Adj.* **anapaestic**. Greek *anapaistos* 'reversed' (an anapaest is a reversed **dactyl**).

anaptyxis /ænəp'tɪksɪs/ *n.* (also **svarabhakti**) A variety of **epenthesis** in which a vowel is inserted between two consonants, as in the pronunciation of *film* as 'fillum', of *athlete* as 'athalete' and of *Henry* as 'Ennery'. The inserted vowel is called an **anaptyctic** vowel, a **parasite vowel** or a **svarabhakti** vowel. *Adj.* **anaptyctic** /ænəp'tɪktɪk/. Ant. **syncope**. Greek *anaptyxis* 'unfolding'.

anataxis /ænə'tæksɪs/ *n.* In **Stratificational phonology**, the phenomenon in which elements occurring in one order at a more abstract level of representation occur in the opposite order at a less abstract level, as when underlying Korean /alh/ + /ko/ is realized as /alkho/. Most other frameworks treat such cases as instances of **metathesis**. *Adj.* **anatactic** /ænə'tæktɪk/. Lamb (1966).

anemometer /ænɪ'mɒmɪtə/ *n.* A device for measuring the velocity of moving air, such as the **hot-wire anemometer** used in instrumental phonetics.

angle(d) brackets /'æŋgl̩(d) brækɪts/ *n. pl.* 1. An **abbreviatory convention** which allows the inclusion in a schema of two or more optional elements which must be either all present or all absent in any one reading. For example, consider a language in which all consonants become palatalized ([+high]) before a high front vowel, and coronal consonants additionally become palato-alveolar ([–ant]). This could be expressed as follows:

$$
\begin{bmatrix} -\text{syll} \\ \langle+\text{cor}\rangle \end{bmatrix} \rightarrow \begin{bmatrix} +\text{high} \\ \langle-\text{ant}\rangle \end{bmatrix} \bigg/ \underline{\quad} \begin{bmatrix} +\text{syll} \\ +\text{high} \\ -\text{back} \end{bmatrix}
$$

By **Proper Inclusion Precedence**, the full expansion, including the material in angle brackets, takes precedence over the expansion without the material in angle brackets, and the two expansions are **disjunctively ordered**. 2. A notational device for setting off **extraprosodic** material in phonological representations.

anglicization /æŋglɪsaɪ'zeɪʃn̩/ *n.* The process of modifying the pronunciation of a word or name from a foreign language so as to produce a version which is more or less compatible with the ordinary phonology of English, as when French *détente* /detãt/ and *déjà vu* /deʒa vy/ are rendered as /deɪtɑːnt/ and /deɪʒa v(j)uː/, or German *Kant* /kant/ is rendered as /kɑːnt/ or /kænt/. Cf. **naturalization**. *V.* **anglicize**.

angma /'æŋmə/ *n.* See **eng**.

anlaut /'anlaʊt/ *n.* The first segment in a word, or less commonly, in a syllable. Cf. **inlaut**, **auslaut**. German: 'on-sound'.

antepenult /æntɪpɪ'nʌlt/ *n.* In a word, the third syllable from the end. Cf. **penult**, **ultima**. *Adj.* **antepenultimate**. Latin *ante* 'before' + *paene* 'almost' + *ultima* 'last'.

anterior /æn'tɪəriə/ *adj.* 1.(**ant**) In the *SPE* feature system, a **distinctive feature** defined as 'produced with an obstruction located in front of the palato-alveolar region'. Thus, labial, dental and alveolar consonants are [+anterior], while palato-alveolars, palatals, velars, uvulars and glottals are [–anterior]. Vowels are assumed to be universally [–ant]. Though arguably derived from the **diffuse/compact** contrast of the **Jakobson–Halle feature system**, this is the most unsatisfactory and controversial of all the *SPE* features, since neither [+ant] nor [–ant] segments ever appear to behave as a natural class, and the definition appears to be little more than an *ad hoc* device for distinguishing alveolars from palato-alveolars. Ant. **non-anterior**. 2. (of a phonation type) Produced exclusively with the front (ligamental) part of the glottis, the back (arytenoidal) part being tightly closed. **Anterior voice** has a hard, sharp quality, and is also called **tense voice**, **sharp voice** or **ligamental voice**. **Anterior creak** and **anterior whisper** are also possible. See Catford (1977) for discussion. *Abstr. n.* **anteriority** /æntɪərɪˈɔːrɪti/. Ant. **posterior**.

anterodorsum /æntɪərəˈdɔːsəm/ *n.* Another name for the **front** of the tongue, preferred by Catford (1988). Cf. **posterodorsum**. *Adj.* **anterodorsal**.

anthropophonics /ænθrəpəˈfɒnɪks/ *n.* [*rare*] The study of the entire range of speech sounds which can be produced by the human vocal apparatus, independently of whether or how the sounds are used for any linguistic purpose in any language. Revived by Catford (1977), this term is nowadays usually avoided in favour of **general phonetics**, though it is occasionally preferred for investigations into such matters as the variation of the vocal tract with sex, age or ethnic background. *Adj.* **anthropophonic**. Baudouin de Courtenay (1881), probably borrowed from Winteler.

anticipation /æntɪsɪˈpeɪʃn̩/ *n.* The phenomenon in which a speaker produces a segment or a feature earlier in an utterance than is necessary or appropriate. The term is applied both to instances of **anticipatory assimilation**, in which it is usually normal, and to **slips of the tongue** such as 'blake fluid' for *brake fluid* and 'bread and breakfast' for *bed and breakfast*. Cf. **perseveration**. *V.* **anticipate**.

anticipatory assimilation /ænˈtɪsɪpeɪtri/ *n.* (also **anticipatory co-articulation**, **regressive assimilation**) The phenomenon in which a phonetic feature spreads from a segment to a preceding segment, as when English /t/ or /s/ is pronounced with lip-rounding when immediately followed by /uː/ or /w/, as in *soon* and *twice*. Cf. **perseverative assimilation**.

antiformant /ˈæntɪfɔːmənt/ *n.* (also **zero**) For a given resonator, such as a particular configuration of the vocal tract, a frequency range in which the system absorbs energy (that is, it exhibits an **anti-resonance**). The result shows up in a **sound spectrogram** as a white space. Ant. **formant**.

antigemination /æntɪdʒemɪˈneɪʃn̩/ *n.* The phenomenon, occurring in certain languages, by which an otherwise regular phonological process is blocked whenever it would lead to the creation of a **geminate**. See McCarthy (1986).

antinode /'æntɪnəʊd/ *n*. In a **standing wave**, any one of the points of maximum displacement. Cf. **node**. *Adj*. **antinodal**.

antiresonance /'æntɪrezənəns/ *n*. The filtering effect of a vibrating chamber which is unable to vibrate at certain frequencies and which hence removes those frequencies preferentially from the source sound. In a **sound spectrogram**, this results in an **antiformant**. Cf. **resonance**.

anywhere rule /'enɪwɛə/ *n*. (also **persistent rule**) In a theory of phonology employing **rule ordering**, a rule which has no place in the order but which applies at any and all stages in the derivation where its structural description is met. Such a rule may therefore apply several times in the course of a single derivation. Chafe (1967); Anderson (1974).

aperiodic wave /eɪpɪərɪ'ɒdɪk/ *n*. An irregular **waveform** in which no consistent pattern of repetition can be observed. Among speech sounds, fricatives provide the clearest examples of aperiodic waves. Cf. **periodic** wave.

Apert's syndrome /'æpət/ *n*. A congenital pathological deformation of the supralaryngeal vocal tract in which the palate lies abnormally far back and the pharynx is constricted. The sufferer is unable to produce the formant frequency range of normal speech and hence cannot produce the ordinary vowel distinctions; high vowels are typically absent entirely.

aperture /'æpətʃə/ *n*. 1. The degree or size of an opening, as of the mouth. 2. [*obsolete*] A synonym for **vowel height**. Translation of German *Schallfülle* 'sonority' (Trubetzkoy 1939). 3. (also **openness**) In **Particle Phonology**, the conventional name for the particle **a**. 4. In some versions of **feature geometry**, a superordinate node governing distinctions of vowel height. Sense 4: Clements (1991).

aperture feature *n*. One of two features invoked to treat differences in **degree of stricture**: stops are [–continuant], fricatives are [+continuant, –sonorant], and approximants are [+continuant, +sonorant]. See Kenstowicz (1994: 503–506). Donca Steriade, unpublished work.

apex /'eɪpeks/ *n*. The **tip** of the tongue. Adj. **apical**; CF **apico-**.

aphaeresis /æ'fɪərəsɪs/ *n*. (also **aphesis** /'æfəsɪs/) The loss or omission of one or more segments from the beginning of a word.

Examples include the reduction of *opossum* to *possum*, *esquire* to *squire*, *nadder* to *adder*, *acute* to *cute*, and *alone* to *lone*, as well as the loss of initial [k] in *knife* and the reduction of *am* and *have* to *'m* and *'ve* in contractions like *I'm* and *we've*. Some sources distinguish **aphesis** (loss of an initial unstressed vowel) from **aphaeresis** (loss of any other initial material), but this distinction is neither usual nor obviously useful. Some would also extend the term to instances of **clipping** like *helicopter* to *copter* and *airplane* to *plane*. *Adj.* **aphetic** or (very rarely) **aphaeretic**. Ant. **prothesis**. Cf. **syncope**, **apocope**, and see also **initial dropping**. The longer form (from Greek *aphairesis* 'a taking away') was used by the Latin grammarians; the shorter form (from Greek *aphesis* 'letting go') was coined by James Murray in 1880 with the intended narrower sense just cited.

aphetic /əˈfetɪk/ *adj.* See under **aphaeresis**.

aphonia /əɪˈfəʊniə/ *n.* The total loss of the ability to use the **vocal folds** to produce phonation. *Adj.* **aphonic** /əɪˈfɒnɪk/. Cf. **dysphonia**.

apical /ˈæpɪkəl/ 1. *adj.* Pertaining to the **tip (apex)** of the tongue. 2. *adj.* (of an articulation) Articulated with the tip of the tongue, as in an **apico-alveolar** segment. 3. *n.* A segment so articulated. In the IPA, an apical articulation may be explicitly represented by the use of the diacritic [ˌ] below the symbol for an alveolar consonant: [t̪], [s̪]. 4. *adj.* A binary **distinctive feature** used in some recent work, chiefly for distinguishing apical segments ([+apical]) from **laminal** segments ([–apical]), and largely replacing for this purpose the feature **distributed** used in the *SPE* feature system. 5. *adj.* In the **Williamson feature system**, one of the three possible values of the feature **apicality**.

apical-dorsal vowel *n.* (also **apical vowel**, **coronal vowel**) A phonetic **vowel** (sense 1) articulated with the tip of the tongue raised sufficiently to produce audible colouring but not friction. Such vowels occur in certain varieties of Swedish and Chinese. See Laver (1994: 319–320).

apicality /æpɪˈkælɪti/ *n.* 1. In the **Williamson feature system**, a **distinctive feature** with the possible values **laminal**, **apical** and **retroflex**. 2. One of the **components** of **Dependency Phonology**, conventionally represented |t|.

apical vowel *n.* See **apical-dorsal vowel**.

apico-alveolar /æpɪkəʊ/ 1. *adj.* (of a segment) Articulated with the tip of the tongue and the alveolar ridge forming the primary occlusion. 2. *n.* A segment so articulated, such as [t d n l] in some languages.

apico-dental 1. *adj.* (of a segment) Articulated with the tip of the tongue and the upper teeth forming the primary occlusion. 2. *n.* A segment so articulated, such as the dental fricatives [θ] and [ð] in Spanish.

apico-labial 1. *adj.* (of a segment) Articulated with the tip of the tongue and the upper lip forming the primary occlusion: one type of **linguolabial**. 2. *n.* A segment so articulated, such as the plosives, fricatives and nasals reported for the South American language Umotina (Ladefoged 1971) and for a number of Pacific languages (Maddieson 1987). In the IPA, an apico-labial may be represented by the use of the diacritic [͙] below the symbol for an alveolar segment: [t̪], [n̪].

apico-post-alveolar 1. *adj.* (of a segment) Articulated with the tip of the tongue forming the primary occlusion just behind the alveolar ridge, one type of **retroflex** articulation. 2. *n.* A segment so articulated, such as [ɹ], the most usual realization of English /r/ in England.

apocope /əˈpɒkəpi/ *n.* (also **apocopation**) The loss or omission of one or more segments from the end of a word, as in the reduction of earlier *singan* to *sing*, *mine* to *my*, *passion* to *pash*, *margarine* to *marge* and *David* to *Dave*, as well as the common reduction of *and* to [ən] and of *first* to [fɜːs] in *first time* [fɜːs taim]. Sometimes the term is extended to cases like Swedish *flicka* 'girl', plural *flickor*, in which the stem-final *-a* is dropped before the plural suffix *-or*. *Adj.* **apocopic** /æpəˈkɒpɪk/. Ant. **paragoge**. Cf. **aphaeresis**, **syncope**. Greek *apokopē* 'a cutting off'.

apophony /əˈpɒfəni/ *n.* A synonym for **ablaut**, but Coates (1994) recommends that this term should be specialized in a synchronic sense to denote internal modification of the stem for exclusively grammatical reasons and as the sole indication of those reasons. *Adj.* **apophonic** /æpəˈfɒnɪk/.

apparent time /əˈpærənt taim/ *n.* The distribution of linguistic forms across age groups in a speech community.

appeal /əˈpiːl/ *n.* 1. One of the three **planes** posited for phonology, with the function of treating such 'expressive' phenomena as exaggerated lengthening and exaggerated pitch differences. Cf.

expression, representation. 2. In the study of **intonation**, a label occasionally applied to certain highly marked patterns with some kind of 'expressive' function.

appendix /ə'pendɪks/ *n*. (pl. **appendices** /ə'pendɪsiːz/) In some analyses of (especially English) **syllable structure**, a consonantal segment which appears in syllable-final position following another consonant, such as the final consonants in *mind*, *begged*, *looked*, *beds*, *fox*, *width*, *strange* and *drinks*. The term is particularly associated with **Metrical Phonology**.

application /æplɪ'keɪʃn̩/ *n*. See **rule application**.

approach /ə'prəʊtʃ/ *n*. (also **closing phase**) In the articulation of a consonant, particularly a **plosive**, the initial stage of the articulation, during which the articulating organs are moving together. Cf. **hold**, **release**.

appropriate order /ə'prəʊpriət/ *n*. [*rare*] See **unmarked order**. Chafe (1967).

approximant /ə'prɒksɪmənt/ *n*. 1. (also **frictionless continuant**) A segment, usually a **consonant** (either sense), articulated with a constriction which is typically greater than that required for a vowel but not radical enough to produce turbulent air flow and hence friction noise, at least when voiced, though a voiceless approximant may involve some friction, and necessarily does so in some definitions. Examples: [w j ʊ ɹ]. Ladefoged (1964, 1971), Abercrombie (1967), Catford (1977) and Laver (1994) offer a range of non-equivalent definitions of the term. Ladefoged's includes lateral resonants (or **lateral approximants**) like /l/, excluded by some others, and also includes *all* vowels, a usage which is elsewhere unknown and which in more recent works he has abandoned (Ladefoged equivocates over [h]); Catford's includes high vowels like [i] and [u], not usually regarded as approximants by other analysts, and also voiceless high-vowel realizations of [h], but excludes non-high vowels and non-high versions of [h]; Laver, uniquely, includes the specification 'non-syllabic' in his definition, thereby including [h] but excluding ordinary vowels. See Laver (1994: 297–306). Ladefoged (1964). 2. In the **Ladefoged feature system**, one of the three possible values of the feature **stop**. 3. In the **Williamson feature system**, one of the five possible values of the feature **stricture**. 4. (**app**) A **distinctive feature** proposed by Clements (1992), by which obstruents and nasals are [–app] while all other segments are [+app].

arbitrariness /ɑːbɪ'trɛərɪnəs/ *n.* The general property of human languages by which there is no necessary, predictable, *a priori* relation between a particular meaning and the phonological form used to represent that meaning in a particular language. Thus English *dog*, French *chien*, German *Hund*, Basque *txakur*, Turkish *köpek*, Arabic *kalb* all express approximately the same meaning, while English *mean*, Welsh *min* 'edge', Basque *min* 'pain', French *mine* '(coal) mine', Arabic *min* 'from', all with roughly the same pronunciation, have quite unrelated meanings. Instances of **iconicity**, such as **onomatopoeia**, constitute partial exceptions to arbitrariness.

arboreal connectedness /ɑːbɔːriəl kə'nektɪdnəs/ *n.* The relation between two elements which are connected by a unidirectional path in a **metrical tree** or a similar representation.

arboreal framework /'freɪmwɜːk/ *n.* (also **arboreal structure**) See **metrical tree**.

arc /ɑːk/ *n.* A directed line in a graph in any of various types of phonological representations but most familiarly in those used in **Dependency Phonology**.

archi- /ɑːkɪ/ A prefix sometimes used in coining convenient labels for particular **archiphonemes**. For example, a segment representing the **neutralization** of three nasal phonemes might be called an 'archinasal'.

archiphoneme /'ɑːkɪfəʊniːm/ *n.* In **Prague School** phonology, the name given to a segment which represents the **neutralization** of two or more phonemes in a specified environment, often conventionally represented by a capital letter. In English, for example, the phonemes /p/ and /b/ contrast in most positions but are neutralized after /s/ in the same syllable; the unaspirated [p] occurring in the word *speak*, for example, would be analysed in the Prague system as containing the archiphoneme /P/, representing the neutralization of /p/ and /b/ in this position: hence /sPiːk/. In terms of **distinctive features**, the archiphoneme corresponds to the matrix of features shared by /p/ and /b/ but excluding those features which otherwise distinguish the two segments. The archiphoneme analysis contrasts strongly with most versions of **classical phonology**, in which the bilabial in *speak* must necessarily be assigned to one or the other of the phonemes /p/ and /b/, most often to /p/. *Adj.* **archiphonemic**. The term was coined by Jakobson (1929), but was given its modern sense by Trubetzkoy (1939).

area function analog /'ɛəriə fʌŋkʃən ænəlɒg/ *n.* An electrical circuit designed to model the vocal tract, consisting of some number of subcircuits each modelling one small part of the tract. Widely used in the 1950s, these circuits were eventually replaced by computer models. See Dunn (1950) and Fant (1960) for descriptions.

areal feature /ɛəriəl/ *n.* A particular phonetic or linguistic characteristic which occurs in a number of (often unrelated) languages in a single geographical region, such as the absence in East Asia of a contrast between lateral and non-lateral liquids, the presence of phonemic tone in West Africa, the presence of click consonants in southern Africa, and the existence of an unusually large number of place contrasts for plosives, nasals and laterals in Australia.

arithmetic conception of quantity /ærɪθ'metɪk kənsepʃən/ *n.* The interpretation of long syllabic nuclei as geminates or other sequences of short elements, sometimes said to be appropriate for languages in which the **mora**, rather than the **syllable**, is the smallest prosodic unit. Trubetzkoy (1939).

arrow /'ærəʊ/ *n.* The symbol →, conventionally used in writing a **phonological rule** to separate the elements to which the rule applies (on the left of the arrow) from the result of the application (on the right).

articulation /ɑːtɪkjuˈleɪʃn̩/ *n.* 1. The use of the organs of speech in the supralaryngeal vocal tract to produce speech sounds. 2. Any particular posture or movement of these organs involved in the production of some particular speech sound; the term is most commonly applied to the production of a **consonant** (sense 1), but is sometimes also applied to the production of a **vowel** (sense 1). See these terms for information on the description and classification of articulations. *Adj.* **articulatory**.

articulation rate *n.* The tempo of performance of all audible speech, including **filled pauses** but excluding **silent pauses**. Cf. **speaking rate**. Laver (1994: 539).

articulation test /test/ *n.* A common but inappropriate name for a **recognition test**.

articulator /ɑːˈtɪkjuleɪtə/ *n.* Any specific part of the **vocal tract** which may be involved in the articulation of a segment, particularly a consonant. See **active articulator**, **passive articulator**.

Articulator Model /'mɒdəl/ *n.* A model of the representation of speech sounds which posits a close relation between phonetics and

phonology, in that it represents the actions of each individual articulator – each movable part of the speech organs – by suitable
distinctive features. It differs from traditional models in that each
feature is associated with some specific muscular activity, rather
than with some configuration of the vocal tract. The model has
been developed by Morris Halle and Elizabeth Sagey in a series
of publications beginning with Halle (1983); **feature geometry** is
a direct outgrowth of this work. See Kenstowicz (1994: 136–168,
ch. 9) for a lengthy presentation with references.

articulatory /ɑː'tɪkjuleɪtri/ *adj.* Pertaining to **articulation(s)**.

articulatory apraxia /eɪ'præksiə/ *n.* (also **articulatory dyspraxia**,
verbal apraxia) A pathological condition characterized by speech
production which is laboured, distorted or impossible, resulting
from damage to specific areas of the brain and not from damage
to motor or sensory faculties.

articulatory complexity /kəm'pleksɪti/ *n.* A proposed parameter
for classifying consonant articulations in terms of departures from
a **default mode of production**; consonants are classified as **basic**,
elaborated or **complex segments**. Lindblom and Maddieson (1988).

articulatory feature *n.* A **distinctive feature** which is related
primarily to some aspect of the posture of the vocal organs during
the articulation of a segment, and not to the acoustic qualities of
the sound produced. The earliest distinctive features were mostly
acoustic in nature, but in 1968 Chomsky and Halle introduced a
new set of articulatory features (the *SPE* **feature system**), including
such features as **coronal**, **anterior**, **rounded**, **nasal** and **lateral**, and
these articulatory features have largely displaced the older ones.

articulatory gesture *n.* See under **gesture**.

articulatory overlap /'əʊvələæp/ *n.* The phenomenon in which the
articulatory posture of a following consonant is formed before
the preceding consonant has been completed. This occurs regularly
in English: e.g., [pt] in *tiptoe*, [tb] in *football*, [sf] in *this fact*.

articulatory perturbation /pɜːtə'beɪʃn̩/ *n.* An experimental technique in which a speaker's articulation is interfered with by mechanical means, such as a **biteblock**, that would prevent an ordinary
articulatory effort from producing the required sounds. Speakers
tend to compensate strongly for the effects of such interference, and
the nature of the compensation is usually the object of investigation.

articulatory phonetics *n.* The branch of **phonetics** which studies the organs of speech and their use in producing speech sounds.

articulatory phonology *n.* An attempt at extending the analytical ideas of **Autosegmental Phonology** to articulatory phonetics. See Browman and Goldstein (1986, 1990) for a presentation, Steriade (1990) and Ladefoged (1990) for critiques.

articulatory place *n.* (also **place**) A **multivalued distinctive feature** used in some systems, notably in the **Ladefoged** and **Williamson feature systems**. Following the traditional description of **place of artic- ulation**, this feature can assume any one of eleven values: (Ladefoged) **bilabial, labiodental, dental, alveolar, retroflex, palato-alveolar, palatal, velar, uvular, pharyngeal, glottal**; (Williamson) **bilabial, labio- dental, dental, alveolar, post-/palato-alveolar, palatal, central, velar, uvular, pharyngeal, glottal**. This feature is intended to supersede the various binary features used for characterizing place of articulation in the *SPE* **feature system**, such as **coronal** and **anterior**.

articulatory posture /ˈpɒstʃə/ *n.* The particular configuration of the organs of speech employed in the **articulation** (sense 2) of some particular segment.

articulatory setting *n.* The overall tendency, on the part of an indi- vidual or of the speakers of a particular language, to maintain the organs of speech in some particular configuration throughout speech, as reflected in such factors as the height of the velum, the degree of lip-rounding and the tension of the tongue and lips. Examples of particular settings include the low velum of some Americans (producing a nasal '**twang**'), the high velum of many speakers in Liverpool (producing '**adenoidal**' speech), the weak-to- nonexistent lip-rounding of some British speakers and the tense oral cavity of many French speakers. Laver (1994: 406–413) distin- guishes *longitudinal*, *cross-sectional* and *velopharyngeal settings*, with further distinctions within each.

artificial larynx /ɑːtɪˈfɪʃḷ/ *n.* A portable device which provides a replacement for the vibration of the vocal cords for a speaker whose larynx has been surgically removed. The user presses the device against the front of her/his throat and speaks as normally as possible. The resulting speech has a rather strange quality but is quite comprehensible.

artificial speech *n.* (also **synthesized speech**) The output produced in **speech synthesis**.

arytenoid cartilage /ærɪ'tiːnɔɪd kɑːtəlɪdʒ/ *n.* Either of the two triangular cartilages located just above the **cricoid cartilage** within the **larynx**, attached to the back of the **vocal folds** and capable of separating the vocal folds or of bringing them partially or wholly together.

Ascendancy Accent /ə'sendənsi/ *n.* In Ireland, a prestigious accent somewhat resembling **Received Pronunciation** but not generally regarded as a norm for Irish pronunciation. From its use by people in positions of power, traditionally known as the 'Ascendancy' in Ireland.

ash /æʃ/ *n.* The symbol ⟨æ⟩, used in various orthographies and transcriptions to represent an unrounded front vowel intermediate in quality between cardinals 3 and 4, as in General American *cat*. The symbol [æ] is so used in the IPA; the character ⟨æ⟩ occurs in the orthographies of Old English and modern Icelandic. The character was invented by the Anglo-Saxon scribes; the name is that of the Old English rune letter representing this vowel.

aspect of articulation /'æspekt/ *n.* Any factor in **articulation** beyond the location and degree of stricture. Laver (1994) recognizes three general classes: **conformational**, **topographical** and **transitional aspects**. Laver (1994); Laver credits Elizabeth Uldall with the term.

aspirata /æspɪ'rɑːtə/ *n.* (*pl.* **aspiratae** /-tiː/) (also **aspirate**) [*obsolete*] A label commonly applied in nineteenth-century philological treatises in an indifferent manner to aspirated voiceless plosives, to murmured plosives ('voiced aspirates') and to fricatives, all of which were regarded as united by the presence of breath in their articulation. Cf. **tenuis**, **media**. Latin *aspirata* 'breathed upon'.

aspirate /'æspərət/ *n.* 1. See **aspirata**. 2. A segment which is **aspirated** (sense 1), such as [pʰ]. 3. See **aspiration** (sense 2).

aspirated /'æspəreɪtɪd/ *adj.* 1. (of an obstruent) Immediately followed by a delay in the onset of voicing; equivalently, followed by a period of voiceless breathing. In the IPA, an aspirated segment is represented by the use of the diacritic [ʰ]: hence [pʰ] represents an aspirated voiceless bilabial plosive. *Abstr. n.* **aspiration**. See also **pre-aspiration**. Ant. **unaspirated**. 2. (**asp**) A **distinctive feature** used in some systems for distinguishing aspirated sounds ([+asp]) from unaspirated ones ([–asp]). This feature is not used in the *SPE* **feature system**, in which aspiration is largely handled with the feature **heightened subglottal pressure**. 3. In the **Ladefoged feature system**, one of the three possible values of the feature **aspiration**.

aspirate mutation *n.* (also **spirantization**) One of the **mutations** of Welsh, in which, in certain grammatical circumstances, a voiceless plosive is converted to the corresponding fricative, and a vowel-initial word acquires a preceding [h]. For example, the possessive *ei* 'her' induces this mutation (*ch, ph* and *th* represent [x], [f] and [θ], respectively): *cath* 'cat', *ei chath hi* 'her cat'; *pen* 'head', *ei phen hi* 'her head'; *tad* 'father', *ei thad hi* 'her father'; *enw* 'name', *ei henw hi* 'her name'.

aspiration /æspə'reɪʃn̩/ *n.* 1. The phonetic phenomenon in which a segment (normally an obstruent) is followed by a period of voiceless breathing, a 'puff of breath'. *Adj.* **aspirated**. See also **voice onset time**, **preaspiration**. See Laver (1994: 348–358). NOTE: Aspiration is simetimes called **voice-onset delay**, but this term is actually of wider applicability than 'aspiration'. 2. (also **aspirate**) A label sometimes applied to the segment [h], the so-called 'voiceless glottal fricative', actually a voiceless vowel. 3. In the **Ladefoged feature system**, a **distinctive feature** invoked to handle distinctions in **voice onset time**; it can assume any of the three values **aspirated**, **unaspirated** or **voiced**. 4. See **lenition** (sense 2). *V.* (all senses) **aspirate**.

ASR /eɪ es 'ɑː/ *n.* See **automatic speech recognition**.

assibilant /ə'sɪbɪlənt/ *n.* [*rare*] An **affricate** whose fricative element is a **sibilant**, such as the affricate [ts].

assibilation /əsɪbɪ'leɪʃn̩/ *n.* The phonological process in which another segment is converted to a **sibilant**. The process t → s / ___ i, for example, occurs in many Pacific languages. *V.* **assibilate**.

assimilated loan /ə'sɪməleɪtɪd/ *n.* A **loan word** which has been completely adapted to the phonological system of the borrowing language. English examples include *music* (all speakers and styles), from French *musique* [myzik], *beret* (when homophonous with *berry*), from French *beret* [beʀɛ], and *tsetse* (when pronounced /'tetsi/), from Tswana *tsetse* [tsɛtsɛ].

assimilation /əsɪmə'leɪʃn̩/ *n.* Any of various phonetic or phonological processes in which one segment becomes more similar to another segment in the same word or phrase. Examples: the pronunciation of *ten pence* as *te*[m]*pence*, in which /n/ assimilates in place to the following /p/; the pronunciation of *has she* as /haʒʃiː/; the pronunciation of *bacon* as /beɪkn̩/; the development of earlier **munθ* into Icelandic *munn*. The first two of these illustrate **anticipatory (regressive) assimilation**, the last two **perseverative (progressive)**

assimilation. Mutual assimilation (assimilation in both directions) is also possible, as when Basque *iduri* 'seem' becomes *üdürü* in the Zuberoan dialect (*ü* is a front rounded vowel). The first four examples also illustrate **contact assimilation** (between adjacent segments); the Basque example illustrates **distant assimilation** (between non-adjacent segments). Some analysts regard **coalescence** as a kind of assimilation. Especially in historical phonology, certain types of assimilation in particular languages have often been given distinctive names such as **affection**, **umlaut**, **metaphony** and **vowel harmony**. Assimilation is usually articulatory in its motivation, but see also **acoustic assimilation**. See Lass (1984: 8.2) for a summary of assimilation types. *V.* **assimilate**; *adj.* **assimilatory**.

assimilation site /saɪt/ *n.* For a segment, a position in which that segment is likely to undergo, or at least capable of undergoing, assimilation. In English, for example, an alveolar consonant may undergo assimilation in place when immediately followed by a bilabial or a velar consonant; this position is an assimilation site for alveolars.

association /əsəʊsi'eɪʃn̩/ *n.* (also **linking**) In **Autosegmental Phonology**, the relation holding between elements which are linked by **association lines** and which are hence to be realized simultaneously in the resulting phonological form. *Adj.* **associated** /ə'səʊʃieɪtɪd/.

Association Convention *n.* A central principle of **Autosegmental Phonology**. It states: when unassociated autosegments and skeletal units appear on the same side of an association line, they will be automatically associated in a one-to-one fashion, radiating outward from the association line. This convention acts as a kind of default, assigning all remaining associations straightforwardly after any special requirements have been met.

association domain *n.* In some analyses of **intonation**, a particular part of an utterance (often a grammatical phrase) over which a single identifiable intonation contour is realized.

association line *n.* 1. In **Autosegmental Phonology**, any one of the arcs connecting an element on one **tier** to an element on another tier. 2. In **Dependency Phonology**, any one of the vertical lines linking a dependency arc to a phonological element.

associative relation /ə'səʊʃiətɪv/ *n.* Saussure's original term for a **paradigmatic relation**.

assonance /'æsənəns/ *n*. 1. Narrowly, the recurrence of the same vowel sound (or sometimes of similar vowel sounds) in two or more words in a phrase or in a poem, as in the phrase *sweet dreams* or in Dylan Thomas's lines *Flash, and the plumes crack,* / *And a black cap of jackdaws.* 2. Broadly, and now more usually, any repetition of the same or similar sounds or sound sequences in a short text, including **consonance** (sense 2) but often excluding both **rhyme** and **alliteration**. *V*. **assonate** /'æsəneɪt/.

asterisk /'æstərɪsk/ *n*. (also **star**) 1. In **historical phonology**, a symbol used to mark an unattested earlier form which has been reconstructed on the basis of some evidence, as when English *father* is derived from an unattested Proto-Germanic **fadar*, or when English *fierce* is traced back to a hypothetical Proto-Indo-European root **ghwer-*. 2. A symbol used to mark a form as either non-existent or impossible. The form /blæk/ is a real English word, while */bræk/ is possible but non-existent and */bnæk/ is impossible; some scholars prefer to write **/bnæk/ for the impossible case, reserving the single asterisk for merely non-existent forms. 3. An *ad hoc* **diacritic** occasionally added to a character in a transcription to represent some segment not otherwise readily representable, such as p* for the 'tense' bilabial plosive of Korean or v* for the labiodental flap of Shona. 4. In a **metrical grid**, the usual device for representing the presence of a **beat** on a syllable; a larger number of asterisks represents a more prominent beat.

asymmetric alternation /eɪsɪ'metrɪk/ *n*. An **alternation** in which a form A alternates with another form B in some words but not in others. For example, in **Received Pronunciation**, the nuclei /uːə/ and /ʊə/ alternate freely in such words as *brewer* and *fluent*, but other words, such as *poor* and *during*, allow only /ʊə/ and never /uːə/. Wells (1982, 1: 56).

asymmetric vowel *n*. A vowel in a particular language which, uniquely among its vowels, undergoes or fails to undergo or to trigger a number of phonological processes. Recognition of asymmetric vowels lies at the heart of **Radical Underspecification** theory.

asymmetry of production and perception /eɪ'sɪmətri/ *n*. Any of various phenomena demonstrating that speakers either can produce distinctions which they cannot hear or can hear distinctions which they cannot produce. See Labov (1994: chs 12–13) for a review.

athematic /eɪθɪ'mætɪk/ *adj.* In the morphologies of certain inflected languages, denoting a lexical item which, in contrast to other items in its class, lacks a **thematic vowel**. Most Latin verbs, for example, are inflected with the use of a thematic vowel: *am-ā-* 'love', *mon-ē-* 'warn', *aud-ī-* 'hear', but the verbs *es-* 'be' and *fer-* 'carry' are athematic. Ant. **thematic**.

atom /'ætəm/ *n.* See **phonological prime**.

Atomic Phonology /ə'tɒmɪk/ *n.* A theory of phonology developed by Daniel Dinnsen in the late 1970s. The framework maintains that all variation requiring differing formulations of phonological rules is predictable from a distinguished set of *atomic rules* and certain universal principles. These atomic rules express basic phonological processes like nasalization and lenition in the least general forms possible; generalizations of these rules (**complement rules**) are permitted only in terms of natural classes. No purely phonological rule may be written which is neither an atomic rule nor a complement rule. The framework is presented in Dinnsen (1978, 1979b); see Wheeler (1985) for a critical view.

atonic /eɪ'tɒnɪk/ *adj.* (of a syllable) Lacking a stress or pitch **accent** (sense 3). *Abstr. n.* **atonicity** /eɪtə'nɪsɪti/. Ant. **tonic**.

ATR /eɪ ti: 'ɑː/ *n.* (also **advanced tongue root**) A **distinctive feature** defined as follows: a [+ATR] segment is articulated with the root of the tongue drawn forward, thus enlarging the pharyngeal cavity, giving the longitudinal profile of the tongue root a tighter curve than otherwise and often raising the body of the tongue. This feature has been invoked specifically to handle the unusual **vowel harmony** systems of some African languages, in which the harmony is based upon two groups of vowels with advanced and retracted tongue root. See Stewart (1967), Ladefoged (1968) and Lindau (1978) for instrumental evidence and discussion, and see Durand (1990) or Laver (1994) for a summary. In the *SPE* **feature system**, the equivalent feature is [**covered**], with [+cov] corresponding to [−ATR]. In much recent work, [ATR] has been interpreted as a successor of the earlier feature [**tense**] and has accordingly been invoked to double the number of vowel heights obtainable from the features [**high**] and [**low**], in most cases without any experimental evidence that the feature is realistic. See also **expanded**, **peripheral**. Ant. **retracted tongue root**. Halle and Stevens (1969).

attested form /əˈtestɪd/ *n.* A form which is explicitly recorded in a text. The term is most commonly used in connection with dead languages and with earlier forms of living languages. Cf. **reconstruction**.

attitudinal function /ætɪˈtjuːdɪnəl/ *n.* The use of some aspect of speech, most commonly an **intonation** pattern, to express a particular attitude, such as doubt or enthusiasm. The existence of such uses is not in doubt, but they have proved extraordinarily difficult to study in a systematic way.

attrition /əˈtrɪʃn̩/ *n.* The phonological phenomenon in which segments or syllables are entirely lost from the pronunciation of a word over time, as in the development of Old English *singan* /siŋgan/ to *sing* /sɪŋ/, of Old English *hlāfdige* to *lady*, of Latin *consobrinum* to French *cousin* /kuzɛ̃/ or of Latin *augustum* to French *août* /u/.

audio band /ˈɔːdiəʊ/ *n.* The range of frequencies of sound waves audible to the human ear, conventionally taken as about 20 Hz to 20,000 Hz (20 kHz), though individuals vary significantly in this respect.

audiogram /ˈɔːdiəgræm/ *n.* A graph recording an individual's ability to hear pure tones of varying frequencies, used to test for and to characterize hearing loss.

audiology /ɔːdiˈɒlədʒi/ *n.* The study of hearing and hearing disorders, including diagnosis and treatment. A practitioner is an **audiologist**.

audiometry /ɔːdiˈɒmətri/ *n.* The measurement of hearing and hearing loss. The instrument used is an **audiometer** /ɔːdɪˈɒmɪtə/.

audition /ɔːˈdɪʃn̩/ *n.* 1. The act of hearing sounds. 2. The sense of hearing.

audition colorée /odisjɔ̃ koloʀe/ *n.* [French: 'coloured hearing'] The phenomenon in which an individual associates particular colours with particular vowels, and occasionally also with particular consonants. Associations vary, but a common pattern is to associate [i] with yellow, [u] with red and [a] with deep blue. First described by the psychologists Stumpf and Köhler, the phenomenon was brought to the attention of linguists by Jakobson (1941). See Fischer-Jørgensen (1967) for an account. (The associations given in Rimbaud's famous sonnet *Voyelles* are anomalous, but are perhaps associations with the shapes of the vowel letters, not with their sounds.)

auditory /'ɔːdɪtri/ *adj*. Pertaining to hearing.

auditory acuity /ə'kjuːɪti/ *n*. An individual's ability to detect sound and to discriminate various types of sounds.

auditory area *n*. (also **auditory cortex** /'kɔːteks/) Either of the two regions of the cerebral cortex of the brain responsible for processing auditory input. The auditory area is located just below the lateral (Sylvian) sulcus and in front of Wernicke's area.

auditory discrimination *n*. The ability of an individual to distinguish sounds with slightly different physical properties; in phonetics, particularly the ability to distinguish speech sounds or words.

auditory feedback /'fiːdbæk/ *n*. The phenomenon in which a speaker hears her/his own speech via the conduction of sound both through the air and through the bones of the head. Such feedback is important in monitoring and controlling speech; loss of feedback, as in severe deafness, may result in abnormal speech. Cf. **kinaesthetic feedback** and see **delayed auditory feedback**.

auditory nerve /nɜːv/ *n*. (also **acoustic nerve**) Either of the two bundles of nervous tissue connecting the **cochlea** of the inner ear to the **auditory area** of the cerebral cortex.

auditory ossicles *n. pl*. The three small bones (the *malleus*, or *hammer*, the *incus*, or *anvil*, and the *stapes*, or *stirrup*) located in the **middle ear**. Vibration of the **eardrum** is transmitted mechanically by the ossicles to the **oval window**; the nature of the linkage is such that it overcomes the mismatch in **acoustic impedance** between the middle and inner ears and amplifies sound pressure by a factor of about 80, or by about 38 **decibels**.

auditory phonetics *n*. The branch of **phonetics** dealing with the way in which the human ear and brain process and interpret speech sounds. See Borden and Harris (1980), Pickett (1980), Denes and Pinson (1993) or Lieberman and Blumstein (1988) for an introduction.

auditory theory /'θɪəri/ *n*. Any theory of the manner in which hearing is performed by the human ear. The accepted theory today is the **place theory of hearing**; obsolete views include the **resonance theory** and the **telephone theory**.

auditory verbal agnosia /vɜːbəl æg'nəʊziə/ *n.* A pathological condition in which the sufferer is unable to recognize speech sounds. Cf. **visual verbal agnosia**. Greek *agnosia* 'lack of recognition'.

augment /'ɔːgment/ *n.* 1. A sequence of one or more segments added to the stem of a word when certain suffixes are added to it. For example, while the pair *music/musical* illustrates the most typical behaviour of the suffix *-al* in English, the pairs *professor/professorial* and *intellect/intellectual* show the use of an augment [i] or [ju] between the stem and the suffix. 2. In the morphologies of certain languages, notably Ancient Greek, a prefix added to a stem in certain formations; for example, the verb *pémpō* 'send', stem *pemp-*, forms aorist *épempon* and pluperfect *épempsa*, both with the augment *e-*.

augmentation /ɔːgmɪn'teɪʃn̩/ *n.* An analytical procedure for adding additional consonants to the margins of syllables, in order to account for consonant clusters in these positions. Steriade (1982).

augmented syllable /ɔːg'mentɪd/ *n.* A syllable which has acquired additional consonants as a result of the loss of a vowel in an adjacent syllable. For example, the common British pronunciations of *correct* and *police* as /krekt/ and /pliːs/ illustrate augmentation of the second syllable. This process can produce consonant clusters not otherwise attested, as when *tomato* is pronounced /t'maːtəʊ/.

auslaut /'aʊslaʊt/ *n.* The last segment in a word, or, less commonly, in a syllable. Cf **anlaut**, **inlaut**. German: 'out-sound'.

automatic alternation /ɔːtə'mætɪk/ *n.* 1. A highly regular morphological **alternation** whose conditioning factors are purely phonological, such as the /s/ ~ /z/ ~ /ɪz/ alternation in the English plural. Bloomfield (1933: 211). 2. An **alternation** which applies exceptionlessly to all morphemes and contexts meeting its structural description. An example is the /r/ ~ ∅ alternation occurring in the speech of those who use the **intrusive** *r*. Ant. **non-automatic alternation**. Wells (1949). NOTE: These definitions are not equivalent.

automatic rule *n.* A rule which expresses an exceptionless phonetic process which takes place below the level of a speaker's awareness, such as (in English) the aspiration of voiceless plosives before stressed vowels or the lengthening of vowels before voiced consonants. These are essentially the **P rules** of **Natural Generative Phonology**. See *veto* **phenomenon**.

automatic speech recognition *n.* (**ASR**) The use of electronic systems to process ordinary speech into a form which is suitable for feeding into a computer program called a 'parser' which can then interpret its grammatical structure and finally its meaning. The successful development of ASR systems will allow human beings to communicate with computers merely by talking to them.

autonomous phoneme /ɔː'tɒnəməs/ *n.* (also **classical phoneme** and, dismissively, **taxonomic phoneme**) The view of the **phoneme** adopted by the **American Structuralists** and also by the British phoneticians, in which the phoneme is regarded essentially as a family of **phones** related by distribution and phonetic similarity. See the discussion under **phoneme**, and see also **systematic phoneme**.

autonomous phonemics *n.* [*rare*] The view that phonology should be independent of grammar; a term of abuse applied by Postal (1968) to (some) **structuralist** approaches.

autosegment /'ɔːtəsegmənt/ *n.* In **Autosegmental Phonology**, any one of the more-or-less independent elements recognized as existing on any one of the various parallel **tiers** posited in that framework, though usually excluding the ordinary **segments** occurring on the **segmental tier**, when such a tier is recognized. *Adj.* **autosegmental**. 'Auto(nomous) segment'.

autosegmental intonation *n.* The analysis of **intonation** within the framework of **Autosegmental Phonology**, typically involving for English only two level tones (High and Low) plus a set of rules for applying these tones to utterances, in contrast to the three or four tone levels posited by most earlier approaches. See Hayes and Lahiri (1991).

autosegmentalization /ɔːtəsegmentəlaɪ'zeɪʃn̩/ *n.* The analytical process of extracting a phonological element, such as [nasal] or [back], from segmental representations and placing it on its own **tier** as an **autosegment**.

Autosegmental Morphology *n.* An extension of the ideas of **Autosegmental Phonology** to morphology, first proposed by McCarthy (1979, 1981) for the **non-concatenative morphology** of Semitic languages and extended by Halle and Vergnaud (1987) to **concatenative morphology**.

Autosegmental Phonology *n.* A major contemporary theory of phonology, one of the most prominent of the frameworks collectively known as **non-linear** approaches. In this framework, a phonological representation takes the form of a **chart** typically consisting of two or more parallel **tiers**; each tier is a linear sequence of elements called **autosegments**, and the autosegments on different tiers are related by **association lines**. The principal tier, variously called the **skeletal tier**, the **CV tier**, the **timing tier** or the **X-tier**, serves as a kind of backbone to which elements on other tiers are associated. Various types of phonological information are distributed among some number of additional tiers, typically including at least the **segmental tier** (ordinary segments) and (in tone languages) the **tonal tier** (tones). The number of distinct tiers recognized is highly variable and analysis-specific; there has been a notable tendency for the number of tiers postulated to increase steadily, and some recent analyses seem to posit a separate tier for every individual distinctive feature. The framework is derivational in conception; phonological processes apply so as to modify particular tiers or so as to modify the associations between tiers. Among the principles of the framework are several **well-formedness conditions**, notably the **Association Convention** and the **No-crossing Constraint**. Autosegmental Phonology, which is in many respects a reincarnation of **Prosodic Analysis**, was originally developed by John Goldsmith as a way of treating tones, which frequently seem to act independently of the segments they are associated with (Goldsmith 1976, 1979); it has been extensively developed by Goldsmith and others, most notably Kahn (1980) and Clements and Keyser (1983). Goldsmith (1990) is the most convenient introduction; Durand (1990) provides a briefer one. Goldsmith (1976).

autotemplatic /ɔːtətem'plætɪk/ *adj.* Denoting an analysis in which no **template** is supplied by the morphology and prosodic structure is projected from the string of segments by syllabification rules. McCarthy and Prince (1991).

auxiliary symbol /ɔːg'zɪliəri/ *n.* Any notational device used in some system of phonological representation which serves only to provide a suitable **environment** for the application of certain rules and never receives any overt phonetic realization of its own, such as the **hash mark** #, representing a **word boundary**, the **plus sign** +, representing a **morpheme boundary**, and the **dollar sign** $, representing a **syllable boundary**.

avoidance of homonymy /ə'vɔɪdəns/ *n.* See **semantic transparency**. Gilliéron (1921).

avoidance of merger *n.* A putative functional principle by which phoneme systems undergoing change tend to resist **mergers** in order to maintain lexical distinctions. Though obviously plausible in motivation, and supported by such data as **chain shifts**, the principle has so far not been constrained sufficiently to account for the numerous mergers which have indisputably occurred, for example in English, Greek and (most spectacularly) Mandarin Chinese. Appeals to **functional load** have clearly not been adequate.

B

babbling /ˈbæblɪŋ/ *n*. The type of sound production characteristic of an infant immediately before the onset of recognizable speech production, typically involving the production of repeated syllables such as [baba] and [dadada]. Cf. **cooing**. Imitative.

baby talk /ˈbeɪbi tɔːk/ *n*. [*non-technical*] 1. Any of the various immature forms of speech used by young children. 2. The distinctive form of speech used by adults in addressing young children, and sometimes also in other circumstances, typically involving short sentences with reduced syntax, exaggerated intonation, limited vocabulary and distinctive lexical items like *bikkie* and *choo-choo*.

back /bæk/ 1. *adj*. (of a vowel) Articulated with the highest point of the tongue at the back of the mouth, as with [u] or [o]. Ant. **front**. 2. *adj*. In the *SPE* **feature system**, a **distinctive feature** defined as 'produced with the body of the tongue retracted from the neutral position'. Back vowels and the glide [w] are [+back], as are velar, velarized, uvular, uvularized, pharyngeal and pharyngealized consonants; other segments are [−back]. 3. *adj*. In the **Ladefoged feature system**, a binary acoustic **distinctive feature** defined 'in terms of the inverse of the difference between the frequencies of formants two and one' and invoked to distinguish front and back vowels. 4. In the **Lindau feature system**, a **distinctive feature** invoked to treat distinctions of backness, with the three possible values *front*, *central* and *back*. 5. *n*. See **dorsum**. *Abstr. n*. (senses 1–4) **backness**.

back-formation /fɔːˈmeɪʃn̩/ *n*. 1. A word formed by the removal from another word of a morph which resembles a familiar affix, e.g., *edit* from *editor*, *sculpt* from *sculptor* and *peddle* from *pedlar*, all by removal of a morph resembling the agent suffix *-er*, as in *writer*. 2. A word formed by the reanalysis of a compound word and the subsequent removal of an affix which was not originally an immediate constituent, such as *sky-dive* from *sky-diving* (originally [*sky*] + [*diving*], but reanalysed as [*sky-dive*] + [*-ing*]). 3. The process of forming a word in either of these ways.

background /ˈbækɡraʊnd/ *n*. In some analyses of **intonation**, notably the **three-tone approach**, any part of an utterance which is marked as being out of focus (not new information) by the absence of any of the distinctive tones associated with material in focus.

backing /'bækɪŋ/ *n.* Any phonological process in which the articulation of a segment, particularly a vowel, is moved backwards within the oral cavity, such as the retraction of /ɪ/ to [ə] in New Zealand and the backing of /e/ to [ʌ] in several northern American cities. *Adj.* **backed**. Ant. **fronting**.

backing diphthong *n.* A **diphthong** in which the second element is further back than the first, such as [ju] or [ew]. Ant. **fronting diphthong**.

backness *n.* 1. The parameter which represents the horizontal dimension within the **vowel space** and which corresponds, at least in principle, to the horizontal location of the highest point of the tongue during the articulation of a vowel. 2. In some versions of **Dependency Phonology**, an element |ɯ| introduced to separate the backness and labiality attributes of the more usual |u|. Lass (1984: 278).

back pressure /'preʃə/ *n.* Resistance to the flow of air through the vocal tract caused by articulatory constriction within that tract.

back slang /slæŋ/ *n.* A type of word play in which words are pronounced as though spelled backwards; a well-known British example is the creation of *yob* from *boy*, while French has *meuf* from *femme*.

ballistic movement /bə'lɪstɪk muːvmənt/ *n.* A single rapid movement by an **active articulator**, most often a part of the tongue, during which the moving articulator is not held in place for any significant length of time. Both **taps** and **flaps** involve such ballistic movements. Greek *ballein* 'throw'.

band-limited signal /'bænd lɪmɪtɪd/ *n.* A signal, such as a sound wave, which contains only those frequencies lying within a specified **bandwidth**. Since the upper limit of the human hearing range lies at about 20 kHz, most high-quality sound reproduction operates with signals limited to the band 0–20 kHz, which makes digital processing easier. An ordinary telephone line is limited to a bandwidth of 0–3.2 kHz.

bandpass filter /'bændpɑːs/ *n.* An electronic circuit which has the property that it allows waves within a certain frequency range (the 'pass band') to pass through undisturbed, while at the same time it drastically reduces the energy contained in higher or lower frequencies and hence selectively filters them out. Such a filter might, for example, have a pass band of 135–180 Hz, giving it a **bandwidth** of 45 Hz. A battery of bandpass filters with adjoining pass bands can be used to analyse a sound wave into components of varying frequencies; this is how a **sound spectrograph** works.

bandwidth /'bændwɪdθ/ *n*. 1. The range of frequencies present in a complex sound wave. High-quality sound reproduction apparatus, for example, normally produces sound waves ranging from 20 Hz to 20,000 Hz (the **audio band**). 2. The range of frequencies passed by a **bandpass filter**, most commonly expressed as a difference. A filter that passes frequencies in the range 135–180 Hz has a bandwidth of 45 Hz.

bandwidth compression /kəm'preʃn̩/ *n*. The operation of converting a signal of a certain **bandwidth** into a form occupying a much smaller bandwidth so that it can be economically transmitted. All systems for doing this necessarily involve some loss of information and require elaborate apparatus for compressing the signal and for reconstructing it at the receiving end. Such compression offers obvious benefits in, for example, maximizing the use of telephone cables.

bare anchor /bɛə(r) 'æŋkə/ *n*. In **Autosegmental Phonology**, a position on the **skeletal tier** which has no material associated with it on other tiers. Cf. **floating**.

barred *i* /bɑːd 'aɪ/ *n*. The symbol [ɨ], used in the IPA to represent a high central unrounded vowel.

barred *u* /juː/ *n*. The symbol [ʉ], used in the IPA to represent a high central rounded vowel.

barrier /'bæriə/ *n*. (also **blocker**) Any **segment** or **boundary** in a phonological form which prevents some otherwise regular phonological process from applying to a domain including it, often especially a process involving two other non-adjacent segments on opposite sides of the barrier.

base /beɪs/ *n*. 1. (also **base form**) In morphology, a morph, variously consisting of a **root**, a **stem** or a word, which serves, upon the addition of a single further morpheme, as the immediate source of some particular formation: thus, for example, *happy* is the base for the formation of both *unhappy* and *happily*, while *unhappy* is the base for the formation of both *unhappily* and *unhappiness*. 2. See **stem**.

base form *n.* 1. (also **basic alternant**) A single, abstract representation of a **morpheme**, in terms of **phonemes** and frequently also **morphophonemes**, posited as the form from which all **allomorphs** of that morpheme can be derived by regular rules or statements. Base forms were used in one form or another by Sapir, Bloomfield and Harris, among others, and are the direct ancestors of the **underlying forms** of **generative phonology**. See Sommerstein (1977: 43–44) for some discussion. 2. See **base** (sense 1).

baseline /ˈbeɪslaɪn/ *n.* In some analyses of **intonation**, a pitch level which acts as a reference level with respect to which heights and contours can be identified; the floor of the current **pitch span**. The baseline is not necessarily of constant pitch throughout an utterance; see **declination**. Cf. **topline**.

basic alternant /ˈbeɪsɪk/ *n.* A former term for the **underlying form** of a morpheme. The term is still sometimes applied to that one alternant of a morpheme which can be identified with the underlying form, if such an alternant exists. Bloomfield (1933).

basic beat *n.* In some versions of **Metrical Phonology**, the name given to a strong **demibeat** – in most cases, simply a stressed syllable.

Basic Beat Rule *n.* In some (especially grid) versions of **Metrical Phonology**, a rule or set of rules with the function of applying to a more elementary representation to pick out the syllables with primary stress.

basic components of speech *n. pl.* The minimal set of physical phenomena without which speech is impossible, identified as **airstream mechanism** (**initiation**) and **articulation** (both obligatory), with **phonation** optionally but frequently also present. Catford (1977).

basic segment *n.* In the **articulatory complexity** model, a segment whose articulation does not depart from the **default mode of production**.

basic stress rule *n.* A set of putative rules for determining the position of the **stress** in English words. For example, Kreidler (1989: 200ff.) presents a set of rules in terms of lexical category, syllable quantity and number of syllables.

basic tone *n.* In some analyses of **intonation**, any one of a small number of **tones** (sense 3) regarded by the analyst as fundamental in that every other tone is analysed as a variant of one of these basic tones.

basilar membrane /bæzɪlə 'membreɪn/ *n.* The membrane running through the length of the **cochlea**, responsible for transmitting vibrations from the **oval window** to the **organ of Corti**.

BBC accent /biː biː 'siː/ *n.* (also **BBC English**) A name formerly given to the type of British English accent usually called **Received Pronunciation**, reflecting the fact that this sort of accent was once regularly used by newsreaders and announcers on the BBC. Today few BBC personnel have such an accent, and the term is no longer appropriate.

bearing unit /'bɛərɪŋ juːnɪt/ *n.* In **Autosegmental Phonology**, any class of autosegments with which some other class of autosegments is most typically associated. For example, in many tone languages, tones are typically phonetically realized on vowels, and hence vowels are tone-bearing units.

beat /biːt/ *n.* 1. The accent, stress or ictus in a metrical **foot**. 2. In grid versions of **Metrical Phonology**, any mark in the grid above the bottom (syllabic) level, representing a metrical unit which is 'strong' at that level. Cf. **demibeat**. Selkirk (1984).

Beat Addition *n.* In some versions of **Metrical Phonology**, a procedure for inserting an extra **beat** into a grid. Hayes (1984).

Beat Movement *n.* See **iambic reversal**.

bedroom voice /'bedruːm/ *n.* [*non-technical*] A semi-jocular label for **whispery voice (murmur)**, applied because such phonation is thought to be particularly appropriate in the bedroom.

bel /bel/ *n.* A unit of sound **intensity**, equal to 10 **decibels**. After Alexander Graham Bell (1847–1922), inventor of the telephone.

Bell–Sweet model /bel swiːt/ *n.* See **tongue-arching model**.

Bernoulli effect /bɜːˈnuːli ɪfekt/ *n.* (also **Bernoulli principle**) The physical phenomenon by which the sideways air pressure on a solid body is reduced when the air is flowing past the body; the faster the air moves, the lower the pressure. Responsible for such effects as the curvature of a pitched baseball and the lift on an airplane wing, the principle is chiefly important in phonetics in causing the vibration of the vocal folds: air flowing upwards forces the vocal folds apart, but, as soon as it flows past them, the pressure drops, and the folds spring back together; the rapid repetition of this sequence constitutes **voicing**. The effect is also crucial in the production of **trills**. After Daniel Bernoulli (1700–1782), Swiss mathematician.

bidental /bar'dentəl/ 1. *adj.* (of an articulation) Produced with the main constriction occurring between the upper and lower teeth. 2. *n.* A segment so articulated. Bidentals are virtually unknown, but Catford (1977: 148; 1988: 85) reports that a voiceless bidental fricative occurs in a dialect of the Caucasian language Adyghe (Circassian); see also Laver (1994: 248). There are no IPA symbols for bidentals.

bidirectional spreading /bardɪ'rekʃənəl/ *n.* The phenomenon in which an **autosegment** or other phonological element, once introduced into a phonological form at any point, is extended both to the left and to the right up to the relevant boundaries. In Akan, for example, the feature [+ATR], once present on any vowel in a root or affix, spreads to every vowel in the phonological word.

bidirectional tone *n.* In **intonation**, a **tone** (sense 3) whose contour involves a change of direction: a fall–rise or a rise–fall.

bilabial /bar'leɪbiəl/ 1. *adj.* (of an articulation) Articulated with both lips; the conventional label for what might more systematically be called 'labio-labial'. 2. *n.* A consonant so articulated, such as [m], [p] or [b]. 3. *adj.* In the **Ladefoged** and **Williamson feature systems**, one of the eleven possible values of the feature **articulatory place**.

bilabialized /bar'leɪbiəlaɪzd/ *adj.* An accurate but rare synonym for **labialized**.

bilateral /bar'lætərəl/ *n.* or *adj.* Denoting a **lateral** consonant in which air flows through openings on both sides of the medial closure, as in most pronunciations of English /l/. Cf. **unilateral**.

bilateral opposition *n.* In **Prague School** phonology, the relation holding between two contrasting segments which are the only ones contrasting along a particular dimension. For example, English /t/ and /d/ represent a bilateral opposition, as do /f/ and /v/, since these pairs contrast in voicing (voiceless vs. voiced), and there is no third member of the opposition exhibiting a third value of voicing. Cf. **multilateral opposition**.

Bill Peters effect /bɪl ˈpiːtəz ɪfekt/ *n.* The phenomenon in which a single speaker consistently produces a conspicuous difference between certain segments in spontaneous speech but pronounces these segments identically, or nearly identically, in self-conscious speech, possibly to the extent of not being able to distinguish them: a special case of **near-merger** apparently resulting from the unconscious acceptance, in adulthood, of an innovating (near-)merger as the norm. Labov (1994: 363): after an individual who showed this phenomenon particularly clearly in respect of the *cot*/*caught* **merger**.

bimodal /baɪˈməʊdəl/ *adj.* (of a phonological property) Capable of being expressed either in articulatory or in acoustic terms. Lass (1984: 177).

bimoraic vowel /baɪməˈreɪɪk/ *n.* A **long** vowel. Cf. **monomoraic vowel, non-moraic vowel**. Hayes (1989).

binarism /ˈbaɪnərɪzm̩/ *n.* (also **binarity**) The use of **binary features**.

binarity /baɪˈnærɪti/ *n.* 1. The property of being binary, as of a **binary feature** or a **foot** with **binary branching**. 2. (also **binarity hypothesis**) The proposal that **distinctive features** should always be **binary**, at least at the phonological level. See Sommerstein (1977: 109–110) for some critical discussion.

binary branching /ˈbaɪnəri/ *n.* 1. The property of a node in a **metrical tree** or other arboreal structure which has exactly two branches. 2. The requirement, advocated by some linguists, that no such node may have more than two branches; some would go further and require every node to have *exactly* two branches.

binary feature *n.* A **distinctive feature** which can assume one of only two possible values; most typically, though not necessarily, the two values are represented as + and −, indicating that the feature in question is present or absent, respectively; two segments which differ only in having the + and − specifications for a single feature represent a **bilateral opposition**. For example, the feature **nasal** is binary in many systems: nasality is either present ([+nasal]) or absent ([−nasal]), and there is no third possibility. Binary features are convenient because (1) they are easy to manipulate, and (2) they impose an explicit decision procedure about whether an input meets the structural description of a rule, and such features as **nasal**,

coronal, **continuant**, **lateral** and **syllabic** have often seemed to be intrinsically binary. However, such parameters as **place of articulation**, **vowel height** and **phonation type** are not obviously binary at all, since they typically allow three or more contrasts along a single dimension; consequently, attempts to treat these parameters in terms of binary features have often led to a good deal of seemingly *ad hoc* manoeuvring. The **Jakobson–Halle feature system** is exclusively binary in principle, though the **sharp/plain/flat** features actually represent a disguised **ternary feature**, and there is the complication that features are sometimes also allowed to assume the third value zero, meaning 'irrelevant'. The *SPE* **feature system** is rigidly binary, but suffers from severe shortcomings, for example in its treatment of vowel height and in its invoking of the highly *ad hoc* feature **anterior**. More recent systems, such as the **Ladefoged** and **Williamson feature systems**, have abandoned binarism and allowed **multivalued features** with any number of possible values; this approach retains phonetic reality and minimizes *ad hoc*-ness, but the resulting features are sometimes cumbersome to manipulate. See also **unary feature**.

binaural /baɪˈnɔːrəl/ *adj*. Involving the use of both ears. Human hearing in ordinary circumstances is binaural, and the slight difference in timing and intensity between the sound waves reaching the two ears is important in locating the source of a sound.

binyan /ˈbɪnjən/ *n*. (pl. **binyanim** /bɪnˈjɑːnɪm/) (rarely also **wazn**) In Semitic languages, one of the systematic sets of derived forms of a verbal root typically expressing distinctions of grammatical categories such as voice. Examples from Arabic: *katab* 'write', *kattab* 'cause to write', *kaatab* 'correspond', *ʔaktab* 'cause to write', *takaatab* 'write to each other', *nkatab* 'subscribe'. See **nonconcatenative morphology**. Hebrew grammar.

bisegmental /baɪsegˈmentəl/ *adj*. Consisting of a sequence of two **segments**. While Russian *tsar*, for example, begins with a single consonant /ts/, the initial [ts-] of English *tsar* must be analysed as bisegmental, since English has no affricate /ts/.

bisyllable /ˈbaɪsɪləbəl/ *n*. See **disyllable**. *Adj*. **bisyllabic** /baɪsɪˈlæbɪk/.

biteblock /ˈbaɪtblɒk/ *n*. A mechanical device which prevents complete closure of the jaw, used in **articulatory perturbation** experiments.

biuniqueness /baɪjʊˈniːknəs/ *n*. The principle, a strengthened form of the **consistency** requirement, that a phonetic transcription of a known language must be uniquely translatable into a phonemic transcription, and vice versa, down to the level of **free variation** – in other words, a given **phone** in a given **environment** must be an **allophone** of one and only one **phoneme**. Acceptance of biuniqueness entails rejection of any analysis involving **complete overlapping**, and typically compels the recognition of extensive **morphophonemic alternation**. First advanced by Bloch (1941), this principle was named by Harris (1944), and it formed a cornerstone of the phonology of the **American Structuralists**. Perhaps more than any of the other structuralist principles, this one obliged its proponents to accept distasteful and counter-intuitive analyses, a fact recognized by Bloch himself. Biuniqueness was the target of **Halle's argument**, and is rejected by all more recent theories of phonology.

blade /bleɪd/ *n.* (also **lamina**) That part of the upper surface of the tongue extending about one centimetre behind the tip. The blade is involved in the most widespread articulations of English [s t n l]. *Adj.* **laminal**. CF **lamino-**.

blade vowel *n.* See **laminal-dorsal vowel**.

blank-filling rule /'blæŋk fɪlɪŋ/ *n.* A rule specifying a non-distinctive phonetic feature of a segment, such as the rule specifying that all English vowels are non-nasal, or the rule specifying that all English non-obstruents are voiced.

bleeding order /'bliːdɪŋ/ *n.* In a system allowing **ordered rules**, an ordering between two rules such that the earlier one destroys some cases to which the later one could otherwise have applied. The first rule is said to *bleed* the second. The opposite order is **counter-bleeding order**. Cf. **feeding order**. Kiparsky (1965, 1968a).

blend /blend/ *n.* (also **portmanteau word**) A word formed by **blending**.

blending /'blendɪŋ/ *n.* The process of word formation by the combination of arbitrary parts of existing words: *smog* (*smoke* plus *fog*), *paralympics* (*parallel* plus *Olympics*), *Oxbridge* (*Oxford* plus *Cambridge*), *chunnel* (*channel* plus *tunnel*). See Bauer (1983) for discussion.

Bloch and Trager system /blɒk ənd 'treɪgə/ *n.* A phonological analysis of the English vowel system presented by Bernard Bloch and George Trager (Trager and Bloch 1941). Bloch and Trager analysed all the vocalic nuclei of English into combinations of just nine elements: six simple vowels and the three prosodies *j*, *w* and *h*. Nuclei were classed into four types: (1) V (short vowels); (2) Vj (diphthongs with fronting offglides); (3) Vw (diphthongs with backing offglides); (4) Vh (both long vowels and diphthongs with centring offglides, the difference being conditioned by the identity of V). The Bloch and Trager system was superseded by the modified version called the **Trager–Smith system**, published in 1951.

block /blɒk/ *n.* Any one of the minimal tone units, each consisting of a single rise or fall, posited in the **Collier–'t Hart analysis** of intonation.

blockage constraint /'blɒkɪdʒ/ *n.* Any **constraint** on the application of a rule of the form 'No form may undergo rule A, even though it meets that rule's structural description, if it has already undergone rule B'. Here rule B is said to *block* rule A. Cf. **precedence constraint**. Sommerstein (1977: 177).

blocker /'blɒkə/ *n.* See **barrier**.

blocking /'blɒkɪŋ/ *n.* 1. The phenomenon in which a particular segment or boundary acts as a barrier to the propagation of **vowel harmony** or **consonant harmony** through a word or morpheme. See **opaque vowel**. 2. In word formation, the phenomenon by which the existence of a regular derived form is apparently prevented by the prior existence of a distinct word, or of a form derived by a less productive path, of identical meaning. Thus, **inhabiter* is blocked by *inhabitant*, **cooker* ('one who cooks') is blocked by *cook*, and **stealer* is blocked by *thief*.

body /'bɒdi/ *n.* 1. The entire mass of the **tongue**. 2. In some analyses of **intonation**, all the syllables occurring between the **head** and the **nucleus**.

borrowing /'bɒrəʊɪŋ/ *n.* The process by which words (or less commonly bound morphemes) which exist in one language are copied into another language; words borrowed in this way are called **loan words**. Extensive borrowing can have significant consequences for the phonology of the borrowing language: English, for example, has largely acquired its phonemes /v/, /ʒ/ and /dʒ/ as a result of borrowings from French like *very*, *pleasure* and *joy*. More recent loans like *pueblo* (Spanish) and *tsunami* (Japanese) have altered the phonotactics of English. See also **coexistent phonemic systems**. *Adj.* **borrowed**.

boundary /'baʊndəri/ *n.* 1. Any of various elements which have often been recognized as separating phonological elements at some level of representation. The **syllable boundary** ($ or .) is unique in having no lexical or grammatical correlate. Others which have often been regarded as universal are the **morpheme boundary** (+), the **single word boundary** (#), the **double word boundary** (##) and the **phonological phrase boundary** (||). Further language-specific boundaries have also been proposed, such as the **equal sign boundary** (=) recognized by Chomsky and Halle (1968) for separating prefixes from roots in certain English words of Latin origin. 2. A proposed multivalued **distinctive feature** invoked to handle phonological boundaries in sense 1, in which the value zero represents no boundary, 1 represents a **morpheme boundary**, and further values are invoked as necessary for distinguishing among further boundaries. Sense 2: McCawley (1968).

boundary signal *n.* (also *Grenzsignal*) The **Prague School** term for the **junction prosody** of **Prosodic Analysis** and the **juncture** of the **American Structuralists**. The notion was little developed by the Prague School theorists. See Fischer-Jørgensen (1975: 40).

boundary tone *n.* In the **generative analysis** of English **intonation**, a special type of **tone** (sense 3) which falls on the very last syllable of a tone-group and handles any tonal movement associated with that syllable. Two types are recognized, denoted H% and L%.

bounded foot /'baʊndɪd/ *n.* In **Metrical Phonology**, a metrical **foot** which is limited to occurring over a specified maximum number of syllables. Ant. **unbounded foot**. See Katamba (1989: 229–231) for discussion.

bound form /baʊnd/ *n.* A **morph** which can never stand alone to make a word but which must always be combined with other material. Examples are the English **derivational** affixes *re-* (as in *rewrite*) and *-er* (as in *writer*), the **inflectional** affixes plural *-s* (as in *dogs*) and *-ing* (as in *writing*), the **clitics** *-'ll* (as in *He'll do it*) and possessive *-'s* (as in *John's book*), the **combining forms** *step-* (as in *stepmother*), *eco-* (as in *ecosystem*) and *-phobia* (as in *arachnophobia*), the Latin verbal **root** *am-* 'love' and the present and perfect stems *ama-* and *amav-* of the same verb (as in *amat* 'he loves' and *amavi* 'I have loved'), the Turkish passive inflection *-n-* (as in *yenmek* 'to be eaten') and the Arabic verbal root *ktb* 'write' (as in *kataba* 'he wrote' and *maktu:b* 'written'). A bound form which is a single morpheme, like most of the examples above, is a **bound morpheme** Cf. **free form**.

braces /'breɪsɪz/ *n. pl.* (also **curly braces, curly brackets**) 1. An **abbreviatory convention** used to combine in a single **rule schema** two or more rules which are identical except for the presence of different elements at one point; the alternative elements are listed within a pair of braces. For example, the two rules [+obstr] → [–voice] / ___ [–voice] and [+obstr] → [–voice] / ___ # could be combined into the schema [+obstr] → [–voice] / ___ {[–voice], #}, indicating that an obstruent is voiceless either before a voiceless segment or word-finally. Cf. **brackets**. 2. A similar notation used to express a **disjunction** of **feature specifications**. For example, the notation

$$\begin{bmatrix} +\text{cor} \\ \left\{ \begin{matrix} -\text{voi} \\ -\text{cont} \end{matrix} \right\} \end{bmatrix}$$

identifies the class of coronals which are either voiceless or noncontinuant (or both). 3. In some contemporary frameworks, the symbols used to enclose the symbols for the **phonological primes** of the system or clusters of such primes; for example, {i}, {u} and {a} are the **components** of **Dependency Phonology** and {i, a} and {a; i} represent various possible combinations of these elements.

Bracket Erasure Convention /'brækɪt ɪreɪʒə/ *n.* In **Lexical Phonology**, the convention by which all internal brackets (morpheme boundaries) are deleted at the end of each level of processing. This principle largely guarantees the modularity of LP by denying later levels of processing access to structural information relevent to earlier levels.

bracketing paradox /'brækɪtɪŋ pærədɒks/ *n.* Any of various phenomena in which the structure required by the phonology is in conflict with the structure required by the morphology. For example, the morphological structure of *ungrammaticality* must be [[[*un-*][*grammatical*]]-*ity*], since *un-* cannot be attached to a noun, but standard views of phonology require the stress-affecting suffix *-ity* to be added before the stress-neutral prefix *un-*.

brackets /'brækɪts/ *n. pl.* (also **square brackets**) 1. The conventional notation for enclosing symbols representing either individual **phones** or sequences of phones in a **phonetic transcription**. Thus, for example, [m] represents a voiced bilabial nasal, [kʰ] represents an aspirated voiceless velar plosive, and [kʰæm] represents a typical pronunciation of English *cam*. Cf. **slashes**. 2. The conventional symbol for enclosing **distinctive features**, with or without their values: [tense], [+coronal], [–voice]. 3. A conventional device for identifying the morphological structure of a form: [[[*un-*][[*know*] [*-ing*]]][*-ly*]]. Such a bracketing is equivalent to a tree. 4. An **abbreviatory convention** which has (very rarely) been used in **generative phonology** for combining two or more phonological rules into a single **rule schema** in the following way: the notation

$$\begin{bmatrix} A \\ B \end{bmatrix} \rightarrow \quad C\, / \underline{\quad} \begin{bmatrix} D \\ E \end{bmatrix}$$

abbreviates the *two* rules A → C / ___ D and B → C / ___ E. That is, the bracket notation requires that *corresponding* elements must be selected from each pair of brackets in any one reading of the schema, and hence any schema involving brackets must contain at least two pairs of brackets. (Note that if the two sets of brackets were replaced by **braces** here, the resulting schema would then abbreviate *four* rules, the two given above and the two additional ones A → C / ___ E and B → C / ___ D.) 5. In **Lexical Phonology**, the conventional device for enclosing material which is accessible during the current cycle or at the current level.

Branching Rhyme Hypothesis /brɑːntʃɪŋ 'raɪm haɪpɒθəsɪs/ *n.* A proposal within **Autosegmental Phonology** for making a principled distinction between **light** and **heavy syllables**. It says: a syllable with a non-branching rhyme is light, while one with a branching rhyme is heavy.

breaking /'breɪkɪŋ/ *n.* (also **fracture**) 1. More generally, any form of **diphthongization** in which a (typically long) vowel acquires a centring off-glide. Such breaking often accompanies the **raising** of a long vowel. See Labov (1994: ch. 5). Ant. **smoothing**. 2. More specifically, this development when it occurs before a following consonant, sometimes still more specifically one in which a front vowel acquires an off-glide before a following velarized consonant. The term in this narrow sense is applied to certain developments in the early history of English, as examplified by the development of **ærm* into *earm* and of **herte* into *heorte*. Translation of German *Brechung*, coined by Jakob Grimm, though Grimm's use of the term was rather wider.

breaking of the voice *n.* See **voice mutation**.

breath /breθ/ *n.* A **phonation type**, involving turbulent, noisy voiceless flow of air through the open glottis, typically at volume velocities above about 200–300 cm³/s; below this rate only **nil phonation**

occurs. Breath is typically used in English for producing aspirated plosives and [h]. Breath differs from **whisper** in that, in breath, the glottis is wide open, the larynx is relaxed, the volume-velocity of air flow is lower and the sound produced is less loud. Breath is one type of **voicelessness**.

breath group /gruːp/ *n.* In principle, a stretch of utterance produced within a single expiration of breath. The notion is not really well defined, but it has often been invoked for various phonological purposes – for example, the breath group has often been said to be the domain of **stress** in French.

breathy voice /ˈbreθi/ *n.* 1. A **phonation type** produced with very low muscular tension in the larynx; the **vocal folds** vibrate but do not meet completely, and the rate of air flow is therefore high, producing a 'breathy' or 'sighing' voice quality. Breathy voice is not known to be used contrastively in any language, but is characteristic of some individuals on some or all occasions. 2. A very common, but erroneous, synonym for **whispery voice**.

breve /briːv/ *n.* The diacritic [˘], used in various orthographies and transcriptions for various purposes. The breve was originally used in classical scansion to mark a short syllable, and is still used in English scansion to mark unstressed syllables. Many dictionary transcriptions of English pronunciation use the breve to mark 'short' (**lax**) vowels. The breve is currently recognized by the IPA for marking **extra-short** vowels. Latin *breve*, neuter of *brevis* 'short'

bright /braɪt/ *adj.* (also **clear**) An impressionistic label occasionally applied to a vowel which is front and unrounded, such as [i] or [e] – roughly, then, to a vowel which is **acute** and non-**flat** in the **Jakobsen–Halle feature system**. Ant. **dark**.

brightening /ˈbraɪtənɪŋ/ *n.* A term used in Germanic phonology for certain instances of the **fronting** of back vowels. The word for 'day' is Gothic *dags*, Old Icelandic *dagr*, Old High German *tag*, but Old English *dæg* and Old Frisian *deg*, the last two exhibiting brightening.

British school of phonetics /ˈbrɪtɪʃ skuːl/ *n.* The name commonly given to the long and continuous tradition of work in phonetics (especially articulatory phonetics) in Britain, particularly in England and most especially in London. Serious work on phonetics began in England as early as the sixteenth century, but the label 'British school' is usually reserved for the work that began in the nineteenth century with A. J. Ellis, A. M. Bell and, most famously, Henry Sweet, one of the originators of the **phoneme principle**. The pivotal figure in the tradition, however, was Daniel Jones, who created the **cardinal vowel system** and established at the University of London the world's premier centre for the study of phonetics; those trained by Jones or by his students include David Abercrombie, A. C. Gimson, J. D. O'Connor, Peter Ladefoged and John Wells. Jones and his successors are variously responsible for such important contributions as *EPD*, *OEP*, the **Gimson–O'Connor system** of transcribing English, the **Ladefoged feature system** and *LPD*.

broad *a* /brɔːd 'eɪ/ *n*. The long low back vowel used in the pronunciation of such words as as *car* and *father*, and also in *dance*, *bath*, *half*, *grass* and *example* by certain speakers of English, notably by speakers of **Received Pronunciation**; other speakers pronounce these words with the short front vowel of *cat*.

broad accent *n*. [*non-technical*] An **accent** (sense 2) which is perceived as rustic, vulgar or difficult to understand.

broad consonant *n*. In Irish, a consonant which is not palatalized and which contrasts with a palatalized ('**slender**') consonant having the same place and manner of articulation: thus *bó* 'cow' /boː/, with a broad plosive, contrasts with *beo* 'alive' /b'oː/, with a slender plosive, and *bád* 'boat' /baːd/ contrasts with *báid* 'boats' /baːd'/.

broad focus *n*. In **intonation**, the case in which the whole of the intonation group is in focus, as typically occurs in an 'out-of-the-blue' utterance. See Cruttenden (1986). Ant. **narrow focus**.

broad transcription *n*. See **phonemic transcription**. Cf. **narrow transcription**.

brogue /brəʊg/ *n*. [*non-technical*] 1. A popular term for a conspicuously Irish speech variety. 2. Occasionally, any conspicuous regional accent. From *brogue*, a type of heavy shoe worn by Irish farmers.

bronchi /'brɒŋkaɪ/ *n. pl.* (also **bronchial tubes**) The two tubes formed by the conjunction of the **bronchioles** at the tops of the lungs; they unite at the base of the **trachea**.

bronchioles /'brɒŋkɪəʊlz/ *n. pl.* The multiply-branching small tubes running throughout the lungs and connecting the **bronchi** to the **alveoli**.

Brooklynese /brʊklɪ'niːz/ *n.* [*non-technical*] A label for the speech
of the borough of Brooklyn in New York City, or often for a stereo-
typed media caricature of such speech. While similar in most
respects to the speech of metropolitan New York generally,
Brooklynese is conventionally characterized by the *oil/earl* merger,
often perceived by outsiders as a reversal of these two nuclei,
leading to such conventional representations of the variety as the
baseball commentator's 'Hoiman hursted to Hoist' for 'Herman
hoisted to Hurst'. This merger is said to be now sharply recessive.

Brummie /'brʌmi/ *n.* [*non-technical*] The traditional label for
the distinctive speech variety of the West Midlands of England,
centred on the city of Birmingham, or for a person who uses this
variety. From *Brummagem*, a representation of the local pronunciation of
'Birmingham'.

buccal /'bʌkəl/ *adj.* 1. A less usual synonym for **oral** (sense 1).
2. More specifically, pertaining to sounds articulated within the
cavity of the cheek(s), as in the buccal speech of Donald Duck.

buccal cavity *n.* See **oral cavity**.

bunched *r* /bʌntʃt/ *n.* See **molar** *r*.

bunching /'bʌntʃɪŋ/ *n.* Any configuration of the tongue in which the
tongue body is held tensely in a position far from its rest position,
as in the production of [i] or [ʃ], or of **molar** *r*. *Adj.* **bunched**.

bundle /'bʌndəl/ *n.* A **segment** regarded as a collection of **feature
specifications**. The view of segments as feature bundles was first
put forward in **Prague School** phonology; it was accepted in all
versions of **generative phonology**, and most contemporary theories
of phonology, in so far as they recognize segments at all, interpret
them as bundles of phonological primitives of one sort or another.

burr /bɜː/ *n.* [*non-technical*] 1. A uvular realization of the phoneme
/r/ in English, such as that found in Northumbria. 2. Occasionally,
a trilled realization of /r/, such as occurs in some Scottish varieties
of English. 3. An accent using one of these pronunciations. Imitative.

burst /bɜːst/ *n.* (also **stop burst**) The small audible explosion which
accompanies the release of a **plosive**, often especially its appearance as a sudden peak of energy in a **sound spectrogram**.

C

c /siː/ *n.* A symbol sometimes used to represent a consonant position in graphical presentations of syllable structure.

C *n.* In phonology, the conventional **cover symbol** for any **consonant**, used in presenting **canonical forms** (as in the CV syllable structure) and in abbreviating **phonological rules** (as in C → ∅ / C ___ C). Often this symbol is restricted to [–syllabic] segments, and hence excludes glides.

cacophony /kəˈkɒfəni/ *n.* Jarring, discordant, unharmonious sound or speech. *Adj.* **cacophonous**.

cacuminal /kəˈkjuːmɪnəl/ *adj.* [*obsolete*] See **retroflex**. Latin *cacūmen* 'point, top'.

cadence /ˈkeɪdəns/ *n.* 1. A rhythmic beat, as in verse or music. 2. A fall in the pitch of the voice at the end of an intonational phrase. 3. In some analyses of intonation, a binary **distinctive feature** in which [+cadence] indicates the presence of a fall. Old Italian *cadenza* 'a fall'; sense 3: Vanderslice and Ladefoged (1972).

caesura /sɪˈzjʊərə/ *n.* (also **cesura**) 1. A pause or break within a line of verse, conventionally indicated by the symbol //, as in Pope's line *To err is human, // to forgive, divine.* 2. The presence of a word boundary within a metrical **foot**. Latin: 'a cutting'.

calque /kælk/ *n.* (also **loan translation**) A lexical item or phrase which is borrowed from another language, not directly, but by translating the foreign item more or less literally, morpheme by morpheme. For example, Greek *sympathia* (literally, 'with-suffering') was calqued into Latin as *compassiō* (also literally 'with-suffering'), and this in turn was calqued into German as *Mitleid* (also literally 'with-suffering'). The entire French phrase *il va sans dire* has been calqued into English as *it goes without saying. V.* **calque**.

Canadian raising /kəˈneɪdiən/ *n.* The phenomenon, occurring in most Canadian and some American accents, by which the first element of the diphthongs /ai/ and /au/ is centralized ('raised') in specified circumstances. Most typically, such raising occurs when the diphthong is immediately followed by an underlyingly voice-less consonant in the same morpheme – hence the famous contrast between *rider* and *writer*, which, thanks to the **tapping** of /t/ and /d/ in these accents, are distinguished phonetically only by the quality of the diphthong: raised in *writer* but not in *rider*. Some speakers, however, also exhibit such raising before certain voiced consonants or before voiced consonants in certain words; thus, *fire*, *file*, *tidy*, *fibre* and *powder* may also show raising. Some speakers additionally exhibit raising in the nucleus /ar/, so that the nuclei of *hard* and *heart*, for example, differ in exactly the same way as those in *ride* and *write*. NOTE: Historically, the term is perhaps a misnomer, since the historical process is probably an absence of lowering.

canonical /kə'nɒnɪkəl/ *adj.* Most frequent, most usual, most typical or least marked (among competing possibilities) in a language or in languages generally.

canonical form *n.* 1. The most general or most typical form of a linguistic element, such as a syllable, a word, a morpheme or a verbal root, usually in terms of its component consonants (C) and vowels (V). For example, the vast majority of Proto-Indo-European roots have the structure CVC, and this is therefore the canonical form of PIE roots; Japanese syllables have the canonical form (C)V(n) – that is, a syllable consists of a vowel optionally preceded by a single consonant and optionally followed by the nasal *n*. 2. The phonetic form of a word when it is spoken carefully in isolation.

cardinal vowel /'kɑːdɪnəl/ *n.* Any one of the reference vowels recognized in the **cardinal vowel system**.

cardinal vowel diagram /'daɪəgræm/ *n.* The conventional graphical device for representing the **cardinal vowels** within the **vowel quadri-lateral**; see the Appendix. The diagram was devised by Daniel Jones, and first appeared in Ward (1929).

cardinal vowel system *n.* A system of conventional, arbitrarily chosen vowel qualities in terms of which actually occurring vowels may be identified. The conventional reference vowels are arranged in a kind of grid (represented graphically by the **vowel quadri-lateral**), and an experienced practitioner can locate a real vowel within this grid in much the same way that points on a map are identified by reference to a superimposed grid. The traditional cardinal vowel system first defines a set of **primary cardinal vowels**;

from this is derived a second set, the **secondary cardinal vowels**. Each of these traditional sets, however, mixes rounded and unrounded vowels, an outcome regarded by some as a descriptive inconvenience, and today it is more usual to regroup the cardinal vowels into rounded and unrounded sets for presentation. See the Appendix for both types of presentation, and see also **Ladefoged experiment**. The idea of a cardinal vowel system was first put forward by A. J. Ellis in the late nineteenth century; the term 'cardinal' was coined by A. M. Bell and was used by Henry Sweet; Daniel Jones was the first to work out a complete system of cardinal vowels (in the first (1917) edition of *EPD* and in the second (1922) edition of *OEP*), and his system is still essentially that in use today.

carrier /'kærɪə/ *n.* In some analyses of certain phonological processes, such as **epenthesis**, a set of features assumed to be added to another single feature which has been introduced into a position where no segment is present in order to yield a pronounceable segment. Lass (1984: 185).

case vide /kaz vid/ *n.* [French: 'empty space'] See **hole in the pattern**.

catachresis /kætə'kriːsɪs/ *n.* See **malapropism**. Greek *katakhrēsis* 'a misusing'.

catalectic /kætə'lektɪk/ *adj.* (of a line of verse) Lacking a final unaccented syllable which is technically required to complete the last foot: *Tyger! Tyger! burning bright*[ ] / *In the forests of the night*[ ]. *Abstr. n.* **catalexis** /kætə'leksɪs/. Ant. **acatalectic**.

categorical perception of speech /kætə'gɒrɪkəl/ *n.* The frequently observed phenomenon in which a speaker perceives both natural speech and synthesized sequences in terms of a small number of discrete categories, most typically the phonemes of the speaker's language. For example, a synthesized sequence showing formant transitions intermediate between those typical of [ba] and those typical of [da] is almost invariably perceived either as an instance of [ba] or as an instance of [da]; very rarely does anyone report hearing something intermediate. This phenomenon is most marked with plosives, less marked with other consonants, and virtually absent with vowels, which are usually perceived on a continuum, like most non-speech sounds. The phenomenon has been invoked as evidence both for the psychological reality of phonemes and for a distinct 'speech mode' of perception which functions differently from the perception of non-speech stimuli.

categorical-phonetic level *n.* In some versions of **generative phonology**, that level of representation having the property that the only rules still to apply are **phonetic rules** and that the last rule to have applied was not a phonetic rule. This is effectively the level of representation, usually still in terms of binary features, at which all information required to produce a careful pronunciation is present. Sommerstein (1974: 72).

categorical property /'prɒpəti/ *n.* Any property characterized by an absolute either/or, yes/no distinction. For example, at the phonological level, nasality is usually regarded as categorical: a segment either is nasal or is not nasal, and no intermediate positions are possible. At the phonetic level, however, since the velum can be raised or lowered along a continuum, any number of degrees of nasality can in principle be distinguished, and nasality is not a categorical property.

categorical view /vjuː/ *n.* The high-level principle that linguistic categories are separated into mutually exclusive sets. While necessary to some degree if any analysis is going to be performed at all, this view, taken to its logical conclusion, has unrealistic consequences: for example, that a given speech variety 'has' a fixed set of phonemes and that a given segment must be unambiguously assigned to one of those phonemes. Such devices as the **morphophoneme**, the **systematic phoneme**, the **archiphoneme** and the recognition of **coexistent phoneme systems** represent varied attempts at forcing recalcitrant data into the categorical view. See Labov (1994: ch. 12) for a critical discussion.

Category Change, Principle of /'kætəgri tʃeɪndʒ/ *n.* A putative principle governing the course of **lexical diffusion**. It says: changes that affect several features of a sound simultaneously proceed by altering the category memberships of individual words. Labov (1994: 603).

Category Stability, Principle of /stə'bɪlɪti/ *n.* The observation that individuals who change their accents on moving to a different speech area tend strongly to preserve the distribution of lexical items among the phoneme categories of the system – that is, while they may change their phonetic realizations, they do not introduce mergers, splits or different distributions of phonemes which are typical of their new area. Labov (1994: 109–111).

Catford classification /'kætfəd/ *n.* A partially distinctive division of the **supralaryngeal vocal tract**, particularly the **oral cavity**, for

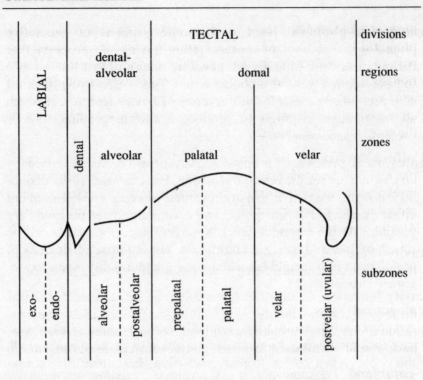

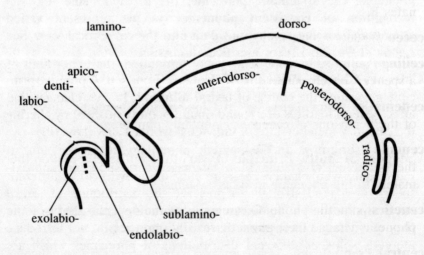

Figure C1 The Catford classification

purposes of labelling the place of articulation of consonants, proposed by J. C. Catford (1977, 1988). See Figure C1. The lower part of the oral cavity is divided more simply (and more traditionally) into the following zones: *labial* (consisting of *exolabial* and *endolabial subzones*), *dental, sublaminal, apical, laminal, anterodorsal* (the front of the tongue), *posterodorsal* (the back of the tongue) and *radical* (the root of the tongue).

Catford–McKinney box /mə'kɪni/ *n.* A box containing a mouthpiece, a flow-transducer, a microphone and a window, allowing an investigator to obtain simultaneously volume-velocities, sound recordings and high-speed films of a subject speaking into the box. After its inventors, J. C. Catford and N. S. McKinney.

cavity /'kævɪti/ *n.* Any more-or-less well-defined empty space within the vocal tract: the **oral cavity**, the **nasal cavity** or the **pharynx**.

cavity feature *n.* In the *SPE* **feature system**, any one of the eleven **distinctive features** invoked for handling variations in the configuration of the supralaryngeal vocal tract: **coronal, anterior, high, low, back, round, distributed, covered, glottal constriction, nasal, lateral**.

c-command /'siːkəmɑːnd/ *n.* A syntactic relation occasionally appealed to in phonology, for example by Kaisse (1985). In a syntactic structure, a node A c-commands a node B iff the lowest branching node which properly dominates A also properly dominates B.

ceceo /θe'θeo/ *n.* See under **seseo**.

ceiling /'siːlɪŋ/ *n.* In some analyses of **intonation**, the upper limit of a speaker's pitch range.

cenematics /siːnə'mætɪks/ *n.* In **Glossematic phonology**, the study of the behaviour of **cenemes**; essentially **phonology**.

ceneme /'siːniːm/ *n.* In **Glossematic phonology**, a minimal unit in the phonological system of a language, corresponding approximately to the **phoneme** in other systems.

cenetics /sɪ'netɪks/ *n.* In **Glossematic phonology**, the study of the phonetic details of **cenemes**; essentially **phonetics**.

central /'sentrəl/ *adj.* 1. (of vowels) Articulated with the highest point of the tongue in neither the front third nor the back third of the oral cavity; in other words, neither **front** nor **back**. Among the central vowels are [ɨ], [ə] and [ɜ]. 2. In the **Williamson feature**

system, one of the eleven possible values of the feature **articulatory place**, identified with central vowels. 3. (of consonants) A synonym for **median**, best avoided because of the possible confusion with sense 1.

central closure *n.* A binary **distinctive feature** proposed by Sommerstein (1977: 103) for distinguishing medial occlusion of the vocal tract from total occlusion, as follows: ordinary plosives are [+occlusive, +central closure, –lateral]; lateral affricates are [+occlusive, +central closure, +lateral]; lateral fricatives and resonants are [–occlusive, +central closure, +lateral]. This feature (which would more properly be called 'median closure') seems never to have been taken up. Cf. **mid-closure**.

centrality /sen'træləti/ *n.* In some versions of **Dependency Phonology**, an element |ə|, posited as a **component** of central and centralized vowels.

centralized /'sentrəlaɪzd/ *adj.* (of vowels) Articulated with the highest point of the tongue somewhat closer to the centre (between front and back) of the mouth than occurs with some standard of comparison. A centralized front vowel is **retracted**; a centralized back vowel is **advanced**; a central vowel cannot be centralized. The diacritic [¨] may be used for representing centralization; equally, the diacritics for retraction and advancement may be used as appropriate. *Abstr. n.* **centralization**.

central release *n.* (also **central plosion**) See **median release**.

central resonant *n.* Any **resonant** which is not a **lateral approximant (lateral resonant)**.

centre /'sentə/ *n.* 1. A label sometimes applied to that part of the upper surface of the **tongue** lying between the **front** and the **back**, that is, that part of the tongue which is highest in the articulation of **central** vowels. 2. See **nucleus**.

centring diphthong /'sentrɪŋ/ *n.* (also **ingliding diphthong**) A **diphthong** during whose articulation the tongue moves toward the central vowel schwa, such as the diphthongs [ɪə], [ʊə] and [ɛə] in **non-rhotic** pronunciations of *beer*, *poor* and *fair*.

cepstral smoothing /sepstrəl 'smuːðɪŋ/ *n.* A procedure for processing a **sound spectrogram** which removes the **voicing ripple** and provides a smooth curve highlighting the frequency bands which are predominantly present.

cerebral /'serəbrəl/ *adj.* [*obsolete*] See **retroflex**. Translation of Sanskrit *murdhanya*.

chain of speech /tʃeɪn/ *n.* See **speech chain**.

chain shift *n.* (also **chaining**, *enchaînement*) Any complex phonological change in which several segments (most often vowels) all change their phonetic realizations, with some segments (**entering elements**) moving into spaces vacated by other segments (**leaving elements**). Two types are recognized: **push chains** and **drag chains**. Chain shifts were championed by Martinet (1955) and·have been most extensively studied by Labov (1994).

change from above /tʃeɪndʒ/ *n.* An innovation introduced by the dominant social class, often with full public awareness, typically appearing primarily in careful speech and reflecting a superposed variety learned after the vernacular is acquired. An example is the self-conscious switch from a **rhotic** to a **non-rhotic accent** in Britain, or the opposite in the United States. Cf. **change from below**. Labov (1966).

change from below *n.* An innovation appearing first in vernacular speech, typically representing the operation of internal linguistic factors, and most often occurring below the level of social awareness, at least until the change has nearly gone to completion. Such a change may be introduced by any social class but is perhaps most typically introduced by members of lower social classes. An example is the spread of **glottal reinforcement** and **glottalling** in England. Cf. **change from above**. Labov (1966).

channel /'tʃænəl/ *n.* 1. In articulation, the passageway through which the airstream flows. 2. A particular, sharply defined **frequency band** through which a signal may be sent.

channel vocoder /'vəʊkəʊdə/ *n.* A type of **vocoder** employing a bank of **filters** with adjacent **frequency bands**. The device transmits only the intensity of activity in each band, together with the fundamental frequency of the vocal folds; at the receiving end, a similar device is used to reconstruct the original speech. Though now little used in telecommunications, the channel vocoder is the basis of the **sound spectrograph**.

characteristic tone /kærəktə'rɪstɪk/ *n.* A system found in some **tone languages** with polysyllabic words in which words are divided into classes, each with its own distinctive tonal pattern. For example, in

LuGanda, there are two classes of verbs, one with sustained high pitch, the other with a falling pitch.

charm /tʃɑːm/ *n.* A fundamental notion in **Government and Charm Phonology**. Each **component** (phonological prime) in this framework is considered to possess exactly one of positive charm, negative charm or no charm. Positive charm corresponds intuitively to a high degree of vowel-like character, and elements of like charm are prohibited from combining. Charm is carried over from elements into segments containing them, and, as a result, most (not all) vowels are considered to be positively charmed, most (not all) obstruents are negatively charmed, and other segments are charmless. These charm properties are appealed to in formulating various principles of the framework, such as phonotactic constraints. By analogy with particle physics, in which charm is a property of certain quarks.

chart /tʃɑːt/ *n.* In **Autosegmental Phonology**, a set of **tiers** along with the **association lines** that relate them.

checked /tʃekt/ *adj.* In the **Jakobson–Halle feature system**, a **distinctive feature** defined as 'involving a higher rate of energy discharge' and associated with **ejective** and **implosive** consonant articulations. In the *SPE* **feature system**, this feature is replaced by the three features **ejection**, **implosion** and **glottal constriction**. Ant. **unchecked**.

checked syllable *n.* See **closed syllable**.

checked vowel *n.* 1. A vowel occurring in a **closed syllable**. 2. A vowel (in a particular language) which can only occur in this position, such as the vowels /e æ ʊ/ in English. Ant. **unchecked vowel** or **free vowel**.

chest pulse /'tʃest pʌls/ *n.* A single contraction of the muscles involved in expelling air from the lungs during speech.

chest-pulse theory of syllable production *n.* The view that every individual **syllable** in speech production is associated with a single respiratory movement. Once widely held, this view is now generally rejected. Stetson (1951).

chest register *n.* (also **chest voice**) The lowest-pitched of the three distinguishable speech **registers** (sense 1), in which the vocal folds are shorter and thicker than in other registers. **Voicing** in chest register is characterized by repeated complete closure of the vocal folds and by a frequency of vibration of about 60–150 Hz (in men), and a **glottal stop** involves a large area of contact between the vocal folds. Chest voice is the register most typically used in ordinary speech. Cf. **mid-register**, **falsetto**.

Chomsky–Halle feature system /tʃɒmski 'hæli/ *n.* See *SPE* **feature system**.

chromatic /krəʊ'mætɪk/ *adj.* In the analysis of vowels in some **privative** systems, especially **Dependency Phonology**, low in **sonority**, such as [i] or [u]. Ant. **achromatic**.

chrone /krəʊn/ *n.* Any positional variant of a **chroneme**. Jones (1950).

chrone language *n.* A language which uses contrastive length of segments (**chronemes**) for phonological purposes, such as those varieties of French in which *mettre* /metr/ 'put' contrasts with *maître* /mɛːtr/ 'master'. Jones (1950), by analogy with **tone language**.

chroneme /'krəʊniːm/ *n.* In some versions of **classical phonology**, a phonological unit, essentially a type of **phoneme**, serving only to lengthen a preceding segment. For example, the five short and five long vowels of Latin (i e a o u iː eː aː oː uː) could be analysed into six phonological units: the five short vowels /i e a o u/ and the chroneme /ː/. Jones (1950).

cineradiography /sɪnɪreɪdi'ɒgrəfi/ *n.* A technique for taking X-ray films of the movements of the organs of speech – exceedingly useful for tracking the movements of organs which are opaque to X-rays or which can be rendered so, as when a chain of tiny lead weights is laid across the upper surface of the tongue.

circumfix /'sɜːkəmfɪks/ *n.* An **affix** which is realized as a combination of a **prefix** and a **suffix**, such as Tigrinya *bi-* ... *-gize* 'at the time when' or the Chukchi 'recessive' *e-* ... *-ke*, the latter illustrated in *e-tejkev-ke it-ek* 'not to fight'; cf. *tejkev-ek* 'to fight'.

circumflex accent *n.* The diacritic ^, used in various orthographies and transcriptions for various purposes. It was first used in Ancient Greek orthography to represent the distinctive rise–fall pitch accent of that language. In Rumanian, the character ⟨î⟩ is used for a vowel distinct from that represented by ⟨i⟩. In French, the circumflex was originally used to mark a lengthened vowel resulting from the loss of a following [s], as in *île* and *bête* (from earlier *isle* and *beste*). The later shortening of these vowels in French has deprived the circumflex of its function, and the French Academy has recently proposed its elimination from most words. This diacritic has no recognized function in the IPA. Cf. **acute accent**, **grave accent**. Latin *circumflexus* 'bent round', from its shape.

citation form /saɪ'teɪʃn̩/ *n*. 1. That particular form of a **lexical item** which is used to name it when talking about it as a linguistic object or when entering it in a dictionary. When a linguistic item has only a single form, like English *under* or *beautiful*, or when it has one form that shows no overt inflection, like *dog*, *big* or *take*, the choice of citation form is obvious (at least to linguists and lexicographers, though native speakers may prefer an inflected form). When a lexical item exists only as a set of overtly inflected forms, however, one of these must somewhat arbitrarily be chosen as the citation form, and different choices are usually possible. For example, the Basque verb meaning 'see' has the root *-kus-*, a bound form; linguists, lexicographers and native speakers have variously used *ikus*, *ikusi* and *ikustea* as a citation form: *ikus* is the morphologically simplest free form, *ikusi* is the most convenient form for predicting the remaining forms, and *ikustea* is semantically the least marked. 2. That particular phonetic form which a **phonological word** assumes when it is pronounced carefully in isolation, typically free of any **reduction**, **assimilation** or **coalescence** which may affect its pronunciation in connected speech.

clash /klæʃ/ *n*. Particularly in **Metrical Phonology**, the occurrence of (usually identical levels of) stress on two consecutive syllables. Some would extend the term to other instances of consecutive identical specifications, such as consecutive high tones. A number of syntagmatic phonological processes are interpreted as repair devices for avoiding such clash, such as the **iambic reversal** of English. Cf. **lapse**.

class I suffix /klɑːs 'wʌn/ *n*. See **primary affix**.

class II suffix *n*. See **secondary affix**.

classical generative phonology /'klæsɪkəl/ *n*. The version of **generative phonology** originally presented in *SPE*; see **generative phonology** for further information.

classical phoneme *n*. See **autonomous phoneme**.

classical phonology *n*. A label sometimes applied to the bulk of the work in phonology between the mid-1920s and the mid-1960s, characterized above all by its emphasis upon the identification of phonetic features which serve, or might serve, to distinguish one word or utterance from another of different meaning, and hence by its emphasis upon **representations**, with a corresponding lack of interest in **rules**.

classificatory function /klæsɪfɪˈkeɪtri/ *n.* The role of a **distinctive feature** in specifying an **opposition (contrast)** between segments, or in formulating a **natural class** of segments. Cf. **phonetic function**.

classificatory matrix *n.* A matrix which displays some or all of the segments of a particular language together with a complete specification of the relevant **distinctive features** of those segments. Such a matrix is in no sense part of the phonology of the language; it serves purely as a convenient summary, for the analyst or the student, of the role of the features in the phonology of that language. Figure C2, for example, is such a matrix for the consonants of a central dialect of Basque.

class node /klɑːs/ *n.* In **feature geometry**, a superordinate node.

clear /klɪə/ *adj.* See **bright**.

clear *l* *n.* A coronal lateral articulated with the back of the tongue held low, and hence without **velarization**. Many speakers in Ireland and Wales use a clear *l* as their realization of /l/ in all positions. Speakers in England typically use a clear *l* for /l/ only before a vowel, using a **dark *l*** elsewhere. Many Scottish and American speakers never use clear *l* at all. Cf. **dark *l***.

cleft lip /kleft/ *n.* (also **hare lip**) A congenital split in the upper lip and/or the upper teeth ridge, often cooccurring with a **cleft palate**. NOTE: The traditional term 'hare lip' is no longer in respectable use.

	p	t	c	k	b	d	ɟ	g	f	ś	s	ʃ	χ	tś	ts	tʃ	m	n	ñ	l	ʎ	ɾ	r
syllabic	−	−	−	−	−	−	−	−	−	−	−	−	−	−	−	−	−	−	−	−	−	−	−
consonantal	+	+	+	+	+	+	+	+	+	+	+	+	+	+	+	+	+	+	+	+	+	+	+
continuant	−	−	−	−	−	−	−	−	+	+	+	+	+	−	−	−	−	−	−	+	+	+	+
sonorant	−	−	−	−	−	−	−	−	−	−	−	−	−	−	−	−	+	+	+	+	+	+	+
voice	−	−	−	−	+	+	+	+	−	−	−	−	−	−	−	−	+	+	+	+	+	+	+
delrel	−	−	−	−	−	−	−	−	+	+	+	+	+	+	+	+	−	−	−	−	−	−	−
coronal	−	+	+	−	−	+	+	−	−	+	+	+	−	+	+	+	−	+	+	+	+	+	+
anterior	+	+	−	−	+	+	−	−	+	+	+	−	−	+	+	−	+	+	−	+	−	+	+
nasal	−	−	−	−	−	−	−	−	−	−	−	−	−	−	−	−	+	+	+	−	−	−	−
lateral	−	−	−	−	−	−	−	−	−	−	−	−	−	−	−	−	−	−	−	+	+	−	−
long	−	−	−	−	−	−	−	−	−	−	−	−	−	−	−	−	−	−	−	−	−	−	+

Figure C2 A classificatory matrix for the consonants of Basque

cleft palate *n.* A congenital permanent opening between the roof of the mouth and the nasal cavity. The sufferer's speech is characterized by strong and persistent nasalization.

click /klɪk/ *n.* 1. A stop consonant produced with a **velaric ingressive** airstream, such as [!] or [ǂ]. Clicks occur as segments only in certain languages of southern Africa, but may occur paralinguistically elsewhere, as in the English use of [!] ('tsk tsk') to express pity or of [ǁ] to make a horse go. See Laver (1994: 174–179, 239) for a summary. In 1989 the IPA replaced its earlier symbols for clicks with those traditionally used by specialists in click languages. Cf. **reverse click**. 2. In the *SPE* **feature system**, an ill-defined feature invoked to distinguish click consonants [+click] from all others [–click]. 3. In the **Ladefoged** and **Williamson feature systems**, one of the two possible values of the distinctive feature **velaric suction** (or **velaric**).

click accompaniment /ə'kʌmpənɪmənt/ *n.* Any of various phenomena which may accompany the articulation of a **click**, such as **affrication**, **aspiration**, **nasal release**, the use of a particular **phonation type**, or the lowering of the **velum** throughout. Ladefoged and Traill (1994).

clipped /klɪpt/ *adj.* 1. [*non-technical*] A label applied to an **accent** (sense 2) which is perceived as being characterized by prominent reduction or loss of syllables. The term is commonly applied by Americans to the speech of southern England, reflecting the striking effect on the American ear of the usual south-of-England pronunciations of such words as *temporarily*, *primarily*, *police* and *geography*. 2. [*non-technical*] A label applied to a speech style which is exceptionally terse, abrupt and close-mouthed, such as the stereotypical speech of British army officers. 3. (of a speech signal) Distorted as a result of overloading of the system. 4. See under **clipping**.

clipping /'klɪpɪŋ/ *n.* The process by which a word is derived from a longer word of identical meaning by the removal of some arbitrary part of the longer word: *bus* from *omnibus*, *phone* from *telephone*, *gym* from *gymnasium*, *porn* from *pornography*, *mike* from *microphone*, *mimeo* from *mimeograph* and *bi* from *bisexual*. Sometimes the term is extended to cases like *Havana* (from *Havana cigar*) and *canary* (from *canary bird*). *Adj.* **clipped**.

clitic /'klɪtɪk/ *n.* An item which exhibits behaviour intermediate between that of a word and that of an affix. Typically, a clitic has the phonological form of a separate word, but cannot be stressed and is obliged to occupy a particular position in the sentence in which it is phonologically bound to an adjoining word, its **host**. A **proclitic** precedes its host; examples include the French subject pronouns *je*, *tu*, etc.: *je vais* 'I'm going', *tu as* or *t'as* 'you have'. An **enclitic** follows its host; examples include the English negative *-n't* (as in *couldn't*) and Basque *be* and Turkish *de*, both meaning 'also': *zu be*, *siz de* 'you too'. See Klavans (1985), Zwicky (1985).

clitic boundary *n.* The type of **boundary** which occurs between a **clitic** and its **host**, often represented as #. Chomsky and Halle (1968).

clitic group *n.* In some versions the **Prosodic Hierarchy** model, a level of the hierarchy posited to account for certain processes which apply when **clitics** are present but not when phonetically similar non-clitics are present, such as the common loss of [v] in *Give me some* but not in *Give Mary some*.

cliticization /klɪtɪsaɪˈzeɪʃn̩/ *n.* Any process by which an independent word is reduced to a **clitic**. See Jeffers and Zwicky (1980).

close /kləʊs/ *adj.* (of vowels) An older synonym for **high** (sense 1), still preferred by some, and officially recommended by the IPA at its **Kiel Convention** in 1989. Ant. **open**.

close approximation *n.* The **degree of stricture** required to produce a **fricative**. Cf. **open approximation**.

closed phase /kləʊzd/ *n.* See **hold**.

closed syllable *n.* (also **checked syllable**) A **syllable** which ends in one or more consonants. All the syllables occurring in the English words *cut*, *aim*, *handle*, *accent* and *companion* are closed; the syllables of *murmur* are closed in a **rhotic accent** but not in a **non-rhotic accent**. See under **ambisyllabic** for the problem posed by words like *ticker* and *petrol*. Ant. **open syllable**.

closed-syllable shortening /ʃɔːtənɪŋ/ *n.* The phenomenon in which an underlying or historical long vowel is shortened when it finds itself in a closed syllable.

closed tone *n.* Any falling **intonation** pattern. Ant. **open tone** (sense 2). Cruttenden (1986).

close juncture *n.* 1. The close phonetic association that exists between consecutive segments not separated by any kind of grammatical boundary, such as between /t/ and /r/ in *nitrate* (as opposed to *night-rate*). 2. A similar phenomenon sometimes taken as typical of **consonant clusters** in certain languages, and realized, for example, by lack of release of the first of two consecutive plosives. English has close juncture: in such words as *apt* and *grabbed*, the first plosive in the cluster is unreleased. Ant. (both senses) **open juncture**.

close-mid *adj*. A synonym for **high-mid**, recommended by the IPA at its **Kiel Convention** in 1989.

close rounding *n*. A variety of **lip-rounding** in which the lips are pursed tightly together, as in a typical articulation of [y]. Ant. **open rounding**.

close transition *n*. The absence of any audible gap between two consecutive consonants, typically characterized by **articulatory overlap** in **heterorganic** sequences (like [kp] in *take part*) and complete continuity in homorganic sequences (like [vf] in *five feet*). Close transition is typical of relaxed English. Ant. **open transition**.

closing diphthong /'kləʊzɪŋ/ *n*. A **diphthong** whose second element is higher (closer) than its first, such as [ei] or [au]. Ant. **opening diphthong**.

closing phase *n*. See **approach**.

closure /'kləʊʒə/ *n*. 1. See **hold**. 2. The maximal **degree of stricture**: a total blockage of air flow in the mouth.

cluster /'klʌstə/ *n*. See **consonant cluster**.

cluttering /'klʌtərɪŋ/ *n*. A pathological disorder of speech, characterized by an intolerable rapidity and hence by frequent loss or distortion of speech sounds and often by abnormal rhythm and sequencing.

Co A frequent symbol for **coda** in representations of **syllable structure**. NOTE: This symbol should not be confused with the notational device C_0, which stands for a sequence of zero or more consonants.

coach test /kəʊtʃ/ *n*. An elaborate procedure for testing whether subjects can distinguish potential **minimal pairs**. A narrative is constructed in which either of the two key items could be sensibly used at one point but the two possibilities lead to radically different interpretations of the narrative; a subject hears the narrative with one or the other item at the crucial point and is then questioned to determine what has been understood. See Labov (1994: 403–406). From a particular narrative involving a football coach.

coalescence /kəʊə'lesəns/ *n.* (also **fusion**) The phonological process in which two segments occurring in sequence in a single linguistic form combine into a single segment, usually one exhibiting some characteristics of both of the original segments. Examples include the historical development of /zj/ into /ʒ/ in English, as in *vision*, the rapid-speech development of English /dj/ into /dʒ/, as in *would you* /'wʊdʒuː/, and the historical development in western varieties of Basque of original /rs/ (with an apical trill and a laminal sibilant) into /ś/ (an apical sibilant), as in western *uso* 'dove, pigeon' vs. eastern *urzo* (orthographic ⟨s⟩ and ⟨z⟩ represent voiceless apical and laminal sibilants, respectively). Some analysts regard coalescence as a variety of **assimilation** and hence call it **coalescent assimilation**. *V.* **coalesce** /kəʊə'les/. Ant. **unpacking**. Cf. **merger**.

coarticulation /kəʊɑːtɪkju'leɪʃn̩/ *n.* 1. (also **double articulation**) Any articulation involving constriction of the vocal tract at two (or rarely more) distinct points. The two constrictions may be equally radical (as in the coarticulated stop [kp]), or one may be less radical than the other (as in the labialized velar plosive [kʷ]). The first type is called 'coordinate coarticulation', the second 'secondary coarticulation', by Catford (1977). 2. See **accommodation** (sense 1). *Adj.* **coarticulated**.

cochlea /'kɒkliə/ *n.* A tightly coiled structure in the **inner ear**, filled with viscous fluid, and containing the **organ of Corti**. The mechanical motion of the **auditory ossicles** in the **middle ear** is transmitted across the **oval window** into the cochlea; it travels through the **basilar membrane** to the organ of Corti, where the mechanical signal is converted into nervous impulses. *Adj.* **cochlear**.

Cockney /'kɒkni/ *n.* [*non-technical*] The traditional label for the distinctive speech variety of the metropolitan London area, centred on the East End of the city, or for a person using this variety. From *coken-ey* 'cock's egg', a label applied originally to a pampered, squeamish or effeminate person, then by countrymen to city-dwellers generally.

cocktail party effect /'kɒkteɪl pɑːti/ *n.* The phenomenon by which an individual surrounded by a large number of people speaking simultaneously can attend selectively to one of them, ignoring the others.

coda /'kəʊdə/ *n.* (**Co**) In most views of **syllable structure**, that part of the syllable which follows the **nucleus** and which contains any syllable-final consonants, such as /t/ in *sit* and /ksθs/ in *sixths*. The nucleus and the coda together constitute the **rhyme**. Hockett (1955): Italian *coda* 'tail', used in music.

coexistent phonemic systems /kəʊɪgˈzɪstənt/ *n. pl.* The phenomenon in which a language exhibits a significant number of loan words whose phonological characteristics are different from those of native words, often particularly in that the loan words show a clear phonemic contrast between segments which in native words are merely allophones of a single phoneme. Turkish is a good example of the phenomenon. In native Turkish words, /k/, /g/ and /l/ are single phonemes exhibiting palatalized allophones in front-vowel words and non-palatalized allophones in back-vowel words: *kar* [kar] 'snow'; *köpek* [k'öpek'] 'dog'; *karga* [karga] 'crow'; *gelmek* [g'elmek'] 'to come'; *yol* [jol] 'road'; *yel* [jel'] 'wind'. Turkish has, however, borrowed many words from Arabic, Persian and French in which palatalized versions of these consonants occur in back-vowel words: *kâr* [k'ar] 'profit'; *gâvur* [g'avur] 'infidel'; *kâbus* [k'abus] 'nightmare'; *lâzïm* [l'aːzïm] 'necessary'; *plan* [pl'an] 'plan'. Fries and Pike (1949).

cognate /ˈkɒgneɪt/ *n.* or *adj.* Any one of two or more words in genetically related languages which áre descended from a single common ancestor in the common ancestral language. For example, English *foot* and German *Fuss* 'foot' are cognate, both being derived from Proto-Germanic **fōt-*, and both are cognate with Spanish *pie*, French *pied* and Ancient Greek *pous*, all being ultimately derived from Proto-Indo-European **ped-*.

cohering affix /kəʊˈhɪərɪŋ/ *n.* An **affix** which is fully integrated into the phonological word of which it forms a part. Ant. **non-cohering affix**. Dixon (1977).

cola /ˈkəʊlə/ *n.* In grid versions of **Metrical Phonology**, a level of representation above the **foot** and below the **word**, sometimes regarded as having theoretical significance. Greek *kōla*, pl. of *kōlon* 'limb'.

cold /kəʊld/ *adj.* 1. (of a feature) In **Government and Charm Phonology**, having an unmarked value. 2. (of a segment) Consisting only of cold features. Ant. **hot**.

collapsing /kəˈlæpsɪŋ/ *n.* See **conflation**. *V.* **collapse**.

Collier–'t Hart analysis /ˈkɒljə tɑːt/ *n.* A model of **intonation** employing a number of building **blocks** which are put together in varying sequences to form the tunes of sentences. Collier and 't Hart (1981).

colon /'kəʊlən/ *n.* 1. The symbol :, occasionally invoked to mark the distinctive type of **boundary** occurring between the elements of a **compound**. McCawley (1968). 2. The symbol [ː], used in the IPA to indicate that a preceding segment is long, as in Finnish /kisːa/ 'cat' (vs. /kisa/ 'game').

coloured vowel /'kʌləd/ *n.* A vowel phoneme in a particular language which contrasts with another vowel phoneme of similar quality by the presence of any of several **secondary articulations** or of a distinctive **phonation type**: **nasalization** (as in French), **rhotacization** (as in American English), **whispery voice** (as in north Indian languages), **creaky voice** (as in Danish), etc. Jones (1950).

combinatorial constraint /kɒmbɪnə'tɔːriəl/ *n.* Any restriction imposed by the **phonotactics** of a language.

combinatory variant /'kɒmbɪneɪtri/ *n.* [*obsolete*] The **Prague School** term for a **conditioned allophone**.

combining form /kəm'baɪnɪŋ/ *n.* 1. A **bound form** of a lexical stem which is used in word formation. For example, Basque *gizon* 'man' has the combining form *giza-* in such formations as *gizajo* 'poor fellow' (suffix *-jo*) and *giza-sorgin* 'sorcerer' (*sorgin* 'witch'). 2. A bound form, usually of Greek or Latin origin, which in word formation behaves as an affix in some respects but not in others: *astro-*, *bio-*, *electro-*, *-crat*, *-phile*, *-phobia*. The difficulty with regarding such forms as affixes is that words can be formed consisting entirely of such combining forms, such as *biocrat* and *electrophile*; if these forms are affixes, then such words contain no root. See Bauer (1983) for discussion.

common core /'kɒmən/ *n.* The set of phonemic contrasts common to all varieties of a language. Cf. **diasystem**. Hockett (1958).

communal change /'kɒmjʊnəl/ *n.* A type of language change in which all or most members of a speech community acquire innovations simultaneously or change their frequency of competing forms in step. Common in lexical and syntactic change, communal change is rare or non-existent in phonological change. Cf. **generational change**. Labov (1994: 84).

commutation /kɒmju'teɪʃn̩/ *n.* Especially, but not exclusively, in **Glossematic phonology**, the **paradigmatic relation** which holds between two segments such that replacement of one by the other in a particular word or morpheme yields a different word or morpheme. For example, the contrast between English *feel* [fiːl] and *veal* [viːl] shows that [f] and [v] stand in the relation of commutation. The notion is essentially the same as the **contrastive distribution** of the **American Structuralists**. See Fischer-Jørgensen (1975: 120–121). *V.* **commute** /kəˈmjuːt/. Hjelmslev (1936).

commutation test *n.* 1. A procedure for demonstrating the existence of a **contrast** between two segments. In a given phonological form, a segment of interest (or zero) is replaced by another segment (or zero); if the result is a different phonological form, the segments in question are shown to **commute** /kəˈmjuːt/ (i.e., to contrast). For example, English has a form *rap* [ræp]; replacing [r] by [l] yields *lap* [læp], which has a different meaning: hence [r] and [l] commute (contrast) in English. Similarly, *clap* [klæp] is different again, showing that [k] commutes with zero. The test does not always yield the desired result. For example, Martinet (1960) points out that English *chip* [tʃɪp] contrasts with both *tip* [tɪp] and *ship* [ʃɪp], showing that both [t] and [ʃ] commute with zero and suggesting that the affricate [tʃ] should be analysed as a sequence of two phonemes, /t/ and /ʃ/. This analysis is, however, to be rejected on independent grounds. Hjelmslev (unpublished work 1941); Fischer-Jørgensen (1956). 2. Any of various adaptations of the preceding designed to examine the speech of an individual for evidence of a contrast, or lack of it, between two potentially different groups of phones. The subject is recorded while reading out a list of words containing the segments of interest, and either the recordings are analysed to find whether a distinction is made or not, or the same or a different subject listens to the recorded items (in a different order) and tries to identify them. See Labov (1994: 356–357).

compact /kəmˈpækt/ *adj.* In the **Jakobson–Halle feature system**, a **distinctive feature** defined as 'exhibiting a concentration of energy in the central area of the spectrum', interpreted as representing an articulation in which the front resonating cavity in the mouth is large compared to the rear cavity, and associated with low vowels and with palatal and velar consonants. The feature [compact] corresponds very roughly to [+low] for vowels and to [−anterior] for consonants in the *SPE* **feature system**. *Abstr. n.* **compactness**. Ant. **diffuse**.

compacting /kəmˈpæktɪŋ/ *n.* See **morphologization**.

comparative reconstruction /kəm'pærətɪv/ *n*. In historical linguistics, a procedure for establishing the forms of words and grammatical morphemes in an unattested ancestral language by comparing the forms found in its several daughter languages. In the most straightforward case, we first identify groups of items from the daughter languages which exhibit **systematic correspondences**, and each systematic correspondence is assumed to represent the development in each daughter of a single ancestral segment.

compatibility /kəmpætɪ'bɪlɪti/ *n*. The degree to which particular articulatory gestures or settings can be produced simultaneously. Those which can be simultaneously produced are **compatible** /kəm'pætɪbəl/; those which cannot, for physiological reasons, are **incompatible**.

compensatory lengthening /'kɒmpənseɪtri/ *n*. Any phonological process in which a vowel is lengthened when a following segment is lost. The most familiar variety involves loss of an immediately following consonant, as when Proto-West-Germanic **yans*, **munθ*, **finf* developed into Old English *gōs* 'goose', *mūθ* 'mouth', *fīf* 'five', with lengthening compensating for the loss of following /n/. Compensatory lengthening can also occur when the vowel of a following syllable is lost, as in the development of Proto-Slavic **bogŭ*, **bobŭ* into pre-Serbo-Croatian *bōg* 'God', *bōb* 'bean'.

complement /'kɒmplɪmənt/ *n*. A synonym for **dependent**, preferred in **Government and Charm Phonology**.

complementary distribution /kɒmplɪ'mentri/ *n*. The relation which holds in a given speech variety between two **phones** which never occur in the same environment. For example, in the English of England, **clear *l*** occurs only before a vowel, while **dark *l*** never occurs before a vowel; in many varieties of English, [h] occurs only before a stressed vowel, while [ŋ] never occurs before a stressed vowel. In each of these cases, the phones in question are therefore in complementary distribution. Providing additional criteria are satisfied, most notably **phonetic similarity**, such segments can be assigned to a single **phoneme**. Clear *l* and dark *l* are accordingly assigned to a single phoneme /l/, while [h] and [ŋ] are not. Complementary distribution is a fundamental notion in **classical phonology**, especially in **American Structuralism**.

complement rule *n*. 1. In **Radical Underspecification** theory, any rule which, for some segments, provides a default value for a feature which is different from the single value which, in this framework, is permitted to be specified underlyingly. Such rules effectively provide unmarked values for features, the marked values being underlyingly specified. 2. In **Atomic Phonology**, any rule which is a generalization of an *atomic rule* constructed by extending the atomic rule in terms of natural classes.

completely specified /kəmpliːtli 'spesɪfaɪd/ *adj.* Of a distinctive feature matrix for a particular segment, having values assigned for all features which are phonetically relevant, including those which are non-distinctive for the segment in question.

completeness /kəm'pliːtnɪs/ *n.* A fundamental **criterion for phonological analysis** by which an analysis must account for all the utterances in the language under investigation. Hockett (1942).

complete overlapping /kəmpliːt əʊvə'læpɪŋ/ *n.* The phenomenon in which two or more **phonemes** receive identical phonetic realizations in identical environments. For example, in German and Russian, both voiced and voiceless obstruents are realized as voiceless obstruents in word-final position: German *Rat* /raːt/ [raːt] 'advice', genitive *Rates* /raːtəs/ [raːtəs]; *Rad* /raːd/ [raːt] 'wheel', genitive *Rades* /raːdəs/ [raːdəs]. Analyses involving complete overlapping (such as the one assumed in the German example) violate the principle of **biuniqueness** and hence were rejected by the **American Structuralists**, even though this rejection frequently led to complex and unsatisfying analyses, as they themselves realized: here they were forced to recognize a **morphophonemic alternation** in which the morpheme for 'wheel' variably exhibits the phonological forms /raːt/ and /raːd/, and the obvious generalization about final devoicing is nowhere expressed. Almost all other approaches to phonology reject biuniqueness and consequently accept analyses with complete overlapping. Cf. **partial overlapping**. Bloch (1941).

complex coda /kɒm'pleks/ *n.* A syllabic **coda** containing more than one consonant.

complex nucleus *n.* A syllabic **nucleus** which is not a **pure vowel** but a **diphthong**, **triphthong** or **tetraphthong**.

complex onset *n.* A syllabic **onset** containing more than one consonant.

complex oral–nasal stop *n.* Any **stop** during the oral closure of which the velum does not remain either closed or open throughout.

Four types exist: a *pre-nasal oral stop*, a *post-nasal oral stop*, a *pre-occluded nasal stop*, and a *post-occluded nasal stop*. See Laver (1994: 227–235) or Herbert (1986). Cf. **simplex stop**.

complex segment *n.* 1. A segment which has two (or rarely more) different specifications for a single feature, where the phonetic correlates of these specifications are taken as appearing in temporal sequence. Such a representation is intended to treat segments whose phonetic character changes during the articulation (**contour segments**); most obviously, an affricate might be analysed as [–+continuant], and a diphthong [ai], if treated as a single segment, might be analysed as [+–low]. Illegal in most conventional feature systems, this idea has frequently been taken up in recent work, especially in **Autosegmental Phonology**. Hoard (1971). 2. By extension of the preceding, an analysis sometimes adopted for certain apparent consonant clusters which are problematic in the description of syllable structure. For example, Selkirk (1982) treats all initial [sC-] clusters in English (such as [st-] in *strip*) as single complex segments. Prenasalized stops like [ᵐp], labialized consonants like [kʷ], coarticulated stops like [kp] and many other such cases have often been treated as complex segments. In Kinyarwanda, even such startling sequences as [tkw] (*tkwaaŋga* 'we hate') and [ndgw] (*kariindgwi* 'seven') have been treated as complex segments, since the language normally allows no consonant clusters. 3. A segment whose articulation involves a **coarticulation**. 4. In the **articulatory complexity** model, a consonant whose articulation involves at least two independent departures from the **default mode of production**, such as a whispery-voiced retroflex.

complex sound *n.* Any sound other than a pure **sine wave**. Virtually all sounds, including speech sounds, are complex even apart from time variation, but every complex sound can be analysed into a number of sine waves of identifiable frequency and amplitude.

complex stop *n.* 1. A **coarticulated** stop, such as [gb]. 2. See **complex oral–nasal stop**.

complex tone *n.* Any **intonation** pattern involving at least one fall and one rise. Cruttenden (1986).

complex wave *n.* Any **wave** other than a **sine wave**. Any sound other than a pure tone is carried by a complex wave.

complication /ˌkɒmplɪˈkeɪʃn̩/ *n.* See **rule complication**.

component /kəm'pəʊnənt/ *n.* (also **element**) In a **privative (holistic)** theory of phonology, any one of the **phonological primes** recognized. Such a component is essentially a **unary feature**, such as [labial], [nasal] or [gravity], which is either present or absent in the specification of a particular segment. The term is particularly associated with **Dependency Phonology** and with **Stratificational phonology**, though the latter framework also uses **phonon**. The early attempts at **distinctive features** proposed by the **Prague School** may also be regarded as components.

componential analysis /kɒmpənentʃḷ ə'nælısıs/ *n.* A label applied to a version of **distinctive feature** analysis advocated by certain **American Structuralists**, notably by Charles Hockett (1947, 1955) and Zellig Harris (1951).

composition /kɒmpə'zıʃn̩/ *n.* The relation which holds between two linguistic levels of representation such that units on the higher level can be analysed as sequences of units on the lower level, as when morphemes are considered to be composed of morphophonemes, or morphs of phonemes. Cf. **representation** (sense 3). Hockett (1961).

compound /'kɒmpaʊnd/ *n.* A word formed by combining two (or rarely more) other words, occasionally with additional affixes: *girlfriend, blackboard, skinhead, voice-over, talking-to, blue-eyed.* See Bauer (1983) for a survey of patterns in English.

compound phonation type *n.* Any **phonation type** in which two or more simple phonation types are produced simultaneously. All of the following are possible: **whispery voice, whispery falsetto, whispery creak, creaky voice, creaky falsetto, breathy voice, whispery creaky voice, whispery creaky falsetto**. Of these, only **whispery voice** and **creaky voice** are known to be used for linguistic purposes.

compound phoneme *n.* [*obsolete*] A sequence of phonemes which patterns like a single phoneme, such as an affricate or a diphthong when these are analysed as sequences. Bloomfield (1933).

Compound Rule *n.* The rule which assigns stress in English compound words like *blackbird* (cf. *black bird*). Chomsky and Halle (1968).

compound sound *n.* See **contour segment**. Ant. **simple sound**. Jones (1950).

compressed /kəm'prest/ *adj.* In the **Lindau feature system**, a **distinctive feature** invoked to treat distinctions of vertical lip-compression (as in Swedish), with the possible values *compressed* and *non-compressed*.

computational phonology /kɒmpjuˈtɛɪʃənəl/ *n.* Any of various applications of computing to the study of phonology. See the special issue of *Computational Linguistics* 20:3 (1994) for a survey.

concatenative morphology /kənˈkætənətɪv/ *n.* Morphological structure of the most familiar type, in which a word is conveniently analysed as a linear sequence of continuous morphemes. Cf. **non-concatenative morphology**.

concomitant feature /kənˈkɒmɪtənt/ *n.* See **redundant feature**.

conditioned allophone /kənˈdɪʃn̩d/ *n.* An **allophone** whose phonetic nature is entirely predictable from the nature of the neighbouring segments.

conditioned alternation *n.* Any **alternation** in which the identity of the variant occurring can be predicted from its environment. For example, the choice between the three regular allomorphs of the English plural morpheme ([s]~[z]~[ɪz]) can be predicted from the phonetic nature of the preceding segment (it is *phonologically conditioned*), while the [k]~[s] alternation observed in cases like *electric* ~ *electricity* can be predicted from the identity of the following suffix (it is *grammatically conditioned*).

conditioned merger *n.* Any phonological change which eliminates a **contrast** (introduces a **neutralization**) between two segments in certain positions only, while leaving the contrast intact elsewhere. For example, /e/ and /ɪ/ merge only before /n/ in many southern American varieties, so that *pen* and *pin* become homophones, while *pet* and *pit* remain distinct.

conditioned variant *n.* An **allophone** or **allomorph** whose form is entirely determined by, and predictable from, the nature of neighbouring segments or morphemes.

conditioning /kənˈdɪʃənɪŋ/ *n.* 1. The selection in a given environment of one particular **allophone** of a **phoneme** in a way which is completely predictable from the phonological context. Such an allophone is a **conditioned allophone**. 2. The selection in a given environment of one particular **allomorph** of a **morpheme**. Such conditioning may be phonological, grammatical or lexical; particularly in the phonological case, the allomorph is a **conditioned variant**.

conditioning factor /'fæktə/ *n.* Any phonetic, phonological, grammatical or lexical element or property whose presence in a particular form is sufficient to determine the realization of some other element also present. For example, in Basque, any plosive, even an underlyingly voiced one, must be voiceless when preceded by a voiceless fricative, and the preceding fricative is therefore the conditioning factor for the realization of the following plosive.

conductive deafness /kən'dʌktɪv/ *n.* Any variety of **deafness** in which sound fails to reach the cochlea. Cf. **sensorineural deafness**.

conflation /kən'fleɪʃn̩/ *n.* (also **collapsing**) The grouping of formally related rules into a **rule schema**, so that those rules become **expansions** of that schema. See the example under **rule schema**. *V.* **conflate** /kən'fleɪt/.

conformational aspect /kɒnfɔː'meɪʃənəl/ *n.* Any aspect of articulation which pertains to the routing of air through the air channel. The chief conformational distinctions are the **oral/nasal** contrast and the **median/lateral** contrast.

congener /kən'dʒiːnə/ *n.* A segment which differs from a second, contrasting, segment only in having a different specification for a single feature: hence English /b/ is the voiced congener of /p/.

conjugate /'kɒndʒəgət/ *adj.* Denoting two objects in a representation which mutually implicate each other's presence.

conjunction /kən'dʒʌŋkʃən/ *n.* Any notational device which requires two or more specifications to be simultaneously present, as in the familiar format [+coronal, +high, –voice], which picks out segments having all three of these specifications at once. Cf. **disjunction**.

conjunctive ordering /kən'dʒʌŋktɪv/ *n.* The relation between two **rules**, especially the **expansions** of a **rule schema**, in which the successful application of one does not prevent the other from applying, if it can. Ant. **disjunctive ordering**.

connected speech /kə'nektɪd/ *n.* Ordinary spontaneous speech, as opposed to the production of individual words or phrases in isolation.

connective /kə'nektɪv/ *n.* An older term for an **empty morph**.

conservative /kən'sɜːvətɪv/ *adj.* In the study of phonological change, denoting a pronunciation which appears to be older with respect to a competing but innovating pronunciation. Ant. **advanced** (sense 2).

conservative RP *n*. In the classification of Gimson (1989: 88), those varieties of **Received Pronunciation** 'used by the older generation and, traditionally, by certain professions or social groups' and contrasting with **general RP** and **advanced RP**.

consistency /kən'sɪstənsi/ *n*. A fundamental **criterion for phonological analysis** – in its simplest form, the requirement that a single phonological representation must receive only a single phonetic representation, excepting only recognized **free variation**. Adding to this the opposite requirement, that a single phonetic representation must correspond only to a single phonological representation, yields the much stronger principle of **biuniqueness**.

consonance /'kɒnsənəns/ *n*. 1. Harmony of sound; **euphony**. Ant. **dissonance**. *Adj*. **consonant**. 2. Especially in verse, the use of words with identical or similar consonants in identical positions but different vowels, as in Shakespeare's *sweet silent thought*, with its *s . . . t s . . . t θ . . . t*, or in Gilbert and Sullivan's *In matters that are animal or vegetable or mineral, I am the very model of a modern major-general*, with its repeated final *l*s. Some people restrict the use of the term to word-final consonants. Consonance was formerly contrasted with **assonance**, but the modern tendency is to regard consonance as a variety of assonance. Cf. **alliteration**.

consonant /'kɒnsənənt/ *n*. 1. (also **contoid**) In phonetics, a segment whose articulation involves a significant obstruction to air flow in the vocal tract. 2. In phonology, a segment which occupies a syllabic **margin**. 3. A letter of the alphabet which, generally or in a particular case, represents a consonant in sense 2. *Adj*. **consonantal**. Ant. (all senses) **vowel**. See also **true consonant**.

consonantal /kɒnsə'næntəl/ *adj*. 1. Pertaining to consonants. 2. Having the nature of a consonant. 3. In the **Jakobson–Halle feature system**, a **distinctive feature** defined as 'exhibiting low total energy' and interpreted as representing an obstruction in the vocal tract. Ant. **nonconsonantal**. 4. (**cons**) In the *SPE* **feature system**, a **distinctive feature** defined as 'involving a radical obstruction in the mid-sagittal region of the vocal tract'. Obstruents, nasals and liquids are [+cons]; vowels and glides (including [h] and [ʔ]) are [–cons]. Ant. **non-consonantal**. Cf. **vocalic**.

consonantal hierarchy *n*. Any of various proposals for ranking consonants according to some intrinsic property or according to their susceptibility to some process. For example, many analysts have proposed a hierarchy of **lenition**, such as *pp* > *p* > *b* > *v* or *pp* > *p* > *f* > *h*, according to which lenition processes in particular languages proceed by shifting segments from left to right along the hierarchy.

consonantality /kɒnsənən'tælɪti/ *n*. In some versions of **Dependency Phonology**, a **component** which is assumed to be present in all consonant segments.

consonant cluster *n*. (also **cluster**) A sequence of two or more **consonants** (especially sense 2) within a single morpheme or word. Languages differ markedly in their tolerance for such clusters: Hawaiian permits no clusters at all; Japanese allows only a very few word-medial clusters; English allows clusters of three consonants word-initially and four word-finally, though with severe constraints on the possible sequences; Georgian allows clusters of up to six consonants. NOTE: It is not proper to apply the term 'consonant cluster' to mere orthographic sequences; the word *scythe*, for example, in spite of its spelling, contains no consonant clusters at all.

consonant harmony *n*. The phenomenon, occurring in certain languages, by which only certain combinations of consonant phonemes are permitted to occur in a specified domain, usually a single phonological word. Basque, for example, has four contrasting voiceless sibilants: the apical ⟨s⟩ and ⟨ts⟩ and the laminal ⟨z⟩ and ⟨tz⟩, two fricatives and two affricates. A single Basque lexical item may contain only apicals or only laminals: *sasi* 'bramble', *itsusi* 'ugly', *itsatsi* 'adhere', *sinetsi* 'believe', *zezen* 'bull', *zortzi* 'eight', *zurtz* 'orphan', *izotz* 'ice'; there are no such words as **sazi* or **itzusi*. Compounds undergo assimilation: thus *sinetsi* 'believe' is derived from *zin* 'oath' + -*etsi* 'consider'. Something similar occurs in Navaho. Consonant harmony is much rarer in the world's languages than **vowel harmony**. See Shaw (1991).

consonantization /kɒnsənəntaɪ'zeɪʃn̩/ *n*. A label occasionally applied to an instance of **fortition** in which a **glide** is strengthened to an **obstruent**. In many varieties of Basque, for example, the historical [j] (as in *jan* 'eat') has been strengthened to [ɟ], [dʒ], [ʒ], [ʃ] or even [χ].

consonant system *n*. The complete set of consonant **phonemes** occurring in a particular language or language variety. Standard varieties of English, for example, exhibit a system of 24 consonants: /p t k b d g tʃ dʒ f θ s ʃ v ð z ʒ h m n ŋ l r w j/. See under **phoneme system** for references.

conspiracy /kən'spɪrəsi/ *n*. The phenomenon in which the phonology of a language exhibits several independently motivated and formally quite distinct rules whose combined effect is to produce a surface generalization which is expressed by none of the rules in question, most often a **phonotactic** one. The classic case is that of Yawelmani (Kisseberth 1970): Kisseberth motivates six distinct rules which have the combined effect of guaranteeing that no Yawelmani syllable can begin or end with more than one consonant. The identification of such conspiracies by the proponents of **generative phonology** has often been interpreted by critics as evidence of a fundamental weakness in such a process-orientated approach and as an argument for approaches to phonology in which **surface phonotactic constraints** can be stated directly. *V.* **conspire** /kən'spaɪə/.

constant opposition /'kɒnstənt/ *n*. In **Prague School** phonology, the relation between two contrasting segments which are never **neutralized** in any position, such as that between /l/ and /r/ in **rhotic accents** of English, or between /b/ and /m/ in all varieties of English. Ant. **suspendable opposition**.

constituent /kən'stɪtʃʊənt/ *n*. In some analyses of phonological structure, particularly of syllable structure, any part of the structure which is dominated by a single node. The concept is particularly important in **Government and Charm Phonology**.

constraint /kən'streɪnt/ *n*. Any statement, in some particular framework or description, which prohibits some derivation, process, structure or combination of elements which would otherwise be allowed.

constricted /kən'strɪktɪd/ *adj*. 1. (of some part of the vocal tract) Characterized by the presence of a **constriction**. 2. See **constricted glottis**.

constricted glottis *n*. (also **constricted**) A binary **distinctive feature** proposed to handle certain aspects of glottal activity and somewhat resembling the *SPE* feature **glottal constriction**. The segments which are [+constricted] are glottal stops, ejectives, implosives, glottalized continuants and creaky-voiced vowels. See Ladefoged (1973) for a critical view. Cf. **spread glottis**. Halle and Stevens (1971); Halle (1972).

constriction /kən'strɪkʃən/ *n*. (also **stricture**) A narrowing or closure of the **vocal tract** at some particular point during an articulation, by the movement of the organs of articulation. See **degree of stricture**.

construction /kən'strʌkʃən/ *n*. In some versions of **Metrical Phonology**, the procedure by which metrical **feet** are built by combining smaller elements according to the principles of the framework and any relevant language-specific parameters.

contact /'kɒntækt/ *n*. 1. The phenomenon in which speakers of one language or dialect encounter speakers of another, as a result of which at least one variety acquires characteristics from the other. 2. The parameter along which **checked vowels** (with 'close contact') are distinguished from **free vowels** (with 'open contact'). Martinet (1964).

contact assimilation *n*. An instance of **assimilation** between two adjacent segments, as when Spanish /n/, which is [n] in most circumstances, is realized as velar [ŋ] before another velar, as in *banco* [baŋko] 'bank'. Cf. **distant assimilation**.

content feature /'kɒntent/ *n*. In some views, any **distinctive feature** which is not a **major-class feature**. Cf. **stricture feature**.

context /'kɒntekst/ *n*. See **environment**.

context-determined neutralization /dɪ'tɜːmɪnd/ *n*. Any **neutralization** determined by the nature of the neighbouring segmental phonemes. Cf. **structure-determined neutralization**. Trubetzkoy (1936).

context-free rule /friː/ *n*. A **phonological rule** for whose application no **environment** is stated, and which hence applies in all environments. For example, the rules p → f and h → ∅ are context-free. Such a rule is said to apply *unconditionally*. Ant. **context-sensitive rule**. *Abstr. n.* **context-freedom** /'friːdəm/.

context-sensitive rule /'sensɪtɪv/ *n*. A **phonological rule** for whose application an **environment** is stated and which applies only in that environment. For example, the context-sensitive rule k → tʃ / ___ V[–back] states that k is palatalized in the context (environment) of a following front vowel. *Abstr. n.* **context-sensitivity** /sensɪ'tɪvɪti/.

contiguous /kən'tɪgjuəs/ *adj*. Of two consecutive consonant articulations, involving adjacent parts of the same articulator, with the consequence that the articulators used in the two segments cannot be manipulated independently. Examples include [bv], [sθ], [tj] and [kj]. Cf. **homorganic, heterorganic**. Catford (1977: 218).

contingent ordering constraint /kən'tɪndʒənt/ *n.* Any **constraint** on **rule ordering** of the general form 'Rules A and B apply in the unmarked order, if there is one; if not, A precedes B'. Such constraints are associated with **local ordering**.

continuant /kən'tɪnjuənt/ 1. *n.* Any segment during whose articulation there is no complete closure in the mouth. 2. *adj.* In the **Jakobson–Halle feature system**, a **distinctive feature** defined as 'lacking any interruption or abrupt transition in the spectrum' and interpreted as representing the absence of any rapid closure and opening of the vocal tract. Ant. **discontinuous**. 3. *adj.* (**cont**) In the *SPE* **feature system**, a **distinctive feature** defined as 'involving a primary constriction which is not narrowed to the point where the air flow past the constriction is blocked'. Plosives, affricates and nasals ('stops') are [–cont]; all other segments are [+cont]. This feature has proved to be problematic; nasals, laterals and trills have all at times been taken as having the opposite value for this feature to that specified in *SPE*, a position entertained for laterals in *SPE* itself. Ant. **non-continuant**.

continuity /kɒntɪ'njuːɪti/ *n.* The degree to which speech is uninterrupted by **pauses**.

continuous palatography /kən'tɪnjuəs/ *n.* A variety of **palatography** involving a false palate with electrodes implanted, allowing palatal contact to be recorded continuously over time during a series of articulations.

continuous speech *n.* Uninterrupted speech by a single individual. Laver (1994: 536) defines it as 'a speaking-turn containing no silent or filled pauses, nor any non-linguistic prolongation of linguistic elements'.

contoid /'kɒntɔɪd/ *n.* (also **non-vocoid**) Any segment which is a plosive, a nasal, a fricative or a lateral resonant – in other words, any segment other than a central resonant. Cf. **vocoid**. This term was proposed by Pike (1947a) as a replacement for **consonant** in the phonetic sense of that term (sense 1) in an effort to avoid the ambiguity between the phonetic and phonological senses of the term; while possibly useful, it has never become established, though it has recently been revived by Laver (1994).

contour analysis /'kɒntuə/ *n.* Any analysis of **intonation** which is constructed in terms of rises and falls as primitives, rather than in terms of jumps between predesignated pitch levels. Cf. **levels analysis**.

contour interaction /ˌɪntəˈrækʃən/ *n.* A name given to a view of intonation in which the basic units are phrase-level (or larger) contours which are overlaid by independent components reflecting such factors as accent, emphasis and emotional colouring. Cf. **tone sequence**. Ladd (1984).

contour segment *n.* (also **compound sound**) A single segment during the articulation of which there is a conspicuous movement of the vocal organs, such as an **affricate** or a **diphthong**, when these are analysed as single segments. Contour segments are sometimes treated analytically as **complex segments**.

contour tone *n.* (also **dynamic tone**, **kinetic tone**, **melodic tone**) In a **tone language**, a single **tone** which is realized as a changing pitch pattern on its syllable: a rise, a fall, a fall–rise, or a rise–fall. Cf. **level tone**.

contraction /kənˈtrækʃən/ *n.* 1. Any phonological process in which a word or (more commonly) a sequence of words is reduced by the removal of some internal material, possibly with the application of some further phonological processes. Paradigm cases include the reduction of *I am* to *I'm*, of *she would have* to *she'd've*, and of *ever* to the 'poetic' *e'er*. The label is often applied also to more complex cases such as the (obligatory) reduction of French *de le* to *du*. 2. The result of such a process. **Clipping** is not properly contraction.

contrast /ˈkɒntrɑːst/ *n.* 1. (also **opposition**) The **paradigmatic relation** between two or more segments which can occur in the same environment to produce different meanings. Such segments must be assigned to different **phonemes**. Since English *fat* [fæt] and *vat* [væt], for example, have different meanings, [f] and [v] exhibit contrast and must belong to different phonemes. Labov (1994: 351) proposes the following account of contrast: two types are in contrast when (a) there is at least one environment where the difference between them is the only difference between two utterances that differ in meaning; (b) the distribution of the two types is not predictable by any general rule; (c) native speakers are sensitive to the difference between the two types, at some level of behaviour, but not to the differences between tokens of the same types. 2. The **syntagmatic relation** between consecutive syllables which differ in **stress**, **pitch** or **tone**. *V.* (both senses) **contrast** /kənˈtrɑːst/; *adj.* **contrastive** /kənˈtrɑːstɪv/. NOTE: The Prague School, especially Martinet, and some American Structuralists use 'opposition' for sense 1 and reserve 'contrast' for sense 2, but most American Structuralists and nearly all generative linguists use 'contrast' in both senses.

Contrast-based Underspecification *n.* See **Contrastive Underspecification**.

contrastive distribution *n.* The relation between two (or more) **phones** in which either can occur in the same position in identical surroundings to produce different meanings. See the examples under **contrast**. Cf. **complementary distribution**, **free variation**.

contrastive stress *n.* 1. **Stress** which is placed on some 'element of an utterance in order to contrast it with some other element, either in the utterance or in the context: *I said ACcept*, not *EXcept*. 2. See **emphatic stress**, and see the remarks there.

Contrastive Underspecification *n.* (also **Contrast-based Underspecification**, **Restrictive Underspecification**) A version of **Underspecification Theory** which holds that a feature specification may be omitted from an underlying representation if the opposite specification would violate some independently determined property of the language (usually, the phoneme inventory). Cf. **Radical Underspecification**. Archangeli and Pulleyblank (1989).

conus elasticus /ˈkəʊnəs ɪˈlæstɪkəs/ *n.* A cone-shaped structure of ligamental tissue extending upward from the top of the **cricoid cartilage** in the larynx; its thickened top edges are the **vocal ligaments**.

convention /kənˈventʃən/ *n.* 1. Any notational or representational device used in some system. 2. Any once-and-for-all statement made in some framework, by which some operation or state of affairs automatically has certain consequences, which need not be spelled out repeatedly. An example is the **Association Convention** of Autosegmental Phonology.

conversion /kənˈvɜːʃən/ *n.* (also **functional shift**, **zero-derivation**) The process in which a lexical item is moved from one part of speech to another, with no overt morphological modifications, as when the nouns *access*, *network* and *napalm* are turned into verbs, the adjectives *goofproof* and *brown* are turned into verbs, and the verbs *wash* and *delay* are turned into nouns.

cooccurrence restriction /kəʊəˈkʌrəns rɪstrɪkʃən/ *n.* Any type of restriction on the ability of phonological elements to occur simultaneously in a single phonological form. Examples include **phonotactic** constraints on permissible sequences of segments, rules of

vowel harmony, limitations on permissible sequences of stressed and unstressed syllables and restrictions on the ability of two **autosegments** to be associated with the same skeletal position.

cooing /ˈkuːɪŋ/ *n.* The earliest identifiable stage in infant vocalization, typically beginning around three months and characterized chiefly by vowel-like sounds of rather indeterminate character. Cooing eventually gives way to **babbling**.

coordination /kəʊɔːdɪˈneɪʃn̩/ *n.* The articulatory relation between consecutive segments in connected speech. Among the various phenomena included under this heading are the **articulatory overlap** of adjacent segments, **initial** and **final devoicing**, **aspiration**, and the various ways of releasing (or failing to release) a plosive. See Laver (1994: 149–151, ch. 12).

core /kɔː/ *n.* See **rhyme**.

core syllable *n.* Any **syllable** which is no more complex than the pattern CCVCC, where the peripheral consonants are less sonorous than the non-peripheral ones. Thus *cat* and *front* are core syllables, but *cats*, *stay* and *stream* are not. Steriade (1982).

cornu /ˈkɔːnjuː/ *n.* (pl. **cornua** /ˈkɔːnjuə/) Any one of the four horn-like projections of the **thyroid cartilage**. The two inferior (lower) cornua form a joint with the cricoid cartilage; the two superior (upper) cornua connect to the **hyoid bone**, providing the upper suspension of the larynx.

coronal /ˈkɒrənəl/ 1. *adj.* (of an articulation) Articulated with the tip or the blade of the tongue. 2. *n.* A segment so articulated, such as [t], [n] or [s]. 3. *adj.* (**cor**) In the *SPE* **feature system**, a **distinctive feature** defined as 'produced with the blade of the tongue raised from its neutral position'. Dental, alveolar, palato-alveolar and retroflex segments are [+cor]; other segments are [–cor]. In post-*SPE* work, palatals have often been taken as [+cor]. 4. [*obsolete*] See **retroflex**. Ant. **non-coronal**. Latin *corōna* 'crown'; the modern sense of the term was apparently established by Bloomfield (1933).

coronal assimilation *n.* The phenomenon in English by which an alveolar consonant is, in certain circumstances, assimilated to a following palato-alveolar, as in *Is she here?* [ɪʒʃiːˈhɪə].

coronal-dorsal *adj.* or *n.* A segment articulated with simultaneous coronal and dorsal constrictions, such as Czech [c].

coronal section /ˈsekʃən/ *n*. In anatomy, a section through the body along a plane which separates the front from the back. Cf. **sagittal section**, **transverse section**. NOTE: In phonetics, a coronal section is often loosely called a **transverse section**.

coronal underspecification *n*. The proposal that **coronal** articulations are unmarked for consonants, and hence that only non-coronal consonants need have their place of articulation underlyingly specified. Paradis and Prunet (1989, 1991).

coronal vowel *n*. See **apical-dorsal vowel**, **laminal-dorsal vowel**.

Corti, organ of *n*. See **organ of Corti**.

cot/caught **merger** /kɒt kɔːt/ *n*. The **merger** of the historically distinct English vowels exemplified by the words *cot* and *caught*. This merger is virtually universal in Canada, has gone to completion in eastern New England, western Pennsylvania and much of the American far west, and is now spreading rapidly across the remainder of North America; it is also widespread in Scotland. Other varieties of English have so far avoided the merger either by raising the vowel of *caught* (as in southern England) or by lowering and unrounding the vowel of *cot* (as in most of the United States). See Labov (1994: 316–319).

counterbleeding order /ˈkaʊntəbliːdɪŋ/ *n*. In a framework allowing **ordered rules**, the opposite order to **bleeding order**. Thus, if rule A bleeds rule B (but not the other way round), then the order 'B precedes A' is counterbleeding order. Kiparsky (1965, 1968a).

counterexample /ˈkaʊntərɪgzaːmpəl/ *n*. Any datum which, superficially at least, appears to be inconsistent with some proposed rule or principle, and which might therefore be interpreted as casting doubt on its validity. The dividing line between counterexamples and mere **exceptions** is far from clear, and is often a subject of controversy.

counterfeeding order /ˈkaʊntəfiːdɪŋ/ *n*. In a framework allowing **ordered rules**, the opposite order to **feeding order**. Thus, if rule A feeds rule B (but not the other way round), then the order 'B precedes A' is counterfeeding order. Kiparsky (1965, 1968a).

coupling /ˈkʌplɪŋ/ *n*. The presence of some kind of connection between two bodies which are capable of vibration, so that vibration of one of them produces vibration of the other. *Adj.* **coupled**.

covered /'kʌvəd/ *adj.* (**cov**) In the *SPE* **feature system**, a **distinctive feature** defined as 'articulated with the pharynx walls narrowed and tensed and the larynx raised'. This feature was introduced specifically to deal with the unusual vowel harmony systems of certain African languages. More recently, it has been generally superseded by the feature [**ATR**], with [+cov] corresponding to [–ATR]. Ant. **non-covered**. From the terminology of singing.

cover feature /'kʌvə/ *n.* 1. Any convenient but somewhat *ad hoc* **distinctive feature** which is invoked to pick out some required **natural class** of segments but which corresponds to no single phonetic parameter. In more straightforward instances, a cover feature represents a bundle of identifiable phonetic features or represents merely the absence of some single phonetic feature; examples are the features **consonantal**, **vocalic** and **syllabic**. In the extreme case, in which the feature corresponds to no identifiable phonetic content of any kind, we speak of an **abstract feature**. Ladefoged (1965). 2. A label occasionally applied to an **acoustic feature** which represents any of several distinct articulations, such as **flat**.

cover symbol *n.* Any symbol used outside a rigorous formalism as a shorthand device for representing any of a variety of possibilities. For example, the symbol **C** is a cover symbol meaning 'any consonant'; C_0 is a cover symbol meaning 'a sequence of zero or more consonants', and C_1^3 is a cover symbol meaning 'a sequence of one to three consonants'.

co-vowel /'kəʊvaʊəl/ *n.* Any of various proposed phonological elements which, in some analyses, can follow a simple (short) vowel to produce a long vowel or a diphthong. Such co-vowels as /ː/, /h/, /r/, /w/ and /y/ (= /j/) are posited in many analyses of the English vowel system, such as the **Trager–Smith system**. Hockett (1955).

crasis /'kreɪsɪs/ *n.* The combination of two vowels across a word boundary into a single long vowel or diphthong. Greek *krāsis* 'mixture'.

crazy rule /'kreɪzi/ *n.* [*informal*] A phonological process, or (more usually) an assembly of phonological processes, in some language, arguably constituting a unitary phenomenon, and possibly even formalizable as such, but none the less consisting of what appear to be highly unnatural phenomena. An example is the treatment of coronal obstruents in standard Japanese, in which the segments /t d s z/, all of which contrast unremarkably before non-high vowels,

undergo the following changes before high vowels: t → tʃ / ___ i;
t → ts ___ / u; d → dʒ / ___ i; d → z / ___ u; s → ʃ ___ i; z → dʒ
/ ___ i. These diverse processes, some of which look very unnatural, can in fact be stated in a single rule schema, though only with
a blizzard of angle brackets and braces. Bach and Harms (1972).

creak /kriːk/ *n.* (also **vocal fry**, **glottal fry**) A simple **phonation type**
produced by holding the entire glottis laterally compressed but
untensed, except for a small opening near the anterior (ligamental)
end, which vibrates very slowly (typically 20–60 Hz), producing a
series of clearly audible taps. The **ventricular folds** are also
adducted and may actually press against the **vocal folds**. Pure creak
is not known to be used phonologically in any language, though it
sometimes occurs paralinguistically; it can often be heard at the
end of an utterance with falling intonation in the speech of a
speaker of **Received Pronunciation**. See Laver (1994: 194–197).
NOTE: The term 'creak' is sometimes used interchangeably with **creaky voice**,
but this usage should be avoided.

creaky falsetto /ˈkriːki/ *n.* A **compound phonation type** in which
falsetto and **creak** are produced simultaneously.

creaky voice *n.* (also **laryngealization**, **voiced creak**) A **compound**
phonation type in which one part of the glottis produces **creak**
while another part of it produces ordinary **voicing**; the precise
mechanism of this is not well understood, and it may well differ
from speaker to speaker. The IPA represents creaky voice with a
tilde placed below the symbol for the corresponding segment with
ordinary voicing. In many languages creaky voice is phonologically
contrastive: Hausa, for example, has creaky-voiced /ḇ ḍ j̰/
contrasting with voiced /b d j/. See Laver (1994: 195–197). Creaky
voice can occur in English in the same circumstances as pure **creak**;
see the remarks under that entry.

crescendo–diminuendo stress *n.* A variety of **stress** in which the
prominence first rises and then falls during the stressed syllable.
Jones (1950); attributed to D. B. Fry.

crescendo diphthong /krɪˈʃendəʊ/ *n.* (also **rising diphthong**) A
diphthong consisting of an **on-glide** followed by a more prominent
second element, such as [ju] or [we]. Ant. **diminuendo diphthong**.

crescendo stress *n.* A variety of **stress** in which the prominence
increases during the the stressed syllable. Ant. **diminuendo stress**.
Jones (1950); attributed to D. B. Fry.

cretic foot /'kretɪk/ *n.* See **amphimacer**.

cricoarytenoid muscle /kraɪkəʊærɪ'tiːnɔɪd mʌsəl/ *n.* A muscle connecting the **cricoid** and **arytenoid cartilages**. When contracted, it pulls the arytenoid cartilages back and down and also rotates them, thus abducting the **vocal folds** and opening the **glottis**.

cricoid cartilage /'kraɪkɔɪd kɑːtəlɪdʒ/ *n.* The large ring-shaped cartilage at the base of the **larynx**, connected to the **trachea** below it; the **arytenoid cartilages** lie just above it, and the **thyroid cartilages** are hinged to it by means of the inferior **cornua**.

cricothyroid muscle /kraɪkəʊ'θaɪrɔɪd/ *n.* A muscle connecting the **cricoid** and **thyroid cartilages**. When contracted, it tilts the thyroid cartilage forward and pulls the **arytenoid cartilages** back; this stretches and tautens the **vocal folds**, increasing their length and tension and hence modifying **phonation**.

cricothyrometer /kraɪkəθaɪ'rɒmɪtə/ *n.* An instrument which uses a small telescope to track and measure vertical movements of the larynx.

criteria for phonological analysis /kraɪ'tɪəriə/ *n. pl.* (sg. **criterion** /-ən/) Any of various putative principles which have been proposed at one time or another for determining or evaluating an analysis of the phonology of a particular language. The identification of such criteria was a major goal of **classical phonology**, and particularly of **American Structuralism**. Among the classical criteria variously proposed for identifying phonemes were **completeness**, **consistency** (and its strong form **biuniqueness**), **complementary distribution**, **phonetic similarity**, **phonetic plausibility** (sense 1), **invariance**, **linearity**, **local determinacy**, **pattern congruity** and **economy**. Postclassical phonologists have, of course, invoked their own rather different criteria; among those associated with **generative phonology** are the **Unique Underlyer Condition**, the principle that every significant generalization should be expressed as a single statement, and a version of **economy** very different from the classical ones.

critical velocity /'krɪtɪkəl vəlɒsɪti/ *n.* The velocity of a moving fluid below which **turbulent** flow changes to **laminar flow** (strictly, the 'lower critical velocity'), or, less usually, the (typically higher) velocity above which laminar flow changes to turbulent flow (the 'upper critical velocity'). Since critical velocity depends on a number of variables, it is usual to characterize a fluid system in terms of an invariant quantity, its critical *Reynolds number*.

Crossing Avoidance, Principle of /ˈkrɒsɪŋ əvɔɪdəns/ *n.* A proposed principle of **Autosegmental Phonology**, a weaker form of the **No-Crossing Constraint**. It says: association lines must not be allowed to cross gratuitously. McCarthy and Prince (1986).

culminative /ˈkʌlmɪnətɪv/ *adj.* (of a prosodic element) Making one syllable more prominent than others; producing **accent** on certain syllables, without necessarily having any contrastive function. Both **stress accent** and **pitch accent** systems are culminative. Martinet (1954).

cupping /ˈkʌpɪŋ/ *n.* Hollowing of the tongue body by allowing the midline of the tongue body to drop lower than the sides, producing a concave hollowed shape. Cupping sometimes, though not always, accompanies the articulation of **retroflex** segments.

curly brackets /ˈkɜːli/ *n. pl.* (also **curly braces**) See **braces**.

cut-glass accent /kʌt ˈɡlɑːs/ *n.* [*non-technical*] A dismissive label sometimes applied to the speech of a person who uses **Received Pronunciation**, sometimes more particularly to the speech of a person whose command of the accent is uncertain. From the association of such accents with wealth and privilege, and perhaps also from the irritating effect of such accents on some non-RP speakers.

CV language /si: ˈviː/ *n.* A language which permits no consonant clusters.

CV phonology *n.* A label applied to versions of **Autosegmental Phonology** positing a **CV tier**. Clements and Keyser (1983).

CV tier *n.* (also **timing tier**) In some versions of **Autosegmental Phonology**, the form taken by the **skeletal tier**, in which that tier contains no information beyond the specification of particular 'slots' as consonants (C) or vowels (V). Cf. **X-tier**.

cycle /ˈsaɪkəl/ *n.* 1. Any single one of the repeated changes in the magnitude of a periodically varying quantity, such as the aperture of the glottis during **voicing**. 2. A mode of rule application favoured in a variety of frameworks for a range of phonological phenomena. The idea is that all relevant rules apply (possibly in some specified order) to the minimal domain, after which all the rules apply again to the next larger domain, and then again to a still larger domain, and so on, until the rules have applied to the maximal domain. 3. Any one application of these rules to a particular domain. Adj. **cyclic**.

cyclic domain /'saɪklɪk, 'sɪklɪk/ *n.* In a framework employing the **cycle** (sense 2), any part of a structure which undergoes a single application of the cycle.

cyclicity /saɪ'klɪsɪti/ *n.* The putative principle by which the phonological rules of a language are all applied (where applicable) first to a smaller domain, then again to a larger domain, then again to a still larger domain, and so on, until the largest domain is reached – hence, for example, first to a morpheme, then to a word containing that morpheme, then to a phrase containing that word. First proposed by Chomsky *et al.* (1956) for English stress assignment, cyclicity was extended by Chomsky and Halle (1968) to all phonological rules and was widely accepted within **generative phonology**. This extension was strongly criticized by Anderson (1974), but cyclicity is still prominent in **Lexical Phonology**. See also **Strict Cyclicity Condition**, **derived environment**.

cyclic rule *n.* A **phonological rule** which applies to representations in the manner of the **cycle**.

D

dactyl /'dæktɪl/ *n.* 1. A metrical **foot** consisting of a stressed syllable followed by two unstressed syllables, or, in **quantitative** verse, of a long syllable followed by two short ones. 2. A word illustrating this pattern, such as *murmuring* or *capital*. *Adj.* **dactylic** /dæk'tɪlɪk/.

damping /'dæmpɪŋ/ *n.* The absorption of energy from a sound wave by the medium carrying it, with consequent reduction in amplitude and blurring of **resonance** peaks. The soft tissues of the **vocal tract** are highly absorbent, and hence the speech wave is highly damped. *Adj.* **damped**.

dangling /'dæŋglɪŋ/ *adj.* [*rare*] See **floating**.

dark /dɑːk/ *adj.* An impressionistic label formerly applied to vowels characterized acoustically by a low second formant, such as [u]. *Ant.* **bright**.

dark *l* *n.* A coronal lateral articulated with the back of the tongue raised towards the velum, represented by the IPA symbol [ɫ]. Except in Ireland and Wales, where dark *l* is generally absent, English /l/ is almost universally realized as a dark *l* when not followed by a vowel; many Scottish and North American speakers use a dark *l* for /l/ in all positions. Cf. **clear *l***.

dB *n.* The abbreviation for **decibel(s)**.

deactivation (of a rule) /diæktɪ'veɪʃn̩/ *n.* See **rule deactivation**.

deafness /'defnəs/ *n.* Partial or total loss of the ability to hear. Total deafness (**anacusis**) is not common, but varying degrees of **hearing loss** can be distinguished. *Adj.* **deaf**.

dearticulation /diːɑːtɪkjʊ'leɪʃn̩/ *n.* The total loss of a segment from a phonological form, often particularly as the final step in a historical process of **lenition**. For example, Proto-Indo-European **k* was lenited in Proto-Germanic to **x*, then further in English to *h*; the final step of dearticulating *h* to zero has occurred in many accents of England. Dearticulation is often accompanied by **compensatory lengthening**. Lass (1984: 179).

debuccalization /dibʌkəlaɪˈzeɪʃn̩/ *n.* See **deoralization**.

decibel /ˈdesɪbel/ *n.* (**dB**) The standard scientific unit for expressing the **intensity** of a sound. Strictly, the decibel scale does not express the absolute intensity of a sound, but only the ratio between its intensity and some reference intensity. In practice, the reference intensity is usually taken to be 10^{-16} watts per square centimetre, the lowest intensity audible to an average human ear. The decibel scale is a logarithmic scale, reflecting the fact that the perceived intensity of a sound is roughly proportional to the logarithm of the physical intensity. If the reference intensity is R, then a sound of intensity S may be expressed on the decibel scale as follows:

intensity in dB = $10 \times \log (S/R)$

Thus, for example, a sound which is 100 times as intense as the reference intensity is expressed as $10 \times \log (100)$ dB, which works out as 10×2, or 20 decibels. From *deci-* 'one-tenth' plus **bel**; a decibel is one-tenth of a **bel**.

declination /deklɪˈneɪʃn̩/ *n.* 1. The gradual lowering of pitch during an utterance; simultaneous lowering of **baseline** and **topline**, often accompanied by a reduction in ′**pitch span**. Cf. **downdrift**, **downstep**. 2. A similar gradual reduction in **loudness** during an utterance.

deep /diːp/ *adj.* (of a level of representation) Remote from the **surface**; requiring the application of **phonological rules** to produce the appropriate surface phonetic form.

default /dɪˈfɔːlt/ *n.* Any phonological element which, in some language, is automatically supplied whenever some element of its class is required. For example, in Basque, an impermissible consonant cluster is always broken up by the insertion of the vowel /e/, the *default vowel* of Basque. Some **tone languages** have a *default tone* which is automatically attached to any syllable lacking a tone.

default mode of production /məʊd/ *n.* The most normal, least marked mode of producing speech sounds. Laver (1994: 575) gives the following characterization of default mode: pulmonic egressive airstream; single stricture; oral and central air flow; active and passive articulators are opposite each other in neutral configuration; no comment required about effect of neighbouring segments (he adds further stipulations for particular classes of segments). Any segment is assumed to be produced in default mode except where otherwise specified.

default rule *n.* (also **default specification**) Any universal or language-specific statement which assigns a **feature specification** which is predictable or **unmarked** in a particular circumstance. For example, the observation that sonorants universally tend to be voiced may be expressed by the default [–obstr] → [+voice], while the absence of front rounded vowels in many languages can be expressed by the default [+syll, –back] → [–round]. A default rule applies automatically unless it is overridden by an explicit statement to the contrary. Default rules have been widely invoked in phonology, but are particularly important in **Underspecification Theory**. Note that in **Radical Underspecification** the term 'Default rules' (usually capitalized) is applied to a much broader class of rules, including **markedness** rules: for example, voiceless obstruents are said to be specified as [–voice] not only in languages which have only voiceless obstruents (as in the ordinary use of default rules), but even in languages with contrasting voiced and voiceless obstruents. This extension is confusing and unfortunate. Cf. **feature co-occurrence restriction**.

defective distribution /dɪ'fektɪv/ *n.* The **distribution** exhibited by a segment which fails to appear in some of the environments occupied by other members of its class. For example, English /ŋ/ has a defective distribution since, unlike the other English nasals, it cannot appear word-initially or after /s/.

defective r *n.* Especially in British English, the realization of /r/ as a labiodental approximant [ʋ], often wrongly perceived as [w]. Best attested among upper-middle-class males, this is perhaps more often an affectation than a true speech defect.

defective segment *n.* In a framework in which **feature matrices** are organized into **submatrices**, a segment containing an empty submatrix. For example, if matrices consist of two parts representing an **oral gesture** and a **laryngeal gesture**, a segment with an empty oral gesture, such as might be proposed for [h] or [ʔ], is a defective segment. Lass (1984: 116).

defective speech *n.* The speech of an individual suffering from a **speech defect**.

defooting /diː'fʊtɪŋ/ *n.* In some versions of **Metrical Phonology**, the process by which an unstressed grammatical word ceases to belong to a **foot** of its own and is incorporated into an adjoining foot, as when the *of* of *lots of people* is shifted into the preceding foot headed by *lots*. Giegerich (1985).

deforestation /diːfɔːrɪsˈteɪʃn̩/ *n*. In some versions of **Metrical Phonology**, the procedure by which, at the beginning of any **cycle**, all prosodic structures are erased in the domain of that cycle. That is, when an affix is added, the existing tree is obliterated, and a new tree is constructed from scratch. Liberman and Prince (1977).

degemination /diːdʒemɪˈneɪʃn̩/ *n*. The phonological process (a form of **lenition**) in which a **geminate** consonant is reduced to a simple one. Degemination is common, for example, in the development of Spanish from Latin: L CUPPA > Sp. *copa* 'wine glass'; L GUTTA > Sp. *gota* 'drop'; L SICCU > Sp. *seco* 'dry'; L OSSU > Sp. *hueso* 'bone'. *V*. **degeminate**. Ant. **gemination**.

degenerate foot /diˈdʒenərət/ *n*. In some versions of **Metrical Phonology**, a **foot** (sense 2) which fails to exhibit **binary branching**, such as a monosyllabic word, or which falls short of the maximal number of elements. See also **zero syllable**.

degree of aperture /dɪˈgriː/ *n*. See **vowel height**.

degree of stricture *n*. The extent to which the vocal tract is obstructed during an articulation. Laver (1994) distinguishes **closure**, **close approximation** and **open approximation**, but some others make finer distinctions.

delabialization /diːleɪbiəlaɪˈzeɪʃn̩/ *n*. Any phonological process in which a segment loses its labial character, such as the development of Latin QUEM /kʷem/ and QUID /kʷid/ to Spanish *quien* /kjen/ 'who?' and *qué* /ke/ 'what?' *V*. **delabialize**.

delateralization /diːlætərəlaɪˈzeɪʃn̩/ *n*. Any phonological process in which a segment loses its lateral character. A common type of delateralization affects a velarized alveolar lateral [ɫ] (**dark *l***), which is reduced to a labial-velar glide [w]; this has occurred in standard Polish and in certain circumstances in English (*walk*, *folk*, *Holborn*); in much of the south of England it applies to all non-prevocalic /l/s: *feel*, *field*, *milk*, *ball*, etc. *V*. **delateralize**.

delayed auditory feedback /dɪˈleɪd ɔːdɪtri fiːdbæk/ *n*. The laboratory technique in which a speaker hears her/his own voice, not directly, but via tape recording which has been deliberately delayed by a fraction of a second. The effect of this is usually devastating:

the speaker is reduced to stammering and stumbling, and is unable to speak fluently.

delayed onset of voicing *n.* An appreciable lapse of time (> 20 ms) after the release of a voiceless consonant before the vocal cords begin vibrating for a following voiced segment.

delayed release *n.* (also **gradual release**) 1. (**delrel**) In the *SPE* **feature system**, a **distinctive feature** defined as '[released with] turbulence ... in the vocal tract', and designed to distinguish affricates [+delrel] from plosives [–delrel]. (In fact, *SPE* introduces two such features, one for primary closures, the other for secondary closures, but the second has attracted little attention.) Ant. **instantaneous release**. 2. In the system of Anderson (1974), a similar feature, but one accompanied by a second feature **instantaneous release**, with unreleased plosives being negatively specified for both. Chomsky and Halle (1968); the authors credit R. Carter with the term.

deletion /dɪ'liːʃn̩/ *n.* The loss of a segment from a word or other phonological form. Named varieties are **aphaeresis**, **syncope** and **apocope**. *V.* **delete** /dɪliːt/. Ant. **epenthesis** or **insertion**.

delinking /diː'lɪŋkɪŋ/ *n.* In some frameworks employing ·**feature geometry**, the procedure by which a feature is 'disconnected' from its superordinate node and hence removed from the phonetic realization of a segment. For example, the three contrasting Thai plosives /b/, /p/ and /pʰ/ are neutralized in final position as unreleased [p]; this is interpreted as delinking of the features [± voice] and [± aspirated] from some superordinate node such as [laryngeal].

demarcative /dɪ'mɑːkətɪv/ *adj.* Serving to indicate the presence of a boundary. For example, stress in a language with **fixed accent** is demarcative with respect to word boundaries.

demibeat /'demibiːt/ *n.* In grid versions of **Metrical Phonology**, any element appearing on the bottom line of the grid, corresponding roughly to a (strong or weak) syllable. Cf. **beat**. Selkirk (1984).

denasalization /diːneɪzəlaɪ'zeɪʃn̩/ *n.* Any phonological process in which a segment loses its nasal character. For example, the nasalized vowels of pre-Basque are reduced to oral vowels in most varieties: *zãi* 'watchful' (preserved in eastern dialects) is *zai* in other varieties. *V.* **denasalize**.

dental /'dentəl/ 1. *adj.* Pertaining to the teeth. 2. *adj.* (of an articulation) Articulated with the primary occlusion involving the teeth.

3. *n.* A segment so articulated, such as English [θ] or [ð] or French [t]. In the IPA, a dental articulation may be represented by the use of the diacritic [ˌ] under the symbol for a dental/alveolar segment: [t̪], [n̪]. 4. *adj.* In the **Ladefoged** and **Williamson feature systems**, one of the eleven possible values of the feature **articulatory place**.

dentalveolar /dentælvi'əʊlə/ *adj.* A convenient cover term embracing all of the more specific terms **dental**, **alveolar** and **post-alveolar** when these are used in labelling **place of articulation**.

denti-alveolar /dentiælvi'əʊlə/ (also **gingival**) 1. *adj.* (of a segment) Articulated at the junction of the upper teeth and the alveolar ridge. 2. *n.* A segment so articulated, such as [s] in Lisbon Portuguese or in some articulations of [s] in English *aesthetic*. The diacritic [ˌ] may be added to a character to represent such an articulation.

denti-labial /denti'leɪbɪəl/ *adj.* 1. (of an articulation) Involving the lower teeth and the upper lip as the primary articulators. Denti-labial segments are not known to occur normally in any language, but Catford (1977: 148) suggests they may sometimes be used in place of **labiodentals** by persons with a projecting lower jaw. 2. An erroneous usage for **labiodental**.

deoralization /diːɔːrəlaɪ'zeɪʃn̩/ *n.* (also **debuccalization**) Any phonological process in which a consonant segment loses its oral articulation. For example, non-prevocalic [s] is deoralized to [h] in many varieties of Spanish: *mismos* 'same' (plural) [mihmoh].

dependency /dɪ'pendənsi/ *n.* (also **government**) A particular type of relation between phonological elements posited in some systems, notably in **feature geometry**, in **Dependency Phonology** and in **Government and Charm Phonology**. The idea is that one element, the 'head', 'governs' one or more other elements, which are in turn 'dependent' on it; in some systems these elements may possibly also appear in left-to-right order (**adjunction**), or they may be realized simultaneously as a single bundle in which the governing element is most prominent (**subjunction**). This idea has been applied to word structure, in which a stressed syllable governs an unstressed syllable, to syllable structure, in which the syllable **nucleus** governs the **margins**, and to the structure of **contour segments** such as diphthongs, in which the more prominent element governs the less prominent. Most notably, though, it has been applied to the analysis of segments: the segment governs **gestures**, which in turn govern **subgestures**, which in turn govern **components**, or **distinctive features**; these features may in turn govern other features, which are therefore not connected directly to the phonological skeleton. There have been attempts to interpret phonological change in terms of dependencies: for example, the common change [ai] → [e] is interpreted as a dependency of [i] upon [a] changing from one of adjunction to one of subjunction, and various other changes are interpreted as the **delinking** of a feature from the dependency structure. See Lass (1984: ch. 11) for an introduction.

Dependency Phonology *n.* (**DP**) A prominent contemporary theory of phonology, a **non-linear** and **privative** framework. Like **feature geometry**, DP aims to account for the composition of all segments; it employs a number of **privative** elements called **components**, which are grouped into dependency structures called **subgestures** and **gestures**. Certain components are scalar (present to varying degrees); others are merely present or absent. In combinations of components, one component may 'preponderate' to a greater or lesser extent. The components recognized in Anderson and Ewen (1987) are as follows: *consonantality* (scalar, ranging from |C| to |V|), *degree of glottal opening* |O| (scalar), *glottalicness* |G|, *velaricness* |K|, *frontness (palatality)* |i|, *lowness (sonority)* |a|, *roundness (gravity)* |u|, *centrality* |ə|, *linguality* |l|, *apicality* |t|, *dentality* |d|, *retracted tongue root* |r|, *advanced tongue root* |ɑ|, *laterality* |λ| and *nasality* |n|. The DP approach may be illustrated by vowel systems: in a Spanish-type five-vowel system, /e/ would be |i,a| (or |i⇔a|); in a seven-vowel Italian-type system, /e/ would be |i;a| (or |i⇒a|) and /ɛ/ would be |a;i|, the semicolon or arrow indicating that the first element is dominant. Similarly, /y/ could be represented as |i;u| and /ø/ as the more complex |i;u|;a|. The DP programme was initiated by Anderson and Jones (1974); its most comprehensive presentation is Anderson and Ewen (1987). Brief introductions can be found in Lass (1984: ch. 11), Clark and Yallop (1990), Carr (1993) and Roca (1994).

dependent /dɪ'pendənt/ *n.* In a framework employing **dependency** relations, an element which is governed by a second element, commonly called the **head**.

dephonologization /diːfənɒlɪdʒaɪ'zeɪʃn̩/ *n.* See **merger**. Ant. **phonologization**. Jakobson (1929, 1931).

depressor consonant /dɪˈpresə/ *n.* In certain tone languages, a consonant which has the effect of lowering the tones of adjacent vowels.

derivation /derɪˈveɪʃn̩/ *n.* 1. The procedure by which an **underlying form** (a **phonological representation**) is converted into a **phonetic form** by the application of relevant **phonological rules**. 2. A particular instance of this process. For example, French *vous écriviez* 'you wrote' might be derived from an underlying form /##vuz# ekriv+i+ez##/ as follows: (by Glide Formation) ##vuz#ekriv+j+ez##/; (by Sonorant Devoicing) /##vuz#ekr̥v+j+ez##/; (by Final Obstruent Deletion) /##vuz#ekr̥iv+j+e##/, yielding the phonetic form [vuzekr̥ivje]. 3. In **word formation**, the process of obtaining new lexical items by adding affixes to existing lexical items, as in the derivation of *happiness* and *unhappy* from *happy* or of *rewrite* and *writer* from *write*. *Adj.* **derivational**.

derivational constraint /derɪˈveɪʃənəl/ *n.* (also **global constraint**) Any constraint by which the applicability or lack of it of a phonological rule can be determined only by reference to earlier stages of the derivation in question. Acceptance of such constraints enormously increases the power of the framework, but it has none the less often been argued that they are inescapable. For example, Kisseberth (1973) notes a rule in Klamath which shortens a long vowel if and only if that vowel is derived from an underlying glide: underlying vowels are not affected.

derivational history /ˈhɪstri/ *n.* For a **derivation** (sense 2) at any given stage, the totality of the preceding stages of that derivation. It has usually been assumed that derivational history is unavailable to a rule about to apply, but see **derivational constraint**.

derivational morphology *n.* (also **lexical morphology**) The branch of **morphology** dealing with **word formation**, particularly (but not exclusively) with **derivation** (sense 3). Cf. **inflectional morphology**.

derivative /dəˈrɪvətɪv/ *n.* (also **derived form**) A word or form which is obtained from another by some morphological process. For example, *happiness* and *unhappy* are both derivatives of *happy*.

derived contrast /dɪˈraɪvd/ *n.* A surface phonetic contrast arising from the presence of a **morpheme boundary**. The contrast between the fricatives of German *kuchen* 'cook', with [x], and *Kuhchen* 'little cow', with [ç], is an example, as the vowel-length contrast in Scottish English between *brood* (short vowel) and *brewed* (long vowel).

Some English speakers have a similar contrast in vowel length in words like *manner* and *scanner*. Harris (1990).

derived environment *n.* A possible situation for one or more segments in a phonological form which is potentially subject to some phonological rule. A segment is in a derived environment with respect to a phonological rule R if either (a) the effects of an earlier phonological rule created the environment that now satisfies that rule or (b) the material that satisfies the environment of rule R belongs to two different morphemes. The notion is important in **Lexical Phonology** in constraining the application of rules. A rule that applies only in a derived environment is a *derived environment rule*. Kiparsky (1973a).

Derived Environment Constraint *n.* An important **constraint** in **Lexical Phonology**. It states: **lexical rules** may apply in **derived environments** only. This is equivalent to the **Revised Alternation Condition**. See **Strict Cyclicity Condition**.

derived form *adj.* 1. A phonological form or segment which is not **underlying** but which is obtained from an underlying form by the application of **phonological rules**. 2. A lexical item which is obtained by the addition of one or more affixes to a simpler lexical item.

descriptive adequacy /dɪ'skrɪptɪv/ *n.* See under **adequacy**.

Designated Terminal Element /'dezɪgneɪtɪd/ *n.* (**DTE**) In tree versions of **Metrical Phonology**, that unique element in a **metrical tree** which is dominated by **s** nodes (strong stress) all the way up the tree.

desyllabification /diːsɪlæbɪfɪ'keɪʃn̩/ *n.* Any process by which a syllabic segment loses its syllabic character, most usually the conversion of a vowel to a glide. *V.* **desyllabify** /diːsɪ'læbɪfaɪ/.

detail rule /'diːteɪl/ *n.* See **phonetic rule**.

devocalization /diːvəʊkəlaɪ'zeɪʃn̩/ *n.* 1. Any phonological process in which a vowel or a glide is converted into a consonant: one form of **fortition**. An example is the process occurring in western varieties of Basque, in which *gau* 'night' and *ao* 'mouth', when combined with the article *-a*, yield *gaba* and *aba*. *V.* **devocalize**. *Ant.* **vocalization**. 2. [*obsolete*] See **devoicing**.

devoicing /diː'vɔɪsɪŋ/ *n.* (formerly also **devocalization**) Any phonological process in which a segment which is historically or underlyingly **voiced** loses its voicing, as when word-final voiced plosives became voiceless in German. See **partial devoicing**, **full devoicing**, **initial devoicing**, **final devoicing**. See Laver (1994: 339–348). *V.* **devoice**; *adj.* **devoiced**. NOTE: The use of the term 'devoiced' in the sense of **voiceless** is an error.

diachronic phonology /daɪəˈkrɒnɪk/ *n.* The branch of historical linguistics dealing with **phonological change**.

diacritic /daɪəˈkrɪtɪk/ *n.* (also [*non-technical*] **accent**) Any one of various written or printed marks which, in some particular system of orthography or transcription, may conventionally be added to a letter, phonetic symbol or other character in order to represent some distinction not otherwise representable in the system being used. Greek *diakritikos* 'distinguishing'

diacritic feature *n.* 1. A **distinctive feature** with no phonetic content which is invoked by the analyst to label instances of a segment which behave exceptionally with respect to other instances of the same segment, or to a morpheme which exhibits anomalous behaviour. For example, *basic* and *strategic* fail to show the regular vowel laxing before *-ic* (cf. *conic*, *manic*). See Sommerstein (1977: 155–159). Cf. **rule feature**, **abstract feature** and see **minor rule**. 2. [*rare*] A **distinctive feature** whose phonetic content cannot be specified in isolation, and which acts only as a kind of 'modifier' of another feature. Examples include **distributed** and **retracted articulation**.

diacritic use of phonological features *n.* The treatment of phonologically irregular forms by the arbitrary use of phonetic features which are non-distinctive for the segments in question. For example, while most English stems undergo **Trisyllabic Laxing** (*sane/sanity*, *serene/serenity*, *divine/divinity*), a few stems fail to undergo it: *obese/obesity*, *pirate/piracy*. We might propose to mark the exceptional vowels with some feature not otherwise required for English vowels, such as [+strident], and then add the specification [–strident] to the trisyllabic laxing rule. Such arbitrary exercises were condemned by Kiparsky (1968), and have usually been avoided in favour of more straightforward devices such as **rule features**. Cf. **phonological use of diacritic features**. Kiparsky (1968).

diaeresis /daɪˈɪərəsɪs/ *n.* (also **dieresis**) 1. (also **trema**; the name **umlaut** is not usual in the function described here) The diacritic ¨, particularly when this is used to show that the second of two consecutive written vowels forms a distinct syllable from the first, as in French (*je*) *haïs* 'I hated', where orthographic *aï* represents two syllables [a.i], as opposed to (*je*) *hais* 'I hate', where the digraph *ai* represents the single vowel [ɛ]. The diaeresis is occasionally found in English in such words as *coöperate* and the name *Zoë*, but its use is not standard in English. Cf. **umlaut** (sense 3). 2. [*rare*] The pronunciation of two consecutive vowels as two syllables. Greek *diairesis* 'separation'

dialect /'daɪəlekt/ *n.* A regionally or socially distinctive variety of a language, differing from other varieties in its grammar and/or lexicon. Cf. **accent**. *Adj.* **dialectal**. NOTE: The form **dialectical* is an error.

dialect atlas /'ætləs/ *n.* A book in which the results of **dialectology** in some area are exhibited in the form of maps showing the regional distributions of various words, forms or pronunciations.

dialect borrowing *n.* (also **dialect mixing** /'mɪksɪŋ/) The putative process by which speakers acquire non-native pronunciations for certain words from speakers of other dialects with significantly different phonological histories, rejecting their own native pronunciations for these words in the process. Though such borrowing no doubt happens, the concept is now in some disrepute because it has been constantly invoked as a near-magical 'explanation' of the innumerable instances of exceptions to the **Neogrammarian Hypothesis** of absolutely regular sound change. See Labov (1994: chs 15–18) for a contemporary view.

dialectology /daɪəlek'tɒlədʒi/ *n.* The branch of linguistics dealing with the distribution of **accents** and **dialects** in space and time. *Adj.* **dialectological**.

diaphone /'daɪəfəʊn/ *n.* 1. (also **diaphoneme**) An abstract phonological unit posited for a language as a whole, represented in each of several distinct varieties of that language as a phoneme with the same distribution but with a significantly different phonetic realization; diaphones are sometimes represented by symbols enclosed in vertical bars. A simple example is English |e|, represented by American /e/ = [ɛ], RP /e/ = [e], and Australian /e/ = [ë], all with essentially the same lexical incidence. A more spectacular example occurs in Basque, in which the diaphone |j| (orthographic ⟨j⟩, as in *jan* 'eat') is realized in various regional dialects as [j], [ʝ], [dʒ], [ʒ], [ʃ] or [χ]. See Jones (1950) for discussion. 2. Any one of the individual realizations of a diaphone in sense 1. *Adj.* **diaphonic**

/daɪə'fɒnɪk/; *abstr.* *n.* **diaphony** /daɪ'æfəni/. Jones (1918 (3rd edn [1932])): Greek *dia* 'across' + **phone**. NOTE: These two senses are conflicting. It is clear that Jones intended the first sense, but, as a result of a misunderstanding, the term has very frequently been used in the second. Later Jones introduced the term 'diaphoneme', also for sense 1, but this term has been little used by anyone. It would be very convenient to use 'diaphone' for sense 2 and to reserve 'diaphoneme' for sense 1, so that we could speak of 'diaphones of a diaphoneme' (on a par with 'allophones of a phoneme'), but this proposal is only partly in accord with observed usage. 3. [*obsolete*] Either of two or more phonemes in an unfamiliar speech variety (or even language) which are identified by an individual with a single phoneme in his own speech. Sense 3: Haugen (1957).

diaphoneme /daɪə'fəuniːm/ *n.* See **diaphone** (senses 1 and 2). Jones (1939).

diaphragm /'daɪəfræm/ *n.* The dome-shaped muscular partition between the chest and the abdomen, partly responsible for contracting the lungs during breathing. During speech, the diaphragm relaxes and is passively pushed against the chest cavity by the contraction of the abdominal muscles.

diastole /daɪ'æstəli/ *n.* [*rare*] The lengthening of a short syllable. Ant. **systole**. Greek *diastolē* 'expansion'.

diasystem /'daɪəsɪstəm/ *n.* (also **overall pattern analysis**) An analysis, particularly a **phoneme system**, which is set up, not for a particular language variety, but for a range of phonetically or phonologically different varieties of the language handled simultaneously. This may involve the use of **diaphones**, or it may involve setting up more phonological units than actually occur in any single variety. A well-known example is the **Trager–Smith system** for treating the vowels of American English. Cf. **common core**. Weinreich (1954).

dichotic listening /daɪ'kɒtɪk 'lɪsnɪŋ/ *n.* An experimental technique for determining which side of the brain is most directly involved in hearing sounds. Typically, different sounds are presented simultaneously to each ear of a subject wearing headphones, and the subject is then asked what she/he has heard. Most speech sounds are heard preferentially by most subjects in the right ear (linked to the left hemisphere of the brain).

diction /'dɪkʃən/ *n.* The degree of clarity with which an individual enunciates when speaking.

diffuse /dɪˈfjuːs/ *adj*. In the **Jakobson–Halle feature system**, a **distinctive feature** defined as 'exhibiting a spread of energy throughout all frequencies of the spectrum' and interpreted as representing high vowels and front consonants. The specification [diffuse] corresponds roughly in the **SPE** system to [+high] for vowels and to [+anterior] for consonants. *Abstr. n*. **diffuseness**. Ant. **compact**.

diffusion /dɪˈfjuːʒn̩/ *n*. The process by which an innovation spreads through a speech community. *V*. **diffuse** /dɪˈfjuːz/.

digital processing /dɪdʒɪtəl ˈprəʊsesɪŋ/ *n*. A technique for transmitting and reproducing complex sounds with very high (in practice, virtually perfect) fidelity. An **analog signal** (an ordinary sound wave) is sampled at very frequent intervals by an **analog-to-digital converter** which produces a set of digits representing the amplitude and frequency of every component; by the *Sampling Theorem*, if the sampling rate is high enough, no information whatever is lost in the resulting digital signal. This digital signal is highly robust; it can be transmitted without interference from the noise found in every transmission system; it can be very easily processed by simple multiplication of frequencies (for example, to amplify the whole signal or to enhance selected frequencies); and it can be converted back into an ordinary analog signal which is indistinguishable from the original. Digital processing is the basis of all modern high-fidelity sound reproduction, and it is increasingly used in sound transmission.

digital signal *n*. The signal produced by **digital processing**, consisting entirely of a stream of numbers. Cf. **analog signal**.

digraph /ˈdaɪɡrɑːf/ *n*. In an alphabetic orthography, a sequence of two letters which conventionally represents a single segment, such as English ⟨sh⟩ for /ʃ/, ⟨ch⟩ for /tʃ/, ⟨ng⟩ for /ŋ/, ⟨th⟩ for /θ/ or /ð/ or ⟨oo⟩ for /uː/, or such as Spanish ⟨ch⟩ for /tʃ/, ⟨ll⟩ for /ʎ/ or ⟨rr⟩ for /r/. Cf. **trigraph**, **tetragraph**. NOTE: The use of the term **diphthong** in this sense is an error.

dimeter /ˈdɪmɪtə/ *n*. A metrical **foot** containing two syllables.

diminuendo diphthong /dɪmɪnjuˈendəʊ/ *n*. (also **falling diphthong**) A **diphthong** consisting of a more prominent first element followed by a less prominent **off-glide**, such as [aj], [aw], [ɛə] or [oj]. Ant. **crescendo diphthong**.

diminuendo stress *n.* A variety of **stress** in which the prominence decreases during the stressed syllable. Ant. **crescendo stress**. Jones (1950); attributed to D. B. Fry.

diphonemic sound /daɪfə'niːmɪk/ *n.* [*rare*] A single phone which, in some analysis, is variously assigned to either of two phonemes even in a single environment. Jones (1950).

diphthong /'dɪfθɒŋ/ *n.* A single syllabic **nucleus** which begins with one vowel quality and changes more or less smoothly to a second quality, as in [ju] and [ai]. Usually one of the two vocalic elements is more prominent than the other, this other consisting only of a preceding glide (an **on-glide**, as in [ju]), or a following glide (an **off-glide**, as in [ai]). The first type is called a **crescendo** (or **rising**) **diphthong**, the second a **diminuendo** (or **falling**) **diphthong**. Diphthongs may be further classified as **wide** or **narrow**, as **closing** or **opening**, or as **backing**, **fronting** or **centring**. Cf. **monophthong**, **triphthong**, **tetraphthong**. NOTE the spelling and the pronunciation of this word. It is an error to use the term 'diphthong' in the sense of **digraph**. Greek *diphthonggos* 'double sound'.

diphthongization /dɪfθɒŋaɪ'zeɪʃn̩/ *n.* Any phonological process in which a simple syllabic nucleus (a **pure vowel**) is converted into a **diphthong**. The history of English, for example, has been characterized by extensive diphthongization, as when the Middle English vowels /iː/ and /uː/ developed into /ai/ and /au/, as in *fine* and *house*. Some particular varieties have special names, such as **breaking**. *V.* **diphthongize**.

diplophonia /dɪplə'fəʊnɪə/ *n.* (also **diplophonic voice** /dɪplə'fɒnɪk/) See **double voice**.

directional clitic /də'rekʃənəl/ *n.* A **clitic** which always binds to a host on one particular side of it, regardless of its grammatical relation to the rest of the sentence. Klavans (1985).

directionality /dərekʃə'nælɪti/ *n.* Particularly in **Autosegmental Phonology**, the parameter by which some phonological property or process, such as tone or syllable formation, must be analysed as proceeding either left-to-right or right-to-left, depending on the language and the property. Analysts invoke a **directionality parameter** to handle differences among languages.

Direct Syntax Hypothesis /də'rekt 'sɪntæks haɪ'pɒθəsɪs/ *n.* The view that syntactic structure directly influences phonology –

reflected, for example, in an analysis in which the applicability or
lack of it of a phonological rule is determined by the presence of
a syntactic constituent boundary. This view has been widely
accepted within **generative phonology** and its successors. Cf.
Indirect Syntax Hypothesis, and see **Prosodic Hierarchy**.

discontinuous /dɪskən'tɪnjuəs/ *adj*. In the **Jakobson–Halle feature
system**, a **distinctive feature** defined as 'exhibiting an interruption
or an abrupt transition in the spectrum' and interpreted as representing rapid closure and opening of the vocal tract, as with
plosives. The specification [discontinuous] corresponds approximately to the *SPE* specification [–continuant]. Ant. **continuant**.

discrete-level tone system /dɪ'skriːt levəl/ *n*. A system of **tones** in
which the pitch values of different tones are maintained in discrete,
non-overlapping pitch ranges throughout an utterance. Navaho is
an example. Welmers (1959).

discreteness /dɪ'skriːtnəs/ *n*. The fundamental property of language
by which continuous speech can be conveniently and insight-
fully analysed into a single linear sequence of elements, with
no intervening material; at the phonetic and phonological
levels, these elements are **segments**. *Adj*. **discrete**. Ant. **non-
discreteness**.

discrimination /dɪskrɪmɪ'neɪʃn̩/ *n*. The ability of an individual to
hear small differences between sounds – in phonetics, of course;
speech sounds.

disharmonic root /dɪshɑː'mɒnɪk/ *n*. In a language with **vowel
harmony**, a **root** (sense 2) which fails to obey the usual harmony
rules, either in containing an **opaque vowel** which blocks the normal
application of vowel harmony, or in combining vowels from the
two harmonic groups.

disjunction /dɪs'dʒʌŋkʃən/ *n*. 1. In a **rule schema**, a listing of two
or more elements or groups of elements such that exactly one of
them must be taken on any one reading of the schema; the elements
in the disjunction are commonly enclosed in **braces**. See **braces**
(sense 1) for an example. 2. In a **feature matrix**, a listing of two
or more **feature specifications** such that exactly one of them
must be taken at any one time; the alternative specifications
are commonly enclosed in braces. For example, the disjunctive specification [[–cor], {[+ant], [+back]}] picks out just those segments
which are either non-coronal and anterior or non-coronal and

back, and hence would pick out the class /p k/ in a language with /p t c k/. *Adj.* **disjunctive** /dɪs'dʒʌŋktɪv/ or **disjoint** /dɪs'dʒɔɪnt/.

disjunctive ordering *n.* The relation that holds between a set of related rules (typically rules combined in a single **rule schema**) such that, as soon as any one of the rules has successfully applied to a phonological form, none of the other rules is permitted to apply to that form, even if its structural description is met. Disjunctive ordering often holds, for example, for a set of rules assigning **stress**: as soon as any one syllable has received stress, no other rules may apply to assign stress to other syllables as well. Disjunctively ordered rules need to be checked for application in some specified order, and general principles must be invoked to determine whether two rules are disjunctively ordered at all. The *SPE* proposal that all and only those rules that can be combined in any kind of rule schema are disjunctively ordered has proved to be inadequate; more successful attempts are represented by **Proper Inclusion Precedence**, the **Elsewhere Condition** and the **Stifling** principle. Ant. **conjunctive ordering**. Chomsky and Halle (1968).

displaced articulation /dɪs'pleɪst/ *n.* Any articulation in which the lower articulator forms a constriction with an upper articulator which is not directly opposite it, and hence in which the lower artic- ulator is displaced from its neutral position. Examples include **labio- dental**, **linguolabial** and **retroflex** articulations. Cf. **place-neutral articulation**.

disproportionation /dɪsprəpɔːʃə'neɪʃn̩/ *n.* A type of phonological change in which a phoneme disappears, some instances of it merging with one other phoneme but other instances with a different phoneme, sometimes in an unpredictable manner. For example, Old Turkish /e/ merged in some cases with /i/ but in other cases with /ɛ/, in a seemingly arbitrary manner, yielding the eight-vowel system of modern Turkish. *V.* **disproportionate**. From chemistry.

dissimilation /dɪsɪmɪ'leɪʃn̩/ *n.* Any of various phonological processes in which one segment changes so as to become less similar to another segment in the same form. For example, Latin *arbor* 'tree' yields Spanish *arbol*, with dissimilation of the second *r* to *l*; the Ancient Greek root **tʰrikʰ-* 'hair' exhibits nominative *tʰriks*, in which the second plosive loses its aspiration regularly before *s*, but genitive *trikʰós*, in which the first plosive loses its aspiration by dissimilation before the second aspirated plosive; Latin *libellum* 'level' yields French *niveau*, in which the first *l* has dissimilated to *n* before the following *ll* (with other later changes producing the modern form). *V.* **dissimilate**; *adj.* **dissimilatory** /dɪ'sɪmɪleɪtri/. Ant. **assimilation**.

dissonance /'dɪsənəns/ *n.* The use or presence of unharmonious sounds. Ant. **consonance** (sense 1) or **euphony**. *Adj.* **dissonant**.

distant assimilation /'dɪstənt/ *n.* Any instance of **assimilation** between segments which are not adjacent, as in **vowel harmony**, or as in Sanskrit, in which a nasal becomes retroflex if the word contains a preceding retroflex sibilant and no coronal segment intervenes.

distinctive feature /dɪ'stɪŋktɪv/ *n.* One of a specified set of **phonological primes** defined in such a way that every **segment** in a language, at least at the phonological level, can be exhaustively characterized as some permitted combination, or 'bundle', of features, each with an associated value. There have been various approaches to defining systems of features. First, a feature may be an **articulatory feature** (defined in terms of the action of the organs of speech), an **acoustic feature** (defined in terms of the physical properties of the speech sound bearing the feature), or a **perceptual feature** (defined in terms of the perception of the associated sound by the ear and the brain). Second, a feature may be **binary** (it can take one of only two possible values, conventionally represented as + and –) or **multivalued** (it can take any one of several possible values). Third, a feature system may be intended as universal (capable of handling all phonological distinctions in all languages) or as language-specific (designed to treat only a single language or variety).

Interest in features grew from the realization that it was often unrealistic to treat segments as phonological primes: many phonological properties and processes are better understood as involving only particular characteristics of segments, and the now fundamental concept of a **natural class** can only be articulated by an appeal to these characteristics. Though the general idea of features can be traced back a long way, it was the **Prague School** which first explicitly introduced features, but without ever developing a fully articulated theory of features. Roman Jakobson pursued the idea in the United States, but his early work focused on language-specific analyses only; Charles Hockett (1942, 1955) also made some proposals in this vein. The first full-blown system was the

Jakobson–Halle feature system of the 1950s, which proposed a rather minimalist set of only twelve features, all of them binary, and all of them defined primarily in acoustic terms, though with articulatory interpretations offered; this set was intended to be universal. The J–H system was followed in 1968 by the very different *SPE* **feature system**, which posited more than two dozen binary features, almost all of them defined in articulatory terms; in spite of some obvious shortcomings, the *SPE* system quickly became orthodox in phonology, though there were endless attempts to improve it by tinkering.

The most serious objections derived from *SPE*'s rigidly binary features, which were awkward or worse in dealing with non-binary parameters like vowel height and place of articulation, and it was Peter Ladefoged who led the reaction in a series of publications, culminating in the **Ladefoged feature system**, which makes liberal use of multivalued features, mostly also articulatory; this system rejects the somewhat *ad hoc* contortions of *SPE* in favour of **hugging the phonetic ground**. Others followed suit, and the **Williamson feature system** constitutes a distinctive development of Ladefoged's ideas, as does the **Lindau feature system** for vowels only. In contrast, the **Wickelgren feature system** represents an unusual attempt at constructing a system based on the perceptual characteristics of sounds.

In all these systems, a segment is regarded as a **feature matrix**, a bundle of feature specifications (features with values) having no internal ordering or structure. Thus, for example, the English phoneme /s/ is represented in the *SPE* system as [+consonantal, –vocalic, –syllabic, –voice, –sonorant, +continuant, +coronal, +anterior, +strident, –nasal, –lateral], in which all these specifications are present simultaneously and there is no more to say (I have omitted a few specifications of minimal significance). More recently, however, there have been two major developments in feature theory.

First, the development known as **feature geometry** introduces considerable structure into feature matrices, in the form of trees: a single feature at the top of the tree governs some other features, each of which in turn may govern further features, and so on.

Second, the various approaches known as **privative** (or **holistic**) frameworks replace conventional binary or multivalued features with **components** (or **elements**), which are in effect **unary features**: features which can take no values, but which can only be present or not. Though such a component as [nasal] may not look different from the conventional [+nasal], the absence of [nasal] is very different from the specification [−nasal]: in the conventional system, [−nasal] can be used to pick out a natural class, but the absence of [nasal] has no such consequence. In holistic frameworks, there is no way of referring to the absence of a component, in principle anyway, though a few versions have tried to sneak this capacity into the system.

See Fromkin and Ladefoged (1981) for an account of the very early history of features, Fischer-Jørgensen (1975: chs 8–9) for a history of features, Sommerstein (1977: ch. 5) for a historical and critical summary, Lass (1984: chs 5–6) for a critical discussion including some original proposals and a review of feature geometry, Anderson (1978) for a survey of the attempts at extending features to the analysis of **tone**, and Singh (1976) for a review of features from a clinical point of view.

distinctness /dɪ'stɪŋktnəs/ *n.* A linguistically significant difference between two segments or two phonological representations. Every theory of phonology is obliged in principle to provide some formal machinery for determining whether two forms are distinct or not. In *SPE*, two segments are distinct if they bear opposed specifications for at least one feature, and two strings are distinct if they are of different lengths or if they contain distinct segments in at least one position. Definitions of distinctness have also been offered for some **non-linear** frameworks, but tend to be more elaborate. *Adj.* **distinct**.

distributed /dɪ'strɪbjʊtɪd/ *adj.* (**dist**) In the *SPE* **feature system**, a **distinctive feature** defined as 'produced with a constriction that extends for a considerable distance along the direction of the air flow'. This feature is primarily invoked to distinguish fricatives, notably bilabials ([+dist]) from labiodentals ([−dist]), laminals ([+dist]) from apicals and retroflexes ([−dist]), and the Polish alveolo-palatal sibilants ([+dist]) from alveolar sibilants ([−dist]), and sometimes also the English alveolar fricatives ([+dist]) from the dental fricatives ([−dist]). Most recent work has eschewed this feature, preferring to handle apical/laminal contrasts in particular by some more direct means, such as a feature **apical(ity)**.

distribution /dɪstrɪ'bju:ʃn̩/ *n.* (also **privilege of occurrence**) The full range of environments in which an element (most often a segment) can occur. See **complementary distribution**, **contrastive distribution**, **free variation**, **defective distribution**.

distributional analysis *n.* An idealized type of phonological analysis suggested by certain **American Structuralists**, in which a complete analysis is performed on a sufficiently large corpus of recorded and transcribed material, without reference to meanings or native speakers. The most determined attempts in this direction were carried out by Bernard Bloch (1948, 1953).

distributional equivalence /ɪˈkwɪvələns/ *n.* The relation between two **phones** which have exactly the same distribution, that is, which exhibit **parallel distribution** in the strict sense. Lyons (1968).

disyllable /ˈdaɪsɪləbəl/ *n.* (also **bisyllable**; formerly also **dissyllable** /ˈdɪssɪləbəl/) A word consisting of two syllables: *money*, *delay*, *trouble*. *Adj.* **disyllabic** /daɪsɪˈlæbɪk/. Greek *di-* 'twice' + *syllabē* 'syllable'.

D-licensing /ˈdiːlaɪsənsɪŋ/ *n.* In **Government and Charm Phonology**, any case of **licensing** which does not fall out of any principles and which must be stipulated by the analyst. Cf. **G-licensing**. From 'direct licensing'.

docking /ˈdɒkɪŋ/ *n.* The process by which a floating autosegment associates with a skeletal position or (in early autosegmental work) with a vowel or a consonant. Goldsmith (1976).

dollar sign /ˈdɒlə saɪn/ *n.* The **auxiliary symbol** $, representing a **syllable boundary** in some frameworks.

domain /dəʊmeɪn/ *n.* The stretch of phonological material to which some rule or constraint applies.

domal /ˈdəʊməl/ *adj.* 1. A cover term for **palatal**, **velar** and **uvular**, when these terms are used to label **place of articulation**. Catford (1977: 142). 2. [*obsolete*] A former synonym for **palatal**. Hockett (1955). 3. [*obsolete*] A former synonym for **retroflex**.

dominant/recessive vowel harmony /dɒmɪnənt rɪˈsesɪv/ *n.* A type of **vowel harmony** occurring in certain languages in which all vowels are divided into two disjoint sets, the **dominant vowels** and the **recessive vowels**. The presence of a dominant vowel at any point in a word, even in an affix, requires all vowels in that word to be dominant, even the vowels in a root which, in isolation, contains only recessive vowels. See Carr (1993: 259–262) for examples from the East African language Kalenjin.

Domino Condition /ˈdɒmɪnəʊ/ *n.* A putative principle by which, when metrical structure is deformed by some process (such as vowel insertion), the deformation is repaired by a complete metrical reorganization of the form from left to right from the point of disruption. Halle and Vergnaud (1987).

Doric /'dɒrɪk/ *n.* or *adj.* [*non-technical*] A popular label for any distinctively rural Scottish speech variety, or less usually for any conspicuously rural speech variety. Coined in contrast to the speech of Edinburgh, the 'Athens of the North', from a supposed resemblance to the Doric accents of Ancient Greek, allegedly regarded as 'rustic' and 'unrefined' by Attic and Ionian speakers.

dorsal /'dɔːsəl/ *adj.* 1. Pertaining to the **back** (**dorsum**) of the tongue. 2. Pertaining to the **body** of the tongue, both front and back. 3. (of a segment) Articulated with the back of the tongue involved in the primary constriction, as in the **dorso-velar** consonants [k], [g], [x] and [ŋ]. 4. (of a segment) Articulated with either the front or the back of the tongue involved in the primary constriction. 5. An occasional synonym for **velar** (senses 2 and 3). 6. In some versions of **feature geometry**, a superordinate **class node** taking the features **high, low** and **back** as dependents. Sense 6: Sagey (1986). NOTE: Senses 1–4 represent conflicting usages; I recommend retaining senses 1 and 3 and avoiding senses 2 and 4.

Dorsey's Law /'dɔːsi/ *n.* In the Siouxan language Winnebago, a rule which inserts a copy of the following vowel within a preceding voiceless-obstruent-plus-sonorant cluster: *ho-š-wažá* → *hošawažá* 'be sick'.

dorso-velar /dɔːsə'viːlə/ (commonly reduced to **velar**) 1. *adj.* (of a segment) Articulated with the **back** of the tongue and the **velum** as the primary articulators. 2. *n.* A segment so articulated, such as [k], [g] or [x].

dorsum /'dɔːsəm/ *n.* 1. *adj.* (also **back**) The back third or so of the upper surface of the tongue. Cf. **front**. 2. In the terminology of Catford (1977, 1988), and of many phonologists, the entire upper surface of the tongue behind the **blade**, including the traditional **front** of the tongue. In Catford's usage, the conventional front and back are called the **anterodorsum** and the **posterodorsum**. *Adj.* **dorsal**. CF **dorso-**. NOTE: These inconsistent usages are most unfortunate; when encountering or using the terms 'dorsum' and 'dorsal', you should take care that the intended sense is clear.

double articulation /'dʌbəl/ *n.* 1. Broadly, a synonym for **coarticulation**. 2. Narrowly, and more usually, an instance of **coarticulation**

in which both constrictions are of equal degree: Catford's 'coordi-nate coarticulation'. Laver (1994) includes vowels in this category, since they involve both tongue and lip action, but this is not usual. See Laver (1994: 314–320) for a survey. Jones (1950). 3. See **duality**. Martinet (1949).

double-bar juncture /'dʌbəlbɑː/ *n*. In some **American Structuralist** analyses, a **juncture phoneme** posited to account for the presence of a rising intonation contour and symbolized as //. Cf. **single-bar juncture**, **double-cross juncture**. Trager and Smith (1951).

double-cross juncture /'dʌbəlkrɒs/ *n*. In some **American Structuralist** analyses, a **juncture phoneme** posited to account for the presence of a falling intonation contour and symbolized as #. Cf. **single-bar juncture**, **double-bar juncture**. Trager and Smith (1951).

doubled consonant or **doubled vowel** /'dʌbəld/ *n*. See **geminate**.

double fricative *n*. A **double articulation** consisting of a fricative made simultaneously at two places of articulation, such as the [s͡x] reported for some varieties of Swedish and the [x͡ɸ] of Urhobo.

double geminate *n*. A sequence of three identical consonants, reported as occurring in certain African languages.

double hash mark *n*. The symbol ##, representing a boundary between two adjacent words. Cf. **hash mark**.

double slashes *n. pl.* 1. A notation sometimes used for enclosing **morphophonemic** representations in frameworks which recognize a distinct morphophonemic level. Thus the German morpheme *Rad* 'wheel' might be represented as //raːT//, variously corresponding to phonemic /raːt/ or /raːd/; see under **complete overlapping** for the point of this, and see Lass (1984: 57–58) for alternative notations. 2. A notation used in marking the **environment** in the **mirror-image convention**. 3. The symbol //, used to mark the end of an **intonational phrase**.

double stop *n*. A **stop** (particularly a **plosive**) whose articulation involves simultaneous complete closure at two positions, such as the [g͡b] in the language name Igbo and the [p͡t] of Bura (West Africa).

doublet /'dʌblət/ *n*. A pair of words in the same language which have the same ultimate origin, or either of the words involved: *faction/fashion* (< Latin *factiō*); *castle/château* (< Latin *castellum*).

Larger groups exist: *hospital/hostel/hotel* (< Latin *hospitalium*); *gentile/genteel/gentle/jaunty* (< Latin *gentilis*).

double voice *n.* (also **diplophonia**, **diplophonic voice**) 1. A complex and highly unusual **phonation type** in which ordinary **voicing** (vibration of the **vocal folds**) is combined with **ventricular voice** (vibration of the **ventricular folds**). Unknown in linguistic usage, double voice is used in certain types of singing in which it allows the simultaneous production of two different notes, as in the chanting of 'certain Tibetan monks' (Catford 1977: 104) and, less melodiously, in the jazz style known as 'scat singing'. 2. A pathological condition resulting from a congenital deformation of the vocal folds, in which the vocal folds vibrate with two different simultaneous fundamental frequencies.

double word boundary *n.* The **boundary** between two consecutive **phonological words**, commonly represented as ##. Cf. **single word boundary**.

downdrift /'daʊndrɪft/ *n.* In some **tone languages**, the phenomenon by which the pitch of high tones is lowered slightly after a low tone, so that the pitch difference between high and low tones becomes steadily smaller during an utterance. Cf. **declination**, **downstep**.

Down East accent /daʊn 'iːst/ *n.* [*non-technical*] The traditional label for the distinctive speech variety of the American state of Maine, the quintessential 'Yankee' accent. The name 'Down East' is applied to Maine in recognition of its geographical position and its low-lying terrain.

downstep(ping) /'daʊnstep(ɪŋ)/ *n.* In some **tone languages**, the phenomenon by which the pitch of high tones is (or may be) steadily lowered even in the absence of intervening low tones, so that the pitch difference between high and low tones becomes steadily smaller during an utterance. Cf. **upstep**, **downdrift**, **declination**. Welmers (1959).

drag chain /'dræg tʃeɪn/ *n.* A putative type of phonological change in which the presence of a **hole in the pattern** induces a nearby segment to undergo phonetic modification so as to move into the hole, with other segments in the system then often undergoing further phonetic changes to fill the new holes which appear. For example, Greek, Swedish, Occitan and the Zuberoan dialect of Basque have all at some time undergone the fronting of *u*, leaving a hole; in all four, the hole has been filled by raising some or all instances of *o* to *u*; in Swedish, *a* has additionally been raised to *o*. The **Great Vowel Shift** of English is perhaps another instance of a drag chain. Cf. **push chain**, and see **paradigmatic imbalance**. Martinet (1955).

drawl /drɔːl/ [*non-technical*] 1. *n.* An impressionistic label for any style of speech which is perceived by the person making the judgement as involving an unusual degree of lengthening of vowels, syllables or words or as merely being unusually slow in tempo. British speakers often regard many North Americans as having a drawl, while northern Americans consider a drawl to be characteristic of southern American accents. 2. *v.* To speak with a drawl. Related to 'draw (out)'.

drift /drɪft/ *n.* The phenomenon in which a linguistic process, or a set of such processes, continues to occur in an identifiable direction over a period of many generations. In one type of drift, sometimes called a **conspiracy**, a number of formally distinct processes, often occurring at different times, combine to produce a single result. It is clear, for example, that all consonants could be distinctively **geminated** in intervocalic position in pre-Basque, but a variety of formally unrelated processes have combined to eliminate all geminate–simplex contrasts except for *r/rr*, which is now isolated and is itself now being eliminated in some varieties, either by loss of *r* or by merger of *r* and *rr*. The overall effect of all these changes is to eliminate geminates from the language, but the process has taken many centuries and is still not quite complete in most varieties. Other types of drift exist, however, such as the centuries-old tendency to diphthongize tense vowels in English. Sapir (1921).

duality /djuˈælɪti/ *n.* (also **double articulation**) The property of human speech by which a small number of meaningless elements (the **phonemes**) can be combined into a limitless number of meaningful expressions (words and sentences). The existence of duality is arguably the single most far-reaching difference between human languages and the signalling systems of other species.

Duke of York derivation /djuːk əv ˈjɔːk/ *n.* A **derivation** in which a form A is converted by rules to a different form B, which is then converted by other rules back to A again. Pullum (1976); from a satirical verse.

dumping /ˈdʌmpɪŋ/ *n.* In **Autosegmental Phonology**, the phenomenon in which an otherwise unassociated ('floating') autosegment is associated with a skeletal position which is already associated with another autosegment on the same tier, as when a second tone is added to a vowel that already bears a tone. Cf. **spreading**.

duplex perception /'djuːpleks/ *n.* A phenomenon in which listeners hear two different signals at different fundamental frequencies simultaneously, each consisting of one or two different **formants** from a single syllable such as [da] or [ga]. What they hear is *two* different sounds at once: the syllable, constructed from its components, and a buzz corresponding to the single formant at one frequency.

duration /djʊ'reɪʃn̩/ *n.* The amount of time occupied by an articulation, usually measured in milliseconds (ms); the primary phonetic correlate of **length** and sometimes one phonetic correlate of **stress**.

dynamic phonetics /daɪ'næmɪk/ *n.* See **parametric phonetics**.

Dynamic Phonology *n.* A label given to an approach to phonology which attempts to integrate **parametric phonetics** into phonological descriptions. The name reflects a statement of intent, rather than a distinct theory of phonology. Griffen (1985).

dynamic tone *n.* 1. See **contour tone**. 2. One of several **prosodic** elements forming a system in a language, resembling **tones** but realized primarily by variations in duration and intensity, rather than by variations in **pitch**. Tsimshian, for example, has a system of three dynamic tones called 'clipped', 'sustained' and 'fading'.

dynamophone /daɪ'næməfəʊn/ *n.* [*rare*] An abstract sound unit whose members are the strong and reduced realizations of a particular segment in a particular word, such as [i] and [ə] in English *the*: one type of **metaphone**. Palmer (1930).

dysperiodicity /dɪspɪəriə'dɪsɪti/ *n.* Any departure from perfectly regular vibration, especially of the vocal folds. *Adj.* **dysperiodic**.

dysphonia /dɪs'fəʊniə/ *n.* The partial loss of the ability to use the **vocal folds** to produce **phonation**. *Adj.* **dysphonic** /dɪs'fɒnɪk/. Cf. **aphonia**.

dysprosody /dɪs'prɒsədi/ *n.* Any pathological disturbance of the ability to produce speech with normal rhythm, intonation or loudness.

E

eardrum /ˈɪədrʌm/ *n.* (also **tympanum, tympanic membrane**) The membrane separating the canal of the **outer ear** from the **middle ear**. Sound waves striking the eardrum cause it to vibrate, and these vibrations are passed across the eardrum to the **auditory ossicles** of the middle ear.

early onset of voicing /ˈɜːli/ *n.* The initiation of **voicing** in a **stop** substantially before the **release**. Cf. **simultaneous onset of voicing, late onset of voicing**.

ear training /ˈɪə treɪnɪŋ/ *n.* The procedure by which students of phonetics learn to identify and characterize a wide range of speech sounds by listening to them.

ease of acquisition /iːz/ *n.* The degree to which a language can be readily learned by children, sometimes cited both as a limiting factor on possible grammars and as a factor in phonological change.

ease of articulation *n.* (also **ease of production**) The degree to which speech sounds, sequences of speech sounds and contrasts between speech sounds may be readily produced by speakers, sometimes cited as a factor in phonological change. This notion underlies the concept of **natural processes**.

ease of perception *n.* The degree to which speech sounds, and contrasts between speech sounds, may be readily and correctly detected by a hearer, sometimes cited as a factor in phonological change.

echolalia /ekəˈleɪliə/ *n.* A pathological condition in which the sufferer automatically repeats, typically without comprehension, part or all of what someone else has just said.

echo word /ˈekəʊ wɜːd/ *n.* A word constructed by repeating an existing word with a fixed alteration (usually to the beginning), as in Yiddish-influenced American English *Jaguar-Schmaguar!*

eclipsis /ɪˈklɪpsɪs/ *n.* 1. The conventional label in Irish for the **mutation** in which, in any of about a dozen specified grammatical circumstances, the initial consonant of a word is affected as follows: a voiceless plosive or /f/ becomes voiced; a voiced plosive becomes a nasal; a vowel-initial word acquires a preceding /n/. Examples: *tigh* [t'ig'] 'house', *an dtigh* [an d'ig'] 'at the house'; *páipéar* [paː'p'eːr] 'paper', *i bpáipéar* [i baː'p'eːr] 'in a paper'; *féar* [fʲiar] 'grass', *sa bhféar* [sa vʲiar] 'in the grass'; *gnó* [gnoː] 'business', *bhur ngnó* [vur ŋnoː] 'your business'; *bó* [boː] 'cow', *féar sé mbó* [fʲiar seː moː] 'the grass of six cows'; *óg* [oːg] 'young', *Tír na nÓg* [t'iːr' na noːg] 'The Land of the Young'. 2. Loss of a segment, especially word-medially. *V.* **eclipse** /ɪ'klɪps/.

economy /ɪ'kɒnəmi/ *n.* Any of various **criteria for phonological analysis**, such as minimization of the number of phonemes or other units, minimization of the number or complexity of descriptive statements or maximal use of distinctive features. These criteria may conflict.

edge /edʒ/ *n.* The position at the left or right extremity of a grammatical **constituent**. The edge position is often important in determining whether some phonological process applies or not. Cf. **flank**.

edge effect *n.* The physical process by which an airstream striking an obstruction produces friction noise. See **obstacle fricative**.

edge-in association *n.* In **Autosegmental Phonology**, the procedure by which some phonological property, such as tone, is 'anchored' at an **edge** by an explicit statement, and is then extended as necessary to the rest of the constituent by spreading or by default.

edge inflection *n.* A bound grammatical morpheme which is always attached to one **edge** of a constituent, regardless of the position of the head of that constituent, such as the English possessive marker -*'s*.

edh /eð/ *n.* See **eth**.

editing /'edɪtɪŋ/ *n.* Monitoring of speech by the speaker. *Covert editing* is carried out below the level of consciousness and produces smooth speech; *overt editing* is performed consciously and is readily detectable by the listener. Hockett (1967).

***e*-grade** /'iːɡreɪd/ *n.* In the phonology of Proto-Indo-European, that form of a root exhibiting the vowel *e*, considered the unmarked form of the root: **yek-* 'speak', **bher-* 'carry', **kleu-* 'hear'. Cf. ***o*-grade**, **zero-grade**.

egressive /ɪ'gresɪv/ *adj.* 1. (of an airstream) Going outward from the body. Ant. **ingressive**. Pike (1943). 2. **(egr)** A **distinctive feature** proposed by Lass (1984: 93): segments with an ingressive airstream are [–egr]; all others are [+egr].

ejection /ɪ'dʒekʃən/ *n.* In the *SPE* **feature system**, a **distinctive feature** defined as 'produced by an upward movement of the glottal closure' and invoked to distinguish **ejective** consonants ([+ejection]) from all other segments.

ejective /ɪ'dʒektɪv/ 1. *n.* or *adj.* (rarely also **recursive**) Any segment, often especially a stop, made on a **glottalic egressive airstream mechanism**. Ejective stops, affricates and fricatives are all attested. The IPA notates ejectives with a following apostrophe: [k'], [s']. 2. In the **Ladefoged** and **Williamson feature systems**, one of the three possible values of the feature **glottalic** (Ladefoged) or **larynx movement** (Williamson).

elaborated segment /ɪ'læbəreɪtɪd/ *n.* In the **articulatory complexity** model, a segment whose production requires one departure from the **default mode of production**, such as a creaky-voiced vowel or a palatalized plosive.

electroaerometry /ɪlektrəʊɛə'rɒmətri/ *n.* (also **aerometry**) The measurement of air flow during speech. The device used is an **(electro)aerometer**.

electroglottography /ɪlektrəglə'tɒgrəfi/ *n.* A technique for examining and recording the movement of the vocal folds in speech, either by passing an electric current across the glottis or by shining a beam of light across it (*photoelectroglottography*). The device is an **electroglottograph**; the printout is an **electroglottogram**.

electrokymography /ɪlektrəkaɪ'mɒgrəfi/ *n.* An instrumental technique employing a face mask connected to instruments which can continuously measure, record and display the velocity and volume-velocity or air flow through the mouth and the nose. The instrument is an **electrokymograph**; the output is an **electrokymogram**.

electrolaryngography /ɪlektrəlærɪŋ'gɒgrəfi/ *n.* See **laryngograph**.

electromyography /ɪlektrəmaɪ'ɒgrəfi/ *n.* **(emg)** A technique for investigating the movements of muscles by using electrodes to detect the firing of motor neurones.

electropalatography /ɪlektrəpælə'tɒgrəfi/ *n.* A version of **palatography** using a false palate implanted with electrodes, so that contact between the tongue and the roof of the mouth may be continuously recorded and displayed. The instrument is an **electropalatograph**; the output is an **electropalatogram**.

element /'eləmənt/ *n.* See **component**.

elicitation /ɪlɪsɪ'teɪʃn̩/ *n.* The technique of obtaining linguistic data from native speakers. In *direct elicitation*, the investigator presents a form or utterance and asks for an opinion; the more exacting, but more reliable, *indirect elicitation* involves a good deal of cunning manoeuvring in order to obtain the required information in the form of spontaneous, unselfconscious utterances. *V.* **elicit** /ɪ'lɪsɪt/.

elision /ɪ'lɪʒn̩/ *n.* Any of various processes in which phonological material is lost from a word or phrase. Specific varieties of elision include **aphaeresis**, **syncope**, **apocope**, **synaeresis**, **synizesis** and **synaloepha**. Not infrequently this name is given to specific processes in particular languages, such as the French process that converts *la* + *amie* to *l'amie* 'the (female) friend', or the Spanish process in which *Santa Ana* 'Saint Anne' is pronounced *Santana*. *V.* **elide** /ɪ'laɪd/. Latin *ēlisiō* 'a striking out'.

elocution /elə'kjuːʃn̩/ *n.* The art of effective public speaking, or training in this art.

Elsewhere Condition /'elswɛə/ *n.* A fundamental, and putatively universal, constraint on the applicability of rules. It says: two rules of the forms (i) A → B / P ___ Q, and (ii) C → D / R ___ S are disjunctively ordered iff (a) the set of strings that match PAQ is a subset of the strings that match RCS, and (b) the structural changes of the two rules are identical or incompatible. In other words, wherever (i) can apply, it does so, and (ii) does not; (ii) applies only 'elsewhere'. Similar, but not identical, to **Proper Inclusion Precedence**, this condition is designed to minimize **extrinsic ordering**. See **Stifling**. Kiparsky (1973b).

elusive /ɪ'ljuːsɪv/ *adj.* (of a segment) Having a somewhat indeterminate and often variable nature, such as English **schwa** or Russian **yers**. Jones (1950).

emg /iː em 'dʒiː/ *n.* See **electromyography**.

emic /'iːmɪk/ *adj.* (of a description) Formulated in terms of a system of relations, contrasts and/or functions, ignoring functionless details. Cf. **etic**. Kenneth Pike, in various works: from **phonemic**.

emphasis /'emfəsıs/ *n.* A very broad and general term applied to any kind of prominence attached to a linguistic element.

emphatic /ım'fætık/ *adj.* 1. Characterized by the presence of some kind of **emphasis**. 2. A traditional label for certain consonants in Arabic which are pharyngealized or velarized and which contrast with other, similar, segments lacking this secondary articulation.

emphatic stress *n.* **Stress** placed on a particular part of an utterance in order to draw attention to it, as in English *I did* NOT *say that*. Cf. **contrastive stress**. NOTE: Many analysts use the terms 'emphatic stress' and 'contrastive stress' interchangeably.

Empty Category Principle /'empti/ *n.* (**ECP**) In **Government and Charm Phonology**, a principle restricting empty positions. It says: a melodically empty slot must be properly governed. Here 'proper government' is a version of **government** meeting certain additional conditions. From a comparable principle in syntax.

empty morph *n.* An overt **morph** which cannot be assigned to any **morpheme**. For example, in Basque *mendietan* 'in the mountains', *mendi* is the noun 'mountain', *-e-* is the usual form of the plural morpheme in oblique cases and *-n* is the usual form of the locative case ending, leaving *-ta-* unassigned as an empty morph. Hockett (1947).

empty nucleus *n.* (also **null vowel**) In some analyses of consonant clusters at syllable margins, a hypothetical vowel which is posited to bear a consonant whose presence is not otherwise permitted in the analysis, as when *depth* is syllabified *dep.θθ*. Kaye (1990).

empty onset *n.* A syllable **onset** containing no material.

e muet /ə mɥe/ *n.* (also **mute** *e*) The name given to **schwa** in French, including instances of 'potential' schwa which are not normally pronounced in standard northern French.

enchaînement /ãʃɛn(ə)mã/ *n.* [French: 'chaining'] 1. See **chain shift**. 2. In French, the phenomenon in which a word-final consonant which is always pronounced is, when preceding a word-initial vowel, pronounced as part of the first syllable of the following word: hence *par* [paʀ] 'by' but *par accident* [pa.ʀak.si.dã] 'by accident'. Cf. *liaison*.

enclitic /ın'klıtık/ *n.* A **clitic** which follows its **host**, such as *-n't* in *couldn't*. Cf. **proclitic**.

encliticization /ɪnklɪtɪsaɪˈzeɪʃn̩/ *n.* The process by which a weak syllable is attached to a strong syllable on its left to produce a metrical **foot**, as when, in the phrase *lots of wine*, the weak syllable *of* is combined with *lots* to form a foot [*lots of*]. According to Giegerich (1985), this is the only possibility in English. Cf. **procliticization**.

endolabial /endəʊˈleɪbiəl/ *adj.* (of an articulation) Involving the inner surfaces of the lips, as in **inner rounding**. Cf. **exolabial**.

eng /eŋ/ *n.* (also **angma**, **tailed** *n*) The name of the character ŋ, used in the IPA to represent a velar nasal consonant, as in English *singing* [ŋ]. Modification of *en* 'n'; the character dates from the seventeenth century, the name from the 1950s.

English Stress Rule *n.* (ESR) In **Metrical Phonology**, the rule posited as accounting for the position of the stress in most English lexical items, essentially a later version of the **Main Stress Rule** and the **Primary Stress Rule**. Liberman and Prince (1977).

enhancement /ɪnˈhɑːnsmənt/ *n.* The phenomenon by which certain articulatory movements increase the acoustic differences between segments. For example, back vowels differ from front vowels in having a lower F2 and F3; lip-rounding further lowers F2, thus enhancing the perceptual distinctness of back vowels. *V.* **enhance**. Stevens and Keyser (1989).

entering element /ˈentərɪŋ/ *n.* In a **chain shift**, a segment which moves into the phonological space formerly occupied by another segment moving out of it, the **leaving element**. Labov (1994: 119).

enunciation /ɪnʌnsiˈeɪʃn̩/ *n.* The articulation of speech, often particularly clear and distinct articulation. *V.* **enunciate**.

environment /ɪnˈvaɪrənmənt/ *n.* (also **context**) The position in the speech chain in which a segment (or sometimes a larger unit) appears; all the preceding and following material within some relevant domain, such as a syllable, a word or a phrase.

environmental context /ɪnvaɪrənˈmentəl/ *n.* The location of a segment expressed in terms of its neighbouring segments. Cf. **structural context**.

environment bar *n.* (also **slash**, **oblique**) In a **phonological rule**, the symbol /, used to separate the **environment** in which a rule applies.

EPD /iː piː ˈdiː/ *n.* (in full, the *English Pronouncing Dictionary*) The most comprehensive and influential pronouncing dictionary of

British English for many years. The first edition appeared in 1917, edited by Daniel Jones, who also edited a number of succeeding editions. The *EPD* **transcription** which it used was long the standard system for transcribing **Received Pronunciation**. After Jones's death, the volume was taken over by A. C. Gimson, and the 14th edition (1977), edited by Gimson and Susan Ramsaran, changed over to the **Gimson–O'Connor transcription**. *EPD* has now been succeeded by *LPD*.

EPD **transcription** (also **Jones transcription** and, among lexicographers, **IPA transcription**) The system used for transcribing the phonemes of English (more precisely, of **Received Pronunciation**) in the first thirteen editions of *EPD* and in most of the published works of Daniel Jones and of other British analysts until 1960 or so, since when the system has been generally superseded by a modified version, the **Gimson–O'Connor system**. The *EPD* system was invented by members of the **International Phonetic Association** early in this century; it became the definitive transcription for English thanks to its use by Daniel Jones, who, however, did not invent it and reportedly didn't even like it much.

epenthesis /e'penθəsɪs/ *n.* The insertion of a segment into a word in a position in which no segment was previously present. The history of English provides examples like the development of *æmtig* into *empty*, with epenthetic *p*, and of *þunor* into *thunder*, with epenthetic *d*. The word *prince* is commonly pronounced like *prints*, with epenthetic *t*. Non-standard pronunciations include 'athalete' for *athlete* and 'fillum' for *film*, with epenthetic vowels. The epenthesis of a vowel is also called **anaptyxis** (or **svarabhakti**), and some linguists restrict the term 'epenthesis' to consonant insertion, while others restrict it to word-medial position. Epenthesis in a specific position is **prothesis** or **paragoge**. *Adj.* **epenthetic** /epen'θetɪk/. Ant. **deletion**. Greek: 'insertion'.

epiglottal /epɪ'glɒtəl/ 1. *adj.* Pertaining to the **epiglottis**. 2. *adj.* (of a segment) Articulated with the primary stricture occurring at the epiglottis. 3. *n.* A segment so articulated, such as the voiceless epiglottal plosive ('epiglottal stop') found in several Caucasian languages and in certain varieties of Arabic and Hebrew (Catford 1988: 101). Epiglottal fricatives are also possible; the IPA provides symbols for all of these.

epiglottis /epɪ'glɒtɪs/ *n.* A spoon-shaped cartilage whose base is attached to the front of the **thyroid cartilage** and whose other end is free. During swallowing, the root of the tongue pushes the epiglottis partially down over the **larynx**, giving limited protection against food entering the trachea. The epiglottis plays a very limited part in speech production. *Adj.* **epiglottal**.

epithesis /e'pɪθəsɪs/ *n.* A rare synonym for **paragoge**. Greek: 'a setting on'.

epitrite /'epɪtraɪt/ *n.* A rare metrical **foot** consisting of three stressed syllables and one unstressed one, or, in **quantitative metre**, of three long syllables and one short one, in any order. Greek *epítritos* 'one-third more'.

equal sign /'iːkwəl saɪn/ *n.* The **auxiliary symbol** =, representing a special type of **boundary** sometimes posited as occurring in English between an original prefix and an original root in a verb of Latin origin: hence *re=sist, de=sign, per=mit, com=pel, trans=fer, inter=sect, com=pre=hend*. The boundary is invoked to handle various peculiarities of these words, including their failure to undergo the **Alternating Stress Rule** and the voicing of *s* in cases like *resist* and *design* (compare *consist* and *consign*). Chomsky and Halle (1968).

Equational Phonology /ɪ'kweɪʒənəl/ *n.* The application of Gerald Sanders's Equational Grammar to phonology. This approach stresses what are regarded as universal natural principles of grammatical function; it restricts the content of descriptions to what are called 'lawlike rules about representational equivalences'; and it is presented in a kind of algebraic formalism. Sanders (1979).

equipollent opposition /ekwɪ'pɒlənt/ *adj.* In **Prague School** phonology, a contrast between two segments which are distinguished neither by the presence or absence of a single feature (as in a **privative opposition**) nor by variation in degree along a single dimension (as in a **gradual opposition**); instead, the two segments differ in respect of multiple phonetic characteristics and must be regarded as logically equivalent: for example, the /p/–/t/ contrast or the /f/–/k/ contrast in English.

esh /eʃ/ *n.* The symbol ʃ, used in the IPA to represent a voiceless palato-alveolar fricative, as in English *ship* /ʃɪp/. By analogy with 'ess' for ⟨s⟩.

esophagus, esophageal, esophagic See **oesophagus**.

ESR /iː es 'aː/ *n.* See **English Stress Rule**.

Estuary English /'estjʊri/ *n.* [*non-technical*] A name sometimes given to a wide spectrum of accents used in southeastern England and falling somewhere between broad **Cockney** at one extreme and unmistakable **Received Pronunciation** at the other. Associated particularly with upwardly mobile working-class speakers, these accents are also adopted by middle-class speakers eager to identify themselves with 'popular' culture. Some observers have suggested that Estuary English may be slowly replacing RP as the prestige accent of southern England. David Rosewarne, *Times Educational Supplement*, 19 October 1984; from its putative origins in the Thames Estuary region.

eth /eð/ *n.* (also **edh**) The character ð, used in the IPA to represent a voiced dental fricative, as in English *this* and *mother*. It was invented and used by the Old English scribes to represent the (single) dental fricative of Old English as an alternative to thorn (þ); it is used in modern Icelandic orthography to represent the voiced dental fricative, with a capital form Đ.

etic /'etɪk/ *adj.* (of a description) Characterized by scrupulous attention to minute detail, without regard to any system of relations or functions. Cf. **emic**. Kenneth Pike, in various works: from **phonetic**.

etymology /etɪ'mɒlədʒi/ *n.* The study of the historical sources of words (lexical items). *Adj.* **etymological**.

etymon /'etɪmɒn/ *n.* (*pl.* **etyma** /'etɪmə/) An ancestral form from which a later form is directly derived. English *father* has the Old English etymon *fæder*, which in turn has the PIE etymon **pətēr*. Cf. **reflex**.

euphony /'juːfəni/ *n.* 1. Attractiveness of sound. 2. [*obsolete* or *non-technical*] Any alteration in the pronunciation of a word which makes it easier to pronounce, such as an **assimilation**.

eurhythmy /juː'rɪðmi/ *n.* (also **eurythmy**) Metrical symmetry; the existence of a highly regular metrical structure in utterances. *Adj.* **eur(h)ythmic**.

evaluation measure /ɪvæljʊ'eɪʃn̩/ *n.* Any mechanical procedure for evaluating either the phonological system of a language or a proposed description of such a system for the purpose of providing a valuation of it in terms of some set of supposedly objective criteria.

Event Perception /ɪ'vent/ *n.* A theory of speech perception which holds that what the hearer perceives is the actions of the speaker's vocal tract. See the special issue of the *Journal of Phonetics* (14:1, 1986) for presentation and discussion.

exception /ɪk'sɛpʃən/ *n.* Any form or datum which is, or appears to be, in conflict with the ordinary rules or constraints constituting the phonology of a language. See *veto* **phenomenon** for an instance. Cf. **positive exception, counterexample**.

exception feature *n.* A more or less *ad hoc* diacritic posited in some analyses as existing on certain morphemes and serving to indicate that those morphemes exceptionally fail to undergo a regular phonological process of the language.

exchange rule /ɪks'tʃeɪndʒ/ *n.* (also **alpha-switching rule, flip-flop rule**) A rule in which the sign attached to a Greek-letter variable in the **alpha notation** is reversed by the action of the rule. For example, Chomsky and Halle (1966: 265) posit the following rule for Early Modern English:

$$
\begin{bmatrix} \alpha \text{ high} \\ -\text{low} \end{bmatrix} \rightarrow [-\alpha \text{ high}] \; / \; \begin{bmatrix} \underline{} \\ +\text{tense} \\ +\text{stress} \end{bmatrix}
$$

This rule exchanges ('flip-flops') high and mid tense vowels under stress.

exclamation mark /eksklə'meɪʃn̩/ *n.* The symbol !, sometimes used in transcribing **tone languages** to mark the onset of **downstepping**.

excrescence /ɪks'kresəns/ *n.* The (usually sporadic) insertion of a plosive into word-final position: *vermin > varmint, no > nope,* Old English *betwihs > betwixt.* This is one type of **paragoge**. *Adj.* **excrescent**.

exolabial /eksə'leɪbiəl/ *adj.* (of an articulation) Involving the outer surfaces of the lips, as in **outer rounding**. Cf. **endolabial**.

expanded /ɪk'spændɪd/ *adj.* 1. In the **Lindau feature system**, a **distinctive feature** invoked to treat differences in the size of the pharynx, with the possible values *expanded, neutral* and *constricted,* only two of which can be used contrastively in a given language. The values *expanded* and *constricted* correspond approximately to the **wide** and **narrow** (respectively) of Ladefoged and to [+ATR] and [–ATR] (respectively). 2. In the **Williamson feature system**, one of the three possible values of the feature **expansion**.

expansion /ɪk'spænʃən/ *n.* 1. (also **subrule**) Any one of the individual **rules** conflated by some **abbreviatory convention** within a

rule schema. 2. In the **Williamson feature system**, a **distinctive feature** with the possible values **expanded**, **normal** and **narrowed**, invoked to handle distinctions of pharynx constriction and covering roughly the same ground as the features **ATR** and **wide** in other systems. 3. A type of phonological change in which the phonological space previously divided between two phonemes is reassigned to a single phoneme, leading to a **merger** of the original phonemes. Sense 3: Labov (1994). *V.* (senses 1 and 3) **expand**.

Expansion Convention *n.* A putative convention governing certain types of sound change. It says: given a process of sound change described by a rule $[z \text{ F}] \rightarrow [z+\alpha x \text{ F}] / \dots$, apply the rule to any one segment by increasing x until a segment bearing $[z+\alpha(x+1) \text{ F}]$ would be non-distinct from another segment, or until $z-\alpha x = 0$. (Here F is any feature, $\alpha = \pm 1$, z is a conservative value for F, and x is an increment to the value of F.) This convention is intended to describe the behaviour of **chain shifts** involved in long-term **drift**. Labov (1994: 264).

experimental phonetics /ɪkspɛrɪ'mɛntəl/ *n.* See **instrumental phonetics**.

experimental phonology *n.* An approach to phonology which attempts to integrate the findings of experimental phonetics and of experimental psychology, in the hope of relating phonological descriptions to observable behaviour. The most prominent advocate is John Ohala: see Ohala (1986) for an introduction and Ohala and Jaeger (1986) for a collection of studies.

expiratory reserve volume /ɪk'spaɪrətri rɪzɜːv vɒljuːm/ *n.* The volume of air which an individual can breathe out beyond the minimum value of the **tidal volume**. Cf. **inspiratory reserve volume**.

explanatory adequacy /ɪk'splænətri/ *n.* See under **adequacy**.

exponent /ɪk'spəʊnənt/ *n.* The phonetic **realization** of a phonological element. The term is particularly associated with **Prosodic Analysis**, but is used elsewhere. *Abstr. n.* **exponence**.

expression /ɪk'sprɛʃn̩/ *n.* One of the three **planes** of phonology. Roughly, the plane of expression includes all those aspects of phonology which express the identity of the speaker: sex, social class, individuality, and so on. Cf. **appeal**, **representation**.

extended articulation /ɪk'stɛndɪd/ *n.* An **articulation** involving a **constriction** which extends for some considerable distance along the axis of the vocal tract. Catford (1977: 194–195).

extended chain shift /ɪk'stendɪd/ *n.* Any **chain shift** involving three or more segments all of which move along a single identifiable trajectory. Labov (1994: 119).

external adequacy /ɪk'stɜːnəl/ *n.* See under **adequacy**.

external evidence /'evɪdəns/ *n.* Any of various types of evidence which can be brought to bear upon a proposed phonological analysis *other than* the characteristics of the analysis itself (economy, generality, simplicity, etc.). Possible sources of external evidence include characteristics of child language, aspects of language pathology, certain types of psycholinguistic experiment, treatment of loan words, conformity to proposed universals, and (in certain circumstances) the orthographic preferences of native speakers. Cf. **internal evidence**.

external open juncture *n.* In **American Structuralist** work, the type of **juncture** which marks either boundary of an utterance. See **juncture phoneme**. Trager and Bloch (1941).

external sandhi *n.* Any form of **sandhi** occurring across word boundaries, such as the process t + j → tʃ in English sequences like *can't you* [kæntʃ uː]. Cf. **internal sandhi**. Hockett (1958).

extra-long /'ekstrə/ *adj.* 1. See **overlong**. 2. In the **Williamson feature system**, one of the four possible values of the feature **length**.

extraprosodicity /ekstrəprɒsə'dɪsɪti/ *n.* (also **extrametricality** /ekstrə-metrɪ'kælɪti/) A device which renders a peripheral (initial or final) element in a phonological form invisible to certain phonological processes, such as tone spreading or stress assignment. An extraprosodic element is conventionally enclosed in **angle brackets**. See Roca (1992) for a historical account. *Adj.* **extraprosodic**. Liberman and Prince (1977).

extra-short *adj.* (of a vowel) Having an unusually short duration while retaining syllabicity. In the IPA, extra-short vowels are marked with a **breve**: [ŭ].

extrasyllabicity /ekstrəsɪlə'bɪsɪti/ *n.* Any of various extensions of **extraprosodicity** to syllable structure. One use of it is to deal with a **latent consonant** in syllable-final position (as in French *mes* 'my'): this is initially assigned to no syllable; unless rescued by a following vowel-initial during a derivation, it receives no phonetic realization. Another is the treatment of Palestinian Arabic *kitábit* 'I wrote', which has stress on the 'wrong' syllable: taking *kitab+t* as the underlying form, with an extrasyllabic affix, allows stress to be assigned correctly. *Adj.* **extrasyllabic**. Clements and Keyser (1983).

extratonality /ekstrətə'næliti/ *n.* In certain **tone languages**, a phenomenon in which a word-final syllable is exempt from the usual rules applying to tones. Myers (1987).

extrinsic allophone /ɪk'strɪnsɪk/ *n.* An **allophone** whose phonetic nature cannot be predicted from its phonetic environment, and which must therefore be stipulated by rule in a description, such as the **dark** *l* which occurs only in non-prevocalic position in the English of England. Cf. **intrinsic allophone**. Wang and Fillmore (1961).

extrinsic ordering *n.* Any version of **rule ordering** in which the order of rules is stipulated by the analyst instead of being derived from universal principles. Ant. **intrinsic ordering** (especially sense 2).

eye dialect /aɪ/ *n.* In writing, the use of non-standard spellings to indicate the use of non-standard speech: *wuz* for *was*, *sez* for *says*, *massa* for *master*.

eye rhyme *n.* In poetry, the occurrence in rhyming position of two words whose spelling suggests that they should rhyme but which do not in fact rhyme, such as *move/love* or *great/meat*.

F

F0 /ef 'zɪərəʊ/ *n.* See **fundamental frequency**.

F1, F2, F3 /ef wʌn, tuː, θriː/ *n.* See **first**, **second**, **third formant**.

facultative /'fækəltətɪv/ *adj.* (of alternative forms) In **free variation**.

fall /fɔːl/ *n.* A lowering of the **pitch** level during an utterance.

falling diphthong *n.* See **diminuendo diphthong**.

falling tone *n.* A **contour tone** characterized by a drop in pitch.

false quantity /fɔːls/ *n.* 1. In **quantitative metre**, the use of a heavy syllable where the metre requires a light one, or vice versa. 2. The pronunciation of an English word of Greek or Latin origin with a long (tense) vowel where the original has a short vowel, or vice versa. For example, Latin *stătus*, with short *a*, 'ought' to yield English *st*[æ]*tus*, with a short vowel, but the pronunciation *st*[eɪ]*tus*, with a false quantity, is both more usual and more prestigious.

false segmentation *n.* The putative process by which speakers insert an apparent **morpheme boundary** into an unjustified position, sometimes posited to account for such data as the *veto* **phenomenon**. Lass (1984: 34).

false step /step/ *n.* In a **derivational** theory of phonology, an intermediate stage of representation which is **ill-formed** in some respect, and which must be corrected by a **rescue rule**, but which is posited in order to make the whole analysis more general or more economical. Zwicky (1973).

falsetto /fɔːl'setəʊ/ *n.* or *adj.* (also **head register**, **head voice**) A distinctive **phonation type** in which the vocal folds are stretched longitudinally, yielding a thin cross-section, and usually leaving the glottis slightly open. The fundamental frequency produced is very much higher than in **modal voice**, typically around three times as high for males; subglottal pressure is lower, and there is often a slight whispery quality as the air leaks through the glottis. Falsetto is not known to be used contrastively in any language, but it has a variety of paralinguistic uses; see Laver (1994: 197–198) for a survey. Since falsetto is typically used for whole utterances rather than for individual segments, Laver (1994) recommends notating it with an F prefixed to the (bracketed) stretch of speech in falsetto. See Hollien (1972) for a detailed description. NOTE: Falsetto has usually been treated as a **register**, but John Laver in recent works prefers to classify it as a **phonation type**.

false vocal cords *n. pl.* See **ventricular folds**.

family universal /'fæmli/ *n.* A phonetic or phonological property uncommon in languages generally but very common in the languages of a particular family or area, such as clicks in southern Africa. Lass (1984: 155).

faucal /'fɔːkəl/ *adj.* 1. Pertaining to the **faucal pillars**. 2. (of a segment) Articulated by means of lateral compression of that part of the pharynx just behind the mouth, bringing the faucal pillars together, often with some raising of the larynx: one type of **pharyngeal** articulation. The Arabic pharyngeal approximants [ħ] and [ʕ] are commonly articulated in this way.

faucalized voice /'fɔːkəlaɪzd/ *n.* A distinctive **voice quality**, sometimes heard from deaf speakers, in which the **faucal pillars** are moved laterally inwards, constricting the **pharynx**.

faucal pillars /'pɪləz/ *n. pl.* The two vertical pairs of muscles which move the **velum** up and down. When they lower the velum, they also tend to narrow the side-to-side diameter of the pharynx.

FCR /ef siː 'aː/ *n.* See **feature cooccurrence restriction**.

feature /'fiːtʃə/ *n.* See **distinctive feature**.

feature bundle /'bʌndəl/ *n.* See **feature matrix**.

feature coefficient /kəʊɪ'fɪʃənt/ *n.* (also **Greek letter variable**) Any of the Greek letters α, β, etc., used as variables in the **alpha notation**.

feature cooccurrence restriction /kəʊə'kʌrəns rɪstrɪkʃən/ *n.* (**FCR**) Any universal or language-specific statement which either requires one feature specification to be accompanied by another or prohibits one specification from being accompanied by another. For example, the universal FCR [+obstr] → [−cons] requires all obstruents to be consonantal; the universal FCR [+high] → [−low] requires all high segments to be non-low; the Basque-specific FCR [+obstr, +cont] → [−voice] requires all continuant obstruents (fricatives) in that language to be voiceless. Some feature systems permit statements like [–obstr] → ~ [delrel], which says that a non-obstruent must carry no specification at all for the feature [delayed release].

feature dependency *n.* An analysis in which some feature, instead of being connected directly to the phonological skeleton, is connected to another feature which is itself connected (directly or indirectly) to the skeleton; the first feature is said to be dependent on the second. Such dependencies underlie the notion of **feature geometry**.

feature disagreement /dɪsə'griːmənt/ *n.* The phenomenon in which the algebraic value of one binary feature must be opposite to that of another, commonly expressed by means of the **alpha notation**. For example, the specification [α ant, –α cor] picks out the class of segments which are either [+ant, –cor] or [–ant, +cor].

feature filling /'fɪlɪŋ/ *n.* In **Underspecification Theory**, the process of filling in feature specifications which are so far blank.

feature geometry /dʒi'ɒmɪtri/ *n.* A theory of **distinctive features** in which features, contrary to the traditional view, are not combined into structureless bundles, but are organized in such a way that some features are grouped together within superordinate nodes called **gestures**. For example, many analysts posit a superordinate feature node {laryngeal} (the **laryngeal gesture**, representing the activity of the larynx) upon which both [±voice] and [±aspirated] are dependent. The logical conclusion of this approach, in which all features are combined in a single structure, is sometimes called the **feature hierarchy**. See Kenstowicz (1994: 136–169, ch. 9) for a detailed account, McCarthy (1988) for a review. Clements (1985).

feature hierarchy *n.* The view, the logical consequence of **feature geometry**, that *all* features are related in a single branching tree, with a single node at the top representing the entire segment, and the daughters of that node dominating high-level features which in turn dominate other features, until every relevant feature appears somewhere in the tree. Figure F1 (p.144), adapted from Roca (1994: 105), shows the structure of an aspirated voiceless plosive.

feature matrix *n.* (also **feature bundle**) A bundle of **feature specifications** (features with values attached), particularly one intended as a representation of a segment. For example, English /k/ might be represented in the *SPE* **feature system** by the following feature matrix:

Feature Minimization Principle /mɪnɪmaɪˈzeɪʃn̩/ *n*. A fundamental principle of **Radical Underspecification**. It states: a grammar is most highly valued when underlying representations include the minimal

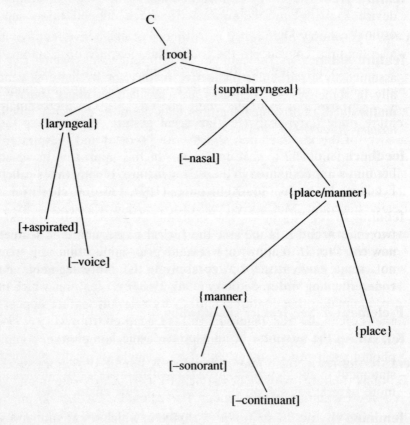

Figure F1 An aspirated plosive in the feature hierarchy

number of features necessary to make different the phonemes of a language. Archangeli (1984).

feature recursion *n.* A device sometimes proposed for treating phonological parameters along which several values need to be distinguished. **Vowel height**, for example, is notoriously difficult to handle with binary features, but, if we posit a single **component** (unary feature) of 'openness' A, we can obtain any number of vowel heights by recursion: /i/ = [ ], /e/ = A, /ɛ/ = AA, /æ/ = AAA, and so on. This is essentially the approach used in **privative theories** of phonology, in which differences are seen as resulting from the presence of differing amounts of a common element.

feature specification *n.* (also **specification, specified feature, valued feature, F-element**) A **distinctive feature** with a legal value assigned to it, such as [+nasal], [–coronal] or [4 height] in various systems.

feature tree /triː/ *n.* In **feature geometry**, the tree-like graphical device showing how subordinate features depend upon superordinate class nodes.

feature valency *n.* The number of different values which can be assumed by a particular **distinctive feature**, or by features generally in some system. Features are classified as **unary, binary** or **multivalued**; multivalued features may be more explicitly labelled *ternary, quaternary*, and so on.

feedback /'fiːdbæk/ *n.* The process by which a speaker is able to hear her/his own speech through the air and through the bones of the head. Feedback is essential in maintaining proper control over speech.

feeding order /'fiːdɪŋ/ *n.* The ordering 'A precedes B' applied to two rules A and B in the case in which the application of A creates new cases for B to apply to, while the prior application of B would not create new cases for A to apply to. Cf. **bleeding order**. Ant. **counterfeeding order**. Kiparsky (1965, 1968a).

F-element *n.* See **feature specification**.

fell swoop /fel 'swuːp/ *n.* An analysis in which some rather complex phonological process is executed by a single (typically elaborate) statement in the description, instead of by a series of simpler and more natural rules applying in order. Cf. **rule chain**. Zwicky (1974).

feminine rhyme /'femənɪn/ *n.* A **rhyme** in which the rhyming words contain one or more unstressed syllables after the stressed syllable:

making/taking; *billion/vermilion*; *pentacle/tentacle*. Cf. **masculine rhyme**.

festination /festɪ'neɪʃn̩/ *n.* A gradual, usually pathological, increase in speed while speaking, characteristic of certain disorders of speaking. Cf. **cluttering**.

field of dispersion /dɪ'spɜːʃn̩/ *n.* For a given phoneme, the area of **phonological space** which is available to provide varying phonetic realizations of that phoneme without intruding upon the space occupied by other phonemes. Cf. **margin of security**. Martinet (1952).

filled pause /fɪld/ *n.* (also **hesitation noise**) A hesitation in speech which is occupied by some non-linguistic material of the sort commonly represented as *um* or *er*. Cf. **silent pause**.

filter /'fɪltə/ *n.* 1. See **acoustic filter**. 2. (also **negative condition**) Any statement whose function is to exclude any phonological structure possessing certain specified characteristics. For example, the filter *[+high, –ATR] disallows any segment with this particular combination of feature specifications, while the filter *[V+V] prohibits a sequence of vowels across a morpheme boundary. Filters have been variously invoked in various frameworks for different purposes; the first example is equivalent to a **feature co-occurrence restriction**, while the second might simply express a **conspiracy** requiring several independent rules to eliminate vowels in hiatus.

filtered speech *n.* Speech which has been passed through an **acoustic filter** which selectively removes certain frequencies. Judicious choice of frequencies can allow effective transmission of speech using a much smaller range of frequencies than is actually used in speech; this happens on an ordinary telephone line.

final /'faɪnəl/ *n.* See **rhyme** (sense 2).

final devoicing *n.* The phenomenon in which an underlyingly voiced segment is pronounced with no voicing during its latter stages, in which the voicing is turned off before the segment has been completed.

final lengthening *n.* The seemingly universal tendency of speakers to lengthen the last one or two syllables before a pause.

final position *n.* The position of the last segment in a word, or sometimes in a syllable, a phrase or an utterance.

fine tuning /faɪn ˈtjuːnɪŋ/ *n.* The putative process by which speakers modify the articulation of particular segments in order to maintain a satisfactory phonetic distance from other, contrasting, segments.

first formant /fɜːst/ *n.* (also **F1**) The lowest in frequency of the **formants** visible in a **sound spectrogram**.

First Germanic Consonant Shift /dʒɜːˈmænɪk/ *n.* (also **Grimm's Law**) The elaborate set of sound changes which affected all the Proto-Indo-European plosives in Proto-Germanic, or the resulting correspondences between Germanic and other IE languages. Using the traditional view of PIE, and ignoring some complications, these changes were as follows:

p → f	b → p	bh → b
t → θ	d → t	dh → d
k → x	g → k	gh → g

Cf. **Second Germanic Consonant Shift**. These correspondences were discovered by Rasmus Rask, but were brought to public attention by Jacob Grimm.

fission /ˈfɪʃn̩/ *n.* 1. See **phonemic split**. 2. Any phonological process which converts a single segment into a sequence of two segments, such as **unpacking** or **diphthongization**.

fixed accent /fɪkst/ *n.* An accentual system in which the accent always falls upon the same syllable of a word, counting either from the beginning or from the end of the word; in the case of a stress accent, this is called *fixed stress*. In Icelandic and Czech, stress always falls on the first syllable; in Polish, it always falls on the penultimate. Cf. **free accent**.

flank /flæŋk/ *n.* That end of a **constituent** at which its head is positioned. A head-initial constituent is 'flank left'; a head-final one, 'flank right'. Cf. **edge**.

flap /flæp/ *n.* 1. (also **flick**) A consonant whose articulation involves an articulator's being withdrawn from its rest position and then moved rapidly back to its rest position in such a way that it strikes another articulator during its trajectory. The most familiar flap is the retroflex flap [ɽ] of many Indian languages; several African languages have a labiodental flap for which Ladefoged has proposed the symbol [ⱱ]. Cf. **tap**. *Adj.* **flapped**. NOTE: Those who, like Laver (1994), prefer to regard a flap as a type of stop use the term **flapped stop** for what most others just call a 'flap'. 2. A frequent but inappropriate alternative term for **tap**, sometimes used as a cover term including both **flap** and **tap**. This usage should be avoided.

flapped /flæpt/ *adj.* In the **Williamson feature system**, one of the three possible values of the feature **posture**.

flapped fricative *n.* A segment which resembles a **flap** except that the brief constriction is not complete, but leaves a small opening through which friction noise can be produced. No language is known to make linguistic use of a flapped fricative. Cf. **tapped fricative**.

flapped lateral *n.* A **flap** in which the moving organ makes only lateral contact with the passive articulator. The alveolar flapped lateral [ɺ] occurs in several languages of India and Africa. See Laver (1994: 311–312).

flapping /'flæpɪŋ/ *n.* 1. The action of producing a **flap**. 2. See **tapping**. NOTE: The second sense is inappropriate and should be avoided.

flat /flæt/ *adj.* In the **Jakobson–Halle feature system**, a **distinctive feature** defined as 'exhibiting weakening or downward shift of the upper frequencies in the spectrum' and interpreted as representing any of lip-rounding, pharyngealization or retroflexion. The use of this feature implies the interesting and controversial claim that no language may contrastively employ more than one of these three phenomena. In the *SPE* system, a number of features are used to cover the same ground: [+round] for lip-rounding, [+low, +back] for pharyngealization and [–anterior, –distributed] for retroflexion. *Abstr. n.* **flatness**. Ant. **plain**. See the remarks under **sharp**. See Ohala (1985) for a review of this feature. Impressionistic; applied by Müller (1855) to non-front vowels; introduced by Trubetzkoy (1939) in its modern sense.

flat fricative *n.* See **slit fricative**.

flexion /'flekʃən/ *n.* See **inflection**.

flick /flɪk/ *n.* See **flap** (sense 1).

flip-flop rule /'flɪpflɒp/ *n.* See **exchange rule**.

floating /'fləʊtɪŋ/ *n.* (also **dangling**) In **Autosegmental Phonology**, a label applied to any **autosegment** which, at some level of representation, is not associated to the skeleton. One may speak of a *floating tone* or even of a *floating segment*.

flow transducer /'fləʊ trænsdjuːsə/ *n.* Any of various devices serving to measure the volume of airflow per unit time (the 'volume-velocity') during speech. An example is the **hot-wire anemometer**.

fluency /'fluːənsi/ *n.* Rapid, smooth, effortless use of language, often particularly of spoken language. *Adj.* **fluent** /'fluːənt/.

folk etymology /'fəʊk etɪmɒlədʒi/ *n.* The process by which a word or phrase, usually one of seemingly opaque formation, is arbitrarily reshaped so as to yield a form which is considered to be more transparent. English examples include *sparrowgrass* (for *asparagus*), *Welsh rarebit* (for *Welsh rabbit*), *crayfish* (from French *écrevisse*) and *past master* (from *passed master*). A particularly striking example is Basque *zainhoria* 'carrot' (literally, 'yellow-root') from Spanish *zanahoria*, of Arabic origin.

foot /fʊt/ *n.* 1. The basic unit of rhythm in poetry, generally consisting of a group of two or more syllables in which one syllable bears the main stress (or, in **quantitative metre**, in which the syllables are **heavy** or **light** in some recognized pattern). Among the commonest types of foot are the **iamb**, the **trochee**, the **dactyl**, the **anapaest** and the **spondee**, though others exist. 2. The fundamental unit of rhythm in phonology, most typically consisting of a sequence of syllables one of which bears a stress or other prosodic element; this notion is of central importance in **Metrical Phonology**. It is not clear whether the notion of a foot can be usefully extended to languages which lack a **stress accent** or which have **syllable-timing**. Sense 2: Abercrombie (1967).

foot formation /fɔː'meɪʃn̩/ *n.* In **Metrical Phonology**, the process, or an analytical formalization of this process, by which a sequence of segments is organized into metrical **feet** in a language.

foot-level shortening *n.* The phenomenon in English by which the addition of an unstressed syllable to a foot shortens the duration of the stressed syllable. Rakerd *et al.* (1987).

forensic phonetics /fə'rensɪk/ *n.* The application of **phonetics** to the investigation of crimes in which recorded voices constitute evidence, most typically in determining the sex, age, social class and geographical background of an unidentified speaker, and hence in identifying that speaker. See Labov (1994: 109–111) for examples.

form /fɔːm/ *n.* 1. Any particular linguistic item, most often one which is longer than a single segment: a syllable, a lexical item, an inflected form of a lexical item, and so on. 2. The relationships between linguistic items, considered independently of the way in which the items are overtly realized. 'Form' in this sense contrasts with **substance**. Sense 2: Saussure (1916).

formal /'fɔːməl/ *adj.* 1. Pertaining to linguistic **forms**, as opposed to the meanings or functions of those forms. 2. (of a description, an analysis or a theoretical framework) Completely explicit; leaving nothing to be filled in by the reader.

formalism /'fɔːməlɪzm/ *n.* Any fully explicit notational device or set of such devices. Most approaches to phonology since the 1960s purport to be formalisms, though some are certainly more explicit and complete than others.

formalization /fɔːməlaɪ'zeɪʃn̩/ *n.* The embedding of a linguistic description into a **formalism**. *V.* **formalize**.

formal universal *n.* A **universal** of language which pertains to the form a description can take. For example, the use of **binary features**, the recognition of the **cycle** and the **Association Convention** of Autosegmental Phonology all represent proposed formal universals. Cf. **substantive universal**.

formant /'fɔːmənt/ *n.* A concentration of acoustic energy within a particular frequency band, especially in speech. Any given configuration of the **vocal tract** produces **resonance**, and hence formants, in certain frequency ranges. During the articulation of a vowel, these formants show up prominently in a **sound spectrogram** as thick dark bars; the three lowest of these, known as the **first**, **second** and **third formants** (**F1**, **F2** and **F3**) are highly diagnostic, and vowels are distinguished acoustically by the positions of these formants. Sonorant consonants produce similar but weaker formants. Plosives can often be distinguished by the characteristic **transitions** which the formants display as the vocal organs move from a plosive to a following vowel.

formant chart *n.* See **vowel chart**.

formative /'fɔːmətɪv/ *n.* 1. A **morpheme** with an explicitly grammatical function, or a particular phonetic form representing such a morpheme. 2. A synonym for **morpheme**. NOTE: The broader second sense is confined to the generative literature, especially Chomsky and Halle (1968); the first sense is more usual elsewhere.

form class *n.* A general term for any class of items sharing morphological, and usually also distributional, characteristics. Examples include the class of nouns in English, the class of -*a*-stem verbs in Spanish and the class of weak adjective forms in German.

form word *n.* See **function word**.

fortis /'fɔːtɪs/ *adj.* 1. (also **intensive**) (of a segment) Articulated in a manner involving more energetic tensing of the articulatory apparatus than a more relaxed but otherwise roughly equivalent segment. In English, for example, voiceless obstruents are fortis while voiced obstruents are not. See Catford (1977: 199–208) for a discussion. 2. (in phonology) In certain languages, such as the Zapotec languages of Mexico, denoting any of a series of consonant phonemes which contrast with a second (**lenis**) series, more or less identical in place and manner, by virtue of a more vigorous articulation. The phonetic correlates of the contrast are rather variable, the fortis consonants variously exhibiting greater duration, greater degree of occlusion, less voicing and more aspiration than their lenis counterparts. See for example Nellis and Hollenbach (1980). 3. A binary **distinctive feature** which is occasionally invoked to handle such contrasts; the feature **tense** is probably more widely used. 4. A binary **distinctive feature** proposed by Ladefoged (1971), defined as 'articulated with increased subglottal pressure'. Unlike the *SPE* feature **heightened subglottal pressure**, Ladefoged's has no correlation with aspiration. This feature was abandoned in the **Ladefoged feature system**. Ant. (all senses) **lenis**.

fortition /fɔː'tɪʃn̩/ *n.* (also **strengthening**) Any phonological process in which some segment becomes 'stronger' (more consonant-like). An example is the development of the glide [j] into some kind of fricative, affricate or plosive in most varieties of Basque. *V.* **strengthen** /'streŋθən/. Ant. **lenition**.

Fourier analysis /'fʊrɪə/ *n.* A mathematical technique by which any complex wave may be analysed into a number of **sine waves**, each with a particular frequency and amplitude.

fracture /'fræktʃə/ *n.* See **breaking**.

free accent /friː/ *n.* An accent system in which the word accent is not fixed upon a particular syllable but may occur on any of several syllables, thus possibly serving to distinguish words or word forms, as in English or Russian. Cf. **fixed accent**.

free autosegment *n.* In some versions of **Autosegmental Phonology**, an **autosegment** which, in lexical representations, is not initially associated with any segments. Most autosegments are free in this sense. Cf. **lexically bound autosegment**. Hyman (1982).

free form *n.* A form which can stand alone as a complete word, such as *book*, *went* or *under*. A free form which is also a morpheme is a *free morpheme*. Cf. **bound form**.

free ride /raɪd/ *n.* In a **derivational** theory of phonology, the phenomenon in which rules posited to account for certain data automatically produce the correct result for other significantly different data for which they were not originally posited; these other data are said to receive a 'free ride'. The statement that maximization of such free rides is desirable is called the **free ride principle**. Zwicky (1970).

free variant *n.* Any one of the segments involved in an instance of **free variation**.

free variation *n.* 1. Most commonly, the phenomenon in which any of two or more **phones** can appear in the same position without any effect upon meaning. For example, a single speaker of English may at various times pronounce the word *eat* with two or more of aspirated [tʰ], unaspirated [t⁼], glottalized [ʔt], or unreleased [t˺]. 2. Less commonly, the phenomenon in which either of two or more **phonemes** may be used in the same position in the same word without affecting meaning, as when *economics* or *evolution* may be pronounced either with initial /iː/ or initial /e/. See **variphone**, **metaphone**.

free vowel *n.* (also **unchecked vowel**) 1. A vowel which occurs in an **open syllable**. 2. A vowel phoneme in a particular language which can occur in this position, such as /iː/ or /aɪ/ in English. Cf. **checked vowel**.

frequency /ˈfriːkwənsi/ *n.* The quantity representing the number of complete **cycles** (sense 1) (oscillations) performed by a given **wave** per unit time, commonly expressed in **Hertz (Hz)** and represented by the symbol *f*. For example, a vibrating violin string that is making 400 complete vibrations in one second is vibrating at 400 Hz. Generally speaking, the higher the frequency of a sound wave, the higher the **pitch** of the perceived sound, though the relationship is not linear.

frequency band *n.* A particular continuous range of frequencies, such as the band 135–180 Hz. The difference between the two extremes is the **bandwidth** of the band.

frequency of occurrence /ə'kʌrəns/ *n.* Any of various measures of the frequency with which some linguistic element occurs in continuous speech or written texts.

fricative /'frɪkətɪv/ *n.* or *adj.* 1. (also **spirant**) A segment whose articulation involves a radical constriction in the vocal tract short of a complete closure but sufficient to produce friction noise as the airstream flows through the constricted opening. Fricatives may be voiced or voiceless; examples include [f v s z]. Since small differences in articulatory posture can produce large differences in the auditory quality of the segment, the number of distinguishable fricatives is quite large, and the IPA provides more distinct symbols for fricatives than for any other manner of consonants. Fricatives are sometimes classified, both phonetically and phonologically, into two groups differing in 'noisiness' by means of such features as [±strident] or [±sibilant]. The most widely occurring fricative in the world's languages is [s], and most languages have one or more fricatives in their phoneme inventory, though some, like Hawaiian and the majority of Australian languages, have none. The combination of a fricative articulation with other independent articulatory gestures allows such segments as a **lateral fricative** or a **fricative trill**. See Laver (1994: ch. 9) for a summary. 2. In the **Ladefoged feature system**, one of the three possible values of the feature **stop**. 3. In the **Williamson feature system**, one of the five possible values of the feature **stricture**. 4. (**fric**) A binary **distinctive feature** proposed by Ladefoged (1971), distinguishing affricates and fricatives ([+fric]) from all other segments ([−fric]).

fricative trill *n.* (also **trilled fricative**) A **trill** whose articulation involves friction noise, at least during the open phases of the trill, and possibly also during the closed phases, if these are less than completely occluded. A lamino-alveolar fricative trill (IPA [r̝]) occurs in Czech, where it is written ⟨ř⟩, as in *Dvořák*.

fricativization /frɪkətɪvaɪ'zeɪʃn̩/ *n.* (also, rarely, **fricatization** /frɪkətaɪ'zeɪʃn̩/) See **spirantization** (sense 1).

friction /'frɪkʃən/ *n.* (also **friction noise**) The auditory effect of air passing turbulently through a small constriction, important in the production of **fricative** and **affricate** consonants. Voiceless friction is perceived as some kind of 'hissing' sound; friction accompanied by **voicing** is heard as some kind of 'buzzing' sound.

frictionless continuant *n.* In general, a synonym for **approximant**, though usage varies as to whether **lateral approximants** (**lateral resonants**) should be regarded as frictionless continuants or not.

front /frɒnt/ 1. *adj.* (of vowels) Articulated with the highest point of the tongue towards the front of the mouth, below the palate, as in [i], [e], [a] and [y]. Ant. **back** (sense 1). 2. *adj.* A **distinctive feature** occasionally invoked, in addition to the established feature **back** (sense 2), for treating languages in which central vowels contrast with both back and front vowels. In such an analysis, front vowels are [+front, −back], central vowels are [−front, −back], and back vowels are [−front, +back]. 3. *n.* (also **anterodorsum**) That part of the upper surface of the tongue lying more or less directly below the palate, usually defined so as to exclude the **tip** and the **blade** (Catford and Ladefoged), but sometimes defined so as to include them (Laver).

fronting *n.* The phonological process in which the articulation of a segment (especially a vowel) moves closer to the front of the mouth. For example, a historical [u] has undergone fronting to [ʉ] or [y] at various times in the history of Greek, Swedish and French, in some dialects of Basque, and in most Scottish and some American varieties of English. *Adj.* **fronted**. Ant. **backing**.

fronting diphthong *n.* A **diphthong** in which the second element is farther front than the first, such as [oj] or [wi]. Ant. **backing diphthong**.

full devoicing /fʊl/ *n.* The phenomenon in which an underlyingly voiced segment loses its voicing completely. Full devoicing is represented in the IPA by the diacritic [̥] below the character.

full form *n.* See **strong form**.

full voicing *n.* The articulation of a segment with voicing throughout its duration. French /b d g/, for example, are usually fully voiced in all positions, while English /b d g/ are partially devoiced initially and finally.

functional change /ˈfʌŋkʃənəl/ *n.* A general term for any historical change in which the phonological status of a segment or a feature is significantly altered, the chief types being called **phonologization** and **dephonologization**.

functional load /ləʊd/ *n.* The degree to which a particular phonological contrast is utilized in a particular language. In English, for example, the voiced/voiceless contrast carries a high functional load, being frequently invoked to carry differences of meaning: *pat*, *pad*, *bat*, *bad*; *safe*, *save*; *race*, *raze*. In Basque, however, the same contrast carries a low functional load, being hardly ever the sole exponent of a difference in meaning, the pairs *ipar* 'north' and *ibar* 'valley' and *ekin* 'continue' and *egin* 'do' being among the handful of minimal pairs in the language distinguished only by voicing. A rough quantitative measure of functional load is given by the number of **minimal pairs** distinguished by the contrast in question, but this measure ignores such factors as the frequency of those items and the likelihood of possible confusion if they should become homophonous by loss of the contrast.

Functionally Constrained Phonology /kən'streɪnd/ *n.* An approach to phonology, proposed by Houlihan and Iverson (1979), which attempts to integrate implicational universals and marking theory into phonological descriptions, particularly for the purpose of accounting for **neutralization**.

functional phonetics *n.* [*obsolete*] A former synonym for **phonology**. Martinet (1949).

functional residual capacity /rɪ'zɪdjuəl kəpæsɪti/ *n.* The volume of air in the lungs at the minimum of the **tidal volume**, consisting of the **expiratory reserve volume** and the **residual volume**.

functional shift *n.* See **conversion**.

function word *n.* (also **grammatical word**, **form word**) A word which has a grammatical function but little lexical content, such as *and*, *of*, *the* or modal *can*. In English, function words are often phonologically reduced, and their **weak forms** are more frequent than their **strong forms**.

fundamental frequency /fʌndə'mentəl/ *n.* (also **F0**) The **frequency** at which a body vibrates when it vibrates in the simplest manner possible, typically the most prominent frequency produced by a vibrating body. Cf. **harmonic**.

fusion /'fjuːʒn̩/ *n.* 1. See **coalescence**. 2. In **Dependency Phonology**, the descriptive procedure by which **components** are combined into phonetic segments, as when li;al is realized as /e/. 3. In **Government and Charm Phonology**, the descriptive procedure by which two **feature matrices** are combined into one, with **hot** (marked) feature specifications overriding **cold** (unmarked) values.

G

GA /dʒiː ˈeɪ/ n. See **General American**.

Garde's Principle /ɡɑːd/ n. A widely accepted principle in historical phonology. It says: mergers are irreversible by linguistic means. See **reversal of merger**. Principle: Garde (1961); name: Labov (1994: 311).

gating experiment /ˈɡeɪtɪŋ/ n. 1. An experimental technique in which subjects are given successively longer stretches of a word, in order to determine the earliest point at which it becomes recognizable. See Frauenfelder and Tyler (1987). 2. An experimental technique for investigating sound changes in progress by exposing listeners to advanced (innovating) pronunciations in isolation, in phrases and finally in complete sentences. Labov (1994: 194, 214).

geminate /ˈdʒemɪneɪt/ n. (also **doubled consonant** or **doubled vowel**) A sequence of two identical segments, especially consonants. Geminate consonants occur in English only at morpheme boundaries: nighttime, bookcase, solely, non-null. Long vowels in some languages are sometimes analysed as geminates, so that [oː], for example, might be analysed as /oo/. Adj. **geminate** or **geminated** /ˈdʒemɪneɪtɪd/.

gemination /dʒemɪˈneɪʃn̩/ n. Any of various phonological processes in which a segment is converted into a **geminate**: Proto-Romance *sapja > Italian sappia 'would know'; Proto-Germanic *sitjan > *sittjan > Old English sittan 'sit'; Sanskrit patra- > pattra- 'leaf'; Latin AQUA [akwa] 'water' > Italian acqua [akkwa]; Latin RE PUBLICA > Italian repubblica 'republic'. Sometimes the term is extended to instances of **total assimilation** like Latin NOCTE > Italian notte 'night'. Ant. **degemination**.

General American /dʒenərəl əˈmerɪkən/ n. (**GA**) The conventional label for the closely related speech varieties typical of the whole of the United States excluding the east coast and the south (that is, excluding the long-settled areas with distinctive and readily identifiable local accents). Krapp (1925).

generalization /dʒenərəlaɪˈzeɪʃn̩/ n. A statement about the phonological facts of a language, or about the facts of languages generally, which holds true in all cases or in nearly all cases. All contemporary theories of phonology consider it a major goal to identify generalizations (at least those which are 'linguistically significant'), to state them within descriptions or within theoretical frameworks, and to explain them as far as possible by deriving them from fundamental principles. It is by no means obvious *a priori*, however, which generalizations are linguistically significant or even which generalizations exist at all; this last point arises partly because linguists disagree about how many exceptions can be tolerated before a proposed generalization must be abandoned and partly because **derivational** theories permit the stating of generalizations which hold at abstract levels of representation but not on the surface.

general phonetics *n.* (also **anthropophonics**). The study of the entire range of speech sounds which can be produced by the human vocal apparatus, independently of whether or how the sounds are used for any linguistic purpose in any language. Cf. **linguistic phonetics**.

general RP *n.* In the classification of Gimson (1989), that variety of **Received Pronunciation** which is most typical and least distinctive and which contrasts with **conservative** and **advanced RP**. This is equivalent to Wells's **mainstream RP**.

generational change /dʒenə'reɪʃənəl/ *n.* A type of language change in which each individual enters the speech community with a characteristic frequency for a particular variable and maintains this value unchanged throughout life, but in which each younger generation enters the community with an increasingly incremented value for the variable, leading to steady change over time. This appears to be by far the most frequent pattern for phonological and morphological change. Cf. **age-grading**, **communal change**. Labov (1994: 84).

generative analysis of intonation /'dʒenərətɪv/ *n.* Any approach to the description of **intonation** which is embedded within the framework of **generative phonology**.

generative phonology *n.* (**GP**) 1. Narrowly, an approach to phonology based upon the setting up of abstract **underlying forms** which are converted by the application of a (possibly long) sequence of **phonological rules** into surface phonetic forms and which are themselves formulated as linear sequences of **segments**:

essentially an elaboration of what had earlier been called **morpho-phonemics**. Generative phonology was adumbrated in Chomsky, Halle and Lukoff (1956) and presented in some detail in Halle (1959); the modified and elaborated version presented in Chomsky and Halle (1968) represented the canonical form of **classical generative phonology**. Deeply influential, this version proved, however, to be excessively unconstrained: there was nothing to prevent underlying representations from being impossibly remote from surface forms, and such devices as **absolute neutralization** were commonplace; **extrinsic rule ordering** and a wide range of **abbreviatory conventions** conferred vast power upon the framework. Attempts at restricting this power included **Natural Generative Phonology** and **Natural Phonology**. In the 1980s the whole approach gave way to the contemporary **non-linear** frameworks, though **Lexical Phonology** still continues the 'feel' of the classical system. 2. Broadly, a label applied to virtually the entire body of work in phonology since about 1960, including not only work referred to in sense 1 but also the various, mostly non-linear, approaches developed in the 1980s. The modern approaches often differ radically from the earlier ones but are united by a recognition that they are continuing the research programme initiated by Chomsky and Halle (1968) (*SPE*).

geno-molar trill /dʒiːnəʊˈməʊlə/ *n.* An unusual type of **trill** produced between the cheeks and the back molar teeth, most readily with a voiceless glottalic egressive airstream, with a distinctive 'rattly' sound. Such trills occur in several Caucasian languages. Catford (1977: 252).

Geordie /ˈdʒɔːdi/ *n.* or *adj.* [*non-technical*] The popular label for the distinctive speech variety of the Tyne and Wear area of north-eastern England, centred on the city of Newcastle, or for a person who uses this speech variety. Diminutive of 'George'; originally a northern dialect word for 'coal-miner'.

gesture /ˈdʒestʃə/ *n.* In some approaches to phonology, any one of the several partly independent components into which the articulation of a segment may be decomposed. One simple approach is to decompose each segment into a **laryngeal gesture**, including everything going on in the larynx, and a **supralaryngeal gesture**, including everything going on in the mouth and the nasal cavity. Most developments of the idea recognize more than two gestures, however, usually including some gestures which are **subgestures** of other superordinate gestures. One typical proposal is to divide a segment into a *categorial gesture*, consisting of *phonatory* and *initiatory subgestures*, and an *articulatory gesture*, consisting of *locational* and *oro-nasal subgestures*; each of the four subgestures is the domain of certain **distinctive features** or **components**. The analysis into gestures underlies **feature geometry** and is also prominent in **Dependency Phonology**. See Lass (1984: chs 5, 11) or Durand (1990: 99–109).

Gimson–O'Connor system /ˈgɪmsən əʊˈkɒnə/ *n.* A conventional system for representing the phonemes of that type of British accent called **Received Pronunciation**, incorporating a particular analysis of the vowel system, one that '**hugs the phonetic ground**'. The Gimson–O'Connor system is identical to the earlier *EPD* **transcription** except in the particular characters used to represent some of the vowel phonemes, which, in line with the general approach characteristic of the system, have been modified to reflect changes in pronunciation. In England this system is almost universally used for transcribing RP in linguistic works; the name used here reflects its use by A. C. Gimson and J. D. O'Connor, two of Jones's successors, in a number of well-known works, of which the various editions of Gimson's standard work (currently Cruttenden 1994) is perhaps the most prominent. The system is also increasingly used in serious dictionaries and in the teaching of English. It is sometimes known as 'modified *EPD*', or, among lexicographers, as 'modified IPA'.

gingiva /ˈdʒɪndʒɪvə/ *n.* See **gum**.

gingival /ˈdʒɪndʒɪvəl/ 1. *adj.* Pertaining to the **gums**. 2. *adj.* [*obsolete*] A former synonym for **alveolar** (sense 2). 3. (also **denti-alveolar**) (of a segment) Articulated with the primary stricture occurring at the point at which the teeth meet the gums. 4. *n.* (also **denti-alveolar**) A segment so articulated, such as [t] and [n] in some varieties of German and Danish.

G-licensing /ˈdʒiː/ *n.* In **Government and Charm Phonology**, one of the two recognized types of **licensing**. A position is G-licensed when it is governed by another position. Cf. **D-licensing**.

glide /glaɪd/ *n.* 1. A very brief phonetic **vowel** (sense 1) which functions in some language as a phonological **consonant** (sense 2); the English glides /j/ and /w/ (as in *yes* and *win*) are brief versions of [i] and [u]. 2. In the *SPE* **feature system**, any segment which is [–cons,

–voc]; this classification includes not only the familiar glides but also [h] and glottal stop, an extension which has met with severe criticism; see, for example, Lass (1976). 3. See **on-glide** and **off-glide**.

global constraint /'gləʊbəl/ *n*. (also **global rule**) See **derivational constraint**.

Glossematic phonology /glɒsɪ'mætɪk/ *n*. The type of phonology associated with the theory of linguistics called *Glossematics*. Glossematics was developed in Denmark between about 1928 and 1953; its chief theorist was Louis Hjelmslev, who sometimes collaborated with H. J. Uldall. Hjelmslev's writings are exceedingly abstract; they bristle with novel and opaque terminology; and they rarely cite linguistic data. As a result, Glossematic work has been seen as arid and baffling, and Hjlemslev has often been perceived by Americans, rightly or wrongly, as the paradigm case of the European armchair theorist who devises magnificent *a priori* theoretical edifices on the basis of no data – though Haugen (1954) argues that Glossematic conceptions are at bottom rather similar to **American Structuralist** ideas. What is clear is that Glossematic phonology absolutely rejects all appeals to psychological reality, to semantics and to phonetic substance. Glossematic phonology, an extreme development of the Saussurean *sign*, deals only with purely linguistic relations in isolation from the rest of the world. In the words of Stephen Anderson, Hjelmslev proposes 'to study systems of correspondence between sound and meaning with methods . . . completely independent of either sounds or meanings' (1985: 147). Almost uniquely among structuralist linguists, however, Hjelmslev pays considerable attention to prosodic phenomena and to syllable structure, thus adumbrating the concerns of contemporary phonologists. Though Hjelmslev's work is often cited with great respect, its impenetrable nature has prevented it from having anything like the influence upon phonological practice which it might have deserved – though **Stratificational phonology**, at least, acknowledges a debt to Hjelmslev. See Fischer-Jørgensen (1975: ch. 7) or Anderson (1985: ch. 6) for an account.

glossolalia /glɒsə'leɪlɪə/ *n*. The peculiar phenomenon, commonly called 'speaking in tongues', in which an individual who has been placed in a kind of trance produces a connected sequence of speech sounds which are clearly not utterances in any language known to her/him. Common among devotees of certain fervent Christian denominations, this behaviour is traditionally regarded by them as representing a God-given ability to speak in a language not known to the performer. Research has failed to support any such interpretation, suggesting instead that the performer merely produces a highly repetitive stream of nonsense syllables, mostly of the form CV, with no discernible structure.

glottal /'glɒtəl/ 1. *adj.* Pertaining to the **glottis**. 2. *adj.* (of an articulation) Articulated with the primary constriction in the glottis. 3. *n.* A segment so articulated, such as [ʔ] or (conventionally) [h]. 4. *adj.* In the **Ladefoged** and **Williamson feature systems**, one of the eleven possible values of the feature **articulatory place**.

glottal constriction *n.* 1. Closure or near-closure of the **glottis**. 2. In the *SPE* **feature system**, a **distinctive feature** defined as 'involving a narrowing of the glottal aperture beyond its neutral position'. The feature is invoked in the feature analysis of **implosives**, of **ejectives**, of certain types of **clicks**, of the tense glottalized stops of Korean, and of the 'laryngealized' or 'creaky-voiced' consonants of some African and Caucasian languages.

glottal fry /fraɪ/ *n.* See **creak**. From a supposed resemblance to the sound of frying food.

glottalic /glə'tælɪk/ *adj.* 1. Pertaining to the **glottis** in its capacity as a producer of an **airstream mechanism**. 2. In the **Ladefoged feature system**, a **distinctive feature** invoked to treat movement of the larynx during articulation; the feature may assume any one of the three values **ejective** (upward motion), **pulmonic** (no motion) or **implosive** (downward motion). This feature is identical to **larynx movement** in the **Williamson feature system**. 3. **(glott)** A **binary distinctive feature** proposed by Lass (1984: 93): segments articulated with a **glottalic airstream mechanism** are [+glott], while all other segments are [–glott].

glottalic airstream mechanism *n.* An **airstream mechanism** produced by closing the glottis more or less tightly and then moving the larynx sharply either upward or downward. Upward movement compresses the air in the mouth, producing a **glottalic egressive** airstream, as in **ejective** consonants; downward movement lowers the pressure in the mouth, producing a **glottalic ingressive** airstream, as in **implosive** and **injective** consonants. See Laver (1994: 171–173, 181–182). Beach (1937); Catford (1939).

glottalic theory of PIE *n.* The proposal that the conventional view of the Proto-Indo-European plosive system, consisting of three series represented by [t d dh], should be re-interpreted on typological grounds as a system containing a series of **ejectives**, most usually [t t' d]. First suggested by Martinet (1953), the glottalic theory has more recently been championed by Gamkrelidze and Ivanov (1973) and Hopper (1973); it has gained some acceptance, though see Szemerényi (1985) for a critical view.

glottalization /glɒtəlaɪ'zeɪʃn̩/ *n.* A very broad term applied loosely to a wide range of phenomena involving some kind of activity in the glottis, including at least **glottalling**, **glottal reinforcement**, the use of **creaky voice**, and the use of a **glottalic airstream mechanism**. *Adj.* **glottalized**. NOTE: This last usage is particularly unfortunate, but it is very widespread.

glottalized /'glɒtəlaɪzd/ *adj.* 1. (of a segment) Produced with **creaky voice**. 2. (of a segment) Produced with a simultaneous glottal stop, as in an **oral–glottal stop**. 3. (of a segment) Produced with a **glottalic airstream mechanism**. NOTE: This last sense is not recommended.

glottalling /'glɒtəlɪŋ/ *n.* 1. The replacement of an oral plosive by a glottal stop, as in the pronunciation of *butter* as ['bʌʔə]. 2. See **glottal reinforcement**.

glottal reinforcement /riːɪn'fɔːsmənt/ *n.* (also **glottalling**) The articulation of an oral plosive with a simultaneous **glottal stop**, as in the pronunciation of *quite good* as [kwaɪʔt gʊd] or of *stop talking* as [stɒʔp tɔːkɪŋ].

glottal state /steɪt/ *n.* In the **Williamson feature system**, a **distinctive feature** with the five possible values **glottal stop**, **laryngealized**, **voiced**, **murmured** and **voiceless**. This feature is identical to **voice** in the **Ladefoged feature system**.

glottal stop *n.* 1. (also **glottal catch** /kætʃ/) A common name for a voiceless glottal plosive (IPA [ʔ]). In some languages, such as Hawaiian and Arabic, the glottal stop functions as an ordinary consonant phoneme; in others, like English and German, it appears phonetically but non-contrastively in certain positions. In singing, the glottal stop is called the **hard attack**. 2. In the **Ladefoged** and **Williamson feature systems**, one of the five possible values of the feature **voice** (Ladefoged) or **glottal state** (Williamson).

glottal stricture *n.* The name used in Ladefoged (1971) for the **distinctive feature** later called **voice** in the **Ladefoged feature system**.

glottal subsystem /'sʌbsɪstəm/ *n.* That part of the **phoneme system** of a language consisting of segments which are distinctively **creaky-voiced** or articulated with a **glottalic airstream mechanism**.

glottal tone *n.* A suprasegmental phenomenon contrastively present on certain segments in a language and resembling a **tone**, but realized by some kind of glottal activity, most usually **creaky voice**, rather than by distinctive pitch. Danish **stød** is an example.

glottal waveform *n.* A representation of the flow of air through a vibrating glottis, typically consisting of a series of sharp peaks separated by flat periods during which no air is flowing.

glottal whistle *n.* A high-pitched sound produced by **voiceless** articulation in the **falsetto** register.

glottis /'glɒtɪs/ *n.* The V-shaped space between the **vocal folds**, opened and closed by the movement of the **arytenoid cartilages**. *Adj.* **glottal** (in most senses), **glottalic** (of an airstream).

glottography /glə'tɒɡrəfi/ *n.* Any of various techniques for investigating the behaviour of the **glottis** during speech. This is variously done by passing weak electric currents across the glottis (*electroglottography*) or by passing light up or down through the glottis (*photoelectric glottography*). *Adj.* **glottographic** /glɒtə'ɡræfɪk/.

gorgia toscana /ɡɔrdʒia tos'kaːna/ *n.* [Italian: 'Tuscan throat'] The phenomenon, typical of the Italian dialects of Tuscany, by which intervocalic voiceless plosives are realized as the corresponding fricatives: [p]*onte* → *i* [ɸ]*onti* '(the) bridge(s)'; [t]*orta* → *la* [θ]*orta* '(the) cake'; [k]*asa* → *la* [h]*asa* '(the) house'.

government /'ɡʌvənmənt/ *n.* (also **governing relation**) A synonym for **dependency**, preferred especially in **Government and Charm Phonology**, in which the notion has been considerably elaborated. See the special issue of *Phonology*, 7:2, 1990.

Government and Charm Phonology *n.* (also **Government Phonology**) A major contemporary theory of phonology, developed by Jonathan Kaye and his colleagues since about 1985. GCP is the most elaborate of the **privative theories**, and it is strongly influenced by ideas from syntax. As its name suggests, it makes heavy use of the concept of phonological **government** (= **dependency**); several different types of government are recognized, and constraints upon these make up much of the content of the framework. It retains the notion of phonological derivations, but dispenses with phonological rules altogether; moreover, it declines to admit such traditional processes as insertion and deletion of segments. It also makes considerable use of a distinctive type of markedness called **charm**. The framework was introduced in Kaye *et al.* (1985); Kaye *et al.* (1990) and Charette (1991) represent major developments and presentations. Brief introductions can be found in Carr (1993: 289–298) and in Roca (1994: 123–132, 159–176).

governor /'gʌvənə/ *n.* A synonym for **head** (sense 2), especially in **Government and Charm Phonology**.

GP /dʒiː 'piː/ *n.* See **generative phonology**.

gradation /grə'deɪʃn̩/ *n.* See **ablaut**.

gradient /'greɪdiənt/ *adj.* In some analyses of **intonation**, denoting an approach in which distinctions (especially of **pitch**) are interpreted as varying continuously along some dimension. Cf. **all-or-none contrast**.

gradual opposition /'grædʒuəl/ *adj.* In **Prague School** phonology, the relation holding between. segments which possess the same property to varying degrees, such as that between [i], [e] and [ɛ], which differ in having varying degrees of **height**. Cf. **privative opposition, equipollent opposition**.

gradual release *n.* See **delayed release**. Anderson (1974).

grammatical conditioning /grə'mætɪkəl/ *n.* (also **morphological conditioning**) 1. The phenomenon in which an **alternation** (sense 1) is determined by the presence of a particular grammatical morpheme: *knife ~ knives* (cf. *knife ~ knife's*, in which a phonologically identical suffix fails to trigger the alternation). 2. The phenomenon in which the course of a phonological change is affected by the grammatical structure of a word. For example, in Scottish English, **Aitken's Law** produces a short vowel in the closed syllable *brood*, while *brewed* retains the long vowel of *brew*: the morpheme boundary prevents shortening.

grammatical prerequisites /pri'rekwɪzɪts/ *n. pl.* In most views of phonology apart from **American Structuralism**, the grammatical information which is required in order to account for observed phonological phenomena. Pike (1947b).

grammatical word *n.* See **function word**.

Grammatischer Wechsel /ɡʀamatɪʃəʀ 'veksəl/ *n.* [German: 'grammatical change'] 1. The originally puzzling set of consonantal alternations occurring in many stems in the older Germanic languages and eventually explained by **Verner's Law**. A few of these survive in English: *was/were, seethe/sodden, lose/forlorn*. 2. By extension, any comparable set of alternations in any language for which the phonological basis is obscure. The term 'grammatical' is used here only in the sense of 'having no obvious phonological conditioning'.

Grassmann's Law /'ɡræsmənz/ *n.* The process, occurring in the histories of Sanskrit and Greek, by which the first of two consecutive aspirations in a word was lost: PIE **dhidhēmi* > Greek *tithēmi* 'put'. This process was bled by the earlier loss of aspiration before /s/, leading to alternations like Greek *thriks* 'hair', genitive *trikhos* (< PIE **dhrighs, dhrighos*). Grassmann (1863).

grave /ɡrɑːv/ *adj.* 1. In the **Jakobson–Halle feature system**, a **distinctive feature** defined as 'exhibiting a concentration of energy in the lower frequencies of the spectrum', interpreted as representing a peripheral (labial, velar, uvular) articulation. The specification [grave] corresponds approximately to the *SPE* specifications [–coronal] for consonants and [+back] for vowels. *Abstr. n.* **graveness** or **gravity**. Ant. **acute**. 2. (also **gravity**) In the **Ladefoged** and **Williamson feature systems**, a similar binary feature, invoked largely to account for such acoustically based historical developments as that of English [x] to [f] in *laugh*. See Lass (1976: 197–207) for an assembly of evidence that the feature grave is indispensable even in an articulatory feature system. Ant. **non-grave**.

grave accent *n.* The diacritic `, used in various orthographies and transcriptions for a variety of purposes. It was first used in Ancient Greek to mark a tone sandhi variant in that language. In French, ⟨è⟩ represents a vowel quality distinct from both ⟨e⟩ and ⟨é⟩. In Italian, the grave accent marks an irregular word-stress. In English, it is occasionally used to mark the unexpected presence of an additional syllable: hence *agèd* (two syllables) versus *aged* (one syllable). In the IPA, the grave accent is used to mark a low level tone. Cf. **acute accent**, **circumflex accent**. Latin *gravis* 'heavy', an impressionistic label for the perceptual effect of the Greek accent.

gravity /'ɡrævɪti/ *n.* 1. The property of a **grave** (both senses) segment. 2. See **grave** (sense 2). 3. (also **backness**) In **Dependency Phonology**, the element {u}, one of the three primary **elements** of vowels in that system. Cf. **palatality**, **sonority**.

Great Vowel Shift /greɪt/ *n.* 1. A series of related phonological developments which affected the **tense (long)** vowels of English from the sixteenth century onward. The two high vowels /iː/ and /uː/ were diphthongized, eventually reaching their modern values /ai/ and /au/, and all the other long vowels were raised. See any history of English for an outline of the process, and see Lass (1976) for a critical examination. 2. (usually **vowel shift**) In some analyses (notably that of Chomsky and Halle (1968)), a postulated synchronic process in English phonology mirroring the action of the historical vowel shift.

Greek letter variable /griːk 'letə/ *n.* See **feature coefficient**.

Grenzsignal /'ɡʀentssɪgnaːl/ *n.* (*pl.* *Grenzsignale* /-lə/) See **boundary signal**.

grid /grɪd/ *n.* See **metrical grid**.

grid-only theory *n.* A version of **Metrical Phonology** which does not recognize any metrical constituents (**feet**).

Grimm's Law /grɪm/ *n.* See **First Germanic Consonant Shift**.

grooved fricative /gruːvd/ *n.* A **fricative** whose articulation involves a longitudinal groove along the upper surface of the tongue, such as [s]. Cf. **slit fricative**.

gum /gʌm/ *n.* (also **gingiva**) Either of the two bony ridges in which the **teeth** are embedded. The upper gum is usually called the **alveolar ridge**.

guttural /'gʌtərəl/ *adj.* or *n.* 1. [*obsolete*] A synonym for **velar** (senses 2 and 3), formerly much used in philological works, where it is sometimes extended to include palatals as well as velars. 2. In some recent work, a cover term for uvulars, pharyngeals and glottals. 3. [*non-technical*] A loose impressionistic label for any consonant produced in the back of the mouth, including velars, uvulars, pharyngeals and glottals. 4. [*non-technical*] A meaningless label typically applied by the linguistically unsophisticated to any unfamiliar language or speech variety that doesn't sound like Italian. Latin *gutturalis* 'throaty'. Note the spelling of this word.

H

hachek /ˈhætʃek/ *n.* (also **wedge**) The diacritic [ˇ], used in various orthographies and transcriptions for various purposes. Czech *hacek* 'little hook'.

half-close /ˈhɑːfkləʊs/ *adj.* (of a vowel) An older synonym for **high-mid**.

half-contrast *n.* See **near-merger**.

half-open *n.* (of a vowel) An older synonym for **low-mid**.

half-rhyme *n.* (also **imperfect rhyme**, **near rhyme**, **oblique rhyme**, **off rhyme**, **pararhyme**, **slant rhyme**) The occurrence in rhyming position in verse of words which do not strictly rhyme in the conventional manner but which exhibit some kind of noticeable similarity of sound: *made/stride*, *late/paid*, *crowd/road*.

Halle's argument /ˈhæli/ *n.* A famous argument advanced by Morris Halle (1959) against the phonological doctrines of the **American Structuralists**, most particularly against **biuniqueness**. Examining Russian, Halle pointed out that Russian obstruents occur in contrasting voiceless/voiced pairs, except for /ts/, /tʃ/ and /x/, which have no voiced counterparts. A word-final obstruent is always voiceless, unless the following word begins with a voiced obstruent, in which case it is always voiced. In order to maintain biuniqueness, therefore, we must make the following statements. (1) No Russian lexical item ends in a voiced obstruent in its citation form. (2) When the following segment is a voiced obstruent, a final voiceless obstruent is replaced by its voiced counterpart (a morphophonemic statement), except for the three segments which have no voiced counterparts; the resulting level of representation is the required **autonomous phonemic** one. (3) A final voiceless obstruent has a voiced allophone before a voiced obstruent (an allophonic statement). This messy analysis conforms to biuniqueness, but it nowhere expresses the obvious generalizations about voicing, which can be readily stated if the autonomous phonemic level is dispensed with. Comparable facts had been noted before, of course, but it was Halle's argument that succeeded in convincing a generation of phonologists that it was more important to write rules expressing generalizations economically than to retain inconvenient levels of representation required only by *a priori* principles. This shift from representations to rules inaugurated the framework later known as **generative phonology**. See Anderson (1985: 318ff.) for a summary, and see Sommerstein (1977: 120–122) for some criticisms of Halle's argument.

Hallidayan analysis /'hælɪdeɪən/ *n.* A distinctive and influential **tone-based** analysis of English intonation presented by Michael Halliday (1963, 1967, 1970) within the framework of **Systemic phonology**. The framework distinguishes **tonality** (sense 3), **tonicity** and **tone** (sense 4).

haplology /hæp'lɒlədʒi/ *n.* 1. The morphological process in which one of two consecutive morphs of identical or similar form is dropped. For example, the Basque word for 'cider', a compound of *sagar* 'apple' and *ardo* 'wine', ought, by the usual rules of word formation, to have the form **sagar-ardo*, but the actual form is *sagardo*, in which one of the *-ar-* sequences has been dropped. 2. The similar phonological process in which one of two consecutive similar syllables is dropped in speech, as in the common pronunciation of *probably* as 'probly'.

hard /hɑːd/ *adj.* [*non-technical*] A traditional impressionistic label applied in an unsystematic and often rather meaningless way to denote one of two different phonetic realizations of a single orthographic character. For example, English ⟨c⟩ and ⟨g⟩ are said to be 'hard' when they represent plosives, as in *cat* and *get*, as opposed to their 'soft' values when they represent affricates or fricatives, as in *centre* and *gentle*. English ⟨s⟩ is similarly said to be 'hard' when it represents a voiceless sibilant, as in *lease*, as opposed to its 'soft' value when it represents a voiced sibilant, as in *ease*. Ant. **soft**.

hard attack /ə'tæk/ *n.* In singing, the use of a **glottal stop** at the beginning of a vowel-initial phrase. Cf. **soft attack**.

hard consonant *n.* In certain languages, notably Russian, in which most consonants occur in pairs, one palatalized and the other not, any one of the non-palatalized consonants. The hard consonants of Russian are usually velarized. The term **broad consonant**, usual in Irish, has the same meaning. Ant. **soft consonant**.

hard mutation *n.* (also **provection**) A rather sporadic phonological process in Welsh, in which a voiced plosive (or, less usually, a voiced

fricative) is devoiced at a morpheme boundary in compound formation, or very rarely in certain other types of formation, sometimes
with reduction of a resulting cluster: *pob-* 'bake' + *ty* 'house' →
popty 'bakehouse'; *dryg-* 'harm' + *hin* 'weather' → *drycin* 'stormy
weather'; *pob* 'every' + *peth* 'thing' → *popeth* 'everything'; *bwyd*
'food' + *-ha* (verb-forming suffix) → *bwyta* 'to eat'; *teg* 'fair' +
-(h)ach '-er' → *tecach* 'fairer'. In spite of its name, hard mutation
is not really a **mutation** in the ordinary sense.

hard palate *n.* See **palate** (sense 1).

hare lip /hɛəˈlɪp/ *n.* See **cleft lip**.

harmonic /hɑːˈmɒnɪk/ *n.* (also **overtone**) In acoustics, any frequency
which is an integral multiple of the **fundamental frequency**. For
example, if the glottis is vibrating at 200 Hz, then 200 Hz is the
first harmonic, 400 Hz is the *second harmonic* (or *first overtone*),
600 Hz is the *third harmonic* (or *second overtone*), and so on. A
vibrating body effectively produces all possible harmonics in some
measure; by the phenomenon of **resonance**, the configuration of
the vibrating body enhances some of these while **damping** others;
the resulting variable intensity distribution of the harmonics is
largely responsible for the characteristic timbre of each musical
instrument and for the existence of **formants** in speech.

harmony /ˈhɑːməni/ *n.* 1. See **vowel harmony** and **consonant
harmony**. 2. In **Prague School** phonology, the presence of a high
degree of symmetry in **phoneme systems**, resulting from the near-
maximal use of distinctive features.

harsh voice /hɑːʃ/ *n.* A **voice quality** characterized by hypertension
in the larynx, resulting in excessive approximation of the **vocal folds**
and sometimes also in vibration of the **ventricular folds**. Vibration
of the vocal folds is irregular both in frequency and in amplitude;
the resulting voice is deep and hoarse to an almost pathological
extent. Harsh voice is notated in Laver's system by a prefixed V!;
see Laver (1980 *passim*). Harshness can also be combined with
falsetto or **creak**.

hash mark /ˈhæʃ mɑːk/ *n.* The symbol #, commonly used to represent a **single word boundary**.

Haskins Laboratories /ˈhæskɪnz ləˈbɒrətriz/ *n.* A laboratory in New
Haven, Connecticut, which has carried out important work in
speech perception and speech synthesis.

h aspiré /aʃ aspire/ *n*. The conventional term in French for a word-initial vowel which, unlike most word-initial vowels, fails to support *liaison* or **elision** of a preceding vowel; *h aspiré* is commonly, though inconsistently, represented orthographically by an initial ⟨h⟩. Examples of words with *h aspiré*: *harpe* 'harp'; *hérisson* 'hedgehog'; *hardware* 'hardware'; *hauteur* 'height'; *onze* 'eleven'. Words with initial orthographic ⟨h⟩ which do undergo liaison normally, such as *herbe* 'grass' and *homme* 'man', are said to have ***h muet***. French: 'aspirated h', reflecting the fact that most such words historically did have an initial [h] which prevented liaison.

***h*-dropping** /ˈeɪtʃ drɒpɪŋ/ *n*. The phenomenon, particularly in English, whereby the phoneme /h/ is lost, so that, for example, *hair*, *heart* and *which* become homophonous with *air*, *art* and *witch*. Such *h*-dropping is exceedingly widespread in England, but is considered standard only before /w/, as in *which*; it occurs sporadically elsewhere, but is virtually unknown in North America, except before /w/.

head /hed/ *n*. 1. At any level of structure in a **metrical tree**, that daughter of a constituent which bears the main stress. Thus, in the phrase *dew-covered lawn*, the syllable *cov* is the head of *covered*, *dew* is the head of *dew-covered*, and *lawn* is the head of the whole phrase. 2. (also **governor**) In a **dependency** relationship, that element which, in some theory-specific sense, takes priority over another associated element, its **dependent** or **complement**. 3. In some analyses of **intonation**, the first accented syllable preceding the **nucleus**, or, alternatively, the entire stretch of speech from this syllable up to (but not including) the nucleus: the **body**.

head-marked notation /ˈhed mɑːkt/ *n*. In **Metrical Phonology**, a notational device in which the node representing a foot constituent is placed directly above the head:

Cf. **s/w notation**.

head register *n*. (also **head voice**) See **falsetto**.

hearing loss /ˈhɪərɪŋ lɒs/ *n*. Partial **deafness**. See **anacusis**.

hearing range /reɪndʒ/ *n*. The range of frequencies over which the human ear functions, typically about 20 Hz to 20,000 Hz.

heavy syllable /'hevi/ *n.* (rarely also **strong syllable**) 1. A **syllable** which ends in any of a long vowel, a diphthong, or one or more consonants, important in languages employing **quantitative metre**. 2. A syllable which ends in one or more consonants. 3. A syllable which ends in two or more consonants. 4. A syllable which contains a long vowel. Ant. **light syllable.** NOTE: The difference among these competing definitions is a matter of controversy and is certainly language-specific, since (C)VC syllables, for example, pattern like heavy syllables in some languages (at least word-finally) but not in others.

height /haɪt/ *n.* 1. See **vowel height**. 2. In the **Ladefoged feature system**, a **distinctive feature** invoked to handle distinctions of vowel height and taking values from 1 (lowest) to 4 (highest).

heightened subglottal pressure /'haɪtn̩d/ *n.* (**hsp**) In the *SPE* **feature system**, an undefined **distinctive feature** related to the presence of tenseness in the subglottal muscles and hence of increased subglottal pressure. Voiceless and voiced aspirated stops are [+hsp], as are the Korean tense unaspirated voiceless stops; other segments are [–hsp]. This feature was quickly abandoned as phonetically unrealistic, and variously replaced by **aspirated** (sense 2) or **spread glottis**.

heptameter /hep'tæmɪtə/ *n.* 1. A line of verse consisting of seven metrical **feet**. 2. A verse pattern consisting of such lines. Heptameter is very rare in English.

Hertz /hɜːts/ *n.* (**Hz**) The standard scientific unit of **frequency**, equivalent to one cycle per second. A glottis vibrating at 200 Hz is thus opening and closing 200 times per second. After Heinrich Hertz (1857–1894), German physicist.

Herzog's Principle /'hɜːtsɒg/ *n.* A putative principle in the **diffusion** of phonological changes. It says: mergers expand at the expense of distinctions. Supported by substantial evidence, this principle is sometimes regarded as a corollary of **Garde's Principle** and is interpreted as demonstrating the purely mechanical nature of sound change. Principle: Herzog (1965); name: Labov (1994: 313).

hesitation /hezɪ'teɪʃn̩/ *n.* Any of various phenomena interrupting the smooth flow of speech, including pauses, **hesitation noises**, repetitions and prolongation of syllables.

hesitation noise *n.* See **filled pause**.

heterograph /'hetərəgrɑːf/ *n.* See under **homograph** and refer to the note there.

heterography /hetə'rɒgrəfi/ *n*. The property of a writing system which, although designed in principle to represent speech sounds, lacks a one-to-one correspondence between sounds and written symbols. English orthography is, of course, a spectacular example of this, but most European orthographies exhibit some degree of heterography. Cf. **homography**. *Adj.* **heterographic**.

heteromorphemic /hetərəmɔ:'fi:mɪk/ *adj.* Belonging to different morphemes.

heteronym /'hetərənɪm/ *n*. 1. Either of two words which are either **homophones** of different spelling (*through/threw*) or **heterophones** of identical spelling (*minute* (60 seconds)/*minute* (tiny)). 2. A frequent but unfortunate synonym for **homograph**.

heterophone /'hetərəfəʊn/ *n*. Either of two words which have the same spelling but different meanings and different pronunciations: *lead* (metal)/*lead* (verb); *unionized* (organized into a union)/*union-ized* (not ionized); *supply* (provide)/*supply* (in a supple manner); *refuse* (say no)/*refuse* (rubbish). A heterophone is a particular type of **homograph**.

heterorganic /hetərɔ:'gænɪk/ *adj.* (of two adjacent consonants) Having different **places of articulation**, such as the /ps/ in *cups* or the /md/ in *mimed*. Cf. **homorganic**, **contiguous**.

heterosyllabic /hetərəsɪ'læbɪk/ *adj.* Occurring in different syllables. Cf. **tautosyllabic**.

heterotopy /hetə'rɒtəpi/ *n*. A speech sound inserted into the wrong position during speech.

hexameter /hek'sæmɪtə/ *n*. 1. A line of verse containing six metrical **feet**. 2. A verse pattern consisting of such lines. Hexameter is rare in English, though Longfellow used it in his poem *Evangeline*.

hiatus /haɪ'eɪtəs/ *n*. The occurrence of two consecutive vowels forming separate syllables, as in *Leo*, *skiing*, *lower* or *playoff*. The vowels in question are said to be **in hiatus**. There is considerable evidence that hiatus is unstable: vowels in hiatus frequently undergo phonological changes which remove the hiatus. Latin *hiatus* 'gap'.

hierarchization of features /haɪərɑːkaɪ'zeɪʃn̩/ *n*. See **feature hierarchy**.

hierarchy /'haɪərɑːki/ *n*. Any of various linear scales along which certain phonetic or phonological elements are ranked with respect to certain properties. A familiar example is the **Sonority Hierarchy**. *Adj.* **hierarchical** /haɪəˈrɑːkɪkəl/.

high /haɪ/ *adj.* 1. (also **close**) (of a vowel) Articulated with the tongue occupying a more-or-less maximally high position in the mouth, as for [i] and [u]. Cf. **high-mid**. 2. In the *SPE* **feature system**, a **distinctive feature** defined as 'produced by raising the body of the tongue above the ... neutral position'. High vowels and palatal, palato-alveolar and velar consonants are [+high]; other segments are [–high]. The combination of this with the feature **low** permits only three vowel heights to be defined, since the combination [+high, +low] is forbidden. 3. A somewhat different feature defined so that all vowels in the top half of the **vowel space** are [+high] while all those in the bottom half are [–high]. The combination of this with the feature **mid** permits four vowel heights to be defined. Wang (1968). 4. In the **Lindau feature system**, a **distinctive feature** invoked to treat distinctions of vowel height, with the four possible values *high*, *upper-mid*, *lower-mid* and *low*.

high fall *n.* A **contour tone** which begins with a high pitch and then falls in pitch.

high key *n.* The use by an individual of a higher than usual part of the ordinary **pitch range**, as may occur during excited or emotional speech. Ant. **low key**.

high-mid *adj.* (also **half-close**, **close-mid**) (of a vowel) Articulated with the tongue slightly higher than its neutral position but not maximally high, as in the vowels [e] and [o]. NOTE: The IPA now recommends the term 'close-mid'.

high tone *n.* A **tone** in a **tone language** which is normally realized with a higher **pitch** than other tones. Ant. **low tone**.

high vowel *n.* In the **Williamson feature system**, one of the five possible values of the feature **stricture**.

historical phonology /hɪˈstɒrɪkəl/ *n.* The study of **phonological change**.

h **muet** /aʃ mɥe/ *n.* See under *h* **aspiré**.

hoarse /hɔːs/ *adj.* (also **husky**) [*non-technical*] (of a voice) Having a rough, rasping quality; characterized by some degree of **harsh voice**.

hold /həʊld/ *n.* (also **closure**, **closed phase**) That part of the articulation of a **stop** consonant during which the airstream is completely blocked within the oral cavity. Cf. **approach**, **release**.

hole in the pattern /həʊl/ *n.* (also *case vide*) In the **phoneme system** of a language, the absence of a phoneme at a point in which the presence of a phoneme would increase the symmetry of the system. For example, the four-vowel system /i e a u/ shows a gap where /o/ would be; if /o/ were to be added to the system, the result would be a more symmetrical five-vowel system. There is evidence that such gaps encourage the occurrence of **chain shifts**. The importance of symmetry in phonological systems was first pointed out by Sapir (1921: 182), but the idea has been developed most vigorously by Martinet (1955).

holistic theory /həʊ'lɪstɪk/ *n.* See **privative theory**.

homeoteleuton /hɒmiəʊte'ljuːtən/ *n.* The relation between two or more words which do not rhyme but which end in identical unstressed syllables: *absurdity/felicity*; *ethical/practical*. Greek *homoisos* 'same' + *teleutē* 'ending'.

homograph /'hɒməgrɑːf/ *n.* (also **heterograph, heteronym**) Either of two words with the same spelling but different meanings and often different pronunciations: *bear* (animal)/*bear* ('carry'); *bark* (of tree)/*bark* (dog noise); *refuse* (say no)/*refuse* (rubbish); *lead* (metal)/*lead* (verb). The last two of these pairs are **heterophones**. Cf. **homophone**. NOTE: The forms 'heterograph' and 'heteronym', though widespread, are etymologically misleading; 'homograph' is preferable.

homography /hə'mɒgrəfi/ *n.* The property of a writing system in which there is a one-to-one correspondence between sounds and written symbols. A **phonemic transcription** has this property. Very few European orthographies are so systematic as this, though Finnish at least comes very close. Cf. **heterography**.

homonym /'hɒmənɪm/ *n.* 1. A cover term for both **homophone** and **homograph**. 2. See **homophone**. *Abstr. n.* **homonymy** /hə'mɒnəmi/. NOTE: The abstract noun 'homonymity' is also used, but is not recommended.

homophene /'hɒməfiːn/ *n.* Either of two words which are pronounced differently but which look identical on the lips, thus posing a problem for deaf individuals relying upon **lip-reading**: *sink/zinc*; *fat/vat*.

homophone /'hɒməfəʊn/ *n.* (also **homonym**) Either of two or more words which have different meanings but identical pronunciations; homophones may or may not be spelled differently. Examples:

flour/flower; *bear* 'large animal'/*bear* 'support'/*bare*; *tide/tied*. *Abstr. n.* **homophony** /həˈmɒfəni/.

homorganic /hɒmɔːˈgænɪk/ *adj.* (of two adjacent consonants) Having the same **place of articulation**, such as the /nd/ in *candy* or the /mp/ in *lamp*. Cf. **heterorganic**, **contiguous**.

horizontal lip-rounding /hɒrɪˈzɒntəl/ *n.* See **inner rounding**. Heffner (1950).

host /həʊst/ *n.* The element to which a **clitic** is bound, such as *should* in *shouldn't*.

hot /hɒt/ *adj.* (of a feature) In **Government and Charm Phonology**, having a specification of marked status which overrides any conflicting specification when feature matrixes are combined ('fused'). Ant. **cold**.

hot-wire anemometer /hɒtˈwaɪə/ *n.* A device which measures the velocity of air flowing past it by the cooling effect of the air on a heated wire and hence on the electrical resistance of the wire.

hugging the phonetic ground /ˈhʌgɪŋ/ *n.* [*informal*] The characteristic of a phonological analysis which, in comparison with other conceivable analyses, is not very **abstract** and which therefore represents the phonetic facts fairly directly, possibly at the expense of theoretical elegance or economy. The treatment of English vowels in the **Gimson–O'Connor system**, for example, may be said to 'hug the phonetic ground' in comparison with the more abstract treatment found in the **Trager–Smith system**. Hockett (1955).

hushing fricative /ˈhʌʃɪŋ/ *n.* A **palato-alveolar** fricative, [ʃ].

husky /ˈhʌski/ *adj.* [*non-technical*] See **hoarse**.

hyoid bone /ˈhaɪɔɪd bəʊn/ *n.* A small V-shaped bone lying just above the **larynx**, which is suspended from it by the superior **cornua** of the **thyroid cartilage**. The only bone in the body which articulates with no other bone, the hyoid is held in place by an array of muscles connected to the skull, the jawbone and the breastbone; contraction of these muscles moves the hyoid, and hence the larynx, up and down.

hypercorrection /haɪpəkəˈrekʃən/ *n.* 1. (also **hyperurbanism** /haɪpəˈrɜːbənɪzm̩/) An error, resulting from an attempt at adjusting one's speech in the direction of a prestige norm, in which a speaker 'overshoots the mark' and introduces a form not found in the prestige norm. For example, an American for whom *dew* is homophonous with *do* might, on attempting to acquire the British pronunciation of *dew*, go too far and also introduce the glide into *do*; or a non-rhotic speaker attempting to acquire a rhotic accent might produce such hypercorrect forms as *avoca*[r]*do*. 2. The phenomenon in which the members of a particular social class, in very formal contexts, produce a higher proportion of prestige variants than the social class just above them. *Adj.* **hypercorrect**.

hypernasality /haɪpəneɪ'zælɪti/ *n.* The presence of excessive nasal resonance in speech, especially when resulting from a clinical condition such as a **cleft palate**. Ant. **hyponasality**.

hyperthesis /haɪ'pɜːθəsɪs/ *n.* 1. The replacement in a line of verse of a metrical **foot** by a mirror-image foot, as of an **iamb** by a **trochee**. 2. A rare synonym for **metathesis**.

hypocorism /haɪ'pɒkərɪzm/ *n.* (also **hypocoristic** /haɪpəkə'rɪstɪk/ or, rarely, **hypocorisma** /haɪpəkə'rɪzmə/) A diminutive, especially one used as an endearment or pet name, such as *Mikey* or *Lucykins*, or as a euphemism, such as *undies* or *hanky*.

hyponasality /haɪpəneɪ'zælɪti/ *n.* The absence of normal nasal resonance in speech, as may occur with someone suffering from a bad head cold. Ant. **hypernasality**.

Hz The abbreviation for **Hertz**.

I

iamb /ˈaɪæm/ *n*. A metrical **foot** consisting of an unstressed syllable followed by a stressed one, or, in **quantitative metre**, of a short syllable followed by a long one. The pattern is illustrated by the words *above* and *below* and by many familiar lines of verse, such as *Rough winds do shake the darling buds of May* and *Mine eyes have seen the glory of the coming of the Lord*. The iamb is the most frequently used foot in English poetry. *Adj.* **iambic** /aɪˈæmbɪk/. Greek *iambos* 'lame'.

iambic lengthening *n*. The phenomenon in some languages whereby a light syllable becomes heavy when it is the head of an **iamb**: LL → LH.

iambic reversal *n*. (also **reversal**, **Rhythm Rule**, **Thirteen-Men Rule**, **Beat Movement**, **stress shift**, **stress retraction**, **stress reversal**) The phenomenon in English in which a stress is shifted from a later to an earlier syllable in a word occurring within a phrase in order to avoid a **clash** between adjacent stresses. Thus, for example, *thirteen* normally has final stress, but it receives initial stress in *thirteen men*; the same is true of *Tennessee* in isolation and in the name *Tennessee Williams*; *good-looking* is normally stressed on *look*, but in *good-looking girl* it is stressed on *good*. Liberman and Prince (1977).

***ich*-Laut** /ˈɪçlaʊt/ *n*. The voiceless front fricative (orthographic ⟨ch⟩) occurring in German word-initially, after front vowels, after consonants, and in the diminutive suffix *-chen*, as in *Chemie* 'chemistry', *ich* 'I', *echt* 'pure', *Bücher* 'books', *durch* 'through', *Mädchen* 'young woman'. The sound is usually described by textbooks as a palatal fricative [ç], but many speakers have alveolo-palatal [ɕ] or even palato-alveolar [ʃ]. The *ich*-Laut is in complementary distribution with the ***ach*-Laut** if morpheme boundaries are taken into account.

iconicity /aɪkəˈnɪsɪti/ *n*. The existence of some kind of direct, motivated, non-arbitrary relation between a phonological form and its meaning. The most familiar example is **onomatopoeia**, but other types exist. *Adj.* **iconic** /aɪˈkɒnɪk/. *Ant.* **arbitrariness**.

ictus /'ɪktəs/ *n.* 1. The position of the metrical or rhythmical beat in a foot or line of verse, typically but not necessarily falling on a stressed syllable: *And I cópied all the létters in a hánd so frée / That nów I am the rúler of the Quéen's Navý* (W. S. Gilbert). 2. The first place in the **foot** (Abercrombie 1991b: ch. 10). Cf. **remiss**. Latin *ictus* 'stroke'.

ideal notation /aɪ'dɪəl/ *n.* In **Glossematic phonology**, an abstract level of representation corresponding roughly to the **underlying forms** of classical generative phonology. Cf. **actualized notation**.

ideal sound *n.* [*obsolete*] A **phoneme**, particularly when regarded as a mental object. Sapir (1925).

identification /aɪdentɪfɪ'keɪʃn̩/ *n.* That aspect of **ear-training** in which the student learns to recognize speech sounds.

ideophone /'aɪdiəfəʊn/ *n.* Any one of an exceptional class of lexical items occurring in certain languages which typically express some particular and distinctive type of sound or movement. In many such languages, ideophones are phonologically exceptional in permitting segments or sequences not occurring elsewhere, and they are very frequently reduplicated. Here are a few of the ideophones in the Carib language Apalai: *kute kute kute* '(frog) croak', *pyh tere* 'jump into canoe', *syrý tope topō* 'falling into the water', *kui kui* 'screaming', *seky seky* 'creep up', *ty ty ty* 'person walking', *wywy-wywy* 'hammock swinging', *uroruro* 'trees falling', *tututututu* 'fast approach'. *Adj.* **ideophonic** /aɪdiə'fɒnɪk/.

idiolect /'ɪdiəlekt/ *n.* The speech of a particular individual. Bloch (1948).

idiophone /'ɪdiəfəʊn/ *n.* [*rare*] A speech sound which is typical of the speech of a particular individual.

ill-formed /ɪl'fɔːmd/ *adj.* (of a phonological form or representation) Not in accordance with all of the requirements of the phonology of the language in question; violating one or more requirements. *Abstr. n.* **ill-formedness**. Ant. **well-formed**.

imperfect diphthong /ɪm'pɜːfɪkt/ *n.* A **diphthong** consisting of a lengthened, fully syllabic vowel preceded or followed by a glide. Jones (1918): 8th edition onwards.

imperfect rhyme *n.* See **half-rhyme**.

implicational relationship /ɪmplɪ'keɪʃənəl/ *n.* Any relationship between two phonetic or phonological characteristics by which the presence of one guarantees the presence or absence of the other.

Some of these are universal: for example, [+high] → [–low] by definition. Others are language-specific: in English, [+lateral] → [+coronal], since English (unlike some other languages) has only coronal laterals.

implicational universal *n.* Any **universal** of the form 'If a language has property *p*, it also has property *q*'. Example: If a language has voiced fricatives, it also has voiceless fricatives.

implosion /ɪmˈpləʊʒn̩/ *n.* In the *SPE* **feature system**, a **distinctive feature** defined as 'involving a glottal closure producing suction'. **Implosives** (and presumably **injectives**) are [+impl]; all other segments are [–impl].

implosive /ɪmˈpləʊsɪv/ *n.* or *adj.* (**impl**) 1. An oral stop articulated with a **glottalic ingressive** airstream, so that outside air is pulled into the mouth upon release of the oral closure. Voiced implosives are fairly common, voiceless ones quite rare. The IPA represents these with a right-curling hook at the top of the symbol for the ordinary plosive: [ɓ ɗ]. See Laver (1994: 172–173, 237–238). 2. Specifically, a voiced implosive, in which lung air leaks up through the vibrating glottis while the larynx is being lowered. In this usage, a voiceless implosive is called an **injective**. NOTE: Before 1989, sense 2 was usual, but since then the IPA has recommended sense 1. 3. In the **Ladefoged** and **Williamson feature systems**, one of the three possible values of the feature **glottalic** (Ladefoged) or **larynx movement** (Williamson).

implosive position *n.* [*obsolete*] (of a consonant) Syllable-final position. In the word *rest*, for example, both [s] and [t] are in implosive position.

impoverishment /ɪmˈpɒvərɪʃmənt/ *n.* In some analyses of prosodic phenomena, the removal from surface syntactic structure of all but a designated set of syntactic constituent boundaries, leaving only these remaining boundaries visible to phonological rules. Selkirk (1986).

impressionistic transcription /ɪmpreʃəˈnɪstɪk/ *n.* A less usual term for **phonetic transcription**.

improper bracketing /ɪmˈprɒpə/ *n.* A **bracketing** involving the partial overlap of pairs of brackets, as in $[_i ci [_j t]_i y]_j$ or $[_i si [_j st]_i er]_j$. Normally regarded as illegal, improper bracketings are occasionally advocated as a way of dealing with **ambisyllabic** consonants.

in absentia /ın æb'sentiə/ *adv.* See **paradigmatic relation**.

inalterability of geminates /ınɔːltərə'bılıti/ *n.* The tendency of **geminates** to escape rules whose application would modify one half of the geminate while leaving the other unchanged.

independent motivation /ındıpendənt məʊtı'veıʃn̩/ *n.* The property of a rule in a particular analysis which is required for the derivation of forms other than those for which the analysis is explicitly being constructed. *Adj.* **independently motivated**.

indeterminacy /ındı't3ːmınəsi/ *n.* See **non-uniqueness**. *Adj.* **indeterminate** /ındı't3ːmınət/.

index /'ındeks/ *n.* See **marker** (sense 2). Abercrombie (1967).

index of oddity /'ɒdıti/ *n.* A putative metric, so far not well articulated, for expressing the extent to which the **phoneme system** of a language departs from universal norms. Lass (1984: 155).

indicator /'ındıkeıtə/ *n.* A **variable** which lies entirely below the conscious awareness of speakers but which nonetheless exhibits social stratification. Cf. **stereotype**, **marker** (sense 3). Labov (1994: 78).

indirect opposition /ındə'rekt/ *n.* A proposed procedure for establishing the presence of a **contrast** between two segments for which no **minimal pair** can be found. For example, the sequence *singer sitter letter leisure* allegedly demonstrates a contrast between English [ŋ] and [ʒ]. See Fischer-Jørgensen (1975: 84) for a demolition of this approach. Trubetzkoy (1939: 32).

Indirect Syntax Hypothesis *n.* The proposal that syntactic structure may be reflected in the phonology only in so far as it influences **prosodic rules**, which in turn may have consequences for ordinary phonological rules. Cf. **Direct Syntax Hypothesis**.

infix /'ınfıks/ *n.* An **affix** which occupies a position in which it interrupts another morpheme. In Tagalog, for example, the verbal root *sulat* 'write' (a single morpheme) exhibits such inflected forms as *sumulat* and *sinulat*, with infixes *-um-* and *-in-*. NOTE: It is an error to apply the term 'infix' to an affix which merely comes between two other morphemes. For example, the Turkish verb stem *ye-* 'eat' forms an active infinitive *yemek* 'to eat' and a passive infinitive *yenmek* 'to be eaten'; in this case the passive marker *-n-* is *not* an infix, but only a suffix which precedes certain other suffixes.

inflection /ɪn'flekʃən/ *n.* (also **inflexion**, **flexion**) 1. The variation in form of a single lexical item for grammatical purposes. 2. A particular word form assumed by a lexical item in some grammatical environment. For example, *gives* and *gave* are two inflections of the verb *give*. 3. A particular bound morph expressing an inflectional distinction, such as the English plural suffix *-s*. *Adj.* **inflectional** (pertaining to inflection), **inflected** /ɪn'flektɪd/ (bearing an inflection); *v.* **inflect**. NOTE: The traditional British spelling *inflexion* has now largely given way to the American spelling *inflection*.

inflectional morphology *n.* The branch of morphology dealing with the variation in the forms of words for grammatical purposes, as in *cat/cats* and *eat/eats/eating/ate/eaten*. Cf. **derivational morphology**.

ingliding diphthong /'ɪnglaɪdɪŋ/ *n.* A less usual synonym for **centring diphthong**.

ingressive /ɪn'gresɪv/ 1. *adj.* (of an airstream) Involving a flow of air from the outside into the vocal tract. 2. *adj.* or *n.* (A segment) produced with such an airstream, such as an **implosive** or a **click**. Cf. **egressive**. Pike (1943).

initial /ɪ'nɪʃl̩/ 1. *adj.* Occurring in first position in a word or syllable. 2. *n.* A segment occurring in this position. 3. *n.* See **onset**.

initial devoicing *n.* The absence of voicing from the first portion of an intrinsically voiced segment, as occurs, for example, with English word-initial /b d g/. *Adj.* **initially devoiced**. Cf. **final devoicing**.

initial dropping /'drɒpɪŋ/ *n.* A type of phonological change in which all or most word-initial consonants, or even word-initial syllables, are lost. Rare in the world's languages, initial-dropping is widespread in certain regions of Australia. For example, Mbabaram shows **gudaga > dɔg* 'dog', **bamba > mba* 'belly', **jawa > wɛ* 'mouth', **naga > ga* 'east', etc. See Dixon (1980: 195–207). Cf. **aphaeresis**.

initial mutation *n.* See **mutation** (sense 2).

initiation /ɪnɪʃi'eɪʃn̩/ *n.* See **airstream mechanism**. Catford (1977).

initiator /ɪ'nɪʃieɪtə/ *n.* That part of the speech organs involved in producing a particular **airstream mechanism**: the respiratory system in **pulmonic** air, the larynx in **glottalic** air and the tongue in **velaric** air. Pike (1943).

initiator power /ˈpɑʊə/ *n.* The rate (expressed in watts) at which an **initiator** does work (delivers energy) in moving air against the **acoustic impedance** of the **vocal tract**, identified by Catford (1977: 84) as the primary phonetic correlate of **stress**.

injective /ɪnˈdʒektɪv/ *adj.* or *n.* A segment articulated with a **glottalic ingressive airstream mechanism** but with no vibration of the vocal folds. Such segments are rare, but see Laver (1994: 173). See under **implosive** for further information.

inlaut /ˈɪnlɑʊt/ *n.* A segment occurring in the middle of a word. Cf. **anlaut, auslaut**. German: 'in-sound'.

inner ear /ˈɪnə/ *n.* The innermost and most complex of the three divisions of the ear, linked to the **middle ear** by the **oval window** and containing the **cochlea**.

inner rounding *n.* (also **horizontal lip-rounding, outrounding**) A version of **lip-rounding** in which the lips are projected forward ('pouted') and the channel between them is formed by their inner surfaces (it is **endolabial**). Inner rounding is typical of rounded back vowels like [u] and [o]. Cf. **outer rounding**. Sweet (1890): the term 'inner rounding' derives from the use of the inner surfaces of the lips; the synonymous 'outrounding' derives from the forward projection of the lips. Both terms are justifiable, but their coexistence is likely to lead to serious confusion.

in praesentia /ɪn praɪˈsentiə/ *adv.* See **syntagmatic relation**.

input /ˈɪnpʊt/ *n.* With reference to a **phonological rule**, the representation to which the rule applies in a particular instance. Cf. **output**.

input conditioning *n.* Any restriction on the application of a **phonological rule** expressed in terms of its **input**. Cf. **output conditioning**. Sommerstein (1977: 73).

inrounded /ˈɪnrɑʊndɪd/ *adj.* **(inr)** A **binary distinctive feature** proposed by Lass (1984: 88): segments with **inrounding** (i.e., **outer rounding**) are [+inr], while segments with **outrounding** (i.e., **inner rounding**) and **unrounded** segments are [–inr]. The feature is specifically designed to handle the three-way contrast in Swedish among /e/ ([–round, –inr]), /ø/ ([+round, –inr]) and /u/ ([+round, +inr]); all three of these have identical height and backness.

inrounding *n.* An unfortunate synonym for **outer rounding**; see the remarks under **inner rounding**.

inseparability of geminates /ɪnsepərə'bɪlɪti/ *n.* The tendency of **geminates** to resist the insertion of an intervening segment.

insertion /ɪn'sɜːʃn̩/ *n.* 1. See **epenthesis**. 2. See **rule insertion**.

inspiratory capacity /ɪn'spaɪrətri/ *n.* The maximum volume of air that can be breathed into the lungs above the minimal value of the **tidal volume**.

inspiratory reserve volume /rɪ'zɜːv vɒljuːm/ *n.* The maximum volume of air that can be breathed into the lungs beyond the maximal value of the **tidal volume**.

instantaneous release /ɪnstən'teɪniəs/ *n.* (also **abrupt release**) In the *SPE* **feature system**, a **distinctive feature** invoked to distinguish affricates ([–abrrel]) from plosives ([+abrrel]). Eventually the feature **delayed release**, with exactly the opposite specifications, came to be the most usual name. Chomsky and Halle (1968); the authors credit R. Carter with the term.

instrumental phonetics /ɪnstrə'mentəl/ *n.* (also **experimental phonetics**) The use of mechanical, electrical or electronic apparatus to investigate any aspect of phonetics.

integration /ɪntɪ'greɪʃn̩/ *n.* In **Prague School** phonology, the property of a phoneme whose presence increases the symmetry of the system and whose absence would leave a **hole in the pattern**. *Adj.* **(well-)integrated**.

intensity /ɪn'tensɪti/ *n.* The amount of energy carried by a sound wave, measured in **decibels**. The perceptual correlate of intensity is **loudness**, but the relationship is far from linear.

intensive /ɪn'tensɪv/ *adj.* See **fortis** (sense 1). Catford (1977).

interconstituent government /ɪntəkən'stɪtʃuənt/ *n.* In **Government and Charm Phonology**, the type of **government** holding between adjacent syllables.

intercostal muscles /ɪntə'kɒstəl/ *n. pl.* Two sets of muscles connecting adjacent ribs within the rib cage. The external intercostals are important in inhalation, while the internal intercostals are important in exhalation.

interdental /ɪntə'dentəl/ 1. *adj.* (of an articulation) Articulated with the tip of the tongue slightly protruding between the upper and lower teeth. 2. *n.* A segment so articulated, such as American

English [θ] or [ð] (many British speakers pronounce these as ordinary dentals, rather than as interdentals).

interference /ɪntə'fɪərəns/ *n.* Imperfections in the use of one language as a result of the influence of another language, such as a 'foreign accent' in speaking a second language.

interfix /'ɪntəfɪks/ *n.* An **empty morph** occurring between a stem and a meaningful suffix, such as the *-o-* in English *kissogram* or the *-ov-* in Russian *Glinkovskij* 'of Glinka', where *Glinka* is a surname and *-skij* is the relational suffix. Dressler (1985).

interlabial space /ɪntə'leɪbiəl/ *n.* The space between the lips, especially when regarded as an articulatory variable.

interlevel /'ɪntələvəl/ *n.* Any level of representation postulated in some analysis as lying between two other levels regarded as more firmly established. The most familiar interlevel is the **morphophonemic** level posited in some analyses between the **morphological** and **phonemic** levels of representation.

interlude /'ɪntəluːd/ *n.* [*rare*] A word-internal **consonant cluster** containing no morpheme boundary. Hockett (1955: 51ff.)

intermediate representation /ɪntə'miːdiət/ *n.* Any level of representation posited, in some analysis, as occurring between the **underlying form** and the surface phonetic form.

intermediate vowel *n.* Any vowel which is not a **cardinal vowel**.

internal adequacy /ɪn't3ːnəl/ *n.* See under **adequacy**.

internal evidence /'evɪdəns/ *n.* Any of several **criteria for phonological analysis** which may be regarded as primarily aesthetic in nature, such as consistency, simplicity, economy, degree of independent motivation (freedom from *ad hoc*-ness) and success in capturing generalizations. Cf. **external evidence**.

internal open juncture *n.* In **American Structuralist** work, a **morpheme boundary** within a word, represented analytically by a **plus-juncture**. Cf. **external open juncture**.

internal reconstruction *n.* In historical linguistics, a procedure for establishing an earlier, unattested stage of a single language without the use of information from related languages. In the simplest case, it involves observing the presence of a pattern with some exceptions and surmising that the exceptions were formerly regular. A famous instance is Saussure's observation that most PIE roots were CVC in form, while some were CV or VC; he proposed that these latter had formerly also been CVC, but that certain consonants had been lost. This **laryngeal** hypothesis was later confirmed by new evidence. Cf. **comparative reconstruction**.

internal rhyme *n.* The rhyming of words within a single line of verse, as in *A maiden from the Bosphorus with eyes as bright as phosphorus / Once wed the wealthy bailiff of the caliph of Khelat.*

internal rounding *n.* The phenomenon in which the perceptual effect of a **rounded** vowel is produced without **lip-rounding** by **sulcalization** of the tongue.

internal sandhi *n.* Any instance of **sandhi** taking place within a single word, such as the change of the [s] in *face* to [ʃ] in its derivative *facial*. Cf. **external sandhi**.

International Phonetic Alphabet /ɪntə'næʃnəl/ *n.* (**IPA**) The most prominent **phonetic alphabet** (sense 1) in contemporary use, first promulgated by the **International Phonetic Association** in 1888 and frequently modified since, the most recent revision being that of 1993. The IPA aims to provide visually distinctive symbols for all speech sounds which are phonologically distinct in any language; preferring to keep the use of **diacritics** to an irreducible minimum, it has introduced a large number of specially designed characters such as [ɔ], [ʃ] and [ŋ]. In spite of the resulting inconvenience in printing, the IPA is now almost universally used in phonetics and linguistics, except in the United States, where it is only slowly gaining ground from the competing **American transcription**; it is also increasingly used in serious dictionaries. See the Appendix for a table of IPA symbols.

International Phonetic Association /əsəusi'eɪʃn̩/ *n.* (**IPA**) An international organization for the study of **phonetics**, founded in France in 1886 by a group of European phoneticians, linguists and language teachers under the leadership of the French linguist Paul Passy and known until 1897 as the Phonetic Teachers' Association. The first and best-known work of the organization was the creation of the **International Phonetic Alphabet**, proposed by the Danish linguist Otto Jespersen and first published in 1888.

interpolation /ɪntɜːpə'leɪʃn̩/ *n.* A putative process by which the value of a phonetic feature is carried from one segment to another, both marked for the feature, across an intervening segment which is unmarked for it, such as when [nasal] is carried across an English vowel from one consonant to another. See Kenstowicz (1994: 521–524). Keating (1988); Cohn (1990).

intervocalic /ɪntəvə'kælɪk/ *adj.* Located between two **vowels**, such as the /t/ in *water* or the /n/ in *winning*.

intonation /ɪntə'neɪʃn̩/ *n.* The use of pitch, and possibly of additional prosodic phenomena such as loudness, tempo and pauses, over a stretch of utterance generally longer than a single word for the purpose of conveying meaning. Intonation is used for a variety of purposes: for marking grammatical boundaries (phrases and clauses), for signalling sentence types (e.g., statements and questions), and for conveying the speaker's attitude (surprise, irony, anger, etc.) Intonation is a complex topic, and a wide variety of approaches has been adopted with varying degrees of success. The study of intonation is **intonology** /ɪntə'nɒlədʒi/. See Cruttenden (1986) for an introduction, and see Laver (1994: 509–510) for a long list of further references. *Adj.* **intonational**.

intonational nucleus *n.* The most prominent syllable within an **intonational phrase**.

intonational phrase *n.* (also **intonation group** /gruːp/, **rhythm unit**) The phonological unit of intonational structure, the longest stretch of speech to which a single intonation pattern applies. In the **Prosodic Hierarchy**, this level is posited as the domain of certain phonological processes, such as the Italian *gorgia toscana*.

intonation language *n.* A language which is neither a **tone language** nor a **pitch language**; a language in which the universally present **intonation** constitutes the only linguistic use of pitch.

intra-oral pressure /ɪntrə'ɔːrəl/ *n.* The pressure of the air within the mouth, or within the **supraglottal vocal tract**.

intrinsic allophone /ɪn'trɪnsɪk/ *n.* An **allophone** whose phonetic character can be entirely explained by its phonetic environment, such as a fronted allophone of /k/ before a front vowel. Cf. **extrinsic allophone**. Wang and Fillmore (1961).

intrinsic duration *n.* The minimal duration which a segment must have in order to 'count' as a segment of its type. For example, a plosive or a vowel must have a certain duration to avoid becoming a tap or a glide, respectively.

intrinsic ordering *n.* 1. Narrowly, the relation between two rules A and B such that A creates all possible inputs to B. In this case, A is intrinsically ordered before B, which otherwise has nothing to do. 2. Broadly, any ordering relation between rules which is derived from some universal principle(s), rather than merely being stipulated by the analyst. Ant. **extrinsic ordering**.

intrinsic pitch *n.* (also **intrinsic F0**) The seemingly universal tendency for high vowels to have a higher **fundamental frequency** than low vowels. Lehiste and Peterson (1961).

intrinsic sonority *n.* The property by which segments are ranked in the **Sonority Hierarchy**.

intrusion /ɪnˈtruːʒn̩/ *n.* Any process in which a segment is added to a word without etymological justification. Word-initially, intrusion is called **prothesis**; medially, **epenthesis**; finally, **paragoge**.

intrusive *r* /ɪnˈtruːsɪv/ *n.* In some **non-rhotic accents** of English, an /r/ which is automatically inserted after any of /ɑː/, /ɔː/, /ɜː/ or /ə/) or after a centring diphthong when one of these occurs before a vowel, regardless of the facts of etymology or spelling, producing such pronunciations as *lawr and order*, *the Shahr of Persia*, *drawring a picture*, *Indiar and Pakistan*, *visar application*, *Philadelphiar Eagles* and (my favourite) the pronunciation of the name of the squash player *Lisa Opie* as *Lisa Ropie*. Intrusive *r* derives from **linking *r*** by **rule inversion**.

invariance condition /ɪnˈvɛəriəns/ *n.* (also, informally, **'once a phoneme, always a phoneme'**) A proposed **criterion for phonological analysis**. Two versions of it have been advocated. Under 'strong' or 'absolute' invariance (also called the **non-intersection condition**), all occurrences of a single phone in a language must be assigned to the same single phoneme – that is, two different phonemes may not overlap at all in their phonetic realizations. This version was adopted by some of the **American Structuralists** (explicitly by Hockett 1942), but it is untenable; see Sommerstein (1977: 25) for a demonstration. Under 'weak' or 'relative' invariance, all occurrences of a single phone *in a given environment* must be assigned to a single phoneme, but identical phones in different environments may be assigned to different phonemes. This version thus permits **partial overlapping** of phonemes. Weak invariance was adopted by Jakobson and by some other American Structuralists, but all versions of invariance were rejected by Chomsky (1964);

the proponents of **generative phonology** preferred to admit analyses involving **complete overlapping**, ruled out even by weak invariance.

inverse voice /'ɪnvɜːs/ *n.* The phenomenon in which, during **glottalic egressive** initiation, air flows downward through the glottis, producing some degree of vibration of the vocal folds.

iotacism /aɪ'əʊtəsɪzm̩/ *n.* Any phonological process in which a different vocalic nucleus develops into the high front vowel [i]. At least eight nuclei which contrasted in Ancient Greek, for example, have merged as [i] in Modern Greek.

IPA /aɪ piː 'eɪ/ *n.* 1. See **International Phonetic Association**. 2. See **International Phonetic Alphabet**.

IPA transcription *n.* 1. Any **phonetic** or **phonemic transcription** using the symbols of the **International Phonetic Alphabet**. 2. (among lexicographers) A synonym for *EPD* **transcription**.

isochrony /aɪ'sɒkrəni/ *n.* (also **isochronism** /aɪ'sɒkrənɪzm̩/) A type of speech **rhythm** in which units of a certain type tend strongly to be produced at regular intervals of time – that is, in which each such unit takes the same length of time to pronounce. The two most widely recognized types of isochrony are **stress-timing** and **syllable-timing**, though in Japanese the **mora** is said to be the unit of isochrony. Instrumental studies have confirmed that isochrony is less a physical reality than a tendency or even a perception of the hearer. *Adj.* **isochronous** /aɪ'sɒkrənəs/.

isodynamic /aɪsədaɪ'næmɪk/ *adj.* Involving the same **initiator power**. Catford (1977: 87) suggests that **feet** in English speech are more accurately described as isodynamic, rather than **isochronous**.

isogloss /'aɪsəglɒs/ *n.* In dialectology, a line drawn on a map to represent the boundary between two competing linguistic forms.

isolated opposition /'aɪsəleɪtɪd/ *adj.* In **Prague School** phonology, a unique contrast between two segments distinguished by a feature which distinguishes no other pair of segments in the language. An example is the English contrast between /r/ and /l/, distinguished by the feature of laterality, which plays no other part in English. Cf. **proportional opposition**.

isophone /'aɪsəfəʊn/ *n.* An **isogloss** which separates two types of pronunciation.

isosyllabicity /aɪsəsɪlə'bɪsɪti/ *n.* See **syllable-timing**.

Item-and-Arrangement /ˈaɪtəm ənd əˈreɪndʒmənt/ *adj.* (**IA**)
Denoting a rigidly distributional approach to phonological description which involves no machinery other than lists of phonological
elements and statements of the positions in which they may occur.
IA prohibits any appeal to phonological processes deriving surface
forms from underlying forms. It was a major feature of most
American Structuralist phonology, but it has been generally
rejected in more recent work, on the ground that it prevents the
formulation of generalizations. Hockett (1954).

Item-and-Process *adj.* (**IP**) Denoting any approach to phonological
description which involves deriving surface forms from underlying
representations by rules. The term was applied to early versions
of **generative phonology** in recognition of the most prominent
difference between it and earlier work by **American Structuralists**;
it is no longer current. Hockett (1954).

iterative rule application /ˈɪtərətɪv/ *n.* The phenomenon in which
a single rule applies repeatedly to a single phonological form
without the intervening application of any other rules. Iterative
application is most commonly invoked in treating **assimilation**
processes like **vowel harmony**, or **voicing** assimilation in **clusters**,
in cases in which the assimilation appears to propagate itself
through a word from left to right or from right to left. Cf. **fell
swoop**.

-ization /-aɪˈzeɪʃn̩/, **-ized** /-aɪzd/ Affixes which are used in phonetics
and phonology in three quite different senses. 1. Statically, to
denote the presence of a secondary articulation. Thus, *palatalization* is the presence during an articulation of the raising of the front
of the tongue (as in [tʲ]), and the segment produced is *palatalized*.
2. Dynamically, to denote the introduction of such a secondary
articulation into a segment which formerly lacked it. Thus, *palatalization* is the conversion of [t] to [tʲ], and the former [t] has been
palatalized. 3. Dynamically, to denote a change in the location of
the primary constriction. Thus, *palatalization* is the conversion of
[t] to [c], and the former [t] has been *palatalized*. NOTE: These
multiple uses are unfortunate, but all are well established, and the context
is usually sufficient to determine which is meant.

J

Jakobson–Halle feature system /jɑːkəbsən 'hæli/ *n*. A major system of **distinctive features**, the first complete system to be proposed. Derived from the earlier ideas of the **Prague School**, the system was developed by Roman Jakobson and his colleagues in the 1950s, notably in Jakobson *et al.* (1952) and Jakobson and Halle (1956); the 1956 version is here taken as canonical. Since these scholars were working at the time with the **sound spectrograph**, the J–H features are explicitly **acoustic**, though all of them are also given articulatory interpretations. In principle, the features are exclusively **binary**, though the **flat/plain** and **sharp/plain** contrasts really disguise a single **ternary** feature, and there is the complication that features are sometimes allowed to take the value zero, meaning 'irrelevant' or 'inapplicable'. The terminology is unusual, in that both values of each feature are given independent names, so that, for example, the specifications [grave] and [acute] are used instead of [+grave] and [–grave]. Only twelve features are recognized, as follows: **vocalic/non-vocalic; consonantal/ non-consonantal; compact/diffuse; tense/lax; voiced/voiceless; nasal/oral; discontinuous/continuant; strident/mellow; checked/ unchecked; grave/acute; flat/plain; sharp/plain**. Though widely used in the 1950s and 1960s, the system suffers from two major problems. First, it fails to capture certain obvious **natural classes**: for example, palatal consonants differ from velars as [compact] vs. [diffuse], but palatalized consonants (including velars) are distinguished from non-palatalized counterparts as [sharp] vs. [plain] – leaving the analyst no way of treating palatal and palatalized consonants uniformly. Second, it unites under a single feature specification quite different articulatory phenomena which have broadly similar acoustic effects. For example, the feature [flat] covers all of lip-rounding, retroflexion and pharyngealization, and hence the system effectively claims that no language can distinctively use more than one of these devices, a claim quickly shown to be false. Under increasing pressure from the proponents of **articulatory features**, the J–H system was eventually superseded in most linguistic usage by the *SPE* **feature system**; nevertheless, certain J–H features, notably [strident] and [grave], have continued in use.

See Fischer-Jørgensen (1975: 154–173) for a summary and critical evaluation of the system.

jitter /'dʒɪtə/ *n.* Irregular variation in the **fundamental frequency** of the **vocal folds**, such as occurs in **harsh voice**. Cf. **shimmer**.

Jones transcription /dʒəʊnz/ *n.* See *EPD* **transcription**.

junction prosody /'dʒʌŋkʃən/ *n.* In **Prosodic Analysis**, any phonological element whose occurrence signals the presence of some kind of boundary. Examples include the word-initial stress of Czech and the occurrence in English of heterorganic plosive–nasal clusters, as in *catnap* and *topmost*, which always fall across morpheme boundaries. In this framework, all such elements are treated as one kind of **prosody**. Junction prosodies represent an elaboration of the **boundary signals** of the Prague School.

juncture /'dʒʌŋkʃə/ *n.* Any phonetic feature whose presence signals the existence of a grammatical boundary. Similar in conception to the Prague School's **boundary signals**, the notion was particularly developed by the **American Structuralists**, who distinguished **close juncture** (normal transitions within words), **internal open juncture** (boundaries within words) and **external open juncture** (at utterance boundaries). Thus *nitrate* has close juncture, while *night-rate* differs in having internal open juncture, and *white shoes* and *why choose* differ in the location of the internal open juncture. See **juncture phoneme**. Trager and Bloch (1941).

juncture displacement /dɪs'pleɪsmənt/ *n.* See **metanalysis**.

juncture phoneme *n.* In **American Structuralist** phonology, any of several putative phonological constructs, having the status of phonemes but lacking any intrinsic phonetic content, set up to account for the observed phonetic differences between apparently identical sequences of segmental phonemes, as in *nitrate* and *night-rate*, or as in *why choose* and *white shoes*. Trager and Bloch (1941) introduced the **plus juncture** to represent *open internal juncture* in such cases, and Trager and Smith (1951) added three varieties of *external open juncture*, distinguished by intonation: **plus**, **single-bar**, **double-bar** and **double-cross junctures**. Juncture phonemes were devised as a means of escaping the unpleasant consequences of the **separation of levels**, by which no grammatical information was available for phonological analysis. See Fischer-Jørgensen (1975: 94–97).

just noticeable difference /dʒʌst nəʊtɪsəbəl 'dɪfrəns/ *n.* (**JND**) The minimum phonetic distinction required to render a phonological contrast perceptible to native speakers – for example, the minimal difference in **duration** which will allow a hearer to distinguish long and short segments.

K

Kazan School /kəzɑːn/ *n.* The name given to the work of the two Polish linguists Jan Baudouin de Courtenay and Mikołaj Kruszewski, who taught at Kazan in southern Russia in the late nineteenth century, and sometimes also to the work of later scholars who were influenced by them. The Kazan School linguists were the first to use the term **phoneme** in roughly its modern sense (they also coined the term **morpheme**); they stressed the importance of **alternations** in illuminating phonological analyses; and they anticipated many of the ideas of Ferdinand de Saussure. Unfortunately, much of their work did not become known in the west until after it had been replicated by other scholars. See Anderson (1985: ch. 3) for an account.

Kensington accent /'kenzɪŋtən/ *n.* See under **Received Pronunciation**.

Kenyon and Knott system /kenjən ənd 'nɒt/ *n.* An analysis of American English vowels proposed by John Kenyon and Thomas Knott (1953). In contrast to the **Trager–Smith system**, Kenyon and Knott analyse most nuclei as single elements. The system is intended to handle all major types of American accent, and hence it sets up 21 distinct nuclei, even though no single American accent distinguishes that many nuclei. Of these, 17 are single elements and only four are diphthongs (those occurring in *buy*, *now*, *boy* and *few*). The system has been highly influential in the United States; with various modifications in its symbols, it can be found in many recent linguistic works. See Kreidler (1989: 298ff.) for a summary.

key /kiː/ *n.* In some analyses of **intonation**, that part of an individual's pitch range in which a particular utterance is made. For example, a shrill, emotionally charged utterance may be said to be in a *high key*. From music.

key susceptible segment /sə'septɪbəl/ *n.* A particular segment whose auditory characteristics are strongly affected by the presence of some **phonetic setting** and which is therefore useful in identifying the presence of that setting. For example, [i] and [s] are key segments for a lip-rounded setting. Laver (1994).

Kiel convention /kiːl/ *n*. The set of recommendations made by the 1989 meeting of the IPA in Kiel, which made substantial changes in the IPA's symbols and terminology.

kiloHertz /'kɪləhɜːts/ *n*. (**kHz**) One thousand **Hertz**.

kinaesthetic /kɪniːs'θetɪk/ *adj*. (also **kinesthetic**) Pertaining to the sensations of one's own movements.

kinaesthetic feedback *n*. (also **kinesthetic**) The ability of a speaker to perceive and monitor her/his own speech by means of sensory stimuli reporting the positions of the organs of speech. Cf. **auditory feedback**.

kinesics /kaɪ'niːzɪks/ *n*. The use of gestures and expressions during speech in order to add meaning or to modify the import of spoken language.

kinetic tone /kɪ'netɪk/ *n*. See **contour tone**.

King's English /kɪŋz 'ɪŋglɪʃ/ *n*. (also **Queen's English**) A name given in Britain to the perceived prestige standard form of English, often particularly to **Received Pronunciation**.

kiss click /kɪs/ *n*. A bilabial **click**. From its resemblance to a kiss.

kymograph /'kaɪməɡrɑːf/ *n*. Any of various mechanical, electrical or electronic devices used to measure and record variations in any of several physical quantities during speech, such as the rate of air flow (the 'volume-velocity'). A modern version is usually called an **electrokymograph**. *Adj*. **kymographic** /kaɪmə'ɡræfɪk/; *abstr. n.* **kymography** /kaɪ'mɒɡrəfi/.

L

labial /'leɪbiəl/ *adj.* or *n.* 1. *adj.* Pertaining to the lips. 2. *adj.* (of a segment) Articulated with the lips. 3. *n.* A segment so articulated, such as [p], [m] or [f]. 4. (**lab**) A **distinctive feature** invoked to distinguish labial segments ([+lab]) from all other segments ([–lab]). Anderson (1971). 5. A different **distinctive feature** invoked to separate labial consonants and rounded vowels and glides (all [+lab]) from all other segments ([–lab]). See Hyman (1975: 53–55) for a discussion of this feature with references. Reighard (1972). 6. In some versions of **feature geometry**, a superordinate feature taking **round** as a dependent. Sagey (1986). 7. See **labiality** (sense 1). Ant. **non-labial**.

labial-alveolar (also **labio-alveolar**, **labio-coronal**) 1. *adj.* (of a segment) Articulated with simultaneous labial and alveolar constrictions of roughly equal degree. 2. *n.* A segment so articulated, such as Margi [pt].

labiality /leɪbi'ælɪti/ *n.* 1. (also **labial**) In the **Ladefoged** and **Williamson feature systems**, a binary **distinctive feature** invoked to distinguish contrasts involving approximation of the centres of the lips. Thus, [kp] is [+lab], while [k] is [–lab]. 2. In **Dependency Phonology** and other privative approaches, the vowel **element** {u}, or, in some versions, {w}.

labialization /leɪbiəlaɪ'zeɪʃn̩/ *n.* 1. The presence in an articulation of some degree of **lip-rounding** as a **secondary articulation**. In the IPA, labialization is represented by a superscript w: hence [sʷ] represents a labialized voiceless alveolar fricative, such as often occurs in English *soon* or *swim*. See Laver (1994: 321–322). 2. Any phonological process by which some segment acquires lip-rounding which was (underlyingly or historically) absent. *V.* **labialize**; *adj.* **labialized**.

labial-palatal 1. *adj.* (of an articulation) Involving simultaneous **labial** and **palatal** strictures of approximately equal degree; one type of **coarticulation**. 2. *n.* A segment so articulated, such as [ɥ] in French *huit* [ɥit] 'eight'.

labial protrusion /prəˈtruːʒn̩/ *n.* Prominent forward extension of the lips during speech, such as occurs in **inner rounding** or as part of the **articulatory setting** of particular speakers or languages.

labial-velar (also **labiovelar, labio-dorsal**) 1. *adj.* (of a segment) Articulated with simultaneous **labial** and **velar** constrictions of approximately equal degree; one type of **coarticulation**. 2. *n.* A segment so articulated, such as [w] or [kp]. A labial-velar articulation differs from a **labialized velar** articulation like [kʷ], in which the **primary articulation** is velar and labialization is a **secondary articulation**.

labio-coronal /ˈleɪbiəʊ/ *adj.* or *n.* See **labial-alveolar**.

labio-coronal-dorsal 1. *adj.* (of a segment) Articulated with simultaneous labial, coronal and velar constrictions. 2. A segment so articulated, such as Kinyarwanda [tkw].

labiodental 1. *adj.* (of a segment) Articulated with the primary stricture involving the lower lip and the upper teeth. 2. *n.* A segment so articulated, such as [f], [v] or [ɱ]. 3. *adj.* In the **Ladefoged** and **Williamson feature systems**, one of the eleven possible values of the feature **articulatory place**.

labiodentalization *n.* The presence, during an articulation, of an incompletely occluded **labiodental** articulation as a **secondary articulation**. Labiodentalized fricatives and affricates occur in a number of African and Caucasian languages (Catford 1977; Ladefoged 1964, 1971). *Adj.* **labiodentalized**.

labio-dorsal *adj.* or *n.* See **labial-velar**.

labiovelar *adj.* or *n.* A traditional and widely used, but nonetheless anomalously formed, term used to label *either* a **labial-velar** articulation (like [w]) *or* a **labialized velar** articulation (like [kʷ]).

labiovelarization *n.* In **Prosodic Analysis**, the **prosody** [ʷ], posited to account for **lip-rounding**. *Adj.* **labiovelarized**.

Lachmann's Law /ˈlækmən/ *n.* The phenomenon in Latin by which an underlyingly short vowel in a verb stem ending in a voiced plosive is lengthened in the participle: *lĕgō* 'read', participle *lēctus*.

Ladefoged experiment /ˈlædɪfəʊgɪd/ *n.* An experiment carried out by Peter Ladefoged (1960) to test how consistently the vowels of an unknown language (Irish) would be characterized by phoneticians in terms of the **cardinal vowel system**. Broadly, the result was

that phoneticians trained in the same tradition exhibited a high
degree of agreement with one another, while those trained in
different traditions agreed less well. This is not to say that consistency implies accuracy in any absolute sense; in any case, the use
of recordings deprived the subjects of a view of the speaker's lips,
which would have provided valuable information. John Laver
(1965) performed a similar experiment testing the consistency of
particular phoneticians over time.

Ladefoged feature system *n.* (also **prime feature system, traditional feature system**) A **distinctive feature system** proposed by
Peter Ladefoged in a series of publications (Ladefoged 1964, 1971,
1975/1982); the 1975/1982 version is here taken as canonical. (Note
that the third (1993) edition of this book does not include the
feature system.) The system employs predominantly **articulatory
features** and allows them to be **multivalued**. There are twenty
features; where the number of possible values is not specified, the
feature is **binary: glottalic** (3 values), **velaric, voice** (5 values), **aspiration** (3 values), **articulatory place** (11 values), **labial, stop, nasal,
lateral, trill, flap** (or **tap**), **sonorant, sibilant, grave, height** (4 values),
back, round, wide, rhotacized, syllabic. Cf. **Williamson feature
system**.

lag /læg/ *n.* A delay in the onset of **voicing** after the release of a
plosive. Cf. **lead**.

lah-di-dah accent /lɑːdiˈdɑː/ *n.* [*non-technical*] See under **Received
Pronunciation**.

Lallans /ˈlælənz/ *n.* [*non-technical*] The popular label for the distinctive speech variety of the lowlands of Scotland, often more particularly for a literary representation of such speech. A representation
of the local pronunciation of 'lowlands'.

lambdacism /ˈlæmdəsɪzm̩/ *n.* (also **lateralization**) Any phonological
process in which a non-lateral consonant is converted to a **lateral**,
as when French *danger* 'danger' and Spanish *naranja* 'orange' are
borrowed into Basque as *lanjer* and *laranja*.

lamina /ˈlæmɪnə/ *n.* The **blade** of the tongue.

laminal /ˈlæmɪnəl/ 1. *adj.* Pertaining to the **blade** of the tongue.
2. *adj.* (of a segment) Articulated with the blade of the tongue
forming the primary stricture. 3. *n.* A segment so articulated,
such as English [t] and [n] for most speakers. In the IPA, a laminal

articulation may be explicitly represented by the use of the diacritic [̪] below the symbol for a dental/alveolar segment: [t̪], [n̪]. 4. *adj.* In the **Williamson feature system**, one of the three possible values of the feature **apicality**.

laminal-dorsal vowel *n.* (also **blade vowel**, **coronal vowel**) A vowel whose articulation involves an approximation of the **blade** of the tongue to the alveolar ridge. Cf. **apical-dorsal vowel**.

laminar flow /'læmɪnə fləʊ/ *n.* Flow, as of air, which is smooth and not **turbulent**. In speech, laminar flow is typical of vowels and voiced approximants.

lamino-alveolar 1. *adj.* (of a segment) Articulated with the blade of the tongue and the alveolar ridge forming the primary occlusion. 2. *n.* A segment so articulated, such as English [t d n l] for most speakers.

lamino-labial *adj.* or *n.* (A segment) articulated with the blade of the tongue and the upper lip forming the primary constriction; one type of **linguolabial** articulation.

language game /'læŋgwɪdʒ geɪm/ *n.* (also **ludling**) Any systematic distortion of the phonological forms of words in speech for purposes of play; a familiar example is **Pig Latin**. Cf. **speech disguise**.

language-specific /spə'sɪfɪk/ *adj.* (also **parochial**) Occurring only in some particular language or languages, but not in languages generally.

lapse /læps/ *n.* Any violation of the **Obligatory Contour Principle** in which too many consecutive syllables lack a certain specification, such as stress. Cf. **clash**.

laryngeal /lə'rɪndʒəl/ (in senses 1–3, also **laryngal** /lə'rɪŋgəl/) 1. *adj.* Pertaining to the **larynx**. 2. *adj.* (of a segment) Articulated with the primary occlusion located in the larynx. 3. *n.* A segment so articulated. Apart from segments which are more narrowly described as **glottal**, laryngeal articulations are highly unusual, but see Catford (1977: 163–164) for a survey. 4. *adj.* In some versions of **feature geometry**, a superordinate **class node** dominating all other features relating to glottal activity. Sagey (1986). 5. *n.* In Indo-European studies, one of several hypothetical consonants which are reconstructed for Proto-Indo-European but which apparently disappeared in all daughter languages except Hittite, though not without affecting the quality and/or quantity of adjacent vowels.

laryngeal gesture *n*. In some analyses of articulation, that part of the articulation of a segment which takes place in the **larynx**. Cf. **oral gesture**. Lass (1984: 115).

laryngealization /lərɪndʒəlaɪˈzeɪʃn̩/ *n*. 1. Narrowly, and most usually, the presence of **creaky voice** during an articulation. Analysts differ as to whether this should be regarded strictly as a **phonation type** or whether it should be considered to involve an articulatory component as well, making it a **secondary articulation**. See **stød**. 2. Loosely, and less commonly, the presence during an articulation of any of several types of activity in the glottis or in the larynx, including at least **creaky voice**, **creak** and a **glottalic airstream mechanism**. *Adj*. **laryngealized**. NOTE: Sense 2, though widespread, is not recommended.

laryngealized *adj*. 1. (of a segment) Characterized by the presence of **laryngealization** (either sense). 2. In the **Ladefoged** and **Williamson feature systems**, one of the five possible values of the feature **voice** (sense 4) (Ladefoged) or **glottal state** (Williamson).

laryngograph /ləˈrɪŋgəgrɑːf/ *n*. (also **electrolaryngograph**) An instrument which records the **fundamental frequency** of the **glottis** during speech. The graphical record produced is a **laryngogram** /ləˈrɪŋgəgræm/. *Adj*. **laryngographic** /lərɪŋgəˈgræfɪk/.

laryngo-pharynx /ləˈrɪŋgə/ *n*. The lower part of the **pharynx**, extending down to the glottis.

laryngoscope /ləˈrɪŋgəskəʊp/ *n*. Any of various devices which permit the inspection or photography of the **larynx** from above during speech. Older versions used a mirror in the mouth; modern types involve an optical fibre inserted through the nasal cavity. *Abstr. n*. **laryngoscopy** /lærɪŋˈgɒskəpi/.

larynx /ˈlærɪŋks/ *n*. (also **voice box**) A complex, mostly cartilaginous, structure connecting the **trachea** to the **pharynx** and acting as a valve through which air must pass during breathing and speech. The upper **thyroid cartilage** is connected to the lower **cricoid cartilage**; in the middle are the **arytenoid cartilages**, which are connected to the **vocal folds** and control their movement. The space between the vocal folds is the **glottis**. *Adj*. **laryngeal**.

larynx-lowering *n*. The lowering of the **larynx** during an articulation, typical of voiced plosives.

larynx movement /ˈmuːvmənt/ *n*. In the **Williamson feature system**, a **distinctive feature** invoked to treat movement of the larynx during articulation, with the possible values **ejective**, **pulmonic** and **implosive**. This is identical to Ladefoged's **glottalic**.

latent consonant /'leɪtənt/ *n*. A **consonant** which is not phonetically present in a word when that word is pronounced in isolation but which appears in certain circumstances in derivatives or in connected speech, such as the final /r/ of *far* in **non-rhotic accents** of English or the final /t/ of French *petit*. *Abstr. n.* **latency** /'leɪtənsi/. Sapir (1925).

latent tone *n*. In some analyses of some **tone languages**, a posited tone which only gets phonetic realization in certain circumstances. See Kenstowicz (1994: 363–369).

late onset of voicing /leɪt/ *n*. The production of an obstruent, especially a plosive, in such a way that **voicing** begins only some considerable way through the articulation of a following voiced segment: often taken as a synonym for **aspiration**.

lateral /'lætərəl/ *adj.* or *n*. 1. (Pertaining to) a consonant whose articulation involves a complete closure somewhere along the median line of the vocal tract while air is allowed to flow through an opening on one side of the occlusion (a **unilateral**) or through openings on both sides of the occlusion (a **bilateral**). Depending on the nature of the opening(s), the resulting articulation may be a **lateral approximant**, a **lateral fricative** or a **lateral affricate**. Dental, alveolar, retroflex and palatal laterals are common; velar laterals occur in a few languages; Catford (1977: 251) reports a remarkable bilabial lateral in a variety of Irish. Ant. **median** or **non-lateral**. NOTE: Some analysts use **central** as the antonym, but this is not recommended. 2. A loose but very common term for **lateral approximant**. 3. In the *SPE* **feature system**, a **distinctive feature** defined as 'involving a lowering of the side(s) of the mid-section of the tongue'. *SPE* explicitly confines the value [+lat] to [+cor] segments, but this is an error: many Caucasian and Papuan languages, and even some varieties of English, have velar laterals with no blade activity. See, however, Levin (1988). 4. See **laterality**.

lateral affricate *n*. An **affricate** in which a complete closure is followed by **lateral** release, such as the alveolar [tɬ] of Nahuatl.

lateral approximant *n*. (also **lateral resonant** and, loosely, but commonly, **lateral**) A segment whose articulation involves a complete **median** closure in the mouth with an opening on one or both sides which is not radical enough to produce friction, such as

[l]. Analysts differ as to whether a lateral approximant should be classified as an **approximant** or not. See Laver (1994: 306–311) for an account.

lateral fricative *n.* A segment whose articulation involves a complete **median** closure in the mouth with an opening on one or both sides radical enough to produce friction noise, such as the [ɬ] of Welsh, as in *Llanelli*.

laterality /lætəˈrælɪti/ *n.* (also **lateral**) In the **Ladefoged** and **Williamson feature systems**, a **distinctive feature** invoked to distinguish **lateral** segments ([+lat]) from all others ([–lat]).

lateralization /lætərəlaɪˈzeɪʃn̩/ *n.* See **lambdacism**.

lateral release *n.* (also **lateral plosion**) The phenomenon in which a **plosive** articulation is released only by dropping one or both sides of the tongue, while retaining a median closure, as often occurs with English *middle*. Lateral release is transcribed in the IPA with a superscript [ˡ], as in [tˡ]. Cf. **median release**.

lateral resonant *n.* See **lateral approximant**.

lax /læks/ *adj.* 1. The opposite of **tense** in most senses of that term; see the discussion under **tense**. 2. In the **Jakobson–Halle feature system**, a **distinctive feature** defined as 'exhibiting low energy, with little spread across the spectrum, and limited duration' and interpreted as representing little deformation of the vocal tract from its rest position. Ant. **tense**.

lax voice *n.* 1. Broadly, a label applied to any **voice quality** characterized by an overall relaxation in muscular tension and hence by some or all of **breathy voice** or **whispery voice**, minimal movement of the tongue, lips and jaw, an unconstricted pharynx, low-pressure air flow, low pitch-range, soft loudness-range and centralization of vowels. The labels **soft voice** and **slack voice** are also applied to some or all of these voice qualities. See Laver (1980: 142–156). Cf. **tense voice**. 2. Narrowly, a distinctive **phonation type** occurring in some languages, notably Javanese. Catford (1977: 106) identifies Javanese lax voice as a type of **whispery voice** involving vibration of the full glottis.

LCPR See **Lexical Category Prominence Rule**.

lead /liːd/ *n.* The time difference between the onset of **voicing** and the following release of a plosive. Cf. **lag**.

leader-timing /ˈliːdə/ *n.* The type of rhythm in which a stressed syllable is perceived as beginning a foot. Cf. **trailer-timing**. Wenk and Wioland (1982).

learnèd form /ˈlɜːnɪd/ *n.* A word or form which has been borrowed from a prestige language (sometimes an earlier form of the borrowing language) and which therefore does not show all of the regular phonological developments of the borrowing language: French *strict* 'strict, narrow', borrowed from Latin *strictus*, which does not show the same developments as *étroit* 'narrow', directly descended from Latin *strictus*.

learnt rule /lɜːnt/ *n.* In some frameworks, notably **Natural Phonology** and **Radical Underspecification**, a language-specific phonological process which can in no way be regarded as natural, but which must be simply stipulated by the analyst and learned by the child. Sommerstein (1977: 235–236) provides a list of ten properties which supposedly differentiate learnt rules from other processes.

Least Effort, Principle of /liːst ˈefət/ *n.* A putative principle of linguistic behaviour, by which speakers attempt to minimize the amount of articulatory effort involved in speaking. Martinet (1960).

leaving element /ˈliːvɪŋ/ *n.* In a **chain shift**, any segment which moves out of the phonological space it formerly occupied, that space being occupied in turn by another segment, the **entering element**. Labov (1994: 119).

lect /lekt/ *n.* Any particular speech variety, considered *per se*, without reference to any social, geographical or other significance which it may possess. Back-formation from **dialect**.

left-capturing /ˈleft kæptʃərɪŋ/ *n.* The phenomenon in which an intervocalic consonant which forms part of a following syllable becomes **ambisyllabic**. Wells (1990b).

left-headed foot /left ˈhedɪd/ *n.* A metrical **foot** in which the most prominent element (its **head**) precedes all other elements. English is commonly described as having left-headed feet. Cf. **right-headed foot**.

length /leŋθ/ *n.* 1. The duration of a syllable, or of the vowel or diphthong it contains, regarded as a phonological characteristic; the phonological correlate of **duration**. In the IPA, a greater value of length is marked by a following ː. 2. (also **quantity**) A phonological element, found in some languages, by which some segments are distinguished from other, similar segments by differences in the amount of time involved in the articulation. Thus, Italian distinguishes /nono/ 'ninth' from /non:o/ 'grandfather'; Swedish distinguishes /je:t/ 'goat' from /jet:/ 'given'; Finnish distinguishes /kisa/ 'a game' from /kis:a/ 'a cat'. Some languages, such as Scots Gaelic and Estonian, reportedly have three degrees of length, and the African language Kamba has been reported as having four. See Laver (1994: 436–445). 3. In the *SPE* **feature system**, an undefined and undiscussed **distinctive feature** suggested for handling contrasts of length in sense 1, later renamed **long**. 4. In the **Williamson feature system**, a similar **distinctive feature** with the possible values **short**, **normal**, **long** and **extra long**.

lengthening /'leŋθənɪŋ/ *n.* Any process which, phonetically or phonologically, increases the duration of a segment, most often a vowel.

Leningrad School /'lenɪngræd sku:l/ *n.* The name given to the approach to phonology developed by a group of linguists based in Leningrad (St Petersburg) throughout the twentieth century and derived chiefly from the ideas of Baudouin de Courtenay. The leading theorist of the school was L. V. Ščerba. See Fischer-Jørgensen (1975: 324–331).

lenis /'li:nɪs/ *adj.* The antonym of **fortis** (all senses); see the discussion under that entry.

lenition /lə'nɪʃn̩/ *n.* 1. (also **weakening**) Any phonological process in which a segment becomes either less strongly occluded or more sonorous, such as [k] → [x], [x] → [h] or [k] → [g]. Often the term is extended to various other processes, such as loss of aspiration, shortening of long segments and monophthongization of diphthongs, which represent 'weakening' in some intuitive sense. See Lass (1984: 177–183). Ant. **fortition**. 2. (also **aspiration**) In Irish, the conventional name for the set of **mutations**, occurring in specified grammatical and lexical environments, in which, in word-initial position, a plosive or /m/ becomes a fricative, /s/ becomes /h/ and /f/ becomes zero: *cloch* /klox/ 'stone', *an chloch* /ən xlox/ 'the stone'; *fear* /f'ar/ 'man', genitive *fhir* /ir/; *mac* /mak/ 'son', *a mhac* /ə vak/ 'his son'.

lento /'lentəʊ/ *adj.* (of speech) Slow and careful, and hence usually not showing the phonological processes typical of rapid speech. Ant. **allegro**. Italian: 'slow'.

level /'levəl/ 1. *adj.* (of a tone) Having a constant **pitch**, with no rise or fall. 2. *n.* [rarely also **stratum**] In **Lexical Phonology**, any one of the domains posited for certain types of process.

levelling /'levəlɪŋ/ *n.* 1. A form of **monophthongization** in which a diphthong is reduced to a pure vowel lying phonetically about halfway between the start point and end point of the original diphthong, as when [ai] is levelled to [e]. 2. See **analogical levelling**.

level one *n.* In **Lexical Phonology**, the **level** at which all processes are carried out which are irregular or not fully productive; this includes word formation (*person/personal/personality*) and irregular inflections like *took* and *children*. Cf. **level two**.

level-ordering *n.* In **Lexical Phonology**, the principle that affixes are grouped into classes called *levels*, such that all affixes in one level must be added to a form before any affixes of the next level can be added.

levels analysis *n.* Any analysis of **intonation** which posits a fixed number of pitch levels (for English, typically four) and interprets all intonational movement as involving jumps from one level to another. See Cruttenden (1986: 3.3). Cf. **contour analysis**.

level stress *n.* A type of **stress** in which there is no perceptible variation in prominence during the articulation of the stressed syllable. Jones (1950: 149).

level tone *n.* See **register tone**.

level two *n.* In **Lexical Phonology**, the **level** at which regular and productive morphological processes are carried out, such as the formation of *cats* and *loved*. Cf. **level one**.

levis /'liːvɪs/ *adj.* An occasional synonym for **lenis**, preferred in some philological works. For example, Spanish /b d g/ are realized intervocalically as continuants [β ð ɣ]; these are sometimes described as 'levis'. Latin *levis* 'light'.

lexeme /'leksiːm/ *n.* See **lexical item**.

lexical accent /'leksɪkəl/ *n.* In some versions of **Metrical Phonology**, a stress which is exceptionally assigned to a particular syllable in the underlying form of a word in order to derive the correct result for a word whose stress pattern is irregular.

lexical blank /blæŋk/ *n.* The absence, in an underlying form, of a **feature specification** whose value can be derived by rule. Kiparsky (1982), though the idea is much older.

lexical category *n.* 1. (also **word class**, **part of speech**) Broadly, and usually, any one of the various classes of lexical items in a language, such as *noun*, *verb*, *pronoun*, *preposition*. 2. Narrowly, a subset of these, including only *noun*, *verb*, *adjective*, *adverb*, but excluding all those categories whose members are primarily grammatical items.

Lexical Category Prominence Rule *n.* (**LCPR**) In some versions of **Metrical Phonology**, a principle invoked in order to derive the stress patterns of polysyllabic English lexical items, including compounds. As a general rule, this principle assigns primary stress to the second foot in such an item, so long as it branches, as in *mortadella*. Liberman and Prince (1977: 270).

lexical conditioning *n.* The use of exceptional **allomorphs** in the presence of specific lexical stems, as in such English plurals as *cacti*, *men*, *sheep* and *children*.

lexical diffusion /dɪˈfjuːʒn̩/ *n.* The process by which a phonological change begins by applying only to certain words and then spreads gradually to other phonologically similar words. In some cases, lexical diffusion stops at some point, leaving all remaining words permanently unaffected; in other cases, the process eventually goes to completion by affecting all remaining words. A famous example is the raising and tensing of /æ/ in Philadelphia. Before final /d/, speakers consistently pronounce a tense vowel in *mad*, *bad* and *glad* but a lax one in *sad*, *had* and *dad*, suggesting that the diffusion has stopped operating only part way through the relevant class of words. In other contexts diffusion appears to be still occurring: only a small minority of speakers have a tense vowel in *manner* and *flannel*, whereas a large majority have one in *planet*. Implicitly or explicitly defended by the nineteenth-century Romance dialectologists and by a number of twentieth-century structuralists, lexical diffusion only became widely accepted after the publication of overwhelming evidence in the 1970s; it is now known to be a major pathway of phonological change, and its existence constitutes a direct refutation of the **Neogrammarian Hypothesis**. See Sommerstein (1977: 251–252) for a historical summary, Chen and Wang (1975) for the classic presentation, and Labov (1994) for extensive discussion. Wang (1969).

lexical incidence /'ɪnsɪdəns/ *n.* (also **lexical distribution**) See **selectional difference**.

Lexicalist Morphology /'leksɪkəlɪst/ *n.* An approach to morphology which holds that morphology is distinct from both phonology and syntax, which introduces much of the machinery of generative grammar, and which stresses a search for morphological universals. See Bauer (1988: ch. 9) for a brief introduction, Scalise (1984) for a more detailed one.

lexical item /'aɪtəm/ *n.* (also **lexeme**) 1. A word regarded as a comparatively abstract object which has a more-or-less consistent meaning or function but which can possibly vary in form for grammatical purposes. For example, the items *dog* and *dogs* are both forms of the lexical item DOG, and *take*, *takes*, *took*, *taking* and *taken* are all forms of the lexical item TAKE. 2. One of a subset of such items, those which are nouns, verbs, adjectives or adverbs, but excluding grammatical items like pronouns and prepositions.

lexicalization /leksɪkəlaɪ'zeɪʃn̩/ *n.* 1. The process by which an underlying phonological representation is converted into a surface phonetic form. 2. The conversion of a compound word or of a phrase into a single unanalysable word, as has happened with English *lord* (formerly *hlāford* 'loaf-ward'). *V.* **lexicalize**.

lexically bound autosegment *n.* In some versions of **Autosegmental Phonology**, an **autosegment** which is represented in the lexicon as permanently bound to its segment, rather than being initially unassociated and then attached to its segment by the **Association Convention**. Cf. **free autosegment**.

lexical matrix *n.* A representation of a **lexical item** in the lexicon in which each segment is represented as a **feature matrix**.

lexical morphology *n.* That part of the morphology which deals with all types of **word formation**.

lexical opposition *n.* For a particular phonological contrast, the number of minimal pairs distinguished only by that contrast: one way of expressing **functional load**. Cf. **lexical predictability**. Labov (1994: 328).

Lexical Phonology *n.* (**LP**) A major contemporary theory of phonology developed in the early 1980s, chiefly by K. P. Mohanan, Paul Kiparsky and Steven Strauss, drawing on earlier work by David Pesetsky. With its emphasis on morphophonology, LP is, of all current frameworks, arguably the one most similar to **classical generative phonology**, and the only one which cannot be described as **non-linear**. On the one hand, LP integrates morphology and phonology into a unified framework; on the other, it divides the process of deriving surface forms into a (possibly unlimited) number of distinct stages (called *levels*) in such a way that all operations must be completed within any given level before any operations can take place at the next level, and it draws a sharp distinction between morphological processes and strictly phonological ones: the former are represented by (cyclic) lexical rules of word formation located in the lexicon, while the latter consist of postlexical rules with access to the phrasal environments of words. Convenient introductions are Kaisse and Shaw (1985), Roca (1994: 246–261) and especially Kenstowicz (1994: 213–243).

lexical predictability /prɪdɪktə'bɪləti/ *n.* For a particular phonological contrast, the extent to which that contrast depends on minimal pairs: one way of expressing **functional load**. If there are few minimal pairs (as, for example, with the /ʃ/–/ʒ/ contrast in English), lexical predictability is high. Labov (1994: 328).

lexical redundancy *n.* The phenomenon in which, in the underlying form of a **lexical item**, certain **feature specifications** are predictable. For example, in any English word beginning with three consonants, the first must be /s/, and hence, in this position, all other specifications are predictable from [–syllabic].

lexical redundancy condition *n.* A generalization of the notion of a **morpheme structure rule** to include statements which cannot be formulated as ordinary phonological rules, such as 'A morpheme may not contain both back and front vowels'. Stanley (1967).

lexical redundancy rule *n.* See **morpheme structure rule**. Chomsky and Halle (1968).

lexical representation *n.* The form in which a **lexical item** is represented in the **lexicon**.

lexical rule *n.* A rule which derives **lexical items** from other lexical items, such as the rule deriving English adjectives from nouns by the addition of the suffix *-al*: *topic/topical*; *transformation/transformational*.

lexical split *n.* A type of phonological change in which a single phoneme undergoes a **split** into two phonemes under typically complex conditions which are partly predictable and partly arbitrary. An example is the split of earlier /æ/ into /æ/ and /ɑː/ in the south of England: the low back vowel is now found in *dance* and *chance* but not in *fancy* or *romance*, in *plant* but not in *ant*, in *class* but not in *bass* (fish), in *sample* but not in *ample*, in *demand* and *slander* but not in *land* or *pander*; the back vowel is variably present in *mass* 'religious service' but never present in *mass* 'material', and it is categorical in *plaster* but uncommon in *plastic*.

lexicon /ˈleksɪkən/ *n*. That part of the complete grammar of a language which contains at least the lexical and grammatical morphemes, including any peculiarities which these may exhibit, and which in ·some frameworks may also contain additional material, such as **lexical rules**.

liaison /liɛzɔ̃/ *n*. In French, the phenomenon in which a word which in isolation ends in a vowel acquires a final consonant in certain circumstances when followed by a vowel-initial word: hence, *petit* [pti] 'little' (masc. sing.) + *ami* [ami] 'friend' yields *petit ami* [ptitami] 'little friend', and *sans* [sɑ̃] 'without' + *oeufs* [ø] 'eggs' yields *sans oeufs* [sɑ̃zø] 'without eggs'. *Liaison* is blocked by *h aspiré*.

licensing /ˈlaɪsənsɪŋ/ *n*. In various frameworks, the analytical procedure by which some phonological element (the *licensee*) is expressly permitted to occur in some position by the presence of some other element elsewhere (the *licenser*). The term is particularly used in **Government and Charm Phonology**, in which it is the fundamental requirement for well-formedness. *V.* **license**.

Licensing Principle *n*. A central principle of **Government and Charm Phonology**. It says: all phonological positions save one must be licensed within a domain; the unlicensed position is the head of this domain.

ligamental voice /lɪɡəˈmentəl/ *n*. See under **anterior** (sense 2).

light diphthong /laɪt/ *n*. A **diphthong** which patterns phonologically like a short vowel, especially in connection with stress assignment. Such diphthongs are reported for Icelandic, among other languages.

light syllable *n*. A **syllable** which is not a **heavy syllable**, in any of the senses of that term; see the remarks under that entry.

lilt /lɪlt/ *n*. [*non-technical*] An impressionistic label sometimes applied to a speech pattern, especially an intonation pattern, perceived as attractively rhythmic or musical: *a Welsh lilt*. *Adj.* **lilting**. Scots *lilt* 'tune'.

Lindau feature system /'lɪndaʊ/ *n.* A system of **distinctive features** for vowels (only) proposed by Mona Lindau (1975, 1978). There are ten features, as follows; the two numbers cited are first the number of possible phonetic values distinguishable and second the maximum number of contrastive values usable by any one language: **high** (4/4), **back** (3/3), **compressed** (2/2), **round** (3/2), **expanded** (3/2), **rhotacized** (4/3), **voice** (5/2), **long** (3/2), **nasal** (2/2), **peripheral** (2/2).

line /laɪn/ *n.* In **Government and Charm Phonology**, the term applied to what is elsewhere called a **tier** or a **plane**.

linear approach to speech segmentation /'lɪniə/ *n.* See **serial approach to speech segmentation**.

linearity condition /lɪni'ærɪti/ *n.* The principle that a linear sequence of phonemes must be realized by a linear sequence of non-null phones occurring in exactly the same order as the phonemes they represent; phonemes and phones must match up one to one, and a phonemic distinction must be represented by a phonetic distinction at the same point. Widely accepted in **classical phonology**, particularly by the **American Structuralists**, this principle was strongly attacked by Chomsky (1964), and it has been rejected by virtually all phonologists since. Hyman (1975: 128) provides a good example of a well-motivated analysis which violates linearity. In Sea Dayak, underlying /naŋa/ 'straighten' is phonetically [nãŋã], while underlying /naŋga/ 'set up a ladder' is phonetically [nãŋa]. Thus the underlying contrast between ∅ and /g/ is realized on the surface only by the nasality or non-nasality of the following vowel, in violation of the linearity condition. Similarly, in some North American accents, the /t/~/d/ contrast of *writer* and *rider* is represented phonetically only by the quality of the diphthong.

linearization /lɪniəraɪ'zeɪʃn̩/ *n.* See **unpacking**. *V.* **linearize**.

Linear Ordering Hypothesis *n.* In a theory of phonology employing **ordered rules**, the theoretical stance that all the rules of a language can be placed in a single unique linear order, and that all rules which apply in a particular derivation must apply in that order, at least within a single **cycle**. Generally accepted in early **generative phonology**, the hypothesis ran into difficulties and was later replaced by more complex views such as **local ordering** and **partial ordering**.

linear vowel system *n.* See **vertical vowel system**.

line conflation *n.* In some versions of **Metrical Phonology**, a process by which adjacent lines of the grid are collapsed by suppression of material on the lower one. This is invoked to treat languages in which a word of any number of syllables has only a single stress. Halle and Vergnaud (1987).

linguagram /ˈlɪŋgwəgræm/ *n.* A photograph of the tongue showing which parts of it have been coloured by contact with the colouring matter applied to the roof of the mouth during a traditional kind of **palatography**.

lingual /ˈlɪŋgwəl/ *adj.* 1. Pertaining to the **tongue**. 2. (of a segment) Articulated with the tongue. 3. (**ling**) A binary **distinctive feature** proposed by Lass (1976: 187–188) and defined as 'articulated with the blade or body of the tongue as primary active articulator'. Coronals, palatals, velars and high vowels are [+ling]; all other segments are [–ling].

lingual airstream *n.* The transient effect in which a large and rapid movement of the tongue briefly causes air flow in the opposite direction to what is otherwise happening. For example, a sequence like [kwa] may briefly induce ingressive air flow into the mouth. Such an airstream has no contrastive use in any language.

linguistic area /lɪŋˈgwɪstɪk/ *n.* (also *Sprachbund*) A geographical region in which several unrelated languages share a number of linguistic features which are not widespread among languages generally or not shared with related languages elsewhere. See **areal feature**.

linguistic phonetics *n.* The study of **phonetics** from the point of view of the ways in which individual languages exploit phonetic distinctions for linguistic purposes. Cf. **general phonetics**.

linguistic pitch range *n.* The range of pitch habitually exploited by an individual speaker in ordinary conversation. Cf. **paralinguistic pitch range**.

linguolabial /lɪŋgwəˈleɪbiəl/ 1. *adj.* (of a segment) Articulated with the tip or blade of the tongue forming a constriction with the upper lip. In the IPA, such sounds are represented by placing the diacritic

[̬] beneath the symbol for a dental/alveolar segment. Where necessary, we may distinguish **apico-labial** and **lamino-labial** sounds
(tip vs. blade). 2. *n.* A segment so articulated, such as the [t̪] of
some Pacific languages.

linking /'lɪŋkɪŋ/ *n.* 1. See **association**. 2. In the **markedness theory**
of *SPE*, the convention by which, when a feature is changed by a
rule, all other features whose markedness values depend on the
changed feature take on their unmarked values at no cost. Thus,
in a language in which /u/ is the only rounded vowel, the appearance of the feature [+round] on a vowel automatically implies the
appearance of [+back, +high].

linking convention *n.* A protocol by which **marking conventions**
apply persistently to the output of language-particular rules, in
order to correct violations of phonotactic or other combinatory
constraints each time they arise. This is an alternative to making
the corrections once and for all at the surface level with some
device such as a **filter** (sense 2). Chomsky and Halle (1968).

linking r *n.* In **non-rhotic accents** of English, the /r/ which surfaces
before a following vowel in words which have lost their historical
final /r/ in isolation: hence *far* /fɑː/ but *far away* /fɑːr əweɪ/. Cf.
intrusive r.

linking sound *n.* Any segment which is absent in words pronounced
in isolation but which is present in certain circumstances in
connected speech: French *il a* 'he has' but *a-t-il?* 'does he have?',
with linking /t/.

lip /lɪp/ *n.* Either of the two fleshy, manoeuvrable organs at the
entrance to the mouth. *Adj.* **labial**; CF **labio-**.

lip compression /kəm'preʃn̩/ *n.* See **outer rounding**. Ladefoged (1971:
62).

lip-reading /'riːdɪŋ/ *n.* (also **speech reading**) A method of interpreting the speech of a speaker one cannot hear, by following the
movements of the mouth. Some deaf people are expert at this.

lip-rounding *n.* Horizontal or vertical compression of the lips.
Where necessary, we distinguish **outer rounding** and **inner
rounding**. See **labialization** (sense 1).

liquid /'lɪkwɪd/ *n.* 1. A conventional label for any non-**nasal sonorant**. The class of liquids includes **lateral approximants** and most

rhotics, especially alveolar and post-alveolar taps, trills and approximants but occasionally certain others. Informally, this is the class of '*l*-sounds' and '*r*-sounds', and membership in doubtful cases is determined chiefly by phonological patterning. In the *SPE* **feature system**, liquids are [+consonantal, +vocalic]. 2. In Lass (1984), any member of a somewhat larger class including the traditional liquids plus the **glides**.

lisp /lɪsp/ *n.* 1. The use of the dental fricatives [θ] and [ð] in place of [s] and [z] in speech, either from a speech defect or as an affectation. 2. [*non-technical*] An impressionistic label applied to the speech of an individual when this is perceived as defective, affected or childish. *Adj.* **lisping**; *v.* **lisp**.

loan translation /'ləʊn trænsleɪʃn̩/ *n.* See **calque**.

loan word *n.* A word which has been copied into a language from another language, as a result of contact, such as French *weekend*, *jogging* and *strip-tease*, all loans from English.

local determinacy /ləʊkəl dɪ'tɜːmɪnəsi/ *n.* A possible **criterion for phonological analysis** by which it must be possible to assign a phone to a phoneme unambiguously by considering only its phonetic form and its phonetic environment: one aspect of **biuniqueness**. Chomsky (1964).

locality /ləʊ'kælɪti/ *n.* Any of various suggested constraints restricting some phonological process to some specified linear domain; the domain in question may be the immediately adjacent segments, a syllable or something else.

local ordering *n.* An elaborate **rule-ordering** hypothesis developed by Stephen Anderson in a series of works, notably Anderson (1974). Abandoning the **Linear Ordering Hypothesis**, local ordering holds that every pair of rules which can possibly interact must be related by exactly one of three types of ordering constraint: (1) an **across-the-board constraint**, (2) a constraint that two rules apply in the 'unmarked order' (i.e., **feeding order** or **counterbleeding order**, defined in terms of an individual derivation), or (3) a **contingent ordering constraint**. Cf. **partial ordering**.

locus /'ləʊkəs/ *n.* In a **sound spectrogram**, the apparent point of origin for a group of **formants**. All the formants of a particular vowel will curve so as to point at the same frequency in an adjoining consonant; this frequency is the locus.

Lombard effect /ˈlɒmbɑːd/ *n.* The tendency of speakers in a noisy environment to adjust the level of their speech to compensate for reduced feedback.

long /lɒŋ/ *adj.* 1. (of a segment) Having a duration which is greater than that of another, similar, segment, especially when the difference is contrastive. See examples under **length**. Ant. **short** (sense 1). 2. A binary **distinctive feature** sometimes invoked to represent contrasts of length, a renaming of the **length** feature of *SPE*. 3. In the **Lindau feature system**, a **distinctive feature** invoked to treat distinctions of vowel duration, with the possible values *short*, *long* and *overlong*, no more than two of which are said to be used by any one language. 4. See **tense** (sense 4).

long component *n.* In some **American Structuralist** phonology, a phonological element which is realized on two or more consecutive segments. Developed chiefly by Zellig Harris (1944, 1951), the long component represents the same idea as the **prosody** of **Prosodic Analysis**, but is more severely constrained in applicability: in particular, only contrastive elements may be so represented, and not purely phonetic ones. See Sommerstein (1977: 56–57) or Fischer-Jørgensen (1975: 99–102) for an account.

loop /luːp/ *n.* In some versions of **Lexical Phonology**, an analytical device by which a representation at some level of a derivation may be fed back into an earlier level. Mohanan (1982).

loss /lɒs/ *n.* A phonological change in which a segment disappears from a word or from a whole class of words, such as the disappearance of initial [k] in English words like *knot* and *know*. See also **rule loss**.

loss of the conditioning factor /ˈfæktə/ *n.* Any phonological change in which, as a result of the disappearance of a phonological environment which had previously induced an allophonic variation in some phoneme, the allophones involved become separate phonemes: a common type of **split**. For example, in several older Germanic languages, /u/ had a fronted allophone [y] when the following syllable contained [i] or [j]; when some instances of the conditioning [i] or [j] were lost, /u/ split into two phonemes /u/ and /y/.

loudness /ˈlaʊdnəs/ *n.* The perceptual correlate of the acoustic **intensity** of a sound. See **subglottal pressure**.

low /ləʊ/ *adj.* 1. (of a vowel) Articulated with the highest point of the tongue more or less maximally distant from the roof of the mouth, such as [a]. 2. In the *SPE* **feature system**, a **distinctive feature** defined as 'articulated with the body of the tongue below the neutral position'. Low vowels and pharyngeal consonants are [+low]; other segments are [–low].

lowered-larynx voice /ləʊəd 'lærɪŋks/ *n.* The **voice quality** in which the larynx is held in an unusually low position throughout speech, typically producing a noticeably low pitch of the voice. Cf. **raised-larynx voice**.

Lower Exit Principle /ləʊər 'eksɪt/ *n.* A putative principle governing the movement of low vowels during **vowel shifts**. It says: in chain shifting, low non-peripheral vowels become peripheral. Labov (1994: 280).

lower-high *adj.* In some descriptions, a label applied to a vowel which is not quite maximally high, such as the vowel of *pit*.

lowering *n.* Any phonological process in which a vowel or diphthong comes to be articulated with the tongue body in a lower position than is historically or underlyingly the case. *Adj.* **lowered**. Ant. **raising**.

low fall *n.* A **contour tone** whose pitch begins low and falls further.

low key *n.* The use by an individual of a lower than normal part of the **pitch range** in order to achieve some special effect. Ant. **high key**.

low-level rule *n.* A rule affecting only the minor phonetic details of the pronunciation of a form. The notion is not well defined.

low-mid *adj.* (also **half-open**, **open-mid**) The second-lowest of the four vowel heights distinguished in the **cardinal vowel system**. The vowels [ɛ] and [ɔ], among others, are low-mid. NOTE: The IPA now recommends the term 'open-mid'.

low tone *n.* A **tone** in a **tone language** which is normally realized with a lower **pitch** than other tones. Ant. **high tone**.

low vowel *n.* In the **Williamson feature system**, one of the five possible values of the feature **stricture**.

LPD /el piː 'diː/ *n.* (in full, the *Longman Pronunciation Dictionary*) The most comprehensive and up-to-date pronouncing dictionary of both British and American English, edited by John Wells (1990a).

ludling /'lʌdlɪŋ/ *n.* See **language game**.

lungs /lʌŋz/ *n. pl.* A pair of spongy, saclike organs located within the chest and playing a vital role in respiration and in providing a **pulmonic airstream** for speech.

Lyman's Law /'laɪmən/ *n.* A phonological process in Japanese by which the voicing induced by *rendaku* is cancelled when the second element contains a voiced obstruent: thus, *kami* 'god' + *kaze* 'wind' yields *kamikaze* 'divine wind', in place of **kamigaze*, because of the /z/ in *kaze*.

M

m In **Metrical Phonology**, a symbol sometimes used in metrical trees for labelling a **phonological word**, or **mot**.

Machine-Readable Phonemic Alphabet /məʃiːn riːdəbl fənetɪk 'ælfəbet/ *n.* (**MRPA**). A phonemic transcription of English (RP) in which every phoneme is represented by a symbol or combination of symbols available on an ordinary keyboard, such as /aa/ for /ɑː/ and /@/ for /ɔː/. The system, designed to be machine-readable, was devised by the Centre for Speech Technology Research at the University of Edinburgh. Terry *et al.* (1986).

macron /'mækrən/ *n.* The diacritic ¯, used for various purposes in various orthographies and transcriptions. It was originally used in classical scansion to mark a long syllable, and it is used in English scansion to mark a stressed syllable. Many English dictionaries have used the macron to mark a 'long' (tense) vowel; this device was used in *SPE* but is not usual in linguistic work. The macron has been used in the IPA to denote a high level tone; since 1989 it officially marks a mid level tone. Other linguistic uses are sporadic and varied; see Pullum and Ladusaw (1986). Cf. **breve**. Greek *makron*, neuter of *makros* 'large'.

macrophoneme /'mækrəfəʊniːm/ *n.* [*obsolete*] An old term for **phoneme**. Cf. **microphoneme**. Twaddell (1935).

Magic Licensing /mædʒɪk 'laɪsənsɪŋ/ *n.* An as yet unexplicated device invoked in **Government and Charm Phonology** to account for the existence of *s* + C onsets, apparently prohibited by the principles of the framework. Kaye (1991–1992).

Main Line accent /meɪn laɪn 'æksənt/ *n.* [*non-technical*] A name sometimes given to a certain sort of American accent, associated particularly with expensive and prestigious private preparatory schools and characterized by marked anglicizing tendencies. From *Main Line*, a nickname given to the fashionable suburban area west of Philadelphia, reflecting the presence there of a major railway line.

mainstream RP /'meɪnstriːm/ *n.* In the classification of Wells (1982, 2: 279ff.), the most typical, most central, least distinctive varieties of **Received Pronunciation**, associated chiefly with well-educated middle-class speakers in England and distinguished from **U-RP**, **adoptive RP** and **near-RP**. This is equivalent to Gimson's **general RP**.

Main Stress Rule /meɪn/ *n.* (**MSR**) The rule proposed by Chomsky and Halle (1968) as the principal rule determining stress in English lexical items. A preliminary formulation (p. 35) is

$$V \rightarrow [1 \text{ stress}] \ / \ X\_\_C_0(W) \ / \ \_\_(\{+\text{affix}, \acute{\Sigma}\})]$$

where W is a weak cluster, C_0 is a string of zero or more consonants, $\acute{\Sigma}$ is a syllable of the form C_0VC_0 (with [1 stress] on V), and *X* does not contain a # boundary internally. After much elaboration, the final version on p. 240 is almost unspeakably complicated. The **Primary Stress Rule** and the **English Stress Rule** represent later versions of the MSR.

maintainability /meɪnteɪnə'bɪlɪti/ *n.* (also **prolongability**) The capacity of an **articulation** (sense 2) to be held for some considerable length of time. This property is associated with all segment types except **glides**, **taps** and **flaps**. Ant. **non-maintainability**.

maintenance of contrast /'meɪntənəns/ *n.* See **semantic transparency**.

major articulator /'meɪdʒə/ *n.* In the **Articulator Model** of **feature geometry**, that articulator which, in a **coarticulated** segment, is viewed as making the primary contribution to the articulation, such as the back of the tongue in [kʷ]. Cf. **minor articulator**.

major-class feature /'meɪdʒə klɑːs/ *n.* Any **distinctive feature** invoked to divide segments into 'major classes', such as **obstruents**, **sonorants**, **vowels**, **nasals**, **liquids** and **glides**. The *SPE* **feature system** uses three such features: **sonorant**, **vocalic** and **consonantal**. The later features **syllabic** and **obstruent** are also of this type.

major pause *n.* See **phonological phrase boundary**.

malapropism /'mæləprəpɪzm̩/ *n.* (also **catachresis**) An error in which an intended word is replaced by a quite different one of similar sound, such as the use of *facilities* for *faculties*, *prostrate* for *prostate* or *epitaph* for *epithet*; a famous literary example is Dogberry's *Comparisons are odorous*. From *Mrs Malaprop*, a character in Sheridan's *The Rivals* much given to such usages, from French *mal à propos* 'inappropriate'.

mandible /'mændɪbl/ *n.* The lower jaw.

mandibular setting /mæn'dɪbjələ/ *n.* Any of various postures which may be assumed by the lower jaw during speech. English, for example, is generally characterized by a close jaw position (so much so that it has been described as 'a language designed for pipe smokers'), while the languages of India are typified by a very open jaw position. See Honikman (1964).

manner of articulation /'mænə/ *n.* In the conventional phonetic system for classifying **consonants** (sense 1), the parameter which treats differences in the activity of the vocal organs. The IPA recognizes the following manners: **plosive**, **affricate**, **fricative**, **nasal**, **trill**, **tap**, **flap**, **lateral fricative**, **lateral approximant** (commonly **lateral**), **approximant**. Though highly convenient in practice, this system suffers from a failure to distinguish the **lateral/median** contrast as a separate parameter, and perhaps also from a failure to distinguish the **nasal/oral** contrast as well. NOTE: Some analysts treat **airstream mechanism** and **phonation type** as aspects of manner, while others regard these as independent parameters.

manner-of-articulation feature *n.* In the *SPE* feature system, either of the features **continuant** and **delayed release**.

margin /'mɑːdʒɪn/ *n.* In syllable structure, a cover term for the **onset** or the **coda**. Hockett (1955).

margin of security /sɪ'kjʊərɪti/ *n.* The degree to which phonemes are phonetically separated within **phonological space**. Martinet (1952).

mark /mɑːk/ *n.* In a **privative opposition**, the feature whose presence or absence is responsible for the opposition: [nasal] for /m/~/b/, [voice] for /b/~/p/, etc.

marked form /'mɑːkt fɔːm/ *n.* 1. In **Prague School** phonology, that member of a **privative opposition** which bears the **mark**. 2. That one of two (or rarely more) contrasting segments which, on any of various grounds, may be regarded as less 'natural' than its unmarked counterpart. Lass (1984: 132) lists the following criteria, not all of which he regards as equally valid. A marked segment (1) is less common cross-linguistically; (2) tends not to appear in positions of neutralization; (3) has lower text-frequency; (4) is later in appearing in language acquisition; (5) tends in cases of phonemic **merger** to be absorbed into its unmarked partner; (6) tends to be less stable historically; (7) tends to imply the existence of its unmarked counterpart. 3. More generally, any linguistic form which is distinguished from an unmarked counterpart on any of various grounds, such as possessing additional morphological material (*hostess* vs. *host*), more narrowly circumscribed use (*brethren* vs. *brothers*; exceptional vs. normal intonation pattern), or lower frequency in languages generally (ejective consonants, nasal vowels). *Abstr. n.* **markedness**. Ant. **unmarked form**. The terms 'marked' and 'unmarked' were introduced by Nikolai Trubetzkoy and Roman Jakobson in the context of the **Prague School**, but the idea goes back into the nineteenth century.

markedness rule /'mɑːkɪdnəs/ *n.* A rule which declares the **unmarked** value of a feature or segment, such as the rule which asserts that a non-high vowel has the same value for [round] that it has for [back].

markedness theory /'θɪəri/ *n.* Any of several approaches which attempt to establish a systematic, principled and (usually) universal distinction between **marked** and **unmarked forms**. The best-known attempt is that in the last chapter of Chomsky and Halle (1968), which argues that, for every feature in every possible environment, one value will be unmarked. This *SPE* approach is not usually regarded as satisfactory. See Lass and Anderson (1975: appendix) for a substantial critique.

marked order of application *n.* In a framework employing **ordered rules**, an ordering of two rules in a particular derivation which prevents maximal use of the rules: **bleeding order** or **counterfeeding order**. Kiparsky (1968).

marked value *n.* In **markedness theory**, that value of a **distinctive feature** which is less natural in a given context and hence not provided by default by a **marking convention**. Ant. **unmarked value**.

marker /'mɑːkə/ *n.* 1. Any piece of morphological material with an identifiable function: for example, English *-s* is a marker of plurality. 2. (also **index**) Any characteristic of speech which conveys information about the personal characteristics of the speaker: sex, age, social class, mood, etc. Laver and Trudgill (1979). 3. A **variable** which lacks a high degree of social awareness but which nevertheless shows consistent stylistic and social stratification. Cf. **stereotype**, **indicator**. Labov (1994: 78).

marking convention /'mɑːkɪŋ kənvenʃən/ *n.* A **markedness rule**, often particularly one expressed in the framework of Chomsky and Halle (1968), such as the following (*u* = 'unmarked'):

$$[u \text{ voice}] \rightarrow [+\text{voice}] \ / \ \left[\begin{array}{c} \underline{} \\ +\text{son} \end{array} \right]$$

masculine rhyme /ˈmæskjəlɪn/ *n.* A **rhyme** between two words which are stressed on the final syllable: *keen/mean*; *rain/remain*; *interfere/appear*. Cf. **feminine rhyme**.

masking /ˈmɑːskɪŋ/ *n.* Interference from background noise which reduces a listener's ability to discriminate speech sounds.

matched-guise technique /mætʃt ˈgaɪz tekniːk/ *n.* An experimental technique used to elicit unconscious social evaluations of speech. Subjects are asked to express opinions about strangers whose voices are heard in recordings; these recordings involve certain individuals speaking the same text more than once using different accents or languages.

matrix /ˈmeɪtrɪks/ *n.* 1. See **feature matrix**. 2. See **classificatory matrix**.

maximally undifferentiated segment *n.* In some analyses, a segment involving no **oral gesture** at all. Thus, [h] and [ʔ] are the maximally undifferentiated fricative and stop, respectively. Lass (1984: 115).

Maximal Onset Principle /ˈmæksɪməl/ *n.* A putative universal principle of syllabification. It says: a consonant which may in principle occupy either rhyme or onset position will occupy onset position. Selkirk (1982).

Maximization of Association, Principle of /mæksɪmaɪˈzeɪʃn̩/ *n.* In some versions of **Autosegmental Phonology**, a principle constraining association lines. It says: associate as many different phonemic melody elements as possible. McCarthy and Prince (1986).

maximum ease of articulation /mæksɪməm ˈiːz/ *n.* A somewhat ill-defined principle sometimes invoked to account for phonological change. One version is: the speaker should articulate in a manner which makes the fewest demands upon the activity of the vocal tract. Carried to extremes, of course, this principle would render speech incomprehensible, and it is counteracted by the next entry.

maximum perceptual separation *n.* A somewhat ill-defined principle sometimes invoked to account for phonological change.

One version is: the speaker should articulate in such a manner that contrasting segments are as perceptually distinct as possible.

McGurk effect /məˈgɜːk ɪfekt/ *n.* The phenomenon in which hearers who see a video of a head saying [ga], [ga], [ga], synchronized with a recording of [ba], [ba], [ba], actually perceive [da], [da], [da].

mean-mid /miːn ˈmɪd/ *adj.* (of a vowel) Exactly midway between maximally **high** and maximally **low**.

Mechanical Principle /məˈkænɪkəl/ *n.* A putative principle governing the course of phonological change. It says: the relative progress of a sound change is determined by phonetic factors alone, without regard to the preservation of meaning. In other words, the principle holds that **avoidance of merger** is not, in general, a primary force in dictating the course of sound change. This is one aspect of the **Neogrammarian Hypothesis**; cf. the **Regularity Principle**. Labov (1994: 603).

media /ˈmiːdiə/ *n.* (pl. **mediae** /ˈmiːdiiː/) [*obsolete*] The term used for a **voiced plosive**, such as [b], [d] or [g], in nineteenth-century philological works. Cf. **tenuis**, **aspirata**. Latin *media* (*littera*) 'halfway letter'; the voiced plosives were regarded as lying halfway between the voiceless plosives and the fricatives.

medial phase /ˈmiːdiəl/ *n.* In the description of a segment in time, the central part of the articulation, during which the target constriction is reached (and possibly held). Cf. **onset phase**, **offset phase**. Laver (1994: 133).

medial position *n.* The position of a segment which is neither at the beginning nor at the end of a word.

median /ˈmiːdiən/ *adj.* 1. Lying along the lengthwise vertical (**sagittal**) plane through the middle of the oral cavity. 2. (also **central**) (of an articulation) Involving either a complete obstruction of the oral cavity or air flow along the median line; non-**lateral**. Ant. **lateral**.

median release *n.* (also **median plosion**, **central release**) A type of **release** for a **plosive** in which all contact is broken off between the articulators, as commonly occurs with both plosives in *bookie*. Cf. **lateral release**, **nasal release**.

mediated relation /ˈmiːdieɪtɪd/ *n.* An indirect relation. For example, the various surface phonetic realizations of a single morpheme are not related directly; instead, their relation is mediated by their common underlying form. Such mediated relations are of central importance in all versions of **generative phonology**.

Meeussen's rule /'meysən/ *n.* A process, found in many Bantu languages, by which the second of two adjacent high tones becomes low.

mel /mel/ *n.* The unit of perceived **pitch**. On a standard scale, 1,000 mels is defined as the pitch of a 1,000-Hertz tone. A pitch of 500 mels is then one which sounds exactly half as high as this, which turns out to represent a tone of about 400 Hz, and a pitch of 2,000 mels is one which is twice as high, approximately 4,000 Hz. (The relation between **frequency** and pitch is far from linear.) Stevens *et al.* (1937).

mellow /'meləʊ/ *adj.* In the **Jakobson–Halle feature system**, a **distinctive feature** defined as 'exhibiting little or no noise in the spectrum'. All segments are [mellow] except for the 'noisy' fricatives like [f v s z]. Ant. **strident** (sense 3).

melodic overwriting /məlɒdɪk 'əʊvəraɪtɪŋ/ *n.* The replacement of one segment by another, in the context of a particular **template**, by a phonological rule. McCarthy and Prince (1986).

melodic tier *n.* See **segmental tier**.

melodic tone *n.* See **contour tone**.

melody /'melədi/ *n.* 1. The sequence of pitch values in a speaker's voice within a particular utterance. 2. In **Autosegmental Phonology**, the material on the **segmental** ('phonemic') **tier**. 3. Any single segment on this tier (or, in other frameworks, any single segment). 4. Broadly, the material on *any* tier.

member (of a phoneme) /'membə/ *n.* A synonym for **allophone** in some versions of **classical phonology**, notably in the work of Daniel Jones.

merger /'mɜːdʒə/ *n.* (also **dephonologization**) Any phonological change in which a previously existing contrast between two or more phonemes is lost. A merger applying only in restricted contexts, thus introducing a **neutralization**, is a **conditioned merger**; one which applies in all contexts, thus reducing the number of phonemes in the language, is an **unconditioned merger**. Labov (1994: 321–323) recognizes three mechanisms by which mergers may occur: in *merger by approximation*, the phonemes gradually become phonetically more similar until they are non-distinct; in *merger by transfer*, lexical items are transferred from one phonemic class to another until one class is empty; in *merger by expansion*, the contrast is abruptly abandoned, and the phonological space formerly occupied by the separate phonemes is reassigned to the single new phoneme. See **near-merger**, **reversal of merger**. *Adj.* **merged**. Ant. **split**.

metacondition /'metəkəndɪʃn̩/ *n.* Any of various **criteria for phonological analysis**, but particularly a very general one such as simplicity, economy or generality.

metanalysis /metə'næləsɪs/ *n.* (also **juncture displacement**) A type of morphological reanalysis in which segments are transferred from the end of a word or morpheme to the beginning of a following one or vice versa. Familiar English examples include the development of earlier *a naddre*, *a napron*, *a noumpere*, *an ewt*, *an ekename* into modern *an adder*, *an apron*, *an umpire*, *a newt*, *a nickname* and the non-standard change of *another* into *a nother*, as in *a whole nother story*. Cf. **pullet surprise**, **folk etymology**. Jespersen (1914).

metaphone /'metəfəʊn/ *n.* Either of two or more **phonemes** which are in **free variation** in a particular word, such as /iː/ and /ai/ in *either* or /iː/ and /e/ in *economics*. Palmer (1930).

metaphony /me'tæfəni/ *n.* 1. A synonym for **umlaut**. 2. Any type of assimilation between non-adjacent vowels in a word, including **vowel harmony** and **umlaut**. The term is applied both to the historical change and to the resulting alternations. 3. A label applied in a quite bewildering fashion to a wide range of historical changes and synchronic alternations involving vowels, including at least **umlaut**, **vowel harmony**, **ablaut** and such vowel alternations as those in Spanish verbs like *poder* 'be able', *puedo* 'I can'. *Adj.* **metaphonic** /metə'fɒnɪk/. NOTE: The term was originally coined in sense 1, but it is perhaps preferable to restrict it to sense 2, as recommended by Lass (1984: 171–172).

metarule /'metəruːl/ *n.* A high-level schema which collapses two or more individual but related rules into a single statement, possibly in a non-standard notation, in order to extract a generalization. For example, the metarule $[V, +\text{height}^n] \rightarrow [+\text{height}^{n-1}]$ uses non-standard notation to express a general process of vowel lowering. Lass (1976: 70).

metathesis /me'tæθəsɪs/ *n.* 1. Narrowly, an exchange in the positions of two segments in a word, either as a historical change or as a synchronic rule. For example, Latin *miraculum* 'miracle' should, by regular phonological change, have yielded Spanish *miraglo, but the actual form is *milagro*, with metathesis of the liquids. The collective derivative of modern Hebrew *seder* 'order' is underlyingly *hit+sadr+ut*, but the surface form is *histadrut* 'organization', with metathesis of *t* and *s*. 2. Broadly, any change in the linear ordering of segments in a word, including also cases like the development of Latin *crocodilus* 'crocodile' into Spanish *cocodrilo*, with metathesis of the *r*. 3. The form resulting from such a process. *V.* **metathesize** /me'tæθəsaɪz/; *adj.* **metathetical** /metə'θetɪkəl/.

metatony /mə'tætəni/ *n.* Especially in Baltic and Slavic languages, any of various processes in which a **pitch accent** or **stress accent** undergoes a change in nature or position. *Adj.* **metatonic**. Saussure (1894).

metre /'miːtə/ *n.* (also **meter**) 1. The rhythmical arrangement of syllables in verse, according to the number and types of **feet** used. For example, *iambic pentameter* employs lines of five feet, each foot an iamb. 2. The rhythm of ordinary speech, especially in a particular analysis. *Adj.* **metrical** /'metrɪkəl/.

metrical constituency /kən'stɪtjuənsi/ *n.* The organization of speech into rhythmic units larger than the syllable, particularly **feet**.

metrical grid *n.* In **Metrical Phonology**, a style of graphical representation which dispenses with **metrical trees**. Instead, a linguistic form is represented as a series of ever-larger constituents, with main stresses at each level being marked by asterisks, as in Figure M1.

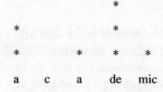

Figure M1 A metrical grid

Metrical Phonology *n.* **(MP)** A major contemporary theory of phonology, introduced by Liberman and Prince (1977) and much developed since. MP is designed primarily to deal with rhythmic (prosodic) phenomena, particularly stress, and it has often focused on the **foot** as a phonological unit. Two major notations exist, the **metrical tree** and the **metrical grid**. See Goldsmith (1990: ch. 4) for a brief introduction, Hogg and McCully (1987) for a more detailed one.

metrical tree /triː/ *n.* (also **arboreal framework**) In **Metrical Phonology**, a type of graphical representation in which the metrical structure of a linguistic form is analysed into smaller and larger constituents. Figure M2 shows an example using the **s/w notation**.

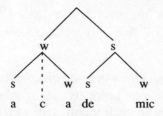

Figure M2 A metrical tree

microphoneme /ˈmaɪkrəfəʊniːm/ *n.* [*obsolete*] An individual occurrence of a **phoneme** in a particular word in a position in which it contrasts with other phonemes. Cf. **macrophoneme**. Twaddell (1935):

mid /mɪd/ *adj.* 1. (of a vowel) Neither **high** nor **low**. Mid vowels are conventionally divided into **high-mid** and **low-mid**. 2. A **distinctive feature** introduced to permit four vowel heights to be defined with only two binary features: [+high, –mid], [+high, +mid], [–high, +mid], [–high, –mid]. This feature is a **diacritic feature** in sense 2, and, though widely used, it has unpalatable consequences for defining natural classes. Wang (1968).

mid-Atlantic accent /mɪdətˈlæntɪk/ *n.* An accent of English which appears to combine features of British and North American accents.

mid-closure *n.* A binary **distinctive feature** proposed by Fant (1971). Plosives, affricates, nasals, laterals and trills are [+mid-closure] (that is, all segments with a **median** closure of the vocal tract), while other segments are [–mid-closure]. Fant argues that the use of this feature would make the feature **consonantal** redundant. Cf. **central closure**.

middle ear /'mɪdl̩/ *n*. One of the three divisions of the ear, an air-filled cavity connected to the **outer ear** by the **eardrum** and to the **inner ear** by the **oval window** and containing the **auditory ossicles**.

Mid Exit Principle /'eksɪt/ *n*. A putative principle governing the raising of mid vowels. It says: in chain shifts, peripheral vowels rising from mid to high position develop inglides (centring glides). Cf. **Lower Exit Principle**, **Upper Exit Principle**. Labov (1994: 284).

mid register *n*. (also **mid voice**) In a traditional conception, one of the three speech **registers**, characterized by vocal fold tension and pitch intermediate between those typical of **chest register** and **falsetto**.

minimal distinctness /mɪnɪməl dɪ'stɪŋktnəs/ *n*. The relation between two segments which differ only in one **feature specification**. *Adj.* **minimally distinct**.

minimal pair /pɛə/ *n*. Two words of distinct meaning which exhibit different segments at one point but identical segments at all other points. The existence of such a pair demonstrates conclusively that the two segments which are different must belong to different phonemes. For example, in English, *fat* [fæt] and *vat* [væt] constitute a minimal pair for [f] and [v], as do also *rifle* ['raɪfl̩] and *rival* ['raɪvl̩], and also *leaf* [liːf] and *leave* [liːv]. Any one of these pairs is sufficient to show that English [f] and [v] must be assigned to different phonemes (conventionally, /f/ and /v/, respectively); each is said to be a minimal pair for /f/ and /v/. A group of three or more words showing a contrast among three or more segments is a **minimal set** – hence *sum*, *sun* and *sung* are a minimal set for /m/, /n/, /ŋ/. Every such set illustrates a **minimal contrast** (a contrast in one segment only).

minimal pair test /test/ *n*. A simple technique for finding out whether two phonetic types are contrastive: a native speaker is asked whether two words constituting a potential **minimal pair** are pronounced identically or differently. See Labov (1994: 353–356) for a detailed description.

minimal word *n*. In some languages, a lower limit upon the length of a lexical item or an inflected form. Some languages permit no words shorter than two moras, or two syllables, though grammatical words may sometimes be exceptional. See Kenstowicz (1994: 640–646).

minor articulator /ˈmaɪnə ɑːˈtɪkjəleɪtə/ _n._ In the **Articulator Model** of **feature geometry**, that articulator which, in a **coarticulated** segment, is viewed as making the secondary contribution to the articulation, such as the lips in [kʷ]. Cf. **major articulator**.

minor rule _n._ A rule which applies only to an arbitrary (and usually small) subset of the forms in a language. An English example is the rule that forms the past tenses of such verbs as _sit/sat_, _sing/sang_, _ring/rang_, _drink/drank_ and _stink/stank_. Lightner (1968), from earlier use in syntax.

mirror-image convention /ˈmɪrər ˈɪmɪdʒ/ _n._ An **abbreviatory convention** of the general form A → B // X ___ Y. This abbreviates the rules A → B / X ___ Y and A → B / Y ___ X, which have mirror-image environments. Cf. **neighbourhood convention**. Langacker (1969).

modal voice /ˈməʊdəl/ _n._ (also **modal register**) The most familiar type of **voicing**, in which the full glottis functions as a single unit, the **vocal folds** vibrate regularly with complete closure on each vibration, and there is no friction noise. Hollien (1974).

modular depotentiation /ˈmɒdjələ diːpətentʃiˈeɪʃn̩/ _n._ A putative type of phonological change in which a maximally strong segment obliged to undergo **fortition** is converted to the weakest segment in the system, as when Spanish [f] (regarded as maximally strong) > [h]. Foley (1977).

modulation /mɒdjəˈleɪʃn̩/ _n._ Systematic variation in the intensity and loudness of a segment (especially a voiced fricative) caused by the opening and closing of the glottis.

module /ˈmɒdjəl/ _n._ In some theories of linguistic structure, any one of several more-or-less independent components of the whole framework, such as the **phonological component** recognized in **classical generative phonology**.

molar _r_ /ˈməʊlə/ _n._ (also **bunched _r_**) A distinctive articulation used by many (not all) American speakers as their realization of the phoneme /r/, in which the tongue body is strongly retracted and bunched up, with the tip held low and well behind the lower teeth while the sides press against the upper molars; the lips are usually noticeably rounded. The resulting sound is perceptually almost indistinguishable from a retroflex approximant, which is the other principal American realization of /r/. Laver (1994: 302) describes this sound as a *voiced labial pre-velar approximant with tongue-tip retraction* and proposes the phonetic symbol [Ψ]. Uldall (1958).

moneme /'mɒniːm/ *n.* A rare synonym for **morpheme**. Martinet (1960).

monometer /mə'nɒmɪtə/ *n.* A line of verse consisting of a single metrical **foot**.

monomoraic vowel /mɒnəmə'reɪɪk/ *n.* A short pure vowel. Cf. **bimoraic vowel, non-moraic vowel**. Hayes (1989).

monophone /'mɒnəfəʊn/ *n.* [*obsolete*] A **phoneme** exhibiting no significant **allophonic variation**. Jones (1950); attributed to H. E. Palmer.

monophonem(at)ic /mɒnəfə'niːmɪk/ /-niː'mætɪk/ *adj.* Constituting a single **phoneme**. The term is commonly applied to **affricates** and **diphthongs** when these are regarded as single phonemes.

monophthong /mə'nɒfθɒŋ/ *n.* A **pure vowel**. Cf. **diphthong, triphthong, tetraphthong**. *Adj.* **monophthongal**.

monophthongization /mənɒfθɒŋaɪ'zeɪʃn̩/ *n.* Any phonological process in which a **diphthong** is converted into a **monophthong**. Examples include the change of Latin /au/ and /ae/ into /ɔ/ and /ɛ/, respectively. *V.* **monophthongize**.

monosegmental /mɒnəseg'mentəl/ *adj.* Consisting of a single segment. The label is applied to such phonetically complex segments as English [tʃ] and Kinyarwanda [tkw], which might in principle be analysed as sequences.

monosyllable /'mɒnəsɪləbəl/ *n.* A word consisting of a single **syllable**: *eat, dog, is, try, black, when, strength*. *Adj.* **monosyllabic** /mɒnəsɪ'læbɪk/. Cf. **disyllable, trisyllable, polysyllable**.

monosystemicism /mɒnəsɪ'stiːməsɪzm̩/ *n.* The analytical stance in which the entire set of phonological phenomena in a language is regarded as constituting a single integrated system. This stance is characteristic of most approaches to phonology. *Adj.* **monosystemic**. Cf. **polysystemicism**.

monovalent feature /mɒnə'veɪlənt/ *n.* See **unary feature**.

mora /'mɔːrə/ *n.* (pl. **moras** or **morae** /'mɔːriː/) (also **weight unit**) A phonological unit larger than a single segment but typically smaller than a syllable. In general, a **light syllable** consists of a single mora while a **heavy syllable** consists of two. The mora appears to be an important rhythmic element in some languages, such as Japanese and Ancient Greek, but is possibly of no relevance in others. Latin: 'pause'.

mora-timing *n.* The type of **rhythm** in which **moras** are produced at approximately regular intervals. A language in which the mora is the primary unit of rhythm, such as Japanese, is a **mora language**.

morph /mɔːf/ *n.* A piece of morphological material, consisting of a sequence of zero or more phonemes, considered *per se*, without any reference to its morphological status. A morph may represent a single morpheme, a sequence of two or more morphemes, a part of a morpheme, or no morpheme at all. For example, the Basque word *mendi* 'mountain' forms a locative plural *mendietan* 'in the mountains'; we can speak of the morph *-etan* occurring in this word without committing ourselves to any particular analysis of it. Hockett (1947).

morpheme /'mɔfiːm/ *n.* The minimal grammatical unit; the smallest unit which plays any part in morphology and which cannot be further decomposed except in phonological terms. A morpheme is an abstract unit which may or may not be realized by a fairly consistent stretch of phonological material. Morphemes may be classified as **free** or **bound**. *Adj.* **morphemic** /mɔː'fiːmɪk/. Cf. **morph**, **allomorph**. The term was introduced by Baudouin de Courtenay (1895); its use has varied considerably, but the modern sense was largely established by Bloomfield (1933).

morpheme alternant *n.* [*obsolete*] See **allomorph**.

morpheme boundary *n.* The division between one **morpheme** and a following morpheme, often represented by a **plus sign** (+), as when *sanity* is represented *sān + -ity*.

morpheme structure rule *n.* (also **morpheme structure condition**, **lexical redundancy rule**, **morphophonotactic rule**) A **phonotactic** constraint which is stated for single morphemes, rather than for entire words. For example, English has the constraint C → [+cor] / aʊ ___ for morphemes, but not for words: *endowment*, *cowboy*. Halle (1959).

morpholexical rule /mɔːfə'leksɪkəl/ *n.* (also **morphological rule**) A phonological rule whose conditioning cannot be stated in purely phonological terms, but which must appeal to some kind of grammatical information. Cf. **morphophonemic rule**. Bloomfield (1933).

morphological conditioning /mɔːfə'lɒdʒɪkəl/ *n.* See **grammatical conditioning**.

morphological rule *n.* 1. A rule pertaining to the organization of morphemes into words, with no phonological character. 2. See **readjustment rule**. Bierwisch (1967). 3. See **morpholexical rule**.

morphologization /mɔːfɒlədʒaɪˈzeɪʃn̩/ *n.* (also **compacting**) The fusion of independent elements into a single morphological form, such as the fusion of Latin phrases like *lenta mente* 'with slow mind' into single adverbs like Spanish *lentamente* and French *lentement* 'slowly'.

morphology /mɔːˈfɒlədʒi/ *n.* The branch of grammar dealing with the analysis of word structure, conventionally divided into **word formation** and **inflectional morphology**. See Matthews (1991), Bauer (1988), Spencer (1991) or Carstairs-McCarthy (1992) for introductions of increasing elaboration. *Adj.* **morphological**.

morphon /ˈmɔːfɒn/ *n.* In **Stratificational phonology**, one of the morphological elements serving as input to the phonological plane, roughly equivalent to the **allomorph**.

morphophoneme /mɔːfəˈfəʊniːm/ *n.* (also **morphoneme** /ˈmɔːfəniːm/) In some analyses, an abstract phonological unit which is realized as one of two or more different **phonemes** in varying conditions, often especially in **neutralization**. For example, German *Bund* 'union' (with final [t]) has genitive *Bundes* (with [d]); if these segments are assigned to separate phonemes /t/ and /d/ (which are elsewhere contrastive in German), then the final segment of *Bund* may be taken as a morphophoneme, notated T or //t//. Morphophonemes were widely invoked by the **Prague School** and by the **American Structuralists**. Coined by H. Ułaszyn, but popularized by Trubetzkoy and by Bloomfield (1939).

morphophonemic alternation /mɔːfəfəˈniːmɪk/ *n.* An alternation between phonemes in a particular position in a particular morpheme in varying contexts. Examples: the /p/~/b/ alternation in Turkish *kitap* 'book', dative *kitaba*; the /s/~/z/~/ɪz/ alternation in the English plural suffix (*cats*, *dogs*, *foxes*); the /k/~/s/ alternation in English *electric*, *electricity*.

morphophonemic rule *n.* (also **MP rule**, **morphophonological rule**) 1. Any rule which accounts for a **morphophonemic alternation**. 2. Especially in **Natural Generative Phonology**, any phonological rule which appeals to morphological information, including boundaries, other rules being termed **phonological rules** in a narrow sense.

morphophonology /mɔːfəfə'nɒlədʒi/ *n.* **(MP)** (also **morpho-phonemics** /mɔːfəfə'niːmɪks/, **morphonology** /mɔːfə'nɒlədʒi/) 1. The description of **morphophonemic alternations**. 2. This sense combined with the description of the phonological structure of morphemes (**morpheme-structure rules**). 3. [*obsolete*] The description of morpheme-structure rules alone. 4. [*obsolete*] The description of **internal sandhi**. 5. The description of morphophonemic alternations by means of **morphophonemes**. NOTE: The term was introduced by Trubetzkoy (1931) in sense 3, but was quickly extended to sense 2 by him. The term 'morphophonemics' was introduced by Bloomfield (1939) and used in sense 4. Some **American Structuralists** used this term in sense 5, such as Harris (1951). Nowadays the term is most widely used in sense 1, less commonly in sense 2.

morphophonotactic rule /mɔːfəfəʊnə'tæktɪk/ *n.* See **morpheme structure rule**.

Moscow School /'mɒskəʊ skuːl/ *n.* The name given to the phonological work done by a group of linguists based in Moscow since about 1920. See Fischer-Jørgensen (1975: 331–335).

mot /məʊ/ *n.* (also **prosodic word**) A synonym for **phonological word**, preferred in **Metrical Phonology**. French: 'word'.

motor theory of speech perception /'məʊtə θɪəri/ *n.* The proposal that a hearer recognizes speech sounds by 'empathically' referring them to the organic mechanism of their production. See Kenstowicz (1994: 185–191) for an introduction, Liberman (1957) and Liberman *et al.* (1963, 1967) for a defence of this interpretation, Liberman and Mattingly (1985) for a revision and Lane (1965) for a critical view. Liberman *et al.* (1963).

MP 1. See **morphophonology**. 2. See **Metric Phonology**.

MP rule /em 'piː/ *n.* See **morphophonemic rule**.

MRPA /em ɑː piː 'eɪ/ See **Machine-Readable Phonemic Alphabet**.

mu /mjuː/ *n.* The symbol μ, used for a **mora** in phonological representations.

multilateral opposition /mʌltɪ'lætərəl/ *n.* In **Prague School** phonology, the relation among three or more segments which contrast along a single dimension, such as that among English /p t k/, which contrast solely in **place of articulation**. Cf. **bilateral opposition**.

multilinear phonology /mʌltɪˈlɪniə/ *adj*. A more accurate but little-used synonym for **non-linear phonology**. Roca (1994).

multi-parametric concept /mʌltɪpærəˈmetrɪk/ *n*. Any concept for a full understanding of which we have to appeal to more than one type of information. For example, **vowel height** involves not only the objective position of the tongue but also acoustic and perceptual properties.

multivalued feature /mʌltɪˈvæljuːd/ *n*. (also **multivalent feature** /mʌltɪˈveɪlənt/, **multinary feature** /mʌlˈtɪnəri/, **n-ary feature**) A **distinctive feature** which can assume any one of three or more values. For example, some analyses take **vowel height** to be a feature with four values ranging from 1 (low) to 4 (high). Cf. **binary feature**, **unary feature**.

murmur /ˈmɜːmə/ *n*. 1. See **whispery voice**. Pandit (1957); popularized by Peter Ladefoged. 2. See **murmured** (sense 2). 3. A **binary distinctive feature** proposed by Lass (1984: 90): **whispery-voiced** segments are [+murmur]; all other segments are [−murmur].

murmured *adj*. 1. (of a segment) Articulated with **whispery voice**. 2. (also **murmur**) In the **Ladefoged** and **Williamson feature systems**, one of the five possible values of the feature **voice** (Ladefoged) or **glottal state** (Williamson).

mutation /mjuːˈteɪʃn̩/ *n*. 1. Any phonological change in which a segment changes its quality under the influence of nearby segments, such as **umlaut**. 2. (also **initial mutation**) Any of various phenomena occurring in certain languages, notably the Celtic languages like Irish and Welsh, in which certain classes of consonants in certain positions (in the Celtic languages, morpheme-initial position) undergo systematic phonological modification in specified grammatical or lexical environments. The two major mutations of Irish are conventionally called **lenition** and **eclipsis** (sense 1); the three major mutations of Welsh are called **soft mutation**, **nasal mutation** and **aspirate mutation**, though Welsh also exhibits a quite distinct process called **hard mutation**. Historically, the Celtic mutations were phonologically conditioned, but phonological loss of the conditioning factors has converted them to grammatically or lexically conditioned alternations. *V.* **mutate**.

mute *e* /mjuːt ˈiː/ *n*. See *e muet*.

mutual assimilation /ˈmjuːtʃuəl/ *n*. Any instance of **assimilation** in which each of two (or more) segments is assimilated to the other.

Examples: modern Greek *tin* 'the' (acc.) + *porta* 'door' > *tim borta*; common Basque *iduri* 'seem' > Zuberoan Basque *üdürü*.

mutual bleeding *n.* The relation between two rules such that, if either one precedes the other in a particular **rule ordering**, it will **bleed** the other (remove some phonological forms from its domain).

myoelastic theory of voice production /maɪəʊɪ'læstɪk/ *n.* See **aerodynamic myoelastic theory of phonation**.

N

N A cover symbol for **nucleus** in syllable structure.

narial /nɛɪriəl/ *adj.* (also, erroneously, **nareal**) 1. Pertaining to the nostrils (nares). 2. (of an articulation) Articulated with the primary constriction at the nostrils. Catford (1977, 1988) points out that the voiceless nasals of Welsh and Burmese could plausibly be described as 'narial approximants', but the term is not in use. Narial fricatives are also possible, but are not known to occur in any language.

narrow /ˈnærəʊ/ *adj.* 1. [*obsolete*] (of a vowel) **Tense**. Sweet (1877). 2. (of a vowel) Articulated without the use of an **advanced tongue root**. See under **ATR**. Ladefoged (1975). 3. (of a constriction or a segment) Involving a comparatively small passageway for air flow. Ant. (all senses) **wide**.

narrow-band spectrogram *n.* A **sound spectrogram** recorded using filters with narrow frequency bands and correspondingly slow sampling times. Such a spectrogram shows the **formants** very clearly but smears the effects of rapid changes in the articulatory configuration. Cf. **wide-band spectrogram**.

narrow diphthong *n.* A **diphthong** whose initial and final elements differ little in tongue height, such as [eɪ] or [ʊw]. Ant. **wide diphthong**.

narrowed *adj.* In the **Williamson feature system**, one of the possible values of the feature **expansion**.

narrow focus /ˈfəʊkəs/ *n.* In **intonation**, the case in which only some part of the intonation-group is in focus. See Cruttenden (1986). Ant. **broad focus**.

narrow transcription *n.* A **transcription** which includes more phonetic detail than is necessary to distinguish phonemes: a **phonetic transcription**.

***n*-ary feature** /ˈenəri/ *n.* See **multivalued feature**.

nasal /ˈneɪzəl/ 1. *adj.* Pertaining to the **nasal cavity**. 2. *adj.* (of a segment or of a voice quality) Articulated with the **velum** lowered, allowing air to pass out through the nasal cavity. 3. *n.* A segment so articulated, most usually a **nasal stop** such as [m] or [n], in which there is a complete occlusion in the mouth. 4. *adj.* In the **Jakobson–Halle feature system**, a **distinctive feature** defined as 'exhibiting additional formants and less intensity in existing formants' and interpreted as representing the coupling of the nasal cavity. Ant. **oral** (sense 3). 5. *adj.* (**nas**) In the *SPE* **feature system**, a **distinctive feature** defined as 'involving a lowered velum'. Ant. **non-nasal**. 6. *adj.* In the **Lindau feature system**, a **distinctive feature** invoked to treat distinctions of nasality in vowels, with the possible values *nasalized* and *non-nasalized*. 7. See **nasality** (sense 2). *Abstr. n.* (all senses) **nasality**.

nasal approximant *n.* 1. An **approximant** articulated with simultaneous air flow through the lowered velum; a nasalized approximant. 2. See **narial**.

nasal cavity *n.* The large cavity lying above the **oral cavity** and connecting the nostrils to the pharynx. When the velum is raised, the nasal cavity is closed off from the rest of the vocal tract.

nasal click *n.* A **click** which is articulated with a simultaneous pulmonic egressive airstream flowing through the lowered velum.

nasal endoscopy /ɪnˈdɒskəpi/ *n.* A technique for inspecting the upper surface of the **velum** during speech by means of an instrument inserted through the nose.

nasal fricative *n.* A **fricative** articulated with simultaneous air flow through the lowered velum; a nasalized fricative.

nasal infix *n.* An **infix** of the form -*n*- which appears in verbal roots in older Indo-European languages: Latin *pingere* 'paint', supine *pictum* (< PIE **peig-*); *tangere* 'touch', *tactum* (< PIE **teg-*).

nasality /neɪˈzælɪti/ *n.* 1. The perceptual effect in speech of a lowered **velum**. 2. A distinctive and perceptually prominent resonance in speech, resembling that of a lowered velum, but produced by any of several quite distinct configurations of the oral cavity. See Laver (1980: 2.3). 3. (also **nasal**) In the **Ladefoged** and **Williamson feature systems**, a binary **distinctive feature** invoked to treat contrasts in velic opening, with the values **nasal** and **oral**.

nasalization /neɪzəlaɪˈzeɪʃn̩/ *n.* 1. The articulation of a segment, particularly one not involving a complete oral closure, with an accompanying lowering of the **velum**, allowing air to pass out through the nose, conveniently if somewhat inaccurately regarded as a **secondary articulation**. The IPA represents nasalization with a tilde: [ã], [ũ]. 2. Any phonological process in which a segment which formerly lacked nasalization in sense 1 acquires it. 3. Any phonological process in which some other segment is converted into a **nasal stop**: Basque *makila* 'stick' < Latin *bacilla* 'sticks'. 4. See **nasal mutation**. *V.* **nasalize**; *adj.* **nasalized**.

nasal mutation *n.* (also **nasalization**) The conventional name for the Welsh **mutation** (sense 2) in which morpheme-initial plosives are converted, in specified grammatical or lexical environments, into the corresponding nasals, voicing and aspiration being preserved: *tad* [tʰaːd] 'father', *fy nhad* [və nʰaːd] 'my father'; *plas* [plas] 'palace', *ym mhlas* [əm mʰlas] 'in the palace'; *blynedd* [bləneð] 'year', *saith mlynedd* [saiθ mləneð] 'seven years'.

nasal release *n.* (also **nasal plosion**) A type of **release** of a **plosive** in which the oral closure is maintained but the velum is lowered, allowing air to escape through the nose, as in the /t/ of *button* for many speakers.

nasal resonance *n.* The distinctive resonance produced by air flow through the **nasal cavity** during speech, as in [n] or [ã].

nasal stop *n.* (commonly shortened to **nasal**) A segment produced with a complete closure in the mouth but with the **velum** lowered, so that air flows out through the nose: [m], [n].

nasal subsystem /ˈsʌbsɪstəm/ *n.* That part of the **vowel system** of a language containing contrastively **nasalized** vowels. Labov (1994: 288–291).

nasal vowel *n.* A **vowel** articulated with the velum lowered and hence accompanied by **nasal resonance**; strictly, a *nasalized vowel*. See Laver (1994: 291–295) for a summary.

naso-pharynx /neɪzəʊˈfærɪŋks/ *n.* That part of the **pharynx** connecting the **nasal cavity**, via the **velopharyngeal port**, to the rest of the vocal tract.

natural /ˈnætʃərəl/ *adj.* (of a phonological process) Easily understood in terms of the physical characteristics of the vocal tract and hence common in languages generally, such as the nasalization of a vowel preceding a nasal consonant. *Abstr. n.* **naturalness**. Ant. **unnatural**.

natural class *n.* 1. Formally, any class which can be characterized using less information than is required to characterize any part of it. Thus, in English, the class of voiceless segments is a natural class, since it is picked out by the single specification [–voice], whereas any subclass of voiceless segments can only be specified by adding further information. In the same way, [+syll, +high, –back] picks out a natural class of segments in French, the high front vowels; to further distinguish [i] from [y] would require additional specifications. 2. Informally, any class of linguistic objects which pattern in the same way and which therefore need to be referred to in a linguistic description as a single unitary class. One of the chief functions of **distinctive features** is to allow us to represent natural classes in the second sense as natural classes in the first sense.

natural frequency *n.* The **frequency** with which a physical system vibrates when allowed to vibrate freely. The **formants** of speech represent the natural frequencies of the air in the vocal tract in a given configuration.

Natural Generative Phonology *n.* (**NGP**) A highly constrained theory of phonology developed in the 1970s as a reaction against the excessive abstractness of **classical generative phonology**, chiefly by Joan Bybee Hooper and Theo Vennemann. Unlike **Natural Phonology**, which stresses the naturalness of rules, NGP stresses the naturalness of underlying representations, generally requiring these to be very close to surface phonetic forms; some versions even deny the existence of underlying forms, requiring all phonological statements to be merely well-formedness conditions on surface phonetic forms. Among the distinctive characteristics of the framework are the **True Generalization Condition**, the **No-Ordering Condition**, and a distinction among strictly phonological rules (**P rules**), rules involving morphological factors (**MP rules**), and the novel conception of **via rules**. The framework is developed in Vennemann (1972b, 1973, 1974) and Hooper (1974a, 1974b); its definitive statement is Hooper (1976); a critical summary is provided in Carr (1993: ch. 7).

naturalization /nætʃərəlaɪ'zeɪʃn̩/ *n.* The process of modifying a **loan word** to make it conform to the phonological patterns of the borrowing language, as when English *helicopter* and *thermostat* are borrowed as Japanese *herikoputaa* and *saamosutatto*. When this is done in English, the process is **anglicization**. Firth (1948).

Natural Morphology *n.* An approach to morphology, derived from **Natural Phonology**, which sets out to provide a theory of what constitutes a natural morphological system. The seminal publications are Wurzel (1984) and Dressler (1985). See Spencer (1991: 125–127) for a summary with references.

Naturalness Condition *n.* A central principle of phonology, which asserts that 'the relation between phonological and phonetic structures must be a natural one' – that is, a phonetic representation is identical to its underlying phonological representation except as required otherwise by phonological rules. In the absence of constraints on the action of those rules, this condition reduces merely to the default statement that any phonological feature not modified by any rules must reach the surface. Postal (1968).

Natural Phonology *n.* (**NP**) A theory of phonology developed by David Stampe and others in the 1970s. NP makes rule naturalness the prime theoretical consideration, distinguishing between *natural processes* and (learned) *rules*. The central idea is that a child is born with a set of universal natural processes (such as obstruent devoicing) and that learning a language consists partly of un-learning these innate processes as required and partly of acquiring the idiosyncratic and largely unnatural rules peculiar to the language being learned (such as **velar softening** in English). NP is presented in Stampe (1969, 1973), Bjarkman (1975) and Donegan and Stampe (1979); a convenient summary is found in Sommerstein (1977: 9.3.3); the framework is criticized by Ohala (1974) and Householder (1979).

natural process *n.* Any phonological process which is readily under-standable in terms of such factors as the anatomy and physiology of the organs of speech and the acoustic characteristics of speech sounds and which is therefore to be expected in languages. While clearly important, the notion has proved difficult to characterize explicitly. See Sommerstein (1977: ch. 9) for a summary of the issues and some attempts at resolving them.

near-merger /'nɪə mɜːdʒə/ *n.* (also **half-contrast**) The phenomenon in which the speakers of a particular language variety consistently produce an objectively observable distinction between the phones (usually vowels) occurring in two sets of words while at the same time they deny the existence of any difference between the phones in question and are usually unable to hear the difference consistently in the speech of their neighbours or in recordings of their own speech. Among the reported examples are *source* and *sauce* in New York City, *pool* and *pull* in Albuquerque, *too* and *toe*, and also *beer* and *bear* in Norwich, *line* and *loin* in Essex, *meat* and *mate* in Belfast, and *ferry* and *furry* in Philadelphia. Such observations suggest that there is a fundamental asymmetry between production and perception. The phenomenon was discovered, and has been chiefly investigated, by William Labov and his colleagues (Labov *et al.* 1972, 1991; Labov 1975, 1994: chs 12–14). Labov (1975) suggests that many problematic historically reported mergers may in fact have been near-mergers of this kind.

near-minimal pair *n.* A pair of words which may be cited to demonstrate the presence of a **contrast** between two segments or sequences of interest but which fall short of being a **minimal pair** by virtue of the presence of an additional difference which is presumed to be irrelevant. An example is *pressure* and *pleasure* for the /ʃ/–/ʒ/ contrast. A near-minimal pair constitutes the clearest type of **analogous environments**.

near rhyme *n.* See **half-rhyme**.

near-RP *n.* In the classification of Wells (1982, 2: 297ff.), a broad and somewhat ill-defined range of accents associated with educated middle-class speakers in England (and possibly elsewhere),. resembling **Received Pronunciation** in most respects but differing from it in the presence of any of a large number of phonetic and phonological characteristics not normally regarded as part of RP.

negative condition /'negətɪv/ *n.* See **filter** (sense 2).

negative operator /'ɒpəreɪtə/ *n.* In some versions of **Dependency Phonology**, a device used to pick out a natural class characterized by the absence of a component, something not normally possible in privative frameworks using components (unary features). Anderson and Ewen (1987).

neighbourhood convention /'neɪbəhʊd/ *n.* An **abbreviatory convention** in which two rules of the form A → B / ___ C and A → B / C ___ are **conflated** into the **rule schema** A → B / C, interpreted as 'A changes to B either before or after C'. This is a special case of the **mirror-image convention**. Bach (1968).

Neogrammarian Hypothesis /niəʊgrə'mɛəriən/ *n.* A major hypothesis about the way in which phonological change proceeds. There are several formulations, of which one is this: sound change proceeds according to laws that admit no exception. In other words, sound change is held to proceed blindly and mechanically, affecting all relevant words simultaneously and without regard for any possible consequences, such as increased homophony or the loss of grammatical distinctions. Even the most extreme proponents of the hypothesis, however, have always admitted certain exceptions, such as nursery words and onomatopoeic words. Formulated in the 1870s, in the teeth of opposition from dialectologists who maintained that 'every word has its own history', this hypothesis has proved to be a powerful methodological principle, in that it forces analysts to search for explanations of apparent exceptions, often with illuminating results, and it has been the backbone of mainstream work in historical phonology ever since. Nevertheless, recent work on sound changes in progress has uncovered such important mechanisms of change as **lexical diffusion**, which are blatantly incompatible with the hypothesis. Labov (1994) decomposes the Neogrammarian Hypothesis into two principles which he calls the **Regularity Principle** and the **Mechanical Principle**. Translation of German *Junggrammatiker* 'young grammarians', originally a term of abuse.

network accent /ˈnetwɜːk/ *n.* [*non-technical*] The type of American accent most commonly used by television newsreaders in the United States, an educated variety of **General American** lacking any regional features.

neuro-chronaxic theory of phonation /njʊərəʊkrɒˈnæksɪk/ *n.* A theory of **phonation** which holds that vibration of the vocal folds is induced by periodic nervous impulses in the muscles located there. Proposed by the French scientist Raoul Husson in the 1950s, this view has been completely abandoned in favour of the **aerodynamic myoelastic theory of phonation**.

neurolinguistic identification /njʊərəʊlɪŋˈgwɪstɪk/ *n.* The last of the seven **phases of speech**, in which incoming nervous signals are identified as speech sounds.

neurolinguistic programming /ˈprəʊgræmɪŋ/ *n.* The first of the seven **phases of speech**, in which the language centres in the brain organize and programme the upcoming nervous impulses.

neuromuscular phase /njʊərəʊˈmʌskjələ/ *n.* The second of the seven **phases of speech**, in which neural impulses induce the contraction of individual muscles.

neuroreceptive phase /njʊərəʊrɪˈseptɪv/ *n.* The sixth of the seven **phases of speech**, in which sound waves are converted by the ear into nervous impulses and transmitted to the brain.

neutral /'njuːtrəl/ *adj.* (of lip position) Neither **spread** nor **rounded**.

neutral affix *n.* 1. An **affix** which has no **morphophonemic** effect upon a form to which it is attached, such as English *-al* (*critic/ critical*); cf. the non-neutral suffix *-ize* (*critic/criticize*). See also **level-ordering**. 2. See **secondary affix**. Chomsky and Halle (1968). NOTE: In English, these two definitions pick out essentially the same set of affixes.

neutral configuration /kənfɪgjə'reɪʃn̩/ *n.* A conventional reference configuration of the vocal tract, defined by Laver (1994: 137) as one in which the vocal tract has a nearly constant cross-section along its length within the mouth, the tongue is in a regularly curved convex shape, the velum is closed, and the lower jaw and the lips are slightly open.

neutralizable opposition /'njuːtrəlaɪzɪbəl/ *n.* See **suspendable opposition**.

neutralization /njuːtrəlaɪ'zeɪʃn̩/ *n.* The disappearance, in a partic-ular position, of a **contrast** between two or more segments which is maintained in other positions. The single segment which appears in the position of neutralization may be phonetically similar to one or other of the neutralized segments; it may be phonetically inter-mediate; or it may have a distinctive phonetic form. For example, English /p/ and /b/ contrast in most positions, but are neutralized after syllable-initial /s/; the contrast between the vowels of *law* and *low* is neutralized for many (not all) speakers before /r/, so that there is no difference between *horse* and *hoarse*; Basque has three contrasting nasals /m n ñ/ before vowels (*ama* 'mother', *Ana* 'Ann', *baña* 'but'), but the three-way contrast is neutralized elsewhere in favour of a nasal which is alveolar before pause and otherwise homorganic with a following consonant. Most versions of **classical phonology** attempt to identify the segment in the position of neutralization with one of the segments contrasting elsewhere, but the **Prague School** treats it as a distinct type of segment, the **archiphoneme**. Trubetzkoy (1931); Trubetzkoy originally only recognized neutralizations between two segments, but this pointless limitation was abandoned after Martinet (1936). *V.* **neutralize**; *adj.* **neutralized**.

neutralization rule *n.* A rule of the form A $\rightarrow$ B / P ___ Q such that, at any stage of a derivation at which it becomes applicable, there exist strings of the form PBQ *not* created by its application. Such rules are important in one formulation of **derivational constraints**. Kiparsky (1973a).

neutral position /pə'zɪʃn̩/ *n.* A putative, more or less universal, position supposedly adopted by the vocal organs when they are not involved in an articulation. The notion is deeply controversial. Chomsky and Halle (1968).

neutral (reference) setting *n.* An arbitrarily defined reference position of the supralaryngeal vocal tract with reference to which any articulatory behaviour may be described. See Laver (1979) for a detailed characterization, Laver (1994: 402–406) for a briefer one.

neutral vowel *n.* 1. See **schwa** (sense 1). 2. In a language with **vowel harmony**, a vowel which fails to participate in the harmony. For example, Hungarian /i iː e eː/ are neutral, appearing in both back-vowel and front-vowel words.

NGP See **Natural Generative Phonology**.

nil phonation /nɪl/ *n.* Silent voiceless flow of air through the **glottis** at volume-velocities below about 200–300 cm³/s. Sometimes the term is extended to cover total closure of the glottis, with no air flow at all. Cf. **breath**.

No-Crossing Constraint /nəʊ'krɒsɪŋ/ *n.* A fundamental principle of **Autosegmental Phonology**. It says: association lines may not cross. See **Crossing Avoidance, Principle of**.

node /nəʊd/ *n.* In a **standing wave**, a point of zero amplitude.

noise /nɔɪz/ *n.* Any undesired sound, particularly that which competes with speech or with the transmission or reproduction of sound signals. A signal-to-noise intensity ratio of 20 dB (i.e., 100:1) has no effect on intelligibility; a ratio of 0 dB (1:1) may reduce intelligibility to 50 per cent, though our ears are very good at tuning in on a directional signal.

non- For any term of the form **non-X** which has no entry of its own, see under the entry for **X**. For example, for *non-coronal* see under **coronal**.

non-automatic alternation *n.* An **alternation** (sense 1) which affects only some morphemes of a particular phonological form, such as the /f/–/v/ alternation occurring in *leaf/leaves* but not in *chief/chiefs*. Ant. **automatic alternation**.

non-cohering affix *n.* An **affix** which is not fully integrated into the phonological word of which it forms a part, which behaves in some

respects like a separate phonological word. Ant. **cohering affix**.
Dixon (1977).

non-concatenative morphology *n.* (also **root-and-pattern morphology**) A type of morphological structure in which a root consists of a kind of skeleton and a word is formed by 'interleaving' the elements of other, discontinuous morphemes. This kind of structure is typical of the Semitic languages. Cf. **concatenative morphology**.

non-consonantal *adj.* In the **Jakobson–Halle feature system**, a **distinctive feature** defined as 'exhibiting high total energy' and interpreted as representing the absence of an obstruction in the vocal tract. Ant. **consonantal**.

non-distinctive *adj.* Not serving to express any contrast between forms or meanings; redundant.

non-intersection condition /nɒnɪntə'sekʃən/ *n.* Another name for the 'strong' version of the **invariance condition**. Hockett (1942).

non-linear phonology /nɒn'lɪniə/ *n.* Any of several theories of phonology in which a phonological representation is viewed as consisting of something other than a single linear sequence of segments. Non-linear approaches have become predominant in phonology since about 1980; the most prominent versions are **Autosegmental Phonology** and **Metrical Phonology**, but many others exist, such as **Particle Phonology**, **Dependency Phonology** and **Government and Charm Phonology**. In many of these, a phonological representation consists of several parallel linear **tiers** with various connections among them; as a result, Roca (1994) suggests that 'multilinear' might be a more accurate label.

non-moraic vowel /nɒnmə'reɪk/ *n.* A **glide**. Hayes (1989).

non-peripheral track *n.* Either of two elongated regions of the **vowel space** located towards the centre of the mouth and posited as significant in certain types of **chain shifts**. Cf. **peripheral track**. Labov (1994: 172).

non-phonetic criteria (for phonological analysis) *n. pl.* In the work of Daniel Jones, any of various criteria other than phonetic facts which might be appealed to in assigning phones to phonemes in doubtful cases. Jones (1950: ch. XIV) cites as examples the usage of other speakers with different pronunciations and the pronunciation which a segment in a given morpheme may receive in a different environment (e.g., change of stress); he rejects all such criteria as inadmissible.

non-rhotic accent *adj.* Any accent of English in which the historical /r/ has been lost everywhere except before a vowel. In such an accent, *farther* is homophonous with *father*, *miner* is homophonous with *mynah*, *star* rhymes with *Shah*, and (usually) *pore* is homophonous with *paw*. Non-rhotic accents are typical of the larger part of England, of Wales, of the east coast and south of the United States, of parts of the West Indies, and of all Southern Hemisphere varieties. See Wells (1982) for an account. Cf. **rhotic accent**, and see **linking *r*, intrusive *r*.**

non-segmental *adj.* See **suprasegmental**.

non-specification *n.* An extension of **underspecification** in which a segment is represented underlyingly by a matrix containing no information at all, all of its phonetic features being provided by default provisions.

non-U *adj.* [*jocular*] Not typical of upper-class speech in England. Ant. **U.** Ross (1954).

non-uniqueness /nɒnjuˈniːknəs/ *n.* (also **indeterminacy**) The phenomenon in which the phonological system of a language admits of more than one possible analysis into **phonemes**. See Sommerstein (1977: 24–35) for a discussion with examples. Chao (1934).

non-verbal *adj.* 1. Pertaining to aspects of communication not involving the vocal tract, such as gestures, postures and expressions. 2. Pertaining to aspects of speech not involving the identification of words, such as utterance accent, intonation and tone of voice.

nonvocalic *adj.* In the **Jakobson–Halle feature system**, a **distinctive feature** defined as 'lacking a sharply defined formant structure' and interpreted as the absence of at least one of voicing and of an unobstructed vocal tract. Ant. **vocalic**.

No-Ordering Condition /nəʊˈɔːdərɪŋ/ *n.* In **Natural Generative Phonology**, the principle that rules may not be extrinsically ordered.

normal /ˈnɔːməl/ *adj.* In the **Williamson feature system**, one of the four possible values of the feature **length** or one of the three possible values of the feature **expansion**.

Northern Cities Shift /nɔːðən 'sɪtiz ʃɪft/ *n.* A major and vigorous **vowel shift** currently affecting up to six vowels in varieties of English spoken in urban areas in a part of the United States ranging from New England to Chicago, in which peripheral vowels are rotating clockwise and non-peripheral vowels are rotating anti-clockwise: /æ/ is being raised towards [i], /aː/ is being fronted, /oː/ is being fronted and centralized, /i/ is being lowered towards [e], /e/ is being lowered and backed, and /ʌ/ is being backed. See Labov (1994: 177–201) for an account. Cf. **Southern Shift**.

Northumbrian burr /nɔː'θʌmbriən/ *n.* See under **burr**.

notation /nəʊ'teɪʃn̩/ *n.* Any conventional written symbol, or set of such symbols, used in representing phonetic or phonological elements or processes.

notational convention *n.* Any notational device which, in some system, is understood as having some particular interpretation. For example, the notation n → ∅ / [+syll, –high] ___ {C, ##} is almost universally understood as meaning 'the consonant *n*, when preceded by a non-high vowel, is lost either before another consonant or in word-final position'.

notational variant /'vɛəriənt/ *n.* Any one of two or more **notational conventions** which are interpreted in the same way.

NSR /en es 'ɑː/ *n.* See **Nuclear Stress Rule**.

nuclear projection government /njuːkliə 'prədʒekʃən gʌvənmənt/ *n.* In **Government and Charm Phonology**, the type of **government** posited as holding between the nuclei of contiguous units equivalent to **feet**.

nuclear stress *n.* (also **sentence stress**) The main stress appearing within a single phrase, the stress that distinguishes *a black bírd* from *a bláckbird*, and that occurs on the pronouns in *John called Mary a Conservative, and then shé insulted hím.*

Nuclear Stress Rule *n.* (NSR) A putative rule of English which assigns stress within phrases (other than compounds) longer than a single word, such as *Lisa's teddy bears*. Chomsky and Halle (1968).

nuclear tone *n.* Any one of the available pitch-patterns which can occur on an **intonational nucleus** in a particular speech variety.

nucleus /'njuːkliəs/ *n.* 1. (also **syllabic nucleus**, **peak**) The most prominent (sonorous) part of a **syllable**, most often a vowel or a diphthong. 2. [*obsolete*] See **rhyme**. Hockett (1955). 3. (also **tonic**) The most prominent pitch-accent within a single **intonation group**. *Adj.* (all senses) **nuclear**.

null element /'nʌl elɪmənt/ *n.* (also **zero**) An element which, in some analysis, is posited as being present at a certain point in a structure even though there is no overt phonetic material there to represent it. An example is the plural marker in the word *sheep*. The Indian grammarian Panini was the first to use null elements, but their modern use derives chiefly from Bloomfield (1933).

null vowel *n.* See **empty nucleus**. Burzio (1988).

numbered brace notation /'nʌmbəd/ *n.* A **notational convention** employing **braces** in the usual sense of 'choose one item', but with the additional requirement that the *same* item must be chosen from all sets of braces bearing the same number. Sommerstein (1977: 136) offers the following rule for English inserting a vowel in certain circumstances between two segments which are either both [–cont] or both [–apic]:

$$\emptyset \rightarrow \textsc{i} \; / \; \begin{bmatrix} -son \\ +cor \\ \left\{ \begin{matrix} -cont \\ -apic \end{matrix} \right\} \\ 1 \quad 1 \end{bmatrix} \quad \# \underline{\quad} \quad \begin{bmatrix} -son \\ +cor \\ \left\{ \begin{matrix} -cont \\ -apic \end{matrix} \right\} \\ 1 \quad 1 \end{bmatrix} \#$$

O

O A symbol for **onset** in representations of syllable structure.

Obligatory Contour Principle /əblɪgətri ˈkɒntʊə prɪnsɪpəl/ *n.*
(OCP) In much recent phonological work, a proposed fundamental
principle governing phonological representations. Essentially, it
prohibits, or at least disfavours, the occurrence of identical feature
specifications on adjacent **autosegments** – that is, it disfavours
clash. It was originally proposed merely for tonal phenomena in
order to account for such widespread processes as the elimination
of HHL sequences, but it has since been extended to to a wide
variety of other phenomena, such as the non-existence in Cantonese
of such syllables as **tup*, in which a rounded vowel is followed
by a labial consonant. It has even been extended to cases involving
non-adjacent segments, such as the Cantonese ban on having
two labial consonants in a single morpheme (**pim*) and the
Arabic ban on having two labial consonants in a single root
(**btf*). See Roca (1994: 269) or Goldsmith (1990: 6.4) for a survey
of the history of this principle, and Kenstowicz (1994: 322–338)
for an account. Idea: Leben (1973); formulation and name: Goldsmith
(1976).

oblique /əˈbliːk/ *n.* 1. See **slashes**. 2. See **environment bar**.

oblique rhyme *n.* See **half-rhyme**.

observational adequacy /ɒbsəˈveɪʃənəl/ *n.* See under **adequacy**.

obstacle fricative /ˈɒbstəkəl/ *n.* Any **fricative** whose noise is chiefly
produced by a jet of air striking an obstacle in front of the constriction; an example is [s], in which the air strikes the teeth. In a
non-obstacle fricative like [θ], the noise is produced at the constriction itself. This is essentially the same as the **sibilant/non-sibilant**
distinction. Shadle (1985).

obstruent /ˈɒbstruənt/ *n.* or *adj.* 1. Any segment whose articulation
involves an obstruction in the vocal tract at least radical enough
to produce friction noise: a **plosive**, an **affricate** or a **fricative**. Note
that **nasal stops** are not classed as obstruents. Ant. **sonorant** or (less
usually) **resonant**. 2. (**obstr**) A **distinctive feature** sometimes used

to distinguish obstruents [+obstr] from all other segments [–obstr]. Sense 2: Lass (1984: 83). *Abstr. n.* **obstruency**.

occlusion /ə'kluːʒn̩/ *n.* 1. A complete closure within the mouth during an articulation, as occurs during a plosive. 2. Complete closure of the jaws, bringing the teeth together.

occlusive /ə'kluːsɪv/ *n.* or *adj.* 1. An older term for **plosive**, or sometimes for **stop**. 2. (**occl**) A **distinctive feature** suggested by Sommerstein (1977: 103) as representing a complete blockage of the airstream within the mouth: the inverse of [**continuant**]. Plosives, affricates and nasals are thus [+occl], while all other segments are [–occl]. The motivation is to clarify the ambiguity over whether nasals, laterals, taps, flaps and trills should be regarded as [+cont] or [–cont]. Cf. **central closure**.

OCP /əʊ siː 'piː/ *n.* See **Obligatory Contour Principle**.

octave /'ɒktɪv/ *n.* The interval between two pitches one of which is exactly double the other.

OEP /əʊ iː 'piː/ *n.* Daniel Jones's book *An Outline of English Phonetics*, first published in 1918 and followed by numerous revised editions, in which Jones presents most of his major ideas about phonetics and phonology.

oesophagic airstream mechanism /iːsə'fædʒɪk/ *adj.* (also **esophagic**) A highly unusual **airstream mechanism** used involuntarily in belching and voluntarily, after training, by individuals whose larynx has been surgically removed. A skilful practitioner, such as the actor Jack Hawkins, can produce something virtually indistinguishable from ordinary pulmonic speech.

oesophagus /ɪ'sɒfəgəs/ *n.* (also **esophagus**) The tube connecting the stomach to the pharynx. *Adj.* **oesophageal** /iːsə'fædʒəl/.

off-glide /ɒf/ *n.* A **glide** occurring at the end of a **diphthong**, such as [j] in [aj]. Ant. **on-glide**.

off rhyme *n.* See **half-rhyme**.

offset phase /'ɒfset/ *n.* The phase in the articulation of a segment during which the articulating organs are moving away from the **medial phase**.

o-**grade** /'əʊ greɪd/ *n.* In the phonology of Proto-Indo-European, that form of a root exhibiting the vowel *o*, considered a modification of the basic *e*. For example, the PIE root **nem-* 'allot' yields Greek *nemein* 'allot', but its *o*-grade **nom-* yields Greek *nomos* 'portion, law'.

'once a phoneme, always a phoneme' An informal label applied to various aspects of **American Structuralist** phonology, especially to **biuniqueness** and the **invariance condition**.

one or two phonemes? (also *un ou deux phonèmes?*) A label applied to the problem of determining whether affricates (like [tʃ]) and diphthongs (like [ai]) should be interpreted as single segments or as sequences. Martinet (1939).

on-glide /ɒn/ *n*. A **glide** occurring at the beginning of a **diphthong**, such as [j] in [ja]. Ant. **off-glide**.

onomatopoeia /ɒnəmætə'piːə/ *n*. 1. Narrowly, and perhaps most appropriately, the coining or use of a word which attempts to represent a non-linguistic sound by a combination of appropriate segments selected from the ordinary phoneme inventory of the language. Familiar English examples include *buzz*, *cock-a-doodle-do*, *rat-a-tat-tat*, *ding-dong*, *meow*, *clink*, *wham*, *kaboom* and *tinkle*. 2. Broadly, any sort of **sound symbolism**. This second use is probably objectionable. *Adj*. **onomatopoeic**. Cf. **phonaesthesia**, **ideophone**, **sound symbolism**. Greek *onomatopoiia* 'name-making'.

onset /'ɒnset/ *n*. (also **initial**) The first part of the syllable, that part preceding the **rhyme** and typically consisting of all consonants preceding the vowel. Hockett (1955).

onset of voicing *n*. In the transition from a voiceless segment to a following voiced one, the precise moment at which vibration of the vocal folds begins.

onset phase *n*. The initial phase of the articulation of a segment, during which the articulators are moving towards the maximal constriction. Cf. **medial phase**, **offset phase**.

opacity /əʊ'pæsəti/ *n*. The property of a phonological rule whose existence is difficult to ascertain from the inspection of surface phonetic forms, for any of various reasons. For example, in an analysis of Basque which posited the (historically accurate) rules (i) $n \rightarrow \emptyset$ / V__V and (ii) $nn \rightarrow n$, rule (i) would be opaque because rule (ii) introduces new surface instances of intervocalic *n*. Ant. **transparency**. *Adj*. **opaque**. Kiparsky (1971, 1973a).

opaque morpheme /əʊ'peɪk/ *n.* A morpheme which exceptionally prevents the **spreading** of some regular phonological process, such as vowel harmony.

opaque rule *n.* A proposed phonological rule which is not a true generalization about surface forms. Cf. **transparent rule**.

opaque vowel *n.* In some **vowel harmony** languages, a vowel which regularly prevents the spread of harmony through it. A root containing such a vowel is a **disharmonic root**.

open /'əʊpən/ *adj.* 1. A synonym for **low** in the description of vowels. Ant. **close**. NOTE: This term is now recommended by the IPA. 2. Denoting a position in which the lips are rather far apart but not **rounded**, as in the vowel of *car*. 3. A multivalued **distinctive feature** proposed by Labov (1994: 258) for treating distinctions of **vowel height**.

open approximation /əprɒksɪ'meɪʃn̩/ *n.* The degree of constriction in the mouth in which air flow is not turbulent, invoked by Laver (1994: 135) as the stricture type for **resonant** segments. Cf. **close approximation**.

opening /'əʊpənɪŋ/ *n.* Any phonological change in which a vowel becomes lower (more open) than formerly.

opening diphthong *n.* A **diphthong** whose second element is more open than its first, such as [ja]. Ant. **closing diphthong**.

open juncture *n.* 1. Originally, any distinctive phonetic characteristics of the beginning or the end of an isolated utterance. Introduced by Trager and Bloch (1941), this was later renamed **external open juncture** and subdivided by Trager and Smith (1951) into **single-bar**, **double-bar** and **double-cross juncture** types. 2. An **internal open juncture**; see **plus-juncture**. Ant. **close juncture**.

open-mid *adj.* See **low-mid**. NOTE: This term is now recommended by the IPA.

openness *n.* See **aperture** (sense 3).

open rounding *n.* A variety of **lip-rounding** in which the space between the lips is fairly large, as in the vowel [œ]. Ant. **close rounding**.

open syllable *n.* (also **unchecked syllable**) A **syllable** which ends in a vowel, with no following consonant; i.e., a syllable which lacks a **coda**, such as all of those in *see*, *veto* and *Malaya*. Ant. **closed syllable**.

open tone *n.* 1. A **tone** in a **tone language** which does not involve any laryngeal activity such as creak; an ordinary tone. Ant. **glottal tone**. 2. Any non-falling **intonation** pattern. Ant. (sense 2) **closed tone**.

open transition *n.* A transition between two consecutive segments which is characterized by a momentary break in articulatory continuity, so that there is no overlap or accommodation between the segments. Ant. **close transition**.

operational definition /ɒpə'reɪʃənəl defɪnɪʃn̩/ *n.* (also **procedural definition**) A definition of a linguistic object in terms of an analytical procedure to be applied to raw data, such as some **American Structuralist** definitions of the **phoneme**.

opposition /ɒpə'zɪʃn̩/ *n.* See **contrast** (sense 1), and refer to the remarks at the end of that entry.

Optimality Theory /ɒptɪ'mælɪti/ *n.* An approach to phonological description pioneered by Alan Prince and Paul Smolensky and developed by them and others in a series of works, most of which remain unpublished. The framework assigns pride of place to the concept of **constraints**, and rests upon the following principles. (1) Universal Grammar largely consists of a set of constraints on representational well-formedness, out of which individual grammars are constructed. (2) In general, the constraints in a grammar are not mutually consistent and are not exceptionlessly true at any level of representation; they often make conflicting requirements. (3) A grammar consists of the constraints together with a general means of resolving conflicts in favour of analyses which best satisfy, or least violate, the conflicting constraints. See Prince and Smolensky (forthcoming) for a detailed account.

oral /'ɔːrəl/ *adj.* 1. (also **buccal**) (of a segment) Articulated within the **oral cavity**. 2. (of a segment) Articulated with the **velum** raised, so that air flow is exclusively through the mouth; non-**nasal**. 3. In the **Jakobson–Halle feature system**, a **distinctive feature** defined as 'exhibiting no additional formants and no reduction in the intensity of existing formants' and interpreted as representing decoupling of the nasal cavity. Ant. **nasal**. 4. A very different **distinctive feature** proposed to distinguish '**laryngeal**' (sense 2) consonants: any segment made in the oral cavity or the pharynx (including a nasal stop) is [+oral]; 'laryngeals' like [ʔ h ɦ] are [–oral]. Lass (1976: ch. 6). 5. In the **Williamson feature system**, one of the two possible values of the feature **nasality**.

oral cavity *n.* That part of the **vocal tract** lying between the pharynx and the lips, containing the tongue and the teeth and bounded on top by the alveolar ridge, the palate and the velum.

oral gesture *n.* In **gesture** theory, all aspects of an articulation taking place above the glottis.

oral–glottal stop *n.* A **coarticulated plosive** in which there is simultaneous closure in the mouth and in the glottis: [ʔp], [ʔk], etc. In many accents of Britain such stops are the usual realizations of intervocalic /p t k/. The less systematic term 'glottalized plosives' is often applied to oral–glottal stops. Catford (1977: 190).

oral–nasal stop *n.* Any **stop** during which the opening and closing of the velum is not synchronized with the closure and release of the oral occlusion. Laver (1994: 227–235) distinguishes *pre-nasal oral stops*, *post-nasal oral stops*, *pre-occluded nasal stops* and *post-occluded nasal stops*.

oral release *n.* (also **oral plosion**) The release of a **plosive** by lowering the velum without releasing the oral occlusion.

order /'ɔːdə/ *n.* [*obsolescent*] A term commonly used in philological works for a group of consonant phonemes in a language which share more or less the same **place of articulation** but differ in **voicing** and/or in **manner of articulation**. For example, English /p b m f v/ would be said to belong to the 'labial order', while /k g ŋ/ would belong to the 'guttural (i.e., velar) order', and so on. Cf. **series**.

ordered rule *n.* One of a set of rules which must be applied to an underlying representation in some particular sequence in order to derive the correct surface form. Ordered rules were used by Bloomfield, but were rejected by the **American Structuralists**; they were reinstated in early **generative phonology**, and have been widely used since.

ordering *n.* See **rule ordering**.

Ordering Hypothesis *n.* The proposal that affixes fall into classes which can only be added to bases in a specified order: *tox-ic-ity-less-ness*, but **tox-ic-less-ness-ity*. Siegel (1974).

ordering paradox /'pærədɒks/ *n.* In a framework employing **ordered rules**, the problematic requirement that two particular rules must apply in one order in some derivations but in the opposite order in others. Some theories of rule ordering, such as **local**

ordering and **partial ordering**, are expressly designed to deal with such paradoxes.

ordering relation /rɪ'leɪʃn̩/ *n.* The particular sequence in which two **phonological rules** apply in some particular analysis.

organic phase /ɔː'gænɪk/ *n.* The third of the seven **phases of speech**, in which the speech organs perform articulations.

organic pitch range *n.* The total range of pitch available to a speaker, constrained only by anatomical and physiological limitations. Laver (1994).

organ of Corti /ɔːgən əv 'kɔːtaɪ/ *n.* A helical structure attached to the **basilar membrane** of the **cochlea** and containing tiny hair cells which convert the mechanical disturbances of the basilar membrane into nervous impulses which are then transmitted along the **auditory nerve**.

organs of speech *n. pl.* See **vocal organs**.

oro-nasal process /ɔːrəʊ'neɪzəl/ *n.* The articulatory parameter by which the **velum** may be either raised, producing an **oral** sound, or lowered, producing a **nasal** (or **nasalized**) sound.

oro-pharynx /ɔːrəʊ'færɪŋks/ *n.* That part of the **pharynx** connecting the back of the oral cavity to the rest of the vocal tract.

orphan /'ɔːfən/ *n.* A syllable or other metrical unit which, in some analysis, is 'left over' after metrical structure is complete by the normal rules and which must be handled by some additional machinery.

orthoepy /'ɔːθəʊepi/ *n.* The study of correct pronunciation.

Oscillomink /ə'sɪləmɪŋk/ *n.* The trade name of a widely used type of ink-writing oscillograph, an instrument which records on paper, as a function of time, several types of information about the acoustic characteristics of the speech wave.

ossicles /'ɒsɪkəlz/ *n. pl.* See **auditory ossicles**.

outer ear /'aʊtə/ *n.* The outermost of the three divisions of the ear, consisting of the external ear, or **pinna**, and the ear canal leading to the **eardrum**. This roughly funnel-shaped structure has a natural **resonance** at around 3,000 Hz, and sounds near this frequency are amplified by as much as ten times before reaching the eardrum.

outer rounding *n.* (also **vertical lip-rounding, lip compression, inrounding**) A type of **rounding** in which the lips are vertically compressed and the channel is made by the outer surfaces of the lips (it is **exolabial**). Outer rounding is typical of front rounded vowels like [y]. Cf. **inner rounding**, and see the remarks there. Sweet (1890).

output /'aʊtpʊt/ *n.* With reference to a rule, the representation which is produced in a particular case by the application of the rule. Cf. **input**.

output conditioning *n.* The property of a rule whose application is constrained by the characteristics of the representation which is its output, such as a rule which is obliged to produce an output conforming to **phonotactic** constraints. Such rules have been little used, except in **Stratificational phonology**, but are now important in **Optimality Theory**. Cf. **input conditioning**.

outrounding /'aʊtraʊndɪŋ/ *n.* See **inner rounding**.

oval window /əʊvəl 'wɪndəʊ/ *n.* The small membrane lying between the **middle ear** and the **inner ear**. The oval window is connected both to the **auditory ossicles** of the middle ear and to the **cochlea** of the inner ear; vibration of the ossicles is transmitted across the oval window to the **basilar membrane** of the cochlea.

overall pattern analysis /əʊvərɔːl 'pætən ənæləsɪs/ *n.* See **diasystem**. Trager and Smith (1951).

overlapping /əʊvə'læpɪŋ/ *n.* 1. Either of **partial overlapping** or **complete overlapping**. 2. See **articulatory overlap**.

overlapping distribution *n.* The relation between two or more phonemes which occur in some, but not all, of the same positions in words – as, for example, the three English nasals.

overlapping morph *n.* See **portmanteau morph**.

overlong /'əʊvəlɒŋ/ *n.* (also **extra long**) Having the greatest of three contrasts of **length**, as in Estonian [jama] 'nonsense', [jaːma] 'of the station' and [jaːːma] 'to the station', [lina] 'flax', [linːa] 'of the town', [linːːa] 'to the town'. An overlong segment is marked by a following [ːː]. *Abstr. n.* **overlength**.

overspreading /'əʊvəspredɪŋ/ *n.* In an analysis involving **spreading** (sense 2), an incorrect result in which the spreading feature spreads over too large a domain.

overtone /'əʊvətəʊn/ *n.* A synonym for **harmonic**, except in numbering: the **fundamental** is the *first harmonic*, so the *first overtone* is the *second harmonic*, and so on.

Oxford accent /'ɒksfəd/ *n.* [*non-technical*] A label occasionally applied to the type of British accent more usually called **Received Pronunciation (RP)**, or sometimes more specifically to a particular variety of RP perceived as typical of elderly academics at Oxford University, allegedly characterized by remarkably great variations in tempo.

oxytone /'ɒksɪtəʊn/ *n.* 1. An Ancient Greek word with an acute accent on the last syllable. 2. In a stress-accented language like English, a word which is stressed on the last syllable: *kangaroo*, *entertain*, *interfere*. Cf. **paroxytone**, **proparoxytone**, **perispomenon**. *Adj.* **oxytone**. Greek *oxys* 'sharp' + *tonos* 'tone'.

P

P1 rule, P2 rule See under **post-lexical rule**.

pair test /ˈpɛə test/ *n.* A procedure for testing for the presence of a phonological **contrast** (sense 1) between two linguistic items. One native speaker is asked to pronounce the two items repeatedly in an arbitrary order selected by the investigator, while a second native speaker tries to identify them. A success rate of around 100 per cent indicates a contrast; a success rate around 50 per cent indicates **free variation**. Cf. **repetition test**. Harris (1951: 32–33).

palatal /ˈpælətəl/ 1. *adj.* Pertaining to the **palate**. 2. *adj.* (of a segment) Articulated with some part of the tongue (usually the front) raised towards the palate. 3. *n.* A segment so articulated, such as [c], [ɟ], [ɲ] or [ʎ]. Sometimes this label is applied loosely to other segments with a palatal element, such as **palato-alveolars** and **palatalized velars**. 4. *adj.* In the **Ladefoged** and **Williamson** **feature systems**, one of the eleven possible values of the feature **articulatory place**.

palatality /pæləˈtælɪti/ *n.* A label commonly applied to the phonological prime {i} or I in various **privative theories** of phonology, especially **Dependency Phonology**. Cf. **gravity**, **sonority**.

palatalization /pælətəlaɪˈzeɪʃn̩/ *n.* 1. The phenomenon in which a segment whose primary articulation is at some other location is articulated with a **secondary articulation** involving the raising of the front of the tongue towards the **palate** or (with back consonants) the moving of the constriction forward towards the palate. Palatalization is transcribed in the IPA by a superscript [ʲ] (e.g., [pʲ], [kʲ]), in American transcription by a superscript [ʸ] (e.g., [pʸ], [kʸ]), and in some specialist traditions by other devices, such as a prime (e.g., [pʼ], [kʼ]). 2. Any phonological process in which a segment which formerly lacked palatalization in sense 1 acquires it. 3. Any phonological process in which a non-palatal segment is converted to a palatal or palato-alveolar segment. *V.* **palatalize**; *adj.* **palatalized**.

palatalized voice *n.* The **voice quality** of an individual who constantly maintains the body of the tongue close to the palate.

palate /'pælət/ *n.* 1. (also **hard palate**) The hard bony structure at the top of the roof of the mouth, just behind the alveolar ridge. 2. [*now rare*] A cover term for the **palate** (sense 1) and the **velum** taken together. *Adj.* **palatal**; CF **palato-**.

palato-alveolar /'pælətəʊ/ (also **postalveolar**, formerly also **alveolo-palatal**) 1. *adj.* (of a segment) Articulated with the primary constriction occupying a (typically extended) region between the **alveolar ridge** and the **palate**. 2. *n.* A segment so articulated, such as the [ʃ] of English *fish* or the [dʒ] of English *judge*. 3. In the **Ladefoged** and **Williamson feature systems**, one of the eleven possible values of the feature **articulatory place**, called **post-/palato-alveolar** by Williamson. Cf. **alveolo-palatal**. NOTE that this term is anomalously formed, and that the IPA now recommends the term 'postalveolar'.

palatogram /'pælətəgræm/ *n.* The picture of the roof of the mouth obtained by **palatography**.

palatography /pælə'tɒgrəfi/ *n.* A technique for determining which areas of the roof of the mouth are touched by the tongue during an articulation. Either the roof of the mouth is coated with a coloured material, or a false palate similarly coated is inserted into the mouth; after the articulation of interest is performed, the mouth or false palate is examined to see where the coating has been removed. See also **continuous palatography**, **electropalatography**, **linguagram**.

paracusis /pærə'kjuːsɪs/ *n.* Any pathological disturbance of the sense of hearing.

paradigm /'pærədaɪm/ *n.* The full set of inflected forms exhibited by some class of lexical items, such as the declensional forms of a class of nouns or the conjugated forms of a class of verbs, often as represented by the forms of a single typical item. *Adj.* **paradigmatic** /pærədɪg'mætɪk/. Greek *paradeigma* 'pattern'.

paradigmatic imbalance /ɪm'bæləns/ *n.* A conspicuous asymmetry in a **phoneme system**, such as the presence of a **hole in the pattern**.

paradigmatic relation *n.* (also **relation** *in absentia*; formerly also **associative relation**) Any relation between two or more linguistic elements which are in some sense competing possibilities, in that exactly one of them may be selected to occupy some position in a structure. Most familiarly, the consonant and vowel phonemes of a language stand in a paradigmatic relation, since only one of them may occupy a given slot in a syllable, a morpheme or a word. Cf. **syntagmatic relation**. Saussure (1916).

paradigm regularity *n.* 1. The presence, in a single **paradigm** or in a set of related paradigms, of a high degree of orderliness and predictability, the extreme case being one in which each morpheme has only a single surface form, with no **allomorphy**. 2. The putative principle that instances of **rule reordering** will normally proceed so as to increase paradigm regularity in sense 1. Sense 2: Kiparsky (1971).

parafix /ˈpærəfɪks/ *n.* A notional **affix** realized as a **reduplication** of some part of a stem. For example, the Tagalog verb stems *sulat* 'write' and *hanap* 'seek' have future forms *susulat* 'will write' and *hahanap* 'will seek', in which the future marker is a parafix consisting of reduplication of the initial CV sequence.

paragoge /pærəˈɡəʊdʒi/ *n.* (also **epithesis**) The addition of one or more segments to the end of a word, as in the derivation of *against* from earlier *again* + genitive *-es*. The addition of a word-final vowel is **proparalepsis**. The addition of a word-final plosive is **excrescence**. Greek *paragōgē* 'addition'.

paralalia /pærəˈleɪliə/ *n.* Any pathological disturbance of speech.

paralanguage /ˈpærəlæŋɡwɪdʒ/ *n.* 1. Narrowly, non-segmental vocal features in speech, such as tone of voice, tempo, tut-tutting, sighing, grunts and exclamations like *Whew!* 2. Broadly, all of the above plus non-vocal signals such as gestures, postures and expressions – that is, all non-linguistic behaviour which is sufficiently coded to contribute to the overall communicative effect. See Crystal and Quirk (1964), Trager (1958), and the references in Laver (1994: 24–25). *Adj.* **paralinguistic** /pærəlɪŋˈɡwɪstɪk/. Trager (1958); Trager credits A. A. Hill with the term.

paralinguistic pitch range *n.* The **pitch range** used by a speaker for signalling attitudes, such as surprise or impatience.

parallel distribution /ˈpærəlel/ *n.* The relation between two or more phones which occur in exactly the same environments, as occurs with English [pʰ], [tʰ], [kʰ]. Some would extend this term to phones which share only some of the same environments. Cf. **complementary distribution**.

parallel segmentation *n.* See **parametric approach to speech segmentation**.

parameter /pəˈræmətə/ *n.* 1. In articulatory phonetics, any category within which a significant degree of variation for linguistic purposes is possible, such as **voicing** or **vowel height**. 2. In some approaches to phonology, a theory-specific variable within which a given language is permitted to choose one of a small number of possibilities, such as the choice between **left-headed** and **right-headed feet** in stress languages. *Adj.* **parametric**.

parametric approach to speech segmentation /pærəˈmetrɪk/ *n.* (also **parallel segmentation**) The analysis of speech in terms of **parametric phonetics**. Cf. **serial approach to speech segmentation**.

parametric phonetics *n.* (also **dynamic phonetics**) An approach to **phonetics** which views speech as consisting, not of a linear sequence of **segments**, but of a set of articulatory **parameters**, or variables, such as tongue height, degree of velic opening, degree of lip-rounding and degree of glottal opening. Each of these variables changes continuously over time in a more or less independent way; their interaction produces a speech wave which is segmented by the listener.

paraphonology /ˈpærəfənɒlədʒi/ *n.* The characteristics of the non-linguistic sounds, such as **filled pauses**, produced during speech. *Adj.* **paraphonological**. Laver (1994: 540).

pararhyme /ˈpærəraɪm/ *n.* See **half-rhyme**.

parasite vowel /ˈpærəsaɪt/ *n.* A vowel inserted in **anaptyxis**. Sweet (1888).

parasitic harmony /pærəˈsɪtɪk/ *n.* (also **parasitic spreading**) A type of **vowel harmony** in which two vowels are required to harmonize for one feature if and only if they also harmonize for another feature. For example, in Ngbaka, if the vowels in a two-syllable word agree in height, then they must also agree in backness; if they do not agree in height, there is no requirement for agreement in backness. Van der Hulst (1989).

paratone /ˈpærətəʊn/ *n.* The largest **intonation** pattern to which an identifiable function can be assigned, often regarded as the spoken equivalent of a paragraph. For example, a newsreader typically introduces a new item by using a wide pitch range, and the pitch range becomes steadily narrower towards the conclusion of the item.

parentheses /pəˈrenθəsiːz/ *n. pl.* (also **round brackets**) 1. An **abbreviatory convention** in which two rules which differ only in that one of them contains an extra term absent from the other are collapsed into a single **rule schema**. For example, in many Canadian accents of English, the diphthong /ai/ is raised to [əi] before a voiceless consonant, as in *write*: ai → əi / ___ [–voi]. For some speakers, the same happens before /n/ followed by a voiceless consonant, as in *pint*: ai → əi / ___ n [–voi]. These can be collapsed as ai → əi / ___ (n) [–voi]. 2. In a phonological representation, a device used to mark material which may be optionally or variably present or absent, as when *fasten* is represented as /fæs(ə)n/.

parochial /pəˈrəʊkiəl/ *adj*. See **language-specific**.

paronomasia /pərɒnəˈmeɪʒə/ *n*. A pun or a play on words.

paronym /ˈpærənɪm/ *n*. Any word derived from a second word or from the same root; a **derivative** or a **cognate**.

paroxytone /pəˈrɒksɪtəʊn/ *n*. or *adj*. In Ancient Greek, a word with an acute accent on the **penult**. Cf. **oxytone**, **proparoxytone**.

parse /pɑːz/ *vt*. 1. To assign a valid phonological structure to (a string of elements in a representation). 2. *vi*. To be assigned such structure. 3. *n*. The phonological structure assigned in such a way.

partial assimilation /ˈpɑːʃəl/ *n*. **Assimilation** in some features only, as when *ten pence* becomes *te*[m] *pence*. Cf. **total assimilation**.

partial devoicing *n*. The absence of vibration of the vocal folds during some part of the duration of an underlyingly voiced segment. There are two types: **initial devoicing** and **final devoicing**. *Adj*. **partially devoiced**.

partial ordering *n*. A theory of **rule ordering** in which rules apply freely whenever their structural description is met except as prevented by **precedence constraints** and **blockage constraints**. Cf. **local ordering**. Sommerstein (1977: 176–180).

partial overlapping *n*. The phenomenon in which two **phonemes** have phonetically identical **allophones** occurring in different environments, but not in the same environment.

partial tone language *n*. A language in which **tones** appear on certain syllables only, such as Norwegian, Lithuanian or Serbo-Croatian.

Particle Phonology /ˈpɑːtɪkəl/ *n*. A **privative (holistic) theory** of phonology developed by Sanford Schane and presented in Schane

(1984a, 1984b). As in other such approaches, segments are built up by recursion of primitive elements called **particles**, so that I = [i], AI = [e], AAI = [ɛ], AAAI = [æ], and so on. The simplest of the holistic theories, Particle Phonology addresses only vowels; it has been eclipsed by more fully elaborated frameworks such as **Dependency Phonology** and **Government and Charm Phonology**.

part of speech /pɑːt/ *n.* See **lexical category** (sense 1).

passive articulator /ˈpæsɪv/ *n.* In the articulation of a consonant, the upper of the two articulators involved in forming the constriction, conventionally regarded as standing still while the lower **active articulator** moves towards it.

path /pɑːθ/ *n.* Any single valid route along the arcs in a **metrical tree**.

patois /ˈpætwɑː/ *n.* [*non-technical*] A regional speech variety of low prestige; the term is dismissive and is never used in linguistic work. French.

pattern congruity /pætən kənˈɡruːɪti/ *n.* Either of two **criteria for phonological analysis** which may be invoked to choose among competing analyses. In the first (**paradigmatic**) version, that analysis is preferred which yields a more symmetric **phonemic system**. In the second (**syntagmatic**) version, that analysis is preferred which yields the simpler or more regular **phonotactics**. The notion is particularly important in **American Structuralism**. Swadesh (1934); derived from Sapir (1925).

pause /pɔːz/ *n.* A short interruption during the production of an utterance. A **silent pause** contains no vocal sound; a **filled pause** is marked by a **hesitation noise** such as *um* or *er*. V. **pause**; *adj.* **pausal**.

peak /piːk/ *n.* 1. A less usual term for the **nucleus** of a syllable. Some analysts distinguish the *nucleus* (the structural place filled by the vowel) from the *peak* (the vowel which fills the nucleus). Hockett (1955). 2. A point of high prominence in a **stress** or **intonation** pattern. Ant. **trough**.

pen-initial /pen/ *adj.* or *n.* (Pertaining to or falling upon) the second syllable of a word. By analogy with **penult**.

pentameter /penˈtæmɪtə/ *n.* A line of verse consisting of five **feet**, the commonest line in English verse, as in *The curfew tolls the knell of parting day*.

penult /pə'nʌlt/ *n.* (rarely also **penultima** /pə'nʌltımə/) The next-to-last syllable in a word. *Adj.* **penultimate**. Latin *paene* 'almost' + *ultima* 'last'.

perceived pitch /pə'siːvd/ *n.* See **pitch**.

perception /pə'sepʃən/ *n.* The process by which an individual detects and interprets information from the external world by means of the organs of sense, the nervous system and the brain. In speech, the term is particularly applied to the way in which acoustic characteristics like **frequency** and **intensity** are registered and interpreted. See **speech perception**. *V.* **perceive**; *adj.* **perceptual**.

perception test *n.* See **recognition test**.

perceptual centre /pə'septʃuəl/ *n.* (also **P-centre**) In the perception of rhythm, the perceptually relevant instant during speech which listeners use to establish a rhythm. This might be the beginning of the first segment of a syllable, the beginning of the nuclear segment, or something else. Morton *et al.* (1976).

perceptual feature *n.* A **distinctive feature** formulated in terms of perception. See **Wickelgren feature system** for examples.

perceptual saliency /'seıliənsi/ *n.* The degree to which a particular segment can be readily distinguished by listeners from contrasting segments in the same language. Stevens *et al.* (1987).

percussive /pə'kʌsıv/ *n.* Any of various sounds made in the oral cavity without the aid of an **airstream mechanism** by moving two organs sharply together or apart. Such sounds do not appear to be used for linguistic purposes. Pike (1943: 103–105).

period /'pıəriəd/ *n.* In wave motion, the time taken to complete one **cycle** of the wave.

periodic /pıəri'ɒdık/ *adj.* (of motion) Occurring at regular intervals.

periodicity /pıəriə'dısıti/ *n.* Particularly in grid versions of **Metrical Phonology**, the more-or-less regular **rhythm** exhibited by stresses at any level of analysis.

peripheral /pə'rıfərəl/ *adj.* 1. (of a vowel) Articulated with the tongue as far as possible from the centre of the mouth. The **cardinal vowels** are peripheral by definition; few vowels in natural languages are strictly peripheral, though the vowels of French come close. 2. In some analyses of English, a label applied to a set of tense non-central vowels and diphthongs which show similar behaviour over time. Labov (1994). 3. In some descriptions, a label applied to any vowel which is either front unrounded, back rounded, or low, regardless of whether it is peripheral in sense 1 – that is, to any vowel with a high degree of **perceptual saliency**. 4. In the **Lindau feature system**, a **distinctive feature** defined as representing the degree of centralization on an acoustic chart and having the possible values *peripheral* and *central*. 5. (of a consonant) Articulated with the main constriction located either towards the front of the oral cavity (bilabials, labiodentals) or towards the back of the oral cavity (velars, uvulars, etc.). 6. In **Prague School** phonology, denoting an element which is not fully integrated into the phonological system of a language. *Abstr. n.* **peripherality** /pərɪfəˈrælɪti/. Ant. **non-peripheral**.

Peripherality Condition *n.* The requirement that **extrasyllabicity** should be confined to segments at one end of the domain. This is an attempt to limit the power of a very powerful device.

peripheral track *n.* In some conceptions of **phonological space**, either of two elongated areas (front and back) occupying the outer region of that space, surrounding the central **non-peripheral tracks**. Labov (1994: ch. 6) argues for the importance of this concept in interpreting a range of sound changes involving vowels.

perispomenon /perɪˈspəʊmənɒn/ *n.* In Ancient Greek, a word bearing a circumflex accent on the last syllable.

perissosyllabic /pərɪsəsɪˈlæbɪk/ *adj.* Of a metrical **foot** in a line of verse, having one or more syllables beyond the number required for scansion.

perseveration /pəsevəˈreɪʃn̩/ *n.* The phenomenon in which a speaker produces a segment or a feature later in an utterance than is necessary or appropriate. The term is applied both to instances of **perseverative assimilation**, in which it is usually normal, and to **slips of the tongue** such as 'bread and brutter' for *bread and butter*. *V.* **perseverate** /pəˈsevəreɪt/. Cf. **anticipation**.

perseverative assimilation /pəˈsevərətɪv/ *n.* (also **progressive assimilation**) Any instance of **assimilation** in which a later segment is assimilated to an earlier one. For example, Basque *egin* 'done' is in many varieties pronounced [eiɲ], in which the palatal quality of the [i] is retained during the following nasal; the phrase *egin da* 'it's been done' in such accents is often [eiɲɟa], in which the palatal quality is carried further to the following plosive. Cf. **anticipatory assimilation**.

persistent rule /pə'sɪstənt/ *n.* See **anywhere rule**. Chafe (1967); Myers (1991).

PF See **phonological form.**

pharyngeal /fə'rɪndʒəl/ (in senses 1–3, also **pharyngal** /fə'rɪŋgəl/) 1. *adj.* Pertaining to the **pharynx**. 2. *adj.* (of a segment) Articulated with the primary stricture occurring in the pharynx. 3. *n.* A segment so articulated, such as Arabic [ħ] or [ʕ]. 4. *adj.* In the **Ladefoged** and **Williamson feature systems**, one of the eleven possible values of the feature **articulatory place**.

pharyngeal expansion *n.* A **distinctive feature** defined as involving 'advancement of the tongue root and lowering of the larynx', thus subsuming two articulations which have otherwise generally been handled with two separate features. Lindau (1975).

pharyngealization /fərɪndʒəlaɪ'zeɪʃn̩/ *n.* 1. The phenomenon in which a segment articulated at some other position is produced with a simultaneous **secondary articulation** in which the root of the tongue is retracted into the **pharynx**. Pharyngealization is transcribed in the IPA with a superscript [ˤ] (e.g., [dˤ]) or with a superimposed tilde (e.g., [ɗ]). The so-called **emphatic** consonants of Arabic are so articulated. See Laver (1994: 326–330) for an account. 2. Any phonological process in which a segment which formerly lacked pharyngealization in sense 1 acquires it. 3. Any phonological process in which a non-pharyngeal segment is converted to a pharyngeal segment. *V.* **pharyngealize**; *adj.* **pharyngealized**.

pharyngealized voice *n.* A **voice quality** characterized by persistent retraction of the tongue body into the pharynx.

pharynx /'færɪŋks/ *n.* The space at the back of the mouth constituting the juncture of the **oral cavity**, the **nasal cavity** and the passageway above the **larynx**, sometimes divided into the **oro-pharynx**, the **naso-pharynx** and the **laryngo-pharynx**. *Adj.* **pharyngeal** or **pharyngal**.

phase /feɪz/ *n.* 1. The timing relation between two simultaneous waves of identical frequency. If they reach their maxima at the same instant, they are *in phase*; if not, they are *out of phase*, and there is a *phase difference* between them. 2. Any distinguishable stage in the articulation of a single segment. A typical segment may be analysed into an **onset phase**, a **medial phase** and an **offset phase**.

phases of speech *n. pl.* The various distinguishable neurological and physical events which occur in sequence during the production and comprehension of speech. Catford (1977: 4–5) distinguishes seven phases: (1) **neurolinguistic programming**; (2) the **neuro-muscular phase**; (3) the **organic phase**; (4) the **aerodynamic phase**; (5) the **acoustic phase**; (6) the **neuroreceptive phase**; (7) **neuro-linguistic identification**.

phon /fɒn/ *n.* A unit of loudness level, defined so that the loudness in phons of any sound is numerically equal to the intensity in deci-bels of a pure 1,000-Hz tone judged to be equally loud. Barkhausen (1926).

phonaestheme /ˈfəʊniːsθiːm/ *n.* A phoneme or cluster in a particular language which recurs repeatedly in words of related meanings, such as English /sl-/ in *slip, slick, slide, slop, slush*, etc. Firth (1930).

phonaesthenia /fəʊniːsˈθiːniə/ *n.* An abnormally weak voice.

phonaesthesia /fəʊniːsˈθiːʒə/ *n.* (also **phonesthesia**, **syn(a)esthesia**) Any direct correspondence between sound and meaning, including **onomatopoeia**, the use of **phonaesthemes**, and such cases as Basque *tximeleta* 'butterfly', whose delicate, fluttery sound appears to mimic the appearance of the insect. *Adj.* **phon(a)esthetic** /fəʊniːsˈθetɪk/.

phonaesthetics /fəʊniːsˈθetɪks/ *n.* (also **phonesthetics**) The study of **sound symbolism**.

phonation /fəʊˈneɪʃn̩/ *n.* 1. [*non-technical*] The act of producing speech sounds. 2. The use of the **larynx**, aided by an **airstream**, to generate an audible source of acoustic energy which can be modified by the rest of the vocal tract. 3. Sometimes more specif-ically a synonym for **voicing** (sense 1). *V.* **phonate** /ˈfəʊneɪt/; *adj.* **phonatory** /ˈfəʊnətri/.

phonation type *n.* (also **phonatory stricture type**) Any of the various distinguishable types of activity in the **glottis** which can produce a stream of air for the organs of articulation. There is some disagreement as to which types should be recognized; here I follow Laver (1994). *Simple* phonation types include **nil phonation**, **breath**, **whisper**, **creak**, **(modal) voice** and **falsetto**, the last three of which provide a *pulsed* airstream. A number of *compound* phonation types are possible, including **breathy voice**, **whispery voice**, **creaky**

voice, **whispery creaky voice**, and similar combinations with *falsetto* in place of *voice*.

phonatory setting *n.* The tendency of an individual to maintain some particular **phonation type** (such as **creaky voice**) throughout speech. See Laver (1994: 414–427) for an account with proposals for transcription.

phone /fəʊn/ *n.* A single phonetic **segment**, viewed in terms of its phonetic character and without regard to its possible phonological status. The term 'phone' is related to **phoneme** in the same way **morph** is related to **morpheme**. Grote (1866); Lloyd (1899); the obsolete terms **sone** and **phthong** were also formerly used in this sense, as was **allophone** for a few years.

phonem /'fəʊniːm/ *n.* An early form of the term **phoneme**, sometimes used also in other senses. See Abercrombie (1985) for an account. Harrington (1912).

phonemateme /'fəʊniːmətiːm/ *n.* In **Glossematic phonology**, a **segment** from the point of view of its phonetic characteristics, as opposed to its place in the system: a **phone**.

phonematic /fəʊnɪ'mætɪk/ *adj.* [*obsolete*] Pertaining to **phonemes**; **phonemic**.

phonematics /fəʊnɪ'mætɪks/ *n.* 1. [*obsolete*] An old synonym for **phonemics** (sense 2). 2. In **Prosodic Analysis**, the study of **phonematic units**. 3. In **Glossematic phonology**, a label applied first to phonology in general and later to that part of phonology dealing with content, rather than with expression; in the second sense, the term contrasts with **cenematics**.

phonematic unit *n.* In **Prosodic Analysis**, any one of the minimally specified segments which can occur in some given position. A phonematic unit represents a kind of skeleton which receives its full phonetic realization only after the application of all relevant **prosodies**. The phonematic units which occur in one position can in no way be identified with those occurring in other positions.

phoneme /'fəʊniːm/ *n.* In many theories of phonology, a fundamental (often *the* fundamental) unit of phonological structure, an abstract **segment** which is one of a set of such segments in the phonological system of a particular language or speech variety, often defined as 'the smallest unit which can make a difference in meaning'. First recognized in the late nineteenth century, the phoneme occupied a more or less central position in every theory of phonology promulgated in the twentieth century, with the sole exception of **Prosodic Analysis**, until the development of **non-linear** approaches in the 1980s; often regarded as the most conspicuous characteristic of **classical phonology**, the phoneme was also important in all earlier versions of **generative phonology**. Two points need to be stressed: (1) the most important property of a phoneme is that it **contrasts** with the other phonemes in the system, and hence (2) we can only speak of the phonemes of some particular speech variety (a particular accent of a particular language). Languages differ in the number of phonemes they distinguish (see **phoneme system**), but every valid word in every language necessarily consists of some permissible sequence of that language's phonemes (see **phonotactics**). Several views of the phoneme have been advanced, chiefly differing first as to whether the phoneme is regarded as a **phonological prime** not capable of further decomposition or as a cluster of more primitive elements, second in the degree of abstractness imputed to it, and finally in whether the phoneme is regarded as a mental reality, a physical unit or merely a convenient analytical fiction. Both the **British school** and the **American Structuralists** regard the phoneme as indivisible and as minimally abstract, a conception often labelled the **autonomous** (or **classical**) **phoneme**. In this view, the phoneme is essentially a structureless object which none the less has identifiable phonetic characteristics; it may be realized in speech by phonetically different **phones** in different environments (its **allophones**), and the allophones of a phoneme are united within it by their shared **phonetic similarity** and by their **complementary distribution**. The view of the **Prague School** differs somewhat in regarding the phonetic characteristics of a phoneme as fundamental, and hence in stressing the way in which phonemes tend to occur in phonetically identifiable patterns. A very different conception, the **systematic phoneme**, was put forward by the early generative phonologists. The systematic phoneme is explicitly regarded, not as a primitive, but as a mere bundle of the real primitives, the **distinctive features**. More importantly, the systematic phoneme is in general a highly abstract object, closely resembling the **morphophoneme** of the American Structuralists; as a result of the application of a long series of ordered rules, a single phoneme may reach the surface in a form which is phonetically utterly different from its canonical form; it may merge with another phoneme into a single segment; it may even disappear altogether. The non-linear approaches which have dominated the field since the 1980s have dispensed with the phoneme altogether, though the term 'phoneme' is still sometimes applied to an autosegment on the **segmental tier** in those versions of **Autosegmental Phonology** which recognize such a tier. See also **diaphone**, **diaphoneme**. *Adj.* **phonemic**, formerly also **phonematic**. The concept of the phoneme was known to the Indian grammarian Patanjali in the second century BC and to the Icelandic First Grammarian in the twelfth century; it was developed with varying degrees of explicitness by a number of nineteenth-century authors, including Odell (1806), Whitney (1843), Müller (in 1843, but published in 1875), Ellis (1844), Pitman (1846), Winteler (1876) and Sweet (1877), but no fully explicit formulation was produced, and no term was available at the time. The term 'phoneme' was coined by the French phonetician A. Dutriche-Desgenettes in a lecture in 1873, but in the sense of **phone** or **segment** – two terms not coined until much later. The term was picked up by others, including Louis Havet and Saussure, both of whom have sometimes been wrongly credited with inventing it. Saussure's famous 1879 paper (actually published in 1878) gave the term wide currency in the earlier sense, and this older sense did not finally disappear until the 1940s, especially in France; it is the only sense attested for 'phoneme' in the first edition of the *OED*. The first fully explicit exposition of the phoneme principle was developed by the **Kazan School**, and the term 'phoneme' was first used in its modern sense by them – though note that the Kazan linguists sometimes also used 'phoneme' in the sense of **morphophoneme**. The Kazan conception was carried to the west by L. V. Ščerba, who introduced the phoneme concept to Daniel Jones in England in 1911. In the United States the phoneme principle was slow to gain acceptance, even though it was championed by Edward Sapir, notably in his classic 1925 paper, in which he argued for the psychological reality of phonemes; Bloomfield accepted the principle in his 1933 book, but as late as 1934 Morris Swadesh could write that the phoneme concept had only recently been accepted. Note also that many American Structuralists, following Bloomfield (1933), regard **prosodemes** (**suprasegmental phonemes**) as phonemes, a position rejected by most others, notably by Daniel Jones, who prefers to speak of **tonemes**, **chronemes** and **stronemes**. For historical accounts, see Fischer-Jørgensen (1975, esp. ch. 6), Anderson (1985, esp. chs 10–11), Abercrombie (1991a: ch. 3), or the appendix to the third (1967) edition of Jones (1950).

phoneme principle *n.* The principle that the sounds of a particular speech variety can be exhaustively assigned to a (usually small) set of **phonemes**.

phoneme system *n.* (also **phoneme inventory**) The complete set of **phonemes** set up for a particular language, especially when presented in an orderly manner, with consonants arranged by place, manner, voicing, etc., and vowels by height, backness, nasality, etc. Beginning with the **Prague School**, phoneme systems have often been regarded as of typological importance. Languages differ widely in the number of phonemes they distinguish: the Brazilian language Piraha% has only 10 (seven consonants and three vowels), while the Khoisan language !Xũ has 119; the average seems to be around 25. Useful surveys can be found in Trubetzkoy (1939), Hockett (1955), Sedlak (1969), O'Connor (1973: ch. 7), Crothers (1978), Nartey (1979), Maddieson (1980a, 1980b, 1984), Lass (1984: ch. 7) and Lindblom (1986).

phonemic clause /fə'niːmɪk klɔːz/ *n.* A single stretch of speech which is planned and executed as an organized piece of behaviour; this may or may not correspond to a syntactic clause. Trager and Smith (1951).

phonemic indeterminacy /ɪndɪ'tɜːmɪnəsi/ *n.* A synonym for **neutralization** used by some **American Structuralists**. Haugen (1969).

phonemicization /fəniːmɪsaɪ'zeɪʃn̩/ *n.* 1. The procedure by which an analyst interprets the sounds of a language as a specified set of **phonemes**. 2. See **phonemic split**. *V.* **phonemicize**.

phonemic long component *n.* A phonetic feature which extends over more than one segment within a single phonological form; the simplest and most obvious type of **prosody**. For example, all obstruents in a cluster in English must agree in voicing; the feature [±voice] might therefore be treated as a phonemic long component extending over the whole cluster, whose members are individually unspecified for voicing.

phonemic overlapping *n.* Any state of affairs in which two or more **phonemes** in a particular language have identical phonetic realizations in certain environments, not necessarily the same environments. See **partial overlapping** and **complete overlapping** for discussion and illustration.

phonemics /fə'niːmɪks/ *n.* [*obsolescent*] 1. Any procedure for identifying the **phonemes** of a language from a corpus of data. 2. (formerly also **phonematics**) A former synonym for **phonology**, often preferred by the **American Structuralists** and reflecting the importance in structuralist work of phonemics in sense 1.

phonemic spelling *n.* (also, commonly but inaccurately, **phonetic spelling**) An alphabetic orthography in which each phoneme is consistently represented by a single letter and each letter consistently represents a single phoneme. This is supposedly the whole basis of an alphabetic orthography, but perhaps no standard orthography achieves the ideal. Among European languages, Finnish and Basque come very close.

phonemic split *n.* (also **split**, **fission**, **phonemicization**) Any historical process in which an original single phoneme gives rise to two (or more) phonemes as descendants. For example, the short /u/ of Middle English has, in most modern varieties, split into the two phonemes /ʊ/ and /ʌ/: *bush* but *mush*, *put* but *putt*, *pull* but *dull*, all of these originally having the same vowel. Split can occur in various ways, of which **loss of the conditioning factor** and **lexical diffusion** are particularly important. If one of the descendants of the original phoneme undergoes **merger** with another pre-existing phoneme, we have **primary split**; if not, we have **secondary split**.

phonemic tier *n.* See **segmental tier**.

phonemic transcription *n.* Any **transcription** of words or connected speech in a particular speech variety in terms of the **phonemes** which have been set up by the analyst for that variety. Such a transcription provides the minimum information necessary to construct a complete pronunciation by rule; it omits all predictable phonetic detail. Cf. **phonetic transcription**.

phonetic /fə'netɪk/ *adj.* 1. Pertaining to speech sounds or to speech. 2. Pertaining to **phonetics**. 3. (of a transcription or representation) Characterized by an abundance of detail beyond that required for strictly linguistic purposes; not **phonemic**.

phonetic alphabet *n.* 1. Any recognized system for transcribing speech sounds onto paper which is sufficiently detailed and complete to provide an unambiguous symbol for every speech sound which needs to be distinguished. The most comprehensive and widely used such system is the **International Phonetic Alphabet**; **American transcription** is still often used in the United States. 2. Any of several recognized systems for spelling out words and names during radio communication. The US Army uses its famous *Able*, *Baker*, *Charlie*, *Dog*, *Easy*, *Fox* system, while shipping and air traffic control use the *Alpha*, *Bravo*, *Charlie*, *Delta*, *Echo*, *Foxtrot* system.

phonetic content *n.* The property of a phonological unit, such as a **distinctive feature** or a **phoneme**, by which it expresses real

information about the phonetic character of associated speech
sounds.

phonetic correlate /ˈkɒrəleɪt/ *n.* Any phonetic property whose
presence is associated with the presence of a phonological characteristic. For example, the phonetic correlates of **stress** may be any
or all of greater loudness, higher pitch or greater duration.

phonetic distance /ˈdɪstəns/ *n.* The inverse of **phonetic similarity**.
See Laver (1994: 392–395) for a proposal based on English.

phonetic drift *n.* An instance of **generational change** involving the
phonetic realization of a phoneme, such as the gradual lowering of
/æ/ in RP during the last several generations.

phonetic feature *n.* Any independently controllable component of
speech.

phonetic form *n.* (also **phonetic representation**) The phonetically
more-or-less fully specified representation of a word or a longer
sequence, often especially when this is contrasted with its **phonological (underlying) form**.

phonetic function *n.* One of the two fundamental functions of a
distinctive feature: the contribution of some significant phonetic
content to the realization of a segment containing it. Cf. **classificatory function**.

phonetician /fəʊnəˈtɪʃn̩/ *n.* A practitioner of **phonetics**.

phonetic illusion /ɪˈluːʒn̩/ *n.* The phenomenon in which a native
speaker insists that two different words which, objectively, are phonetically identical nevertheless sound different, as a consequence of
their having different underlying forms. The classic case is the Sarcee
speaker who insisted that *dìní* 'this one' (underlying *dìní*) sounded
different from *dìní* 'it makes a sound' (underlying *dìnít*). Sapir (1933).

phonetic motivation /məʊtɪˈveɪʃn̩/ *n.* The property of a **phonological rule** which is easy to understand in phonetic terms, such as
the nasalization of a vowel before a nasal consonant. Phonetically
motivated rules are commonly called **natural** rules.

phonetic plausibility /plɔːzɪˈbɪlɪti/ *n.* 1. In **American Structuralist**
phonology, a **criterion for phonological analysis** by which different
phones may be assigned to a single phoneme only if the phonetic
variation of the resulting phoneme can be explained in terms of
natural phonetic processes. 2. The property of a **phonological rule**

whose presence makes either production or perception of speech easier in some identifiable respect. Sommerstein (1977: 14–15).

phonetic representation *n.* See **phonetic form**.

phonetic rule *n.* (also **detail rule**) In any approach to phonology employing rules, a particular type of rule whose function is, in some sense, no more than producing the correct phonetic detail in the pronunciation of a linguistic form: a **low-level rule**. Its precise characterization is controversial; Anderson (1975), as interpreted by Sommerstein (1977), suggests the following: a rule is a phonetic rule iff (1) it makes no reference to any non-phonological feature; (2) it makes no reference to any boundary weaker than a word-boundary; and (3) it does not change the specification of any feature which is underlyingly distinctive for any segments affected by the rule. See Sommerstein (1977: 9.1) for discussion, and see also **P-rule**.

phonetics /fə'netɪks/ *n.* (formerly also **phonology**) The scientific study of speech, conventionally divided into **articulatory phonetics** (the study of the organs of speech and their use in producing speech sounds), **acoustic phonetics** (the study of the physical properties of the sounds produced in speaking) and **auditory phonetics** (the study of the processing and interpretation of speech sounds by the ear, the nervous system and the brain); **instrumental phonetics** is the study of any of these by means of instruments to measure, record or analyse data. **Anthropophonics** (or **general phonetics**) considers the total range of speech sounds producible by the human vocal apparatus, independently of any real or possible linguistic use; **linguistic phonetics** examines the speech sounds occurring in particular languages or in languages generally. Phonetics is commonly regarded as a distinct discipline from linguistics, the two together being labelled the *linguistic sciences*. For an introduction, see Laver (1994), Ladefoged (1975 [1993]), or Clark and Yallop (1990). *Adj.* **phonetic**. The ancient Indian grammarians were sophisticated phoneticians; their work was not equalled anywhere before the nineteenth century. The Greeks and the Chinese made only very limited progress in phonetics; the Icelandic First Grammarian and the medieval Arabs were very much better, but still not up to Indian standards. The modern tradition of phonetics began in England in the sixteenth century and led, through the work of such scholars as Ellis, Bell, Sweet and Jones, to the establishment of the **British school of phonetics**. See Robins (1990) for an account. NOTE: See the comments under **phonology**.

phonetic setting *n*. The tendency on the part of a given speaker to maintain a particular configuration or state of the vocal apparatus throughout speech. See Laver (1994: 394–427) for an account with proposals for transcription.

phonetic similarity /sɪmɪ'lærɪti/ *n*. An important but elusive **criterion for phonological analysis**. The idea is that two phones which are in **complementary distribution** can be assigned to a single phoneme if they are 'phonetically similar', but this notion is difficult to make explicit. One approach is to demand that such segments should share more phonetic features with each other than either does with any other segment. In English, for example, unaspirated [p⁼] is in complementary distribution with each of [pʰ], [tʰ] and [kʰ] (which themselves contrast), but [p⁼] clearly shares more features with [pʰ] than either does with any of the others, and so [p⁼] and [pʰ] can be assigned to a single phoneme /p/. On the other hand, English [h] and [ŋ] are in complementary distribution, but they share no features at all beyond [–syllabic], which they also share with all other English consonants, and hence they should not be assigned to a single phoneme. See Fischer-Jørgensen (1975: 25–26, 84–86) for discussion, and see Hyman (1975: 64–65) for a problematic example.

phonetic specification *n*. The determination, in terms of some system of description, of the phonetic characteristics of a speech sound.

phonetic spelling *n*. See **phonemic spelling**.

phonetic transcription *n*. Any **transcription** of words or connected speech which represents speech sounds in some considerable phonetic detail, often including some detail which is predictable by rule from other information. Such a transcription can be provided by any competent phonetician, even in the absence of any phonological analysis of the speech variety represented and even when the phonetician has no idea what the utterance means. Cf. **phonemic transcription**.

phonetic universal *n*. Any **universal** which pertains primarily to the phonetic characteristics of segments. See Fischer-Jørgensen *et al.* (1979).

phoniatrics /fɒni'ætrɪks/ *n*. The diagnosis and treatment of pathological disorders of speech. A practitioner is a **phoniatrist** /fə'naɪətrɪst/.

phonic /'fɒnɪk/ *adj.* 1. Pertaining to speech sounds. 2. Using speech sounds as a medium; oral.

phonics /'fɒnɪks/ *n.* A method of teaching spelling and reading which concentrates on breaking a word down into a sequence of graphic elements and assigning pronunciations to these.

phonic substance *n.* (also **phonetic substance**) Speech regarded as consisting of a set of physical properties, either articulatory or acoustic.

phonological /fəʊnə'lɒdʒɪkəl/ *adj.* 1. Pertaining to **phonology**. 2. (of some linguistic phenomenon) Belonging properly to the domain of phonology, rather than to some other domain, such as phonetics, morphology or syntax.

phonological change *n.* 1. Broadly, any historical change which has perceptible consequences for the pronunciation of a language. 2. More narrowly, a historical change which has consequences for the phonological structure of language, such as a change in the number or distribution of phonemes, in the way the phonemes are related, or in the number, nature or ordering of phonological rules. In this narrower sense, the term excludes purely phonetic changes in which nothing happens beyond fairly small changes in the phonetic realizations of certain segments. See Fischer-Jørgensen (1975: 102–104) for a brief summary with references, and see Moulton (1967) for a classification of types of phonological change.

phonological component *n.* 1. In some comprehensive theories of grammar, notably in transformational grammar and its descendants, that part of the framework which deals with relating phonological representations and their corresponding phonetic realizations. 2. See **component**.

phonological conditioning *n.* The selection of an **allomorph** on the basis of its phonetic environment, as when the English plural marker appears as [s] after a voiceless segment but [z] after a voiced one. Cf. **grammatical conditioning**, **lexical conditioning**.

phonological form (PF) *n.* In some theory or analysis, a representation of a linguistic object (a word, a phrase, etc.) in terms of the phonological elements recognized in that framework. The term is particularly associated with early versions of **generative phonology**, where it is applied to a rather abstract level of representation which has not yet been converted by rules to its corresponding **phonetic form**.

phonological phrase *n.* (also **prosodic phrase**) In some analyses, a posited level of phonological structure which is larger than a **phonological word** but smaller than an **intonational phrase**. This construct is particularly associated with the **Prosodic Hierarchy** model, in which it is taken, for example, as the domain within which **iambic reversal** applies in English.

phonological phrase boundary *n.* (also **major pause**) A boundary separating units which form the maximal domain within which any phonological processes can apply, generally identified as a single intonation contour and often represented by the symbol //. No rule can ever apply across such a boundary.

phonological position *n.* In some analyses, a position in a morpheme which is underlyingly empty of phonological material but which must be filled by some segment in any phonetic form involving that morpheme. For example, the Hebrew definite article is sometimes represented underlyingly as *haX*, in which *X* represents an empty position. This position is filled by gemination of a following consonant, if possible; if the following consonant is one that cannot be geminated in Hebrew, the position is filled instead by gemination of the preceding vowel: hence *melex´* 'king', *hammelex* 'the king', but *ʔiiš* 'man', *haaʔiiš* 'the man' (/ʔ/ cannot be geminated).

phonological prime *n.* (also **phonological primitive**, **atom**) In a given theory of phonology, any one of the minimal phonological elements in terms of which the theory operates and which can in no way be decomposed into simpler elements. Most versions of classical phonology took the **phonemes** as primes; the Prague School (arguably) and classical generative phonology (certainly) took the **distinctive features** as primes. Many contemporary theories of phonology take as their primes **components** or **autosegments** which are rather similar to **unary features**. See Fudge (1967).

phonological representation *n.* A representation of the sound structure of a linguistic form which excludes phonetic information predictable by rules, such as a **phonemic transcription**.

phonological rule *n.* (also **P-rule**) In the broadest sense, any rule which, in some analysis, is posited as involved in deriving a pronunciation from an underlying phonological representation. In this conception, both rules appealing to morphological and lexical information and purely phonetic rules are included. Very frequently, however, this label has been restricted to some proper subset of such rules. Some would exclude rules appealing to morpholexical information like 'preterite' or 'ablauting verb' while including rules appealing to major word classes like 'noun' or 'Latinate vocabulary'; others would exclude all such rules; both groups might, independently, include or exclude purely phonetic (allophonic) rules. Some would exclude purely **morphophonemic rules**, while others would apply the term 'phonological rules' *only* to such rules, excluding all other types. In **Natural Generative Phonology**, the term is applied *only* to phonetic (allophonic) rules, all other types being excluded.

phonological scaling /ˈskeɪlɪŋ/ *n.* The setting up of phonological **hierarchies**, such as that based on **phonological strength**, in the hope of deriving **universals** of phonological behaviour.

phonological space /speɪs/ *n.* An abstract conception of the total range of possibilities available for distinguishing one **segment** from another. The familiar **vowel quadrilateral** represents a simple two-dimensional section of that space (tongue height vs. backness), but a full representation of phonological space would be a multi-dimensional space involving such additional factors as lip-rounding, velic position and tongue configuration. Only a subset of these parameters is ever considered at one time, most often in connection with vowels (the **vowel space**).

phonological strength *n.* (also **strength**) An abstract dimension, or rather one of several abstract dimensions, along which **segments** can be hierarchically ordered with respect to their behaviour in the phonological processes of **lenition** and **fortition**. A familiar example is the dimension of *openness*, along which segments may be ranked Stop > Fricative > Approximant > Zero, corresponding to a common direction of change in intervocalic position. See Lass (1984: 177–183).

phonological universal *n.* Any **universal** of fundamentally phonological character, such as one constraining **phoneme systems**. See Greenberg (1978). Cf. **phonetic universal**.

phonological use of diacritic features *n.* The use of **diacritic features** to distinguish segments which undergo some phonological process from otherwise identical segments which fail to undergo the process. For example, some Spanish verbs with infinitives in

-cer (/θer/) and *-cir* (/θir/) acquire a /k/ in the first-person singular present indicative while others do not: *conocer* 'know', *conozco* 'I know', but *mecer* 'stir', *mezo* 'I stir'; *conducir* 'drive', *conduzco* 'I drive', but *esparcir* 'spread', *esparzo* 'I spread'. A suitable diacritic feature might be added to one group or the other, and the /k/-insertion rule could be formulated only to apply in the presence (or absence) of that feature. This device has usually been regarded as quite legitimate within **generative phonology**. Cf. **diacritic use of phonological features**. Kiparsky (1968).

phonological utterance *n*. See **prosodic utterance**.

phonological weight *n*. See **syllable weight**.

phonological word *n*. A particular phonological unit which is the domain of certain phonological processes in a given language. In the unmarked case, the phonological word is identical to the morphological word. But it may be larger: in many languages, a group of clitics forms a single phonological word with the associated host, as in French *je te le donnerai* 'I'll give it to you'. Or it may be smaller: in Turkish, compound words are not subject to the usual word-based rules of vowel harmony and stress assignment, and apparently consist of two phonological words. The concept has been particularly developed within the **Prosodic Hierarchy**; a rather similar notion within **Metrical Phonology** is called the **mot** or the **prosodic word**.

phonologist /fə'nɒlədʒɪst/ *n*. A practitioner of **phonology**.

phonologization /fənɒlədʒaɪ'zeɪʃn̩/ *n*. Any phonological change in which an allophonic variation becomes phonemic (contrastive): phonemic **split**. An example is the split of Old English /f/, with conditioned allophones [f] and [v], into the modern English phonemes /f/ and /v/.

phonology /fə'nɒlədʒi/ *n*. 1. The branch of linguistics dealing with the relations among speech sounds in particular languages and in languages generally, and contrasting with **phonetics**. Though the creation of alphabetic writing necessarily required some intuitive grasp of phonology, the subject only began to be distinguished from phonetics in the late nineteenth century, and the distinction was not firmly established until well into this century, particularly as a result of the work done by the **Prague School**, which popularized the term 'phonology'. Most approaches to phonology before the 1960s were centred on the **phoneme** and attached great importance to **distribution**, to **contrast** and to **representations**, with little interest in phonological processes; this **classical phonology** embraced the work of the **American Structuralists** and of the **British school of phonetics**, as well as that of **Glossematic phonology** and that of the more divergent Prague School. The highly divergent **Prosodic Analysis** of the 1950s, though not widely influential, adumbrated many ideas of the 1980s. In the 1960s the classical version of **generative phonology** revolutionized phonological thinking. This approach emphasized the role of phonological processes; abstract **underlying forms** formulated in terms of **systematic phonemes** were converted by elaborate sequences of **phonological rules** into surface phonetic forms, and the phonemes themselves were decomposed into bundles of **distinctive features**. The framework quickly proved to be excessively unconstrained, and both **Natural Phonology** and **Natural Generative Phonology** were developed to curb these excesses, while an exuberant range of proposals such as **Stratificational phonology**, **Upside-down Phonology** and **Atomic Phonology** failed to attract wide support. Around 1980, several linguists began independently to develop **non-linear** views of phonology involving much more elaborate representations of phonological structure. **Autosegmental Phonology** was developed mainly to handle tonal phenomena but was rapidly expanded into a comprehensive theory, while **Metrical Phonology** has largely remained a method for dealing with word accent, particularly stress. Meanwhile, a range of increasingly elaborate **privative** (or **holistic**) frameworks was being developed, including **Particle Phonology**, **Dependency Phonology** and **Government and Charm Phonology**. In contrast, **Lexical Phonology** retains much of the spirit of classical generative phonology, in that it concentrates on the same kinds of phenomena. See Householder (1979) for a critical overview of some modern approaches to phonology, and see Goldsmith (1995) for a comprehensive review of current work. 2. The entire phonological system of a particular language: *the phonology of French*. 3. [*obsolete*] In the work of many **American Structuralists**, a label applied to the totality of phonetics and 'phonemics' ('phonology' in the modern sense). 4. [*obsolete*] A label once applied specifically to the phonological ideas of the **Prague School**. 5. [*obsolete*] In British usage, a frequent synonym for **historical phonology**. 6. [*obsolete*] In the nineteenth century, a frequent term for **phonetics**, sometimes extended or specialized to denote any of speech physiology, the study of pronunciation in general, the pronunciation of a particular language, or the sound system of a particular language. *Adj.* **phonological**. NOTE: The modern distinction between 'phonetics' and 'phonology' was not well established before the 1950s; see Abercrombie (1991b: ch. 2) for a brief historical survey. The term 'functional phonetics', coined by André Martinet, has often been used in preference to 'phonology', and is not quite dead even today in some quarters.

phonology–syntax interface /ˈɪntəfeɪs/ *n.* The putative boundary between the domains of phonology and syntax. The nature and location, and even the very existence, of this boundary have often been vexed questions. The **American Structuralists**, with their doctrine of the **separation of levels**, refused to admit *any* grammatical information, even morphological facts, into phonology, but all other frameworks have accepted that phonological rules (in the broad sense) must be sensitive at least to the presence of morphological and syntactic boundaries, and sometimes also to additional grammatical information, such as the identity of a syntactic category. The issue of whether syntactic rules can have access to phonological information has been deeply controversial. See Pullum and Zwicky (1988) for a review with references.

phonometer /fəˈnɒmɪtə/ *n.* An instrument for measuring or recording the **intensity** of sound. *Adj.* **phonometric** /fɒnəˈmetrɪk/; *abstr. n.* **phonometry** /fəˈnɒmətri/ or **phonometrics** /fɒnəˈmetrɪks/.

phonon /ˈfəʊnɒn/ *n.* In **Stratificational phonology**, any one of the **unary features** (**components**) which are the minimal phonological units in that framework, such as *vocalic*, *labial* or *voiceless*.

phonostylistics /fəʊnəstaɪˈlɪstɪks/ *n.* The study of the aesthetic or expressive functions of sound(s). *Adj.* **phonostylistic**.

phonotactically motivated rule /fəʊnətæktɪkli ˈməʊtɪveɪtɪd/ *n.* A **phonological rule** which has the effect of bringing phonological forms into line with the **phonotactics** of the language. A 'positively motivated rule' removes or alleviates violations; a 'negatively motivated rule' applies *except* when its application would produce a violation. Sommerstein (1977: 197).

phonotactic range /fəʊnətæktɪk ˈreɪndʒ/ *n.* The total set of contexts in which a particular segment can occur.

phonotactics /fəʊnəˈtæktɪks/ *n.* In a given language, the set of constraints on the possible sequences of consonant and vowel phonemes within a word, a morpheme or a syllable. For example, an English word can have a maximum of three consonants before the first vowel; if three occur, the first must be /s/, the second must be a voiceless plosive /p t k/, and the third must be a liquid or glide /l r w j/. *Adj.* **phonotactic**.

Phrasal Stress Rule /'freɪzəl/ *n.* (**PSR**) In some analyses, the distinctive stress rule which assigns stress in compounds like *pregnancy test* and *driving licence*.

phthong /fθɒŋ/ *n.* [*obsolete*] An early synonym for **phone** or **segment**. Carruthers (1900).

physical phonetics /'fɪzɪkəl/ *n.* The detailed description, usually by means of instruments, of the phonetic characteristics of individual utterances. Cf. **systematic phonetics**. Chomsky (1964).

Pig Latin /'pɪg lætɪn/ *n.* An English **language game** in which each word of an utterance is deformed by having its initial consonant(s) (if any) moved to the end and followed by the diphthong /ei/, or by /wei/ if the word has no initial consonant: *Yntactic-say Uctures-stray as-way itten-wray y-bay Oam-Nay Omsky-Chay in-way ineteen-nay ifty-fay even-say*.

Pike heresy /'paɪk herəsi/ *n.* The view, advanced by Kenneth Pike (1947b and elsewhere), that the phonology of a language cannot be adequately analysed without reference to grammatical facts, and more generally that no aspect of a language can be studied without taking other aspects into account. This rejection of the **separation of levels** was regarded as heretical by the **American Structuralists** of the time.

pinna /'pɪnə/ *n.* The fleshy part of the **outer ear** lying outside the head; the 'ear' in everyday usage.

pitch /pɪtʃ/ *n.* 1. (also **perceived pitch**) The perceptual correlate of the **frequency** of a sound – in speech, of the **fundamental frequency** of the vocal folds. The higher the frequency (that is, the more rapid the vibration), the higher the pitch, but the correlation is far from linear: at higher frequencies (though not at lower), the pitch is roughly proportional to the logarithm of the frequency. (See Denes and Pinson 1993: 104.) The unit of pitch is the **mel**. 2. In the *SPE* **feature system**, a group of six **distinctive features** (*high, low, elevated, rising, falling, concave*) provisionally suggested (p. 300) but not defined or elaborated.

pitch accent *n.* 1. A type of **word accent** occurring in some languages, in which the syllables (or moras) of each word must exhibit one of the permitted sequences of **pitches**. Standard Japanese, for example, shows such contrasts as *shiro* (HL) 'white' and *shiro* (LH) 'castle', *ame* (HL) 'rain' and *ame* (LH) 'candy', *sakura* (LHH) 'cherry', *zakuro* (HLL) 'pomegranate' and *kokoro* (LHL) 'heart'. A pitch accent differs from a **tone** system in that the pitches of only certain syllables need be specified, the rest being predictable by rule: in Japanese, for example, only the position of the pitch fall need be marked, all other pitches then being completely determined. In a tone language, in contrast, the tone of every syllable usually has to be independently specified. 2. [*rare*] See **sentence stress**.

pitch contour *n.* The shape of the **pitch** value within the duration of the syllable bearing it.

pitch height *n.* The exact placement of the **pitch** of a syllable within a given **pitch span**.

pitch language *n.* A language in which each word has a characteristic pitch contour, so that each syllable receives a particular pitch level depending on its place in the word and on the contour assigned to that word. In the canonical case, the pitch of every syllable is predictable from just one specification. In the pitch language Japanese, for example, the pitch of every syllable is predictable from a specification of the location of the pitch fall in the word. Cf. **tone language**.

pitch obtrusion /əbˈtruːʒn̩/ *n.* A rapid and wide departure of pitch from a smooth or undulating contour, often regarded as a major means of making a syllable prominent in English. Bolinger (1958).

pitch prominence *n.* The phenomenon in which an accented syllable stands out within a word by having a noticeably higher or lower **pitch** than neighbouring syllables.

pitch range /reɪndʒ/ *n.* The limits within which an individual produces or uses variations in **pitch**. Laver (1994: 155) distinguishes among the *organic pitch range* (the limits imposed by the individual's physiology), the *linguistic pitch range* (the range of pitch used in ordinary speech) and the *paralinguistic pitch range* (the extended range used for paralinguistic purposes).

pitch setting *n.* The use of pitch by a particular speaker: mean value, overall range and degree of fluctuation.

pitch span /spæn/ *n.* The difference in pitch height between a local maximum and a local minimum in speech.

Pitmatic /pɪt'mætɪk/ *n.* [*non-technical*] The local name for the distinctive speech variety of County Durham in northern England. Presumably from *pitman* 'coal-miner'.

place /pleɪs/ *n.* 1. See **place of articulation**. 2. See **articulatory place**. 3. In some versions of **feature geometry**, a superordinate **class node** dominating all features pertaining to place of articulation.

place-neutral articulation *n.* Any articulation in which the **active articulator** forms a constriction with the **passive articulator** which is most directly opposite it, such as a bilabial, an apico-dental, a lamino-alveolar or a dorso-velar. Cf. **displaced articulation**.

place of articulation *n.* (also **place**) In the description of consonants, the parameter along which differences in the location of the **constriction** are recorded. A large number of such places can be linguistically distinguished; these are denoted by such labels as *bilabial*, *(lamino-)alveolar* and *velar*.

place theory of hearing *n.* A theory of hearing which holds that sound waves of different frequencies stimulate nerve receptors at different points along the **basilar membrane**, thus allowing complex sounds to be analysed into their components; the greater the amplitude of the sound, the more intense the nervous response. This theory is now universally accepted. Cf. the **telephone** and **resonance theories of hearing**.

plain /pleɪn/ *adj.* In the **Jakobson–Halle feature system**, a **distinctive feature** invoked somewhat anomalously as the opposite of both **flat** and **sharp**. A [plain] consonant, therefore, is one which is not [flat] (that is, not characterized by a downward shift of formants in the spectrum, and hence not lip-rounded, not pharyngealized and not retroflexed) and also not [sharp] (that is, not characterized by an upward shift of the upper frequencies in the spectrum, and hence not palatalized). Effectively, [flat], [plain] and [sharp] constitute the three values of a single **ternary feature**. Most of the 'ordinary' consonants of English and other languages are [plain].

planar phonology /'pleɪnə/ *n.* Any approach to phonology which views phonological structure as consisting of a number of more-or-less autonomous planes of representation all attached to a single skeleton, rather like the pages of a book. See Roca (1994: 255–260).

plane /pleɪn/ *n.* 1. Any one of the three aspects of phonology distinguished by Karl Bühler: **representation**, **expression**, **appeal**. Bühler

(1934). 2. In **planar phonology**, any one of the autonomous levels posited. Each plane corresponds to a **tier** in the more familiar representation.

plane conflation *n*. In some versions of **planar phonology**, a process by which two independent planes are combined into a single level of representation at some stage in a derivation. McCarthy (1986).

plane copying /'kɒpiɪŋ/ *n*. In some versions of **planar phonology**, a procedure by which the information present in one plane is copied onto a second plane carrying different information so that phono-logical processes can apply to a representation containing both types of information. Halle and Vergnaud (1987).

plateau /'plætəʊ/ *n*. See **topline**. Vaissière (1983).

plateauing *n*. A tone assimilation phenomenon, occurring in some tone languages, in which non-high tones are assimilated to adja-cent high tones, as when the sequence HLH is assimilated to HHH.

Plato **phenomenon** /'pleɪtəʊ/ *n*. See *veto* **phenomenon**.

plethysmograph /plə'θɪzməgrɑːf/ *n*. A device, consisting of a tank enclosing the entire body below the neck, for measuring the expansion and contraction of the chest during speech. *Abstr. n.* **plethysmography** /pləθɪz'mɒgrəfi/.

plosion /'pləʊʒn̩/ *n*. The **release** stage of a **plosive** consonant, during which the built-up air pressure is released. Several types are possible: **median oral release**, **lateral release** and **nasal release**.

plosive /'pləʊsɪv/ *n*. or *adj*. A consonant segment, one type of **oral stop**, whose articulation involves a complete closure of the vocal tract held long enough for air pressure to build up, followed by a sudden release of the trapped air; examples include [p d g q]. The term is commonly restricted to segments made with a **pulmonic egressive airstream mechanism**, the terms **injective**, **ejective**, **implo-sive** and **click** being used for comparable articulations made with other airstream mechanisms. See **plosive theory**.

plosive theory *n*. The analysis of the articulation of a **plosive** con-sonant into three phases: the **approach**, the **hold** and the **release** (or **plosion**).

plummy /'plʌmi/ *adj*. [*non-technical*] A dismissive label occasionally applied to the speech of an individual who uses **Received Pronunciation**, especially **U-RP**, by a hearer who finds such an accent unattractive. According to Wells (1982: 283), the distinctive voice quality of this sort of accent is produced by lowering the larynx and expanding the oro-pharynx. From the jocular suggestion that such an individual appears to speak with 'a plum in the mouth', reflecting the rather small degree of movement of the lips and tongue characteristic of such an accent.

plurisegmental /pluərıseg'mentəl/ *adj.* See **suprasegmental**.

plus-juncture /plʌs/ *n.* In some **American Structuralist** work, a type of **juncture**, represented by the symbol +, posited as occurring internally in words like *night-rate* (*night+rate*) to account for the phonetic contrast with words like *nitrate*, not containing the juncture. The plus juncture is the source of the **morpheme boundary** symbol later used by generative phonologists. Trager and Smith (1951).

plus sign /saın/ *n.* The **auxiliary symbol** +, commonly used to represent a **morpheme boundary**, as when the underlying form of *divinity* is represented as #divi:n + iti#.

pneumograph /'nju:məgrɑ:f/ *n.* A device for measuring expansion of the chest during speech, consisting of a taut belt around the chest whose expansion is recorded. *Abstr. n.* **pneumography** /nju'mɒgrəfi/.

pneumotachograph /nju:mə'tækəgrɑ:f/ *n.* An instrument which measures airflow through the mouth and the nose simultaneously and independently. *Abstr. n.* **pneumotachography** /nju:mətə'kɒ-grəfi/.

polar chart /'pəulə/ *n.* A distinctive graphical device for representing the **vowel space**, differing from the usual **vowel quadrilateral** in having the shape of a circular arc exceeding 90°. It has the advantage of allowing the description of vowels to be unified with the description of consonants. See Figure P1. Catford (1977).

pole /pəul/ *n.* In **Dependency Phonology**, any one of the positions defined by the **elements** of the framework.

polysyllable /'pɒlisıləbəl/ *n.* A word consisting of two or more syllables. Cf. **monosyllable**. *Adj.* **polysyllabic** /pɒlisı'læbık/.

polysystemicism /pɒlisı'sti:məsızm̩/ *n.* The view that there is no such thing as a single phonological system for an entire language, but that different phonological systems must be recognized for different purposes, such as for different strata of vocabulary,

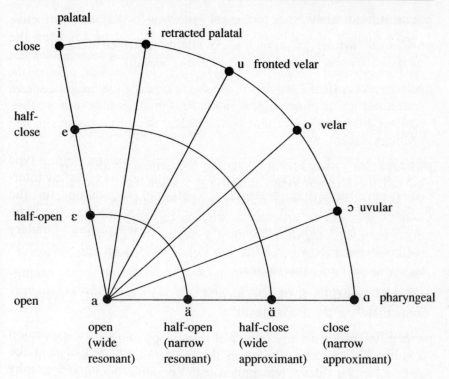

Figure P1 A polar chart

different positions within a word or morpheme, and even for different parts of speech. Though both **Prague School** phonologists and those **American Structuralists** who recognized **coexistent phonemic systems** admitted some degree of polysystemicism, the principle was most fully developed within **Prosodic Analysis**, whose proponents adopted the extreme position that the phonological units occurring in one position or context could absolutely not be identified with those occurring in another. *Adj.* **polysystemic** /pɒlɪsɪˈstiːmɪk/. Ant. **monosystemicism**.

portmanteau morph /pɔːtˈmæntəʊ/ *n.* (also **overlapping morph**) A single **morph** which represents two or more **morphemes**. An example is the morph *-o* in the Latin verb form *amo* 'I love': here *am-* is the verb root, and *-o* simultaneously expresses the categories first person, singular, present, active, indicative, most of which are in general overtly and separately marked on Latin verb forms. Hockett (1947).

portmanteau word *n.* A less usual synonym for **blend**.

positional variant /pə'zɪʃənəl/ *n.* An **allophone** which is conditioned by its environment, as opposed to a **free variant**.

positive exception /'pɒzɪtɪv/ *n.* A phonological form which undergoes a particular **phonological rule** even though it fails to meet the **structural description** of that rule – hence, the very opposite of an ordinary **exception**.

postalveolar /pəʊstælvi'əʊlə/ 1. *adj.* Pertaining to the region just behind the **alveolar ridge**. 2. *adj.* (of a segment) Articulated with the primary constriction occurring just behind the alveolar ridge. 3. *n.* A segment so articulated, such as the post-alveolar approximant used for English /r/ by most speakers in England. 4. *adj.* See **palato-alveolar**. NOTE: The IPA now recommends **postalveolar** in place of the traditional term **palato-alveolar**.

postconsonantal /pəʊstkɒnsə'næntəl/ *adj.* (of a segment) Occurring immediately after a consonant.

postcyclic rule *n.* In any theory of phonology employing the **cycle**, a rule which is not included in the cycle but which applies only after all cyclic rules have applied to all possible domains.

posterior /pɒ'stɪərɪə/ *adj.* (of a phonation type) Produced exclusively with the back (arytenoidal) part of the glottis, the front (ligamental) part being tightly closed. Posterior phonation is possible, but perhaps not used in any language. See Catford (1977: 103). Ant. **anterior**.

posterodorsum /pɒstɪərə'dɔːsəm/ *n.* Another name for the **back** of the tongue, preferred by Catford (1977, 1988). *Adj.* **posterodorsal**.

postlexical rule /pəʊst'leksɪkəl/ *n.* A phonological rule which applies to sequences of words already embedded in a syntactic structure, such as the rule of **tapping** in American English – essentially, a phonological rule applying to phrases. The notion has been particularly well developed within **Lexical Phonology**. Kaisse (1985, 1987) distinguishes **postlexical 1 rules (P1 rules)** from **postlexical 2 rules (P2 rules)**: P1 rules require access to grammatical information, may apply cyclically, may be restricted to applying at word boundaries, and may have lexical exceptions; P2 rules (postlexical rules as earlier conceived) are totally automatic and exceptionless and are typically below the threshold of consciousness. See also **prosodic rule**.

post-nucleus *n.* Any material following the **intonational nucleus** within an **intonational phrase**.

post-tonic *adj.* (of a syllable or segment) Occurring after the position of the **stress**, sometimes more specifically immediately after the stress.

posture /'pɒstʃə/ *n.* In the **Williamson feature system**, a **distinctive feature** with the possible values **flapped**, **steady** and **trilled**.

postvelar /pəʊst'viːlə/ *adj.* or *n.* See **uvular**.

postvocalic /pəʊstvə'kælɪk/ *adj.* (of a segment) Occurring immediately after a vowel.

potential pause /pə'tenʃəl/ *n.* A notion formerly much invoked, particularly by the **American Structuralists**, as a way of identifying **word boundaries**: a word boundary is a point at which a speaker might in principle pause during speech.

Prague School /'prɑːg skuːl/ *n.* The name commonly given to the work done by linguists associated with the Prague Linguistic Circle in the 1920s and 1930s. The Prague School, whose leading theorists were Nikolai Trubetzkoy and Roman Jakobson, is best known for its work in phonology. Though in many respects Prague School analyses were typical of **classical phonology**, and hence broadly similar to those of the **American Structuralists**, the school also introduced a number of strikingly original ideas, many of which have proved to be of lasting influence. Among these ideas were the **archiphoneme**, the concepts of **neutralization** and **markedness**, an early version of **distinctive features** and an associated classification of **oppositions**, and an emphasis on **typology** and on phonological **universals**; Jakobson also did pioneering work in the **acquisition of phonology**. The major synthesis of Prague School phonology was Trubetzkoy (1939); soon after its publication, Trubetzkoy died at the hands of the Gestapo, while Jakobson fled to the United States. There he introduced Praguian ideas; with Morris Halle, he championed the linguistic use of the **sound spectrograph**, developed the first full-blown **distinctive feature system** (the **Jakobson–Halle feature system**), and exerted considerable influence upon the development of **generative phonology**. Some later European linguists were also notably influenced by Prague School ideas, perhaps most notably the French linguist André Martinet, who developed in Martinet (1955) a 'neo-Praguian' view of phonological change. Accounts of Prague School phonology can be found in Vachek (1966), Krámský (1974: 32–76), Fischer-Jørgensen (1975: ch. 3), Sommerstein (1977: 45–53), Sampson (1980: ch. 5), Lepschy (1982: ch. 3), Lass (1984: ch. 3), and Anderson (1985: chs 4–5). *Adj.* **Praguian** /ˈprɑːgiən/.

preaffrication /priːæfrɪˈkeɪʃn̩/ *n.* The phenomenon in which a consonant (most usually a voiceless plosive) is preceded by a brief period of friction noise, as in [aˣk]. See Laver (1994: 373–374). *Adj.* **preaffricated** /priːˈæfrɪkeɪtɪd/.

preaspiration /priːæspɪˈreɪʃn̩/ *n.* The phenomenon in which a consonant (most usually a voiceless plosive) is preceded by a period of voiceless breathing. This occurs with voiceless plosives in certain circumstances in Icelandic, so that *uppi* 'up' is pronounced [uʰpi] and *batna* 'improve' is pronounced [baʰtna]. See Laver (1994: 356–358). *Adj.* **preaspirated** /priːˈæspɪreɪtɪd/.

precedence /ˈpresɪdəns/ *n.* The occurrence of one element before another in left-to-right order. *V.* **precede** /prɪˈsiːd/.

precedence constraint *n.* Within the **partial ordering** hypothesis of rule application, any constraint upon rule application of the following form: Where the same form meets the structural description of both rule A and rule B, only rule A is applied, though this does not in itself preclude rule B from applying later in the derivation. Here rule A is said to *take precedence over* rule B, or, in a somewhat special sense, to *precede* rule B. For example, underlying Menomini /oeːkeoam/ meets the structural description of both Glide Formation, which converts certain vowels to glides, and Epenthesis, which inserts [j] between adjacent vowels; since the phonetic form is [weːkewam], clearly Glide Formation takes precedence over Epenthesis. Cf. **blockage constraint**. Sommerstein (1977: 177).

preconsonantal /priːkɒnsəˈnæntəl/ *adj.* (of a segment) Occurring immediately before a consonant. Both the /ɪ/ and the /l/ in *milk* are preconsonantal.

predorsal /priːˈdɔːsəl/ *n.* or *adj.* A rare synonym for **laminal**.

preferential environment /prefəˈrenʃəl/ *n.* A particular position in which, universally or language-specifically, a particular phonological process is most likely to occur. For example, intervocalic position is almost universally a preferential environment for the **lenition** of consonants. Lass (1984: 181).

prefix /'pri:fɪks/ *n.* An **affix** which precedes the root, stem or base to which it is bound, such as the English derivational prefixes *re-* and *un-*, the Japanese honorific *o-* or any of the large set of inflectional affixes found in Swahili.

pre-head /'pri:hed/ *n.* In those treatments of **intonation** which recognize a **head**, any sequence of unstressed syllables preceding the head.

premature release /'premətʃə/ *n.* (**premrel**) A **distinctive feature** proposed for treating contrasts of **aspiration**: aspirated segments are [+premrel], unaspirated ones are [–premrel]. Lass (1984: 91).

prenasalization /pri:neɪzəlaɪ'zeɪʃn̩/ *n.* The articulation of a segment, most often a plosive, with an initial brief period of air flow through the nasal cavity, as in the segment [ᵐb]. *Adj.* **prenasalized**.

pre-nucleus /'pri:nju:kliəs/ *n.* Any material preceding the **intonational nucleus** within an **intonational phrase**.

preoccluded /pri:ə'klu:dɪd/ *adj.* (also **preploded** /pri:'pləʊdɪd/) (of a segment other than a plosive) Articulated with an initial brief total blockage of the air flow, as in [ᵇm]. *Abstr. n.* **preocclusion** /pri:ə'klu:ʒn̩/ or **preplosion** /pri:'pləʊʒn̩/.

prepalatal /pri:'pælətəl/ *adj.* or *n.* A segment articulated at the front part of the **palate**. NOTE: This term is sometimes used more broadly to denote **alveolo-palatal** or even **palato-alveolar** articulations, but Laver (1994: 136) recommends the narrower use.

preruptive /prɪ'rʌptɪv/ *n.* or *adj.* [*rare*] Any unaspirated voiceless obstruent. Latin *praeruptus* 'broken off abruptly'.

prespecification /pri:spesɪfɪ'keɪʃn̩/ *n.* In some analyses, especially of **reduplication** involving fixed elements in the reduplicated forms, the analytical procedure of inserting information into the template before copying. Cf. **melodic overwriting**. Marantz (1982).

pressure /'preʃə/ *n.* In the *SPE* **feature system**, either of the two features **velaric pressure** and **ejection** (glottal pressure).

pretonic /pri:'tɒnɪk/ *adj.* (of a syllable or a segment) Occurring before the position of the **stress**.

prevelar /pri:'vi:lə/ *n.* or *adj.* A segment articulated at the front edge of the **velum**; a palatalized velar.

prevocalic /pri:və'kælɪk/ *adj.* (of a segment) Occurring immediately before a vowel.

prevoicing /priːˈvɔɪsɪŋ/ *n*. The occurrence of a brief period of pulmonically initiated voicing before a voiceless segment produced with another airstream mechanism, as in the !Xũ segment [ᵈtʃ']. *Adj*. **prevoiced**.

primacy of phonemes /ˈpraɪməsi/ *n*. The view that **phonemes** are the fundamental **phonological primes**, accepted in most versions of **classical phonology** but generally rejected since the introduction of **distinctive features** in early **generative phonology**.

primary affix /ˈpraɪməri/ *n*. (also **stress-shifting suffix**, **Class I suffix**) An **affix** which is counted in determing the position of stress, such as English *-ic*, *-al* or *-ous*: *pýramid* vs. *pyrámidal*, *hómophone* vs. *homóphonous*. Such affixes have other properties, such as triggering **Trisyllabic Laxing** (*sane/sanity*) and **velar softening** (*electric/electricity*). Cf. **secondary affix**. Chomsky and Halle (1968).

primary articulation *n*. (also **primary stricture**) In a segment which is articulated with constrictions at two different locations, that constriction which is more radical (that is, which involves the tighter closure), the other being treated as a **secondary articulation**. It is the primary articulation which determines the choice of symbol for representing the segment, secondary articulations being indicated by diacritics. Hence [tʷ] is a labialized voiceless alveolar plosive, while [mʲ] is a palatalized bilabial nasal.

primary cardinal vowel *n*. In the traditional version of the **cardinal vowel system**, any one of the eight peripheral vowel qualities set up initially as arbitrary reference points: [i e ɛ a ɑ ɔ o u]. From these the **secondary cardinal vowels** are derived by reversing the lip-rounding in each case.

primary phoneme *n*. In some versions of **American Structuralism**, an ordinary segmental **phoneme**. NOTE: The contrasting term, **secondary phoneme**, has been replaced by **suprasegmental phoneme**.

primary split *n*. A type of **phonemic split** in which one of the descendants of the single original phoneme simultaneously undergoes **merger** with another pre-existing phoneme. For example, pre-Latin /s/ became [r] between vowels, thereby merging with existing /r/, while other instances of /s/ were unaffected. Cf. **secondary split**. Hoenigswald (1960).

primary stress *n*. The position of the single most prominent **stress** in a polysyllabic word. In the IPA, primary stress is indicated by a

raised vertical bar preceding the syllable with primary stress: hence
vaccination would be [ˌvæksɪˈneɪʃn̩]. When ordinary orthography is
used, the primary stress is often marked with an **acute accent**:
vàccinátion. Cf. **secondary stress**.

Primary Stress Rule (PSR) A putative rule which assigns
primary stress to the majority of English nouns. Various formulations exist; the one below is taken from Hogg and McCully
(1987: 14):

$$V \rightarrow [\text{1stress}] / \underline{\quad} C_0(V(C))(VC_0)]_N$$

The rule applies disjunctively, starting with the longest environment
matched by the string in question. Halle (1973).

prime /praɪm/ *n.* See **phonological prime**.

prime feature system *n.* See **Ladefoged feature system**.

primitive /ˈprɪmɪtɪv/ 1. *n.* See **phonological prime**. 2. *adj.* (of a
segment or a phonological system) Very early; characteristic of
a language at the earliest stage of it which can be reconstructed.
Sense 2: French *primitif* 'early, original'.

Prince language /prɪns/ *n.* A language in which the consonants in
a cluster must agree in place of articulation. After Prince (1984).

privative opposition /ˈprɪvətɪv/ *n.* In **Prague School** phonology, a
contrast between two segments one of which (the **marked** member)
is characterized by the presence of a property which is absent from
the other (the **unmarked** member). An example is the /p/–/b/
contrast in English, in which /b/ is marked by the presence of **voice**,
absent from /p/, there being no other differences between the two.
Privative oppositions are fundamental in a number of current
theories of phonology, such as **Particle Phonology**, **Dependency
Phonology** and **Government and Charm Phonology**. Cf. **gradual
opposition**, **equipollent opposition**.

privative theory *n.* (also **holistic theory**) Any approach to
phonology which functions in terms of **unary features** (variously
called **components** or **elements**) which can only be present or
absent and which cannot take values. Examples include **Particle
Phonology** and **Dependency Phonology**. See Roca (1994: 114–132)
for a comparative review of several such approaches.

privilege of occurrence /ˈprɪvɪlɪdʒ/ *n.* See **distribution**.

procedural definition /prə'siːdʒərəl defɪnɪʃn̩/ *n*. See **operational definition**.

process /'prəʊses/ *n*. Any phonological statement which is expressed in the form of a rule which applies to one representation and converts it into a different representation. Though rejected by certain frameworks (most notably by the **American Structuralists**), processes have been accepted as indispensable by most twentieth-century theories of phonology; their use was developed to an extreme degree by **classical generative phonology**.

process morphophonemics *n*. A label sometimes applied to the particular version of **morphophonology** advocated by Leonard Bloomfield, in which **processes** were recognized to treat morpho-phonological alternations. See Lass (1984: 59–62).

process phonology *n*. Any theory of phonology in which phono-logical **processes** are recognized as playing a central part.

proclitic /prəʊ'klɪtɪk/ *n*. A **clitic** which is phonologically bound to a following **host**, such as French *je* 'I' in *je vais* 'I'm going'. Cf. **enclitic**.

procliticization /prəʊklɪtɪsaɪ'zeɪʃn̩/ *n*. Any process by which some element is converted into a **proclitic**. *V*. **procliticize**.

production /prə'dʌkʃən/ *n*. See **speech production**.

productive /prə'dʌktɪv/ *adj*. (of a phonological or morphological process or alternation) Applying freely to new instances of words, forms or utterances of the appropriate type. For example, the rule that inserts an /e/ before a word-initial sibilant–plosive cluster in Spanish is still productive, as evidenced by such recent loan words as *estéreo* 'stereo'. Ant. **unproductive**.

progressive assimilation /prə'gresɪv/ *n*. See **perseverative assimila-tion**. NOTE: Some people apply this term instead to **anticipatory assimilation**; this is not recommended.

projection /prə'dʒekʃən/ *n*. 1. In some versions of **non-linear** phonology, most notably **Government and Charm Phonology**, a level of representation obtained by extracting the elements of a certain type from another level, often for the purpose of making adjacency statements between elements which are not strictly adjacent in the original level. For example, the vowels alone might be projected from a CV representation in order to state rules of **vowel harmony**. 2. In frameworks employing the **X-bar structure**, the relationship which holds between a head and its mother (or its mother's mother). For example, a syllable is regarded as the maximal projection of its nucleus.

Projection Principle *n.* A central principle of **Government and Charm Phonology**. It says: governing relations are defined at the level of lexical representation and remain constant throughout a phonological derivation.

prolongability /prəʊlɒŋə'bɪlɪti/ *n.* See **maintainability**.

prolongation /prəʊlɒŋ'geɪʃn̩/ *n.* Unusual or abnormal lengthening of a sound during speech.

prominence /'prɒmɪnəns/ *n.* 1. The property of a syllable which stands out from adjoining syllables by virtue of any of several phonetic characteristics, such as greater loudness, greater duration, higher or lower pitch, greater **syllable weight**, or greater excursion of the vocal tract from its neutral position. The phonological use of such prominence is **accent** (senses 3–4). 2. [*rare*] See **sonority** (sense 2).

prominence theory of syllable production *n.* The view that a **syllable** is phonetically a peak in prominence resulting from a combination of stress, length, pitch and intrinsic sonority. The difficulty is that such a notion of 'prominence' is impossible to define objectively.

promotion /prə'məʊʃn̩/ *n.* The replacement of a primary place feature by a secondary one, as when PIE *[kʷ] becomes Greek [p] or pre-Basque *[tʲ] becomes Basque [c]. *V.* **promote** /prə'məʊt/. Clements (1991).

pronouncing dictionary /prənaʊnsɪŋ 'dɪkʃənri/ *n.* A reference book which gives the preferred pronunciations of a wide range of words and proper names. Daniel Jones's *EPD* was long the standard for British English; John Wells's *LPD* is now the definitive work for both British and American pronunciation.

pronunciation /prənʌnsi'eɪʃn̩/ *n.* [*non-technical*] The manner in which speech sounds, especially connected sequences, are articulated by individual speakers or by speakers generally. This everyday term is little used in phonetics and phonology, in which a particular style of speaking is called an **accent** (sense 1), and more specific terms are applied to distinguishable aspects of pronunciation. *V.* **pronounce** /prə'naʊns/.

proparalepsis /prəʊpærə'lepsɪs/ *n.* The addition of a vowel to the end of a word, a particular form of **paragoge**. Ant. **apocope**.

proparoxytone /prəʊpə'rɒksɪtəʊn/ *n.* In Ancient Greek, a word with an acute accent on the **antepenult**. Cf. **oxytone**, **paroxytone**.

proper analysis /'prɒpə/ *n.* See **structural description**.

Proper Inclusion Precedence /prɒpə ɪn'kluːʒn̩/ *n.* An important principle governing the priority of application of phonological rules, variously invoked to avoid statements of **extrinsic rule ordering** or to assign precedence in cases of **disjunctive ordering**. Several versions exist; the following is taken from Sommerstein (1977: 186): if every logically possible form meeting the structural description of rule A also meets the structural description of rule B, and the converse is not the case, then rule A has precedence over rule B. (In other words, A applies before B, or, if they are disjunctively ordered, instead of rule B.) In plain English, the special case takes precedence over the more general one. Cf. **Elsewhere Condition**. Koutsoudas *et al.* (1974).

properispomenon /prəʊperɪ'spəʊmənɒn/ *n.* In Ancient Greek, a word with a circumflex accent on the **penult**. Cf. **perispomenon**.

proportional opposition /prə'pɔːʃənəl/ *adj.* In **Prague School** phonology, a contrast which applies identically to two or more pairs of segments – for example, the voicing contrast distinguishing English /p/–/b/, /t/–/d/, /k/–/g/. Cf. **isolated opposition**.

proprioception /prəʊprɪə'sepʃən/ *n.* A speaker's own awareness of her/his articulations by means of **kinaesthetic feedback**. *Adj.* **proprioceptive** /prəʊprɪə'septɪv/.

prosodeme /'prɒsədiːm/ *n.* See **suprasegmental phoneme**.

prosodic /prə'sɒdɪk/ *adj.* 1. Narrowly, pertaining to distinctions of **prominence** in speech, particularly as realized phonetically by variation in **pitch** and **loudness**, or phonologically by the use of **tone**, **pitch accent** or **stress**. 2. Broadly, pertaining to any phonetic or phonological variable which can only be described with reference to a domain larger than a single segment; **suprasegmental**. NOTE: Laver (1994: 450) recommends restricting this term to sense 1, reserving **suprasegmental** for the broader sense including also metrical and temporal organization of utterances, but sense 2 is none the less widespread.

Prosodic Analysis *n.* A highly distinctive approach to phonology developed in London by J. R. Firth and his students, chiefly in the 1950s. Whereas other approaches had often emphasized the **paradigmatic** aspects of phonology, prosodic analysis concentrated on the **syntagmatic** aspects. Not only **phonemic long components**, but a wide range of other phonetic and phonological characteristics, were extracted from phonological representations and regarded as **prosodic elements**, or **prosodies**, overlying a skeleton of minimally specified segments called **phonematic units**; even properties of single segments were treated as prosodies if their presence could be associated with an aspect of the syntagmatic structure. Moreover, the framework was characterized by an extreme version of **polysystemicism** in which it was considered impossible to identify any of the phonological units occurring in one context or position with those occurring in another. Prosodic Analysis never received a clear and comprehensive presentation from Firth or anyone else, and in practice the principles of the framework have largely had to be reconstructed by examining the various specific analyses that were published. Never influential outside of England, the framework all but disappeared with the retirement of Firth's students. Ironically, however, many aspects of the prosodic approach championed by the Firthians have recently been reinvented by proponents of various contemporary frameworks, most particularly **Autosegmental Phonology**. Accounts of Prosodic Analysis are given in Langendoen (1968), Fischer-Jørgensen (1975: ch. 5), Sommerstein (1977: ch. 3), Lass (1984: 10.2) and Anderson (1985: ch. 7).

prosodic circumscription /sɜːkəmˈskrɪpʃən/ *n.* An analytical device by which a single phonological form is 'cut' into two pieces, so that certain phonological or morphological processes can apply to just one of the pieces before the two are put back together again. This device is useful in treating such things as reduplication, infixation and the Arabic broken plurals. See Kenstowicz (1994: 633–640). McCarthy and Prince (1990).

prosodic constituency *n.* The organization of speech into several levels of **prosodic domains** of increasing size, as in the **Prosodic Hierarchy**.

prosodic domain *n.* Any unit of phonological structure larger than a single segment, such as a **syllable**, a **word** or a **phonological phrase**, when such a unit is deemed to be phonologically significant for certain purposes. The **Prosodic Hierarchy** constitutes an attempt at providing an integrated treatment of all such domains.

prosodic feature *n.* 1. See **suprasegmental**. 2. Any **distinctive feature** invoked in some feature system to treat contrasts involving units larger than a single segment. *SPE*, for example, uses a feature called *stress* which, exceptionally in that system, can take any number of values; *SPE* also cites, but does not discuss, a feature *length* and six *pitch* features called *high, low, elevated, rising, falling, concave*. The various types of **boundary** or **juncture** recognized in some systems are also sometimes treated by means of distinctive features: *SPE*, for example, treats boundaries as [+unit, –segment].

Prosodic Hierarchy *n.* An approach to phonological organization which holds that phonological phenomena involving structures larger than a single segment can be linearly ordered into types applying to different **prosodic domains** such that each smaller domain is properly included within the next larger one. The domains commonly recognized, from smallest to largest, include the **mora**, the **syllable**, the **foot**, the **phonological word**, the **clitic group**, the **phonological phrase**, the **intonational phrase** and the **prosodic utterance**. Some versions omit certain of these domains. The Prosodic Hierarchy can be viewed as an attempt at providing a principled account of the **phonology–syntax interface**, replacing the earlier approach, typical of **classical generative phonology**, in which the interface was treated as a direct mapping of syntactic constituent boundaries onto phonological boundaries. For discussion, see the papers in *Phonology Yearbook* 4 (1987). Selkirk (1981).

prosodic level *n.* In tree versions of **Metrical Phonology**, any one of several designated levels of organization, including the **mot**, the **foot** and the **syllable**. These levels are sometimes represented graphically by horizontal lines cutting across trees.

Prosodic Licensing, Principle of *n.* A universal condition on the well-formedness of phonological representations. There are various formulations; a simple one is: all phonological units must be part of prosodic structure. This principle imposes a requirement of **prosodic constituency** at some level of representation (most often the phonetic level). See Kenstowicz (1994: 285–291). Itô (1986).

Prosodic Morphology Hypothesis *n.* The hypothesis that morphological operations which are sensitive to the phonological form of the base (reduplication, infixation, truncation, addition of the

English comparative suffix *-er*, etc.) can be fully described by appealing only to such prosodic units as the foot and the syllable, without invoking powerful new types of rule. The idea has been developed by McCarthy and Prince (1986, 1990, 1991). See Kenstowicz (1994: ch. 11).

prosodic phonology *n.* That part of **phonology** which treats phonological phenomena whose domain is some unit larger than a single segment. With the major exception of **Prosodic Analysis**, prosodic phonology received much less attention than segmental phonology before the 1980s, since when it has been increasingly regarded as central. Selkirk (1972) is the ground-breaking work.

prosodic phrase *n.* See **phonological phrase**.

prosodic rule *n.* A proposed type of **postlexical rule** which is intermediate between **P1** and **P2 rules**: like P2 rules, such rules are automatic and exceptionless; unlike P2 rules, they are sensitive to *certain* aspects of syntactic structure. Selkirk (1986).

prosodic utterance *n.* (also **phonological utterance**) In some versions of the **Prosodic Hierarchy**, the largest domain of any phonological significance, posited for example as the domain of [r]-insertion in RP English: *That's a nice ca*[r]: *is it yours?* Nespor and Vogel (1986).

prosodic word *n.* See **mot**.

prosody /ˈprɒsədi/ *n.* 1. The study of poetic metre and of versification. 2. The study of stress, pitch and intonation. 3. A phonological element which is realized phonetically on more than one segment, including for example (in certain circumstances in certain languages) lip-rounding, backness or nasalization. The extended realization of height, backness, lip-rounding or ATR in **vowel harmony** languages is an outstanding example. 4. (also **long component**) A phonological element which can only be described with reference to a domain longer than a single segment, including all those mentioned in sense 3 and also **suprasegmental** elements like stress and tone. 5. In **Prosodic Analysis**, a similar but much broader notion which includes everything in sense 4 but also **boundary signals**, **phonotactics** and anything else which can conceivably be described in terms of something larger than a single segment. Such prosodies are superimposed upon a skeleton of **phonematic units**.

protected environment /prə'tektɪd/ *n.* An environment in which a segment is much less likely than elsewhere to undergo some phonological process, often especially lenition or loss.

prothesis /'prɒθəsɪs/ *n.* (also, less usually, **prosthesis** /'prɒsθəsɪs/) The addition of a segment to the beginning of a word, as in the development of Latin *stannum* 'tin' to Spanish *estaño*, the borrowing of Latin *regem* 'king' into Basque as *errege*, or the development of pre-Motu *au 'me' to Motu *lau*. Some linguists restrict this term to the addition of initial vowels. *Adj.* **prothetic** /prə'θetɪk/. Ant. **aphaeresis**. Greek *prothesis* 'a placing before'; the variant form is from Greek *prosthesis* 'addition'.

protocol /'prəʊtəkɒl/ *n.* A chart designed for the annotation of the settings of articulation, phonation, overall muscular tension and prosodic behaviour in the speech of an individual. The completed protocol is the speaker's **vocal profile**. See Laver (1994: 154) for an example.

provection /prəʊ'vekʃən/ *n.* 1. See **hard mutation**. 2. More generally, any phonological process in which voiced obstruents are devoiced, particularly in Celtic languages. 3. The transfer of a segment (usually a consonant) from the end of one word to the beginning of a following word; one type of **metanalysis**: earlier *for then once* to modern *for the nonce*; *an other* to *a nother*, leading to such locutions as *a whole nother story*. Latin *prōvectiō* 'advancement'.

P-rule /'piː ruːl/ *n.* A synonym for **phonological rule**, used especially in **Natural Generative Phonology** for the narrow class of rules recognized as phonological in that framework.

pseudo-boundary /'sjuːdəʊ baʊndəri/ *n.* A hypothetical, etymologically invalid **morpheme boundary** which is occasionally posited in the middle of a single morpheme in order to account for some kind of exceptional behaviour, as for example in the *veto* **phenomenon**. Lass (1984: 34–38); Lass credits A. J. Aitken with the idea.

PSR /piː es 'ɑː/ *n.* 1. See **Phrasal Stress Rule**. 2. See **Phrasal Stress Rule**.

public school pronunciation /'pʌblɪk skuːl/ *n.* [*non-technical*] Daniel Jones's original label for the type of British accent now usually called **Received Pronunciation**, reflecting the importance of the 'public schools' (prestigious and expensive private boarding schools) in the creation and maintenance of this accent. Jones (1917).

pullet surprise /ˈpʊlɪt səˈpraɪz/ *n.* [*jocular*] A phrase, especially a comical one, derived by mishearing an ordinary phrase, such as *four-stair system* for *forced-air system* and the classic *The cost of this government project has been calculated with a sly drool* (sc. *slide rule*). Occasionally one of these achieves permanent status, as when the earlier *spit and image* was converted to *spitting image*. Cf. **folk etymology, metanalysis**. Self-referential, from *Pulitzer Prize*.

pulmonic /pʊlˈmɒnɪk/ *adj.* 1. Pertaining to the action of the **lungs** in speech production. 2. (of a segment) Articulated with a **pulmonic airstream mechanism**. 3. In the **Ladefoged** and **Williamson feature systems**, one of the three possible values of the feature **glottalic** (Ladefoged) or **larynx movement** (Williamson).

pulmonic airstream mechanism *n.* The **airstream mechanism** which uses the respiratory system as the initiator of air movement (loosely, which uses 'lung air'). The **pulmonic egressive airstream** forces lung air up through the larynx; this is the principal airstream mechanism in all languages and the only one used in most languages. The **pulmonic ingressive airstream**, in which outside air is sucked into the lungs, is virtually never used for linguistic purposes, but may be used paralinguistically. See Laver (1994: 162–171) for an account. Beach (1937); Catford (1939).

pulsed input /pʌlst/ *n.* The delivery of energy to the vocal tract in a rapid sequence of short bursts, such as occurs whenever the vocal folds are vibrating in one way or another. See **phonation type**.

punctual tone /ˈpʌŋkʃuəl/ *n.* A rare synonym for **register tone**.

pure vowel /pjʊə/ *n.* (also **monophthong**) A vowel whose quality does not change perceptibly during its articulation. Cf. **diphthong**.

push chain /pʊʃ/ *n.* A type of **chain shift** in which the shift is instigated by a segment which, in phonological space, begins to move into the space occupied by another segment, forcing that segment to move out of the way in order to maintain its distinctness, possibly forcing further moves for the same reason. It is sometimes thought that the **First Germanic Consonant Shift** was a push chain in which the loss of aspiration by the PIE **voiced aspirates** threatened a merger with the existing voiced stops, which devoiced in response, forcing the existing voiceless plosives to become first aspirated and then fricatives. Labov (1994: ch. 6) presents evidence that some parts of the **Northern Cities Shift** involve a push chain, notably the backing of /e/ towards /ʌ/ and the (consequent) backing of /ʌ/. Cf. **drag chain**.

Q

quadrangular vowel system /kwə'dræŋgjʊlə/ *n.* A **vowel system** consisting of pairs of front and back vowels of equal height.

quality /'kwɒləti/ *n.* 1. Broadly, the sum of the perceptual characteristics of a single speech sound, derived from the **acoustic spectrum** of that sound; its characteristic resonance. 2. See **vowel quality**.

quantal theory of speech /'kwɒntəl/ *n.* A theory of speech, based upon the observation that acoustic patterns and auditory responses tend to change sharply from one state to another as the articulatory pattern is varied continuously. Such 'quantal' relations are held to be a major factor in determining the articulatory and acoustic attributes used to signal distinctions in language. See the special issue of the *Journal of Phonetics* 17:1/2 (1989) for an extended discussion. Stevens (1972).

quantal vowel *n.* A vowel whose acoustic qualities are little affected by variation in its articulation and whose perception is little affected by variation in its acoustic quality: one of [i u a]. Stevens (1972).

quantitative metre /'kwɒntɪtətɪv/ *n.* (also **quantitative verse** /vɜːs/) A type of rhythm based on the **phonological weight** of syllables and not upon stress, typical of verse in Ancient Greek and Classical Latin.

quantity /'kwɒntɪti/ *n.* See **length** (sense 2).

quantity-sensitivity /sensɪ'tɪvɪti/ *n.* The phenomenon, occurring in some languages, in which the position of the word accent is partly determined by the **quantity** of some syllable(s). *Adj.* **quantity-sensitive** /'sensɪtɪv/.

quasi-RP /'kweɪsaɪ/ *n.* A label applied by Wells (1982, 2: 285) to a type of accent resulting from poor speech training and characterized by an RP-like distribution of phonemes but a strongly unnatural distribution of allophones, such as the use of median oral release for /t/ in all environments.

quaternary feature /kwə'tɜːnəri/ *n.* A **distinctive feature** which may assume one of exactly four values.

Queen's English /kwiːnz/ *n.* See **King's English**.

R

R In some versions of **Dependency Phonology**, a **component** invoked to characterize tongue-root retraction in pharyngealized consonants. Cf. **alpha** (sense 2). Anderson and Ewen (1987).

raddoppiamento sintattico /raddɔppiamɛnto sin'tattiko/ *n.* [Italian: 'syntactic doubling'] The phenomenon in Italian by which, in certain grammatical circumstances, a word-initial consonant is pronounced long: *Maria è più* [kː]*alda che mai* 'Maria is hotter than ever'; *Mario ha* [fː]*atto tutto* 'Mario has done everything'.

radical /'rædɪkəl/ *adj.* 1. Pertaining to the **root** of the tongue. 2. (of a constriction) Involving a complete or nearly complete obstruction of the vocal tract, as in the articulation of an obstruent. 3. In some analyses, a superordinate feature of which [ATR] is a dependent.

Radical Underspecification *n.* (**RU**) A version of **Underspecification Theory** which holds that, in every phonological position, one value or the other of each feature is the unmarked value, and that the unmarked value cannot be specified underlyingly; hence all underlying feature specifications are of (contextually) marked feature values. RU was proposed in Archangeli (1984) and defended in Archangeli (1988) and Archangeli and Pulleyblank (1989). See Roca (1994: 62–77) for a summary. Cf. **Contrastive Underspecification**.

radiography /reɪdi'ɒgrəfi/ *n.* The use of X-rays to take photographs of the vocal tract during the production of speech sounds. Cf. **cineradiography**. *Adj.* **radiographic** /reɪdiə'græfɪk/.

radix /'rædɪks/ *n.* The **root** of the tongue. *Adj.* **radical**; CF **radico-**.

raised /reɪzd/ *adj.* 1. (of a vowel) Having undergone earlier **raising** within the time span under consideration, such as the raised /æ/ found in many urban American accents. 2. A label formerly applied to [+ATR] vowels in African languages showing **ATR** vowel harmony.

raised-larynx voice *n.* A **voice quality** characterized by persistent raising of the larynx during speech; such speech often sounds rather strained and is always characterized by an elevated pitch unless steps are taken to compensate for this. Cf. **lowered-larynx voice**.

raising /ˈreɪzɪŋ/ *n.* Any phonological process in which the articulation of a vowel is moved to a higher point in the mouth. Several of the developments in the English **Great Vowel Shift** involved raising, such as the shift of [eː] to [iː]. Raising can also be a synchronic process, as in the raising of mid vowels before low vowels in Basque: *etxe* 'house' and *asto* 'donkey', when followed by the article -*a*, are pronounced *etx*[i]*a* and *ast*[u]*a*. Ant. **lowering**.

random sequential rule application /rændəm sɪˈkwenʃəl/ *n.* A rarely espoused theory of **rule ordering**, in which rules apply one at a time but any rule whose structural description is met may apply at any given point, and a rule may apply more than once. Sommerstein (1977: 184).

rate /reɪt/ *n.* 1. (also **tempo**) The pace of the delivery of speech. Laver (1994: 158) distinguishes between **articulation rate** and **speaking rate**. See Laver (1994: 540–545) for a discussion with references. 2. A **distinctive feature** proposed in Ladefoged (1971) for treating contrasts of length, with the four values [rapid], [normal], [long] and [extra long], essentially identical to **length** in the **Williamson feature system**. This feature was abandoned in Ladefoged (1975).

***r*-coloured** /ˈɑːkʌləd/ *adj.* See **rhotacized**.

re-adjustment component /riːəˈdʒʌstmənt/ *n.* That part of a complete description including the **re-adjustment rules**.

re-adjustment rule *n.* In some views of phonology, particularly those in which a fully elaborated syntactic structure is taken as the input to the phonological rules, a somewhat *ad hoc* type of rule which applies to the syntactic representation *before* any phonological rules proper apply, in order to provide a structure to which the phonological rules can apply to produce the correct output. Most commonly, such rules weaken or remove syntactic boundaries which would block certain necessary phonological processes – for example, by reducing certain pronouns or particles to clitics. Re-adjustment rules are chiefly associated with **classical generative phonology**; the development of more sophisticated theories of the **phonology–syntax interface**, such as the **Prosodic Hierarchy**, has largely rendered such *ad hoc* devices unnecessary. See Sommerstein (1977: 115) for a brief account.

realization /ˌrɪəlaɪˈzeɪʃn̩/ *n.* 1. The phonetic form of a phonological representation. Most familiarly, an **allophone** is a realization of a **phoneme** in some particular context. 2. By extension, any representation of a linguistic form which is less abstract (closer to the phonetics) than some other representation. For example, the phoneme sequence /kæt/ realizes the English morpheme {cat}. Prague School.

realizational difference /ˌrɪəlaɪˈzeɪʃənəl dɪfrəns/ *n.* A difference between two or more **accents** (sense 1) consisting merely of different phonetic realizations of a single phoneme. For example, English /l/ is realized as **clear *l*** in all positions by most Welsh and (southern) Irish speakers, as **dark *l*** in all positions by most Scottish and North American speakers, and as clear *l* prevocalically but as dark *l* elsewhere by many speakers in England. Cf. **systemic difference**, **selectional difference**, **structural difference**.

Received Pronunciation /rɪˈsiːvd/ *n.* (**RP**) A certain accent of British English (or more precisely a group of closely related accents). Though used by perhaps no more than 3 per cent of the British population, RP is generally acknowledged as the prestige standard in England and also by certain social groups in the rest of the United Kingdom and in the British Commonwealth; it is the type of pronunciation most frequently taught to foreign learners of English in Britain. RP has long been associated with wealth, privilege and power; it is (or was) used by the royal family, by the landed aristocracy, by army officers, by Oxbridge academics, by senior politicians, by BBC newsreaders, by successful actors, and by anyone wishing to penetrate the upper echelons of British society. RP is usually described as having no regional associations, even though in most respects it exhibits the structural features of the accents of the southeast of England, from which it differs primarily in its phonetic details. Several varieties of RP may be distinguished: Gimson (1989) recognizes **conservative**, **general** and **advanced** varieties, while Wells (1982) distinguishes **mainstream RP**, **U-RP** and **adoptive RP**. RP continues to be influential today; speakers of regional varieties in England and Wales often adjust their speech in the direction of RP, producing the kind of accent called **near-RP** by Wells (1982), and upwardly mobile working-class speakers in the southeast of England are increasingly exhibiting a comparable shift, resulting in the spectrum of accents collectively dubbed **Estuary English**. On the other hand, the use of RP has become somewhat less frequent on the BBC and in the media generally, and it is far less prominent than formerly in the universities, in the House of Commons and even among army officers. Moreover, RP itself is showing striking signs of evolution: even some younger members of the royal family now show a degree of **glottalling** not previously typical of RP but widespread in regional accents. RP was originally called **public school pronunciation** by Daniel Jones, and it has sometimes also been called a **BBC accent** or an **Oxford accent**; those who dislike it may call it a **plummy**, **lah-di-dah**, **Kensington** or **cut-glass accent**. See McArthur (1992) for a historical summary, Gimson (1989) for a detailed characterization and Wells (1982) for an account of variation in RP; Wells (1990a) is an up-to-date RP pronouncing dictionary. Jones (1917) established the name in its modern sense; the term had earlier been used without capitals to denote 'correct' pronunciation in general.

recessive accent /rɪ'sesɪv/ *n.* Movement of the **word accent** (see **accent**, sense 3) towards the beginning of the word, or the tendency for this to occur. This is a powerful tendency in English nouns: such words as *research*, *detail*, *cigarette*, *magazine* and *ice cream*, all formerly with final stress, are now widely pronounced with initial stress.

recessive rule *n.* In some theories of **rule ordering**, notably **partial ordering**, a rule which fails to apply when its structural description is met if there is another rule taking precedence over it whose SD is met at the same time. Sommerstein (1977: 179).

recessive vowel *n.* In a language with **dominant/recessive vowel harmony**, any one of the vowels which are automatically replaced by their dominant partners in the appropriate circumstances.

recognition test /rekəg'nɪʃn̩ test/ *n.* (also **perception test**, **articulation test**) A standard test of speech perception, in which a set of spoken words is presented and a listener is asked to repeat, write down or otherwise respond to the test items. The percentage of words correctly perceived is the measure of intelligibility.

reconstruction /riːkən'strʌkʃən/ *n.* 1. (also **reconstructed form** /riːkən'strʌktɪd/, **unattested form**) A hypothetical form which is nowhere attested but which is posited, on the basis of some evidence, as having existed in some earlier or ancestral form of a language. Such a form is conventionally marked with an asterisk. For example, Spanish *aguijada* 'goad' is derived from a reconstructed Latin *AQUILEĀTA, and English *book* is derived from a reconstructed Proto-Germanic *bōkō* 'beech'. 2. The process of constructing such forms.

recoverability condition /rɪkʌvərə'bɪlɪti/ *n*. In some versions of **Metrical Phonology**, the requirement that the locations of the metrical constituent boundaries and the locations of the heads must be unambiguously recoverable from each other. Halle and Vergnaud (1987).

recursion /rɪ'kɜːʃn̩/ *n*. The re-application of some process to its own output. Recursion is explicitly invoked in some phonological frameworks, as for example in the association of particles in **Particle Phonology** to yield successively the vowels I ([i]), AI ([e]), AAI ([ɛ]), AAAI ([æ]). *V.* **recurse** /rɪ'kɜːs/; *adj.* **recursive** /rɪ'kɜːsɪv/.

recursive /rɪ'kɜːsɪv/ *n*. or *adj.* [*rare*] A segment produced with a **glottalic airstream mechanism**; an **ejective** or **voiced implosive**. From Latin *recursiō* 'a running back'.

Redefinition Principle /riːdefɪ'nɪʃn̩/ *n*. A putative principle of phonological change. It says: peripherality is defined relative to the vowel system as a whole. In other words, the peripheral/non-peripheral contrast among vowels is not merely a matter of objective phonetics, but may be substantially determined by phonological changes. Labov (1994: 285).

reduction /rɪ'dʌkʃən/ *n*. Any process in which a segment or a sequence of segments is, in some sense, 'weakened'. The term is applied, for example, to the centralization or loss of unstressed vowels (as in *collect* and *medicine*), to the lenition or loss of consonants (as in the lenition of [p] to [v] in the development of Latin RIPA 'riverbank' to French *rive*) and to the simplification of a consonant cluster by the loss of a consonant (as in the loss of /ð/ from *clothes* and of /k/ from *knife*. Some phonologists extend the term to instances of **neutralization** in favour of the 'weaker' member of a contrast. *Adj.* **reduced** /rɪ'djuːst/.

redundancy /rɪ'dʌndənsi/ *n*. The central property of speech and language by which more information is provided than is strictly necessary for the message to be understood, so that, if some information is lost or misheard, the remaining information will still often be sufficient for the message to be received correctly. *Adj.* **redundant** /rɪ'dʌndənt/.

redundancy rule *n*. Any rule which states that some feature or behaviour is entirely predictable from the presence of something else. For example, the English rule [+voi] → [–asp] states that voiced segments are predictably unaspirated, while the rule [+Germanic] → [–Velar Softening] states that no native English word or morpheme ever undergoes **velar softening**.

redundancy rule ordering constraint *n.* In some versions of **Underspecification Theory**, the requirement that a redundancy rule supplying a feature value αF must apply before any rule referring to αF in its structural description. This constraint is designed to prevent the misuse of blanks. Archangeli (1984).

redundant feature *n.* (also **concomitant feature**) A feature which, although phonetically present, is non-distinctive for a particular segment, in a particular language, or universally by definition. The feature [voice], though generally distinctive for Arabic obstruents, is redundant for /b/, which has no voiceless counterpart; the feature [nasal] is redundant for English vowels; the feature [low] is redundant for all [+high] segments by definition.

reduplication /rɪdjuːplɪˈkeɪʃn̩/ *n.* The morphological process in which some phonological material is repeated within a single form for lexical or grammatical purposes. Reduplication is a common phenomenon in the languages of the world, taking a variety of forms and serving a variety of purposes. Malay, for example, uses reduplication for adverb formation (*baik* 'good', *baik-baik* 'well'), for indefinite plurality (*bunga* 'flower', *bunga-bunga* 'flowers') and for word formation (*mata* 'eye', *mata-mata* or *memata* 'policeman'). Certain Latin verbs form their perfect stems by reduplication: *curr-* 'run', perfect stem *cucurr-*. Chukchi derives certain absolutive case forms by reduplication: *nute-* 'tundra' (stem), absolutive *nutenut*. Tagalog uses reduplication in its verbal inflection: *sulat* 'write', future *susulat*. Turkish uses it to express 'and so forth': *Ali-Mali* 'Ali and the others'. Yiddish-influenced American English uses it to express dismissal: *Jaguar-Schmaguar!* V. **reduplicate** /rɪˈdjuːplɪkeɪt/; *adj.* **reduplicative** /rɪˈdjuːplɪkətɪv/.

reflex /ˈriːfleks/ *n.* In historical phonology, a form or segment in a particular language which is historically derived from a form or segment in an ancestral form of the language, its **etymon**. Thus, English *father* is the reflex of Old English *fæder*, and English /f/ is the reflex of Proto-Indo-European /p/.

register /ˈredʒɪstə/ *n.* 1. The natural pitch range available to a particular speaker or singer for anatomical reasons such as the size and thickness of the vocal folds; in singing, registers are denoted by such labels as *soprano, contralto, tenor*. 2. Any one of different pitch ranges available to a single speaker or singer by modification of the tension in the vocal folds. It is traditional to distinguish *chest voice* (ordinary speech) from *head voice* (**falsetto**); professional singers reportedly learn an intermediate *middle voice* to smooth the abrupt transition between these two. If falsetto is regarded as a **phonation type** (as is now common), the concept of register becomes unnecessary in phonetics.

register tone *n.* (also **punctual tone, level tone, static tone, stepping tone**) A particular **tone** in a **tone language** which is realized by an unvarying level pitch on its syllable, with no upward or downward movement. A tone language which uses such tones exclusively is a *register tone language*. Cf. **contour tone**.

regressive assimilation /rɪ'gresɪv/ *n.* See **anticipatory assimilation**. NOTE: Some people apply this term instead to **perseverative assimilation**; this is not recommended.

regularity /regju'lærəti/ *n.* 1. Any phonological or morphological pattern which constitutes the normal state of affairs in a language, which is in no way exceptional within that language. 2. A **phonological change** which applies to all instances of a given sound in a given set of environments, without exception. *Adj.* **regular** /'regjʊlə/.

Regularity Principle *n.* A putative principle governing the course of phonological change. It says: sound change is a change in the phonetic realization of a phoneme, without regard to lexical identity. A central component of the **Neogrammarian Hypothesis**, this principle is falsified by the occurrence of **lexical diffusion**. Cf. the **Mechanical Principle**. Labov (1994: 603).

relaxation pressure /riːlæk'seɪʃn̩/ *n.* The pressure in the lungs and airways produced by non-muscular forces, the elastic and mechanical recoil factors in the lungs, chest, diaphragm and abdomen.

release /rɪ'liːs/ *n.* (also **plosion**) The final stage in the articulation of a **plosive**, in which the closure is released and the articulating organs move apart. Cf. **approach, hold**.

relic form /'relɪk/ *n.* A linguistic form which preserves an archaism otherwise generally lost in the language, such as the pair *was ~ were*, which uniquely preserves the ancient /z/~/r/ alternation.

remiss /rɪ'mɪs/ *n*. The second place in a **foot**. Cf. **ictus** (sense 2). Abercrombie (1991b: ch. 10), after Joshua Steele.

rendaku /rendaku/ *n*. The phenomenon in Japanese compound formation by which the initial consonant of a second element undergoes voicing: *ami* 'net' + *to* 'door' → *amido* 'screen door'; *ori-* 'fold' + *kami* 'paper' → *origami* 'paper-folding'; *omocha* 'toy' + *hako* 'box' → *omochabako* 'toy box' (Jap. *h* < **p*). Cf. **Lyman's Law**.

Rennison framework /'renɪsən/ *n*. A **privative** theory of phonology developed by J. R. Rennison (1987, 1991) which uses elements, but not government, opting instead for 'visibility' relations between stacked tiers.

reordering /riː'ɔːdərɪŋ/ *n*. See **rule reordering**.

repair mechanism /rɪ'pɛə mekənɪzm̩/ *n*. Any of various devices postulated as acting to correct violations of some principle, especially the **Obligatory Contour Principle**. See Paradis (1988–1989).

repetition test /repə'tɪʃn̩ test/ *n*. A procedure for checking for the reality of a **contrast** between two putatively contrasting items. The two items are recorded and then played back to a native speaker a number of times in random order; the speaker is asked to repeat each item. A success rate of 90 per cent or better in reproducing the features in question indicates a genuine contrast. Cf. **pair test**. Contreras and Saporta (1960).

rephonologization /riːfənɒlədʒaɪ'zeɪʃn̩/ *n*. A type of phonological change in which the relations among phonemes are changed but not the number of phonemes or their distribution. For example, some Slavic languages formerly had three velar phonemes /k g x/, in which /k/ but not /x/ had a voiced counterpart; the development of /g/ into /ɣ/ reversed this situation. The **First Germanic Consonant Shift** provides a more elaborate example of rephonologization. Jakobson (1931).

replacive morph /rɪ'pleɪsɪv/ *n*. In some versions of **American Structuralism**, an element posited as being substituted for another element within a morpheme, as in plural *geese*, in which /iː/ replaces /uː/. Nida (1948); Bloomfield (1933) had earlier called this a 'substitution-alternant'.

representation /reprɪzən'teɪʃn̩/ *n*. 1. Any conventional rendering of a piece of speech with a set of symbols or linguistic objects appropriate to some particular level of analysis. For example, the word *cats* might be represented morphemically as {cat} + {Plural}, phonemically as /kæts/ or /kætz/ (depending on one's view of phonemes), or phonetically as [kʰæts]. 2. One of the **planes** (sense 1) of phonology, that one handling the purely linguistic content of expressions: **phonology** in the ordinary sense. 3. In some **American Structuralist** work, the relation which holds between certain linguistic elements: morphemes are represented by morphs and morphophonemes are represented by phonemes. Cf. **composition**. Sense 3: Hockett (1961).

rescue rule /'reskjuː/ *n.* A rule which applies to the result of a **false step** to produce a well-formed result, often especially such a rule which has no other function. Zwicky (1973).

residual volume /rɪ'zɪdjuəl/ *n.* The volume of air remaining in the lungs after all possible air has been expelled by expiration.

resonance /'rezənəns/ *n.* 1. The physical phenomenon in which some body which is capable of vibration prefers to vibrate at certain frequencies rather than others, thereby favouring and enhancing those frequencies while suppressing others. The **formants** of speech represent the resonant frequencies of the vocal tract in a given configuration; changing the shape of the vocal tract alters its resonant frequencies and hence the positions of the formants. Cf. **damping**. *Adj.* **resonant** /'rezənənt/. 2. Any distinguishable element in speech which can be ascribed to some prominent modification in the shape of the vocal tract, such as the nasal resonance heard when the velum is lowered.

resonance theory of hearing *n.* A theory of hearing, proposed by Hermann von Helmholtz, in which the **cochlea** is presumed to contain a range of taut, tuned fibres resembling piano strings, with each fibre resonating at a different particular frequency. This theory is now known to be wrong. Cf. **place theory of hearing**.

resonant /'rezənənt/ *n.* 1. See **sonorant**. 2. Any segment made with **open approximation**: a vowel, an approximant, a lateral approximant, [h] or [ʔ]. This is the usage of Laver (1994). 3. In the usage of Catford (1988), any non-high vowel. This usage is anomalous. 4. See **sonant**.

respiratory cycle /rɪ'spɪrətri/ *n.* The pattern of breathing in (inspiration) and breathing out (expiration) characteristic of ordinary breathing.

respiratory tract /trækt/ *n.* (also **respiratory system**) The entire passage, from the lungs up to the lips and nose, through which air flows during breathing and speech.

Restrictive Underspecification /rɪ'strɪktɪv/ *n.* See **Contrastive Underspecification**.

restructuring /riː'strʌktʃərɪŋ/ *n.* The putative process in which a child learning a first language posits **underlying forms** which are different from those of the earlier generation and much closer to the surface phonetic forms of the items in question, supposedly because the length and complexity of derivations from the older underlying forms have become too great to allow the child to recover the older forms.

resyllabification /riːsɪlæbɪfɪ'keɪʃn̩/ *n.* In some approaches, a process which applies during a derivation to move segments from one syllable to another. For example, when French *bête* 'beast' [bɛtə] loses its schwa, the [t] must be moved from the second syllable to the first.

retracted /rɪ'træktɪd/ *adj.* 1. (of a segment) Articulated at a position slightly further back than another, similar segment taken as a reference point. In the IPA, a retracted segment is marked by an underbar: thus [a̠] represents a retracted variety of [a]. 2. (of the tongue) Pulled back so as to narrow the **pharynx**. *Abstr. n.* **retraction** /rɪ'trækʃən/.

retracted articulation *n.* (**retrart**) A **distinctive feature** proposed by McCawley (1966) to distinguish the contrasts bilabial/labiodental, interdental/dental, dental/alveolar, retroflex/palatal, and velar/uvular, the second item in each case being [+retrart]. Early drafts of *SPE* had posited an identical feature called *proximal*.

retracted tongue root The opposite of **advanced tongue root**.

retroflex /'retrəʊfleks/ *adj.* or *n.* 1. A traditional but unsystematic label conventionally applied to any of various consonant and vowel articulations in which the tip of the tongue is bent back and up to some extent; the articulations in question might in principle be given more explicit labels, such as 'apico-post-alveolar' or 'sublamino-prepalatal', but these systematic labels are rarely used in practice. The IPA has a full set of symbols for retroflex consonants ([ʈ], [ɖ], etc.). 2. In the **Ladefoged feature system**, one of the eleven possible values of the feature **articulatory place**. 3. In the **Williamson feature system**, one of the three possible values of the feature **apicality**. 4. In Laver (1994), a label applied to any conformation of the tongue in which the tip is bent up and back, but not used to label a place of articulation. Latin *retrōflexus* 'bent backward'.

retroflexed *adj.* (of a vowel) A common but not strictly accurate synonym for **rhotacized**.

reversal /rɪ'vɜːsəl/ *n.* See **iambic reversal**.

reversal of merger *n.* (also **unmerger**) The phenomenon in which the speakers of a language in which an earlier distinction between two segments has disappeared as a result of a **merger** re-introduce the earlier distinction. By **Garde's Principle**, reversal of merger is theoretically impossible, but a number of apparent cases of it have been described in the literature, such as the reversal of the merger of the vowels of *mate* and *meat* in English. Three types of explanation have been advanced for these cases. (1) The merger genuinely occurred, but just one of the merged segments had a distinctive phonological role in the language, and speakers were later able to distinguish instances of the merged result which bore this role from those which did not. This is the interpretation offered by Michelena (1957; 1977: 194–195) for the merger of /ʃ/ (resulting from the strengthening of /j/) with pre-existing /ʃ/ in the Gipuzkoan dialect of Basque, followed by a reversal in which /ʃ/ derived from earlier /j/ developed to /χ/ while original /ʃ/ did not. All instances of original /ʃ/, like all palatal and palato-alveolar consonants in Basque, had a clear 'expressive' function, serving only to form diminutives and hypocorisms. Instances of /ʃ/ derived from /j/ lacked this expressive function and hence could be separated out from instances of original /ʃ/. (2) The merger took place in the prestige variety but not in other varieties, and a change in the prestige of the competing varieties shows up in the record as an apparent reversal, since only prestige varieties tend to be well recorded. This is the view famously presented by Weinreich *et al.* (1968). (3) The merger never really occurred; instead, there was only a **near-merger** resulting in the usual failure of speakers to observe the objectively real contrast. This view is championed by Labov (1975; 1994: ch. 13).

reverse click /rɪ'vɜːs/ *n.* A consonant produced with a **velaric egressive airstream mechanism**. Such sounds are not known to be used in any language.

Revised Alternation Condition /rɪ'vaɪzd/ *n.* A principle formulated to constrain abstract analyses and specifically to prohibit the use of **absolute neutralization**. It says: an obligatory neutralization rule may apply only in a derived environment. A reformulation of the earlier **Alternation Condition**, this principle helped pave the way for **Lexical Phonology**. See **derived environment**. Kiparsky (1973b).

rhotacism /'rəʊtəsɪzm̩/ *n.* 1. Any phonological process in which another segment develops into a **rhotic**, such as the development of early Latin intervocalic *s*, or of pre-Basque intervocalic *l*, into *r*. 2. A synonym for **defective *r***, used by clinicians.

rhotacized /'rəʊtəsaɪzd/ *adj.* 1. (also ***r*-coloured**, **retroflexed**) (of a vowel) Having a distinctive acoustic quality, the lowering of the third formant, produced by articulating the vowel either with a **retroflex** tongue position or with a 'bunched' tongue, as in a **molar *r***. Rhotacized vowels occur in American English (as in *bird*) and in Mandarin Chinese. In the IPA, rhotacized vowel is transcribed with a following hook, as in [ɚ] for the vowel of *bird*. *Abstr. n.* **rhotacization**. 2. In the **Ladefoged feature system**, a **distinctive feature** defined as 'exhibiting a lowered frequency for the third formant'. 3. In the **Lindau feature system**, a **distinctive feature** defined as involving a retracted tongue root and invoked to treat distinctions of *r*-colouring in vowels; it has the possible values *strongly rhotacized*, *rhotacized*, *weakly r-coloured* and *plain*, no more than three of which can be contrastively used by one language.

rhotic /'rəʊtɪk/ *n.* or *adj.* Any member of a particular group of phonetically heterogeneous segments which for various phonological reasons are conveniently treated as a class – informally, the class of 'r-sounds'. The most familiar rhotics are the alveolar and post-alveolar taps, trills and approximants, but various retroflex and uvular segments, as well as the American **molar *r***, are also included. See Lindau (1985) for a (generally negative) survey of attempts to identify the class of rhotics in acoustic terms.

rhotic accent *n.* Any accent of English in which the historical /r/ is overtly realized as a constriction in non-prevocalic position. For a rhotic speaker, *farther* is not homophonous with *father* and *far* does not rhyme with *Shah*. Rhotic accents are typical of most of Canada and the United States (apart from the east coast and the south), of much of the Caribbean, of Scotland, of Ireland and of the south-west of England and parts of the north. Cf. **non-rhotic accent**, and see Wells (1982) for details. According to Abercrombie (1975), coined by John Wells.

rhyme /raɪm/ *n*. 1. Either of two or more words which have identical nuclei in their stressed syllables and identical sequences of segments after these nuclei: *bear/care*; *plate/berate*; *utter/butter*; *vision/collision*; *heinous/Coriolanus*. True rhymes are divided into **masculine** and **feminine rhymes**. Rhymes with identical consonants preceding the rhyming nuclei are said to exhibit *rich rhyme*: *line/malign; team/steam*. Homophones are sometimes said to exhibit *identical rhyme*: *bare/bear*. Cf. **homeoteleuton**. 2. (also **rime**, **final**, **core**) That part of a **syllable** consisting of the **nucleus** and the **coda** – in other words, the entire syllable except for the **onset**.

rhyming slang /'raɪmɪŋ slæŋ/ *n*. A playful speech device typical of the **Cockney** speech of the London area. A word is replaced by a rhyming phrase, which in many cases is then reduced to its initial (non-rhyming) element. For example, *head* is replaced by *loaf of bread*, which is then reduced to *loaf*, as in the phrase *Use your loaf!*

rhythm /'rɪðm̩/ *n*. The perceptual pattern produced in speech or poetry by the occurrence at regular intervals of prominent elements; these elements may be stresses (as in English), syllables (as in Spanish), heavy syllables (as in Ancient Greek) or moras (as in Japanese). See Laver (1994: 533) for references. *Adj*. **rhythmic** /'rɪðmɪk/.

Rhythm Rule *n*. See **iambic reversal**.

rhythm unit *n*. A synonym for **intonational phrase**, used by some **American Structuralists**. Pike (1945).

right-headed foot /raɪt'hedɪd/ *n*. In **Metrical Phonology**, a **foot** whose most prominent element (its *head*) comes last. Cf. **left-headed foot**.

rim /rɪm/ *n*. The front part of the edge of the **tongue**.

rime /raɪm/ *n*. See **rhyme**.

***r*-insertion** *n*. The use of **intrusive** *r*.

rise /raɪz/ *n*. An increase in pitch. The term is chiefly used in labelling **contour tones**, as in *fall–rise* and *rise–fall*. *Adj*. **rising**. Ant. **fall**.

rising diphthong *n.* See **crescendo diphthong**.

rising tone *n.* A **contour tone** characterized by a sustained increase in pitch.

roll /rəʊl/ *n.* A less usual synonym for **trill**. *Adj.* **rolled**.

root /ruːt/ *n.* 1. (also **radix**) That part of the **tongue** which lies furthest back and lowest, in front of the **laryngo-pharynx** and the **epiglottis**. *Adj.* **radical**; CF **radico-**. 2. In morphology, the simplest possible form of a lexical morpheme, with no affixes, such as Latin *am-* 'love' or Arabic *ktb* 'write'. Cf. **stem**, **base**. 3. In some versions of **feature geometry**, a superordinate **class node** which dominates all other features and which typically marks a single segment. Sense 3: Sagey (1986).

root-and-pattern morphology /ruːt ənd 'pætən/ *n.* See **non-concatenative morphology**.

root constraint *n.* A seemingly arbitrary restriction upon the co-occurrence within a single root of certain segments. Thus, a Japanese root may not contain two voiced obstruents, while an Arabic root may not contain two labials.

root-marker theory *n.* An analysis of **vowel harmony** in which each root is lexically marked with an arbitrary feature specification which is later converted by rules into phonological forms, much as roots in gender languages are marked as having some gender. Lightner (1965).

rough breathing /rʌf 'briːðɪŋ/ *n.* 1. In Ancient Greek, the presence of an aspiration [h] at the beginning of a word. 2. The diacritic ʻ, used to represent this aspiration. Cf. **smooth breathing**.

round(ed) /raʊnd(ɪd)/ *adj.* 1. (of an articulation) Characterized by the presence of **rounding** (sense 1). In the IPA, rounded and unrounded vowels have their own distinct symbols; in American transcription, only one vowel symbol is provided at each position, and the less usual value of rounding at that position is indicated by the diacritic ¨ : hence ü for IPA y. For rounding of consonants, see under **labialization**. Ant. **unrounded** (of a segment), **spread** (of a lip position); a segment is either rounded or unrounded, but lips can be any of rounded, neutral or spread. 2. In the *SPE* **feature system**, a **distinctive feature** defined as 'articulated with a narrowing of the lip orifice'. Rounded vowels and labialized consonants are [+round]; other segments are [−round]. This feature partly replaces the feature **flat** in the **Jakobson–Halle feature system**. 3. In the **Lindau feature system**, a **distinctive feature** invoked to treat distinctions of lip protrusion, with the possible values *round*, *neutral* and *spread*, no more than two of which may be contrastive in any one language. 4. See **rounding** (sense 2).

round brackets *n. pl.* See **parentheses**.

rounding *n.* 1. The presence during an articulation of protrusion of the lips (**inner rounding**) or of horizontal compression of the lips (**outer rounding**). *Adj.* **rounded**. 2. (also **round**) In the **Ladefoged** and **Williamson feature systems**, a binary **distinctive feature** invoked to treat distinctions of lip-rounding.

RP /ɑː ˈpiː/ *n.* See **Received Pronunciation**.

rule /ruːl/ *n.* Any statement which, in some analysis, is intended to express a generalization about the facts of the language being described. Rules can be expressed in words, but in phonology it is more usual to express them with the aid of various **abbreviatory conventions**.

rule activation *n.* In some theories of **rule ordering**, the phenomenon in which, by some principle or circumstance, a rule is finally permitted to apply to a form from which it had earlier been prevented from applying even though its structural description might have been met. *V.* **activate** /ˈæktɪveɪt/. Ant. **rule deactivation**.

rule addition *n.* A type of **rule change** in which a new rule is introduced into the grammar so that it applies after all previously existing rules. Such a rule can have a dramatic effect upon the output, as with the rule deleting all word-final consonants introduced into many Polynesian languages. Cf. **rule insertion**.

rule application /æplɪˈkeɪʃn̩/ *n.* In any approach to phonology involving **derivations**, the notional process by which a particular rule acts upon some representation to produce a different representation in line with the requirements of the rule.

rule chain *n.* A sequence of simple and natural rules which achieves the same effect as a single highly complex rule. Cf. **fell swoop**. Zwicky (1974).

rule change *n.* Any of various types of phonological change in which a rule is introduced, lost or modified, or in which the order of two rules changes. See King (1969), Kiparsky (1971) or Sommerstein (1977: ch. 10).

rule complication /kɒmplɪ'keɪʃn̩/ *n.* A type of **rule change** in which a rule becomes more complex than previously. This is not usually regarded as a primary form of change, but as an indirect effect of other changes. See Bach and Harms (1972).

rule deactivation /diːæktɪ'veɪʃn̩/ *n.* In some frameworks, the phenomenon in which a rule which would otherwise apply is prevented from applying ('turned off') in some specified domain, most usually a grammatical one. Ant. **rule activation**.

rule feature *n.* A note on a lexical entry stipulating that that item does not undergo a rule to which it would otherwise be subject, a common way of treating items which are phonologically exceptional. For example, *veto* and *Plato* might be marked [–Tapping] in American English, since they exceptionally fail to undergo **tapping**.

rule-governed /'ruːl gʌvənd/ *adj.* Denoting the presumed property of human linguistic behaviour, or of some part of it, by which most phenomena can be seen as instances of the interaction of a relatively small number of generalizations expressible by rules.

rule insertion *n.* A putative type of **rule change** in which a new rule is added to the grammar, not at the end, but at an earlier point, so that it has an effect upon the operation of later rules. There appear to be no certain cases of rule insertion, and many linguists would deny its existence. Cf. **rule addition**.

rule inversion /ɪn'vɜːʃn̩/ *n.* A type of **rule change** in which a rule is replaced by one operating in the opposite direction – that is, the original derived form is taken as underlying, and the original underlying form is derived by rule. For example, in pre-Basque, the segment *l* uniformly became *r* in intervocalic position but remained *l* elsewhere, producing such alternations as *euskara* 'Basque language' (< **euskala*), *euskaldun* 'speaker of Basque'. But the Latin word *sagmarius* 'beast of burden' was borrowed into Basque as *zamari* 'horse'; this forms derivatives such as *zamaldun* 'horseman', showing that the original rule converting *l* to *r* between vowels has been inverted: *r* is now taken as underlying, and the rule converts *r* to *l* before a consonant. The **intrusive** *r* of some English accents results from another case of rule inversion. Vennemann (1972a).

rule loss *n.* A type of **rule change** in which a rule which was formerly present disappears from the language. For example, all southern varieties of German historically acquired a rule devoicing final obstruents. Standard German still has this rule, which is responsible for such alternations as *Bund* [bunt] 'league', genitive *Bundes* [bundəs] (cf. *bunt* [bunt] 'mottled', genitive *buntes* [buntəs]). But many Swiss German and Yiddish varieties have lost the devoicing rule, producing [bund], [bundəs] 'league' but [bunt], [buntəs] 'mottled'; the former presence of the rule is shown by the continued devoicing in forms which do not alternate, such as *weg* [vek] 'away'.

rule ordering *n*. The property of a grammar in which **phonological rules** act on underlying forms to derive surface forms, but in which these rules do not apply simultaneously. Rule ordering may be **intrinsic** or **extrinsic**; a number of theories of rule ordering have been put forward, including **linear ordering**, **partial ordering**, **local ordering** and **unordered semisimultaneous ordering**.

rule reordering /riː'ɔːdərɪŋ/ *n*. A type of **rule change** in which the order of two rules is reversed, thus changing the output. For example, some Bizkaian dialects of Basque have one rule which raises a mid vowel before a non-high vowel and a second rule which raises /a/ to /e/ before /a/. In varieties with the original ordering, underlying /ea/ becomes [ia], while underlying /aa/ becomes [ea]; some varieties, however, have reordered the two rules, so that /ea/ and /aa/ are both realized as [ia].

rule schema *n*. (also **schema**) Any statement which collapses two or more rules by means of some **abbreviatory convention**; the collapsed rules are **subrules** or **expansions** of the schema. See examples under **braces**, **parentheses**.

rule simplification /sɪmplɪfɪ'keɪʃn̩/ *n*. A type of **rule change** in which, by the removal of some conditions on its operation, a rule comes to apply either to a wider range of cases or in a more uniform manner than previously.

S

s A symbol used to mark a strong foot or syllable.

sagittal section /'sædʒɪtəl sekʃən/ *n*. A planar section through the body which separates the left side from the right side. The familiar diagram of the vocal tract is a sagittal mid-section (that is, a sagittal section midway through the body). Cf. **coronal section**, **transverse section**.

salience /'seɪliəns/ *n*. The property of being the first syllable in a **foot**, the syllable on which the **beat** of **stress-timing** falls. Abercrombie (1991b: ch. 10).

Salience, Principle of *n*. A putative principle governing the effect of phonological change on inflectional morphology. It says: the more prominent an inflectional marking is (that is, the more phonetic substance associated with it), the greater the tendency to retain the inflection in the face of sound changes tending to reduce it. Lemle and Naro (1977).

Sammy /'sæmi/ *n*. A jocular term for a **sagittal section** of the upper part of the human vocal tract, the familiar diagram in every phonetics textbook.

sandhi /'sændi/ *n*. Any of various phonological processes applying to sequences of segments either across morpheme boundaries (**internal sandhi**) or across word boundaries (**external sandhi**). Examples of the first are the devoicing of English plural /z/ in *cats* and the **velar softening** of /k/ to /s/ in *electric/electricity*; examples of the second are Sanskrit *sa:* 'she' + *u:vača* 'spoke' > *sovača* 'she spoke' and *tat* 'this' + *mama* 'of mine' > *tan mama* 'this of mine', plus **linking *r*** and **intrusive *r*** in **non-rhotic accents** of English. See Allen (1962) for an account. Sanskrit grammar: *sam* 'together' + *dhi* 'put'.

satellite /'sætəlaɪt/ *n*. [*obsolete*] See **onset**. Hockett (1955).

scalar feature /'skeɪlə/ *n*. A **distinctive feature** which can assume three or more values.

scansion /'skænʃən/ *n*. 1. The analysis of the metrical structure of verse. 2. In **Metrical Phonology**, the analysis of metrical structure (stress patterns).

schema /'skiːmə/ *n.* See **rule schema**.

schwa /ʃwɑː/ *n.* (also **shwa**) 1. The unrounded mid central vowel [ə], the **neutral** vowel produced with the tongue and lips in their rest positions. Schwa is the most frequent vowel in English, occurring for example in the first syllable of *about* and in the second syllable of *carrot*. 2. The symbol [ə], used in the IPA to represent this vowel. 3. See **centrality**. Hebrew grammar.

Scots /skɒts/ *n.* A name applied collectively to the distinctive regional varieties of English spoken in the lowlands of Scotland. While sharing some characteristics with the English of northern England, Scots is distinguished from all other varieties (except the Scots-influenced English of Northern Ireland) by a number of independent developments. Scots must be distinguished from *Scottish Standard English*.

Scouse /skaʊs/ *n.* [*non-technical*] The traditional name for the distinctive speech variety of the Merseyside area of northwestern England, centred on the city of Liverpool. See Wells (1982) for a summary, Knowles (1974) for a detailed description. **Scouser**: one who speaks Scouse. From *lobscouse*, a kind of stew traditionally served in Liverpool waterfront cafes.

secondary /'sekəndri/ *adj.* (of a form or segment) In **historical phonology**, derived by phonological change from an earlier form or segment.

secondary affix *n.* (also **stress-neutral suffix**, **neutral affix**, **Class II suffix**) In English, a suffix whose addition has no effect upon the location of the primary stress, such as *-ness*: *meaningless, meaninglessness*. Cf. **primary affix**.

secondary aperture *n.* A cover term for the nasal/non-nasal and lateral/non-lateral distinctions. Chomsky and Halle (1968: 316).

secondary articulation *n.* 1. Narrowly, any articulation which accompanies another (**primary**) articulation and which involves a less radical constriction than that primary articulation, such as **labialization** or **velarization**. 2. Broadly, and perhaps more usually, any of various independent articulatory gestures which can be performed simultaneously with another articulation, including the two just mentioned as well as **nasalization**, **palatalization**, **glottalization** and others. See Laver (1994: 320–335).

secondary cardinal vowel *n.* In the **cardinal vowel system**, any one of the eight reference vowels derived from the **primary cardinal**

vowels by reversing the lip-rounding. Secondary vowels numbers 1–5 are thus rounded, while 6–8 are unrounded.

secondary phoneme *n.* [*obsolete*] See **suprasegmental phoneme**. Bloomfield (1933).

secondary split *n.* An instance of **phonemic split** in which the total number of phonemes is increased, as when Old English /θ/ split into modern /θ/ and /ð/. Cf. **primary split**. Hoenigswald (1960).

secondary stress *n.* In English and some other languages, a degree of **stress** which is less than **primary stress** but greater than that found on unstressed syllables, as in the first syllable of *kangaroo* or in the last syllable of *formaldehyde*.

second formant /'sekənd/ *n.* (also **F2**) The second-lowest of the **formants** visible in a **sound spectrogram**, typically lying between about 800 Hz and 2,400 Hz. The second formant of a vowel is particularly sensitive to the place of articulation of a neighbouring consonant, and its characteristic *second-formant transitions* are a major acoustic cue in identifying place of articulation, especially for plosives.

Second Germanic Consonant Shift /dʒɜːˈmænɪk/ *n.* A related series of sound changes affecting obstruents which applied to High German but not to other Germanic languages. Briefly, /p/ → /pf/ or /f/ (English *plum*, German *Pflaume*; *apple*, *Apfel*; *deep*, *tief*); /t/ → /ts/ or /s/ (*ten*, *zehn*; *water*, *Wasser*; *foot*, *Fuss*); /k/ → /x/ (in some circumstances) (*make*, *machen*); /d/ → /t/ (*day*, *Tag*; *ride*, *reiten*; *good*, *gut*); /θ/ → /d/ (*thick*, *dick*; *brother*, *Bruder*; *oath*, *Eid*). Cf. **First Germanic Consonant Shift**.

segment /'segmənt/ *n.* 1. A single speech sound; any one of the minimal units of which an utterance may be regarded as a linear sequence, at either the phonetic or phonological level, such as [a], [s], [k] or [m]. The segment is broadly conceived of as a period of speech during which the organs of articulation are more or less unmoving; however, since the speech organs are actually in constant and largely independent motion during speech, phoneticians have long stressed that the segment is (phonetically, at least) a fiction, but it is none the less a very convenient fiction, and such varied evidence as alphabetic writing and slips of the tongue show that the segment is linguistically real. 2. A bundle of **distinctive features** which is fully specified and hence capable of receiving a phonetic interpretation in a particular language. 3. (**seg**) In the *SPE* **feature**

system, a **distinctive feature** invoked to distinguish segments ([+seg]) from **boundaries** ([–seg]). 4. In **Autosegmental Phonology**, a frequent shorthand for **autosegment**. *Adj.* **segmental**. Scott (1941); popularized by Pike (1943).

segmentalization /segmentəlaɪˈzeɪʃn̩/ *n.* See **unpacking**.

segmental phoneme /segˈmentəl/ *n.* The label used by most **American Structuralists** for a **phoneme** in the ordinary sense, as opposed to a **suprasegmental phoneme**. Bloomfield (1933) had called this a *primary phoneme*.

segmental susceptibility /səseptəˈbɪlɪti/ *n.* The degree to which a particular segment is affected by a particular **phonetic setting**.

segmental tier *n.* (also **melodic tier**, **phonemic tier**) In some versions of **Autosegmental Phonology**, a **tier** on which individual segments are located. Most recent versions of the framework decompose this tier into several distinct tiers.

segmentation /segmenˈteɪʃn̩/ *n.* The division of a piece of speech into a linear sequence of identifiable elements. In phonetics and phonology, these elements are most usually **segments** (either **phones** or **phonemes**).

segmentator /ˈsegmenteɪtə/ *n.* An instrument which allows a very short stretch of tape-recorded speech to be played back for analysis.

selectional difference /səˈlekʃənəl/ *n.* (also **lexical incidence**, **lexical distribution**) A difference between two **accents** (sense 1) of a language which share the same set of phonemes (in the relevant domain) but which use different phonemes in particular words. For example, some accents of English have *pass*, *dance*, *bath* with the vowel /æ/ of *cat*, while others have them with the vowel /ɑː/ of *father*.

semantic transparency /sɪˈmæntɪk/ *n.* (also **avoidance of homonymy**, **maintenance of contrast**) A putative principle which is sometimes invoked to explain unusual or irregular phonological developments in cases in which the usual or regular developments would have led to increased homophony, thereby perhaps interfering with communication.

semiconsonant /ˈsemɪkɒnsənənt/ *n.* [*obsolete*] A segment which can function either as a syllabic **margin** or as an on-glide or off-glide to the **nucleus**, but not as a nucleus. Cf. **semivowel**. Hockett (1955).

semi-phoneme /'semifəuniːm/ *n.* [*obsolete*] A phonetically distinctive segment which arises only as a **conditioned alternant** of a phoneme, such as Menomini [uː], which occurs only as a predictable variant of /oː/. Bloomfield (1939); Max Wheeler (p.c.) has suggested that this term might be usefully revived for cases like English schwa, representing the neutralization of several phonemes in a form not close to the other allophones of any of them.

semivowel /'semivɑuəl/ *n.* A non-syllabic segment which has the phonetic characteristics of a vowel but the phonological behaviour of a consonant, most usually a **glide**.

sensorineural deafness /sensərɪ'njuərəl/ *n.* A type of **deafness** arising from a malfunction of the **cochlea**. Cf. **conductive deafness**.

sentence stress /'sentəns/ *n.* 1. (also **tonic stress, accent, pitch accent**) Prominence attached to a single syllable in a single word of a complete sentence in an unmarked style of pronunciation – in English, normally to the last lexical item: *Janet lóves it* vs. *Janet loves her fóod*. 2. See **emphatic stress**. 3. See **nuclear stress**. NOTE: These usages conflict; sense 1 is recommended.

separation of levels /sepə'reɪʃn̩/ *n.* A putative principle of linguistic analysis by which no morphological analysis may be undertaken until the phonological analysis is complete, and so on for other levels of analysis. Acceptance of this principle denies the phonologist all access to grammatical or lexical information. Embraced by most **American Structuralists**, this principle frequently compelled exceedingly counterintuitive analyses and led to the introduction of such devices as **juncture phonemes**; it was attacked by Kenneth Pike in a famous article (Pike 1947b), and it has probably not been seriously maintained by anyone since the 1960s.

sequence /'siːkwəns/ *n.* The linear ordering of elements, most often segments, within a phonological form. Constraints on permissible sequences are the domain of **phonotactics** and have been treated in various ways, such as by **morpheme structure rules**.

serial approach to speech segmentation /'sɪərɪəl əprəutʃ tə spiːtʃ segmenteɪʃn̩/ *n.* (also **linear approach to speech segmentation**) The most familiar method of segmenting speech into smaller units, in which the continuum of speech is exhaustively divided into a single linear sequence of consecutive adjoining units, the **segments**. Cf. **parametric approach to speech segmentation**.

series /'sɪəriːz/ *n.* A label used in philological works, and still sometimes today, for a group of consonant phonemes in a language which share both **voicing** (sense 2) and **manner of articulation** but which differ in **place of articulation**. For example, English has a series of voiceless plosives /p t k/, a series of voiced plosives /b d g/, a series of nasals /m n ŋ/, and so on. (Philological works do not generally use these modern phonetic labels, preferring such traditional names as **tenues**, **aspiratae** and **mediae**.) Cf. **order**.

seseo /se'seo/ *n.* In Spanish, the merger as a sibilant [s] of the two fricatives which are distinguished in standard European Spanish as /s/ and /θ/: hence /'kasa/ for both *casa* 'house' and *caza* 'hunting', distinguished in standard European Spanish as /'kasa/ and /'kaθa/, respectively. Seseo is universal in American Spanish and widespread in southern Spain. In some areas of southern Spain, the result of the merger is a strongly fronted dental variety of [s] perceptually resembling [θ]; this type of pronunciation is called **ceceo**.

setting /'setɪŋ/ *n.* See **phonetic setting**.

sharp /ʃɑːp/ *adj.* In the **Jakobson–Halle feature system**, a **distinctive feature** defined as 'exhibiting an upward shift of the upper frequencies in the spectrum' and interpreted as palatalization of the segment in question. Only palatalized consonants are [sharp]. Ant. **plain**. Cf. **flat**.

sharpening /'ʃɑːpənɪŋ/ *n.* In some early Germanic languages, the reinforcement of geminate glides with plosives, as in the Gothic development of *ww* to *ggw* and of *jj* to *ddj*.

sharp voice *n.* A distinctive **voice quality** involving bright, ringing, penetrating tones, approximately the *voix blanche* of singing, and possibly sometimes identical to **tense voice**. There are different views as to how this is achieved; see Laver (1980: 142–146). Chiba and Kajiyama (1958).

shibilant /'ʃɪbɪlənt/ *n.* or *adj.* [*non-technical*] A semi-jocular label occasionally applied to a **palato-alveolar fricative**, especially to voiceless [ʃ]. By analogy with **sibilant** for [s].

shimmer /'ʃɪmə/ *n.* Irregular variation in the **intensity** (volume) of an individual's voice, such as occurs during **harsh voice**. Cf. **jitter**.

short /ʃɔːt/ *adj.* 1. (of a segment) Having less duration than some other segments, especially than another segment which is otherwise similar. Ant. **long** (sense 1). 2. In the **Williamson feature system**, one of the four possible values of the feature **length**.

shortening /'ʃɔːtənɪŋ/ *n.* Any phonological process in which a **long** segment loses its distinctive length. For example, the long vowels of Old English were at various times shortened before certain consonant clusters and in antepenults: *gōd-spell* > *god-spell* 'gospel', *cēpte* > *cepte* 'kept', *Hlāf-mæsse* > *Hlammæsse* 'Lammas', *sūþerne* > *suþerne* 'southern'.

shwa /ʃwɑː/ *n.* A less usual spelling of **schwa**.

sibilance /'sɪbɪləns/ *n.* 1. The distinctive acoustic property of a **sibilant**, essentially **stridency** (sense 2). Often treated phonologically as a binary, either–or property, sibilance is more realistically regarded as a continuum. 2. (also **sibilant**) In the **Ladefoged** and **Williamson feature systems**, a binary **distinctive feature** invoked to distinguish sibilant fricatives (like [s]) from non-sibilant fricatives (like [θ]).

sibilant /'sɪbɪlənt/ *n.* or *adj.* (**sib**) 1. A **fricative** or **affricate** produced with a concentration of energy at high frequencies, usually by means of a groove in the tongue, and having a characteristic hissing sound. The term is most usually applied to [s], but is sometimes extended to [z] and other segments. 2. A binary **distinctive feature** sometimes invoked to distinguish **obstacle fricatives** ([+sib]) from non-obstacle fricatives ([–sib]): essentially the same feature as **strident** (senses 3–4). Ant. **non-sibilant**. Ladefoged and Maddieson (1986). 3. See **sibilance** (sense 2).

sigma /'sɪgmə/ *n.* The symbol σ, used to label a **syllable** node in tree representations of syllable structure.

signal /'sɪgnəl/ *n.* In the transmission or reproduction of information, such as by sound waves or by electronic means, the information which is intended to be transmitted or reproduced, as opposed to any accompanying **noise**.

silent letter /saɪlənt 'letə/ *n.* A letter in the conventional spelling of a word which has no overt phonetic realization, such as *w* in *write*, *k* in *knife*, *l* in *walk*, *gh* in *right*, *t* in *castle*, *b* in *lamb* and *e* in *mile*.

silent pause *n.* A hesitation in speech containing nothing but silence, sometimes operationally defined as lasting at least 200 ms. Cf. **filled pause**.

silent stress *n*. In English, a pause which occupies a position which needs to be occupied by a stress in order to maintain **stress-timing**. See Abercrombie (1971).

simple sound /'sɪmpəl/ *n*. A segment during whose articulation the organs of speech do not move appreciably, such as a pure vowel or a fricative. NOTE: The antonym **contour segment** is now preferred to the earlier **compound sound**. Jones (1950).

simplex stop /'sɪmpleks/ *n*. An ordinary **plosive** or **nasal stop** throughout which the velum is maintained either open or closed. Cf. **complex oral–nasal stop**.

simplicity /sɪm'plɪsɪti/ *n*. A possible **criterion for phonological analysis**. Simplicity has often been invoked in defending particular analyses, but it is very difficult to attach any clear and consistent content to the term, and in any case an analytical decision which results in simplification in one area may produce greater complexity elsewhere. Attempts to construct *simplicity metrics* for evaluating analyses were highly unsuccessful and have now been largely abandoned.

simplicity–generality criterion /dʒenə'rælɪti/ *n*. A cover term for the criteria taken as paramount in evaluating analyses in **classical generative phonology**, by which the most highly valued analysis consisted of maximally general rules each containing a minimal number of specifications. This criterion placed no constraints upon the degree of abstraction of underlying representations, which tended to become absurdly remote from their surface realizations (in spite of the presence of the **Naturalness Condition**), a state of affairs attacked by Kiparsky (1968) and addressed by **Natural Generative Phonology**.

simultaneous context /sɪməl'teɪniəs/ *n*. A notational device indicating that a **phonological rule** applies to a segment when some feature is present on that same segment. For example, the following rule lengthens a stressed vowel:

$$V \rightarrow [+\text{long}] / \left[\begin{array}{c} \underline{\hspace{2cm}} \\ [+\text{stress}] \end{array} \right]$$

simultaneous iterative rule application /'ɪtərətɪv/ *n*. A mode of **rule ordering** in which, at each stage of the derivation, all rules whose structural description is met apply simultaneously, and a given rule can re-apply as many times as its SD is met. Sommerstein (1977: 171).

simultaneous (once-only) rule application /wʌns ˈəʊnli/ *n.* A mode of **rule ordering** in which, at each stage of the derivation, all rules which have not previously applied but whose structural descriptions are met apply simultaneously, but no rule can apply more than once in a single derivation. Sommerstein (1977: 171).

simultaneous onset of voicing *n.* The circumstance in which vibration of the vocal folds begins within ±20 ms of the release of a preceding voiceless consonant.

sine wave /saɪn/ *n.* The simplest possible type of **wave**, represented by an equation of the form $y = sin\ x$. A sound wave of this type is a pure tone, such as that produced by a tuning fork.

single-bar juncture /ˈsɪŋgəl/ *n.* In some **American Structuralist** work, a type of **juncture** posited as occurring at the end of an intonation contour ending in a level tone. Cf. **double-bar juncture**, **double-cross juncture**. Trager and Smith (1951).

single word boundary *n.* A type of **boundary** which is stronger than a **morpheme boundary** (+) but weaker than a full word boundary, or **double word boundary** (##). Represented as #, the single word boundary is often taken as the kind of boundary separating a **clitic** from its **host**.

singulary feature /ˈsɪŋgjʊləri/ *n.* See **unary feature**.

skeletal tier /skəˈliːtəl/ *n.* (also **skeleton** /ˈskelətən/, **timing tier**) In **Autosegmental Phonology**, the central **tier**, the one which is minimally specified for information of its own and which provides anchor points (*slots*) for the autosegments on all other tiers. This tier is also called the **CV tier** or the **X-tier**, especially when a particular view is held as to what information (if any) is specified there.

Skeleton Satisfaction Condition /sætɪsˈfækʃən/ *n.* In some versions of **Autosegmental Phonology**, a proposed constraint on well-formedness. It says: all skeletal positions must be exhausted. This constraint prevents positions in the **skeletal tier**, of whatever origin, from receiving no melodic content. McCarthy and Prince (1986).

slack (vocal cords) /slæk/ *n.* A **distinctive feature** proposed by Halle (1972), interpreted as representing low tension in the vocal folds, and intended to provide a unified characterization for both low pitch and voicing: both low-pitched and voiced segments are to be classified as [+slack], allowing the pitch-lowering effect of voiced consonants to be interpreted as assimilation. Cf. **stiff (vocal cords)**.

slack voice *n.* See under **lax voice**. Halle and Stevens (1971).

slant rhyme /slɑːnt/ *n.* See **half-rhyme**.

slash /slæʃ/ *n.* See **environment bar**.

slashes *n. pl.* (also **slant brackets** /slɑːnt/, **obliques**) The usual notational device for enclosing **phonemes**, either single phonemes, such as English /k/, /æ/ and /t/, or sequences of phonemes, such as /kæt/ 'cat'. Cf. **brackets** (sense 1).

slender consonant /'slendə/ *adj.* In Irish, a **palatalized** consonant. Such consonants contrast systematically with non-palatalized counterparts; see the examples under **broad consonant**.

slip of the tongue /slɪp/ *n.* Any speech error in which a segment or a feature occurs in an unintended position: 'bread and breakfast' for *bed and breakfast*, 'piss and stretch' for *pitch and stress*, 'pig and vat' for *big and fat*.

slit fricative /slɪt/ *n.* (also **flat fricative**) Any **fricative** produced with a more or less flat lower articulator and hence a wide, flat channel for air flow. An example is [θ]. Cf. **grooved fricative**.

smooth breathing /smuːð 'briːðɪŋ/ *n.* 1. In Ancient Greek, the absence of aspiration at the beginning of a vowel-initial word. 2. The diacritic ', used to represent this.

smoothing /'smuːðɪŋ/ *n.* A type of **monophthongization** in which an off-glide is simply lost, as when Old English *ēa* and *ea* were reduced to *ē* and *e*, respectively. Ant. **breaking**. Sweet (1888).

social stratification /səʊʃḷ strætɪfɪ'keɪʃn̩/ *n.* The phenomenon in which different speech varieties are used by different social classes within a single speech community.

soft /sɒft/ *adj.* [*non-technical*] The opposite of **hard**; see the remarks under that entry.

soft attack /ə'tæk/ *n.* (also **smooth attack**) In singing, the absence of a glottal step at the beginning of a vowel-initial phrase. Cf. **hard attack**.

soft consonant *n.* In certain languages, notably Russian, in which most consonants occur in pairs, one palatalized and the other not, any one of the palatalized consonants. The term **slender consonant**, usual in Irish, has the same meaning. Ant. **hard consonant**.

soft mutation *n.* (also **lenition**) A **mutation** in Welsh by which, in specified grammatical circumstances, voiceless plosives become voiced, voiced plosives become fricatives (or zero in the case of /g/), /m/ becomes /v/, and (in some circumstances) voiceless liquids become voiced: *tref* 'town', *y dref* 'the town'; *desg* 'desk', *y ddesg* 'the desk' (*dd* = [ð]), *mam* 'mother', *y fam* 'the mother' (*f* = [v]), *pont yr afon* 'the river bridge', *dros bont yr afon* 'over the river bridge', *Glyn Ebwy* 'Ebbw Vale', *i Lyn Ebwy* 'to Ebbw Vale', *llyfr* 'book' (*ll* = voiceless lateral), *Dyma lyfr da* 'Here's a good book'.

soft palate *n.* 1. See **velum**. 2. In some analyses, a superordinate **class node** governing the feature [nasal]. Sense 2: Sagey (1986).

soft universal *n.* See **statistical universal**.

soft voice *n.* See under **lax voice**.

Sonagraph /ˈsəʊnəɡrɑːf/ *n.* The trade name of a widely used variety of **sound spectrograph**.

sonant /ˈsɒnənt/ *n.* or *adj.* (also **resonant**) Any voiced sound capable of acting as a syllabic **nucleus**: a vowel, liquid or nasal. The term is particularly used in Indo-European studies.

sone /səʊn/ *n.* 1. The unit of perceived loudness. A 1,000-Hz tone which is 40 dB above the listener's threshold frequency has a loudness of one sone. Stevens (1957). 2. An older synonym for **phone** or **segment**. Harrington (1912). 3. An apparent phonetic unit in a dead language recorded only in writing.

soneme /ˈsəʊniːm/ *n.* An apparent phonemic unit in a dead language recorded only in writing.

sonorant /ˈsɒnərənt/ *n.* or *adj.* (**son**) 1. (also **resonant**) A consonant which is not an **obstruent** – that is, a **liquid**, a **nasal** or an **approximant**. 2. In the *SPE* **feature system**, a **distinctive feature** defined as 'produced with a configuration of the vocal tract cavity in which spontaneous vocal cord vibration is possible'. Obstruents are [−son]; all other segments are [+son], including [h] and [ʔ] and all vowels. This definition in terms of 'spontaneous voicing' has been shown to be unworkable. Many analysts have preferred to rename this feature **obstruent**, with exactly the opposite specifications, though many now prefer to regard [h] and [ʔ] as [+obstr]. Ant. **non-sonorant** or **obstruent**. 3. In the **Ladefoged feature system**, a **distinctive feature** defined as 'possessing a high amount of acoustic energy' and specifically designed to pick out segments which are capable of being syllabic. Hence vowels, nasals and liquids are [+son], while obstruents and glides are [–son]. NOTE that these definitions are not equivalent.

sonorant obstruent *n.* A label suggested for an **obstruent** in some language which patterns in some respects like a **sonorant**, such as the voiced plosives which alternate with nasals in the Celtic languages. Rice (1993).

sonorant voice *n.* (also **spontaneous voice**) (**SV**) A **distinctive feature** proposed by Rice and Avery (1989) and Rice (1993). The proposal is that the traditional feature of **voice** (interpreted as 'laryngeal voice') is found only in **obstruents**, while sonorant voice (regarded as differing in some unspecified phonetic respect) is found in **sonorants** (including vowels) but may also occur in **sonorant obstruents**. The idea is to capture certain generalizations involving obstruents (especially plosives) and sonorants, such as the voiced plosive/nasal alternations occurring in some languages.

sonority /sə'nɒrəti/ *n.* 1. [*obsolete*] A synonym for **vowel height**. Trubetzkoy (1939). 2. A particular sort of prominence associated with a segment by virtue of the way in which that segment is intrinsically articulated. Sonority is an elusive notion. One approach holds that it is a measure of the output of periodic acoustic energy associated with the production of a particular segment, and hence of its intrinsic loudness: the greater such output, the greater the sonority of the sound. Others would associate sonority chiefly with the degree of aperture of the vocal tract. 3. In **Dependency Phonology** and some other privative theories, the vowel element {a}.

Sonority Dispersion Principle /dɪ'spɜːʃn̩/ *n.* A putative principle governing syllabification. It says: the sonority should slope maximally from onset to nucleus and minimally from nucleus to coda. This principle is held to integrate a number of observations about syllable structure; see Kenstowicz (1994: 283). Clements (1990).

Sonority Hierarchy *n.* A putative ranking of segment types in order of their intrinsic sonority. Views differ, but a common ranking is (from least to most sonorous) oral stops > fricatives > nasals >

liquids > glides > vowels. Some would add further elaborations, such as voiceless plosives > voiced plosives and high vowels > low vowels. The idea goes back at least to Whitney, Sievers, Jespersen and Saussure, but modern formulations date from a revival in the 1970s by Zwicky, Hooper, Vennemann and others.

Sonority Sequencing Principle /'siːkwənsɪŋ/ *n.* (also **sonority cycle**) A widely accepted constraint on syllable structure. It says: the sonority profile of the syllable must slope outwards from the peak. In other words, the level of sonority must rise as we proceed from the beginning of the syllable to the peak and fall as we proceed from the peak to the end, in accordance with the **Sonority Hierarchy**. This principle is designed to block such putatively 'impossible' syllables as [ndu] and [spidz]. Note, however, that the second actually occurs in English.

sound change /'saʊnd tʃeɪndʒ/ *n.* (also **sound law** /lɔː/, **sound shift** /ʃɪft/) Any phonological change in which certain segments are systematically converted into phonetically different segments.

Sound Pattern of English, The /'pætən/ *n.* See **SPE**.

sound spectrograph /'spektrəgrɑːf/ *n.* Any of various devices which accept a stretch of speech (or other sounds) as input and produce as output a recording or display representing an analysis of the input, usually a graph with frequency on the vertical axis and time on the horizontal axis, with the darkness of the graph at any point representing the intensity of the sound. Such a graph is a **sound spectrogram** /'spektrəgræm/; it exhibits clearly the frequencies and intensities of the components as a function of time, the periods of voicing and voicelessness, the high-frequency noise of certain fricatives, and the **formant** structure of each part of the utterance.

sound symbolism /'sɪmbəlɪzm̩/ *n.* Any of various types of iconic (non-arbitrary) relations between the sound of a word and its meaning, such as **onomatopoeia** and **phonaesthesia**.

sound system *n.* 1. Narrowly, the **phoneme system** of a language. 2. Broadly, the entire **phonology** (sense 2) of a language.

sound wave *n.* (also **acoustic wave**) A **wave** that propagates sound.

source /sɔːs/ *n.* That part of a sound-generating system which provides the required input of energy. In speech, the **larynx** is commonly taken as the source.

source feature *n.* In the *SPE* **feature system**, any of the several features invoked to treat differences in the source of the acoustic output: **voiced**, **strident** and **heightened subglottal pressure**. Apart from the first, these features have been repeatedly modified and replaced in various ways in the literature.

source/filter theory of speech production *n.* The universally accepted theory of speech production, in which the vibrating larynx serves as a source of energy and the supralaryngeal vocal tract acts as an acoustic filtering system modifying that energy. See Fant (1960), Flanagan (1965), Fry (1979), Lieberman and Blumstein (1988) or Kent and Read (1992).

Southern Shift /'sʌðən ʃɪft/ *n.* A general type of **vowel shift** which has affected, or is currently affecting, most varieties of English spoken in the southern United States, in southern England and in all Southern Hemisphere countries. High and mid vowels are fronted, while low vowels are raised and backed. See Labov (1994: 201–218) for an account. Cf. **Northern Cities Shift**.

span /spæn/ *n.* In speech, a period of measurable duration during which the articulatory organs maintain a more or less steady state. Each span is separated from the next by some kind of **transition**. Catford (1977: 227).

SPE /es piː 'iː/ *n.* (in full, *The Sound Pattern of English*) The major work published by Noam Chomsky and Morris Halle in 1968. In the guise of a detailed description of the phonology of English, *SPE* was the first substantial presentation of the **classical** version of **generative phonology**. The work introduced the *SPE* **feature system** and introduced or elaborated nearly all the principal ideas of generative phonology; it is the most influential publication in phonology in modern times. The title is a bow to Edward Sapir's classic but long-neglected 1925 paper 'Sound patterns in language'; the book ends with an in-joke: its final line, the strange-looking rule $\bar{a} \rightarrow \bar{a}$, is a duplicate of the final line of Pāṇini's great grammar of Sanskrit.

speaking rate /'spiːkɪŋ/ *n.* The overall tempo of a particular piece of speech, including any **filled pauses**. Cf. **articulation rate**.

specification /spesɪfɪ'keɪʃn̩/ *n.* See **feature specification**.

specified feature /'spesɪfaɪd/ *n.* See **feature specification**.

spectrograph *n.* See **sound spectrograph**.

spectrum /'spektrəm/ *n.* (pl. **spectra** /'spektrə/) See **acoustic spectrum**.

speech chain /'spiːtʃ tʃeɪn/ *n.* (also **chain of speech**) The entire sequence of events linking the speaker's brain to the hearer's brain during speech. For a possible analysis, see the **phases of speech**.

speech defect /dɪ'fekt/ *n.* (also **speech impediment** /ɪm'pedɪmənt/) A minor, involuntary, consistent departure from the pronunciation norms of a language, such as a **lisp** or a **defective** *r*.

speech disguise /dɪs'gaɪz/ *n.* A systematic phonological deformation of words resembling a **language game** but typically used to hide speech from outsiders with a limited command of the language. See Kenstowicz (1994: 408–409) for a striking example from Hijaazi Arabic.

speech error /'erə/ *n.* Any utterance which deviates in some way from the intended utterance, such as a **slip of the tongue**. See Fromkin (1973 or 1980).

speech organs *n.* See **vocal organs**.

speech perception *n.* The process by which a hearer extracts identifiable linguistic elements from the continuous acoustic signal of speech.

speech production *n.* All those activities involved in the uttering of speech, usually including the contributions of the brain and nervous system.

speech reading /'riːdɪŋ/ *n.* See **lip reading**.

speech recognition /rekəg'nɪʃn̩/ *n.* The task performed by a computer program which can respond appropriately to human speech.

speech science /'saɪəns/ *n.* The study of all the factors involved in producing, transmitting, perceiving and comprehending speech, including all relevant aspects of anatomy, physiology, neurology and acoustics, as well as phonetics.

speech sound *n.* An individual phonetic segment; a particular pronunciation (**token**) of a consonant or vowel.

speech stretcher /'stretʃə/ *n.* An instrument which allows a stretch of recorded speech to be played much more slowly than at normal speed but without distortion, useful for certain analytical purposes.

speech surrogate /'sʌrəgət/ *n.* A non-vocal system of sounds for transmitting speech, such as **whistled speech** or **talking drums**. See Stern (1957).

speech synthesis /'sɪnθəsɪs/ *n.* The process of producing, usually by electronic means, artificial speech which can be understood by humans. A device which does this is a **speech synthesizer**; the speech produced is **synthetic speech**. *Speech synthesis by rule* is a procedure for converting written texts into intelligible speech.

speech therapy /'θerəpi/ *n.* The diagnosis and treatment of disorders of spoken language.

SPE **feature system** *n.* (also **Chomsky–Halle feature system**) A system of **distinctive features** introduced in Chomsky and Halle (1968). The features in this system are all **binary** and are nearly all **articulatory**; they are grouped into several classes. The **source features** are **voiced**, **strident** and **heightened subglottal pressure**. The **major-class features** are **sonorant**, **consonantal** and **vocalic** (the last quickly replaced by **syllabic**). The **manner features** are **continuant**, **delayed release**, **velaric suction**, **velaric pressure**, **implosion**, **ejection** and **tense**. The **cavity features** are **coronal**, **anterior**, **high**, **low**, **back**, **round**, **distributed**, **covered**, **glottal constriction**, **nasal** and **lateral**. A few **prosodic features** are mentioned but not discussed: *stress*, *length* and several *pitch* features. The framework rapidly replaced the earlier **Jakobson–Halle feature system** as the standard feature system, and it proved highly successful in some respects. None the less, it was criticized on several grounds: the phonetic unreality of some of its definitions, the *ad hoc* nature of certain features (notably **anterior**), and its cumbersome and inadequate treatment of obviously non-binary parameters like **vowel height**. A large number of modifications were proposed, both redefinitions of features and totally new features, but only a few of these ever won general acceptance, and the *SPE* system is still essentially the one used by phonologists who use binary features at all (many phonologists now prefer **unary features**).

spelling pronunciation /'spelɪŋ/ *n.* A pronunciation of a word which has not developed in a historically regular way but which has been strongly affected by the conventional spelling of the word. Examples include the common British pronunciation of *missile* as /'mɪsaɪl/ and the pronunciation of *often* with a [t] in it.

spirant /'spaɪrənt/ *n.* or *adj.* An older term for **fricative**.

spirantization /spaɪrəntaɪˈzeɪʃn̩/ *n.* 1. (also **fricativization**) Any phonological process in which a **plosive** is converted to a **fricative**: one type of **lenition**. Examples include the development of Proto-Indo-European voiceless plosives into Proto-Germanic fricatives (PIE **peisc-* > English *fish*, **trei-* 'three' > Eng. *three*) and the development of Latin intervocalic voiced plosives into Romance fricatives (Latin *habēre* 'have' > French *avoir*, Italian *avere*, Latin *ripa* 'riverbank' > French *rive*). 2. See **aspirate mutation**.

spirometer /spaɪˈrɒmɪtə/ *n.* Any of various devices for measuring the volume of air expelled during speech. *Abstr. n.* **spirometry**.

split /splɪt/ *n.* See **phonemic split**.

spondee /spɒnˈdiː/ *n.* A metrical **foot** consisting of two stressed syllables, or, in **quantitative metre**, of two long syllables: *feline*, *spondee*, *good news*. *Adj.* **spondaic** /spɒnˈdeɪɪk/. Greek *spondeios pous* 'foot of libation', from its use in libation songs.

spontaneous speech /spɒnˈteɪnɪəs/ *n.* Ordinary, unselfconscious speech; the speech we produce when we are not thinking of the effect of our speech upon hearers.

spontaneous voicing *n.* 1. In Chomsky and Halle (1968), a phonetically questionable notion invoked to distinguish sonorants from obstruents; the idea is that vibration of the vocal folds occurs spontaneously when the vocal folds are suitably positioned and there is no obstruction in the vocal tract to raise the air pressure there (producing a sonorant); some different mechanism is assumed to produce voicing in obstruents. 2. See **sonorant voice**.

spoonerism /ˈspuːnərɪzm̩/ *n.* The transposition of segments between the words of a phrase, as in *slow and sneet*, *our queer old dean*, *a blushing crow*, *The Lord is a shoving leopard*, and the classic if doubtless apocryphal *You have hissed all my mystery lectures and tasted the whole worm*. After the Reverend W. A. Spooner of New College, Oxford, who was reportedly much given to this sort of error.

Sprachbund /ˈʃpraxbʊnt/ *n.* [German: 'language union'] See **linguistic area**.

spread /spred/ *adj.* Denoting a configuration of the lips in which the corners are extended outward from the neutral position. *Ant.* **rounded**.

spread glottis *n.* A **distinctive feature** proposed to define the class of 'breathy' segments: aspirated consonants, voiceless vowels and

[h] are [+spread]; all other segments are [–spread]. Cf. **constricted glottis**. Halle and Stevens (1971).

spreading /'spredɪŋ/ *n.* 1. The use of a **spread** lip position. 2. The phenomenon in which a phonetic feature occurring intrinsically on one segment or in one morpheme, such as nasality or high tone, is realized phonetically over a longer stretch of material.

square brackets /skwɛə/ *n.* See **brackets**.

SSC /es es 'siː/ *n.* See **Stress Subordination Convention**.

stability /stə'bɪləti/ *n.* In **Autosegmental Phonology**, the principle by which the deletion of an autosegment on one tier has no effect upon associated autosegments on other tiers. For example, if a tone is associated with a vowel, either may disappear while the other remains.

stacking /'stækɪŋ/ *n.* In some versions of **Autosegmental Phonology**, an arrangement in which some tiers are directly dependent upon other autosegmental tiers, rather than upon the **skeletal tier**. Rennison (1987).

stammer(ing) /'stæmər(ɪŋ)/ *n.* Abnormal hesitation in speech; difficulty in speaking continuously and smoothly. This may result from a speech defect or from strong emotion. Cf. **stutter(ing)**. *V.* **stammer**.

standing wave /'stændɪŋ/ *n.* A type of **wave**, found in a vibrating body such as an air column or a drumhead, which results from the superposition of two identical waves travelling in opposite directions. Certain points (the **nodes**) are not displaced at all, while others (the **antinodes**) exhibit maximum displacement.

star /stɑː/ *n.* See **asterisk**.

starred form /stɑːd/ *n.* A form marked with an **asterisk** to show that it is a hypothetical reconstructed form or to show that it is ill-formed or impossible.

static tone /'stætɪk/ *n.* See **register tone**.

statistical universal /stə'tɪstɪkəl/ *n.* (also **soft universal**) A **universal** which holds for the great majority of languages but not for all. Examples: voiced obstruents imply voiceless ones; if a language has one front rounded vowel it will be /y/.

steady /'stedi/ *adj.* In the **Williamson feature system**, one of the three possible values of the feature **posture**.

steady state /steɪt/ *n*. Any stage during the production of speech during which the organs of articulation briefly remain more or less motionless, as during the **hold** phase of a **plosive**.

stem /stem/ *n*. In morphology, a bound form of a lexical item which typically consists of a **root** to which one or more **affixes** have been added and which serves as the immediate **base** for the formation of grammatical words. For example, the Latin verb *amare* 'love' has the root *am-*, from which are derived the imperfect stem *amab-*, the perfect stem *amav-*, the supine stem *amat-*, and so on.

stepping tone /'stepɪŋ/ *n*. See **register tone**.

stereotype /'steriətaɪp/ *n*. A **variable** which is the overt topic of social comment in a community and which typically shows conscious correction and **hypercorrection**. Cf. **marker** (sense 3), **indicator**. Labov (1994: 78).

stiff (vocal cords) /stɪf/ *n*. A **distinctive feature** proposed to treat distinctions of tension in the vocal folds: [+stiff] is associated with voicelessness and high pitch; [–stiff] with voicing and low pitch. The feature has the advantage of allowing the familiar tendency of a voiced consonant to lower a following tone as an assimilation, but it is not without problems: see Ladefoged (1973), Sommerstein (1977: 106). Cf. **slack (vocal cords)**. Halle and Stevens (1971).

stiff voice *n*. See **tense voice**. Halle and Stevens (1971)

Stifling /'staɪflɪŋ/ *n*. A proposed unification of **Proper Inclusion Precedence** and the **Elsewhere Condition**, as follows. Given two rules of the form (i) A → B / P___Q and (ii) C → D / R___S, such that the set of strings that fit P[+seg]Q is a proper subset of the set that fit R[+seg]S, and the structural changes of the two rules are either identical or incompatible, and (ii) is not a phonetic rule, then a representation that meets the structural description of both (i) and (ii) may not undergo (ii), either immediately or later. Hastings (1974).

stød /stød/ *n*. A highly distinctive **suprasegmental** occurring in Danish, derived from an earlier **tone** related to the **accent I** of Norwegian and Swedish. Stød is realized phonetically as **creaky voice** on the stressed syllable; its presence is not wholly predictable, and it is sometimes contrastive. For example, the following pairs of words are homophonous apart from the presence of stød in the first but not the second: *hund* 'dog'/*hun* 'she'; *mand* 'man'/*man* 'one' (impersonal); *bønder* 'peasants'/*bønner* 'beans'; *tanken* 'the tank'/*tanken* 'the thought'; *banken* 'the bank'/*banken* 'the knocking'. See Fischer-Jørgensen (1985) or Laver (1994: 330–331).

stop /stɒp/ *n.* 1. [*rare*] An older synonym for **plosive**. 2. A general label for any segment whose articulation involves a complete oral closure. In this sense, the class of stops includes **nasals** ('nasal stops') as well as **plosives** and **affricates** ('oral stops'). Laver (1994) extends the term to include **flaps**, **taps** and **trills**, all of which involve momentary closures, but this wider use is not standard. 3. In the **Ladefoged feature system**, a **distinctive feature** invoked to handle distinctions in degree of occlusion, with the three possible values *stop*, *fricative* and *approximant*. 4. In Ladefoged (1971), a quite different binary **distinctive feature** with the possible values 0 (no complete closure) and 1 (complete closure). 5. In the **Williamson feature system**, one value of the feature **stricture**.

stop burst *n.* See **burst**.

strangulated /'stræŋgjuleɪtɪd/ *adj.* [*non-technical*] (of speech) Produced with abnormal constriction of the throat, whether from strong emotion, pathological causes or physical strangling.

Stratificational phonology /strætɪfɪ'keɪʃənəl/ *n.* The type of phonology practised within *Stratificational Grammar*. A series of planes, or *strata*, relates the conceptual end of a linguistic form to its phonetic realization; within each plane, the *tactics* of that plane define the elements available on that plane and their possible combinations. The *morphotactics* handles the combinations of *morphemes*, which are realized as **morphons** (roughly, allomorphs); morphons consist of *phonemes* (roughly, the morphophonemes of earlier approaches), whose combinations are treated by the *phonotactics*; phonemes consist of **phonons** (unary features). See Sommerstein (1977: ch. 4) for a brief introduction, Lockwood (1972, especially ch. 6) for a more detailed one. Lamb (1966).

stratum /'streɪtəm/ *n.* (*pl.* **strata** /-tə/) 1. Any one of the planes of representation recognized in **Stratificational phonology**. 2. [*rare*] See **level** (sense 2).

stray consonant /streɪ/ *n.* A consonant occupying a marginal position in a syllable in which it cannot be straightforwardly parsed, such as /m/ in *rhythm* and /n/ in *damn* (cf. *damnation*).

Stray Erasure Convention /ɪˈreɪʒə/ *n.* An earlier version of the principle of **Prosodic Licensing**. It says: erase segments and skeleton slots unless attached to higher levels of structure. Steriade (1982).

strength /strɛŋθ/ *n.* See **phonological strength**.

strengthening /ˈstrɛŋθənɪŋ/ *n.* See **fortition**.

stress /strɛs/ *n.* 1. A certain type of **prominence** which, in some languages, is present upon certain syllables. Native speakers and phoneticians usually find it easy to determine which syllables bear stress, and even to distinguish varying degrees of stress, but the phonetic characterization of stress is exceedingly difficult: stress is variously associated with greater loudness, higher pitch and greater duration, any of which may be most important in a given case, and sometimes also with vowel quality. Earlier attempts to identify stress with greater intensity of sound are now discredited, and current thinking holds that stress is primarily a matter of greater muscular effort by the speaker, and that hearers take advantage of several types of information to identify that effort. Jones (1950) distinguishes four phonetic types of stress: **level**, **crescendo**, **diminuendo** and **crescendo–diminuendo**. See Laver (1994: 533) for references. See **word stress**, **sentence stress**, **emphatic stress**, **nuclear stress**. 2. In the *SPE* **feature system**, an undefined and undiscussed **distinctive feature** invoked to handle contrasts of stress in sense 1. Attempts at developing this feature quickly revealed that it was fundamentally different from all other *SPE* features (see Roca 1994: 208–209), and the search for a better alternative led to the development of **Metrical Phonology**.

stress accent *n.* A type of **word accent** in which certain syllables are made more prominent than others by the presence of **stress**. Cf. **pitch accent**.

stressed *adj.* (of a syllable or a word) Bearing a **stress**.

Stress Erasure Convention /ɪˈreɪʒə/ *n.* In some versions of **Metrical Phonology**, a convention which prevents one application of the **cycle** from having access to information derived from earlier cycles. One version is: all existing metrical structure is erased at the start of each cycle. Halle and Vergnaud (1987).

stress foot *n.* A **foot** in a **stress language**: a prosodic unit consisting of one stressed syllable and some number of unstressed syllables.

stress language *n.* A language with a prominent **accent** (sense 3) realized as strong **stress** (sense 1), such as English, Spanish or Russian. In some stress languages, such as English and Russian, unstressed syllables undergo reduction; in others, such as Spanish, they do not. Cf. **pitch language**.

stress-neutral suffix *n.* See **secondary affix**.

stress retraction *n.* 1. (also **stress reversal**, **stress shift**) See **iambic reversal**. 2. The phenomenon in English in which the primary stress occurs earlier in a word than is usual, as in *catamaran* and *mulligatawny*. Several versions of a **Stress Retraction Rule** appear in the literature to account for this, including the *Long, Alternating, Weak* and *Strong Stress Retraction* rules. See Hogg and McCully (1987) for a survey.

stress-shifting suffix /'ʃɪftɪŋ/ *n.* See **primary affix**.

Stress Subordination Convention /səbɔːdɪ'neɪʃən/ *n.* (**SSC**) In many analyses of English stress, the convention by which the assignment of primary stress at some stage of an analysis automatically reduces all existing stress levels by one within the current domain. For example, the primary stress assigned earlier to the first syllable of *player* is reduced one level when primary stress is assigned to the first element in *baseball player*.

stress-timing *n.* The type of speech **rhythm** in which stressed syllables occur at approximately equal intervals, with any number of unstressed syllables allowed to occur between the stresses. Stress-timing is often said to be characteristic of English, though objective measurement shows that the occurrence of stresses at equal intervals is more an ideal than a reality. *Adj.* **stress-timed**. Cf. **syllable-timing**. The term was coined by Pike (1947a), but the idea goes back to Joshua Steele in the eighteenth century.

Strict Cyclicity Condition /saɪ'klɪsɪti/ *n.* Especially in **Lexical Phonology**, a proposed constraint upon cyclic rules. It says: cyclic rules may apply in derived environments only. In other words, a cyclic rule can only effect a change in an input which has been created within the current cycle. This condition does essentially the same work as the **Revised Alternation Condition** and the **Derived Environment Constraint**. Mascaró (1976); Kaisse and Shaw (1985).

Strict Layer Hypothesis /'leɪə/ *n.* In the **Prosodic Hierarchy** model, the requirement that all material on a given level must be exhaustively dominated by the nodes of the next higher level. Among other things, this requirement rules out improper bracketings, such as ambisyllabic consonants.

stricture /'strɪkʃə/ *n.* 1. See **constriction**. 2. In the **Williamson feature system**, a **distinctive feature** with the possible values **stop**, **fricative**, **approximant**, **high vowel** and **low vowel**. 3. A **distinctive feature** proposed by Lass (1984: 110), with six values ranging from *plosive* to *low vowel*.

stricture feature *n.* A rare synonym for **major-class feature**. Cf. **content feature**.

stricture type *n.* Any one of the different ways of forming a **constriction** in order to produce a speech sound (especially a consonant). Catford (1988) distinguishes stops, fricatives, approximants, resonants and trills (the maintainable types), plus taps, flaps and semi-vowels (the momentary types). The notion of sticture type is similar to that of **manner of articulation**, but narrower in excluding such things as laterality, velic attitude (nasality) and fricative release.

strident /'straɪdənt/ *adj.* (**stri**) 1. [*non-technical*] (of a sound) Loud or harsh. 2. (also **sibilant**) (of a fricative) Characterized by a large amount of energy at high frequencies; intense and high-pitched, such as [s]. See Laver (1994: 260–263). 3. In the **Jakobson–Halle feature system**, a **distinctive feature** defined as 'exhibiting high-intensity noise' and interpreted as involving a 'rough-edged' effect at the point of articulation. Ant. **mellow**. 4. In the *SPE* **feature system**, a similar **distinctive feature** defined as 'marked acoustically by greater noisiness [than a non-strident counterpart]' and associated with turbulent air flow over a surface, the turbulence being caused by any or all of a rough surface, a high rate of flow or a steep angle of incidence. Contrasts of stridency are possible only for affricates, fricatives and 'non-vocalic liquids'; all other segments are non-strident. The feature is variously invoked to distinguish [f] ([+stri]) from [ɸ] ([–stri]), [s] ([+stri]) from [θ] ([–stri]), [ʃ] ([+stri]) from [ç] ([–stri]) and the Czech fricative trill [r̝] ([+stri]) from [r] ([–stri]). This acoustic (or perceptual?) feature is unusual in the articulatorily based *SPE* feature system, and in most cases it could be replaced by the *SPE* feature **distributed**. Cf. **sibilant** (sense 2). *Abstr. n.* **stridency** /'straɪdənsi/. Ant. **non-strident**.

Strine /straɪn/ *n.* [*non-technical*] A jocular label for the distinctive speech variety of Australia, especially for its less well-educated varieties. Morrison (1965): a representation of the local pronunciation of 'Australian'.

strone /strəʊn/ *n.* [*rare*] Any particular phonetic realization of a **stroneme**. Jones (1950).

stroneme /'strəʊniːm/ *n.* [*rare*] A unit of phonological **stress**, regarded as a kind of phoneme. Jones (1950).

strong /strɒŋ/ *adj.* (of a **secondary articulation**) Present to a high degree: *strong nasalization, strong palatalization.*

strong consonant *n.* [*informal*] A consonant which is low in **sonority**, such as a voiceless plosive, and which may therefore undergo **lenition** or be the target of **fortition**. Ant. **weak consonant**.

Strong Domain Hypothesis *n.* In **Lexical Phonology**, a proposed mode of rule application. It says: all rules are free to apply at the earliest lexical level (unless barred by an independent constraint). The idea is that each rule applies from the initial level onward, until at some point stipulated by the analyst it ceases to apply (it is *deactivated*), after which it may not be activated again. (**Structure Preservation**, of course, bars many rules from lexical application, so that they cannot apply before the postlexical level.) Kiparsky (1985).

strong form *n.* (also **full form**) One of two (or more) possible pronunciations of a given word in connected speech, the one which occurs when the word is stressed, such as *can* in *I CAN do it* (/kæn/). Ant. **weak form**.

strong syllable *n.* A less usual term for **heavy syllable**.

strong verb /vɜːb/ *n.* In English and other Germanic languages, a verb which forms its past tense and past participle by vowel change: *sing/sang/sung; write/wrote/written.* Cf. **weak verb**.

structural change /'strʌktʃərəl/ *n.* (**SC**) In a **phonological rule**, the string of elements which is produced from a given input when the rule succeeds in applying – in the traditional notation, the output between the arrow and the environment bar plus the environment on the right of the bar. Thus, the rule A → B / C___D (equivalently, CAD → CBD) yields the SC CBD. Cf. **structural description**.

Structural Compensation, Principle of /kɒmpən'seɪʃn̩/ *n.* A putative functional principle of language change. It says: when the rate of deletion of a meaningful feature of a language increases, the frequency of features that redundantly carry this meaning will increase. Labov (1994: 604).

structural context *n.* A possible position for the occurrence of a segment, in terms of syllables, morphemes or words. For example, English /h/ occurs only syllable-initially. Cf. **environmental context**.

structural description /dɪ'skrɪpʃən/ *n.* (**SD**) (also **proper analysis**) In a **phonological rule**, the string of elements which must be matched by a representation in order for the rule to apply to it – in the traditional notation, the input on the left of the arrow plus the environment on the right of the environment bar. Thus, the rule A → B / C___D (equivalent to CAD → CBD) has the SD CAD. Cf. **structural change**.

structural difference /'dɪfrəns/ *n.* A difference between two **accents** (sense 1) of a language which permit different sequences of phonemes. For example, **rhotic accents** of English differ from **non-rhotic** ones in permitting /r/ before a vowel or pause.

structuralism /'strʌkʃərəlɪzm̩/ *n.* 1. Any approach to linguistic description which views the structure of a language primarily as a system of relations. Structuralism in this sense derives chiefly from the work of the Swiss linguist Ferdinand de Saussure. Virtually all twentieth-century approaches to phonology are structuralist in this sense, as opposed to earlier atomistic approaches, which regarded the phonology of a language as a collection of elements. 2. See **American Structuralism**.

structural set /set/ *n.* Any subset of the **phonemes** of a language which share a common distribution, such as English /r l w j/ (can follow a plosive in a word-initial cluster) or /ɪ e æ ʌ ɒ ʊ/ (can only occur in a closed syllable). Bloomfield (1933).

structure /'strʌkʃə/ *n.* The relation between elements which are all present simultaneously and which form part of some complex object. Cf. **system**.

structure-determined neutralization /dɪ'tɜːmɪnd/ *n.* A **neutralization** which occurs in some **structural context**, such as word-finally. Cf. **context-determined neutralization**. Prague School.

Structure Preservation /prezə'veɪʃn̩/ *n.* In **Lexical Phonology**, a constraint upon lexical rules. It says: lexical rules do not introduce distinctions not present in lexical entries. See **Strong Domain Hypothesis**. Kiparsky (1985).

stutter(ing) /'stʌtər(ɪŋ)/ *n.* The unintentional repetition of segments or syllables in speech, especially word-initial consonants, either from a speech defect or from strong emotion: *G-G-G-Good morning*. The cartoon character Porky Pig has a prominent stutter. Cf. **stammer**. *V.* **stutter**.

subgesture /'sʌbdʒestʃə/ *n.* In a representation of segments in terms of **gestures**, a gesture which is a subordinate part of another gesture. Thus, the *oro-nasal subgesture* is one aspect of the *articulatory gesture*.

subglottal pressure /sʌb'glɒtəl/ *n.* The air pressure in the pulmonic airstream just below the vocal folds, the primary determinant of perceived **loudness**.

subjunction /səb'dʒʌŋkʃən/ *n.* In **Dependency Phonology**, the relation between two elements one of which directly dominates the other. For example, the representations

i and a

a   i

might be used for [e] and [æ], while **i:a** might be used for [ɛ], the first two showing subjunction. *V.* **subjoin** /səb'dʒɔɪn/.

sublamina /sʌb'læmɪnə/ *n.* See **underblade**.

sublamino-prepalatal 1. *adj.* (of an articulation) Involving the **underblade** of the tongue and the front part of the **palate** as the primary articulators; one type of **retroflex** articulation. 2. *n.* A segment so articulated, such as the retroflex consonants of southern India.

submatrix /'sʌbmeɪtrɪks/ *n.* A **matrix** which is part of a larger matrix. The term is used particularly in the **gesture** analysis of articulations.

subphonemic /sʌbfə'niːmɪk/ *adj.* Pertaining to phonetic details which are not contrastive; **allophonic**.

subrule /'sʌbruːl/ *n.* See **expansion** (sense 1).

substance /'sʌbstəns/ *n.* The physical material – speech sounds – representing some linguistic object. Cf. **form** (sense 2). Saussure (1916).

substantive universal /səb'stæntɪv/ *n.* Any formal object which is universally present in languages, or at least universally available, such as the feature [nasal]. Cf. **formal universal**.

substrate /'sʌbstreɪt/ *n.* (also **substratum** /'sʌbstreɪtəm/) An indigenous language upon whose speakers a second, more prestigious, language is imposed. Cf. **superstrate**.

suction /'sʌkʃən/ *n.* Another name for an **ingressive airstream mechanism**. Catford (1939).

suffix /'sʌfɪks/ *n.* An **affix** which follows the root in the form containing it, such as English plural *-s* in *cats* and both agent *-er* and *-s* in *writers*. *Adj.* **suffixal** /'sʌfɪksəl/.

sulcalized /'sʌlkəlaɪzd/ *adj.* Concave; hollow. The term is applied to the upper surface of the tongue in a configuration in which the **tip** and the **back** are both raised but the **front** is lowered, yielding a concave outline, as in the articulation of a **dark** *l* or in **internal rounding**. *Abstr. n.* **sulcalization**. Latin *sulcus* 'furrow'.

superficial /suːpə'fɪʃl̩/ *n.* Pertaining to the **surface** phonetic form of a linguistic item.

superfix /'suːpəfɪks/ *n.* (also **suprafix**) A suprasegmental (stress or tone) distinction which serves as the sole exponent of a grammatical distinction. See Trask (1993: 270) for examples.

superfoot /'suːpəfʊt/ *n.* In **Metrical Phonology**, a unit posited in order to combine two **feet** in a word which contains three or more feet. Selkirk (1980).

superheavy syllable /'suːpəhevi/ *n.* In some languages, a syllable type which contrasts with ordinary **light** and **heavy syllables** in being heavier than both. In Cairene Arabic, for example, a syllable ending in two consonants or a long vowel plus a consonant is superheavy and is treated differently in stress assignment from a heavy syllable (ending in one consonant or a long vowel) and from a light syllable (ending in a short vowel).

superjump /'suːpədʒʌmp/ *n.* A hypothetical type of phonological change in which the phonetic realization of a phoneme leaps discontinuously from one point to another in phonological space, passing over in the process another phoneme with which it does not merge – for example, a shift of /ɔ/ from [ɔ] to [u] in which an intervening /o/ ([o]) is unaffected. There seems to be little hard evidence for the reality of such shifts. Labov (1994: 147).

superstrate /'suːpəstreɪt/ *n.* A language which is imposed upon the speakers of a different, less prestigious, language. Cf. **substrate**.

suppletion /sə'pliːʃn̩/ *n*. The use of two or more distinct stems for forming the inflections of a single lexical item: *go/went, person/ people, bad/worse. Adj.* **suppletive**.

suppletive alternation /sə'pliːtɪv/ *n*. **Alternation** between phonologically unrelated forms, as in the English plural morphs found in *cats, oxen* and *radii*. Bloomfield (1933).

supported /sə'pɔːtɪd/ *adj.* (of an element of linguistic structure) Accompanied in the stream of speech by other sources of the information that it carries. Ant. **unsupported**. Labov (1994: 589).

suprafix /suːprəfɪks/ *n*. See **superfix**.

supraglottal /suːprə'glɒtəl/ *adj.* Pertaining to that part of the **vocal tract** above the **glottis**, that is, to the pharynx, the oral cavity or the nasal cavity.

supralaryngeal /suːprələ'rɪndʒəl/ *adj.* In some versions of **feature geometry**, a class node dominating all phenomena within the oral and nasal cavities.

supralaryngeal gesture *n*. In some analyses of articulation, that part of the articulation of a segment which takes place in the **supralaryngeal vocal tract**. Cf. **laryngeal gesture**.

supralaryngeal vocal tract *n*. (also **supraglottal vocal tract**) That part of the vocal apparatus lying above the larynx (or glottis): the **vocal tract** in common parlance.

suprasegmental /suːprəseg'mentəl/ *adj.* or *n*. (also **non-segmental**, **plurisegmental**) (Pertaining to) a phonological element whose domain is something larger than a single segment and whose phonetic realization can only be described by reference to adjoining domains in the same utterance. The most familiar such elements are **stress** and **tone** (or **pitch**), though others are sometimes recognized. Suprasegmental elements are essentially the same as **prosodic** elements. The term was introduced by the **American Structuralists** but is still in widespread use.

suprasegmental phoneme *n*. (also **prosodeme, secondary phoneme**) In some analyses, notably those of the **American Structuralists**, a **suprasegmental** element when this is regarded as a **phoneme**, more or less on a par with ordinary segmental phonemes. Bloomfield (1933) had earlier called these *secondary phonemes*, using *primary phonemes* for segmental phonemes.

surd /sɜːd/ *n.* [*obsolete*] Any voiceless segment. Latin *surdus* 'muffled'.

surface /'sɜːfɪs/ *n.* The level of **phonetic** representation of words or utterances. *Adj.* **superficial**.

surface phonotactic constraint *n.* A constraint upon the permissible sequences of segments which applies to phonetic forms, but not necessarily to underlying representations. Sommerstein (1977: 195).

surface representation *n.* See **phonetic form**.

susceptibility /səseptɪ'bɪlɪti/ *n.* The degree to which the articulation of a particular segment is influenced by a speaker's use of a particular **phonetic setting**. For example, vowels are highly susceptible to the use of **palatalized voice**, while plosives are little affected.

suspendable opposition /sə'spendəbəl/ *n.* (also **neutralizable opposition**) In **Prague School** phonology, the relation between two segments which contrast in some positions but which are **neutralized** in other positions. Ant. **constant opposition**.

svarabhakti /svɑːrə'bɑːkti/ *n.* See **anaptyxis**. Sanskrit *svārabhakt* 'vowel-separation'.

s/w notation /es 'dʌbəljuː/ *n.* In **Metrical Phonology**, a notation for **feet** in which each syllable is explicitly marked as *s* ('strong') or *w* ('weak'). Cf. **head-marked notation**.

syllabic /sɪ'læbɪk/ *adj.* 1. Constituting a syllable, or (more usually) the **nucleus** of a syllable. *Abstr. n.* **syllabicity** /sɪlə'bɪsɪti/. 2. Pertaining to a syllable or to syllables. 3. (**syll**) A **distinctive feature** proposed by Chomsky and Halle (1968: 354) (who credit the idea to an unidentified 'Milner and Bailey'), not as part of the canonical *SPE* **feature system**, but as a suggested revision. Defined as 'constituting a syllabic peak', this feature is intended as a replacement for the feature **vocalic**: vowels and syllabic consonants are [+syll]; all other segments are [−syll]. Though widely used, this feature suffers from the absence of any phonetic correlate: syllables are undefined in Chomsky–Halle framework and play no part in **classical generative phonology**. 4. A similar binary **distinctive feature** in the **Ladefoged feature system**.

syllabic consonant *n.* A segment which has the phonetic characteristics of a **consonant** (sense 1) but which, in a particular case, functions as a syllabic **nucleus**, such as the /n/ in *button* or the /l/ in *bottle* (in most accents) or Czech /l/ in *vlk* 'wolf'. See Laver (1994: 239–241, 264–265) for a catalogue.

syllabic margin *n.* Either edge of a **syllable**.

syllabic nucleus *n.* See **nucleus**.

syllabification /sɪlæbɪfɪˈkeɪʃn̩/ *n.* Any analytical procedure for dividing a phonological representation into a well-defined sequence of **syllables**. *V.* **syllabify** /sɪˈlæbɪfaɪ/.

syllable /ˈsɪləbəl/ *n.* A fundamental but elusive phonological unit typically consisting of a short sequence of segments, most typically a single vowel or diphthong possibly preceded and/or followed by one or more consonants. Although native speakers usually find it easy to decide how many syllables are present in a given word or utterance, although syllable-based writing systems have been in use for thousands of years and although speech errors provide abundant evidence for the mental reality of syllables, the syllable has proved exceedingly difficult to define. There have been various attempts to define the syllable phonetically: as a single respiratory movement (the **chest-pulse theory**), as a single opening and closing of the vocal tract, as a single peak of prominence in the soundstream resulting from a combination of stress, pitch, length and intrinsic sonority (the **prominence theory**). See Kloster Jensen (1963) for a survey. None of these has proved adequate, and a few workers have concluded that the syllable is no more than a convenient fiction. Such pessimism has proved unsustainable, since a large number of phonological processes appear to operate in terms of syllables. Today two approaches dominate: (1) the syllable is a unit of neural programming which can be reconstructed by the hearer from a variety of clues, in spite of the absence of any single phonetic correlate; (2) the syllable is a purely phonological unit consisting of a single peak of intrinsic sonority, though with qualifications for cases like English *spit*, which has two peaks. It is now usual to subdivide the syllable into an **onset** and a **rhyme**, with the rhyme further divided into a **nucleus** (or **peak**) and a **coda**. In much contemporary work, syllables are regarded as more fundamental than segments.

syllable adjunction *n.* A proposed analytical procedure for introducing into syllables segments whose presence violates the **Sonority Sequencing Principle**, such as the sibilants of English *stops*. Levin (1985).

syllable-based tone *n.* The type of **tone** system in which each syllable is assigned its own independent tone, as in Chinese or west African languages. Cf. **word-based tone** (sense 2).

syllable boundary *n.* The **boundary** between two adjacent **syllables**, often represented as . or $.

Syllable Integrity Principle /ɪn'tegrɪti/ *n.* In some versions of **Metrical Phonology**, a proposed constraint upon prosodic structure. It says: prosodic constituent structure cannot violate syllable structure. Prince (1980).

syllable quantity *n.* See **syllable weight**.

syllable structure *n.* In a particular language, or in languages generally, the requirements and constraints which determine the shapes of possible syllables, usually formulated in terms of sequences of consonants and vowels, but also in terms of **onset** plus **rhyme**, or **onset** plus **nucleus** plus **coda**. See **canonical form**.

syllable template *n.* In **Autosegmental Phonology**, a **template** invoked to account for **syllable structure**. The idea was introduced by McCarthy (1979) for **non-concatenative morphology** and extended by Itô (1986).

syllable-timing /'taɪmɪŋ/ *n.* (also **isosyllabicity**) A type of rhythm in which each syllable in an utterance takes roughly the same amount of time to produce. This sort of rhythm is reported for many languages, such as Spanish and Vietnamese. *Adj.* **syllable-timed**. Cf. **stress-timing**. Pike (1947a).

syllable weight *n.* (also **weight, phonological weight, syllable quantity**) A metrical property by which syllables are divided into two (rarely three) classes differing in the number of **moras** they contain and hence in their degree of metrical prominence. In terms of weight, **light syllables** differ from **heavy syllables** (and rarely also from **super-heavy syllables**); the difference is fundamental in many languages.

symbol /'sɪmbəl/ *n.* 1. Any conventional character which is not a letter of the alphabet, such as 5 or $. 2. Any character used in a **phonetic alphabet** (sense 1) to represent some **phone** or **phoneme**, such as [k] or /θ/.

synaeresis /sɪ'nɪərəsɪs/ *n.* (also **syneresis**) The combining of two adjacent vowels within a single word into a single syllable, as in the usual pronunciations of *familiar* and *righteous*. Greek *synaíresis* 'a taking together'.

synaesthesia /sɪniːs'θiːziə/ *n.* The subjective sensation of a sense other than the one being stimulated, as in *audition colorée*.

synaloepha /sɪnə'liːfə/ *n.* The coalescence of two syllables into one across a word boundary by reduction or loss of the first vowel, as in *Th'Almighty*. Greek *synaloiphé* 'a coalescing'.

synchronic /sɪŋ'krɒnɪk/ *adj.* Pertaining to the development of language over time. Cf. **diachronic**. *Abstr. n.* **synchrony** /'sɪŋkrəni/. Saussure (1916).

syncope /'sɪŋkəpi/ *n.* (also **syncopation** /sɪŋkə'peɪʃn̩/) The loss of a segment from the interior of a word. The term is most commonly applied to vowel loss, as in the common British pronunciations of *medicine* as /'medsɪn/ and of *library* as /'laɪbri/, but is sometimes extended to consonant loss, as in *ever > e'er* and *boatswain > bosun*. *Adj.* **syncopated**. *Ant.* **syncope**. Greek *synkopē* 'a cutting off'.

syncretism /'sɪŋkrətɪzm̩/ *n.* 1. The morphological phenomenon in which two or more morphosyntactically distinct forms of a lexical item are formally identical. In Latin, for example, genitive and dative case forms are usually distinct (*amicus* 'friend', genitive *amici*, dative *amico*), but in -*a*-stem nouns they exhibit syncretism (*puella* 'girl', genitive/dative *puellae*). 2. In **Glossematic phonology**, the unit which appears in a position of **neutralization**. *Adj.* **syncretic** /sɪŋ'kretɪk/. Greek *synkrētismos* 'alliance of Cretans'.

synizesis /sɪnɪ'ziːsɪs/ *n.* (also **synecphonesis**) The fusion of two syllables into one by the coalescence of two adjacent vowels without the formation of a recognized diphthong. Greek *synízēsis* 'a collapse'.

syntactic feature /sɪn'tæktɪk/ *n.* An element which is primarily syntactic in motivation, such as [noun] or [past +]; such features must sometimes be invoked in phonological descriptions.

syntactic stress *n.* A rare type of **stress** used for making grammatical distinctions. The Brazilian language Terena does this: *Kúti otopíko* 'Who chopped?' vs. *Kúti otópiko* 'What did he chop?'

syntagmatic relation /sɪntæg'mætɪk/ *adj.* (also relation *in praesentia*) Any relation holding between two elements which are simultaneously present in a single structure. Cf. **paradigmatic relation**.

synthesized speech /'sɪnθəsaɪzd/ *n.* (also **speech synthesis**) See **artificial speech**.

synthetic speech /sɪn'θetɪk/ *n.* The artificial speech produced in **speech synthesis**.

system /'sɪstəm/ *n*. A set of linguistic elements which stand in a **paradigmatic relation** (that is, they represent choices), together with the relations among them. We may speak, for example, of the **phoneme system** or the *tone system* of a language. The items in a system stand in a relation of *systemic contrast* to one another. The conception of a language as a system, or rather as a system of systems, is the fundamental insight of **structuralism**. Cf. **structure**. *Adj*. **systemic**. The idea was stressed by Saussure, but the term was particularly promoted by Firth.

systematic correspondence /sɪstə'mætɪk/ *n*. In historical linguistics, the pattern in which a segment X in language A is found to be consistently matched by segment Y in language B in the same position in words of identical or similar meaning. For example, English *t* corresponds systematically to German *z* (= [ts]) in word-initial position: *ten/zehn*, *to/zu*, *tooth/Zahn*, *tide/Zeit* 'time', *toe/Zehe*, *tell/zählen* 'count', *two/zwei*. The existence of significant numbers of such correspondences not attributable to borrowing is commonly taken as substantial evidence for a genetic relationship between the languages in question.

systematic gap /gæp/ *n*. The absence from a language of an entire class of phonological forms as a consequence of some constraint, most often a **phonotactic** one, such as the absence from English of forms with initial /sr-/ or /zd-/. Cf. **accidental gap**.

systematic phoneme *n*. The name given to the highly abstract conception of the **phoneme** favoured in **classical generative phonology**, as opposed to the comparatively non-abstract **autonomous phoneme** favoured in most earlier work.

systematic phonemic representation *n*. A phonological representation in terms of **systematic phonemes**, in early generative phonology the input to the phonological rules.

systematic phonetic representation *n*. In early generative phonology, the output of the phonological rules, commonly regarded as a set of instructions issued by the central nervous system to the articulatory apparatus.

systematic phonetics *n*. A somewhat abstract conception of **phonetics**, defined by Ladefoged (1972: 277) as 'that level which specifies all the targets necessary for the description of a particular language as opposed to all other languages, but contains no information of the kind that is used simply to specify one speaker of that language as opposed to other speakers'. Cf. **physical phonetics**. Chomsky (1964).

systemic difference /sɪˈstiːmɪk/ *n.* A difference between two **accents** (sense 1) of a language in which one accent possesses one or more phonemes absent from the other. For example, the RP phoneme /ɒ/ is absent from American accents, and words which have /ɒ/ in RP variously have /ɑː/, /ɔː/ or /ʌ/ in American English.

Systemic phonology *n.* The type of phonology practised by adherents of *Systemic Grammar*, an explicit continuation of some aspects of **Prosodic Analysis** incorporating many of the tools of Systemic Grammar. As expected, Systemic phonology emphasizes the study of connected speech, and it makes heavy use of hierarchies of phonological units. See Tench (1992) for an introduction.

systole /ˈsɪstəli/ *n.* [*rare*] The shortening of a long syllable. Ant. **diastole**. Greek *systolē* 'contraction'.

T

tail /teɪl/ *n*. In some analyses of **intonation**, any syllables that come between the nuclear syllable and the end of the tone unit. In English, the tail always continues the final pitch direction of the nucleus.

tailed *n* /teɪld en/ *n*. See **eng**.

talking drums /tɔːkɪŋ 'drʌmz/ *n*. A system of transmitting speech using drums whose pitch can be changed at will; linguistic pitch and rhythm can be represented so effectively that messages can be understood even in the absence of segmental information.

tamber /'tæmbə/ *n*. See **timbre**. According to Jones (1950), invented by the poet Robert Bridges.

tap /tæp/ *n*. 1. A segment in whose articulation the moving articulator is moved rapidly from its rest position so as to lightly strike a second, stationary articulator and is then returned to its starting position. The most familiar tap is the alveolar tap [ɾ], as in Spanish *pero* 'but' and in a typical American pronunciation of *Betty*. A tap is sometimes regarded as the limiting case of a **trill**, with only a single vibration, but this is phonetically dubious, since the **Bernoulli effect** plays no part in producing a tap. See Laver (1994: 224–227) for a survey. Cf. **flap**. NOTE: Those who, like Laver (1994), prefer to regard taps as stops, use the term 'tapped stop' for what is more usually just called a 'tap'. 2. In the **Ladefoged feature system**, a **distinctive feature** somewhat hesitantly proposed to distinguish taps (and flaps?) ([+tap]) from all other segments ([–tap]) and partly replacing Ladefoged's earlier feature of **rate**. In the **Williamson feature system**, the same work is done by the feature **posture**.

tapped fricative /tæpt/ *n*. A segment articulated like a **tap** except that the maximum constriction is not a complete closure, but only a constriction sufficient to produce frication. The Nigerian language Etsako has a phonemic voiceless tapped alveolar fricative, and some American speakers use a similar sound as their realization of intervocalic /t/, as in *city*.

tapping /'tæpɪŋ/ *n*. 1. The articulation of a **tap**. 2. (also **flapping**) The phenomenon, occurring in many varieties of English, in which

/t/ or /d/ in intervocalic position is realized as a tap [ɾ], as in the familiar American pronunciation of *butter* or *wedding*. NOTE: Though widespread, the use of 'flapping' in this sense is inaccurate and should be avoided.

target /'tɑːgɪt/ *n.* 1. In phonetics, a slightly idealized configuration of the speech organs at which the speaker 'aims' when producing a speech sound. 2. In the study of **speech errors**, an utterance which is intended by a speaker who makes an error.

tautomorphemic /tɔːtəmɔːˈfiːmɪk/ *adj.* Belonging to the same **morpheme**. Cf. **heteromorphemic**.

tautosyllabic /tɔːtəsɪˈlæbɪk/ *adj.* (of a segment) Belonging to the same **syllable** (as another segment).

taxonomic phoneme /tæksəˈnɒmɪk/ *n.* A dismissive synonym for **autonomous phoneme**.

taxonomy /tækˈsɒnəmi/ *n.* A classification; in particular, any approach to linguistic description in which classification is considered to be a primary goal. *Adj.* **taxonomic**.

TBU See **tone-bearing unit**.

tectal /'tektəl/ 1. *adj.* Pertaining to the **tectum**. 2. *n.* In philological works, an occasional term for any **palatal** or **velar** obstruent

tectum /'tektəm/ *n.* The roof of the mouth, usually including but sometimes excluding the upper teeth and the **alveolar ridge**. *Adj.* **tectal**. Malone (1923): Latin *tectum* 'roof'.

teeth /tiːθ/ *n. pl.* (sg. **tooth** /tuːθ/) The enamelled bony structures set in two curving lines in the upper and lower gums. The upper teeth (and rarely the lower teeth) may serve as passive articulators. *Adj.* **dental**; CF **denti-**.

telephone theory of hearing /'telɪfɪʊn/ *n.* A theory of hearing which holds that neurons transmit electrical signals unchanged from the **cochlea** to the brain, where all processing is performed. This theory is now known to be wrong.

telephone voice *n.* A distinctive style of speaking used by some people when using the telephone, often characterized by a reduction in **rate** (sense 1) and noticeably increased formality.

telescoping /'telɪskəʊpɪŋ/ *n.* A complex type of language change in which some intermediate stages in a series of natural changes get lost, leaving behind a phonetically bizarre set of alternations. For example, a certain Basque morpheme has the alternants /e/ ~ /i/ ~ /χ/ as a result of the loss of several intermediate steps.

template /'templeɪt/ *n.* In phonology or morphology, a general, schematic, skeletal representation of some class of forms consisting of a set of positions or 'slots' into which elements of specified types may be inserted to produce valid forms. Templates are widely used in contemporary phonology and also in describing **non-concatenative morphology**. *Adj.* **templatic** /tem'plætɪk/.

templatic syllabification *n.* The analytical procedure of constructing syllables by **templates**, rather than by rules. Itô (1986, 1989).

tempo /'tempəʊ/ *n.* See **rate**.

tense /tens/ *adj.* 1. A frequent but exceedingly ill-defined label applied to certain segments in particular languages which contrast with other, similar, **lax** segments in a complex manner. The general idea is that tense segments are characterized by greater muscular tension, more extreme movements of the vocal organs, greater duration and greater subglottal air pressure than their lax correlates, but there is frequently little or no evidence for such phonetic correlates, though a few languages, such as Korean, genuinely do appear to possess contrasting consonants which can be realistically described as tense and lax. Tense consonants are also called **fortis**; tense vowels were formerly called **narrow**, and are now often labelled [+**ATR**]. In recent years there has been a marked tendency to try to interpret the tense/lax distinction in terms of glottal and subglottal activity. See Lass (1976: ch. 1, Appendix) and especially Catford (1977: 199–208) for a critical examination of the use of this term, and Wood (1975b) for a defence. 2. In the **Jakobson–Halle feature system**, a **distinctive feature** defined as 'exhibiting high energy with greater spread across the spectrum and longer duration', and interpreted as representing greater deformation of the vocal tract from its rest position. 3. In the *SPE* **feature system**, a **distinctive feature** defined as 'produced with a deliberate, accurate, maximally distinct gesture that involves considerable muscular effort'; tense segments are also said to be relatively long. Often invoked in a seemingly arbitrary manner, especially for the purpose of doubling the number of vowel heights available, this feature suffers from the same problems cited in sense 1, and it has now been replaced by the feature **ATR**, itself suspect for similar reasons, in connection with vowels, while **constricted glottis** and **spread**

glottis are often invoked for distinguishing tense and lax consonants. See Sommerstein (1977: 104–105) for a critical survey of this
feature. 4. (also **long**) In the phonology of English, a conventional
label for all vowels and diphthongs derived from the long vowels
of Middle English. Some treatments would also include /æ/ in the
tense vowels, even though it is descended from an original short
vowel. *Abstr. n.* **tenseness**. Ant. (all senses) **lax**.

tense voice *n.* (also **stiff voice**) 1. Broadly, a label applied to any
of various **voice qualities** involving an overall increase in muscular
tension and hence some or all of **anterior** (sense 2) voice, **harsh
voice**, **ventricular voice**, vigorous and extensive movements of the
tongue, lips and jaw, constriction of the larynx and the pharynx,
heightened subglottal air pressure, and elevated pitch and volume.
Cf. **lax voice**. 2. See **anterior voice** (under **anterior**, sense 2).

tensing *n.* Any phonological change in which a **lax** vowel becomes
tense, such as the change of /æ/ to /æː/ in some American cities.

tension /'tenʃən/ *n.* 1. A stretching or stiffening of an elastic organ,
such as the tongue or the vocal folds, as a result of muscular effort.
2. A ternary **distinctive feature** proposed by Ladefoged (1971),
resembling the **expansion** (sense 2) feature of the **Williamson
feature system** and designed to do roughly the same work as **ATR**.
Tension was replaced in the **Ladefoged feature system** by the binary
feature **wide**.

tenuis /'tenjʊɪs/ *n.* (*pl.* **tenues** /'tenjuːz/) [*obsolete*] An older term
for a **voiceless plosive**, such as [p], [t] or [k], sometimes especially
(as in Ancient Greek) for an **unaspirated** one. This term was widely
used in the nineteenth-century philological literature. Cf. **media**,
aspirata. Latin *tenuis* 'thin', translation of Greek *psilos* 'plain'.

terminal feature /'tɜːmɪnəl/ *n.* In **feature geometry**, a feature which
occurs at the bottom of a tree, so that no other features depend
upon it.

terminal juncture *n.* In the analysis of Trager and Smith (1951),
any of several **juncture phonemes** posited to account for differences in phrase-final intonation. There are three types: **single-bar**,
double-bar and **double-cross junctures**.

ternary feature /'tɜːnəri/ *adj.* A **distinctive feature** which may
assume any one of exactly three values.

terraced-level /'terəst/ *adj.* (of an utterance) Showing **tone terracing**.

tertiary stress /ˈtɜːʃəri/ *n.* In some analyses of English stress, a third level of stress recognized as being less prominent than both **primary** and **secondary stress** but still not completely unstressed. For example, the word *decontamination* has primary stress on its fifth syllable and secondary stress on its first syllable; tertiary stress is sometimes posited for the third syllable.

tessitura /tesɪˈtʊərə/ *n.* The characteristic pitch range used by an individual in ordinary speech, or sometimes by the speakers of a particular language. Italian: 'texture'; borrowed from musical usage.

tetragraph /ˈtetrəgrɑːf/ *n.* In an alphabetic writing system, a sequence of four letters which conventionally represents a single phoneme. Tetragraphs are rare, but German ⟨tsch⟩ for /tʃ/, as in *deutsch* 'German', is an example, if /tʃ/ is a single segment. Cf. **digraph**, **trigraph**.

tetrameter /teˈtræmɪtə/ *n.* A line of verse containing four metrical **feet**.

tetraphthong /teˈtræfθɒŋ/ *n.* A single syllabic **nucleus** in which four different vowel qualities can be sequentially distinguished. Tetraphthongs are vanishingly rare, but Wells (1982, 3: 538–539) reports hearing [bræɪæʊn] for *brown* from a woman in Mississippi. Cf. **monophthong**, **diphthong**, **triphthong**.

***t*-glottalling** *n.* The phenomenon, occurring in many varieties of English, in which the phoneme /t/ is realized in certain positions either as an **oral–glottal plosive** [ʔt] or simply as a **glottal stop** [ʔ].

thematic /θɪˈmætɪk/ *adj.* (of a word or a class of words in some language) Lacking a **thematic vowel** in its inflected forms. Ant. **athematic**.

thematic vowel *n.* In certain languages, such as Spanish and Latin, a linking vowel which occurs between a root or stem and a following affix. For example, Latin *mon-* 'advise' has thematic vowel *-e-*: *mon-e-ō* 'I advise', *mon-e-t* 'he advises', *mon-e-nt* 'they advise', etc. Such languages usually have several classes of words with different thematic vowels.

theme /θiːm/ *n.* An older synonym for **base** (both senses), now little used.

third formant /θɜːd/ *n.* (also **F3**) The third of the **formants** visible in a **sound spectrogram**, typically lying above 2,000 Hz.

Thirteen-Men Rule /θ₃ːtiːn 'men/ *n*. See **iambic reversal**.

thoracic cavity /θɔːˈræsɪk/ *n*. The chest cavity, containing the **lungs** and bounded by the rib-cage and the **diaphragm**.

three-tone approach /θriː/ *n*. An approach to English intonation which recognizes just three tonal distinctions: fall, rise, fall–rise. See Cruttenden (1986: 117–119). Gussenhoven (1983).

thyroid cartilage /ˈθaɪrɔɪd kɑːtəlɪdʒ/ *n*. The largest of the cartilages making up the **larynx**. Suspended from the **hyoid bone** and pivoted upon the lower **cricoid cartilage**, the thyroid has a snowplough-shaped forward projection which is responsible for the **Adam's apple**.

tidal volume /ˈtaɪdəl/ *n*. The volume of air breathed in and out during the **respiratory cycle**.

tier /tɪə/ *n*. In **Autosegmental Phonology**, any one of the several linear sequences of elements of some specified kind whose combination constitutes a phonological representation. One of these, the **skeletal tier**, is designated as the 'backbone' to which elements on all other tiers are **associated** (see under **association**).

tier conflation *n*. In some versions of **Autosegmental Phonology**, an analytical procedure by which two **tiers** are combined into one at some stage in a derivation. McCarthy (1986).

tilde /ˈtɪldə/ *n*. The diacritic ~, conventionally used in various orthographies and transcriptions for various purposes. In Spanish and Basque, the character ñ represents the palatal nasal /ɲ/. In the IPA, a tilde above a character represents **nasalization**: hence [ã] represents a nasalized [a].

timbre /ˈtɪmbə/ *n*. (also **tamber**, **tonality**) The perceptual tonal qualities which distinguish one sound (especially a vowel) from another.

timing tier /ˈtaɪmɪŋ/ *n*. See **skeletal tier**.

tip /tɪp/ *n*. (also **apex**) The forwardmost extremity of the **tongue**, often used as an active articulator. *Adj*. **apical**; CF **apico-**.

token /ˈtəʊkən/ *n*. A single pronunciation of a linguistic form by a particular individual on a particular occasion. Cf. **type**.

tonal default /ˈtəʊnəl/ *n*. In some **tone languages**, a tone which is automatically assigned to any syllable not assigned tone by any other process.

tonal displacement /dɪs'pleɪsmənt/ *n.* An analytical procedure by which a **tone** which is intrinsically attached to an affix is assigned instead to a root. Pulleyblank (1986).

tonal feature *n.* See **tone feature**.

tonality /tə'nælɪti/ *n.* 1. See **timbre**. 2. The use of **tones**. 3. In the **Hallidayan analysis** of intonation, the system of options for dividing an utterance into **tone groups** (intonational phrases). Cf. **tonicity**.

tonality feature *n.* In the **Jakobsen–Halle feature** system, any of the features [grave]/[acute], [sharp]/[plain] or [flat]/[plain].

tonal morpheme *n.* A morpheme which is realized exclusively as a tone, and which contains no segments. For example, the Recent Past suffix in Tiv consists only of a high tone: *vèndè* 'refuse' has recent past *vèndé*, with a final high tone.

tonal particle /'pɑːtɪkəl/ *n.* A grammatical morpheme realized entirely as a **tone**, with no segments of its own.

tonal sandhi *n.* Variation in the phonetic realization of **tones** due to the contextual influence of neighbouring tones in connected speech.

tonal stability /stə'bɪlɪti/ *n.* The phenomenon in tone languages in which a tone remains undeleted when its associated vowel is deleted. Goldsmith (1976).

tonal tier *n.* In **Autosegmental Phonology**, the **tier** on which **tones** are located.

tone /təʊn/ *n.* 1. The phenomenon, occurring in many languages, in which words of different meaning which consist of identical sequences of consonants and vowels are distinguished merely by contrasts of **pitch**. 2. Any one of the lexically contrastive pitches occurring in such a system. Mandarin Chinese, for example, has four tones: level, rising, falling and falling–rising. Examples: *shū* 'write', *shú* 'sorghum', *shù* 'technique', *shŭ* 'category'. See Laver (1994: 462–483) for an introduction, Fromkin (1978) for a detailed survey. 3. In some analyses of **intonation**, an individual pitch regarded as one of the units from which intonation patterns are built up. 4. In the **Hallidayan analysis** of intonation, the system of choices of the type of pitch pattern on an intonational **nucleus**. *Adj.* **tonal** /'təʊnəl/.

tone assimilation *n.* Any of various phenomena in **tone languages** in which the realization of a tone is affected by a neighbouring tone, such as High–Low → High–Falling.

tone-based *adj.* Denoting an approach to **intonation** in which contours are analysed into sequences of discrete pitch-levels, as in the **tone sequence** model. This approach has been widely used in the United States, and is increasingly influential in Britain. Cf. **tune-based**.

tone-bearing unit *n.* **(TBU)** In **Autosegmental Phonology**, any element on the **segmental tier** which is capable of bearing a **tone** – most often a syllabic nucleus.

tone feature *n.* (also **tonal feature**) 1. A **distinctive feature** invoked to treat distinctions of tone in **tone languages**. Among those widely used (all binary) are (with conventional diacritics) [high] (´), [mid] (ˉ), [low] (ˋ), [rising] (ˇ), [falling] (ˆ), [fall–rise] (˜). 2. A **distinctive feature** invoked to treat distinctions of **intonation**. For example, Vanderslice and Ladefoged (1972) propose the features [accent], [intonation], [cadence], [endglide] and [emphasis].

tone group *n.* The fundamental unit of **intonation**, the stretch of utterance to which a single intonational contour applies.

tone language *n.* A language in which **tones** can be used to distinguish words consisting of identical segments, such as Chinese, Yoruba or Norwegian. Sometimes the term is restricted to languages in which virtually every syllable receives a tone, such as Chinese, while those in which only certain syllables receive tone are **partial tone languages**. In the canonical case, the tone on each syllable is independent of the tones on other syllables and hence the tone of each syllable must be specified separately. Cf. **pitch language**.

toneless *adj.* (of a syllable or an affix in a **tone language**) Lacking any intrinsic tone.

tone letter /ˈletə/ *n.* A graphical symbol for representing a **tone**, such as ⊣ for a mid level tone. See Laver (1994: 476). Chao (1930).

toneme /ˈtəʊniːm/ *n.* Any one of two or more distinctive **tones** in a particular language which can serve alone to distinguish words. By analogy with **phoneme**; according to Daniel Jones (1950 [1967]: 262), he himself coined the term in 1921, and it was later re-invented by Kenneth Pike and others.

tonemics /tə'niːmɪks/ *n. pl.* A synonym for **tonology**, preferred by the **American Structuralists**.

tone of voice *n.* The use of phonetic features with no linguistic function by a speaker in order to express particular attitudes (confidentiality, anger, scepticism, etc.).

tone polarity /pə'lærɪti/ *n.* In a **tone language** with just two tones, the presence of a morpheme (usually a bound morpheme or a clitic) which has no intrinsic tone of its own but which always assumes the opposite tone to the neighbouring syllable. For example, Margi /a/ 'present tense', takes a high tone before a verb with a low tone and vice versa.

tone sandhi *n.* (also **tonal sandhi**) A change in the phonetic realization of a **tone** under the influence of a neighbouring tone; sometimes more specifically the replacement of one **toneme** by another in such circumstances. Pike (1947b).

tone sequence /'siːkwəns/ *n.* A **tone-based** approach to intonation which incorporates all intonational phenomena into a single sequence of pitch movements. Cf. **contour interaction**. Ladd (1984).

tone terracing /'terəsɪŋ/ *n.* Any of various phenomena in **tone languages** in which the absolute pitches realizing particular tones change in a systematic way during an utterance: **downdrift, downstep, upstep**.

tonetics /tə'netɪks/ *n. pl.* The phonetic details of the realization of **tones** in speech. *Adj.* **tonetic**. By analogy with **phonetics**.

tongue /tʌŋ/ *n.* The flexible muscular organ occupying the lower part of the **oral cavity**, the single most important organ of articulation. The tongue is a nearly globular mass of densely interlocking muscles, and is described by Laver (1994: 121) as resembling 'three quarters of a tennis ball, with a very highly extensible and manoeuvrable tip'. Its upper surface is conventionally divided into the **tip**, the **blade**, the **front**, the **back** (or **dorsum**) and the **root**; some phoneticians, however, apply the term **dorsum** to the combined front and back, which are then sometimes distinguished as **anterodorsum** and **posterodorsum**. *Adj.* **lingual**; CF **linguo-**.

tongue-arching model /'tʌŋɑːtʃɪŋ/ *n.* (also **Bell–Sweet model**) The conventional, but controversial, view of vowel quality, in which the primary determinant of vowel quality is taken to be the location of the highest point of the tongue. See Catford (1981) for a history, Lindau (1975), Wood (1975a) or Lass (1984: 6.6) for critical discussion.

tongue-body feature *n.* Any **distinctive feature** invoked to treat differences of the position of the body of the tongue within the oral cavity during an articulation. The most familiar such features are **high**, **low** and **back**.

tongue-fronted voice *n.* A **voice quality** characterized by persistent fronting of the tongue during speech.

tongue-raised voice *n.* A **voice quality** characterized by persistent raising of the tongue during speech.

tongue-retracted voice *n.* A **voice quality** characterized by persistent retraction of the tongue during speech.

tongue-twister /'twɪstə/ *n.* Any phrase, especially a deliberately constructed one, containing a sequence of segments which makes it very difficult to pronounce accurately at normal speed: *The sixth sheik's sixth sheep's sick.*

tonic /'tɒnɪk/ 1. *adj.* (of a syllable or a vowel) Bearing the word accent (pitch or stress). Ant. **atonic** /'eɪtɒnɪk/. 2. See **nucleus** (sense 3).

tonicity /tə'nɪsɪti/ *n.* In the **Hallidayan analysis** of intonation, the system of options for the location within the **tone group** (intonational phrase) of the **intonational nucleus**. Cf. **tonality**.

tonic stress *n.* See **sentence stress**.

tonogenesis /təʊnə'dʒenəsɪs/ *n.* Any process of phonological change by which **tones** are acquired by a language which formerly lacked them.

tonology /tə'nɒlədʒi/ *n.* The phonological study of **tones**. *Adj.* **tonological** /təʊnə'lɒdʒɪkəl/.

topline /'tɒplaɪn/ *n.* (also **plateau**) The pitch value forming the upper limit of the current **pitch span**. Cf. **baseline**.

topographical aspect /tɒpə'græfɪkəl/ *n.* Any aspect of an articulation involving a departure of the tongue from its neutral configuration.

total assimilation /'təʊtəl/ *n.* An instance of **assimilation** in which one segment becomes identical to another, as when Latin ECLIPSE 'eclipse' developed into Italian *eclisse*.

total lung capacity /kə'pæsɪti/ *n.* The volume of air in the lungs after a maximal inspiration.

trachea /'treɪkiə/ *n.* (also **windpipe**) The cartilaginous channel connecting the lungs to the **larynx**, through which air passes in breathing and speaking. *Adj.* **tracheal** /'treɪkiəl/.

traditional feature system /trə'dɪʃənəl/ *n.* See **Ladefoged feature system**.

Trager–Smith system /treɪgə 'smɪθ/ *n.* An analysis of the English vowel system proposed by George Trager and Henry Smith (1951), an elaborated version of the earlier **Bloch and Trager system**. The system posits twelve units: nine simple vowels (with three degrees each of height and backness) and three off-glides (high front *y*, high back *w* and centring/lowering *h*); each of the off-glides is sometimes interpreted as length: /iy/ = [iː], /uw/ = [uː], /ah/ = [aː]. Four types of vocalic nucleus are recognized: V, Vy, Vw, Vh. This gives a total of 36 possible nuclei, and Trager and Smith claim that all of these occur in some varieties of English. Of course, no single accent of English exhibits anything like 36 distinct nuclei, and the Trager–Smith system is therefore a **diasystem**, rather than a description of a single variety of English. Nevertheless, the system cannot handle the contrast between [ɔə] and [ɔː] found in some non-rhotic varieties of English, as in *lore* and *law*. Once almost universal in the United States, the Trager–Smith system is now little used, but its policy of analysing tense nuclei as sequences of elements is still widespread in American analyses (though not in British analyses). See Kreidler (1989: 300ff.) for a summary of the system. Cf. **Kenyon and Knott system**.

trailer-timing /'treɪlə/ *n.* A type of rhythm in which a **foot** is perceived as beginning with an unstressed syllable. Cf. **leader-timing**. Wenk and Wioland (1982).

transcription /træn'skrɪpʃən/ *n.* 1. Any conventional system for representing speech or language in writing *other than* one which is customarily employed for ordinary writing, most usually one which attempts to render pronunciation in a consistent manner, and commonly excluding mere **transliteration**. Two types are linguistically important: **phonetic transcription** and **phonemic transcription**. 2. Any particular example of such a representation. *V.* **transcribe** /træn'skraɪb/.

transderivational constraint /trænzderɪ'veɪʃənəl/ *n.* A **constraint** on the application of a rule in one derivation which depends upon the properties of an entirely different derivation. Wilkinson (1976) cites a neutralization rule in Terena which applies if and only if its application does not result in homophony – that is, it fails to apply only if, as a result, two different derivations would have the same output.

transfer problem /'trænsfɜː/ *n.* In the analysis of **reduplication**, the phenomenon by which prosodic information, such as vowel length, must sometimes be copied from a base to a reduplicating affix. Clements (1985).

transfix /'trænsfɪks/ *n.* A discontinuous affix which combines with a discontinuous base. For example, the Arabic root *ktb* 'write' appears in such forms as *katab* 'he wrote', *jiktib* 'he will write', *kitaab* 'book', *kaatib* 'clerk', *maktuub* 'written' and *maktaba* 'book-shop', each of which illustrates a different transfix.

transglottal airflow /trænz'glɒtəl/ *n.* The flow of air through the **glottis** during speech.

transient /'trænziənt/ *n.* A very brief disturbance in the form of a sound wave.

transition /træn'zɪʃn̩/ *n.* 1. Any movement of the vocal organs during speech from one more-or-less steady position to another. 2. The acoustic effect of such a movement, particularly as revealed in the upward or downward movement of the **formants** in a **sound spectrogram**.

transitional aspect *n.* Any aspect of an articulation involving something other than a steady state during the medial phase of the segment in question. **Taps**, **flaps** and **trills** are intrinsically transitional.

Translation Theory /trænz'leɪʃn̩/ *n.* An approach to the physiological control of speech in which representations in terms of linguistic units are considered to form the input to the speech mechanism. See Nolan (1982) or Laver (1989), and cf. **Action Theory**.

transliteration /trænzlɪtə'reɪʃn̩/ *n.* Any conventional system for representing in one orthography a language which is ordinarily written in a different orthography, normally by merely replacing each character of the ordinary orthography in a uniform manner by some character or sequence of characters in the orthography being used, with no attempt at providing a phonetic or phonemic **transcription**. For example, the Russian word Честолюбие 'ambition' might be transliterated into the Roman alphabet as *chestoljubije*. *V.* **transliterate**.

transparency /træns'pærənsi/ *n.* 1. The property of a **transparent rule**. Ant. **opacity**. Kiparsky (1971, 1973a). 2. The property of a segment which does not prevent some phonological process, such as assimilation, from applying right across it without being itself affected. *Adj.* (both senses) **transparent**.

transparent rule *n.* A phonological rule whose existence can easily be inferred from inspection of surface phonetic forms. Roughly speaking, such a rule states a true generalization about surface forms. An example is a rule devoicing final consonants in a language in which all final consonants are voiceless. Cf. **opaque rule**.

transverse section /trænz'vɜːs/ *n.* A planar section through the body which separates the top of the head from the soles of the feet. Cf. **coronal section**, **sagittal section**. NOTE: Phoneticians frequently but erroneously apply this term to what is properly called a **coronal section**.

trema /'triːmə/ *n.* See **diaeresis**.

triangular vowel system /traɪ'æŋgjʊlə/ *n.* A **vowel system** in which all vowels except the lowest occur in front–back pairs.

trigraph /'traɪgrɑːf/ *n.* In an alphabetic orthography, a sequence of three letters which conventionally represents a single segment, such as German ⟨sch⟩ for /ʃ/ or French ⟨eau⟩ for /o/. English makes no regular use of trigraphs, though the British spelling *manoeuvre* exceptionally uses the trigraph ⟨oeu⟩ for /uː/. Cf. **digraph**, **tetragraph**.

trill /trɪl/ *n.* 1. (also **roll**) A segment whose articulation involves the repeated rapid striking of one flexible organ against another (flexible or rigid) organ, as a result of the **Bernoulli effect**. The most familiar trill is the alveolar trill [r], as in Spanish *perro* 'dog'. See Labov (1994: 218–221). Cf. **tap**, **flap**. *Adj.* **trilled**. 2. In the **Ladefoged feature system**, a binary **distinctive feature** invoked to distinguish trills ([+trill]) from all other segments ([–trill]), and replacing Ladefoged's earlier **vibration** feature. In the **Williamson feature system**, the same work is done by the feature **posture**.

trilled /trɪld/ *adj.* 1. (of a segment) Having the nature of a **trill**. 2. In the **Williamson feature system**, one of the three possible values of the feature **posture**.

trilled fricative *n.* See **fricative trill**.

trimeter /ˈtrɪmɪtə/ *n.* A line of verse consisting of three metrical **feet**.

triphthong /ˈtrɪfθɒŋ/ *n.* A single vocalic nucleus which begins with one vowel quality, moves to a second quality, then finishes with a third quality. Examples include the [aɪə] of *fire* and the [aʊə] of *flour* in many varieties of RP. Cf. **monophthong**, **diphthong**, **tetraphthong**. *Adj.* **triphthongal**.

Trisyllabic Laxing /traɪsɪlæbɪk ˈlæksɪŋ/ *n.* (also **Trisyllabic Shortening**) 1. The historical process in English by which tense (long) vowels underwent laxing (shortening) whenever followed by two or more further syllables in the word. This process is responsible for such modern alternations as *sane/sanity*, *divine/divinity* and *profound/profundity*. 2. In some descriptions of English, a synchronic rule posited to account for these alternations.

trisyllable /ˈtraɪsɪləbəl/ *n.* A word consisting of three **syllables**, such as *kangaroo* or *happily*.

trochee /ˈtrəʊkiː/ *n.* A metrical **foot** consisting of a stressed syllable followed by an unstressed syllable, or, in **quantitative metre**, of a long syllable followed by a short. English examples: *better*, *money*. *Adj.* **trochaic** /trəʊˈkeɪɪk/. Cf. **iamb**.

trough /trɒf/ *n.* A point of low prominence in **stress** or **intonation** during an utterance. Ant. **peak**.

true consonant /truː/ *n.* In the *SPE* **feature system**, any segment which is [+consonantal] and [–vocalic]: an **obstruent** or a **nasal**.

True Generalization Condition *n.* The principle, associated with **Natural Generative Phonology**, that no statement is truly phonological unless it holds for all surface phonetic representations. Acceptance of this principle renders impossible that very large number of analyses in **classical generative phonology** employing abstract underlying representations and ordered rules.

truncation /trʌŋˈkeɪʃn̩/ *n.* Any phonological process which removes one or more segments from the end of a word. *V.* **truncate**.

tune /tjuːn/ *n.* In some analyses of **intonation**, a sequence of pitches regarded as one of the units from which intonation patterns are built up. The minimal tune, containing a single **nucleus**, is a *nuclear tone*; the maximal tune, consisting of several nuclear tones, is a *whole tune*. See Cruttenden (1986).

tune-based *adj.* Denoting an approach to **intonation** which analyses all patterns as variations upon a very small number of contrastive **tunes**, as in the **contour interaction** model. This approach has been particularly influential in England and France, especially in language-teaching; it has also been adopted by some phonological theorists. Cf. **tone-based**.

turbulence /'tɜːbjʊləns/ *n.* Irregular air flow, usually caused by obstruction of the flow and often perceived as some kind of hissing noise. Turbulence is most conspicuously a property of fricatives like [s]. *Adj.* **turbulent**.

twang /twæŋ/ *n.* [*non-technical*] An impressionistic label applied to an accent of English which is characterized by an unusually high degree of **nasalization**.

two-level phonology /tuː 'levəl/ *n.* A theory of phonology developed by the Russian linguist S. K. Šaumjan in the 1950s and 1960s, drawing together a number of ideas from such western scholars as Saussure, Trubetzkoy, Hjelmslev and Jakobson. The framework recognizes a (more abstract) *level of constructs* and a (less abstract) *level of observation*; it resembles **Glossematic phonology** in setting up a large number of abstract constructs couched in opaque terminology. See Fischer-Jørgensen (1975: 341–360).

tympanum /'tɪmpənəm/ *n.* (also **tympanic membrane** /tɪmpænɪk 'membreɪn/) See **eardrum**.

type /taɪp/ *n.* 1. A single abstract linguistic object, such as a **phoneme**. Cf. **token**. 2. In **typology**, a constellation of structural features which pattern together so frequently in languages that they may all be regarded as aspects of a single linguistic pattern.

typology /taɪ'pɒlədʒi/ *n.* The classification of languages, or of subsystems in languages, according to structural characteristics, together with the identification of principles determining the possible types. In phonology, a familiar example is the classification of **vowel systems** into such types as **triangular** and **quadrangular**, together with statements about the permitted types.

U

U /juː/ *adj.* Typical of upper-class British speech. Ant. **non-U**. Ross (1954).

ultima /ˈʌltɪmə/ *n.* (rarely also **ult**) The final syllable of a word. Latin *ultima*, feminine of *ultimus* 'last'.

umlaut /ˈʊmlaʊt/ *n.* (in senses 1 and 2, also **metaphony**) 1. A type of phonological change in which a vowel assimilates in quality to a following vowel, as when pre-Old-English *muːsiz (the plural of *muːs* 'mouse') developed into *myːsiz (the ancestor of modern *mice*). The term is particularly used with Germanic languages. See also **affection**. 2. A synchronic alternation in vowels deriving from such a change, as in English *mouse/mice*. 3. A **diaeresis**, especially when this diacritic is used to indicate the presence of an umlauted sound, as in German *fünf* 'five'.

un- For any term of the form **un-X** which has no entry of its own, see under the entry for **X**. For example, for *unvelarized* see under **velarized**.

unarism /ˈjuːnərɪzm̩/ *n.* The use of **unary features**.

unary feature /ˈjuːnəri/ *n.* (also **monovalent feature**, **singulary feature**) A phonological element which resembles a **distinctive feature** but which can take no values: that is, it can only be either present or absent. If [nasal] is taken as a binary feature, then [−nasal] defines a natural class just as effectively as [+nasal]; but, if [nasal] is taken as unary, then there is no way of referring to the absence of [nasal], and hence no equivalent of [−nasal]. Unary features were invoked with varying degrees of explicitness in much work preceding the introduction of binary features in the 1950s; the **phonons** of **Stratificational phonology** were perhaps the first explicit use of unary features, and the **components** or **elements** of contemporary **privative theories** of phonology are unary features.

unaspirated /ʌnˈæspɪreɪtɪd/ *adj.* 1. Lacking **aspiration**, such as English /p/ in *spin* or any voiceless plosive in Spanish or Italian. 2. In the **Ladefoged feature system**, one of the possible values of the feature **aspiration**. Ant. **aspirated**.

unattested form /ʌnəˈtestɪd/ *n.* See **reconstruction**.

unbounded foot /ʌnˈbaʊndɪd/ *n.* A **foot** containing an arbitrarily large number of syllables. English is sometimes held to have such feet, but the claim is controversial. Ant. **bounded foot**.

unchecked /ʌnˈtʃekt/ *adj.* In the **Jakobson–Halle feature system**, a **distinctive feature** defined as 'exhibiting a lower rate of energy discharge' and interpreted as representing an absence of glottalization. Ant. **checked**.

unchecked syllable *n.* See **open syllable**.

unchecked vowel *n.* See **free vowel**.

unconditioned merger /ʌnkənˈdɪʃənd/ *n.* Any phonological change in which the contrast between two phonemes disappears in all positions, thereby reducing the number of phonemes in the system. An example is the merger of Old Spanish /z/ with /s/. Cf. **conditioned merger**.

underbar /ˈʌndəbɑː/ *n.* The diacritic [ˍ], used in the IPA to mark a **retracted articulation**.

underblade /ˈʌndəbleɪd/ *n.* (also **sublamina**) That part of the lower surface of the **tongue** extending about one centimetre behind the **tip**. *Adj.* **sublaminal**; CF **sublamino-**.

underdot /ˈʌndədɒt/ *n.* The diacritic [ˌ], placed under a character in various transliterations for various purposes, such as for representing the emphatic consonants of Arabic and the retroflex consonants of Sanskrit. It has no IPA use.

underlyer /ʌndəˈlaɪə/ *n.* See **underlying form**. Coates (1977).

underlying form /ʌndəˈlaɪɪŋ/ *n.* (also **underlying representation**, **underlyer**) A more or less abstract phonological representation of a segment, a morpheme, a word or a phrase which is posited by an analyst and from which corresponding surface forms, including any variant realizations, are derived by the application of rules. Underlying forms may be more or less abstract, depending upon the theoretical preferences of the analyst. NOTE: Though the ancient Indian grammarians made extensive use of underlying forms, both the concept and the term were introduced into modern linguistics by Bloomfield (1933). American Structuralists generally rejected the idea, though Swadesh, Pike, Nida and Hockett all made use of it. With the rise of generative phonology, underlying forms became central to phonological analysis.

underspecification /ˌʌndəspesɪfɪˈkeɪʃn̩/ *n.* The analytical procedure of omitting from underlying representations some information, usually the values of distinctive features, which will have to be 'filled in' later in order to obtain the surface form.

Underspecification Theory *n.* A group of related approaches to phonological description based upon the idea that the values of certain distinctive features need not be underlyingly specified, but can be predicted by rule during derivations. Based upon earlier work by Paul Kiparsky, the idea has been variously developed by Diana Archangeli, Douglas Pulleyblank and others. Two main versions are distinguished: **Contrastive Underspecification** and **Radical Underspecification**. See Carr (1993: 181–187) or Kenstowicz (1994: 506–521) for a brief introduction, and see the special issue of *Phonology*, vol. 5, 1984.

underspreading /ˈʌndəspredɪŋ/ *n.* In **Autosegmental Phonology**, the failure of a position on the **skeletal tier** to be properly associated with an element on some other tier.

unexploded /ˌʌnɪkˈspləʊdɪd/ *adj.* (of a plosive) Lacking any audible release. The term is commonly used as a synonym for **unreleased**, but is perhaps more appropriate for labelling a plosive which is released inaudibly because of the previous formation of another closure, as with [k] in *tact*.

Uniformity Condition /juːnɪˈfɔːmɪti/ *n.* In some versions of **Autosegmental Phonology**, a proposed constraint upon rule application, often invoked especially to account for the resistance of **geminates** to phonological processes. It says: in order to change the feature content of a segment [A], every skeletal slot linked to [A] must satisfy the rule. Hayes (1986), Schein and Steriade (1986).

unilateral /juːnɪˈlætərəl/ *n.* or *adj.* A **lateral** segment in which air passes along only one side of the median closure. Cf. **bilateral**.

Unique Underlyer Condition /juːˈniːk/ *n.* (**UUC**) The principle that every non-suppletive alternation is to be accounted for by assigning to each morpheme a single, phonologically specified underlying representation, with the allomorphy derived by general (preferably phonologically specified) rules. Name: Lass (1984), but the principle was widely accepted in classical generative phonology.

unit /ˈjuːnɪt/ *n.* In a phonological representation, any item which is either a segment or a boundary – in other words, any item which represents some kind of phonological material. Chomsky and Halle (1968).

universal /juːnɪˈvɜːsəl/ *n.* or *adj.* 1. Narrowly, a property which is shared by all languages, which is part of the definition of a human language: an **absolute universal**. 2. Broadly, any property found in most, but not all, languages: a **statistical universal**. See also **implicational universal**.

universal syllable structure *n.* The syllable structure CV, the only syllable type which seems to occur in all languages.

universal tendency /ˈtendənsi/ *n.* A statement which is true for the overwhelming majority of languages, but not for all. For example, nasals and liquids universally tend to be voiced, yet a few languages, such as Welsh and Burmese, have contrastive voiceless nasals and/or liquids.

unmarked form /ʌnˈmɑːkt/ *adj.* The opposite of a **marked form** (especially sense 2).

unmarked order of application *n.* (also **appropriate order**) Within the **local ordering** hypothesis, the order of application of two rules which allows them to apply more freely than the opposite order. Kiparsky (1968).

Unmarking Principle /ʌnˈmɑːkɪŋ/ *n.* A putative principle of phonological change. It says: In chain shifts, elements of the marked system are unmarked. For example, in chain shifts, nasalized vowels may become oral vowels, but not normally the other way round. Labov (1994: 288–291).

unmerger /ʌnˈmɜːdʒə/ *n.* See **reversal of merger**.

unordered semisimultaneous rule application /ʌnɔːdəd semi-sɪməlteɪniəs/ *n.* A mode of **rule ordering** in which all rules whose structural description is met apply simultaneously to a representation, after which all rules whose SD is met apply simultaneously again to the output, and so on, until no rule has its SD met. This is the simplest and least constrained type of rule ordering possible. Pullum (1975).

un ou deux phonèmes? [French: 'one or two phonemes?'] See **one or two phonemes?** Martinet (1939).

unpacking /ʌnˈpækɪŋ/ *n.* (also **segmentalization**, **linearization**) The phonological process in which a single segment in a particular environment develops into a sequence of two segments, each of the new segments typically retaining some of the features of the original segment. For example, the historical palatal nasal /ɲ/ of Basque has developed in some northern dialects into the sequence /in/, so that, for example, earlier *baño* /baɲo/ 'than' has become *baino* /baino/ in these dialects. Ant. **coalescence**. Cf. **phonemic split**.

unreleased /ʌnrɪ'liːst/ *adj.* (of a plosive) Lacking an audible release of the closure.

unrounded /ʌn'raʊndɪd/ *adj.* (of an articulation) Unaccompanied by **rounding** of the lips. Unrounded segments may have **neutral** or **spread** lip positions.

unsupported zero /ʌnsə'pɔːtɪd/ *n.* The total absence of any overt marking of a linguistic category, as in the plural *sheep*. Labov (1994: 589).

unvoiced /ʌn'vɔɪst/ *adj.* See **voiceless**.

Upper Exit Principle /ʌpə(r) 'eksɪt/ *n.* A putative principle of phonological change applying to high tense vowels in **chain shifts**. It says: in chain shifts, the first of two high moras may change peripherality, and the second may become non-peripheral. This principle is designed to account for changes like [iː] > [əɪ́] in the English Great Vowel Shift. Cf. **Mid** and **Lower Exit Principles**. Labov (1994: 281–284).

UPSID /'ʌpsɪd/ *n.* (in full, the *UCLA Phonological Segment Inventory Database*) A database listing the **phoneme systems** of 317 languages chosen for typological diversity; it is published as Maddieson (1984).

Upside-Down Phonology /ʌpsaɪd 'daʊn/ *n.* A highly distinctive approach to phonology, proposed by W. R. Leben and O. W. Robinson (1977), in which words are represented in the **lexicon** in their surface phonetic form and phonological rules 'run backward' in order to convert surface forms into underlying forms which can then be directly related to other underlying forms. For example, *capricious* has the surface form [kə'prɪʃəs]; this is converted by successive rules to [kə'prɪʃjəs], [kə'prɪsjəs], and finally [kə'priːsjəs], which can be directly related to the underlying form of *caprice* ([kəpriːs]) by the morphological rule [NOUN-(j) əs]$_{ADJ}$.

upstep /'ʌpstep/ *n.* The phenomenon in certain tone languages, such as Zulu, by which the pitch of high tones rises throughout an utterance. Cf. **downstep**.

U-RP /juː ɑː 'piː/ *n.* (also **upper-crust RP**) In the classification of Wells (1982), those varieties of **Received Pronunciation** associated with upper-class speakers and typically distinguished from **mainstream RP** by such phenomena as the diphthongization of /æ/, very back realizations of /uː/, /ɔː/ and notably /ʌ/, a very low off-glide in words like *near* and *where*, a very low vowel in words like *nurse*, a very low realization of the final vowel in *city*, tapping or even loss of intervocalic /r/, lengthening of post-tonic consonants like the /f/ in *awfully*, and a tendency to pronounce trochees like *water* with a short first syllable and a long second syllable.

utterance /'ʌtərəns/ *n.* Any single piece of speech produced by a particular individual on a particular occasion. *V.* **utter** /'ʌtə/.

utterance accent *n.* A **stress** which occurs in some position in an utterance for any reason at all: normal word or sentence stress, contrast, emphasis, etc. The example *They repórted him? No, they depórted him* shows an utterance accent in an unusual position for purposes of contrast.

utterance-marginal lengthening *n.* The tendency, in English and other languages, for the first and last syllables of an utterance to be pronounced more slowly than other syllables.

UUC /juː juː 'siː/ *n.* See **Unique Underlyer Condition**.

uvula /'juːvjʊlə/ *n.* The small flap of muscular tissue dangling from the back of the **velum**. *Adj.* **uvular**. Diminutive of Latin *ūva* 'grape'.

uvular /'juːvjʊlə/ (also **postvelar**) 1. *adj.* Pertaining to the **uvula**. 2. *adj.* (of a segment) Articulated with a constriction between the back of the tongue and the uvula. 3. *n.* A segment so articulated, such as the uvular fricative [χ] of Arabic, Dutch and southern German. 4. In the **Ladefoged** and **Williamson feature systems**, one of the eleven values of the feature **articulatory place**.

uvularization /juːvjʊləraɪ'zeɪʃn̩/ *n.* 1. A **secondary articulation** in which the back of the tongue is raised towards the uvula. 2. Any phonological process in which a segment at another place of articulation is converted into a **uvular**. *Adj.* **uvularized**.

V

v /viː/ *n.* A conventional symbol for a **vowel**, particularly in analyses of **syllable structure**.

V /viː/ *n.* In phonology, the conventional **cover symbol** for any **vowel**, used in presenting **canonical forms** (as in the CV syllable structure) and in abbreviating **phonological rules** (as in V → ∅ / ___ #, which states that a final vowel is lost).

vacuous application /'vækjuəs/ *n.* The phenomenon in which a **phonological rule** applies to a form which meets its **structural description** but produces no change as a result, the output being identical to the input. For example, the rule [+obstr] → [–voice] / ___ # makes a word-final obstruent voiceless; it necessarily applies vacuously to a word-final obstruent which is voiceless to begin with. Vacuous application is universally admitted because it both simplifies rules and permits generalizations to be stated – for example, the rule above expresses the generalization 'A word-final obstruent is voiceless', which would be impossible if vacuous application were prohibited.

valency /'veɪlənsi/ *n.* The number of distinct **values** which can be assumed by a **distinctive feature**. A two-valued feature is **binary** or **bivalent**; a feature with three or more possible values is **multivalued**, **multivalent**, or ***n*-ary**. Specifically three-valued or four-valued features are **ternary** or **quaternary**. A feature which can take no values, but which can only be present or absent, is **unary** or **mono-valent**; the phonological **components** of many contemporary frameworks are of this sort.

value /'væljuː/ *n.* A specification which can (and must) be added to any **distinctive feature**, except a **unary** one, in a particular instance in order to represent the contribution which that feature is making to the nature of the segment containing it: hence, [+coronal] or [3 height]. It is customary to write the value before the feature name, though the reverse order may also be encountered: [coronal+].

valued feature /'væljuːd/ *n.* See **feature specification**.

variable /'vɛəriəbəl/ *n.* 1. In a **phonological rule**, any element whose value can be different in differing circumstances, such as a Greek letter used in the **alpha notation**. 2. Any phonological element, most often a segment, which can receive different phonetic realizations within a single speech community, and even from a single speaker, possibly with social significance attached to each realization. An example is the [t]~[?] variation for /t/ in certain positions in many varieties of English.

variable constraint *n.* Any factor which favours or disfavours some particular realization of a **variable** (sense 2).

variable rule *n.* A statement couched in a format resembling that of an ordinary **phonological rule**, expressing a process which is possible but not obligatory in some speech variety, and often including some mention of factors which favour or disfavour the process. An example: [–cont] → ⟨∅⟩ / [+cons] ___ ## ⟨–syll⟩. This says that a stop is deleted in word-final position after a consonant; the first angle brackets mean that the process is optional (variable), the second that the presence of a following non-syllabic segment favours the process. Labov (1972).

variable stress *n.* The property of a language in which **stress** is free to appear on different syllables, as in Spanish: *término* 'conclusion', *termíno* 'I finish', *terminó* 'he finished'. Cf. **fixed accent**.

variant /'vɛəriənt/ *n.* 1. Any phonetically distinguishable variety of a **phoneme**; an **allophone**. 2. Any of two or more equivalent forms or pronunciations in a language which either are in **complementary distribution** or are used by different speakers or even by the same speaker on different occasions, particularly one which is not regarded as the standard or canonical form.

variation /'vɛəri'eɪʃn̩/ *n.* Any of various phenomena involving departure from a single type of pronunciation for a linguistic form. Individuals may exhibit **free variation** in particular forms and may also show variable pronunciations correlated with **rate** (**tempo**) or style; speech communities may exhibit variation correlating with such factors as sex, age or social class (see **social stratification**).

varichrone /'vɛərɪkrəʊn/ *n.* The set of phonetically different **chrones** used by the speakers of a language to represent a single **chroneme**. Jones (1950).

variphone /'vɛərɪfəʊn/ *n.* 1. One of two or more phonetically distinct segments or segment sequences used interchangeably by a single speaker in the same environment; the use of variphones constitutes the most familiar type of **free variation**. For example, some midland speakers in England have [ŋ] and [ŋg] alternating freely in words like *sing* and *singer*. 2. A single abstract unit of which a set of interchangeable variphones in sense 1 are the possible realizations. Jones (1929); Jones appears to have meant the term in sense 2, but it has been more commonly used in sense 1, a usage promoted by Haugen (1957).

vdH theory of vocalic representations /vi: di: 'eɪtʃ/ *n*. A highly distinctive version of **Dependency Phonology** presented by Harry van der Hulst (1988, 1989); a summary is presented in Carr (1993: 11.4).

velar /'viːlə/ 1. *adj*. Pertaining to the **velum** as an articulator. Cf. **velic**, **velaric**. 2. *adj*. (of an articulation) Articulated with the main constriction involving the velum as the upper articulator; in this sense, usually equivalent to the more explicit **dorso-velar**. 3. *n*. A segment so articulated, such as [k], [g], [x] or [ŋ]. 4. *adj*. In the **Ladefoged** and **Williamson feature systems**, one of the eleven possible values of the feature **articulatory place**.

velaric /viː'lærɪk/ *adj*. 1. Pertaining to the **velum** in its role of providing an **airstream mechanism**. 2. See **velaric suction** (sense 2). 3. In the **Ladefoged feature system**, a binary **distinctive feature** invoked to distinguish **clicks** from all other segments. 4. A similar **distinctive feature** invoked by Lass (1984: 93) to distinguish segments produced with a **velaric airstream mechanism** ([+velaric]) from all others ([–velaric]).

velaric airstream mechanism *n*. An **airstream mechanism** in which air is trapped in the mouth between two closures, one made by the back of the tongue against the velum, the other made further forward. Backward movement of the velar closure lowers the pressure of the trapped air, producing a **velaric ingressive** segment (a **click**) when the front closure is released; forward movement compresses the trapped air, producing a **velaric egressive** segment, or **reverse click**. See Laver (1994: 173–179) for an account. Beach (1937); Catford (1939).

velaric pressure *n*. In the *SPE* feature system, an undefined **distinctive feature** suggested to deal, if required, with the apparently unattested use of **velaric egressive** segments ('reverse clicks').

velaric suction *n*. (**velsuct**) 1. In the *SPE* feature system, an undefined **distinctive feature** introduced to distinguish **clicks** ([+velsuct]) from all other segments ([–velsuct]). 2. (also **velaric**) In the

Ladefoged and **Williamson feature systems**, a similar **distinctive feature** invoked to distinguish clicks ([+click]) from all other segments ([–click]).

velarization /viːləraɪˈzeɪʃn̩/ *n.* 1. The presence during the articulation of a segment of the raising of the back of the tongue towards the velum as a **secondary articulation**. Velarization is represented in the IPA by a following superscript [ɣ], as in [lˠ]; it was formerly represented by an overprinted tilde, as in [ɫ]. See Laver (1994: 325–326) for an account. 2. Any phonological process in which such an articulation is introduced into a segment which formerly lacked it. *V.* **velarize** /ˈviːləraɪz/; *adj.* **velarized**.

velarized voice *n.* A **voice quality** characterized by persistent retraction and raising of the back of the tongue towards the velum during speech, as in the speech of Liverpool, Birmingham or New York.

velar lateral *n.* A rare type of **lateral resonant** in which the back of the tongue forms a lateral contact with the velum. This segment is found in the Papuan language Kanite; the IPA symbol is [ʟ]. Ladefoged *et al.* (1977).

velar softening /ˈsɒfənɪŋ/ *n.* The process in English by which a velar plosive is converted in certain environments to a fricative or an affricate: *critic*/*criticize* ([k]→[s]); *analogue*/*analogy* ([g]→[dʒ]).

velic /ˈviːlɪk/ *adj.* Pertaining to the **velum** in its role of opening and closing the passage between the **nasal cavity** and the rest of the vocal tract.

velic attitude /ˈætɪtjuːd/ *n.* In articulatory phonetics, the parameter representing the various possible positions of the **velum**. In reality, this parameter represents a continuum ranging from maximally closed to maximally open, but for phonological purposes it is commonly analysed as a binary distinction between 'closed' ('raised') and 'open' ('lowered'). Lass (1984: 174).

velic opening *n.* The lowering of the **velum**, permitting air to flow out through the **nasal cavity**.

velopharyngeal port /ˈviːləfərɪndʒəl ˈpɔːt/ *n.* The opening between the **pharynx** and the **nasal cavity**, opened and closed by the **velum**.

velum /ˈviːləm/ *n.* (also **soft palate**) The flexible sheet of muscular tissue which makes up the rear part of the roof of the mouth, just behind the **palate**. It is connected to the palate by a hinge which allows it to be raised and lowered; when raised, it closes off the **nasal cavity** from the **oral cavity**; when lowered, it allows air from the **pharynx** to flow into the nasal cavity. The velum also serves as the upper articulator in the production of **velar** consonants and it plays a crucial role in producing the **velaric airstream mechanism**. *Adj.* **velar** (in relation to articulations), **velic** (in relation to opening and closing), **velaric** (in relation to an airstream). Latin: 'veil'.

ventricular folds /ven'trɪkjʊlə fəʊldz/ *n. pl.* (also **false vocal cords**) A pair of fleshy folds of tissue, somewhat resembling the **vocal folds** and lying just above them. Their precise function is unknown, but they appear to make no contribution to **phonation** in ordinary circumstances. They can, however, be approximated to produce **ventricular whisper**; they can be set in vibration to produce **ventricular voice**; and they can be completely closed to produce a **ventricular stop**. Catford (1977: 104) reports that ventricular fricatives, trills and stops have phonemic status in several Caucasian languages.

ventricular voice *n.* An unusual **phonation type** produced by vibration of the **ventricular folds**. With practice, it is possible to combine ventricular voice with ordinary **voicing** to produce **double voice**.

Venturi tube /ven'tjʊəri tju:b/ *n.* A tube containing a constriction through which a fluid flows. The constriction both constrains the flow and increases its velocity. The larynx, when the vocal folds are approximated (as in voicing), constitutes a Venturi tube. After G. B. Venturi (1746–1822), Italian physicist.

verbal apraxia /'vɜːbəl eɪ'præksiə/ *n.* See **articulatory apraxia**.

Verner's Law /'vɜːnə/ *n.* An important sound change in Proto-Germanic by which voiceless obstruents were voiced in certain positions, leading, for example, to Old English *fadar* 'father' (cf. Latin *pater*). Verner (1875).

vertical lip rounding /'vɜːtɪkəl/ *n.* See **outer rounding**. Heffner (1950).

vertical vowel system *n.* (also **linear vowel system**) A **vowel system** whose members are distinguished only by **height**, such as the /ɨ əa/ system of the Caucasian language Adyghe.

***veto* phenomenon** /'viːtəʊ/ *n.* (also ***Plato* phenomenon**) The phenomenon, occurring for many North American speakers of English, by which the word *veto* (and, for some speakers, also the word *Plato*) behaves as though it consisted of two stressed phonological words: the first vowel has a duration typical of word-final vowels, and the /t/ absolutely cannot undergo **tapping**, in contrast to what happens with such apparently similar words as *meaty*, *motto* and *ditto*. These words appear to constitute flagrant exceptions to the ordinarily automatic phonetic rules of American English and they have accordingly been much discussed.

via rule /'vaɪə/ *n.* A statement which directly expresses a relationship between surface forms which are not derived from a common underlying form. For example, the via rule [aɪ] ↔ [ɪ] expresses the vowel **alternation** in pairs like *divine*/*divinity* and would be stored in the **lexicon** next to each such pair. Via rules are particularly associated with **Natural Generative Phonology**; their status is controversial, since it is not clear that they are **rules** in the ordinary sense of the term. Hooper (1976).

vibrant /'vaɪbrənt/ *n.* (rarely also **vibrative**) 1. A cover term for **taps** and **trills**. 2. [*rare*] A less usual synonym for **trill**.

vibration /vaɪ'breɪʃn̩/ *n.* (**vibr**) A **distinctive feature** proposed by Ladefoged (1971) to distinguish **taps**, **flaps** and **trills** ([+vibr]) from all other segments ([–vibr]), further distinctions being handled by the feature **rate**. In the **Ladefoged feature system**, this feature is abandoned in favour of the features **flap** and **trill**.

vibrato /vɪ'brɑːtəʊ/ *n.* Rapid slight variation in the pitch and volume of the voice, characteristic of a professional singing voice. Italian.

visible speech /'vɪzɪbəl/ *n.* Any graphical or manual system for representing speech or speech sounds *other than* a standard writing system. The term is most often applied to various systems devised for teaching deaf or handicapped persons to speak, but has sometimes also been applied to **sound spectrograms**. Bell (1867).

visual verbal agnosia /vɪʒuəl vɜːbəl æg'nəʊziə/ *n.* A pathological condition in which the sufferer is unable to recognize written words. Cf. **auditory verbal agnosia**.

vital capacity /'vaɪtəl kəpæsɪti/ *n.* The maximum volume of air that an individual can expel after a maximal inspiration, consisting of the **inspiratory reserve volume**, the **tidal volume** and the **expiratory reserve volume**.

vocal–auditory channel /vəʊkəl 'ɔːdɪtri/ *n.* The conventional name for the ordinary medium of speech: the production of sounds in the **vocal tract**, the transmission of those sounds through the air, and the reception and interpretation of those sounds by the ears and the brain. Sign language and writing constitute two ways of transferring speech out of the vocal–auditory channel into other media.

vocal cords /ˈvəʊkəl kɔːdz/ *n. pl.* See **vocal folds**. NOTE: The spelling 'vocal chords' is an error.

vocal folds /fəʊldz/ *n. pl.* (also **vocal cords**) A symmetrical pair of tissues located in the **larynx**, consisting of the **vocal ligaments** and the **vocalis muscle** with a covering of mucous membrane. Triangular in cross-section, the vocal folds are connected in front to the **thyroid cartilage** and in back to the **arytenoid cartilages**. Rotation of the arytenoids moves the edges of the vocal folds together or apart, thus allowing the production of various **phonation types**. The opening between the vocal folds, with its continuation between the arytenoids, constitutes the **glottis**.

vocal fry /fraɪ/ *n.* A synonym for **creak** or, less appropriately, for **creaky voice**. From a supposed resemblance to the sound of frying food.

vocalic /vəʊˈkælɪk/ *adj.* (**voc**) 1. Pertaining to **vowels**. 2. Having the nature of a vowel. 3. In the **Jakobson–Halle feature system**, a **distinctive feature** defined as 'exhibiting a sharply defined formant structure' and interpreted as representing a voiced sound with air flowing without obstruction through the vocal tract. Cf. **consonantal**, and see the remarks there. 4. In the *SPE* **feature system**, a **distinctive feature** defined as 'involving a constriction in the oral cavity which does not exceed that of a high vowel, with the vocal folds in a position to allow spontaneous voicing'. **Vowels** and **liquids** are [+voc]; **true consonants** and **glides** are [–voc]. Essentially only a re-interpretation of the earlier J–H feature, [vocalic] has generally been dropped in practice in favour of the non-equivalent feature **syllabic**. Cf. **consonantal**. *Abstr. n.* **vocalicity** /vəʊkəˈlɪsɪti/. Ant. (senses 2–4) **non-vocalic**.

vocalis muscle /vəʊˈkeɪlɪs mʌsl̩/ *n.* Either of two bands of muscular tissue running parallel to the **vocal ligaments** and constituting part of the **vocal folds**, thought to be important in controlling the tension of the vocal folds.

vocalization /vəʊkəlaɪˈzeɪʃn̩/ *n.* 1. The act of producing speech sounds. 2. Any phonological process in which a **consonant** is converted into a **vowel**, or sometimes into a **glide**, as when *field* is pronounced as [fiwd]. *V.* **vocalize**. Ant. **devocalization**.

vocal ligaments /'lɪɡəmənts/ *n. pl.* The upper edges of the **conus elasticus**, constituting part of the **vocal folds**.

vocal nodule /'nɒdjuːl/ *n.* (also **vocal node** /nəʊd/) A small swelling on the **vocal folds**, typically caused by excessive straining of the voice and resulting in a hoarse voice quality.

vocal organs /'ɔːɡənz/ *n. pl.* (also **speech organs, organs of speech**) All those parts of the body involved in producing speech sounds, from the lungs to the lips and nose, but usually excluding the brain and the nervous system.

vocal processes /'prəʊsesəz/ *n. pl.* The anterior projections of the **arytenoid cartilages**, to which the rear ends of **vocal folds** are attached.

vocal profile /'prəʊfaɪl/ *n.* A detailed description of an individual's **phonetic settings** for articulation, phonation, overall muscular tension and prosodic behaviour, typically constructed by filling in a **protocol**. See Laver (1994: 154) for an example.

vocal tract /trækt/ *n.* The entire length of the pathway through which air flows or can flow during the production of speech, running from the **lungs** through the **trachea**, the **larynx** and the **pharynx** and out through the **oral** and **nasal cavities**. That part of it lying above the larynx is called the **supralaryngeal** (or **supraglottal**) **vocal tract**. NOTE: Many analysts restrict the use of the term 'vocal tract' to the supralaryngeal vocal tract, and a few further exclude the nasal cavity from the vocal tract proper, but these restrictions do not appear to be helpful.

vocoder /'vəʊkəʊdə/ *n.* Any of various devices which allow speech to be transmitted over a limited **bandwidth** by extracting selected frequencies from the total signal. From 'voice coder'.

vocoid /'vəʊkɔɪd/ *n.* 1. A synonym for **vowel** in the phonetic sense of that term (sense 1), introduced in an effort to remove the ambiguity between the phonetic and phonological senses of 'vowel'. While possibly useful, the term has never become established. Pike (1943). 2. More narrowly, a vocoid in sense 1 which is also **syllabic**: a true vowel, as opposed to a **glide** or **approximant**. Sense 2: Laver (1994).

vocoid chart *n.* See **vowel chart**.

vocoid space *n.* See **vowel space**.

voice /vɔɪs/ *n.* 1. The natural and distinctive tone of the speech sounds produced by a particular person. 2. Broadly, any **phonation type** involving vibration of the vocal folds; **voicing**. The term is most commonly used in combination in such labels as **creaky voice** and **whispery voice**. 3. Narrowly, the **phonation type** involving vibration of the focal folds with no whisper or creak: essentially **modal voice**, though such modified versions as **anterior voice** and **tense voice** are recognized. 4. In the **Ladefoged feature system**, a **distinctive feature** invoked to treat distinctions of glottal activity, with the five possible values **glottal stop, laryngealized, voice, murmur** and **voiceless**. Ladefoged had earlier called this feature **glottal stricture**; the equivalent feature in the **Williamson feature system** is **glottal state**. 5. In the **Lindau feature system**, a **distinctive feature** invoked to treat distinctions in the shape of the glottis, with the possible values *glottal stop*, *creaky voice*, *voice*, *murmur* and *voiceless*, no more than two of which are said to be used contrastively in a given language.

voice box /bɒks/ *n*. See **larynx**.

voice compass /'kʌmpəs/ *n*. The range of pitch stretching one standard deviation on either side of a speaker's mean pitch. Eady (1982).

voiced /vɔɪst/ *adj*. 1. (of a segment, in phonetics) Accompanied by **voicing**, that is, by vibration of the **vocal folds**. 2. (of a segment, in phonology) Regarded as being in principle (underlyingly) accompanied by such vibration, whether or not it is phonetically present. For example, English /b d g/ often lack phonetic voicing in final position, but are still regarded as phonologically voiced. 3. In the **Jakobson–Halle feature system**, a **distinctive feature** defined as 'exhibiting periodic low-frequency excitation', and associated with vibration of the vocal folds. 4. In the *SPE* **feature system**, a **distinctive feature** defined as 'involving sufficient narrowing of the glottis to make vocal-fold vibration possible', whether or not such vibration actually occurs. 5. (also **voice**) In the **Ladefoged** and **Williamson feature systems**, one of the possible values of the feature **voice** (Ladefoged) or **glottal state** (Williamson). 6. In the **Ladefoged feature system**, one of the possible values of the feature **aspiration**. Ant. (senses 1–3 and, informally, sense 4) **voiceless**.

voiced aspirate *n*. A segment, especially a plosive, articulated with **whispery voice** (**murmur**). *Abstr. n*. **voiced aspiration**.

voiced click *n*. A **click** whose articulation is accompanied by simultaneous **voicing** – in effect, by a simultaneous [g]. A voiced alveolar click is notated [g!], and similarly for other voiced clicks.

voiced creak *n*. See **creaky voice**.

voiced *h* *n.* A somewhat informal label for the segment [ɦ], the **whispery-voiced** counterpart of [h].

voiced implosive *n.* A stop consonant articulated with a glottalic ingressive airstream with simultaneous voicing provided by a pulmonic egressive airstream, such as [ɓ] or [ɗ]. Since voiced implosives are far commoner than voiceless ones, voiced implosives are often just called 'implosives'. See Greenberg (1970) or Laver (1994: 179–181) for a survey.

voice dynamics /daɪ'næmɪks/ *n.* A cover term for a range of vocal effects in speech other than the phonological characteristics of the language spoken, including such factors as **rate (tempo)**, **rhythm**, **register** and **loudness** but usually excluding **voice quality**.

voiceless /'vɔɪsləs/ *adj.* (also **unvoiced**) 1. (of a segment) Articulated without vibration of the **vocal folds**. Three types of voiceless speech are distinguished: **whisper**, **breath** and **nil phonation**. *Abstr. n.* **voicelessness**. Ant. **voiced**. 2. In the **Jakobson–Halle feature system**, a **distinctive feature** defined as 'not exhibiting periodic low-frequency excitation' and interpreted as representing an absence of vocal-fold vibration. Ant. **voiced**. 3. In the **Ladefoged** and **Williamson feature systems**, one of the five possible values of the feature **voice** (Ladefoged) or **glottal state** (Williamson).

voiceless vowel *n.* A vowel whose articulation is unaccompanied by vibration of the vocal folds. See Laver (1994: 295–297).

voice mutation *n.* (also **breaking of the voice**) The phenomenon, usually occurring around the onset of puberty, in which, as a result of rapid growth of the larynx, an individual's voice changes from that of a child to that of an adult. The process takes several months to complete, and is particularly noticeable in boys, in whom the pitch of the voice typically drops by about an octave.

voice onset *n.* With respect to the **closure** and **release** of a **stop** consonant, the point at which **voicing** (vibration of the vocal folds) begins.

voice-onset delay *n.* A less usual term for **aspiration**.

voice onset time *n.* (**VOT**) The time which elapses between some articulatory event, most often the **release** of a **plosive**, and the point at which the vocal folds begin to vibrate. VOT is important in many languages in determining whether a segment is perceived as **voiced** or **voiceless**. For a voiced consonant, VOT may have a negative value.

voiceprint /'vɔɪsprɪnt/ *n*. A **sound spectrogram**, or any similar visual display of the acoustic features of an individual's voice, when such a display is regarded as a reliable guide to identifying the individual whose voice is exhibited, as is sometimes claimed to be possible in **forensic phonetics**. By analogy with 'fingerprint'.

voice quality *n*. The characteristic auditory colouring of an individual's voice, derived from a variety of laryngeal and supralaryngeal features and running continuously through the individual's speech. Though a variety of impressionistic terms for particular voice qualities have been used, voice quality can in fact be precisely characterized in terms of **phonetic settings**. See Laver (1994: ch. 13) for a survey, Laver (1980) for a detailed account and Laver (1991: Part II) for discussion of some particular points.

voice range /reɪndʒ/ *n*. The range of frequency or pitch used by a particular speaker or by speakers generally. The average fundamental frequency is about 120 Hz for men, 225 Hz for women and 265 Hz for children. The total range of fundamental frequencies encountered in speech runs from about 60 Hz to about 500 Hz. Each individual normally uses not more than one octave, always in the lower part of her/his range. A professional soprano can reach 1,024 Hz, or exceptionally 2,048 Hz, in singing.

voicing /'vɔɪsɪŋ/ *n*. 1. (also **voice**) The presence during an articulation of vibration of the **vocal folds**. Normal voicing is **modal voice**, but **creak**, **creaky voice** and **falsetto** may also be regarded as distinctive varieties of voicing. 2. The parameter along which **voiced** and **voiceless** segments (and possibly other **phonation types**) are distinguished. 3. Any phonological process in which a formerly or underlyingly voiceless segment becomes voiced.

voicing lag *n*. Retardation of the onset of **voicing**, such as occurs in the production of **aspirated** plosives.

voicing ripple /'rɪpəl/ *n*. The vertical striations visible in a **sound spectrogram**, particularly in a **wide-band spectrogram** reflecting the rapid rise and fall in intensity produced by the opening and closing of the glottis.

voix blanche /vwa blɑ̃ʃ/ *n*. [French: 'white voice'] In singing, the use of clear, bright, ringing tones, reportedly achieved by lifting and tensing of the velum.

VOT /viː əʊ 'tiː/ *n*. See **voice onset time**.

vowel /'vɑʊəl/ *n.* 1. (also **vocoid**) In phonetics, a segment whose articulation involves no significant obstruction of the airstream, such as [a], [i] or [u]. Strictly speaking, a **glide** such as [j] or [w] may also be regarded as a (brief) vowel in this sense. 2. In phonology, a segment which forms the **nucleus** of a **syllable**. 3. Any letter of the alphabet which, generally or in a particular case, represents a vowel in sense 2. *Adj.* **vocalic**. Ant. (all senses) **consonant**.

vowel chart *n.* (also **formant chart**, **vocoid chart**) A graphical device for showing the locations of vowels within the **vowel space**, most often in terms of the first and second **formants**. Figure V1 shows the vowel chart of Les Branson of Norwich.

vowel classification /klæsɪfɪ'keɪʃn̩/ *n.* 1. The description of **vowels** in terms of phonetic parameters, most often **height**, **backness** and **rounding**, and sometimes also further parameters such as **length** or **nasalization**. 2. The representation of vowels in terms of **distinctive features**.

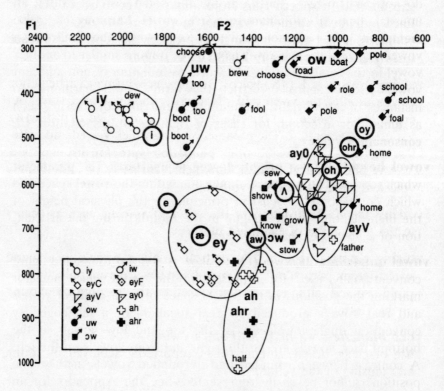

Figure V1 The vowel chart of Les Branson, 42, of Norwich (1971)

vowel echo *n.* The phenomenon in which an underlyingly unspecified vowel automatically takes on the identity of the vowel in an adjoining syllable. For example, Klamath has a causative prefix *snV-* whose vowel is always identical to the vowel in the next syllable: *sne-ge:jiga* 'makes tired', *sno-bostgi* 'makes something turn black', *sni-nklilk'a* 'makes dusty', and so on.

vowel gradation /grəˈdeɪʃn̩/ *n.* See **ablaut**.

vowel harmony *n.* (also **harmony**) 1. The phenomenon, occurring in some languages, in which only certain combinations of the language's vowel phonemes are permitted to occur within some specified phonological domain, most usually a single phonological word; the permitted combinations are usually those which agree (harmonize) in respect of one or more phonetic features, such as [back], [round] or [ATR]. Turkish is a famous example: in Turkish, a word must consist entirely of front vowels or entirely of back vowels, and an unrounded vowel cannot be followed by a rounded vowel. Some vowel-harmony systems contain **neutral vowels** which do not participate in the harmony, and some systems exhibit an unusual type of **dominant/recessive vowel harmony**. 2. (also **metaphony**) Any phonological process in which the quality of a vowel is altered in such a way as to make it more similar to another vowel in the same phonological word: **assimilation** of non-adjacent vowels. Some analysts restrict the term 'vowel harmony' to instances of left-to-right assimilation, preferring other terms, such as **umlaut** or **affection**, for cases of right-to-left assimilation. Cf. **consonant harmony**.

vowel height *n.* (also **height**, **degree of aperture**) The parameter which represents the vertical dimension within the **vowel space** and which corresponds, at least in principle, to the physical height of the highest point of the tongue in the mouth during the articulation of a vowel. Cf. **backness** (sense 1).

vowel quadrilateral /kwɒdrɪˈlætərəl/ *n.* A stylized four-sided figure conventionally used for representing the **vowel space** and for marking the positions in the vowel space of both **cardinal vowels** and real vowels produced by real speakers of a language. By convention, high vowels are at the top and low vowels at the bottom; back vowels are on the right and front vowels on the left. A contrast between rounded and unrounded vowels in the same position cannot be easily represented. See the Appendix for an illustration.

vowel quality *n.* The totality of those distinguishing characteristics of a particular vowel which result from the positions of the tongue and the lips during its articulation, but excluding such features as pitch, loudness, duration and usually also phonation type. Analysts differ as to whether they regard nasalization and its absence as part of the vowel quality or as an independent characteristic; the IPA transcription of vowels effectively adopts the second position, while acoustic analysis in terms of formants favours the first.

vowel reduction *n.* Any phonological process in connected speech which makes a vowel shorter, less loud, lower in pitch or more central in quality, or which neutralizes some vowel contrasts in unstressed syllables.

vowel shift /ʃɪft/ *n.* 1. Any phonological development in a language in which a whole class of vowels undergoes a systematic change in quality, such as the **Great Vowel Shift** of English. 2. See **Great Vowel Shift** (sense 2).

Vowel Shift Principle *n.* A putative principle governing the course of **vowel shifts**. It says: in chain shifts, peripheral vowels become more open and non-peripheral vowels become less open. Labov (1994: 601).

vowel space /speɪs/ *n.* (also **vocoid space**) The space available within the **oral cavity** for the production of **vowels** (sense 1), variously conceived as a physiological reality, as a somewhat stylized abstraction (as in the **vowel quadrilateral**), or as a highly abstract set of axes (as in some **privative theories** of phonology).

vowel system *n.* The total inventory of the vowel **phonemes** of a particular language or language variety, especially when presented in an orderly manner more or less corresponding to the positions of those vowels within the **vowel quadrilateral**. Symmetrical vowel systems are often classified according to the approximate shape of the figure produced when the vowels are so displayed: hence **vertical**, **triangular**, **quadrangular**, etc., vowel systems. See under **phoneme system** for references.

W

w In some approaches to phonology, notably **Metrical Phonology**, a conventional label for a weak (unstressed) **foot**.

wave /weɪv/ *n.* An oscillation propagated through a medium in such a way that energy is periodically interchanged between two kinds of disturbance. In the case of a sound wave travelling through air, the disturbance takes the form of alternating compressions and rarefactions of the air along the line of transmission.

wave equation /ɪ'kweɪʒn̩/ *n.* The fundamental equation describing the behaviour of all **waves**: $v = f\lambda$. Here **v** is the **velocity** of the wave, f is the **frequency** and λ is the **wavelength**.

waveform /'weɪvfɔːm/ *n.* The shape of a **wave** as shown by plotting the value of some oscillating quantity against time.

wavelength /'weɪvleŋθ/ *n.* The distance, measured in the direction of propagation, between two points in the same phase in consecutive cycles of a wave. Symbol: λ.

wazn /'wɒzn/ *n.* See **binyan**. Arabic grammar.

weak consonant /wiːk/ *n.* A **consonant** which is high in **sonority**, such as an **approximant**, and which may serve as the target of **lenition**. Ant. **strong consonant**.

weakening /'wiːkənɪŋ/ *n.* See **lenition** (sense 1).

weak form *n.* A pronunciation of a word, typically occurring in unstressed position, in which one or more segments are reduced to central vowels or to zero: [ən] or [n̩] for *and*, [ðən] for *than*, [ðəm] or [əm] for *them*, [əv] or [v̩] for *have*, [kən] or [kn̩] for *can*. Ant. **strong form**.

weak syllable *n.* A less usual term for **light syllable**.

weak verb /vɜːb/ *n.* In English and other Germanic languages, a verb which forms its past tense and past participle by suffixation: *live/loved/loved*. Cf. **strong verb**.

wedge /wedʒ/ *n.* See **hachek**.

weight /weɪt/ *n.* See **syllable weight**.

weight-by-position *n.* In some analyses, an analytical procedure by which a segment which would not ordinarily constitute a **mora** is assigned a mora in certain specified positions – for example, a consonant in syllable-final position. Hayes (1989).

weight unit *n.* A less usual term for **mora**.

well-formed /wel'fɔːmd/ *adj.* (of a phonological form or representation) In accordance with all the requirements of the phonology of the language in question; violating no requirements. *Abstr. n.* **well-formedness**. Ant. **ill-formed**.

well-formedness conditions *n. pl.* (**WFC**) Any of various conditions which must be met by a phonological representation, usually as formulated within the confines of a particular theory of phonology, in order for that representation to be admissible within the phonology of the language in question. Most theories of phonology impose various such conditions as part of their content.

whisky voice /'wɪski/ *n.* Any of several complex and distinctive **phonation types** exhibited by individuals who are heavily under the influence of alcohol, perhaps most commonly **whispery creaky voice**.

whisper /'wɪspə/ *n.* A simple **phonation type** characterized by complete closure of the anterior (ligamental) part of the glottis combined with a broad triangular opening in the posterior (arytenoidal) part. Air flowing through the opening produces friction noise and hence the distinctive 'whisper' sound quality. Whisper differs from **breath** in that, in whisper, the larynx is tense, the glottis is partly closed, the volume-velocity of the air flow is greater, and the sound produced is louder.

whispery creak /'wɪspəri/ *n.* A complex **phonation type** in which the ligamental portion of the vocal folds produces **creak** while the arytenoid cartilages are simultaneously spread, producing **whisper** as the air flows through the opening.

whispery creaky falsetto *n.* A highly complex **phonation type** in which all of **whisper**, **creak** and **falsetto** are produced simultaneously. This is physiologically possible, but it is not known to be used linguistically or paralinguistically anywhere.

whispery creaky voice *n.* (also **whispery voiced creak**) A complex **phonation type** in which all of **whisper**, **voicing** and **creak** are simultaneously produced by the glottis: a common variety of **whisky voice**.

whispery falsetto *n.* A complex **phonation type** in which the anterior part of the glottis produces **falsetto** while the arytenoidal part produces **whisper**.

whispery voice *n.* (also **murmur** and, erroneously, **breathy voice**) A complex **phonation type** in which **voicing** (sense 1) and **whisper** are produced simultaneously by the glottis. Most commonly, perhaps, this is done by having the posterior (arytenoidal) part of the glottis wide open as in whisper while the anterior (ligamental) part vibrates as is usual in voicing, but it is also possible to have the entire glottis vibrating in such a way that the vocal folds do not meet completely, so that noisy air flow occurs continuously through the glottis. Whispery voice ('murmur') is linguistically contrastive in many languages, such as those of north India. Officially, the IPA represents it with a double dot placed below the phonetic character, as in [b̤], but various other devices are also in use. NOTE: Both Catford (1977) and Laver (1979) reject the term 'breathy voice' in this sense as a misuse of terminology, but it is nevertheless widely used.

whistle /'wɪsl̩/ *n.* A shrill, high-pitched noise produced by passing breath through a narrow constriction. The two most familiar types of whistle involve pursing the lips and approximating the tip of the tongue to the alveolar ridge, but whistle may also be produced inadvertently during certain articulations, notably during the production of retroflex fricatives.

whistled speech *n.* A transferred type of 'speech' used by certain communities, in which the speech melody, including intonation and possibly tones, is whistled. See Laver (1994: 481–482) for references.

whistling fricative /'wɪslɪŋ/ *n.* A **fricative** whose articulation is consistently accompanied by a perceptible **whistle**. The famous whistling fricatives of Shona are described by Ladefoged (1971: 60) as labial-lamino-alveolar fricatives.

white noise /waɪt/ *n.* A sound which consists of a mixture of all audible frequencies, either in equal proportion or rising by six decibels every octave; the second type sounds more uniform to the ear. White noise is heard as a featureless hiss. By analogy with white light, which is a mixture of all visible colours.

whole-segment process /həʊl/ *n.* Any of various phonological processes in which one or more complete segments are inserted, deleted or moved to different positions, such as **epenthesis** or **metathesis**. Lass (1984: 183).

Wickelgren feature system /'wɪkəlgrən/ *n.* A system of **distinctive features** proposed by Wickelgren (1966). The system is defined only for English consonants and is unusual in being justified on perceptual grounds. The features, facetiously known as 'Wickelphones', are four in number. The features *voicing* and *nasality* are binary and have the values 0 and 1, assigned in an obvious way. The feature *openness* has the value 0 for plosives, affricates and nasals, 1 for fricatives, and 2 for liquids, glides and /h/. The feature *place* has the value 0 for labials (including /w/), 1 for interdentals, /t/, /d/ and /n/, 2 for /s/, /z/ and /l/, 3 for palato-alveolars and /j/, and 4 for velars and /h/.

wide /waɪd/ *adj.* 1. [*obsolete*] (of a vowel) A former term for **lax**. Ant. **narrow**. Sweet (1877). 2. (also **width** /wɪdθ/) In the **Ladefoged feature system**, a **distinctive feature** invoked to treat differing degrees of expansion of the pharynx, roughly equivalent to the **ATR** feature of other systems.

wide-band spectrogram /'waɪdbænd/ *n.* A **sound spectrogram** produced using filters with a large frequency bandwidth but rapid sampling. The result shows the formants smeared out vertically, but is very sensitive to changes over time; **voicing ripple** is prominent. Cf. **narrow-band spectrogram**.

wide diphthong *n.* A **diphthong** involving a large movement between its initial and final elements, such as [ai]. Ant. **narrow diphthong**.

Williamson feature system /'wɪljəmsən/ *n.* A **distinctive feature system** proposed by Kay Williamson (1977). Like the rather similar **Ladefoged feature system**, it consists mostly of **articulatory features** and allows them to be **multivalued**; it also permits sequential feature specifications for single segments to handle such phenomena as **aspiration** and **prenasalization** (see **complex segment** (sense 1) for an example of this approach). There are fifteen features: **larynx movement** (3 values), **velaric suction** (2), **glottal state** (5), **articulatory place** (11), **labiality** (2), **apicality** (3), **stricture** (5), **nasality** (2), **laterality** (2), **posture** (3), **length** (4), **sibilance** (2), **gravity** (2), **rounding** (2) and **expansion** (3).

windpipe /'wɪndpaɪp/ *n.* See **trachea**.

word /wɜːd/ *n.* A label applied in linguistics to any of several rather different conceptions of a unit which is typically larger than a morpheme but smaller than a phrase and which shows a high degree of internal coherence. In phonology, the **phonological word** is the most important conception.

word accent *n.* See **accent** (sense 3).

word-based tone /'wɜːdbeɪst/ *n.* 1. A less usual term for **pitch accent**. 2. The type of **tone** system in which only one syllable in a word can bear a tone, as in Swedish. Cf. **syllable-based tone**.

word boundary *n.* Either end of a **word** in any sense of that term. Word boundaries are of considerable importance in phonology, where they are conventionally represented by **hash marks**.

word class *n.* 1. See **lexical category**. 2. Any group of words in a language united by lexical or grammatical properties, such as the class of nouns, the class of transitive verbs, or the class of -*a*-stem verbs in Spanish. 3. In historical phonology, all the words which contained some particular segment of interest at an earlier stage of a language, such as the class of words which contained /oː/ in Middle English, which includes the ancestors of modern *moon*, *good*, *blood* and *floor*.

word formation /fɔːˈmeɪʃn̩/ *n.* The entire set of processes by which lexical items are derived from or related to other lexical items. In English, the principal such processes are **compounding** and **derivation** (sense 3), though others exist.

word-formation bracket *n.* In **Lexical Phonology**, one of a pair of brackets placed around the domain to which the current **level** is applying and erased at the end of this level. Thus *personality* would be bracketed [[[pɜːsən]æl]ɪti]. These brackets replace the various **boundaries** of earlier **generative phonology**.

word-formation rule *n.* In some approaches to **word formation**, a rule which is posited within that component of the grammar dealing with word formation and which serves to identify a (typically partially productive) process involved in the formation of certain words. The following rule states the use of the English agent suffix -*er*, as in *writer*, *singer*, *rider*:

$$[[X]_V \#er]]_N \text{ 'one who Xs habitually, professionally } \ldots\text{'}$$

Halle (1973); developed by Aronoff (1976) and Scalise (1984).

word stress *n.* The presence within a single word, especially in isolation but usually also in connected speech, of **stress** on some particular syllable or syllables. Word stress is characteristic of **stress languages** like English and Spanish.

word terminus /'tɜːmɪnəs/ *n.* (pl. **termini** /'tɜːmɪnaɪ/) A boundary between syntactic constituents. A **phonological word** is a sequence bounded by word termini and containing no internal word termini. Chomsky and Halle (1968).

X

X-bar structure /eks 'bɑː/ *n*. In some analyses, a view of syllable structure closely parallelling the X-bar structure of syntactic theory. In this view, a syllable is interpreted as N″, the maximal projection of the **nucleus** N; a syllable has the form N″ → **onset** + N′, and N′ has the structure N (nucleus) + **coda**. Levin (1985).

X-tier /'eks tɪə/ *n*. In **Autosegmental Phonology**, a synonym for **skeletal tier**, preferred for versions in which the positions on this tier are specified for no information at all. Cf. **CV tier**.

Y

Y In some versions of **Dependency Phonology**, a superordinate **component** governing |i| and |u| and relating to tongue-body constriction. Ewen and van der Hulst (1988).

yeismo /je'izmo/ *n*. In Spanish, the merger as some kind of non-lateral palatal segment of the two consonants which in standard European Spanish are distinguished as /ʎ/ and /j/, and hence the merger of such pairs as *mallo* 'mallet' and *mayo* 'May', which in standard European Spanish are distinguished as /'maʎo/ and /'majo/, respectively. Yeismo is typical of almost all of American Spanish and of the southern half of Spain, including Madrid, and it appears to be gaining ground in northern Spain. The phonetic realization of the merged sound varies widely; both voiced and voiceless affricates and fricatives can be heard.

yer /jɛə/ *n*. (also **jer**) Any of certain unusual vowels occurring in Slavic languages. Historically, they were apparently extra-short or weak vowels which were phonetically lost in most cases, but, since their effect is still often visible in alternations in the modern languages, they are often posited as abstract underlying vowels in these.

Z

zero /'zɪərəʊ/ *n*. 1. See **antiformant**. 2. See **null element**.

zero-alternant *n*. See **zero morph**. Bloomfield (1933).

zero-derivation *n*. See **conversion**.

zero grade /greɪd/ *n*. In an **ablaut** system such as that of Proto-Indo-European, that form of a morpheme in which the vowel is absent. For example, the PIE root **men-* 'think' shows its zero grade **mn̥-* in Greek *mnasthai* 'remember'.

zero morph *n*. An element containing no phonetic material but recognized, in some analysis, as representing some morpheme. For example, *sheep* has a plural *sheep* which is commonly regarded as consisting of {*sheep*} + {Plural}, with a zero morph representing the morpheme {Plural}. Concept: Bloomfield (1933); term: Hockett (1947).

zero notation *n*. The notation Z_0 (where Z is any valid phonological object), used in **phonological rules**, especially in **classical generative phonology**, in which it can be matched by any of the following: zero (the absence of anything), Z, or an uninterrupted sequence of any number of items of the form Z.

zero phoneme *n*. A putative **phoneme** posited, in some analysis, which has no intrinsic phonetic content, such as a **juncture phoneme**. Harris (1951: 81).

zero syllable *n*. In some versions of **Metrical Phonology**, a second syllable posited as existing within a monosyllabic word for the purpose of maintaining **binary branching** and avoiding **degenerate feet**. Giegerich (1985).

Appendix: the International Phonetic Alphabet (revised to 1993)

CONSONANTS (PULMONIC)

	Bilabial	Labiodental	Dental	Alveolar	Postalveolar	Retroflex	Palatal	Velar	Uvular	Pharyngeal	Glottal
Plosive	p b			t d		ʈ ɖ	c ɟ	k ɡ	q ɢ		ʔ
Nasal	m	ɱ		n		ɳ	ɲ	ŋ	N		
Trill	B			r					R		
Tap or Flap				ɾ		ɽ					
Fricative	ɸ β	f v	θ ð	s z	ʃ ʒ	ʂ ʐ	ç ʝ	x ɣ	χ ʁ	ħ ʕ	h ɦ
Lateral fricative				ɬ ɮ							
Approximant		ʋ		ɹ		ɻ	j	ɰ			
Lateral approximant				l		ɭ	ʎ	L			

Where symbols appear in pairs, the one to the right represents a voiced consonant. Shaded areas denote articulations judged impossible.

CONSONANTS (NON-PULMONIC)

Clicks	Voiced implosives	Ejectives
ʘ Bilabial	ɓ Bilabial	ʼ as in:
ǀ Dental	ɗ Dental/alveolar	pʼ Bilabial
ǃ (Post)alveolar	ʄ Palatal	tʼ Dental/alveolar
ǂ Palatoalveolar	ɠ Velar	kʼ Velar
ǁ Alveolar lateral	ʛ Uvular	sʼ Alveolar fricative

VOWELS

Where symbols appear in pairs, the one to the right represents a rounded vowel.

OTHER SYMBOLS

ʍ Voiceless labial-velar fricative

w Voiced labial-velar approximant

ɥ Voiced labial-palatal approximant

ʜ Voiceless epiglottal fricative

ʢ Voiced epiglottal fricative

ʡ Epiglottal plosive

ɕ ʑ Alveolo-palatal fricatives

ɺ Alveolar lateral flap

ɧ Simultaneous ʃ and x

Affricates and double articulations can be represented by two symbols joined by a tie bar if necessary.

k͡p t͡s

SUPRASEGMENTALS

ˈ Primary stress	ˌfoʊnəˈtɪʃən
ˌ Secondary stress	
ː Long	eː
ˑ Half-long	eˑ
˘ Extra-short	ĕ
. Syllable break	ɹi.ækt
ǀ Minor (foot) group	
ǁ Major (intonation) group	
‿ Linking (absence of a break)	

TONES & WORD ACCENTS

LEVEL		CONTOUR	
e̋ or ˥	Extra high	ě or ˇ	Rising
é ˦	High	ê ˆ	Falling
ē ˧	Mid	e᷄ ˎ	High rising
è ˨	Low	e᷅ ˏ	Low rising
ȅ ˩	Extra low	e᷈ ˜	Rising-falling
ꜜ Downstep		↗ Global rise	etc.
ꜛ Upstep		↘ Global fall	

DIACRITICS

Diacritics may be placed above a symbol with a descender, e.g. ŋ̊

̥ Voiceless	n̥ d̥	̤ Breathy voiced	b̤ a̤	̪ Dental	t̪ d̪
̬ Voiced	s̬ t̬	̰ Creaky voiced	b̰ a̰	̺ Apical	t̺ d̺
ʰ Aspirated	tʰ dʰ	̼ Linguolabial	t̼ d̼	̻ Laminal	t̻ d̻
̹ More rounded	ɔ̹	ʷ Labialized	tʷ dʷ	̃ Nasalized	ẽ
̜ Less rounded	ɔ̜	ʲ Palatalized	tʲ dʲ	ⁿ Nasal release	dⁿ
̟ Advanced	u̟	ˠ Velarized	tˠ dˠ	ˡ Lateral release	dˡ
̠ Retracted	i̠	ˤ Pharyngealized	tˤ dˤ	̚ No audible release	d̚
̈ Centralized	ë	̴ Velarized or pharyngealized	ɫ		
̽ Mid-centralized	e̽	̝ Raised	e̝ (ɹ̝ = voiced alveolar fricative)		
̩ Syllabic	n̩	̞ Lowered	e̞ (β̞ = voiced bilabial approximant)		
̯ Non-syllabic	e̯	̘ Advanced Tongue Root	e̘		
˞ Rhoticity	ə˞	̙ Retracted Tongue Root	e̙		

References

Abbreviations

CLS n   Papers from the nth Regional Meeting of the Chicago
         Linguistic Society. Chicago: University of Chicago.
IJAL   International Journal of American Linguistics
JASA   Journal of the Acoustical Society of America
JL   Journal of Linguistics
JP   Journal of Phonetics
Lg   Language
LI   Linguistic Inquiry
NLLT   Natural Language and Linguistic Theory
TCLP   Travaux du cercle linguistique de Prague

Note: The periodical *Phonology* is a continuation of *Phonology Yearbook* after volume 3.

Note: Dutch surnames of the form *van der Hulst* are listed under *van*.

Abercrombie, David. 1967. *Elements of General Phonetics*. Edinburgh: Edinburgh University Press.
—— 1971. 'Some functions of silent stress'. In A. J. Aitken, A. McIntosh and H. Pálsson (eds), *Edinburgh Studies in English and Scots*. London: Longman. Reprinted in Abercrombie (1991b), pp. 71–80.
—— 1975. 'The accents of standard English in Scotland'. Unpublished paper. Reprinted in A. J. Aitken and T. McArthur (eds) (1979), *The Languages of Scotland*. Edinburgh: Chambers. Reprinted in D. Abercrombie (1991), *Fifty Years in Phonetics: Selected Papers*, pp. 54–70. Edinburgh: Edinburgh University Press.
—— 1985. 'Daniel Jones's teaching'. In V. A. Fromkin (ed.), *Phonetic Linguistics: Essays in Honor of Peter Ladefoged*, pp. 15–24. Orlando: Academic Press. Reprinted in D. Abercrombie (1991), *Fifty Years in Phonetics: Selected Papers*, pp. 37–53. Edinburgh: Edinburgh University Press.

—— 1991a. 'Phoneme, the concept and the word'. In D. Abercrombie, *Fifty Years in Phonetics: Selected Papers*, pp. 22–26. Edinburgh: Edinburgh University Press.

—— 1991b. *Fifty Years in Phonetics: Selected Papers*. Edinburgh: Edinburgh University Press.

Aitken, A. J. 1962. 'Vowel length in modern Scots'. Unpublished paper, Department of English Language, University of Edinburgh.

Allen, W. S. 1962. *Sandhi*. The Hague: Mouton.

Anderson, John and Colin J. Ewen. 1987. *Principles of Dependency Phonology*. Cambridge: Cambridge University Press.

Anderson, John and Charles Jones. 1974. 'Three theses concerning phonological representations'. *JL* 10: 1–26.

Anderson, Stephen R. 1969. *West Scandinavian Vowel Systems and the Ordering of Phonological Rules*. Bloomington: Indiana University Linguistics Club.

—— 1971. 'On the description of "apicalized" consonants'. *LI* 2: 103–107.

—— 1974. *The Organization of Phonology*. New York: Seminar Press.

—— 1975. 'On the interaction of phonological rules of various types'. *JL* 11: 39–62.

—— 1978. 'Tone features'. In Victoria A. Fromkin (ed.) *Tone: a Linguistic Survey*, pp. 133–176. New York: Academic Press.

—— 1985. *Phonology in the Twentieth Century: Theories of Rules and Theories of Representations*. Chicago: University of Chicago Press.

Archangeli, Diana. 1984. 'Underspecification in Yawelmani phonology and morphology'. Unpublished Ph.D. dissertation, MIT.

—— 1988. 'Aspects of underspecification theory'. *Phonology* 5: 183–207.

Archangeli, Diana and Douglas Pulleyblank. 1989. 'Yoruba vowel harmony'. *LI* 20: 173–217.

Aronoff, Mark. 1976. *Word Formation in Generative Grammar*. Cambridge, MA: MIT Press.

Asher, R. E. and Eugénie J. A. Henderson (eds) 1981. *Towards a History of Phonetics: Papers Contributed in Honour of David Abercrombie*. Edinburgh: University of Edinburgh Press.

Bach, Emmon. 1968. 'Two proposals concerning the simplicity metric in phonology'. *Glossa* 2: 128–149.

Bach, Emmon and Robert T. Harms. 1972. 'How do languages get crazy rules?' In R. P. Stockwell and R. K. S. Macaulay (eds),

Linguistic Change and Generative Theory, pp. 1–21. Bloomington: Indiana University Press.

Barkhausen, H. 1926. *Zeitschrift für technische Physik* VII: 601.

Baudouin de Courtenay, Jan. 1881. *Podrobnaja Programma Lekcij* ['A detailed programme of lectures']: Kazan–Warsaw.

—— 1895. *Versuch einer Theorie der phonetischen Alternationen*. Strasburg.

Bauer, Laurie. 1983. *English Word-formation*. Cambridge: Cambridge University Press.

—— 1988. *Introducing Linguistic Morphology*. Edinburgh: University of Edinburgh Press.

Beach, D. M. 1937. *Phonetics of the Hottentot Language*. Cambridge: Heffer.

Bell, Alexander Melville. 1867. *Visible Speech or Self-interpreting Physiological Letters for the Writing of All Languages in One Alphabet*. London: Simpkin & Marshall.

Bickerton, Derek. 1971. 'Inherent variability and variable rules.' *Foundations of Language* 7: 457–492.

Bierwisch, Manfred. 1967. 'Syntactic features in morphology: general problems of the so-called pronominal inflection in German'. In *To Honor Roman Jakobson*, vol. 1, pp. 239–270. The Hague: Mouton.

Bjarkman, P. C. 1975. 'Toward a proper conception of processes in natural phonology'. *CLS* 11: 60–72.

Bloch, Bernard. 1941. 'Phonemic overlapping'. *American Speech* 16: 278–284. Reprinted in Martin Joos (ed.) (1957), *Readings in Linguistics I*, pp. 93–96. Chicago: Chicago University Press. Also reprinted in V. B. Makkai (ed.) (1972), *Phonological Theory: Evolution and Current Practice*, pp. 66–70. New York: Holt, Rinehart & Winston.

—— 1948. 'A set of postulates for phonemic analysis'. *Lg* 24: 3–46. Reprinted in Valerie Becker Makkai (ed.) (1972), *Phonological Theory: Evolution and Current Practice*, pp. 167–199. New York: Holt, Rinehart & Winston.

—— 1953. 'Contrast'. *Lg* 29: 59–61. Reprinted in Valerie Becker Makkai (ed.) (1972), *Phonological Theory: Evolution and Current Practice*, pp. 224–225. New York: Holt, Rinehart & Winston.

Bloomfield, Leonard. 1933. *Language*. New York: Holt, Rinehart & Winston.

—— 1939. 'Menomini morphophonemics'. *TCLP* 8: 105–115. Reprinted in Valerie Becker Makkai (ed.) (1972), *Phonological*

Theory: Evolution and Current Practice, pp. 58–64. New York: Holt, Rinehart & Winston.

Blumstein, Sheila E. and Kenneth N. Stevens. 1981. 'Phonetic features and acoustic invariance in speech'. *Cognition* 10: 25–32.

Bolinger, Dwight L. 1951. 'Intonation: levels versus configuration'. *Word* 7: 199–210.

—— 1958. 'A theory of pitch accent in English'. *Word* 14: 105–149.

Borden, G. J. and K. S. Harris. 1980. *Speech Science Primer: Physiology, Acoustics and Perception of Speech*. Baltimore: Williams & Wilkins.

Browman, C. P. and L. M. Goldstein. 1986. 'Towards an articulatory phonology'. *Phonology Yearbook* 3: 219–252.

—— 1990. 'Tiers in articulatory phonology, with some implications for casual speech'. In J. Kingston and M. Beckman (eds), *Papers in Laboratory Phonology: Between the Grammar and the Physics of Speech*, pp. 341–376. Cambridge: Cambridge University Press.

Bruck, A., R. A. Fox and M. W. La Galy (eds) 1974. *Papers from the Parasession on Natural Phonology*. Chicago: Chicago Linguistic Society.

Bühler, Karl. 1934. *Sprachtheorie: die Darstellung-funktion der Sprache*. Jena. 2nd edn. (1992), Stuttgart: Fischer. English translation by D. F. Goodwin (1990), *Theory of Language: the Representational Function of Language*, Amsterdam: Benjamins.

Burzio, Luigi. 1988. 'English stress'. In P. M. Bertinetto and M. Loporcaro (eds), *Certamen phonologicum: Papers from the 1987 Cortona Phonology Meeting*, pp. 63–76. Turin: Rosenberg & Sellier.

Carr, Philip. 1993. *Phonology*. Basingstoke: Macmillan.

Carruthers, S. W. 1900. 'Contribution to the mechanism of articulate speech'. *Edinburgh Medical Journal*, September–October–November.

Carstairs-McCarthy, Andrew. 1992. *Current Morphology*. London: Routledge.

Catford, J. C. 1939. 'On the classification of stop consonants'. *Le Maître Phonétique*, 3rd series 65: 2–5. Reprinted in W. E. Jones and J. Laver (eds) (1973), *Phonetics in Linguistics: a Book of Readings*, pp. 43–46. London: Longman.

—— 1977. *Fundamental Problems in Phonetics*. Edinburgh: Edinburgh University Press.

—— 1981. 'Observations on the recent history of vowel classification'. In R. E. Asher and E. J. A. Henderson (eds), *Towards a*

History of Phonetics: Papers Contributed in Honour of David Abercrombie, pp. 19–32. Edinburgh: Edinburgh University Press.

—— 1988. *A Practical Introduction to Phonetics*. Oxford: Clarendon Press.

Chafe, Wallace. 1967. 'The ordering of phonological rules'. *Project on Linguistic Analysis* 2. Reports. Phonological Laboratory, Department of Linguistics, University of California at Berkeley, pp. 1–42. Reprinted (1968) in *IJAL* 34: 115–136.

Chao, Yuen-ren. 1930. 'A system of tone letters'. *Le Maître Phonétique* 30: 24–27.

—— 1934. 'The non-uniqueness of phonemic solutions of phonetic systems'. *Bulletin of the Institute for History and Philology (Academia Sinica)* 4: 363–397. Reprinted in Martin Joos (ed.) (1957), *Readings in Linguistics I*, pp. 38–54. Chicago: Chicago University Press.

Charette, Monik. 1991. *Conditions on Phonological Government*. Cambridge: Cambridge University Press.

Chen, Matthew Y. and William S.-Y. Wang. 1975. 'Sound change: actuation and implementation'. *Lg* 51: 255–281.

Chiba, T. and M. Kajiyama. 1958. *The Vowel: its Nature and Structure*. Tokyo: Phonetic Society of Japan.

Chomsky, Noam. 1957. *Syntactic Structures*. The Hague: Mouton.

—— 1964. *Current Issues in Linguistic Theory*. The Hague: Mouton.

Chomsky, Noam and Morris Halle. 1968. *The Sound Pattern of English*. New York: Harper & Row.

Chomsky, Noam, Morris Halle and Fred Lukoff. 1956. 'On accent and juncture in English'. In M. Halle, H. G. Lunt, H. McLean and C. H. van Schooneveld (eds), *For Roman Jakobson: Essays on the Occasion of his Sixtieth Birthday*, pp. 65–80. The Hague: Mouton.

Clark, John and Colin Yallop. 1990. *An Introduction to Phonetics and Phonology*. Oxford: Blackwell.

Clements, George N. 1985. 'The problem of transfer in nonlinear generative phonology'. *Working Papers in Linguistics* 5: 38–73. Ithaca, NY: Cornell University.

—— 1990. 'The role of the sonority cycle in core syllabification'. In J. Kingston and M. Beckman (eds), *Papers in Laboratory Phonology: Between the Grammar and the Physics of Speech*, pp. 283–333. Cambridge: Cambridge University Press.

—— 1991. 'Vowel height assimilation in Bantu languages'. *Working Papers of the Cornell Phonetics Laboratory* 5: 37–76.

—— 1992. 'Phonological primes: features or gestures?' *Phonetica* 49: 181–193.

Clements, George N. and Jay Keyser. 1983. *CV Phonology: a Generative Theory of the Syllable*. Cambridge, MA: MIT Press.

Coates, Richard A. 1977. 'The status of rules in historical phonology'. Unpublished Ph.D. thesis, University of Cambridge.

—— 1994. 'Morphophonemics'. In R. E. Asher (ed.), *The Encyclopedia of Language and Linguistics*, vol. 5, pp. 2602–2612. Edinburgh: Pergamon Press.

Cohn, Abigail. 1990. 'Phonetic and phonological rules of nasalization'. *UCLA Working Papers in Phonetics* 76.

Collier, R. and J. 't Hart. 1981. *Cursus Nederlandse Intonatie*. Louvain: Acco.

Contreras, H. and Sol Saporta. 1960. 'The validation of a phonological grammar'. *Lingua* 9: 1–5.

Coseriu, E. 1954. *Forma y sustancia en los sonidos del lenguaje*. Montevideo: Universidad de la República.

Crothers, John. 1978. 'Typology: universals of vowel systems'. In Joseph H. Greenberg (ed.), *Universals of Human Language*, vol. 2: *Phonology*, pp. 93–152. Stanford: Stanford University Press.

Cruttenden, Alan. 1986. *Intonation*. Cambridge: Cambridge University Press.

—— 1994. *Gimson's Pronunciation of English*, 5th edn. London: Edward Arnold.

Crystal, David. 1987. *The Cambridge Encyclopedia of Language*. Cambridge: Cambridge University Press.

Crystal, David and Randolph Quirk. 1964. *Systems of Prosodic and Paralinguistic Features in English*. The Hague: Mouton.

Dell, François. 1980. *Generative Phonology*. Cambridge: Cambridge University Press.

Denes, Peter B. and Elliot N. Pinson. 1993. *The Speech Chain: the Physics and Biology of Spoken Language*, 2nd edn (1st edn 1973). New York: W. H. Freeman.

Dinnsen, Daniel. 1978. 'Some formal and empirical issues in Atomic Phonology'. *Communication and Cognition* 11: 427–440. Reprinted in D. L. Goyvaerts (ed.) (1979), *Recent Advances in Phonological Theory*, pp. 143–156. Ghent: Story-Scientia. Also reprinted in D. L. Goyvaerts (ed.) (1981), *Phonology in the 1980s*, pp. 143–156. Ghent: Story-Scientia.

—— (ed.) 1979a. *Current Approaches to Phonological Theory*. Bloomington: Indiana University Press.

—— 1979b. 'Atomic Phonology'. In Daniel Dinnsen (ed.), *Current Approaches to Phonological Theory*, pp. 31–49. Bloomington, IN: Indiana University Press.

Dixon, Robert M. W. 1977. 'Some phonological rules in Yidin^y. *LI* 8: 1–34.

—— 1980. *The Languages of Australia*. Cambridge: Cambridge University Press.

Donegan, Patricia J. and David Stampe. 1979. 'The study of natural phonology'. In Daniel Dinnsen (ed.), *Current Approaches to Phonological Theory*, pp. 126–173. Bloomington: Indiana University Press.

Dressler, Wolfgang U. 1985. *Morphonology: the Dynamics of Derivation*, ed. Kenneth C. Hill. Ann Arbor, MI: Karoma.

Dunn, H. K. 1950. 'The calculation of vowel resonances and an electrical vocal tract'. *JASA* 22: 740–753.

Durand, Jacques. 1990. *Generative and Non-Linear Phonology*. London: Longman.

Eady, S. J. 1982. 'Differences in the FØ patterns of speech: tone language versus stress language'. *Language and Speech* 25: 29–42.

Ellis, A. J. 1844. *The Alphabet of Nature*, Part 1. Bath.

Ewen, C. and H. van der Hulst. 1988. '[high], [low] and [back] or [I], [A] and [U]?' In P. Coopmans and A. Hulk (eds), *Linguistics in the Netherlands 1988*, pp. 49–57. Dordrecht: Foris.

Fant, Gunnar M. 1960. *Acoustic Theory of Speech Production*. The Hague: Mouton.

—— 1971. 'Distinctive features and phonetic dimensions'. In G. E. Perren and J. L. M. Trim (eds), *Applications of Linguistics*, Cambridge: Cambridge University Press. Reprinted in G. M. Fant (1973), *Speech Sounds and Features*, pp. 171–191. Cambridge, MA: MIT Press

Firth, J. R. 1930. *Speech*. London: Ernest Benn. Reprinted in J. R. Firth (1964), *The Tongues of Men and Speech*, ed. P. Strevens. London: Oxford University Press.

—— 1948. 'Sounds and prosodies'. *Transactions of the Philological Society*, pp. 127–152. Reprinted in V. B. Makkai (ed.) (1972), *Phonological Theory: Evolution and Current Practice*, pp. 252–263. New York: Holt, Rinehart & Winston.

Fischer-Jørgensen, Eli. 1956. 'The commutation test and its application to phonemic analysis'. In M. Halle, H. G. Lunt, H. McLean and C. H. van Schooneveld (eds), *For Roman Jakobson: Essays on the Occasion of His Sixtieth Birthday*, pp. 140–151. The Hague: Mouton. Reprinted in Valerie Becker Makkai (ed.) (1972), *Phonological Theory: Evolution and Current Practice*, pp. 582–592. New York: Holt, Rinehart & Winston.

—— 1967. 'Perceptual dimensions of vowels'. In *To Honor Roman Jakobson*, vol. 1, pp. 667–671. The Hague: Mouton.

—— 1975. *Trends in Phonological Theory: a Historical Introduction*. Copenhagen: Akademisk Forlag.

Fischer-Jørgensen, E., J. Rischel and N. Thorsen (eds) 1979. *Proceedings of the Ninth International Congress of Phonetic Sciences*, 2 vols. Copenhagen: Institute of Phonetics, University of Copenhagen.

Flanagan, J. L. 1965. *Speech Analysis, Synthesis and Perception*. Berlin: Springer.

—— 1972. *Speech Analysis, Synthesis and Perception*, 2nd edn. New York: Springer.

Foley, J. 1977. *Foundations of Theoretical Phonology*. Cambridge: Cambridge University Press.

Fowler, C. A. 1980. 'Coarticulation and theories of extrinsic timing control'. *JP* 8: 113–133.

Fowler, C. A., P. Rubin, R. E. Remez and M. T. Turvey. 1980. 'Implications for speech production of a general theory of action'. In B. Butterworth (ed.), *Language Production*, vol. I: *Speech and Talk*, pp. 373–420. London: Academic Press.

Frauenfelder, U. H. and L. K. Tyler (eds) 1987. *Spoken Word Recognition*. Cambridge, MA: MIT Press.

Fries, Charles C. and Kenneth L. Pike. 1949. 'Coexisting phonemic systems'. *Lg* 25: 29–50.

Fromkin, Victoria A. (ed.) 1973. *Speech Errors as Linguistic Evidence*. The Hague: Mouton.

—— (ed.) 1978. *Tone: a Linguistic Survey*. New York: Academic Press.

—— (ed.) 1980. *Errors in Linguistic Performance: Slips of the Tongue, Ear, Pen, and Hand*. New York: Academic Press.

—— (ed.) 1985. *Phonetic Linguistics: Essays in Honor of Peter Ladefoged*. Orlando, FL: Academic Press.

Fromkin, Victoria A. and Peter Ladefoged. 1981. 'Early views of distinctive features'. In R. E. Asher and E. J. A. Henderson (eds), *Towards a History of Phonetics: Papers Contributed in Honour of David Abercrombie*, pp. 3–8. Edinburgh: Edinburgh University Press.

Fry, D. B. 1979. *The Physics of Speech*. Cambridge: Cambridge University Press.

Fudge, Erik C. 1967. 'The nature of phonological primes'. *JL* 3: 1–36. Reprinted in Valerie Becker Makkai (ed.) (1972), *Phonological Theory: Evolution and Current Practice*, pp. 500–521. New York: Holt, Rinehart & Winston.

—— (ed.) 1973. *Phonology: Selected Readings*. Harmondsworth: Penguin.

Gamkrelidze, Thomas V. and V. V. Ivanov. 1973. 'Sprachtypologie und die Rekonstruktion der gemeinidg. Verschlüsse'. *Phonetica* 27: 150–156.

Garde, Paul. 1961. 'Réflexions sur les différences phonétiques entre les langues slaves'. *Word* 17: 34–62.

Giegerich, Hans J. 1985. *Metrical Phonology and Phonological Structure: German and English*. Cambridge: Cambridge University Press.

Gilliéron, Jules. 1921. *Pathologie et thérapeutique verbales*. Paris: Champion.

Gimson, A. C. 1989. *An Introduction to the Pronunciation of English*, 4th edn, revised by Susan Ramsaran (1st edn 1962). London: Edward Arnold.

Goldsmith, John A. 1976. 'An overview of autosegmental phonology'. *Linguistic Analysis* 2: 23–68. [This paper is an edited version of Goldsmith (1979).]

—— 1979. *Autosegmental Phonology*. New York: Garland. [This is the author's 1976 MIT Ph.D. thesis; it was circulated by the Indiana University Linguistics Club and is sometimes cited with that date.]

—— 1990. *Autosegmental and Metrical Phonology*. Oxford: Blackwell.

—— (ed.) 1995. *The Handbook of Phonological Theory*. Oxford: Blackwell.

Grassmann, Hermann. 1863. 'Über die Aspiraten und ihr gleichzeitiges Vorhandensein im An- und Auslaute der Wurzeln'. *Zeitschrift für vergleichende Sprachforschung auf dem Gebiete des Deutschen, Griechischen und Lateinischen* 12 (2): 81–138. English translation 'Concerning the aspirates and their simultaneous presence in the initial and final of roots', in Winfred P. Lehmann (ed.), *A Reader in Nineteenth-Century Historical Indo-European Linguistics*, 1967, pp. 109–131. Bloomington: Indiana University Press.

Greenberg, Joseph. 1970. 'Some generalizations concerning glottalic consonants, especially implosives'. *IJAL* 36: 123–146.

—— (ed.) 1978. *Universals of Human Language*, vol. 2: *Phonology*. Stanford: Stanford University Press.

Griffen, Toby D. 1985. *Aspects of Dynamic Phonology*. Amsterdam: Benjamins.

Grote, J. 1866. *Journal of Philology* IV: 55.

Gussenhoven, C. 1983. 'Focus, mode and the nucleus'. *JL* 19: 377–417.

Halle, Morris. 1959. *The Sound Pattern of Russian*. The Hague: Mouton.
—— 1962. 'Phonology in generative grammar'. *Word* 18: 54–72.
—— 1972. 'Theoretical issues in phonology in the 1970s'. In *Proceedings of the Seventh International Congress of Phonetic Sciences*. The Hague: Mouton.
—— 1973. 'Prolegomena to a theory of word-formation'. *LI* 4: 3–16.
—— 1983. 'On distinctive features and their articulatory implementation'. *NLLT* 1: 91–105.
Halle, Morris and Kenneth N. Stevens. 1959. 'Analysis by synthesis'. In W. Wathen-Dunn and L. E. Woods (eds), *Proceedings of the Seminar on Speech Compression and Processing*. AFCRC-TR-59-198, December 1959, vol. II, paper D[7].
—— 1969. 'On the feature "advanced tongue root"'. *Quarterly Progress Report 94*, Cambridge, MA: Research Laboratory of Electronics, MIT, pp. 209–215.
—— 1971. 'A note on laryngeal features'. *MIT Quarterly Progress Report* 101: 198–213.
—— 1972. 'Theoretical issues in phonology in the 1970s'. *Proceedings of the Seventh International Congress of the Phonetic Sciences*. The Hague: Mouton.
Halle, Morris and Jean-Roger Vergnaud. 1987. 'Stress and the cycle'. *LI* 18: 45–84.
Halliday, Michael A. K. 1963. 'The tones of English'. *Archivum Linguisticum* 15: 1–28.
—— 1967. *Intonation and Grammar in British English*. The Hague: Mouton.
—— 1970. *A Course in Spoken English: Intonation*. London: Oxford University Press.
Harrington, John P. 1912. 'Notes on certain usages relating to linguistic work'. *American Anthropologist* 14.
Harris, John. 1990. 'Derived phonological contrasts'. In S. Ramsaran (ed.) (1990), *Studies in the Pronunciation of English: a Commemorative Volume in Honour of A. C. Gimson*, pp. 87–105. London: Routledge.
Harris, Zellig S. 1944. 'Simultaneous components in phonology'. *Lg* 20: 181–205. Reprinted in Martin Joos (ed.) (1957), *Readings in Linguistics I*, pp. 124–138. Chicago: University of Chicago Press. Also reprinted in V. B. Makkai (ed.), *Phonological Theory: Evolution and Current Practice* (1972), pp. 115–133. New York: Holt, Rinehart & Winston.
—— 1951. *Methods in Structural Linguistics*. Chicago: University of Chicago Press.

Hastings, A. J. 1974. *Stifling*. Bloomington: Indiana University Linguistics Club.

Haugen, Einar. 1954. Review of Hjelmslev's *Prolegomena*. *Lg* 39: 69–96.

—— 1957. 'The phoneme in bilingual description'. Unpublished paper.

—— 1969. 'Phonemic indeterminacy and Scandinavian umlaut'. *Folia Linguistica* III: 107–119.

Hayes, Bruce. 1984. 'The phonology of rhythm in English'. *LI* 15: 33–74.

—— 1986. 'Inalterability in CV phonology'. *Lg* 62: 321–351.

—— 1989. 'The prosodic hierarchy in meter'. In P. Kiparsky and G. Youmans (eds), *Rhythm and Meter*, pp. 201–260. Orlando: Academic Press.

—— 1990. 'Precompiled phrasal phonology'. In S. Inkelas and D. Zec (eds), *The Phonology–Syntax Connection*, pp. 85–108. Chicago: University of Chicago Press.

Hayes, Bruce and Aditi Lahiri. 1991. 'Bengali intonational phonology'. *NLLT* 9: 47–96.

Heffner, R. M. S. 1950. *General Phonetics*. Madison: University of Wisconsin Press.

Herbert, R. K. 1986. *Language Universals, Markedness Theory, and Natural Phonetic Processes*. New York and Amsterdam: Mouton de Gruyter.

Herzog, Marvin I. 1965. *The Yiddish Language in Northern Poland*. Bloomington: Indiana University Press.

Hjelmslev, Louis. 1936. 'On the principles of phonematics'. *Proceedings of the Second International Congress of Phonetic Sciences*, pp. 49–54. Cambridge: Cambridge University Press. Reprinted in L. Hjelmslev (1973), *Essais linguistiques* II, TCLC XIV. Copenhagen.

Hoard, James E. 1971. 'The new phonological paradigm'. *Glossa* 5: 222–268. Reprinted in D. L. Goyvaerts and G. K. Pullum (eds) (1975), *Essays on the Sound Pattern of English*, pp. 25–61. Ghent: Story-Scientia.

Hockett, Charles F. 1942. 'A system of descriptive phonology'. *Lg* 18: 3–21. Reprinted in Martin Joos (ed.) (1957), *Readings in Linguistics I*, pp. 97–108. Chicago: University of Chicago Press. Also reprinted in Valerie Becker Makkai (ed.) (1972), *Phonological Theory: Evolution and Current Practice*, pp. 99–112. New York: Holt, Rinehart & Winston.

—— 1947. 'Problems of morphemic analysis'. *Lg* 23: 321–343.

Reprinted in Martin Joos (ed.) (1957), *Readings in Linguistics I*, pp. 229–242. Chicago: University of Chicago Press.

—— 1954. 'Two models of grammatical description'. *Word* 10: 210–233.

—— 1955. *A Manual of Phonology*. Baltimore: Indiana University Publications in Anthropology and Linguistics, Memoir II.

—— 1958. *A Course in Modern Linguistics*. New York: Macmillan.

—— 1961. 'Linguistic elements and their relations'. *Lg* 37: 29–53.

—— 1967. 'Where the tongue slips, there slip I'. In *To Honor Roman Jakobson*, vol. 2, pp. 910–936. The Hague: Mouton.

Hoenigswald, Henry. 1960. *Language Change and Linguistic Reconstruction*. Chicago: University of Chicago Press.

Hogg, Richard and C. B. McCully. 1987. *Metrical Phonology: a Coursebook*. Cambridge: Cambridge University Press.

Hollien, H. 1972. 'Three major vocal registers: a proposal'. In *Proceedings of the Seventh International Congress of Phonetic Sciences* (Montreal), pp. 320–331. The Hague: Mouton.

—— 1974. 'On vocal registers'. *JP* 2: 125–143.

Honikman, B. 1964. 'Articulatory settings'. In D. Abercrombie, D. B. Fry, P. A. D. MacCarthy, N. C. Scott and J. L. Trim (eds), *In Honour of Daniel Jones*, pp. 73–84. London: Longmans Green.

Hooper, Joan Bybee. 1974a. *Aspects of Natural Generative Phonology*. Bloomington: Indiana University Press.

—— 1974b. 'Rule morphologization in natural generative phonology'. In A. Bruck, R. A. Fox and M. W. La Galy (eds), *Papers from the Parasession on Natural Phonology*, pp. 160–170. Chicago: Chicago Linguistic Society.

—— 1976. *An Introduction to Natural Generative Phonology*. New York: Academic Press.

Hopper, Paul J. 1973. 'Glottalized and murmured occlusives in IE'. *Glossa* 7: 141–166.

Houlihan, Kathleen and Gregory K. Iverson. 1979. 'Functionally-constrained phonology'. In Daniel Dinnsen (ed.), *Current Approaches to Phonological Theory*, pp. 50–73. Bloomington: Indiana University Press.

Householder, Fred W. 1979. 'How different are they?' In D. Dinnsen (ed.), *Current Approaches to Phonological Theory*, pp. 252–265. Bloomington: Indiana University Press.

Huddleston, Rodney. 1972. 'The development of a non-process model in American structural linguistics', *Lingua* 30: 333–384.

Hyman, Larry M. 1973. 'The role of consonant types in natural tonal assimilations'. In L. M. Hyman (ed.), *Consonant Types and Tone*,

Southern California Occasional Papers in Linguistics 1, Department of Linguistics, UCLA.

—— 1975. *Phonology: Theory and Analysis*. New York: Holt, Rinehart & Winston.

—— 1982. 'The representation of nasality in Gokhana'. In H. van der Hulst and N. Smith (eds), *The Structure of Phonological Representations*, vol. 1, pp. 111–130. Dordrecht: Foris.

Hyman, Larry and Russell G. Schuh. 1974. 'Universals of tone rules: evidence from West Africa'. *LI* 5: 81–115.

Ingram, David. 1989. *Phonological Disability in Children*, 2nd edn (1st edn 1976). London: Edward Arnold.

Itô, Junko. 1986. 'Syllable theory in prosodic phonology'. Ph.D. thesis, University of Massachusetts at Amherst. Published 1988: New York: Garland.

—— 1989. 'A prosodic theory of epenthesis'. *NLLT* 7: 217–259.

Jakobson, Roman. 1929. 'Remarques sur l'évolution phonologique du russe comparée à celle des autres langues slaves'. *TCLP* II. Reprinted in Roman Jakobson (1962), *Selected Writings*, vol. 1, pp. 7–116. The Hague: Mouton.

—— 1931. 'Prinzipien der historischen Phonologie'. *TCLP* IV: 247–267. Reprinted in Roman Jakobson (1962), *Selected Writings*, vol. 1, pp. 202–220. The Hague: Mouton. French translation appended to N. S. Trubetzkoy (1949), *Principes de phonologie*. Paris: C. Klincksieck.

—— 1941. 'Kindersprache, Aphasie und allgemeine Lautgesetze'. Reprinted in Roman Jakobson (1962), vol. 1, pp. 328–401.

—— 1962. *Selected Writings*. Five vols. The Hague: Mouton.

Jakobson, Roman, Gunnar Fant and Morris Halle. 1952. *Preliminaries to Speech Analysis*. Cambridge: MIT Press.

Jakobson, Roman and Morris Halle. 1956. *Fundamentals of Language*. The Hague: Mouton.

Jeffers, Robert J. and Arnold M. Zwicky. 1980. 'The evolution of clitics'. In E. C. Traugott, R. Le Brum and S. Shepherd (eds), *Papers from the Fourth International Conference on Historical Linguistics*, pp. 221–231. Amsterdam: Benjamins.

Jespersen, Otto. 1914. *A Modern English Grammar on Historical Principles*. New York: Barnes & Noble.

Jones, Daniel. 1917. *An English Pronouncing Dictionary*. London: Dent. [This book has since appeared in many revised editions.]

—— 1918. *An Outline of English Phonetics*. Cambridge: W. Heffer. [This book has since appeared in many revised editions.]

—— 1929. 'Definition of a phoneme'. *Le Maître Phonétique* 28: 43–44.

—— 1939. *Proceedings of the Third International Congress of the Phonetic Sciences* 6. Ghent.

—— 1950. *The Phoneme: its Nature and Use*. Cambridge: W. Heffer. 3rd edn, revised and expanded, 1967.

—— 1957. 'The history and meaning of the term "phoneme"'. Supplement to *Le Maître Phonétique*. Reprinted as Appendix to the third (1967) edition of Daniel Jones (1950), *The Phoneme: its Nature and Use*, pp. 253–269. Cambridge: W. Heffer. Also reprinted in E. C. Fudge (ed.) (1973), *Phonology: Selected Readings*, pp. 17–34. Harmondsworth: Penguin.

Joos, Martin (ed.) 1957. *Readings in Linguistics I*. Chicago: University of Chicago Press.

Kahn, Daniel. 1980. *Syllable-based Generalizations in English Phonology*. New York: Garland.

Kaisse, Ellen 1985. *Connected Speech: the Interaction of Syntax and Phonology*. New York: Academic Press.

—— 1987. 'Rhythm and the cycle'. *CLS* 23 (2): 199–209.

Kaisse, Ellen and Patricia Shaw. 1985. 'On the theory of lexical phonology'. *Phonology Yearbook* 2: 1–30.

Katamba, Francis. 1989. *An Introduction to Phonology*. London: Longman.

Kaye, Jonathan D. 1990. '"Coda" licensing'. *Phonology* 7: 301–330.

—— 1991–1992. 'Do you believe in magic? The story of *s* + C sequences'. In A. Görkel and E. Parker (eds), *SOAS Working Papers in Linguistics and Phonetics*, pp. 293–313. London: School of Oriental and African Studies.

Kaye, Jonathan D., J. Lowenstamm and J.-R. Vergnaud. 1985. 'The internal structure of phonological elements: a theory of Charm and Government'. *Phonology Yearbook* 2: 305–328.

—— 1990. 'Constituent structure and government in phonology'. *Phonology* 7: 193–231.

Keating, Patricia. 1988. 'Underspecification in phonetics'. *Phonology* 5: 275–292.

Kenstowicz, Michael. 1994. *Phonology in Generative Grammar*. Oxford: Blackwell.

Kent, R. D. and C. Read. 1992. *The Acoustic Analysis of Speech*. San Diego: Singular.

Kenyon, John S. and Thomas A. Knott. 1953. *A Pronouncing Dictionary of American English*. Springfield, MA: Merriam.

King, Robert D. 1969. *Historical Linguistics and Generative Grammar*. Englewood Cliffs, NJ: Prentice-Hall.

Kingston, J. and M. Beckman (eds) 1990. *Papers in Laboratory*

Phonology: Between the Grammar and the Physics of Speech.
Cambridge: Cambridge University Press.

Kiparsky, Paul. 1965. 'Phonological change'. Ph.D. dissertation,
Cambridge, MA, MIT.

—— 1968a. 'Linguistic universals and linguistic change'. In E. Bach
and R. T. Harms (eds), *Universals in Linguistic Theory*,
pp. 171–202. New York: Holt, Rinehart & Winston.

—— 1968b. *How Abstract is Phonology?* Bloomington: Indiana
University Linguistics Club. Reprinted in O. Fujimura (ed.)
(1974), *Three Dimensions of Linguistic Theory*, Tokyo: TEC.

—— 1971. 'Historical linguistics'. In W. O. Dingwall (ed.), *A Survey
of Linguistic Science*, College Park: University of Maryland.

—— 1973a. *Abstractness, Opacity and Global Rules*. Bloomington:
Indiana University Linguistics Club. Reprinted in O. Fujimura
(ed.) (1974), *Three Dimensions of Linguistic Theory*, pp. 57–86.
Tokyo: TEC.

—— 1973b. '"Elsewhere" in phonology'. In S. Anderson and
P. Kiparsky (eds), *A Festschrift for Morris Halle*, pp. 93–106. New
York: Holt, Rinehart & Winston.

—— 1982. 'Lexical phonology and morphology'. In I. S. Yang (ed.),
Linguistics in the Morning Calm, pp. 3–91. Seoul: Hanshin.
Abridged version published as 'From cyclic to lexical phonology',
in H. van der Hulst and N. Smith (eds) (1982), *The Structure of
Phonological Representations*, vol. 1, pp. 131–175. Dordrecht: Foris.

—— 1985. 'Some consequences of Lexical Phonology'. *Phonology
Yearbook* 2: 83–138.

Kisseberth, Charles. 1970. 'On the functional unity of phonological
rules'. *LI* 1: 291–306. Reprinted in Erik C. Fudge (ed.) (1973),
Phonology: Selected Readings, pp. 257–274. Harmondsworth:
Penguin.

—— 1973. 'On the alternation of vowel length in Klamath: a global
rule'. In M. Kenstowicz and C. Kisseberth (eds), *Issues in
Phonological Theory*, pp. 9–26. The Hague: Mouton.

—— 1976. 'The interaction of phonological rules and the polarity of
language'. In A. Koutsoudas (ed.), *The Application and Ordering
of Grammatical Rules*, pp. 41–54. The Hague: Mouton.

Klavans, Judith L. 1985. 'The independence of syntax and phonology
in cliticization'. *Lg* 61: 95–120.

Kloster Jensen, M. 1963. 'Die Silbe in der Phonetik und Phonemik'.
Phonetica 41: 150–174.

Knowles, Gerald O. 1974. 'Scouse: the urban dialect of Liverpool'.
Unpublished Ph.D. thesis, University of Leeds.

Koutsoudas, Andreas, Gerald Sanders and Craig Noll. 1974. 'On the application of phonological rules'. *Lg* 50: 1–28.

Krámský, J. 1974. *The Phoneme*. Munich: Wilhelm Funk.

Krapp, G. P. 1925. *The English Language in America*, 2 vols. New York: Century.

Kreidler, Charles W. 1989. *The Pronunciation of English: a Course Book in Phonology*. Oxford: Blackwell.

Labov, William. 1966. *The Social Stratification of English in New York City*. Washington, DC: Center for Applied Linguistics.

—— 1972. *Sociolinguistic Patterns*. Philadelphia: University of Pennsylvania Press.

—— 1975. 'On the use of the present to explain the past'. In L. Heilmann (ed.), *Proceedings of the Eleventh International Congress of Linguists*, pp. 825–851. Bologna: Il Mulino.

—— 1994. *Principles of Linguistic Change*, vol. 1: *Internal Factors*. Oxford: Blackwell.

Labov, William, Mark Karen and Corey Miller. 1991. 'Near-mergers and the suspension of phonemic contrast'. *Language Variation and Change* 3: 33–74.

Labov, William, Malcah Yeager and Richard Steiner. 1972. *A Quantitative Study of Sound Change in Progress*. Philadelphia: US Regional Survey.

Ladd, D. R. 1984. 'Declination: a review and some hypotheses'. *Phonology Yearbook* 1: 53–74.

Ladefoged, Peter. 1960. 'The value of phonetic statements'. *Lg* 36: 387–396.

—— 1962. *Elements of Acoustic Phonetics*. Chicago: University of Chicago Press.

—— 1964. *A Phonetic Study of West African Languages*. Cambridge: Cambridge University Press.

—— 1965. 'The nature of general phonetic theories'. *Georgetown University Monograph Series on Language and Linguistics* 18: 27–42.

—— 1968. 'Linguistic aspects of respiratory phenomena'. In A. Bouhuys (ed.), *Sound Production in Man*, Annals of the New York Academy of Sciences, vol. 155, art. 1, pp. 141–151.

—— 1971. *Preliminaries to Linguistic Phonetics*. Chicago: University of Chicago Press.

—— 1972. 'Phonetic prerequisites for a distinctive feature theory'. In A. Valdman (ed.), *Papers in Linguistics and Phonetics to the Memory of Pierre Delattre*, pp. 273–285. The Hague: Mouton.

—— 1973. 'The features of the larynx'. *Journal of Phonetics* 1: 73–83.

—— 1975. *A Course in Phonetics*. New York: Harcourt Brace Jovanovich. 2nd edn 1982; 3rd edn 1993.

—— 1979. 'Phonetic specification of the languages of the world'. *Revue de Phonétique Appliquée* 49/50: 21–40.

—— 1990. 'On dividing phonetics and phonology: comments on the papers by Clements and by Browman and Goldstein'. In J. Kingston and M. Beckman (eds), *Papers in Laboratory Phonology: Between the Grammar and the Physics of Speech*, pp. 398–405. Cambridge: Cambridge University Press.

Ladefoged, Peter, A. Cochran and S. Disner. 1977. 'Laterals and trills'. *Journal of the International Phonetic Association* 7: 46–54.

Ladefoged, Peter and Ian Maddieson. 1986. 'Some of the sounds of the world's languages: preliminary version'. *UCLA Department of Linguistics Working Papers in Phonetics* 64.

Ladefoged, Peter and A. Traill. 1994. 'Clicks and their accompaniments'. *JP* 22: 33–64.

Lamb, Sidney. 1966. *Outline of Stratificational Grammar*. Washington, DC: Georgetown University Press.

Lane, H. H. 1965. 'The motor theory of speech perception: a critical review'. *Psychological Review* 72 (4): 275–309.

Langacker, Ronald W. 1969. 'Mirror-image rules II: lexicon and phonology'. *Lg* 45: 844–862.

Langendoen, D. Terence. 1968. *The London School of Linguistics*. Research Monograph no. 46. Cambridge, MA: MIT Press.

Lass, Roger. 1974. 'Linguistic orthogenesis? Scots vowel quantity and the English length conspiracy'. In J. M. Anderson and C. Jones (eds), *Historical Linguistics: Proceedings of the First International Conference on Historical Linguistics*, vol. 2, pp. 311–352. Amsterdam: North-Holland.

—— 1976. *English Phonology and Phonological Theory: Synchronic and Diachronic Studies*. Cambridge: Cambridge University Press.

—— 1984. *Phonology: an Introduction to Basic Concepts*. Cambridge: Cambridge University Press.

Lass, Roger and John M. Anderson. 1975. *Old English Phonology*. Cambridge: Cambridge University Press.

Laver, John. 1965. 'Variability in vowel perception'. *Language and Speech* 8: 95–121.

—— 1979. 'The description of voice quality in general phonetic theory'. *Edinburgh University Department of Linguistics Work in Progress* 12: 30–52. Reprinted in John Laver (1991), *The Gift of Speech: Papers in the Analysis of Speech and Voice*, pp. 184–208. Edinburgh: Edinburgh University Press.

—— 1980. *The Phonetic Description of Voice Quality*. Cambridge: Cambridge University Press.

—— 1989. 'Cognitive science and speech: a framework for research'. In H. Schnelle and N.-O. Bernsen (eds), *Logic and Linguistics*, vol. 3: 37–69. Reprinted in John Laver (1991), *The Gift of Speech: Papers in the Analysis of Speech and Voice*, pp. 92–128. Edinburgh: Edinburgh University Press.

—— 1991. *The Gift of Speech: Papers in the Analysis of Speech and Voice*. Edinburgh: Edinburgh University Press.

—— 1994. *Principles of Phonetics*. Cambridge: Cambridge University Press.

Laver, J. and P. Trudgill. 1979. 'Phonetic and linguistic markers in speech'. In K. R. Scherer and H. Giles (eds), *Social Markers in Speech*, pp. 1–32. Cambridge: Cambridge University Press. Reprinted in John Laver (1991), *The Gift of Speech: Papers in the Analysis of Speech and Voice*, pp. 235–264. Edinburgh: Edinburgh University Press.

Leben, William R. 1973. 'Suprasegmental phonology'. Unpublished Ph.D. dissertation, MIT.

Leben, William R. and Orrin W. Robinson. 1977. '"Upside-down" phonology'. *Lg* 53: 1–20.

Lehiste, Ilse and G. E. Peterson. 1961. 'Some basic considerations in the analysis of intonation'. *JASA* 33: 419–425.

Lemle, Miriam and Anthony Naro. 1977. *Competencias básicas do portugues*. Rio de Janeiro: MOBRAL.

Lepschy, Giulio. 1982. *A Survey of Structural Linguistics*, 2nd edn (1st edn 1970). London: André Deutsch.

Levin, Juliette. 1985. 'A metrical theory of syllabicity'. Unpublished Ph.D. thesis, MIT.

—— 1988. 'A place for lateral in the feature geometry'. Unpublished paper, Austin: University of Texas.

Liberman, A. M. 1957 'Some results of research on speech perception'. *JASA* 29: 117–123.

Liberman, A. M., F. S. Cooper, K. Harris and P. E. McNeilage. 1963. 'A motor theory of speech perception'. In G. Fant (ed.), *Proceedings of the Speech Communications Seminar*, vol. 2. Stockholm: Royal Institute of Technology.

Liberman, A. M., F. S. Cooper, D. P. Shankweiler and M. Studdert-Kennedy. 1967. 'Perception of the speech code'. *Psychological Review* 74: 431–461.

Liberman, A. M. and I. G. Mattingly. 1985. 'The motor theory of speech revised'. *Cognition* 21: 1–36.

Liberman, Mark and Alan Prince. 1977. 'On stress and linguistic rhythm'. *LI* 8: 249–336.

Lieberman, Philip and Sheila E. Blumstein. 1988. *Speech Physiology, Speech Perception, and Acoustic Phonetics*. Cambridge: Cambridge University Press.

Lightner, Theodore M. 1965. 'On the description of vowel and consonant harmony'. *Word* 21: 224–250.

—— 1968. 'On the use of minor rules in Russian phonology'. *JL* 4: 69–72.

—— 1975. 'The role of derivational morphology in generative grammar'. *Lg* 51: 617–638.

Lindau, Mona. 1975. 'Features for vowels'. *UCLA Working Papers in Phonetics* 30.

—— 1978. 'Vowel features'. *Lg* 54: 541–563.

—— 1985. 'The story of /r/'. In Victoria A. Fromkin (ed.), *Phonetic Linguistics: Essays in Honour of Peter Ladefoged*, pp. 157–168. Orlando, FL: Academic Press.

Lindblom, Björn. 1986. 'Phonetic universals in vowel systems'. In John J. Ohala and Jeri J. Jaeger (eds), *Experimental Phonology*, pp. 13–44. Orlando, FL: Academic Press.

Lindblom, Björn and Ian Maddieson. 1988. 'Phonetic universals in consonant systems'. In L. M. Hyman and C. N. Li (eds), *Language, Speech and Mind: Studies in Honor of Victoria Fromkin*, pp. 62–80. New York: Routledge.

Lloyd, R. J. 1899. *Northern English*. Leipzig.

Locke, John L. 1983. *Phonological Acquisition and Change*. New York: Academic Press.

Lockwood, David G. 1972. *Introduction to Stratificational Linguistics*. New York: Harcourt Brace Jovanovich.

Lyons, John. 1968. *Introduction to Theoretical Linguistics*. Cambridge: Cambridge University Press.

Maddieson, Ian. 1980a. 'A survey of liquids'. *UCLA Working Papers in Phonetics* 50: 93–112.

—— 1980b. 'Vocoid approximants in the world's languages'. *UCLA Working Papers in Phonetics* 50: 113–119.

—— 1984. *Patterns of Sounds*. Cambridge: Cambridge University Press.

—— 1987. 'Linguo-labials'. *UCLA Working Papers in Phonetics* 68: 87–99.

Makkai, Valerie Becker (ed.) 1972. *Phonological Theory: Evolution and Current Practice*. New York: Holt, Rinehart & Winston.

Malone, Kemp. 1923. *The Phonology of Modern Icelandic*. Menasha, WI: Collegiate Press.

Marantz, Alec. 1982. 'Re reduplication'. *LI* 13: 435–482.

Martinet, André. 1936. 'Neutralisation et archiphonème'. *TCLP* VI: 46–57.

—— 1939. 'Un ou deux phonèmes?' *Acta Linguistica* 1: 94–103. Reprinted in A. Martinet (1968), *La Linguistique synchronique: études et recherches*, 2nd edn, pp. 109–123. Paris: Presses Universitaires de France.

—— 1949. 'Phonology as functional phonetics'. *Publications of the Philological Society*: 1–27.

—— 1952. 'Function, structure and sound change'. *Word* 8: 1–32.

—— 1953. 'Remarques sur le consonantisme sémitique'. *Bulletin de la Société Linguistique de Paris* 49: 67–78.

—— 1954. 'Accents et tons'. *Miscellanea Phonetica* 2: 13–24. Reprinted in André Martinet (1968), *La Linguistique Synchronique*, 2nd edn (1st edn 1965), pp. 141–161. Paris: Presses Universitaires de France.

—— 1955. *Economie des changements phonétiques*. Bern: Editions A. Francke.

—— 1960. *Elements of General Linguistics*. London: Faber & Faber.

—— 1968. *La Linguistique synchronique*, 2nd edn (1st edn 1965). Paris: Presses Universitaires de France.

Mascaró, Joan. 1976. *Catalan Phonology and the Phonological Cycle*. Bloomington: Indiana University Linguistics Club.

Matthews, Peter. 1991. *Morphology*, 2nd edn (1st edn 1974). Cambridge: Cambridge University Press.

McArthur, Tom (ed.) 1992. *The Oxford Companion to the English Language*. Oxford: Oxford University Press.

McCarthy, John 1979. *Formal Properties of Semitic Phonology and Morphology*. Bloomington: Indiana University Linguistics Club. Also published (n.d.) New York: Garland.

—— 1981. 'A prosodic theory of nonconcatenative morphology'. *LI* 12: 373–418.

—— 1986. 'OCP effects: gemination and antigemination'. *LI* 17: 207–263.

—— 1988. 'Feature geometry and dependency: a review'. *Phonetica* 43: 84–108.

McCarthy, John and Alan Prince. 1986. 'Prosodic phonology'. Unpublished paper, University of Massachusetts, Amherst.

—— 1990. 'Foot and word in prosodic morphology: the Arabic broken plural'. *NLLT* 8: 209–284.

—— 1991. 'Lectures on prosodic morphology'. LSA Summer Institute, University of California at Santa Cruz.

McCawley, James D. 1966. 'Further revisions in Finnish rules'. Unpublished paper, University of Chicago.

—— 1968. *The Phonological Component of a Grammar of Japanese*. The Hague: Mouton.

McMahon, April M. S. 1991. 'Lexical phonology and sound change: the case of the Scottish vowel length rule'. *JL* 27: 29–53.

Michelena, Luis. 1957. 'Las antiguas consonantes vascas'. In *Miscelánea homenaje a André Martinet*, vol. 1, pp. 113–157. La Laguna. Reprinted in L. Michelena (1988), *Sobre historia de la lengua vasca*, vol. 1, pp. 166–189, San Sebastián. English translation by R. L. Trask, 'The ancient Basque consonants', in J. I. Hualde, J. A. Lakarra and R. L. Trask (eds) (1995), *On the History of the Basque Language: Studies in Basque Historical Linguistics*. Amsterdam: John Benjamins (CILT).

—— 1977. *Fonética histórica vasca*. 2nd edn (1st edn 1961). San Sebastián: Publicaciones del Seminario Julio de Urquijo de la Excma. Diputación de Guipúzcoa.

Miller, G. A. and P. E. Nicely. 1955. 'An analysis of perceptual confusions among some English consonants'. *JASA* 27: 338–352.

Mohanan, K. P. 1982. *Lexical Phonology*. Bloomington: University of Indiana Linguistics Club.

Morrison, Alistair [writing as Afferbeck Lauder]. 1965. *Let Stalk Strine*. Sydney.

Morton, J., S. Marcus and C. Frankish. 1976. 'Perceptual centres (P-centres)'. *Psychological Review* 83: 405–408.

Moulton, William G. 1947. 'Juncture in modern standard German'. *Lg* 23: 212–226. Reprinted in Martin Joos (ed.) (1957), *Readings in Linguistics I*, pp. 208–215. Chicago: University of Chicago Press.

—— 1967. 'Types of phonemic change'. In *To Honor Roman Jakobson*, vol. 2, pp. 1393–1407. The Hague: Mouton.

Müller, Max. 1855. *The Languages of the Seat of War in the East*, 2nd edn. London: Williams & Norgate.

—— 1875 [written 1843]. *Lectures on the Science of Languages* 2. London: Longman.

Myers, S. 1987. 'Tone and the structure of words in Shona'. Ph.D. dissertation, University of Massachusetts, Amherst. Published by Garland Press, New York, 1990.

—— 1991. 'Persistent rules'. *LI* 22: 315–344.

Nartey, J. N. A. 1979. 'A study in phonemic universals – especially concerning fricatives and stops'. *UCLA Working Papers in Phonetics* 46.

Nellis, D. G. and B. E. Hollenbach. 1980. 'Fortis versus lenis in

Cajonos Zapotec phonology'. *IJAL* 46: 92–105.

Nespor, Marina and Irene Vogel. 1982. 'Prosodic domains of external sandhi rules'. In H. van der Hulst and N. Smith (1982), pp. 225–255.

—— 1986. *Prosodic Phonology*. Dordrecht: Foris.

Newton, B. E. 1971. 'Ordering paradoxes in phonology'. *JL* 7: 31–53.

Newmeyer, Frederick J. 1986. *Linguistic Theory in America*, 2nd edn (1st edn 1980). New York: Academic Press.

Nida, Eugene A. 1948. 'A system for the identification of morphemes'. *Lg* 24: 414–441.

Nolan, Francis. 1982. 'The role of Action Theory in the description of speech production'. *Linguistics* 20: 287–308.

O'Connor, J. D. 1973. *Phonetics*. Harmondsworth: Penguin.

Odell, J. 1806. *An Essay on the Elements, Accents and Prosody of the English Language*. London.

Ohala, John J. 1974. 'Phonetic explanation in phonology'. In A. Bruck, R. A. Fox and M. W. La Galy (eds), *Papers from the Parasession on Natural Language*, pp. 251–274. Chicago: Chicago Linguistic Society.

—— 1985. 'Around *flat*'. In Victoria A. Fromkin (ed.), *Phonetic Linguistics: Essays in Honour of Peter Ladefoged*, pp. 223–241. Orlando, FL: Academic Press.

—— 1986. 'Consumer's guide to evidence in phonology'. *Phonology Yearbook* 3: 3–26.

Ohala, John J. and Jeri J. Jaeger (eds) 1986. *Experimental Phonology*. Orlando, FL: Academic Press.

Palmer, H. E. 1930. *Principles of Romanization*, II. Tokyo: Maruzen Company.

Pandit, P. B. 1957. 'Nasalisation, aspiration and murmur in Gujarati'. *Indian Linguistics* 17: 165–172.

Paradis, Carole. 1988–1989. 'On constraints and repair strategies'. *The Linguistic Review* 6: 71–97.

Paradis, Carole and Jean-François Prunet. 1989. 'On coronal transparency'. *Phonology* 6: 317–348.

—— (eds) 1991. *Phonetics and Phonology*, vol. 2: *The Special Status of Coronals*. San Diego: Academic Press.

Paul, Hermann. 1886. *Principien der Sprachgeschichte*, 2nd edn. Halle: Max Niemeyr.

Pickett, J. M. 1980. *The Sounds of Speech Communication*. Baltimore: University Park Press.

Pike, Kenneth L. 1943. *Phonetics: a Critical Analysis of Phonetic Theory and a Technic for the Practical Description of Sounds*. Ann

Arbor: University of Michigan Press.

—— 1945. *The Intonation of American English*. Ann Arbor: University of Michigan Press.

—— 1947a. *Phonemics: a Technique for Reducing Languages to Writing*. Ann Arbor: University of Michigan Press.

—— 1947b. 'Grammatical prerequisites to phonemic analysis'. *Word* 3: 155–172. Reprinted in Valerie Becker Makkai (ed.) (1972), *Phonological Theory: Evolution and Current Practice*, pp. 153–165. New York: Holt, Rinehart & Winston. Also reprinted in Erik C. Fudge (ed.) (1973), *Phonology: Selected Readings*, pp. 115–135. Harmondsworth: Penguin.

Pitman, Isaac. 1846. *The Phonotypic Journal* 5.

Postal, Paul M. 1968. *Aspects of Phonological Theory*. New York: Harper & Row.

Prince, Alan. 1980. 'A metrical theory for Estonian quantity'. *LI* 11: 511–562.

—— 1984. 'Phonology with tiers'. In M. Aronoff and R. T. Oehrle (eds), *Language Sound Structure*, pp. 234–244. Cambridge, MA: MIT Press.

Prince, Alan and Paul Smolensky. Forthcoming. *Optimality Theory: Constraint Interaction in Generative Grammar*. Cambridge, MA: MIT Press.

Pulleyblank, Douglas. 1986. *Tone in Lexical Phonology*. Dordrecht: Reidel.

Pullum, Geoffrey K. 1975. 'Rule interaction and the organization of a grammar'. Ph.D. thesis. Published 1979: New York: Garland.

—— 1976. 'The Duke of York gambit'. *JL* 12: 83–102.

Pullum, Geoffrey K. and William A. Ladusaw. 1986. *Phonetic Symbol Guide*. Chicago: University of Chicago Press.

Pullum, Geoffrey K. and Arnold M. Zwicky. 1988. 'The syntax–phonology interface'. In F. J. Newmeyer (ed.), *Linguistics: the Cambridge Survey*, vol. 1: *Linguistic Theory: Foundations*, pp. 255–280. Cambridge: Cambridge University Press.

Rakers, B., W. Sennett and C. A. Fowler. 1987. 'Domain-final lengthening and foot-level shortening in spoken English'. *Phonetica* 44: 147–155.

Ramsaran, Susan (ed.) 1990. *Studies in the Pronunciation of English: a Commemorative Volume in Honour of A. C. Gimson*. London: Routledge.

Reighard, J. 1972. 'Labiality and velarity in consonants and vowels'. *CLS* 8: 533–543.

Rennison, J. R. 1987. 'Vowel harmony and tridirectional features'.

Folia Linguistica XXI/2–4: 337–354.

—— 1991. 'On the elements of phonological representations: the evidence from vowel systems and vowel processes'. *Folia Linguistica* XXIV: 175–224.

Rice, Keren D. 1993. 'A reexamination of the feature [sonorant]: the status of sonorant obstruents'. *Lg* 69: 308–344.

Rice, Keren D. and Peter Avery. 1989. 'On the interaction between sonorancy and voicing'. *Toronto Working Papers in Linguistics* 10: 65–82.

Robins, R. H. 1990. *A Short History of Linguistics*, 3rd edn (1st edn 1967). London: Longman.

Roca, Iggy. 1992. 'Constraining extrametricality'. In W. Dressler, H. Lüschutzky, O. Pfeiffer and J. Rennison (eds), *Phonologica 1988*, pp. 239–248. Cambridge: Cambridge University Press.

—— 1994. *Generative Phonology*. London: Routledge.

Ross, Alan S. C. 1954. *Neuphilologische Mitteilungen* 55.

Sagey, E. 1986. 'The representation of features and relations in non-linear phonology'. Unpublished Ph.D. dissertation: MIT.

Sampson, Geoffrey. 1980. *Schools of Linguistics: Competition and Evolution*. London: Hutchinson.

Sanders, Gerald A. 1979. 'Equational rules and rule functions in phonology'. In Daniel Dinnsen (ed.), *Current Approaches to Phonological Theory*, pp. 74–105. Bloomington: Indiana University Press.

Sapir, Edward. 1921. *Language*. New York: Harcourt Brace.

—— 1925. 'Sound patterns in language'. *Lg* 1: 37–51. Reprinted in D. Mandelbaum (ed.) (1949), *Selected Writings of Edward Sapir in Language, Culture and Personality*, pp. 33–45. Berkeley: University of California Press. Also reprinted in Martin Joos (ed.) (1957), *Readings in Linguistics I*, pp. 19–25. Chicago: University of Chicago Press. Also reprinted in Valerie Becker Makkai (ed.) (1972), *Phonological Theory: Evolution and Current Practice*, pp. 13–21. New York: Holt, Rinehart & Winston. Also reprinted in Erik C. Fudge (ed.) (1973), *Phonology: Selected Readings*, pp. 101–114. Harmondsworth: Penguin.

—— 1933. 'The psychological reality of phonemes'. Reprinted in D. Mandelbaum (ed.), (1949), *Selected Writings of Edward Sapir in Language, Culture, and Personality*, pp. 46–60. Berkeley: University of California Press. Also reprinted in Valerie Becker Makkai (ed.) (1972), *Phonological Theory: Evolution and Current Practice*, pp. 23–31. New York: Holt, Rinehart & Winston.

Saussure, Ferdinand de. 1879. *Mémoire sur le système primitif des voyelles dans les langues indo-européennes*. Leipzig.

—— 1894. *Mémoires de la Société Linguistique de Paris* VIII: 429.

—— 1916. *Cours de linguistique générale*. Paris: Payot.

Scalise, Sergio. 1984. *Generative Morphology*. Dordrecht: Foris.

Schane, Sanford A. 1984a. 'Two English vowel movements: a particle analysis'. In M. Aronoff and R. T. Oehrle (eds), *Language Sound Structure*, pp. 32–51. Cambridge, MA: MIT Press.

—— 1984b. 'The fundamentals of Particle Phonology', *Phonology Yearbook* 1: 129–155.

Schein, Barry and Donca Steriade. 1986. 'On geminates'. *LI* 17: 691–744.

Scott, N. C. 1941. 'Broad transcription'. Le Maître Phonétique 76: 48–51.

Sedlak, P. 1969. 'Typological considerations of vowel quality systems'. *Stanford Working Papers on Language Universals* 1.

Selkirk, Elisabeth O. 1972. 'The phrase phonology of English and French'. Ph.D. thesis, MIT. Published 1980: New York: Garland.

—— 1980. 'The role of prosodic categories in English word stress'. *LI* 11: 563–605.

—— 1981. 'On prosodic structure and its relation to syntactic structure'. In T. Fretheim (ed.), *Nordic Prosody II*, pp. 111–140. Trondheim: TAPIR.

—— 1982. 'The syllable'. In H. van der Hulst and N. Smith (eds), *The Structure of Phonological Representations*, 2 vols, part II, pp. 337–383. Dordrecht: Foris.

—— 1984. *Phonology and Syntax: the Relation Between Sound and Structure*. Cambridge, MA: MIT Press.

—— 1986. 'On derived domains in sentence phonology'. *Phonology Yearbook* 3: 371–405.

Shadle, C. H. 1985. 'The acoustics of fricative consonants'. Ph.D. dissertation, Cambridge, MA, MIT.

Shaw, Patricia D. 1991. 'Consonant harmony systems: the special status of coronal harmony'. In Carole Paradis and Jean-François Prunet (eds) (1991), *Phonetics and Phonology*, vol. 2: *The Special Status of Coronals*, pp. 125–157. San Diego: Academic Press.

Siegel, D. 1974. *Topics in English Morphology*. New York: Garland.

Singh, Sadanand. 1976. *Distinctive Features: Theory and Validation*. Baltimore: University Park Press.

Smith, Neil V. 1973. *The Acquisition of Phonology: a Case Study*. Cambridge: Cambridge University Press.

Sommerstein, Alan H. 1974. 'On phonotactically motivated rules'. *JL* 10: 71–94.

—— 1977. *Modern Phonology*. London: Edward Arnold.

Spencer, Andrew. 1991. *Morphological Theory*. Oxford: Blackwell.

Stampe, David. 1969. 'The acquisition of phonetic representation'. *CLS* 5: 443–454.

—— 1973. 'A dissertation on natural phonology'. Unpublished Ph.D. dissertation, University of Chicago.

Stanley, Richard. 1967. 'Redundancy rules in phonology'. *Lg* 43: 393–435.

Stark, Bruce R. 1972. 'The Bloomfieldian model'. *Lingua* 30: 385–421.

Steriade, Donca. 1982. 'Greek prosodies and the nature of syllabification'. Unpublished Ph.D. thesis, MIT.

—— 1990. 'Gestures and autosegments: comments on Browman and Goldstein's paper'. In J. Kingston and M. Beckman (eds), *Papers in Laboratory Phonology: Between the Grammar and the Physics of Speech*, pp. 382–397. Cambridge: Cambridge University Press.

Stern, T. 1957. 'Drum and whistle languages: an analysis of speech surrogates'. *American Anthropologist* 59: 487–506.

Stetson, R. H. 1945. *Bases of Phonology*. Oberlin, OH: Oberlin College.

—— 1951. *Motor Phonetics*, 2nd edn (1st edn 1928). Amsterdam: North-Holland.

Stevens, Kenneth N. 1972. 'The quantal nature of speech: evidence from articulatory–acoustic data'. In E. E. David and P. B. Denes (eds), *Human Communication: a Unified View*, pp. 51–56. New York: McGraw-Hill.

Stevens, Kenneth N. and Sheila E. Blumstein. 1981. 'The search for invariant acoustic correlates of phonetic features'. In P. D. Eimas and J. L. Miller (eds), *Perspectives on the Study of Speech*. pp. 1–38. Hillsdale, NJ: Lawrence Erlbaum.

Stevens, Kenneth N. and Samuel Jay Keyser. 1989. 'Primary features and their enhancement in consonants'. *Lg*. 65: 81–106.

Stevens, Kenneth N., Samuel Jay Keyser and H. Kawasaki. 1987. 'Toward a phonetic and phonological theory of redundant features'. In J. S. Perkell and D. H. Klatt (eds), *Symposium on Invariance and Variability*, pp. 426–449. Hillsdale, NJ: Lawrence Erlbaum.

Stevens, S. S., J. Volkmann and E. B. Newman. 1937. 'A scale for the measurement of the psychological magnitude pitch'. *JASA* 8: 185–190.

—— 1957. 'On the psychophysical law'. *Psychological Review* 64: 153–181.

Stewart, J. M. 1967. 'Tongue root position in Akan vowel harmony'. *Phonetica* 16: 185–204.

Swadesh, Morris. 1934. 'The phonemic principle'. *Lg* 10: 117–129. Reprinted in Martin Joos (ed.) (1957), *Readings in Linguistics I*, pp. 32–37. Chicago: University of Chicago Press. Also reprinted in Valerie Becker Makkai (ed.) (1972), *Phonological Theory: Evolution and Current Practice*, pp. 32–39. New York: Holt, Rinehart & Winston. Also reprinted in Erik C. Fudge (ed.) (1973), *Phonology: Selected Readings*, pp. 35–46. Harmondsworth: Penguin.

—— 1935. 'Twaddell on defining the phoneme'. *Lg* 11: 244–250. Reprinted in Valerie Becker Makkai (ed.) (1972), *Phonological Theory: Evolution and Current Practice*, pp. 41–44. New York: Holt, Rinehart & Winston.

Sweet, Henry. 1877. *Handbook of Phonetics*. Oxford. Reprinted 1970. College Park, MD: McGrath.

—— 1888. *A History of English Sounds*, 2nd edn. Oxford: Clarendon Press.

—— 1890. *A Primer of Phonetics*. Oxford: Clarendon Press.

Szemerényi, Oswald J. L. 1985. 'Recent developments in Indo-European linguistics'. *Transactions of the Philological Society*: 1–71.

Tench, Paul. 1992. *Studies in Systemic Phonology*. London: Pinter.

Terry, M., S. Hiller, J. Laver and G. Duncan. 1986. 'The AUDLAB interactive speech analysis system'. *Proceedings of the IEE Conference on Speech Input/Output*, 258: 263–265. London: IEE Publications.

Trager, George L. 1958. 'Paralanguage: a first approximation'. *Studies in Linguistics* 13: 1–12.

Trager, George L. and Bernard Bloch. 1941. 'The syllabic phonemes of English'. *Lg* 17: 223–246. Reprinted in Valerie Becker Makkai (ed.) (1972), *Phonological Theory: Evolution and Current Practice*, pp. 72–89. New York: Holt, Rinehart & Winston.

Trager, George L. and Henry L. Smith. 1951. 'An outline of English structure'. *Studies in Linguistics: Occasional Papers* 3.

Trask, R. L. 1993. *A Dictionary of Grammatical Terms in Linguistics*. London: Routledge.

Trubetzkoy, Nikolai. 1931. 'Die phonologischen Systeme'. *TCLP* IV: 96–116.

—— 1936. 'Essai d'une théorie des oppositions phonologiques'. *Journal de Psychologie* 33: 6–18.

—— 1939. *Gründzüge der Phonologie*. Travaux du Cercle Linguistique de Prague VII. English translation (1969), *Principles of Phonology*, Berkeley: University of California Press.

Twaddell, W. Freeman. 1935. 'On defining the phoneme'. *Language Monograph* 16. Reprinted in Martin Joos (ed.) (1957), *Readings in Linguistics I*, pp. 55–80. Chicago: University of Chicago Press.

Uldall, E. 1958. 'American "molar" *r* and "flapped" *t*'. *Revista do Laboratório de Fonética Experimental da Faculdada de Letras da Universidade de Coimbra* 4: 3–6.

Vachek, Josef. 1966. *The Linguistic School of Prague*. Bloomington: Indiana University Press.

Vago, Robert. 1973. 'Abstract vowel harmony systems in Uralic and Altaic languages'. *Lg* 49: 579–605.

Vaissière, J. 1983. 'Language independent prosodic features'. In A. Cutler and D. R. Ladd (eds), *Prosody: Models and Measurements*, pp. 53–66. Berlin: Springer.

van den Berg, J. 1958. 'Myoelastic-aerodynamic theory of voice production'. *Journal of Speech and Hearing Research* 1: 227–244.

—— 1968. 'Mechanism of the larynx and the laryngeal vibrations'. In B. Malmberg (ed.), *Manual of Phonetics*, pp. 278–308. Amsterdam: North-Holland.

van der Hulst, Harry. 1988. 'The geometry of vocalic features'. In H. van der Hulst and N. Smith (eds), *Features, Segmental Structure and Harmony Processes*, pp. 77–125. Dordrecht: Foris.

—— 1989. 'Atoms of segmental structure: components, gestures and dependency'. *Phonology* 6: 253–284.

van der Hulst, Harry and Norval Smith (eds) 1982. *The Structure of Phonological Representations*, 2 vols. Dordrecht: Foris.

Vanderslice, R. and Peter Ladefoged. 1972. 'Binary suprasegmental features and transformational word-accentuation rules'. *Lg* 48: 819–838.

Vennemann, Theo. 1972a. 'Rule inversion'. *Lingua* 29: 209–242.

—— 1972b. 'Phonological uniqueness in natural generative grammar'. *Glossa* 6: 105–116.

—— 1973. 'Phonological concreteness in natural generative grammar'. In R. Shuy and C.-J. N. Bailey (eds), *Toward Tomorrow's Linguistics*, pp. 202–219. Washington: Georgetown University Press.

—— 1974. 'Words and syllables in natural generative grammar'. In A. Bruck, R. A. Fox and M. W. La Galy (eds), *Papers from the Parasession on Natural Phonology*, pp. 346–374. Chicago: Chicago Linguistic Society.

Verner, Karl. 1875. 'Eine Ausnahme der ersten Lautverschiebung'. *Zeitschrift für vergleichende Sprachforschung* 23: 97–130. English translation 'An exception to Grimm's Law' in W. P. Lehmann (ed.)

(1967), *A Reader in Nineteenth-century Historical Indo-European Linguistics*, Bloomington: Indiana University Press. Translation also in P. Baldi and R. N. Werth (eds) (1978), *Readings in Historical Phonology: Chapters in the Theory of Sound Change*, pp. 32–63. University Park: Pennsylvania State University Press.

Wang, William S.-Y. 1968. 'Vowel features, paired variables, and the English vowel shift'. *Lg* 44: 695–708.

—— 1969. 'Competing sound changes as a cause of residue'. *Lg* 45: 9–25.

Wang, W. S.-Y. and C. J. Fillmore. 1961. *Journal of Speech and Hearing Research* 4.

Ward, Ida C. 1929. *The Phonetics of English*. Cambridge: W. Heffer. 3rd (revised) edn 1939.

Weinreich, Uriel. 1954. 'Is a structural dialectology possible?' *Word* 10: 388–400.

Weinreich, Uriel, William Labov and Marvin I. Herzog. 1968. 'Empirical foundations for a theory of language change'. In W. P. Lehmann and Y. Malkiel (eds), *Directions for Historical Linguistics*, pp. 95–188. Austin: University of Texas Press.

Wells, John C. 1982. *Accents of English*, 3 vols. Cambridge: Cambridge University Press.

—— 1990a. *Longman Pronunciation Dictionary*. London: Longman.

—— 1990b. 'Syllabification and allophony'. In S. Ramsaran (ed.), *Studies in the Pronunciation of English: a Commemorative Volume in Honour of A. C. Gimson*, pp. 76–86. London: Routledge.

Wells, Rulon. 1949. 'Automatic alternation'. *Lg* 25: 99–116.

Welmers, William. 1959. 'Tonemics, morphotonemics, and tonal morphemes'. *General Linguistics* 4: 1–9.

Wenk, B. J. and F. Wioland. 1982. 'Is French really syllable-timed?' *JP* 10: 193–216.

Wheeler, Max. 1985. 'On some claims of Atomic Phonology'. *JL* 21: 139–148.

Whitney, William Dwight. 1843. 'On Lepsius's standard alphabet'. *The Journal of the American Oriental Society* 7: 229–232. Reprinted in M. Silverstein (ed.) (1971), *Whitney on Language: Selected Writings of William Dwight Whitney*. Cambridge, MA: MIT Press, pp. 215–248.

Whorf, Benjamin Lee. 1938. 'Language: plan and conception of arrangement'. Unpublished ms., Yale University. Reprinted in J. B. Carroll (ed.) (1956), *Language, Thought and Reality: Selected Writings of Benjamin Lee Whorf*, pp. 125–133. Cambridge, MA: MIT Press.

Wickelgren, Wayne A. 1966. 'Distinctive features and errors in short-term memory for English consonants'. *JASA* 39: 388–398.

Wilkinson, R. W. 1976. 'A homonymy-avoiding transderivational constraint in Terena'. *IJAL* 42: 158–162.

Williamson, Kay. 1977. 'Multivalued features for consonants'. *Lg* 53: 843–871.

Winteler, J. 1876. *Die Kerenzer Mundart des Kanton Glarus*. Leipzig.

Wood, S. 1975a. 'The weakness of the tongue-arching model of vowel articulation'. *Working Papers in Linguistics* 11: 55–108. Lund: Phonetics Laboratory, Lund University.

—— 1975b. 'Tense and lax vowels: degree of constriction or pharyngeal volume?' *Working Papers in Linguistics*, Lund University, pp. 109–134.

Wurzel, W. 1984. *Flexionsmorphologie und Natürlichkeit*. Berlin: Akademie Verlag. English translation *Inflectional Morphology and Naturalness*, 1989, Dordrecht: Reidel.

Yeni-Komshian, Grace H., James F. Kavanagh and Charles A. Ferguson (eds) 1980. *Child Phonology*, 2 vols. New York: Academic Press.

Zwicky, Arnold. 1970. 'The free-ride principle and two rules of complete assimilation in English'. *CLS* 6: 579–588.

—— 1973. 'Taking a false step'. *Ohio State University Working Papers in Linguistics* 14: 100–112.

—— 1974. 'Homing in: arguing for remote representations'. *JL* 10: 55–70.

—— 1985. 'Clitics and particles'. *Lg* 61: 283–305.